The Art of the Mantua-Maker: 1870 - 1879
Fashion, Sewing, and Clothes Care Advice

Compiled from Original Sources

Edited by Deb Salisbury

Editor of
Elephant's Breath & London Smoke:
Historic Colour Names, Definitions & Uses

Fabric à la Romantic Regency:
A Glossary of Fabrics from Original Sources 1795 – 1836
and
Victorian Bathing and Bathing Suits:
The Culture of the Two-Piece Bathing Dress from 1837 – 1901

The Mantua-Maker Historical Sewing Patterns
Abbott, Texas
2014

The Art of the Mantua-Maker: 1870 - 1879
Fashion, Sewing, and Clothes Care Advice

is a new work, first published by The Mantua-Maker Historical Sewing Patterns in 2014. All new text, the selection and arrangement of period text, and revised versions of period materials are protected by copyright. They may not be reproduced or transmitted in any form without prior written arrangement from The Mantua-Maker Historical Sewing Patterns, except in the case of brief quotations embodied in critical articles and reviews.

The Mantua-Maker Historical Sewing Patterns
100 PR 232
Abbott, TX 76621
deb@mantua-maker.com
http://www.Mantua-Maker.com

Cover illustration from *Peterson's Magazine*, July 1872

Table of Contents

Introduction 1

Dressmaking and Fashion Advice 3
   1870 3
   1871 39
   1872 64
   1873 87
   1874 108
   1875 138
   1876 159
   1877 180
   1878 221
   1879 256

Washing and Repair Advice 285
   1870 285
   1871 285
   1872 285
   1873 286
   1874 287
   1875 287
   1876 288
   1877 290
   1878 301
   1879 305

Bibliography 306

About the Author 307

Dedicated to my mom, Dona Salisbury,
and my friend, Karen "Oma",
in thanks for their kindness and continued support.

Introduction

After all, the most important thing to be observed in dress is whether a particular style, shape, or color, suits the wearer's age, figure, height, or complexion. The present fashions are most varied, and every woman ought to be able to discover the one most suited to improve instead of to uglify her appearance. There is a greater art in dressing well than many would suppose;
Peterson's Magazine, April 1870

The art of the mantua-maker was practiced by every woman who wanted to create her own wardrobe. Fashion magazines were studied and dissected, scoured for details on how each effect was created, how many seams were used, and where the pleats were used. They learned why changes were made, when they went out of date, and how to recreate the styles they liked.

All females with any pretense of belonging to society were expected to follow the current trends, within certain bounds. She was expected to look good in whatever she wore, which could be a problem when fashion clashed with her body type or skin coloring. Learning to modify the fashionable styles became an art form in itself – unless one was able to afford a good modiste who could modify the fashions and make the needed changes to the patterns. And of course, everyone followed the fashions of Paris.

As to the Berlin fashions, which some of our contemporaries have been trying to introduce, they are unutterably ugly. Paris is, and must always remain, the fountain-head of fashion. Nobody, with any pretentions to style, will dress after any other mode.
Peterson's Magazine, May 1871

Period sewing patterns did not give voluminous instructions. In fact, the seamstress was expected to understand and reproduce a garment from the most basic description and sketch, such as this one.

These sleeveless jackets, which have been worn abroad for two years and more, and of which we have, from the first, given illustrations, are, at last, becoming very popular in this country also. Accordingly, we give an engraving of one, and also a diagram of it.

These jackets should be made either of the same material as the skirt, or that of the tunic; for unless they match some part of the dress, they look patchy, and are out of taste. Our pattern consists of four pieces, viz.

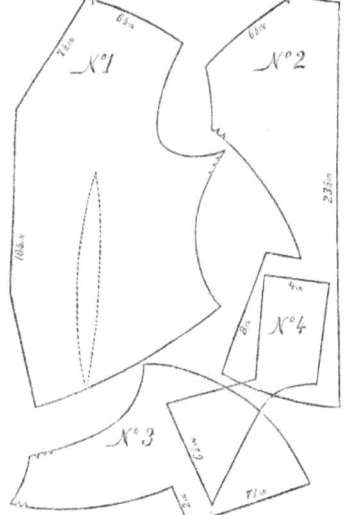

No. 1. Front.
No. 2. Side-piece.
No. 3. Half of Back.
No. 4. Half of Revers and Collar.
Peterson's Magazine, November 1872

I've included as many of these tiny patterns as I could find. Some give measurements and other dressmaking hints. All show an illustration of the garment they were intended to create.

This book compiles sewing and fashion advice given in books and magazines during the 1870s, given in the words of writers of that time. Each entry shows the name and date of the periodical quoted. It has three sections:
     1) Sewing tips and fashion advice
     2) Fabric cleaning and care.
     3) Bibliography of magazines and books I found useful.

I've included over 740 black and white period engravings to help show the details of their work.

To Dress Out of Fashion is to make one's self the subject of remark, a contingency which every woman ought to avoid. How would even a man like to go down the street, in knee-breeches, and with powdered hair, as his great-grandfather did? For a woman to be behind the fashion is absurd. To make one's self conspicuous, in any way, is a mistake.
Peterson's Magazine, September 1872

Change in fashion is simply the expression of an awakened intellect, groping in small things as in great for something better than it has known; and the use for a manual of fashion, such as we offer is, not to dictate to women any rule which they must blindly follow, but to afford such knowledge of varying costumes, and the manner of making them, that each may clothe herself appropriately, according to her appearance of age, or even mood.

Why should not a woman's purity of mind, her quick eye for color, her aesthetic sense of fitness, be disclosed in her attire as well as in the pictures on her walls or her garden? Very few of us will ever carve a great statue, or paint a great picture but we all have clothes to wear; and it is a duty we owe to ourselves and those around us, to so drape the bodies God has given us, as to make no discord in this beautiful, pleasant word. All of us have friends, or, it may be, children, with whom we would have a fair and tender memory. Carelessness and bad taste in dress, so far from being indicative of strength of mind, argues a certain vulgarity of feeling, just as vanity and foppery, on the other hand, prove a weak brain. Wise men or women make their dress so thoroughly in accordance with their person and character, that nobody notices it any more than the frame of a picture; but to be clothed shabbily, in the hopes that our inner perfections will overshadow our dress, is but the extreme of vanity.
Peterson's Magazine, June 1873

A lady, unless she wishes to be eccentric, must follow the fashions, at least in a modified degree. The first requisite to dressing well yourself, is to know what is going to be worn. You may then adapt the style to suit your complexion, etc. But you cannot entirely ignore it.
Peterson's Magazine, October 1875

Formerly fashion was absolute and exclusive; there was *one* pattern, and one pattern only, for all dresses, mantles, bonnets, etc.; now there are different patterns for all dresses to be worn on different occasions. Thus there is the *robe de chambre,* the home dress, the walking costume for the morning, the dress for calling and driving out in the afternoon, the toilet for the theatre or concert, and lastly for small or large parties.
Godey's Lady's Book, July 1877

In a word, the conclusion to which Mrs. Oliphant comes is that which has always been maintained in these pages; it is, that the art of dressing well consists in knowing the prevailing fashions, and adapting them to your particular style. What suits one will not always look beautiful on another. There should be discrimination, the result of a cultivated taste. To deviate from the prevailing *mode* entirely is, on the other hand, a grave blunder; for anything odd makes a lady a laughing-stock, and the dress quite out of the fashion is, therefore, to be avoided.
Peterson's Magazine, June 1879

Dressmaking and Fashion Advice

1870

We begin with a plaid walking-dress, suitable for a best dress. The material should be either a woolen plaid, or any one-colored woolen stuff goods. It will require about eighteen yards of single width, or fourteen yards of double width material; and can be made both fashionably, and at the same time comparatively inexpensively.

The under-skirt has one gored width in front, and if the material is of double fold, the side gores come off of the front width. By observing to cut the skirt in this way, much material can be saved; then add two full widths in the back; cut the flounce a quarter of a yard in depth, and bias, and put it on as seen in the design, either with a band of black velvet one inch wide, or with worsted braid, or even with bias bands of black alpaca, stitched down by the sewing-machine. The upper-skirt is short, and even all round, (trimmed also with a bias ruffle six inches deep,) being simply looped up in the middle of the back with a large bow of the material of the dress.

For the jacket, cut out a simple straight sack, short, only a little below the waist; then slit it up the back, as seen in the engraving; trim with the same width ruffle as on the upper-skirt, and with a narrow quilling around the armholes and at the hands. Such a dress, made of ordinary woolen reps, or plaids, at seventy-five cents per yard, and trimmed with the bias bands of black alpaca, ought not to cost over fifteen dollars, including all trimmings.

...

New Trimmings. – Velvet is the material most used for trimming; *gros grain* is the second choice; satin has fallen somewhat into disfavor. Bands of bias velvet, cut from the piece in varied widths from two inches to a quarter of a yard, are place straight around the skirts, the narrow bands as headings to flounces, wider ones in conjunction with *ruches*, lace, or fringe. Velvet, of the same shade of the dress, is preferable, though black and contrasting colors are used. Ribbon velvet, both wide and narrow, fills the space between flounces. *Gros grain* is seen as bias bands piped with satin, or notched with saw-teeth, or edged with passementerie or fringe; also, as puffs, quillings, and flounces. Satin is most used in thick cable cords, in facings, and narrow pipings. Straight flounces in large plaits, all turned one way, are seen in profusion on silk and woolen dresses; but few box-plaits are made. Gathered flounces, hitherto thought unsuitable for thick materials, are found even on velvet garments – a scant velvet full piped with satin and *faille* being prettier than one would imagine. The new passementerie or crocheted gimp in lace patterns of points and scallops, forms a beautiful edging. Thick, oval ornaments, like elongated buttons and shoulder-knots, or frogs of passementerie, add a dressy appearance to plain cloth suits. Large buttons of satin and velvet rings and crocheted centers are placed in double rows down the front of redingotes, and fastened by double loops of thick cord. Chenille fringe is on many of the new suits; also bullion fringe of thick cable cord, and a heavy fringe of detached tassels. The appropriate trimmings for cloth and woolen materials are velvet, *gros grain*, and fringe; for silks, flounces of the same with velvet bands; for velvet, *gros faille* facings, satin pipings, passementerie, and lace.

...

Flounces and quillings are in greater vogue than ever, without causing any prejudice to cross strips and rouleaux; all this is mixed together upon modern dresses, and fringes and fancy braid are added besides.

...

Long dresses, even when looped up, are rarely worn. Ladies have come to the very just conclusion, that it is impossible to loop up gracefully the train of a dress. For walking, the costume must be short, made expressly to favor the free motion of the feet, and give the wearer an easy and graceful carriage. Long dresses, however, will continue to be worn in-doors, especially at evening parties and grand dinners.

...

The Empress Jacket is the newest thing in Paris. It is short, wide, and cut with four large basques, which are bordered with Venetian point sewn on plain. The guipure is carried up the back in a point, and the whole is embellished at the edge with narrow gold braid.

...

Black velvet sacques are the style this winter. They are made long, so as to dispense with the tunic, and are to be worn over silk petticoats, for in this way there can be great variety in the toilet, as the petticoat can easily be changed.

...

WALKING-DRESS.

Fig. VI. – Walking-Dress of Black Cashmere. – The under-skirt has two fluted flounces, the upper one of which is trimmed with a band of black velvet. The upper-skirt, which is looped up at the sides, and falls in a deep puff at the back, is trimmed to correspond with the lower-skirt. The basque has a rolling-collar of black velvet, is slit at the sides, and is trimmed with black velvet and fringe. ←

Peterson's Magazine, January 1870

STYLE OF MAKING.

Ball dresses have a distinct style of their own this season, since they alone are made with the low-necked, almost sleeveless corsages that are banished from dinner and soirée toilettes. Pointed, round, and basque waists are all represented in ball costumes, with the neck cut extremely low in front and back, and filled out to a decorous height by Medici frills of fluted lace or several *plissés* (pleatings) of the trimming arranged standing, and to lean outward from the wearer. Berthas are also worn, but the frills are most stylish. Other corsages are straight around the top, falling very low off the shoulders. In some cases there are no shoulder-straps, the tiny sleeves along passing over the arm. Thinnest tulle and gauze corsages have the material laid plainly over silk lining. Pointed corsages fasten behind and are laced by a silken string.

Skirts are of a length easily managed in the rapid dances now in vogue. The longest trains worn in the ball-room measure fifty-four inches; the majority are shorter than these, and many skirts merely lay a few inches on the floor behind without being train-shaped. The last are gored in the usual way, but resemble in effect the round skirts worn before trains came in. Short skirts of walking-length are worn by very young ladies. Those who are more mature wear a short skirt with a trained tunic or court train, and make the most elegant ball toilettes of the season.

A tunic, either short or trained but always very bouffant, is a part of every ball toilette. The shape of these was described by our Parisian correspondent in the last *Bazar*, and illustrations will be found in the present Number. The handsomest trained tunics are of China crape, royale velvet, or heavy brocaded silk of the color of the dress worn beneath it, which is of tulle with many flounces, or else satin trimmed with rich lace. The train should be widely faced with silk and trimmed to match the dress. Some modistes put in hooks along the edge of the train to fasten in silk loops on the side of the skirt and prevent the train from flying back. Shorter tunics are either made with apron fronts, or are turned back *en revers*. White tulle tunics over colored silk skirts are made long enough to veil the entire skirt, and are then draped and festooned with flowers. Silk or satin tunics, either short or trained, are worn with white tarlatan and tulle dresses. Black satin tunics with gilt trimmings are admired for stylish ladies.

...

TRIMMINGS FOR BALL AND EVENING DRESSES.

The trimmings here given are intended for white or colored dresses of light material, such as muslin, mull, tarlatan, crape, gauze, etc.

Fig. 1. – This trimming is of pink tarlatan pinked on the edges, and arranged on a foundation of white tarlatan. It consists of two downward ruffles, each three inches wide, and arranged in close box-pleats each two-fifths of an inch wide. The second of these ruffles lies half-way over the first ruffle. Two similar ruffles are turned upward, as shown by the illustration. Between these is set a ruche, which consists of a strip of the material two inches and a half wide, and arranged in threefold box-pleats. An inch above the upward ruffles arrange a flounce five inches wide; above this is another flounce six inches wide. The upper flounce lies over the under one, and is sewed on with a head an inch wide. Nearly an inch above this last flounce sew six ruffles, each two inches wide, and arranged in box-pleats two-fifths of an inch wide; each of these ruffles covers the seam made by setting on the preceding one. After every twelve inches space these ruffles are ornamented with a threefold bias strip of tarlatan two inches wide, which is edged with narrow blonde insertion, and sewed diagonally over the pleats. Above this

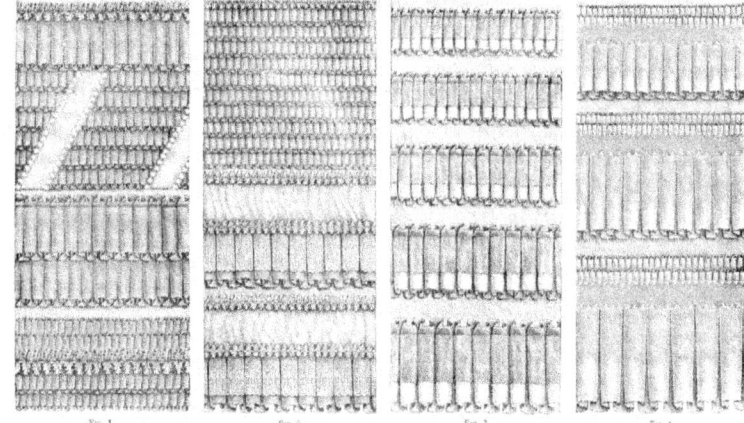

sew a flounce five inches wide arranged in box-pleats an inch wide and a quarter of an inch apart; head this with a double box-pleated ruche an inch and a half wide.

Fig. 2. – This trimming is of green and white tarlatan and white blonde lace two inches and a half wide, and is arranged on a foundation of white tarlatan. Trim the under edge with a pinked flounce of green tarlatan six inches wide, which is laid in box-pleats an inch wide with a fifth of an inch space between. The strip which forms the flounce is covered plainly with blonde lace, beginning two inches from the upper edge, and extending nearly to the under edge. A third of an inch above the flounce set a green tarlatan puff three inches wide (the strip of stuff designed for this must be four inches wide). Finish each edge of the puff with a double box-pleated ruche of white tarlatan two inches wide. An inch above this repeat the same arrangement; after this follow ten ruffles, each two inches and a quarter wide, and made of a strip of green tarlatan pinked on the under edge and arranged in box-pleats two-fifths of an inch wide, with a fifth of an inch space between. Each ruffle heads the preceding one, and the last is headed with a white ruche an inch and a half wide.

Fig. 3. – This trimming is made of blue and white tarlatan on a foundation of white tarlatan. It consists of five ruffles of double material, each separated from the next by an inch and a half space. Each ruffle is made of a white and a narrower blue strip. Both strips are pinked on each side, and laid with the upper edges together. With a quarter of an inch space between arrange the strips in box-pleats an inch wide, in such a manner that the upper edge shall form a head. The under ruffle is seven inches wide including the head, which is an inch wide, each succeeding ruffle is three-quarters of an inch narrower, and the heads are narrower in proportion.

Fig. 4. – The ruffles of this trimming are of white tulle; the strips which cover the places where the narrow upward ruffles are set on are of threefold pink tulle. The under flounce consists of a strip seven inches wide, pinked on the under edge, and laid in close box-pleats an inch and a quarter wide. An inch and a half above the wide flounce sew on the two narrow ruffles, each of which is an inch and a half wide, and is pinked on the under edge, and laid in close box-pleats a third of an inch wide. The under one of the two upward ruffles heads the upper one. The flounce and the next upward ruffle are covered with the pink strip two inches and a quarter wide, which is edged on both sides with narrow blonde insertion. With an inch and a half space between repeat this arrangement twice; the following flounce is five inches and a half wide, and the upper one four inches wide, while the pink strips and upward ruffles are narrower in proportion.

...

Fig. 1. – Low Blouse Waist with Peplum. – Front.
Fig. 2. – Low Blouse Waist with Peplum. – Back.

➜

Harper's Bazar, January 29, 1870

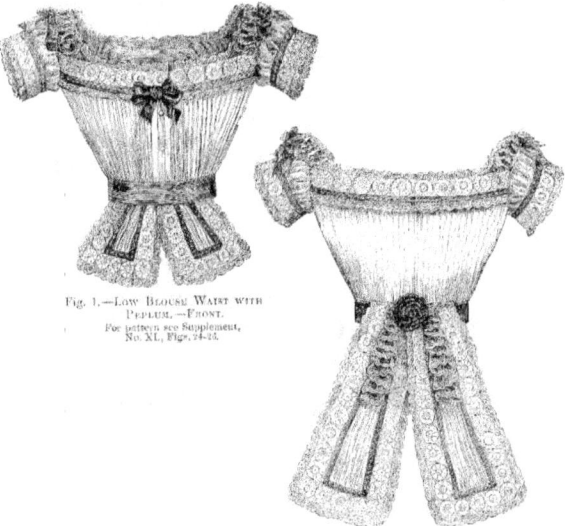

Fig. 1.—Low Blouse Waist with Peplum.—Front. For pattern see Supplement, No. XL, Figs. 74-75.

Fig. 2.—Low Blouse Waist with Peplum.—Back.

3. – Evening Toilets.

1. Dress of straw-coloured silk, with a long train, trimmed with a flounce gathered and edged with a thick pinked out ruche, forming a puff at the back and looped up on both sides with a long garland of red roses and natural foliage. Silk bodice with points in front and at the lack, chemisette of pleated tulle and garland of roses round the bodice, and falling over the skirt. Diadem of red roses with a long spray at the back. Artistic jewels.

2. Dress of white tarlatan, with two skirts. The first trimmed round the bottom with flounces, alternately plain and scalloped out. Second skirt plain, and looped up at the side. Bodice of white silk with long basques in front and at the back. Berthe and basque are ornamented with moss silk trimmings, strips, and buttons of satin. Bunch of flowers at the side. Muslin fichu inside the bodice. Locket fastened round the neck with a black ribbon velvet.

...

For more ordinary walking dresses those in real cloth, or fabrics imitating good cloth, are now the *fureur* in Paris. They are composed of a skirt, with one or several flounces, a tunic caught up at the back, and a short paletot, lined with fur. These dresses, which are in a high degree convenient, should be accompanied by a muff, made of the same material as the dress, with bands of fur running round it, and boots to match. English furriers should at once take up this notion, and boot-makers likewise, for cloth boots well made, and trimmed at the top with fur, would be exceedingly acceptable to ladies in these days of short dresses, and when there is every disposition to show and see a lady's feet. The shades of cloth most liked are dark green (bottle green), dark brown (chestnut), and bronze; these make up into costumes of very considerable distinction. German velvet, very pretty, is much more dressy, of course, and ladies can wear this when calling, or at the theatre, and it is not out of place at a dinner. For ladies of taste, and who can appreciate a good dress, can be recommended: – Underskirt trimmed at the bottom with a flounce in thick folds; jacket with revers over a satin waistcoat of the same colour, made in such a way that it can be readily replaced by a muslin chemisette, trimmed with lace, which will give sufficient lightness and elegance to the costume to make it allowable to be worn to the ordinary theatre.

...

Toilets, taken as a whole, and in the best circles, are and will be considerably simpler this winter. Tunics worn without waistband, the corsages with basques and points are being worn instead of the exaggerated bows which were the fashion last year, and which it cannot be denied, considerably detracted from the elegance of a lady's figure. The voluminous tournures, so to speak, are going or are gone out, or at any rate have become so moderate in size that there is not much to talk about. The old cage crinoline, which is nevertheless very useful in the street, is replaced by stiff petticoats of horse-hair or other material starched or stiffened. No more ruches or bouillons to trim the bodies or the skirts, but flat trimmings almost entirely. The under skirts, to be elegant, are trimmed at the bottom, with a gathered flounce about nine inches wide, surmounted by three or four rows of piping. This new style of petticoat maybe confidently recommended to ladies of good style.

...

Cage crinolines are, for indoors, replaced by hair or stiff petticoats trimmed, at the bottom, with bouillons and flounces. Peculiar shapes are necessary for these to set well, to be graceful, and to be of the necessary volume. A single garment is sufficient, when well made, to support the shape of a robe. For long trains, the stiff petticoat must be longer. For the street, the *Eugénie* and the *Régente* cages are very good. Modified according to present necessities, these two are very comfortable to wear. Skilfully disposed, the hoops hold up the bottom of the petticoat, and keep them from the dirt. They are white or coloured. We prefer them in red cashmere, that being the prettiest colour and the least likely to soil. Of the stiff petticoats for indoors, the Impératrice and La Valliere are good.

The Milliner and Dressmaker, January 1870

HOUSE OR CARRIAGE-DRESS.

Fig. VIII. – House-Dress of Blue Silk. – The skirt is only of medium length, and is trimmed with one deep flounce, headed with two narrow bands of silk. Upper-skirt of blue and white striped silk, also trimmed with a flounce and two bias bands of the blue silk. This skirt is made like a polonaise at the waist, and is seen in front beneath the blue cape, which opens there in two points. The sleeves, pannier at the back, and bows, are all of the plain blue silk. The upper-skirt reaches to the top of the flounce in front.

...

We give here two patterns for borders for jackets, opera-cloaks, chemise Russe, etc., etc. The first, printed above, may be worked in white or gold-colored silk; or silks of various colors may be employed, according to taste. Cashmere is the ground usually selected.

The second, printed below, is an arabesque pattern, of the full size, [3 1/2" x 1 3/8"] worked in chain-stitch of yellow silk cordon, with white knots in the middle. The stars are raised embroidery, alternately blue, green, lilac, and red. The three loose stitches are also alternately worked in the same colors.

...

PATTERN FOR AN ALL-ROUND SKIRT.
By Emily H. May.

As All-Round Skirts are now so universally worn, a pattern of one will be found useful to our subscribers. These skirts are now trimmed in various ways, the newest style being a flounce from twelve to sixteen inches in depth, according to the height of the wearer. If the flounce is plaited, the folds all fall in the same direction in the Russian style: if gathered, either a heading or a ruche is added to the flounce.

Our pattern consists of four pieces: – Half of the front breadth, half of back breadth, and two side breadths. The order in which the pieces join will be known by the notches on the side of the diagram, which must correspond. The front breadth as a single notch on the side on which it joins to the next breadth. The back breadth has three notches. The two front breadths are sewn plain to the waistband, if the figure is slight, but they must be somewhat eased, should the figure be stout. The remaining breadths are gathered. It has recently become fashionable to wear a train-skirt over a short All-Round one, and the style of the newest creation is given in the accompanying illustration. This train, which can be slipped on and off at pleasure, imparts a very dressy appearance to the toilet for either in-door or out-door wear. By the aid of this diagram, most ladies can make the skirt themselves.

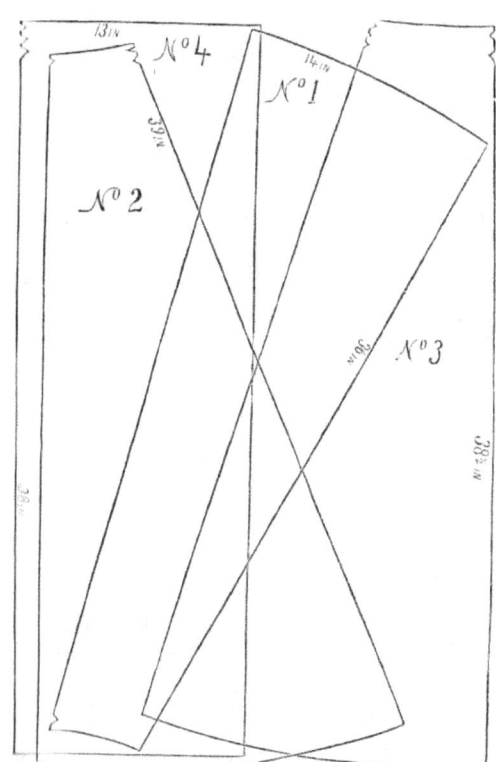

The Watteau style continues to reign; *paniers* at the back, skirts looped up at the sides, and richly trimmed petticoats, are still as popular as last winter. Some of the sleeves of these dresses are of the coat shape, with deep cuffs, others loose, of the old pagoda shape, over a close sleeve.

Over-skirts are more worn than ever. The most graceful style for upper-skirts, with apron fronts, is to make them as long as the under-skirt, and drape them in deep plaits on the hips, making them only short enough to show the trimming of the under-skirt beneath. Scallops, or castellated points, or else flat bands, trim upper-skirts better than frills that rumple easily.

The most fashionable costumes are made with a tunic, forming at once a bodice and mantle. Pointed waists are becoming more and more popular, and for any, save the slightest figures, they are infinitely the most becoming, though much more difficult to fit nicely than the round waist. All skirts are draped; for ball-dresses, a thin over-dress is always draped over a silk, or over a satin, which is much more lustrous.
Peterson's Magazine, February 1870

The often thankless task of combining elegance with economy is the business of modistes to perform, and they may suggest to ladies a plan which even in these times of reckless extravagance may allow of following the fashions without incurring unreasonable expense.

Ladies who are in the habit of going out much or little of an evening probably possess a number of light-coloured dresses of satin, silk, foulard, or silk gauze, which, not being worn as frequently as others, get out of fashion before they are faded or spoilt, and therefore become incumbrances, which they do not like to throw away, but do not know what to do with.

The present fashion of wearing dresses of two different materials and colours, affords a resource in such cases. The bright-coloured dress of a past season can easily be made use of as an under-dress. Should it even be gored and quite plain, it can still be made up to suit the present fashion by being shortened, and by that means increased in fullness at the top; to shorten the skirt, the material must be cut off from the upper part, which will allow of all the fullness of the gored train being taken into the back part of the skirt. In front the skirt may be quite plain, and short enough for the toes to show without the dress being looped up. To such a skirt a square, plain, low bodice being added, a fashionable under-dress will be obtained.

For the trimming, should it be possible to obtain any of the same material, it may be disposed in ruches or flutings, arranged in the shape of an apron, as only the front part of the skirt is meant to show. Sufficient material for a trimming of this sort is often procured by the piece cut off at the top, in the case of train-shaped skirts. The ruches or flutings may be merely pinked at the edges, or they may be edged with lace or bound with satin; this must depend upon the quality of the material; glacé silk and foulard look best pinked out, silk gauze and satin edged with lace, and *gros-grain* or *faille* silk bound with satin of a darker or contrasting colour.

If there is not a sufficient quantity of the same material as the dress for the trimming, lace, or satin, or velvet may be used instead. Satin and lace look well in ruches or flutings, upon any material; and velvet is rich and elegant for a heavy satin or gros-grain silk dress. The low bodice and waist-band should be trimmed to correspond with the skirt.

Of course an under-dress of this sort composes but one half of the toilet. To complete it there must be a train-shaped skirt and a bodice, high at the back, but remaining entirely open in front. Several of our engravings have given elegant models of this style of open tunic-dress.

A coloured dress of a former season may also frequently be made use of for the upper-dress, but it should always be darker than the under one, and, of course, well matched in colour.

For instance, violet will look well with mauve, pale yellow, or pearl grey; deep blue, with light blue, pale pink, or white; green, with rose-colour, maize, or mauve; ruby, or garnet, or plum-colour, with faint pink, blue or green, or dust grey; and golden brown with buttercup-colour; while with black any colour looks well.

The tunic should not only be of a darker colour than the underskirt, it should be also of a thicker material; thus, a velvet tunic looks best over satin, *gros-grain,* or *faille* silk; while satin, or thick silk can be worn over glacé silk, foulard, or gauze. In either case it can be made quite plain, and there is no need to overload it with velvet or flowers, though this is often done to suit particular tastes. A handsome lace trimming is the only one which is in fact a desideratum in such a toilet; and, if such cannot be procured, it is best to dispense with any ornament whatever. The full, sweeping train is in itself most elegant and graceful, and the *chiffonné* style, or ruched trimmings, looks best upon the under-dress. The tunic-bodies should open squarely upon the low under-bodice, quite in the Medicis style, and be finished off with a handsome standing-up ruffle of point-lace, or guipure d'art. We advise a black velvet tunic-dress as a most desirable article in a lady's wardrobe, as it makes up a handsome toilet with an under-dress of any colour.

As for ball-dresses, the first condition of their elegance is extreme freshness, and therefore there is little to be done in their case towards turning an old dress into a new one. Of all light materials *crêpe de Chine* is the only one which wears at all well, and bears cleaning and dyeing without losing all its beauty. But *crêpe de Chine* has but lately come into fashion again; and besides, it is so expensive as not to be within the reach of many fortunes. Tarlatans, tulle, and gauze never look well a second year, and can, in fact, barely be worn three or four times, nor would it be well-understood economy to have them done up again several times, since the making and trimming are always the most expensive part of such toilets, while the material itself costs but very little, and is pretty only when quite new and fresh.

Many of the most elegant modern ball-dresses are made with looped-up tunic-dresses of silk or satin, over underdresses of some light material. The tunic-skirt is open in front, draped and looped up with bows, while at the back it is very much puffed out; for we seem to be getting more and more into the style of the Louis the XVI. toilets, and the real *panier tournure* of that time is apparently not far off. We have already the double dress, train-shaped at the back, plain in front, and short enough to show the high-heeled shoes matched in colour to the dress, the square low bodice, the pleated fichu, the high coiffure. Will fashion adopt once more the hooped petticoats, the powdered wig, and patches?

...

Balls, parties, and soirees, have scarcely begun than the great success which all kinds of lace are to have is at once apparent. It will be worn everywhere this year. Already walking and visiting dresses are trimmed with it profusely. Lace, worn low on the dresses, is disposed in ruches or scallops, whilst folds above form elegant tunics, gracefully draped and relieved by velvet or satin bows on materials like satin or velvet. We advise the employment of guipure Louis XIII. Placed flat in large revers, it has a very aristocratic appearance. As to black lace dresses, and white lace, over transparent colours, these should be found in the wardrobes of every lady pretending to elegance in dress. These contribute the bases of a good array of toilets quite indispensable to those who go most into the world. No trousseaux are of any pretention which have not two skirts of lace, and flounces of point de Chantilly and point d'Angleterre. At this moment may be seen in the best magasins a great variety, and many complete new sets of muslin, comprising stomachers, neckerchiefs, and chemisettes, ornamented with revers or pipings of Valenciennes, with sleeves to match, which sit on the arm, and are as beautifully cut as they are pretty. For more dressy toilets, these muslin sets are repeated in tulle and application d'Angleterre. To ladies of taste they will be very welcome. No lady can have so great a chance of looking charming as when lace fabrics, and all their attendant lightness and airiness, are in the ascendant.

...

Complete costumes of a uniform colour are much preferable to parti-coloured toilets, even if the latter are richer in quality. A simple whole toilet lends distinction to the wearer, and faults in point of taste are more difficult to avoid when the skirt, mantle, and bonnet are of different tints.

...

The most elegant toilets are now trimmed with feathers, and it is impossible to too highly approve this innovation or rather resurrection. The pheasant, jay, pintado, and grey partridge yield beautiful feathers which make the most lovely trimmings, and are neither so hot or heavy as fur. The most charming of these we have seen are of peacock's feathers; not the eye which has become so common, but the throat, with all the shotted shades of the most adorable blue. Bands and tufts bordered a tunic of faille, peacock colour, and formed the revers of a small and entirely velvet paletot in velvet of the same changing colours. The bonnet of faille, velvet and feathers to match, was ornamented at the side by a white satin magnolia. Muff of peacock's throat feathers, bound with white satin bands. A small peacock setting its tail; emeralds and sapphires in each ear.

...

Although the task of the Milliner And Dressmaker is to seek out incessantly whatever may appear new in fashion, it is not necessary to advise ladies, however, to implicitly follow all the changes which occur in order to keep within the pale of modern fashion. Thus, draped dresses are still in very great favour; the double or triple skirt of gauze, tarlatan, or crape de Chine, looped up with flowers or bows, upon a slip of silk or satin, are as yet the most graceful that have been found for ball toilets. Sometimes a train of silk material is added, which renders the dress more rich and elegant. The tournure in every case is always very much puffed out at the back.

...

Dress With Reference To Weight. – A mode in which many violate the health-laws relating to dress, is, in having their clothes unnecessarily heavy, long, flowing drapery which in all civilized countries is generally considered an essential part of woman's dress, must be very heavy and encumbering; but it need not be nearly as much so as it generally is now. We have lately taken the trouble to weigh a linsey dress, a thick cloth cloak, a scarlet flannel upper petticoat, a steel skeleton skirt, a flannel under petticoat, and all the rest of the clothing worn in winter by a young lady of eighteen, of the average height: the weight of the whole was fourteen pounds and a quarter. This may be considered as below, rather than above, the average weight of the clothing worn by most women in winter, for there are few who do not wear more petticoats, and wrap more in every way, than this young lady. Few of us have enough to do with weights and scales to have a very clear idea of the weight represented by fourteen pounds. We would recommend those of our readers who are not learned in this matter, to carry, on the first opportunity, a seven pound weight in each hand up and down the room for five minutes; they will then assuredly need no argument to convince them that such a weight is far too great to be carried about all day in the shape of clothes. There is no doubt that it greatly wastes our strength, so that there is much less left for our work. It makes us unable to walk nearly so far as we could if we carried no needless weight, and often makes walking, which is the best of all kinds of exercise, only a misery to those who are very weak and delicate. This is a very serious thing for working women, though very little to the rich lady, who drive everywhere with her brougham and pair of greys.

The Milliner and Dressmaker, February 1870

LOW BODICE AND PANNIER TUNIC.
By Emily H. May.

This pattern is one of the latest novelties from Paris, and can be made up in a variety of styles – in white tarlatan, with satin braces of some bright color, and edged with blond; in silk, with velvet braces; or again, in velvet, with lace braces. In one and all of these materials it looks remarkably well. It is, of course, for evening wear.

We give a diagram, from which to cut it out, on the next page.

It consists of five pieces – three for the bodice and two for the tunic. The front and back and one brace form the pattern of the bodice; four braces will be required, as there are two in front and two at the back; but as all four are cut exactly the same, only one has been given. The small holes that mark the darts show the front of the bodice; the position for the brace is marked in a similar manner on both the front and the back. The braces may be either cut in one piece for each back and front, or joined on the shoulder, as most convenient. The two pieces for the tunic now remain. The front is the smaller one; it turns back with a *revers*, the two notches indicate how it is to be joined to the corresponding two notches on the *panier*. The edge of the side of the *panier* is to be gathered and sewn to the side of the front. The back is to be bunched up according to the illustration, and a short, wide sash added over it. Ruches, plaited ribbon, lace, feathers, and fringe, may be used for trimming; the selection to be ruled by the material used. The whole costume is an exceedingly stylish one.

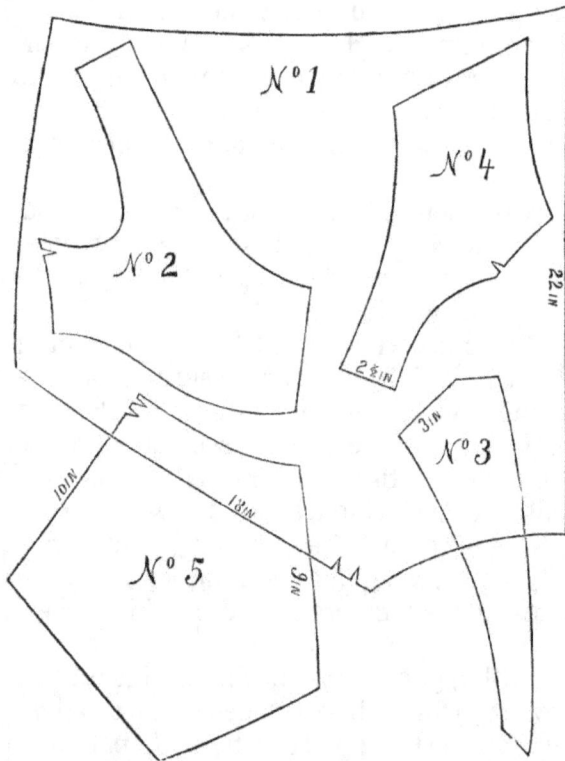

Ball and party dresses are, perhaps, less coquettish, but more beautiful, than last year. The Medici collarettes will be adapted to low dresses. Bows of ribbon and voluminous waistbands will be worn by young girls only. We should advise, for very slender ladies, corsages with basques falling over a puffed tunic; this will give them more volume. Rather stout ladies ought, in their turn, to avoid all kinds of dresses and trimmings which increase their bulk; they should chose flat trimmings rather than ruches and puffings. By endeavoring to lengthen themselves as much as possible, they will diminish the effect which their stoutness would otherwise produce.

...

We repeat what we have often said before: the rich costumes or dresses we describe, may always be copied in less expensive materials. It is the style, not necessarily the material, that you must follow.

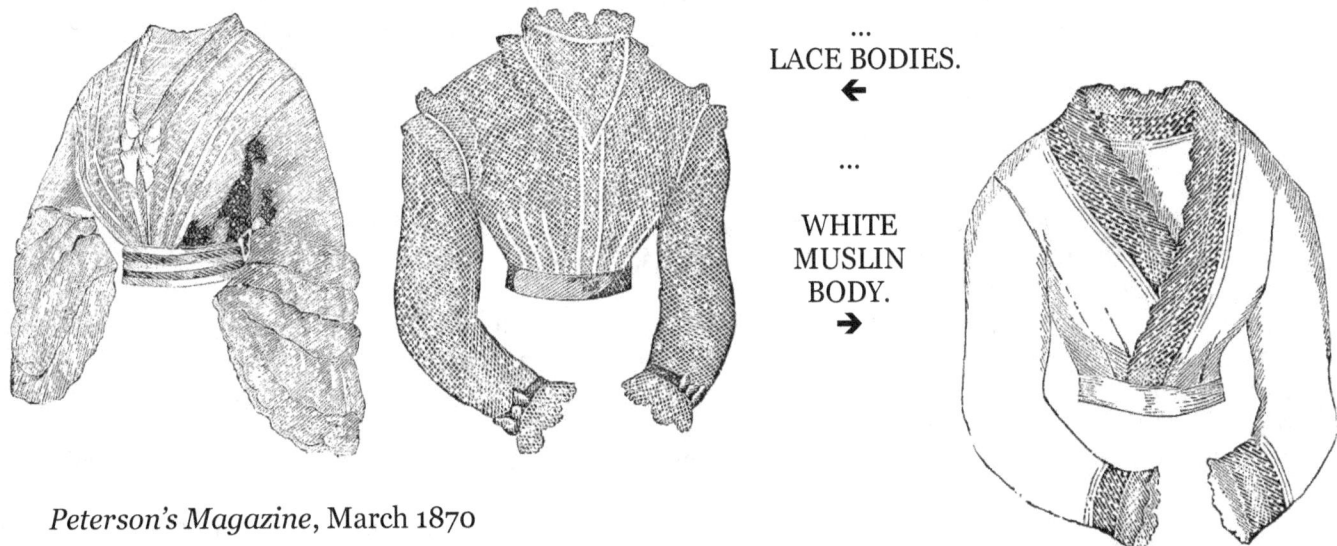

...

LACE BODIES.
←

...

WHITE
MUSLIN
BODY.
→

Peterson's Magazine, March 1870

Jacket bodices are made to open in front like a coat, while the basques at the back are puffed out; in front the bodice is in the shape of a waistcoat; sometimes the jacket is merely simulated by the trimming, and is in reality all of the same piece with the front waistcoat part.

The complete costume is not now as exclusively made of but one colour as it was last year; on the contrary, it is often of two different tints.

For instance, a costume of pearl-grey *poult-de-soie* is trimmed with a gathered flounce, cut on the cross, above which there are three bands of brown velvet. The second skirt is also trimmed with a similar flounce and three velvet bands – it is looped up on one side with a chatelaine band of *poult-de-soie* and velvet. A velvet trimming is put on in a square outline upon the high bodice; the sleeves are tight, with three velvet bands forming bracelets. Loose paletot, quilted, open at back, with lappels trimmed, like all the rest of the paletot, with bands of brown velvet, to which is added a short crimped fringe of the same colour. A sash with four wide loops at the back, forming a puff; and the sleeves, in the pagoda style, are trimmed to correspond.

...

Complete costumes are evidently to continue their success during the *demi-saison* and all the Spring at least. They will be varied, however, by being made of two materials, two tints, and also two colours. In the latter case, *modestes* should bid ladies beware of glaring contrasts and unharmonizing shades. The mixture of colours has always been a stumbling-block in the toilet, and perhaps for that reason, it is said so often of several people that they are never so well-dressed as when they are in mourning. Better a hundred times uniformity than badly matched colours, and a plain black preferable to a great variety of tints.

A good theory and simple, is this: There should never be more than two positive colours in a lady's toilet; black and white not being reckoned as such. The two colours must harmonize well together. If one is neutral, let the other be well defined; if one is dark, let the other possess a certain brightness. This year, in toilets of two colours, the under skirt and mantle will be made of one colour, the dress of another. The flounces, of the same material as that part the dress of which they form the trimming, will be edged with cross-strips or pipings of the other colour. This will not be universal fashion, great numbers will be made of one tint, and many of two shades of the same colour.

...

Young ladies' dresses are uniformly made very simple, of tarlatan, with draperies and narrow flounces. They are either all white, all pink, or light blue or green.

Married ladies, on the contrary, continue to dress elaborately. The tunic does not exclude flounces, nor a double skirt, nor a train, and the under skirt is always very much trimmed.

Very frequently the toilet is composed of a light dress placed over a slip of silk, all the front part covered with light trimmings, flowers and lace. You see also the train-shaped skirt which is made so as to be able to carry it over the arm; this dress is of rich silk, and not much trimmed, excepting with cross-strips, loops or pleated ruches of the same material; for ladies find that light trimmings soon get spoiled at balls where the crowd is great. The low bodice opens in front upon a plastron of lace, to correspond with the under skirt.

This train thrown over the arm is apt to daunt young ladies, and it requires a graceful carriage. For those who fear this duchess-like fashion, trains are made to be looped up at pleasure by a very easy process.

...

With the present dresses the greatest possible care is necessary, *modistes* should inform their patronesses, in the manner of arranging the petticoats. The skirt question is of great importance regarded from the point of elegance.

The petticoats from the establishment of Messrs. Bandolier and Roche are perfect in style. First, there is the "Metternich" crinoline, which is only 68 inches round, and is open at the knees to permit sitting down with facility; the crinoline "Louis XV.," larger at the hips than below, is very suitable for stout figures. Petticoats with steels are intended to be worn with short costumes.

To support the trains of long dresses this house makes the tunic "*vert-vert*" in muslin, with one flounce all round, and a series of flounces superposed. Under this skirt ought to be worn a petticoat of thick corded muslin, with a double flounce round the bottom. For an indoor toilette, or for the theatre, are worn the crinoline petticoat without steels, with *tournure* independent, the *tournure,* "Grande Duchesse" and the half-skirt with *tournure,* or puff.

The Milliner and Dressmaker, March 1870

WALKING-DRESS.

Fig. VII. – Dress of Brown Silk, trimmed round the bottom with three flounces, two striped with black satin and a plain one in the middle. Casaque ornamented like the skirt, rounded in front and with revers trimmed with a ruche and flounce, and looped up in the middle of the back. Bonnet of brown velvet and black lace. Long feather forming a diadem.

...

Only the smallest kind of crinoline or hoop is worn, just enough to make a person walk comfortably, if the dress be either long or short; the hoops should in no instance meet in front, either at the top or bottom.

...

TRIMMING FOR DRESSES.

...

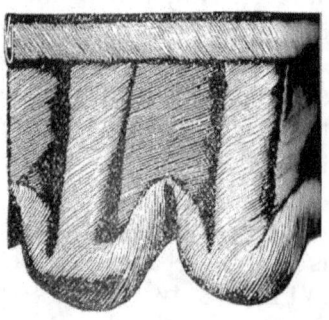

BLACK SILK UNDER-SKIRT.

A very useful under-skirt, which may be put on under almost any dress, is represented in an engraving in the front of the present number. This under-skirt is made of black silk, and it trimmed with a deep puffing, fastened down with a narrow scalloped-out edge, and with a flounce put on with a heading and scalloped out on both sides. All the scallops are edged with black satin. The shape and style of this under-skirt may be copied in a cheaper material, if wished.

...

For the street, the lower-skirt is trimmed with either one deep ruffle, or several narrower ones, or with puffings, quillings, etc., as the fancy may dictate.

...

HOUSE-DRESS.

Fig. VIII. – Gray Silk Dress, trimmed in front with a deep flounce surmounted by a wide velvet cross-strip. Long tunic forming a train behind. Corsage with long basques in front. Short basque behind laid in three wide plaits. The corsage opens shawl-fashion, and the basques are trimmed with a wide satin cross-strip. Sleeves plain to the elbow, with a satin cross-strip and bow; wide on the fore-arm, slit up and trimmed with deep, white lace. ➜

...

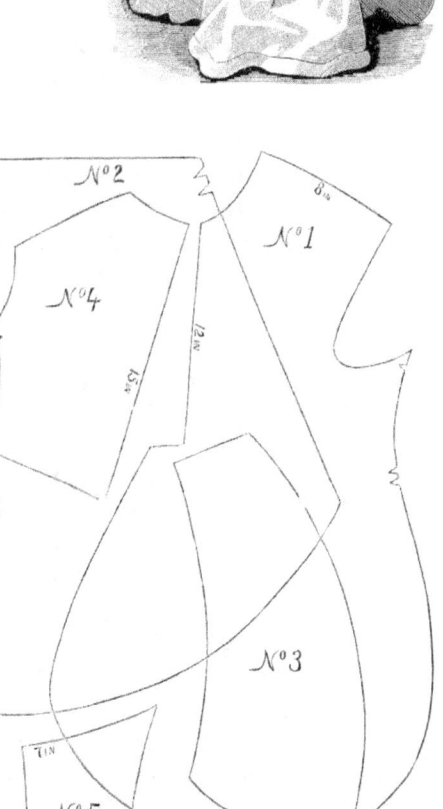

THE CHEVALIER CASAQUE.
By Emily H. May.

We give here an engraving and diagram of one of the newest and prettiest affairs of the season.

It is called "The Chevalier Casaque," and the pattern consists of five pieces, which represent half of the Casaque: Front, back, pannier, sleeve, and gauntlet.

Our model is trimmed with lace and *ruche*. The trimming is laid on the bodice to simulate a square-cut one.

The front joins to the back according to the notches at the edges of the paper. The *panier* is gathered into the back of the waist; the sides of the *panier* are likewise gathered, and the sides of the fronts wrap over the *panier*, and are fastened with either a bow or a gimp ornament. A waistband and short, bunchy sash complete the *Casaque*, which is just the thing for out-of-door wear in the spring.

Very short jackets, slit up the back and under the arms, so as to give room for the pannier, and with long flowing sleeves, will also be worn on the street.

...

JACKET: FRONT AND BACK.

... a fine white jacket for the house, and to be made without sleeves. This jacket is trimmed with a row of velvet all around, and with two other rows at the bottom; the back of the jacket is slit up behind; and it has a black velvet collar, and is fastened in front by one large button.

Peterson's Magazine, April 1870

The costumes *camaïeux,* that is to say, Cameo Dresses, (Cameo meaning two layers of different tones), in two shades of the same colour, are very much in fashion this Spring. Here are some new models, not yet out, which merit special attention, and which are the novelties of the season.

A visiting costume in *poult de soie,* mastic grey and light Havannah brown. The under skirt is trimmed round the bottom with a pleating in Havannah *poult de soie.* Above this pleating, which does not measure much more than three inches in depth, is another flounce, ten inches deep, in the mastic grey *poult de soie.* This flounce is composed of large pleats and of smaller ones, alternately, at equal distances. Above this flounce, a small pleating in Havannah brown, forming a double heading. A very narrow piping serves for the upper skirt, trimmed like the under one; *pouf* gathered at the sides and back, and raised in the middle. Pointed body, *moyen age* style, open in front *en châle,* trimmed with two pleatings, one Havannah brown, and one mastic grey; Postillion with large pleatings behind. Sleeves plain to the elbow and terminating in large pleats, which fall open in order to let the under sleeves of lace appear. ...

Another new style: the under skirt very much trimmed round the bottom, long upper skirt, open in front, and raised at the back and sides. This tunic is trimmed with a ruche of silk and a deep fringe; it is worn without a ceinture. Ceintures, or sashes, are, indeed, every day going more and more out of fashion; the corsage with a basque, and corsages tightfitting, are preferred. The voluminous bows so much worn last year, and which seemed indispensable with the short costumes, are replaced by a very modest bow, which is placed at the waist, but *in front* now instead of *behind.* This new fashion of placing the bow, not having yet scarcely appeared, if at all, we hasten to apprise our readers of it. Fewer square bodies are worn also, or bodies trimmed squarely; the vest form, with basques, is adopted, and all dressy corsages are opened *en châle* – that is to say, heart or V-shaped.

...

For walking costumes, either silk, poult de soie, poplin, cashmere, or fancy stuffs, are better of one plain colour than striped patterns, or figured, which are preferable for summer wear, or evening or dinner dresses. Almost all the costumes consist of a first skirt trimmed with small or large flounces (the latter are prettier, with a tight tunic forming a second skirt, coquettishly raised), or of a first skirt always flounced, and of a second skirt forming three pouffs, with a body with basques, piped in front and plain behind. Sometimes these basques, very long in front, form a Louis XV. vest, whilst a big bow with wide, short ends, is placed at the back of the waist. Basques of all sizes and kinds this season, bodies with waistcoats open, heart-shaped, showing pipes of muslin, or a waistcoat with a Eabrielle [sic: Gabrielle] collarette.

As trimming for poult de soie costumes, we know nothing prettier than ravelled-out ruches of the same material (we employ the term as being the most intelligible). This ravelled silk as a ruche produces a feathery effect, very soft and not easily understood – indeed, this is the advantage of its originality. Below these ruches, a silk fringe or a border of lace about four inches wide, and you have the most charming trimming for a dress that can possibly be imagined.

Muslin pleats, trimmed with Valenciennes, not only for going round bodies, or for stomachers, cuffs, &c., but for a double flounce round the hem of the first skirts of costumes, round tunics, and second skirts of silk or foulard. With light colours, these white trimmings, a trifle below the hem, will be charming; and with darker colours, they will be very stylish.

The Milliner and Dressmaker, April 1870

We give, first, a walking-dress of buff or white pique. The under-skirt is cut with the front width gored, two side widths, also gored, and two plain widths for the back. The back widths to be gathered in large French gathers. This skirt is trimmed with a flounce nearly three-eighths of a yard in depth – quite that deep, including the heading. Top and bottom of the flounce are scalloped out, and trimmed with black velvet ribbon, or, what is better for washing, alpaca braid or narrow mantua ribbon. Five widths of the pique will make fullness sufficient. Upper tunic is cut perfectly straight all round, and long enough to touch the top of the flounce; three widths, two in the back, and the front one cut in half, and gored; put on a separate band, baking it long enough to clasp a little in front. Scallop out to match the flounce, and loop at the sides. Plain, high bodice, and coat-sleeves, trimmed to match. Small cape, with basque ends, to cross in front under the waistband. From fourteen to fifteen yards of pique with be required for this dress.

...

The fashion of wearing two skirts may be turned to good account, however, by those who possess a number of light-colored dresses of thin material; since by cutting the gored skirts shorter they can be made fuller at the waist, and the piece taken off the top will form a trimming for the front of the under-skirt. A tunic or train, open in the front, displaying the under-skirt very long, and disposed in short puffs, *en panier*, at the back, with a low or square bodice, will form a toilet at once fashionable and effective. The upper-dress may be of the same color as the under one, but always of a darker shade. ...

Married and single ladies' toilets differ considerably, according to the latest styles, and this is no more than they ought to do. Young ladies' dresses are uniformly made very simple, of tarlatan, with draperies and narrow flounces. They are either quite white, or quite pink, or light-blue or green. The toilets of married ladies, on the contrary, are rich and elaborate. The tunic does not exclude flounces, nor a double skirt, nor a train, and the under-skirt is always very much trimmed. Most frequently the toilet is composed of a light dress, placed over a slip of silk, all the front part of which is covered with light trimmings, flowers and lace; then with a second dress, the train-shaped skirt of which is made so as to be able to carry it over the arm; this second dress is of rich silk material, and is not much trimmed, excepting with cross-strips, loops, or pleated ruches of the same materials; for ladies have experienced that light trimmings become far too much spoiled in balls, where the crowd is almost always too great. The low bodice opens in front upon a plastron of lace, to correspond with the under-skirt. This train, thrown over the arm, very much frightens many young ladies, it, in fact, requires much grace. For those who do not feel the courage to adopt this duchess-like fashion, trains are made to be looped up at pleasure, by a very easy process.

Peterson's Magazine, May 1870

No. 959 B. – No. 1. Visiting Dress. – Green *poult de soie* skirt, plain and train-shaped, plain in front and gathered at the back. Bodice with vest in front, postillion at back, lace *collarette* and *jabot*. Coat-sleeves trimmed with satin of the same shade. Black cachemire paletot trimmed with a wide silk biais. The paletot is open high at the back and sides, and trimmed with a headed fringe, wide page sleeves. The paletot is slightly shorter in front than behind. Bonnet of black tulle, forming half-cap, lace ruches arranged as a diadem, and curtain, with bouquet of flowers forming the shape of the bonnet.

No. 2. Walking Dress. – Grey sultane of two skirts; the first trimmed with two flounces composed of one fluted flounce, of a ravelling, and two crossway strips forming the heading. Second skirt composed of three widths, two wide ones at the sides, and one shorter behind. The tunic has two long points at each side; it is trimmed with a ravelling, surmounted by a niche like the first skirt; and round berthe and wide sleeves. Shorter basques in front to the corsage. Pleated muslin collarette and sleeves.

Jacket bodies are quite come back into fashion again, but *sans exclusion* of round waists. Bodies with points are also in favour once more, so that every lady may choose for herself what best suits her figure. Almost all dressy toilets are made with a bodice open in front, either in a pointed or square shape, and the great *luxe* of modern toilets is the elaborate chemisette, fully trimmed with embroidery and lace.

Never, indeed, were the triumphs of our lingeries so great as this year. The plain linen collar is quite given up. In these days there is an end to simplicity, the merest morning toilet is now adorned with frill and ruching of dainty Valenciennes lace.

The flowing peignoirs – in winter of soft quilted cashmere, in summer of clear muslin trimmed with Valenciennes and bows of coloured ribbon – are things essentially French, and they are veritably charming. The French lady will wear her *costume de matinée* in perfect style, and all beautifully matched, from the coquettish little cap to the dainty fairy slipper, and including the smallest details of trimmings, ribbons, ruches, or pipings. In this way there is a very large business to be done by English houses, if they can get public taste directed properly through the magazines which are received in society – such as the "Englishwoman's Domestic Magazine," and others.

In *robes de chambre,* we have seen a pretty new model. The dress is made princess fashion, but fitted in at the waist, and with a postillion basque at the back, while in the front it is trimmed all the way down with cross-way bands and small bows. The model was of pearl grey *toile de laine.* The cross-way bands and bows of the same material were all piped round with cerise-coloured silk, and the basque and waistband were piped to correspond. This would also look very pretty, with a blue or mauve trimming.

For the summer, the *robe de chambre, or matinée* as it is now called, is of white cambric muslin over the pink or mauve silk; strips of insertion edged with lace, take the place of the cross-way bands above described, Valenciennes lace edging that of the pipings, and the bows are of ribbon to match with the silk lining.

...

The camaïeux costumes, or cameo dresses, which we noted last month, are worn very much at present; they are made in two shades of the same colour, light green and dark green, light blue and dark blue, mastic grey and light Havannah brown. The under skirt is in the dark shade, the tunic or upper skirt in the lighter; corsage in the dark and sleeves in the light shade. It is the fashion at present that the sleeves should be different from the corsage. Thus, with a dress striped black and white, the body will be in black *poult de soie,* and the sleeves striped like the *jupe.* This fashion may be adopted with dresses of every shade and colour, and produces, in the hands of a skilful artist, a not inharmonious effect. But there are dangers in this kind of dress to those who have not a good eye for colour, or possess but indifferent taste.

...

White bodices are much gone out of fashion, being exchanged for pretty chemisettes to accompany low dresses or those that are open in front. These chemisettes, embroidered and trimmed with lace, are a luxury in good taste. For some time past, as noted, ruches of tulle, clear muslin, or lace, have taken the place of plain collars. This is extremely becoming. Another pretty fashion is that of muslin fichus, trimmed with embroidery and Valenciennes lace, worn with low dresses. These are the real coquettish *fichus menteurs* of the last century, and it is a fashion very becoming to thin ladies.

While recommending to them these fichus, they may be warned against the bodices cut low and square in front; this style of bodice has the effect of showing the chest narrower, and is suitable only to stouter persons.

When a lady has a perfectly good figure, she may wear any thing she chooses; but when, which oftener happens, let it be whispered, she has an excess of thinness or of embonpoint, certain details it is well to observe to her.

To ladies gifted with embonpoint may be suggested dark materials, long waists, but few flounces, and those placed very low down, the train-shaped tunic rather than the double skirt, no puff, at the utmost a wide sash, the loop of which puffs out the tournure a little behind.

Thin ladies may allow themselves many more complications in trimming, draperies and puffs; fichus, chemisettes with thick bouillons, flowing lace, light or white materials, all these suit them beautifully. They may also wear with advantage, the small loose flowing jacket, slit open at the seam, and half-open in front to show the chemisette and its ruffles. It is really not because Parisians wear toilets more beautiful or rich than those of ladies of other lands, that they always look so nicely dressed, but because they almost all possess the art of dressing according to their own peculiar figure, tournure, and countenance.

This is an art which every lady should endeavour to acquire, and her dressmaker should be her teacher, for she is in the position of the artist who poses and drapes his model.

...

No. 41. – Dress of maroon mohair and light Havannah silk. The skirt is trimmed at bottom with three flounces – two silk ones, and the middle one maroon mohair; the top flounce is scalloped and ornamented with a button in each point. Plain bodice of mohair under a tunic of Havannah silk. This tunic is scalloped all round, open in front, rounded at each side, and looped up in the middle of the back. Deep scalloped cuff of silk on the plain mohair sleeve. Bonnet of *crêpe de chine,* havannah, and maroon, adorned with a tuft of feathers of both shades. Maroon parasol.

Costume of foulard. The under-skirt is made of violet and white striped, and trimmed with two cross-cut bands. Upper skirt of crêpeline, the same shade of violet as the stripe; this skirt is trimmed with a flounce bouillonné and a fluted heading. Bodice of striped foulard, with plain pointed basque in front; the revers and long hanging sleeves are of crêpeline trimmed to match the upper skirt. The basque of bodice forms a postillion behind. Collarette of fluted muslin.

The Milliner and Dressmaker, May 1870

Summer toilets exhibit quite a marked change from those of the six months preceding. The short overskirts, very *bouffant paniers,* and short, bunched-up sashes, although seen, perhaps, more extensively than ever upon the street, are giving way, in more private circles, to softer, more flowing and graceful styles.

The introduction of *crêpe de Chine* as one of the most important fabrics for dressy toilets, has created, or revived the taste for yielding, delicate materials, and supplanted the stiff stuffs, which hardly required the addition of patent linings, to make them take any shape or form required.

The change is decidedly advantageous, so far as simplicity, and the quantity of material required, are concerned. Overskirts are longer; but they do not cut up, or cut into, or waste the material in bunching up, as the short ones did. Moreover, they are more confined to ceremonious toilets – the outside garment simulating an overskirt upon walking-dresses.

Very elegant dresses are now made of white, pink, or blue *faille* (corded silk), trimmed upon the front *en tablier,* and having a long overskirt of the China *crêpe,* the shade of the silk, bordered with crimped fringe to match. The low bodice is trimmed with fold of China *crêpe,* and fringe.

Quite an innovation is announced in Paris by the new leader of fashion, Mme. Ollivier – that of high-necked dresses for evening wear. The lady, it is said, not only wears them herself, but has intimated her desire that ladies who frequent her *salons* should follow her example.

Such a style, should it become general, would cause nothing less than a social revolution abroad, where low necks, for "full" dress, have been as long and as firmly established as class distinctions. Here we are only just acquiring, through the influence of the imitative, traveled class, all the bad habits which, with them, have been the growth of centuries, and should have less difficulty in getting rid of them.

GEORGETTE SASH.

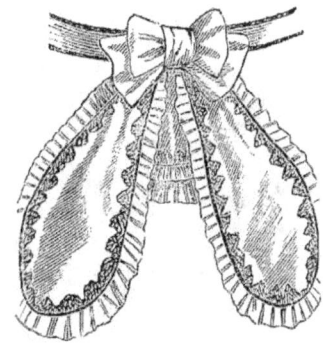

A stylish sash of silk, trimmed with a ruching of the same and black lace, separated by satin piping. The ends are sixteen inches long, by seven inches wide at the broadest part, and are set slightly apart on the belt, so as to show a box-plaited postillion, eight inches long by eleven inches wide, which is placed underneath.

THE ELFRIDA BASQUE. – (*Front and Back Views.*)
Our model for this stylish basque is made in heavy black *gros-grain*, trimmed with satin folds, and leaves of *gros-grain* bound with satin, having in addition, on the back of the basque, *guipure* lace falling from under the points. It would be a very appropriate style for any other goods, without the lace, and with folds and bindings of silk.

...

The fashionable Polonaise opens in front, is rounded off only a very little, and is full at the back, which is cut out separate from the waist, and gathered into the sides so as to form side *paniers*. The sash fills up the space at the back. Twelve or fifteen yards will make a suit of this description, unless much trimming is required.

Flat braids trim linen and *pique* very nicely – are very cheap, easily done up, and wear as long as the material – so, of course, they must continue to be the most popular finish.

Embroidered ruffling, unbleached *guipure*, and black velvet, undoubtedly produce more distinguished effects, but they are too costly for ordinary wear, by ordinary people.

...

THE AMARANTH.

A walking-costume, to be made in *chene* mohair, trimmed with bindings and folds of brown silk, edged with white silk star braid. The skirt is ornamented with two bias flounces, the lower one five, and the upper one ten inches deep, each bound with silk. The lower flounce is finished at the top with a fold of silk, and the upper one forms a ruffled heading above a similar fold. A series of ruffles about five inches wide (including heading) are arranged diagonally on the skirt, commencing about six inches above the heading of the upper flounce, and continuing about the same distance on the flounce. These ruffles are trimmed to correspond with the flounces, and are finished at each end with bows. The front ruffles are continued up to the waist, being slightly graduated toward the top. Waist high, with a pointed cape simulated by a ruffle surmounted by three folds of silk. Postillion sash trimmed to match, and ornamented with bows.

...

ZENOBIA BASQUE.

This is a convenient arrangement, by which a round waist may be transformed into a suitable outer garment for a walking-costume. The waist is ornamented with *revers* and a sailor collar, which may either be placed on or simply outlined by the trimming. It will be noticed that the *revers* commence at the belt, so as to give the appearance of a vest underneath. The waistcoat-shaped basque in front, and the postillion at the back, are attached to a belt, and left slightly apart at the sides. We give two views of the economical arrangement, so that it can easily be copied from the illustrations.

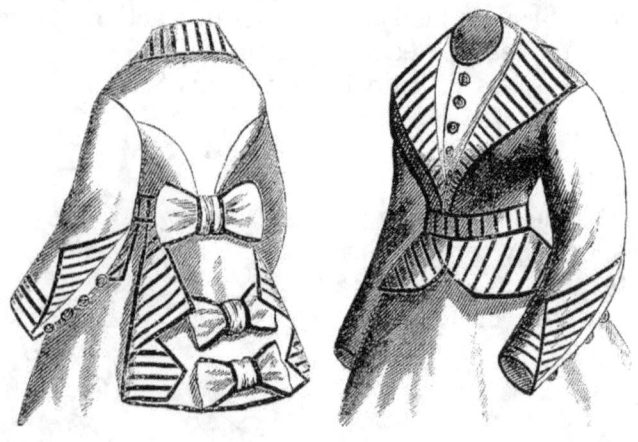

THE VERONICA SLEEVE.

A graceful combination of the close with the flowing sleeve. The lower part is trimmed with a bias band of the material edged with black velvet, and the upper part with machine-fluted ribbon. Two bows of the material, also edged with velvet, are placed on the upper part of the sleeve.

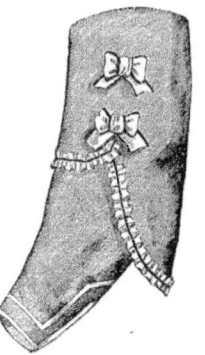

THE VERONICA SLEEVE.

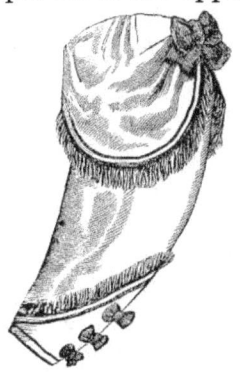

JENNIE SLEEVE.

JENNIE SLEEVE.

A plain coat sleeve, with deep cap cut round, caught up on the top with bow and short ends. The cuff at the wrist is very deep and pointed, and has three bows on the back. The whole trimmed with heavy fringe, edged with two rows of velvet or braid.

THE "PURITAN" SLEEVE.

This is a good sleeve in alpaca, shepherd's check, or French poplin. It is trimmed with flat plaitings of the material, inclosed between rows of machine-fluted ribbon. In all-wool back and white check, with quilling of black velvet, it is very effective.

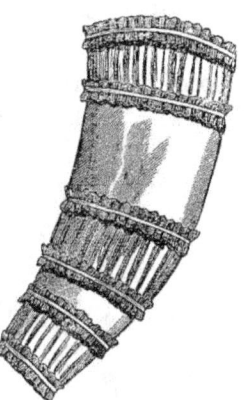

THE "PURITAN" SLEEVE.

THE OLLIVIER SLEEVE.

A plain coat sleeve, trimmed, on the outer side, with bands of velvet or silk, in the manner shown in our illustration. It is a very pretty sleeve, suitable for a walking-costume or any plain house-dress.

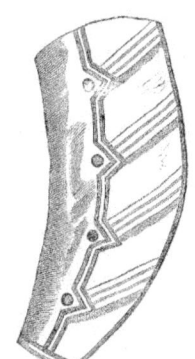

THE OLLIVIER SLEEVE.

CASTLEREIGH SLEEVE.

A plain coat sleeve, trimmed at the bottom with a box plaited ruffle four and a half inches wide, held in place by a cuff cut in squares about two and a half inches wide, turned up from the bottom of the sleeve. The ruffle and cuff are bound with velvet, or trimmed to correspond with the dress. A cap at the top to match the lower part of the sleeve, only a little deeper.

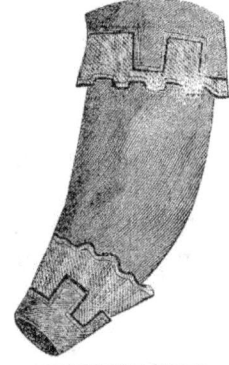

CASTLEREIGH SLEEVE.

THE "LÆTITIA".

A particularly graceful sleeve, suitable for thin goods. It descends nearly to the wrist, and is just flowing enough to be comfortable and not in the way. The puffs are each eight inches deep, including the narrow ruffle at the edges, and are, of course, a little narrower at the inner seam. The space between them is five inches, and the ruching, with which it is ornamented, the same width. The width of the flounce at the bottom, including the narrow ruffle, is five and a half inches.

THE "LÆTITIA."

"Dear Demorest – 1st. I have a very handsome blue silk to make for spring wear, and twelve yards of knotted fringe to match. How would I best cut it so as to be able to wear it for four or five years? Would it not be best to cut the skirt plain – not gored – and of moderate length, with coat sleeves and plain waist? If so, how trim it?

"2d. How do you put wiggan in the skirt? and what depth?

"3d. In cutting a dress gored in front, with plain widths behind, do you round the plain widths *at the bottom*, to form a train, or have them straight, and turn down the top so as to form it?

"4th. Are walking-dresses made with plain widths behind? and if so, how do you make them hang gracefully?

"5th. Is white striped muslin made into suits for summer wear – and how made? when worn?

"6th. When are black silk overskirts worn – and what kind of body accompanies them? Are they worn with low bodices on the street, and to church? or are they reserved for evening wear? M.R.P."

Ans. 1st. You can gore the front and side breadths by turning them in, without cutting. Train the skirt moderately, and make a short overskirt, which trim with the fringe. Make the body high and plain, and trim it either to form bretelles, with fringe and feathered-out ruches of the silk, or a very low square. Coat sleeves somewhat loose at the wrist, and worn with lace undersleeves. Sash – the ends trimmed with fringe and ruches.

2d. Cut it to fit, and put it between the silk and the outside lining to the depth of a quarter of a yard.

3d. Round them off at the bottom.

4th. There is no difficulty, especially as almost every lady wears a small *tournure*.

5th. Yes. Exactly like other thin and some thick suits. Trim with ruffles.

6th. Black silk overskirts are worn with all sorts of dresses, at all sorts of times, and upon all sorts of occasions. They are sometimes worn in the evening, but are so useful in dressing up a plain toilet, for home and ordinary wear, that they are generally employed for this purpose, and more fancy colored silk, satin, or white muslin overdresses reserved for evening.

...

LIDA OVERSKIRT.

A tasty overskirt, easily arranged, and appropriate for almost any material. The back is formed of two full widths, thirty-one inches long, looped carelessly in the back, and gathered all the way to the waist on the sides, where they are attached to side gores. It has no apron front, but there are two sash-shaped gores on each side – the back ones measuring twenty-one inches to the extremity of the points, fourteen inches where they are joined to the back widths, and twelve inches where they are joined to the front gores. They measure nine inches across the widest part, and slope to four inches at the waist. The front gores are of the same width as the back ones, but about two inches shorter, and are rounded off in the front to the waist, where they just meet.

...

Scarfs are just now more fashionable at the neck than ribbon bows. They are knotted, and the ends tucked in like those of a gentleman. Netting silk scarfs tied in a bow, with fringed ends, are also worn. ...

"French waists" are made plain upon the shoulders, and gathered, back and front, into a belt. They are not lined, and are finished with a narrow ruffle of lace or of the material, and are closed at the neck with a brooch. Your striped goods would form the *under* dress better than the overdress; the latter should be of plain material. A walking-skirt should clear the ground.

Demorest's Monthly Magazine, June, 1870

For travelling costumes, small tight-fitting jackets are very convenient, as they are the more comfortably worn under the useful waterproof – the indispensable companion of all who travel.

Among new trimmings are ruches composed of strips of silk, unravelled, so as to form a fringe, up to two-thirds of their depth, which varies from three to four; placed double, these ruches resemble the trimmings of curled feathers worn this winter. They are put on as heading to flounces, or round the edge of tunics and double skirts.

...

The new printed muslins are very pretty, in patterns of flowers, of natural colours, thrown upon a white ground; or again, flowers *en camaïeu,* with foliage of the same colour as the pleats. They are trimmed with flounces headed with ruches of self-coloured cambric, matching the principal colour of the dress; these ruches are pinked or trimmed with narrow Valenciennes lace.

...

Dresses of unbleached foulard, and also of the unbleached linen so much patronized for summer toilets by Parisians, are now trimmed with point-lace work; muslin dresses are also ornamented with this style of work, which many ladies delight in making.

A very pretty dress of cambric muslin, trimmed in this style, is made with a jacket, and a small pelerine, open at back. The skirt is trimmed round the bottom with a muslin flutting [sic]; above which, there is a deep border of point-lace work, and the work is continued *en tablier* over all the front part of the dress. The jacket is merely edged with a muslin fluting, but the pelerine is entirely made of point-lace work, with a vandyked edge. The sleeves are demi-wide, and ornamented with a fluting and work to correspond. Such a dress looks sweetly pretty upon an underslip of coloured silk, with sash to correspond. It is a lovely morning toilet for the summer.

...

And now to turn again to the subject of the new summer costumes. The first thing to be remarked is, that the second skirt is extremely short; it is, in most cases, open in front and puffed out at the back to make a full *tournure*. The jacket bodice is often preferred to the round-waisted corsage, and the *confection* is most frequently half-fitting, and very much cut out and slit open in different places to show the trimmings of the dress. These trimmings are most elaborate. A mere flounce is considered no trimming at all: it must itself be trimmed with flutings, pipings, cross-way bands, fringe, lace, and what not – a flounce is in itself quite a study for the couturiere, and even for an under skirt it is put on with two or three fluted headings, scalloped out and piped, and finished off with something or other.

The new costumes are extremely elegant. Light-coloured silks compose under skirts trimmed with piped flounces, divided by draperies or scallops, which form a very handsome *tout ensemble,* even without the help of lace. The upper skirts are often made of black *faille,* trimmed with flutings piped of the colour of the under skirt. But by far the most graceful style is that of the second skirt, thrown back at the side, slightly looped up in some places, and coming down rather low behind, where it is still open in the middle. These upper skirts are often made of grey *poult de soie;* they join on to a high bodice without sleeves. Such upper dresses look extremely well upon under skirts of cerise, blue, or orange silk, in which case the toilet becomes very dressy.

...

We see many wide and demi-wide sleeves, though tight ones are also frequently worn. In this, as in everything, each modiste can follow her own taste, but of course the sleeve should correspond in shape to the style of the dress.

...

The strangest thing of all is, that while most toilets imitate the Lous [sic] XV. style, with looped-up skirts, aprons, and tunics, draped with large bows, the headdresses partake rather of the modes of the First Empire, though on a reduced and modified scale, happily, so far.

Thus there is a want of harmony in present fashions, but they are altogether so fanciful that they may be forgiven for not adhering to any general rules.

And yet there are a few rules to be observed; that of the *tournure* is one of the most important. It must be full and *bouffante,* but this should be managed with the jupon, over which the dress has then only to fall in full pleats and gathers. The best tournure is that of white horsehair, arranged in a number of puffs, and finished off with a flounce. This tournure should be worn over a scant jupon, having only a few steel or whalebone circles round the bottom. To wear with train-shaped dresses a flounce should be adapted to the jupon, cut on the cross, gored and lengthened at the back so as to support the train. This flounce can be buttoned on so as to be taken off at pleasure, for with the walking costume of course the short jupon is more convenient. Two skirts, a plain one and a flounced one, are required to wear over the jupon. Under dresses of light material, the second skirt should be of starched muslin, with a deep flounce. Of course, if an under skirt form part of the costume, it is sufficient to wear one plain skirt under it.

For demi-toilette there are very nice skirts of a somewhat stiff light woollen material, striped grey and white, which would look well with almost any dress. They are made with a gathered flounce, put on with a double-fluted heading. The same model in percale, striped black or lilac blue, or red and white, is also very nice for summer wear.

The new skirts of white alpaca, trimmed with flutings edged with black, or with any colour to match with the dress, are much admired. But the complete costume is now so almost exclusively fashionable that there is not so much variety in under skirts as there used to be.

Flounces are not now considered in themselves sufficient trimming; they must be completed by fluted headings, crossway bands, bows and loops of ribbon. Never were trimmings more elaborate than they are now.

Plate No. 961.

Travelling Toilet of Belgian material. The skirt trimmed with a deep flounce, the heading composed of a bouillon with a fluted edging, similar to the dress, and of two cross strips of crêpe de Chine of a rather dark colour, with fringe to match. The skirt forms a puff looped up at the side with a scarf of brown crepe de Chine. Bodice with plain basques, forming- a waistcoat in front, trimmed with a cross strip of crepe, with fringe and a fluting of the same material. Round berthe formed by the trimming, Wide sleeves trimmed with a flounce, a cross strip of crêpe de Chine and fringe. ...

Dressy Country Toilet of Pompadour foulard. First skirt trimmed with a high fluting at intervals. Second skirt shorter in front, longer at the back, and draped at the sides, forming a puff behind. The trimmings consist of slightly waved flounces of cherry-coloured silk covered with flounces of black lace. Jacket bodice with waistcoat. The jacket forms two long basques, rounded off on both sides with large pleats en *postillion* at the back.

...

In costumes there is the Camargo, very charming in deep blue poult de soie, with first skirt just touching the ground, trimmed with a deep flounce cut on the cross, and with an apron of small pinked-out flounces. Over this first skirt falls a tunic, cut out into points, ornamented with flounces of unbleached Valenciennes lace. The bodice of the tunic is a jacket, with simulated waistcoat of unbleached Valenciennes lace. Bows of blue ribbon complete the trimming.

And the Pompadour costume of unbleached twilled foulard, composed of two skirts and a jacket elegantly embroidered with garlands of flowers in all their natural tints. These flowers vary according to taste; they are roses, or violets, or convolvulus, or field-flowers mixed with the unripe wheatears: all look fresh and pretty.

For the country, dresses of unbleached linen are in great favour. They are now trimmed with borders in point-lace work. This modern point-lace is preferred to all other kinds of lace for trimming the pretty dresses of unbleached *toile d'Irlande* now so fashionable. The point-lace borders, worked with braid outlines filled up with lace stitches, are put on plain above the hem of the skirt; patterns are sometimes made to come up over each width, or else to cover the front of the dress only, *en tablier*. Again, on some of the dresses the point-lace border simulates a tunic, or a double skirt and a plastron or braces upon the bodice. In our wholesale warehouses they sell trimmings of what they call *dentelle Anglaise;* this is, in fact, an imitation of point-lace work. It is done by machine, not by hand, and is not, of course, nearly so pretty as the delicate work of lace stiches which English ladies are said to be so clever in producing. We say English ladies, for French ones, or at least Parisians, though they admire the work, do not seem to possess sufficient patience or industry to apply themselves to it, so they procure it readymade, or, as it is very expensive, are content with an imitation which falls far short of the original patterns.

...

TRIMMINGS.

The extraordinary quantity and variety of Trimmings used upon modern dress is not likely to diminish until "costumes" become a thing of the past. The costume, whether black or coloured, demands and requires not only ruches and gimps, passementerie and headings, but ornaments – agrémens, as our French neighbours term the adornment complete in itself, now so much in vogue upon all toilettes with any pretence at fashion or richness. To name the well-known house of Richard Evans and Co., of Watling-street, appears all but superfluous, so accustomed are large mercers and mantle houses to connect this name with the best and newest trimmings of every kind. Still lesser stars in the drapery world, and our foreign and colonial subscribers, will gladly read of the novelties manufactured and imported by this noted firm, which is always foremost in following the capricious footsteps of Parisian fashion.

Four large houses are devoted to the display of a large and well-arranged stock, which is kept in perfect order, and for selection is most convenient.

The black and coloured dress and mantle fringes are headed with passementerie and various headings, and are either crepe or crimped, and plain. Fancy crimped tassels and agrémens are also in endless variety. Another heading for fringes is a satin rouleau or band; and another fringe is called the *effilé* from its appearance of being ravelled out from rich *poult de soie*. Beaded gimp headings are placed above plain fringes with great effect, and the fringed braids and scintillating fringes are among the newest kinds.

Satin trimmings of every kind and class of exquisite design and finish are made in all colours, shades of colour, and in black. Lace fringes form another trimming department, where all lace suitable for mantle houses is edged with short or long, plain or ravelled, fringes.

The black and coloured buttons in passementerie and gimp, the netted buttons and crape ornaments, the handsome fringed agrémens now used to raise the artistic folds of all stylish mantles and dresses, the jet and fancy ornaments, form several departments. The coloured St. Etienne trimmings, the satin and rep St. Etienne, occupy warehouses exclusively devoted to these deservedly favourite trimmings. For braids, Messrs. Richard Evans offer some very cheap lines of Llama, mohair, fancy mohair, and cotton braids, these last being both white and coloured, as well as an immense selection of Hercules and Breton and Adelaide fringed cotton braids.

No. 52. – Toilets For Flower Shows, Visiting, &c.

1. Dress of green *poult de soie*. The train skirt is trimmed with two gathered flounces. The second one is shorter, and has a fluted heading. Plain bodice and coat sleeves. Low tunic without sleeves, made of silk grenadine with satin spots. This tunic is long at each side, forms a Watteau behind and fitted to the waist in front by a band passed under the Watteau pleats; it is trimmed with a band of satin and lace flounce. Hat of English straw, lined and bound with black velvet. A green feather is placed at the back.

2. Dress of unbleached twilled foulard, trimmed with bands of maroon crêpeline placed lengthwise on the bodice and skirt to simulate a tunic with fringed ends. The bands are longer behind, trimming the skirt nearly to the bottom of the train.

The Milliner and Dressmaker, June 1870

The modistes and coutureures agree that the prettiest costumes of the season, either of silk or fancy material, or both combined, are made with a jacket bodice, the basques of which are elaborately trimmed. No mantle is required. The trimming often simulates an open jacket, or rather *coat,* in the Louis XV. style.

The most fashionable of all trimmings this summer is white lace. Old point-lace stands first on the list, then point Duchesse then guipure d'art, and imitations of old point-lace. Next to lace, the favourite trimmings are bands of English embroidery, and flutings of white gauze or muslin – either plainly hemmed or edged with Valenciennes lace.

Unbleached lace, whether Valenciennes or other, is used to trim dresses of the colour of unbleached linen – *écru* – which are much in vogue this summer. Thus, not only the dresses of unbleached linen or foulard, but those of a number of fancy materials of that colour are ornamented with strips of insertion and edgings of the *dentelle écrue*.

Thus, there is making, a costume of Indian silk of the *ècru* colour, trimmed round the bottom with a deep gathered flounce; the skirt is covered from the waist down to the heading of the flounce with bands of pleated white muslin, divided by strips of unbleached lace insertion edged with narrow borders to match; the last (upper) band, however, which is deeper than the others, is not pleated, but merely gathered round the top. Short loose paletot, with wide open sleeves, forming a deep point at the back. The paletot is covered with white muslin, which however, is pleated round the edge only, and ornamented with unbleached lace insertion and edging. Lappets of similar lace are placed upon the epaulettes.

Another pretty costume is made of mouse-grey *mousseline de soie*. The under skirt is trimmed with a deep flounce put on with a heading, the upper skirt is looped up on both sides. Jacket bodice, loose and slit open at the back, tight-fitting and open *en châle* in front, fitted to the waist with a sash, the long rounded lappets of which fall at the side. The wide open sleeves, the outline of the jacket bodice, and the sash, are all trimmed round with Cashmere pattern of many colours worked in Indian embroidery. A straw hat trimmed with a bouquet of various flowers, and a gray silk gauze scarf completes this elegant country toilet.

...

Plate No. 965b.

1. Sea-side Costume of white foulard, spotted with black. The skirt trimmed at the edge with a deep flounce, with a double heading composed of two cordings of cerise foulard, separated by three rows of black velvet. Bodice without sleeves, open in front *en cœur,* and showing a Louis XV. waistcoat. This bodice has long basques forming a tight-fitting casaque; the trimming is of black velvet with a heading of cerise foulard, and forms a puff at the back. Chemisette with collar of cambric, with Valenciennes jabot, with sleeves to correspond. Hat of English straw; the brim raised on one side with, *crêpe de chine* scarf, and spray of wild flowers, and ears of corn arranged as an aigrette.

2. Costume of Green And Gray. – The first skirt is plain, and of green foulard, second skirt of grey silk is trimmed with a pleated flounce, headed by a green ruche; the skirt is slightly raised on each side. Louis XV. bodice, cut low, square, and with deep basques, trimmed with a grey ruche, with crossway rouleau of green foulard in the centre, cambric collar with jabot, and sleeves of Valenciennes lace.

...

Another tasteful costume for the country or seaside is one of white chaly; first skirt scalloped out, and bound with black velvet, second skirt very short, bridled in front, and rounded off at the sides. This second skirt is scalloped out and bound with velvet like the first, but it is more over-trimmed with a deep flounce of black lace, *dentelle des Indes,* which is put on just under the edge of the scallops. The bodice is a very short, loose, and rounded off jacket, trimmed exactly like the second skirt; the sleeves, very wide and rounded off to the elbow, have a double trimming of velvet scallops and black lace border. The short upper skirt is fastened behind with a large bow of black *crêpe de Chine* with long lappets edged with lace. A chemisette and under sleeve of Bruges lace give a nice finish to the dress.

The *costume complet* is also made of the richest materials, and trimmed with the best point-lace, for elegant visiting or reception dresses. Few have trains; when they have, the train is independent, and is put on under the second skirt, forming a *manteau de cour.*

...

Foulard toilets are much more prized in France than in England. A very young married lady has ordered for the country one of twilled foulard with cherry and white stripes; the skirt, bordered with a narrow flounce, in hollow plaits, white, with a fringe, and surmounted by two cherry cross-strips; apron fixed by bows, half-white, half-cherry, which are repeated on the sleeves; these last are rather wide, but taken in just below the elbow by three hollow plaits. Basque very full and raised to the hips, trimmed with a deep white fringe having a gimp head as light as guipure. High boots to match the dress. Almost a basket of cherries on the head. Bonnet of English straw, with brims turned up. No strings, but wide lace barbs, proceeding from behind the head and fastened on the breast by a bouquet of cherries.

...

At our good *couturières,* travelling and seaside costumes form the main attractions, and these may be subdivided under many other appellations – the excursion, the Alpine, the waterside, and the railway costume – the costume for the short, easy journey, which is but a party of pleasure, and the costume for the real serious *voyage,* which should be comfortable, and proof against rain and dust. Again, for the seaside, there are walking, driving, riding, and bathing costumes; the costume for the *matinee* on the beach, and the costume for the evening, for the concerts and balls in the casino or *salon de conversation.*

The style of costume which appears to us the most to be recommended for travelling is that in which all elaborate trimmings in the way of flutings and ruches are eschewed. Trimmings are liable to catch dust, very liable also to get caught in odd nails and cranks about railway platforms or steamboat decks and cabins: those who have known such a trial will shudder at the remembrance.

Plain *toile de laine* costumes, trimmed with wide bands of velvet, are about the most appropriate dresses of all for anything like a lengthy or continued journey.

Many ladies prefer black silk to anything else for a journey. It is ladylike, certainly, but has one great drawback; black silk shows dust more than anything else, with the exception, indeed, of black cashmere or other woollens.

Now, as dust is the very greatest enemy of our ladies' toilets during the hot summer weather, it is best to choose for a travelling costume its own colour, dust-grey, which is indeed very fashionable this season. If a lady wish it to be very elegant, she may have her costume of twilled foulard. It is a most pleasant material to wear in summer – very cool, very light, and not liable either to tear or to crumple. ...

The most fanciful travelling, or rather excursion costumes, are very generally of some pretty fanciful material, much trimmed with flutings and crossway bands, with silk pipings of a darker shade. It is, in fact, much akin to the walking costume. The dress is made with a jacket bodice, dispensing with any separate *confection.* The basque of the jacket is often lengthened into coat lapels, or else it is a postillion, while the front part is made like a Louis XIV. waistcoat, with a double-fluted jabot in front.

For excursions in the mountains, a special costume has been decreed by fashion – it is called the Alpine. The costume is made of fine white woollen serge. There is a short skirt, trimmed with five rows of dark blue velvet, of graduated widths. A second skirt is short and bridled in front; it is long behind, but very gracefully looped up with a scarf of blue grosgrain silk, which is also put on over the bodice, across the left shoulder, The bodice is high and plain with a double row of blue velvet buttons down the front, and a band of blue ribbon, put on so as to simulate an open jacket, rounded off at the sides, and continued behind, round the edge of a postillion basque. This basque forms two double pleats, fastened down with buttons. The sleeves are tight, and trimmed with bracelets of blue velvet, and a ruche of old guipure lace. A similar ruche is placed around the neck.

This costume, completed by a Tyrolese hat of white straw, turned up with blue velvet, and trimmed with bluish-black feathers, is quite *distingué.* With it ladies use the long walking-stick for climbing mountains, with sunshade of unbleached foulard at the top. Another article of the costume, though it should be invisible, must be mentioned; it is the *pantalon,* of the same material as the dress, which is worn underneath, and comes down almost to the ankle.

...

No. 59. – Walking Toilets.

1. Dress of pearl-grey twilled foulard, with plain train skirt, Bodice with plain basque in front, and postillion behind, trimmed with black velvet and pearl-grey fringe. Mantle of a new shape, forming a small Arabian hood. This mantle is made of white velvet, and trimmed with rouleaux of black satin and wide broom fringe. Hat of grey straw, trimmed with pearl-grey ribbon, and a tuft of flowers placed in the centre.

2. Dress just touching the ground of thin buff-coloured woollen material, trimmed with gathered flounces bound with black velvet, and surmounted with a wide heading, composed of a fluting turned

down, a bouillon and two flutings standing upward. Second skirt very short, of light maroon foulard, trimmed with cross-cut bands piped with black, and a maroon fringe. Short paletot open behind and at the sides, and large sleeves cut up to the elbow. This paletot is trimmed like the upper-skirt with bands and fringe. Oval hat entirely covered with field-flowers. Unbleached silk parasol.

...

The most remarkable novelties of the season are the white trimmings in muslin, embroidery, and lace, which are put upon coloured silk and fancy material dresses. Fringes are also very fashionable – knotted fringes, with a network heading filling up the intervals between the Vandykes or round scallops in which the material is cut.

...

No. 60. – Evening Toilets.

1. Dress of white tarlatane, with a deep pleated flounce round the bottom. Long tunic, draped and looped up in several places with sprays of lilac. Waistband of grosgrain silk, fastened behind with a spray of lilac. Low round bodice, buttoned in front, and ornamented with a drapery of tarlatane and sprays of lilac on each shoulder; very short sleeves. Diadem of lilac, with long spray falling on the chignon.

2. Dress of maize silk, with plain skirt. Tunic of *crêpe de chine* of the same shade as the dress: it is very short in front, with train behind, and trimmed with Bruges lace surmounted with black velvet and a fluting of silk. Three velvet bows ornament each side, and join the front of the tunic to the back Two very large sash-ends are trimmed to match the tunic, and form a second skirt over the train. Bodice open in Louis XV. style, trimmed with velvet and lace. Large pagoda sleeves, with bracelet above the elbow of velvet and lace, and fastened with a velvet bow. Maize satin shoes.

...

No. 65.—Model Of La Czarina Costume, showing mode of arranging drapery. (See No. 67.)

...

No. 67. – La Czarina Costume. A rich costume designed and executed by the noted house of MM. Jourdan & Aubry, for the lady of a South American President. The skirt and bodice are of a rich grey *poult de soir*. The second skirt which forms a train, and drapes the shoulders, is composed of black *drap de France velouté*. This costume is trimmed with black lace of four different widths, of the same pattern. Grelots of artistically carved jet, half hidden in the folds of lace, produce a brilliant effect. At the edge of the first skirt of grey *poult de soie,* is placed a pleated flounce, with a corded heading and bouillonné. Bodice with short basques at the back, and with waistcoat in front, sash with long ends of the same shade as the first skirt. Bonnet of English straw entirely covered with flowers, diadem of flowers, and gauze scarf of the same colour as the

costume. No. 65 shows the mode of arranging the Czarina upon the shoulders, where it is kept in position by two buttons placed on each side of the upper part of the arm.

...

In spite of the outcry against crinoline, it is still, in a modified form, *de rigueur*. Completely absent for a few months from the salon and from the promenade, two causes have conspired to reproduce the mode, and to establish a moderate-sized skirt apparently *en permanence*. One of these causes may be found in the exceedingly awkward gait induced by the embarrassment occasioned by the clinging drapery of jupons and costumes; the other is to be seen in the very excellent model of crinolines supplied to modistes by first-class manufacturers of corsets and crinolines.

The Milliner and Dressmaker, July 1870

PATTERNS FOR BRAIDING
By Mrs. Jane Weaver.

We give, in the front of the number, three different patterns for braiding on pique dresses; with black, white, or colored binding. All are new and tasteful patterns.

...

Thin ladies may allow themselves a great many more complications in trimming, draperies, and puffs; fichus, chemisettes with large bouillons, flowing lace, light or white materials, all this suits them beautifully. They may also wear with advantage, the small, loose, flowing jacket, slit open at the seam, and half open in front, to show the chemisette and its ruffles. It is not because Parisians wear toilets more beautiful or rich than those of other ladies that they always look so nicely dressed; it is because they almost all possess the art of dressing according to their own peculiar figure, *tournure*, and countenance. This is an art which every lady should endeavor to acquire.

Peterson's Magazine, August 1870

A black grenadine dress is a great resource, to modistes who have to dress with both elegance and simplicity. The grenadine dress should be worn over a black silk skirt with low silk bodice, to be truly elegant. A very pretty toilet of this sort was seen lately in the Champs Elysees, trimmed with a number of narrow flounces, put on with a heading, and edged on either side with a narrow rouleau of black satin. The high bodice was very slightly opened, *en châle,* on the bosom, edged with a ruche, bound with satin, and *inside,* a border of Bruges lace, rendering the opening so small that it was almost entirely filled up with a large locket in gold and enamel, suspended by a double gold chain, joined together at equal distances by gold and enamel balls to match with the locket. A pleated basque at the back of the bodice, edged with a flounce similar to those upon the skirt.

...

The Froufrou muslin dresses are tasteful and coquettish. The muslin is white, with a very small pattern of coloured flowers, rosebuds, Parmese violets, blue cornflowers, pansies, daisies, and so on; and there are bands for the trimmings with garlands of flowers of a larger size, *à disposition.* The skirt is trimmed with a number of flounces; the tunic or second skirt with one flounce or fluting. This second skirt is generally bridled a little in front, looped up with bows or rosettes at the sides, and longer behind, with a full tournure at the top.

In plain white muslin we have the Merveilleuse dress, trimmed with flounces, and the loose paletot to match, with cutout square basques, and edged all round with a fluting. ...

Flutings of white muslin are put on us a trimming to silk dresses; they are placed rather wide apart, so as to show the silk material between. These flutings are sometimes merely hemmed round; sometimes they are edged with narrow Valenciennes lace.

Flounces or richly embroidered muslin are placed upon silk dresses, rose-coloured, pale blue, mignonette green, mauve, maize, or cerise; each flounce is headed with a ruche imitating the petal of some flower according to its colour – cornflowers, peonies, dahlias, variegated carnations, and so on. The flounces cover the lower half of the skirt, and the bodice, open in front *à la Raphael* – that is, in a square or *en châle* – is lengthened into *gilet* basques, and a postillion at the back. ...

The Empress, at her last ball, wore a pink dress of extreme simplicity, arranged in a manner quite novel. No paniers behind, but only a wide waistband of pink moire attached to her toilet with infinite grace. On the front of the dress, a rounded apron of pink China crape, trimmed with three rows of silk ruches and white lace. Ruches and lace at the bottom of the dress. Round her neck a black velvet sparkling with diamonds; in her hair light clusters of pink flowers

...

Plate No. 966.

Dinner Dress of black crape, or with crossways of green silk over a foundation of the same silk. The train-skirt is trimmed in front and all round with white lace and crossways of silk, covered with bows placed at short distances. Bodice low and square, with short sleeves, and basque rounded in front, and with a puff of green silk at the back. Both bodice and sleeves are trimmed, and match the skirt. An aigrette, placed at the side of a diadem of green ribbon, forms the coiffure.

Toilet for Seaside and Watering-Places. – Skirt of mauve foulard trimmed at the edge with three gathered flounces, edged by a small flounce. Serve tunic of striped grenadine, raised on each side, and at the back, and trimmed with fringe. The revers trimmed to match; sleeves tight to the elbow, and wide at the wrist. High collarette.

...

The Watteau style still prevails indeed in our fashions. Our *grandes dames* dress themselves like marquises or like Florian's shepherdesses. We see none but materials of insipid colours – the *ecru* tints, more or less golden, pale yellows, water greens, frosted lilacs and pinks, azure blues, and then the whole collection of grey tints, fawn-colour, light browns, orange shades, apricotine, lavender, *aventurine,* and so on. Such shades are pretty in silk, crape, crêpeline, and foulard, but they are not very suitable to cheap materials, and seem made only for elegant and well-trimmed dresses.

We must, however, make an exception in favour of the unbleached Irish linen and batiste, which are much sought after; but can we indeed place such materials among cheap ones? scarcely. In good quality such unbleached tissues are of rather a high price, and if one considers the elaborate trimmings with which they are overloaded, one will soon perceive that this style of toilet is still somewhat of a luxury.

Our *élégantes* place this summer their dresses of unbleached batiste amongst their freshest and prettiest toilets.

...

No. 70. – Walking Toilets For The Country.

1. Toilet of pearl-grey mohair, under-skirt quite plain, upper-skirt forming a pouff behind, is trimmed with a deep flounce, bows of black velvet on each side, and a broad velvet band across the apron front. Bodice with short round basques; the revers and waistband are of black velvet. Rice-straw bonnet with turned-up brim, trimmed with white lace, bows of black velvet, and a tuft of pearl-grey feathers.

2. Dress of Havannah-coloured foulard. The skirt is trimmed behind with four flounces headed with a pouff. On each side a trimming of unbleached foulard simulates a drapery fastened at equal distances with bows of Havannah ribbon. A very deep flounce ornaments the front, headed with a drapery to match the sides, and a fluted heading. Half-fitting casaque open in front, and the basque cut up under the arm. This casaque is edged with a narrow gathered flounce of unbleached foulard. Pagoda sleeves with *creves,* slashes at the back to show puffs of unbleached foulard ornamented with three Havannah ribbon bows. Very small hat of Havannah straw adorned with tea-roses.

No. 74. – Visiting Toilets.

1. Dress of lilac foulard, with train tunic, plain behind and trimmed in front with violet fringe headed by a coquillée ruche of the same shade to simulate an apron; casaque bodice with pouff behind. This bodice is open *en châle;* the basques are rounded and trimmed with a ruche and fringe fastened at each side by a bow. Fichu of Bruges lace, coat-shaped sleeve. Hat of rice-straw, bound with black velvet and ornamented with violet feathers flowing behind.

2. Dress of nankeen and Havannah foulard; the first skirt of Havannah colour is trimmed round the bottom with two gathered flounces of nankeen, three narrow Havannah ones, and a fluted heading of nankeen-coloured foulard. Plain tunic of nankeen, long behind, very short in front, and forming points on each side. Bodice of nankeen, with long basque trimmed with a gathered flounce, three folds of Havannah, a fluted heading, and a bow with flowing ends joined to the tunic. Sleeve trimmed with a flounce and Havannah folds to match. Charlotte Corday fichu of nankeen foulard, with folds of Havannah getting gradually narrower towards the front, where it is fastened by a bow.

The Milliner and Dressmaker, August 1870

We give next a very pretty and inexpensive home-dress. It is to be made of striped mohair or poplin: mohair is the cheapest material; the best is double width, and cost from forty to seventy-five cents per yard. Poplins are more expensive, costing from a dollar to a dollar and fifty for one of a good quality. Fall "reps" sell for about sixty-two cents. Any of these materials are suitable for early fall wear, and about twelve yards are required. The waist is a plain, round one, and trimmed in the front to simulate a surplice. The trimmings are all of black silk, consisting of a bias fold upon the bottom of the skirt, which fold should be lined with black crinoline, as it makes the silk look thicker, and consequently makes a richer-looking trimming. The fold is from two to three inches in width: and the "bows" are to be made also of the bias silk, (lined,) around the bottom of the skirt they are placed at intervals of nine inches. The cuff and piece for the body may easily be cut from the engraving. A sash of blue ribbon (or one made of the silk is less expensive) completes the dress. There is little if anything new in the cut of skirts; the front breadth gored, and the side breadths; fullness at the back, which seems to be indispensable.

NEW MODE OF LOOPING UP A SKIRT.
By Emily H. May.

In the front of the number, we give two engravings, showing a new mode of looping up a skirt. To loop up a skirt in the manner seen in these illustrations, sew a number of small rings down each side on the wrong side, and draw through these rings a silk cord on either side, by means of which the skirt is taken up. The rings must be sewn on at intervals of about four inches. One end of the cord is fastened below the lowest circle; the other end is drawn through a slit made in the skirt in front at the waistband on the right-hand side of the skirt; sew on tassels or buttons at the ends of the cord, so as to prevent its sliding back through the slit. This manner of taking up dresses is very suitable for such as short trains only. If the train of the dress be very long, two other

cords must be drawn though two other rows of brass rings in the middle of the back, taking the cords double. All these cords are drawn at the same time though the slit at the side of the skirt, fastening likewise tassels or buttons at the ends. The process is both simple and effective.

...

The Short Skirt, we are glad to chronicle, still holds its own, at least for walking-dresses. It is too comfortable to be given up without a struggle. The most simply constructed upper-skirts are most stylish. There should be no set pieces at the sides trimmed all round, and no panier puffs behind. They should be very long, fuller than the under-skirt, and are frequently only draped at the sides, the back hanging plainly, or being opened in the center and trimmed to the belt. Forty inches is the average length of the back of over-skirts. This is, in many cases, as long as the lower-skirt, consequently the upper-skirt must be draped by tapes attached under the belt and buttoned over loops half-way down the seams. Square tunic-skirts are made of four straight widths of three-quarter materials shaped longer toward the back, left plainly open in front, simply trimmed all around, and draped in the way just described. Apron fronts are now made of a straight width of three-quarter materials, and a single side-gore rounded up to the belt. The front width is not sloped in the least, is scantily gathered to the belt, extending far back on the sides, while the narrow side-gore is very full at the belt. The long back widths are then sewed to the sides, where the only drapery is made by gathering up the side-seam from three fingers below to a very small space just beneath the belt. This give the increased size necessary on the hips. If it produces a fold or two, or wrinkles across the lower part of the apron, these or not objectionable.

...

SLEEVELESS JACKET AND TUNIC.
By Emily H. May.

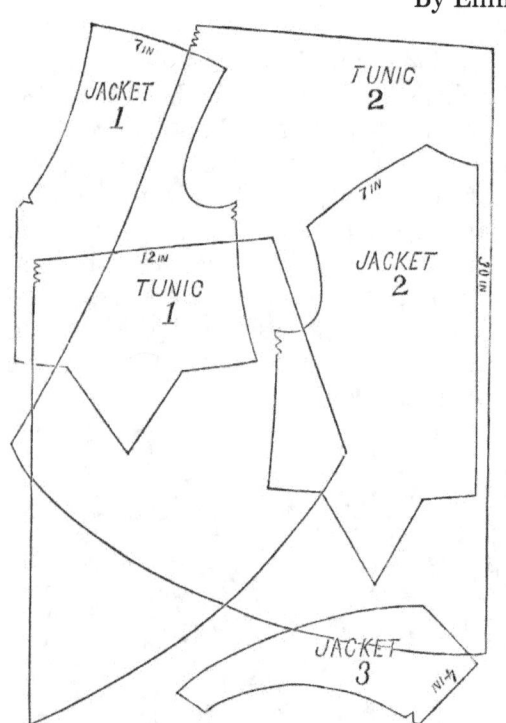

In the front of the number, we give another engraving of a full-length figure, show two articles, a Sleeveless Jacket and a Tunic, both intended for morning wear, and for washing materials, although the jacket could also be made in scarlet flannel or bright velvet, and braided with either gold or *soutache*. There are three pieces for the jacket, as will be seen from the diagram annexed, Nos. 1, 2, and 3, representing the front, half of back, and *revers* and collar combined. These represent one-half of the jacket. There is one notch in the front, and a corresponding notch on the *revers*, showing how the latter is to be laid on the jacket, which, as seen in the engraving, is open at the throat. There are two notches under the arm, indicating how the back and front are joined; the back is straight, and there is no necessity for a join down the center. If made of *pique* or brown Holland, the whole should be edged with Madeira work, the frill round the armhole being made to fall upward over the jacket, instead of downward over the sleeve. For mohair or alpaca, the jacket should be edged with fringe.

There are two pieces for the tunic, for which also see the diagram tunic, Nos. 1 and 2. The front is the smaller piece; it has three notches on the side, indicating how it is to be joined to the corresponding notches on the back breadth. The tunic is open in front, and at the side-seam a casing is run on the wrong side; a tape is fastened at the lower edge of the tunic, and carried through the casing to the waist. This tape can be drawn up according to taste, and be let down when the dress is to be washed. The skirt is trimmed (see engraving) with Russian plaitings, headed with bands of the same, or with braid. The bodice is plain, and the coat-sleeve is trimmed at the wrist to correspond with the skirt.

Peterson's Magazine, September 1870

Plate No. 971 B.

1. Alpaca Travelling Dress. – The skirt is trimmed with scalloped bands and narrow crossway band of violet silk ribbon. The scallops are notched. The tunic is open in front, gathered at the back, and raised by a trimming formed of a flounce edged and headed by notched scallops similar to those on the skirt. Half-fitting paletot bodice; the back is raised at the sides, and forms a puff at the back, ornamented with the same trimming. Bonnet of English straw, with tuft of feathers and ribbons, to match the shades of the toilet.

2. Visiting Costume of grey and black silk. Skirt of grey silk, trimmed with alternate flounces of black and grey. Tunic fitting to the figure, open at the sides, raised, and edged with pointed scallops of black silk. Tunic-sash of black silk cut out in deep points. Bonnet of grey *crêpe de chine,* trimmed with black ribbon, and with a tuft of grey and black feathers.

...

Sashes have much diminished in volume, often indeed none are worn with costumes which have tunics. The double skirts are now exchanged for dresses with jacket bodices, the basques of which, very much trimmed and draped, take the place of a second skirt. A great many tunics of white muslin over a skirt of coloured glacé silk or foulard are still to be seen trimmed with narrow flounces. The tunic is ornamented with fluting edged with narrow lace and with strips of Valenciennes lace insertion or embroidery. For the autumn, these tunics will be made of white woollen tissue; they are drawn tight across in front, and are draped into a puff at the back. The bodice is slightly open in the shape of a heart. These tunics are often trimmed with black lace, sometimes there is besides a handsome llama fringes, with tassels and a network heading. White jackets and mantles, trimmed in black or colours, are still the most in vogue for the country or sea-bathing places.

...

No. 81. – VISITING AND COUNTRY TOILETS.

1. Dress with train skirt of maroon foulard, trimmed with wide and narrow bouillonnés divided by unbleached Cluny lace. Tunic of unbleached foulard, without sleeves, entirely edged with Cluny lace to match the skirt. Maroon sleeves, with frill and bouillonné at the bottom trimmed to correspond. Bonnet of maroon gauze with ribbon strings of the same shade. It is ornamented with an unbleached feather placed on the top.

2. Toilet for a young lady in white mohair. Under-skirt trimmed with a wide pleating. Upper-skirt rounded in front and behind, very short at the sides, and edged with pleating. Bodice with basque cut in square tabs, and trimmed with narrow pleating. Hat of English straw with turned up brim, lined with black velvet. A tuft of blue feathers is placed at the side and flows behind.

...

In the making of dresses there is also an important change. It is no longer the two skirts and bodice, it is the skirt much trimmed, and the jacket bodice. What is now called the tunic is, in fact, a jacket bodice with long basques.

...

Then the *gilet,* or waistcoat, is coming into fashion again, to wear with the jacket bodice, open in front. The lace ruffle and jabot will be *de rigueur,* and form a very elegant finish to the toilet, together with the lace cuffs to match, falling over the hand. ...

It is strange to note the influence of great events upon even the smallest of trifles. The war will not be without effect upon our fashions. ... Even in our *grandes dames'* most elegant toilets a great many models savour of the warlike propensities of the times, and the most successful at this moment are the Franc-tireur blouse, or tunic, the Tyrolienne vest, and the Cantinière jacket.

The Franc-tireur blouse is of white cashmere, richly trimmed with coloured velvet and embroidery; it is worn as a tunic over a silk dress.

The Tyrolienne is a gracefully-cut jacket of coloured cashmere cloth, elaborately braided with silk soutache of a darker shade.

And the Cantinière jacket of dark blue *taupeline,* piped with black faille silk and satin, is tight-fitting at the back, half-fitting in front, and cut out into separate square basques; it is lined with fine red flannel, and sometimes ornamented with black silk braid-work. ...

The Franc-tireur blouse is also made sometimes of white muslin trimmed with Mechlin or Valenciennes lace. It is also made of cambric, trimmed with English embroidery, of grenadine, with silk cross-strips and fringe, and of foulard with guipure d'art or Bruges lace.

...
No. 82. – COUNTRY AND SEASIDE TOILETS.
1. Dress of mauve sultana. The first skirt is trimmed with a wide pleated flounce, ornamented with festoons of violet ribbon, and bows on the heading. Tight-fitting casaque, forming a round apron in front and skirt behind, trimmed with a flounce to match the under-skirt. Similar trimming forms the round berthe, with bows on the shoulders and wrists. Hat of English straw, bound with black velvet, and ornamented with a garland of ivy falling over the chignon.

2. Toilet of stone drab and maroon. The skirt is trimmed at the bottom with bands of maroon, placed slanting. Upper-skirt plain behind, with striped side-piece and sash to match. Bodice with basque, long in front and short behind, and bound with maroon. Pagoda sleeves with striped cuffs. Maroon cravat. Rice-straw hat, ornamented with autumn foliage. A maroon frou-frou gauze scarf, and ribbon string of the same shade tied on the chignon.

The Milliner and Dressmaker, September 1870

Materials and Trimmings, formerly confined to evening toilets, now appear in full daylight. Even the simplest costumes, that is, those which, by their material, pretend to be no more than demi-toilet, have most elaborate patterns and trimmings. Velvet ribbon is profusely used for trimmings on all materials, and one of the newest styles of making deep flounces, is to place perpendicular bands of velvet ribbon of any width that suits the taste (it should not be less than one inch in width, however,) between the plaitings of the flounces. A very little gold is sometimes used on black trimmings, but it is not in good style to use it too lavishly. Fringes are very much used, and nothing can be prettier than the little narrow moss-fringe, which is so soft, and can either be used alone, are as the heading of a longer fringe.

Peterson's Magazine, October 1870

Crinoline skirts are made about two yards round at base, with very large tournures. Corsets are longer at waist, and slender sizes are manufactured in large quantities by first-class houses. There has been observable of late years a tendency to return to the stern lacing of "Puritanic stays," and now that the world of fashion is deprived of its leader the ex-Empress of the French, all eyes turn to the Empress of Austria, whose known beauty and devotion to *modes artistiques* point her out as the next in command. As for Berlin taking the place of Paris in matters of fashion and dress, the idea is preposterous. Should the Empress of Austria accept the vacant throne of *La Mode,* we may indeed look for tight-lacing with a vengeance, and our manufacturers must be prepared to supply twelve and sixteen inch corsets. The cestus of gold worn by the Empress of Austria shown at a recent international exhibition measured under fifteen inches.

No. 101. – Indoor Toilets.

1. Dress of grey poplin, with five flounces of different widths, edged with a fancy satin trimming. Upper-skirt cut in deep points, edged with satin, and ornamented with bows. Bodice open *en châle,* and edged with satin. Hanging sleeve, trimmed with a flounce and satin heading; two rows of trimming simulate an epaulette.

2. Dress of blue silk, just touching the ground, trimmed with deep fringe and scalloped bands of the same material, edged with black velvet and arranged in Vandykes. Tunic upper-skirt, forming a Vandyke on each side, and flowing behind; it is trimmed with fringe and scalloped bands to match. Bodice open *en châle,* and trimmed with fringe and bands to correspond with the skirt.

...

Fashion being, to a certain extent, "the reflection of the times," it can hardly be supposed that the present war will be without its influence on styles of dress. What that influence may be cannot be immediately discerned. Parisians at this time are occupied for the most part with other thoughts than those pertaining to the latest modes; yet a reference to our illustrations will show that the designs brought out are eminently graceful. Heaven be thanked for the instinct of the carrier-pigeons and the service of balloons. Well, in the future, shall we use fashions *à la militaire*? We opine not. When the present contest is over, the world will only be too glad to throw away warlike considerations. The genius of France, so conspicuous in art, design, and manufactures, will shine with a purer lustre. Germany never yet made any contribution to fashion. She has appropriated and adopted French modes – and that is all. At the present moment the fashions of Paris prevail in Berlin, as at Brussels, St. Petersburgh, London, and New York. France has much to give, nothing to receive, and the world must continue her debtor. The Tartar hordes that swept, centuries ago, over Europe, introduced certain features of Eastern costume yet observable among the races of Russia, with its blended European and Asiatic ideas. The Moors introduced into Spain gorgeous barbaric vestments, indicative of barbaric taste, which looks mainly to richness of material for asserting social rank; and the rich ecclesiastical vestments of Spain, and the gifts at Catholic shrines now being scattered to the four winds of heaven, bear tokens of her influence. Only gradually is the world educated to those high ideal tastes of which Parisian fashions are the most exquisite exponents. If we may venture on a prophecy for the future, we would say that when the tide of Prussian invasion which has paralysed the industry of France, shall have rolled back, and the arts of peace again resume ascendency, we shall witness possibly more subdued, but not less elegant styles than those which have hitherto prevailed. Nothing can be more charming than the fashions of the present month.

...

No. 104. – Indoor Toilets.

1. Dress of violet cashmere, with long train under-skirt; upper-skirt, forming tabs of different lengths, trimmed with fluted flouncing and bands of satin. High bodice, with long hanging sleeves trimmed to match; waistband fastened with a double bow of black velvet. Coiffure cap of point d'Angleterre, ornamented with velvet ribbon.

2. Dress of green Irish poplin, trimmed with a deep flounce, and headed with a bouillonne. Bodice cut square in front, trimmed with point-lace and black velvet. A pleated muslin fichu is worn inside; sleeve with frill at the wrist, and cuffs underneath; bands of black velvet are worn round the head, and fastened on the top with a rosette.

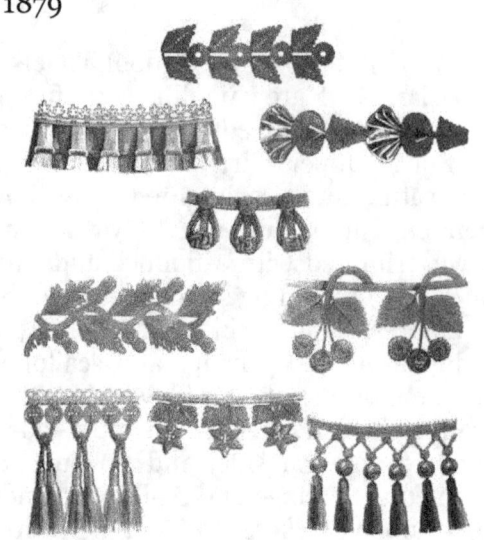

No. 106. – Dress And Mantle Trimmings.

We are indebted to the house of Messrs. Barnett, Druiff, and Co. for these designs in trimmings.

No. 1 consists of a green fringe of silk, edged with velvet and headed by fringe lace of the colour.

No. 3 is a satin and silk cord dress trimming.

Nos. 2 and 4 are varieties of handsome passementerie.

Nos. 5, 6, and 8 are further varieties of the same class, jet being introduced in No. 8.

No. 7 is a handsome ball-headed fringe composed of tassels.

No. 9 is a tassel fringe with rich passementerie heading.

SKIRTS.

The newest modes in crinolines and over-skirts are extremely graceful. It is impossible that a modiste can succeed with costumes unless the under-skirts are arranged in accordance with the last modes. Many milliners, and indeed, most dressmaking houses of any pretensions to elegance, send out with their costumes, tournures and skirts. The house of Messrs. Sage and Hart, of 30A, Old Change, is noted for a constant succession of the newest modes in this *genre,* and the models now showing are certainly most elegant, The Austrian skirt is composed of horsehair crinoline, and is a demi-skirt with large train tournure to button on *à volonté*: the base of this graceful skirt is trimmed with a gathered flounce, which gives a soft appearance to the folds of the dress. The newest demi-jupon of Messrs. Sage and Hart is also composed of horsehair, and consists of a tournure and skirt in one, with bands of the same material in place of the tapes usually employed in demi-skirts: the base of this beautifully shaped skirt is covered with round flutings of horsehair at the sides and back; in front quite plain, in accordance with *la mode*. Every kind and class of tournure and panier is to be seen here, from the simple single flounced improver to the latest French model tournure, with its three deep flounces arranged on a fluted foundation.

The Milliner and Dressmaker, October 1870

No. 2 is a skirt of satin cloth richly braided and flounced. ... ↗

No. 5. Violet cloth jupon with deep flounce arranged vandyked box-plaits, with violet velvet trimming and velvet buttons; or can be had trimmed with plain braid and buttons. →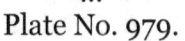

...

Plate No. 979.

Visiting Toilet. – Bonnet of black lace and black satin. The lace entirely surrounds a large handsome rose. The strings of this elegant bonnet are of satin and are tied beneath the chin. A plain satin dress. Tight-fitting bodice with open sleeves. Velvet casaque forming tunic and trimmed with fans satin, gold buttons and silk tassels richly headed. If this *confection* made in cloth instead of velvet, it must be trimmed with gold tassels or with gold fringe.

Indoor Toilet. – Dress of mauve grey faille, with high bodice, trimmed with black lace. Berthe, round in front and caught up at the back. Long plain shirt, the back of which is trimmed with a lace flounce rounded on each side, and caught up at the waist. The half-open sleeve is trimmed with lace falling over the hand, and raised to a point on the elbow.

No. 110. – Evening Dresses.

1. Young lady's dress of clear muslin; the skirt is round in front, and train-shaped at the back. Two tunics are worn, each crossing over in front, forming scallops and floating over the train at the back. Low corsage with velvet bretelles and waistband, bows on the short sleeve. Fluted tucker, gold and velvet ribbon aigrette in the hair. Necklace of gold cord and tassels loosely tied. Artistic bracelets and antique fan.

2. Married lady's dress of faille silk, trimmed with rich lace, forming jabot; trimming at the sides and arranged as a flounce on the long train. Deep puff and basques trimmed with lace flounces and ruchings, and forming tunic skirt raised by bows at the back. Low bodice and very short sleeves trimmed with lace. Jet earrings, necklace, pendants, and bracelets. Tropical foliage in the hair.

← No. 111. – Indoor Toilets.

1. Dress of grey poplin trimmed with a flounce, two rows of pleating and putting between; long upper-skirt, trimmed with a pleating. Jacket bodice cut in tabs, and trimmed to match the upper-skirt.

2. Dress of ruby silk rep, trimmed with three flounces, divided by wide bands of black velvet. Tunic skirt with square apron, trimmed with a flounce and bands of velvet. High bodice and large open sleeves, trimmed to correspond.

The Milliner and Dressmaker, November 1870

Frills and flounces are not quite so much used now for trimming costumes as they were in the summer. Plain bands, rouleaux, and fringes are preferred for edging the pannier and tablier, as well as the jacket of winter costumes, always made of thick and rather unmanageable fabrics. The underskirt, however, is still most generally trimmed with either a headed flounce or a very deep plissé of the material – sometimes with two plissés.

Cloth can with difficulty be gathered into flounces, but it forms very nice plissés, which we think our readers know means a strip of material arranged in close flat pleats all lying the same way, arranged, in fact, like the folds of little boys' skirts in Scotch costumes.

Velvet and velveteen costumes do not require flounces or plissés of any kind, a very narrow band of dark fur or sealskin is the trimming which suits them best. It is put on much as it was last winter, upon the edges of both skirt and jacket.

Serge costumes may be trimmed with velvet, or with very wide ribbed braid. Serge is such a nice strong material, and so cheap withal, that it is still much worn, although French *drap de dame* is more fashionable. Very dark green, bronze, prune, chestnut, slate, felt, garnet, and claret colour, and various shades of brown, violet, and grey are the favourite tints this winter for both serge and cloth costumes.

The upper skirt or tunic almost invariably forms the rounded-off apron in front and the pannier at the back, while the underskirt is trimmed in various ways, according to the material, or left plain, if preferred.

The bodice is very frequently open in front, either in a square or pointed shape, even for morning dresses, or else the trimming simulates such an opening. Very deep fringe is the most elegant of all trimmings. It is often placed in two or three rows instead of flounces. Rows of fringe headed with a ribbon or silk ruche form a very pretty ornament for silk poplin and cashmere dresses. Both ruche and fringe should be of the same colour as the dress, though they may be of a darker shade. Sometimes the fringe is made in the following manner: the silk is cut in strips from six to twelve inches wide, and is ravelled out till only an edge of two-fifths of an inch is left. This makes an extremely light fringe, which is especially adapted to light-coloured fabrics, and therefore to evening dresses. ...

For a dress of woollen material we find it much preferable to put the trimming only on the skirt, so as to simulate an apron, while at the back there is really a double piece which is puffed out into a pannier. We have seen a very pretty camlet dress made in this way. The trimming was a narrow fluting of silk of the same colour; two rows of it were put on to form a rounded *tablier* in front, and two rows were put on round the pannier, which was divided in the middle so as to form two points. One row of the fluting simulated the outline of a square low *corslet* upon the high bodice, and also went round the throat and wrists, the sleeves being tight. The bodice had a round waistband finished off behind with a number of loops of ribbon. The skirt of this pretty dress was trimmed with two flounces about two inches deep, put on with headings piped with silk.

For walking costumes there is nothing more tasteful and ladylike than the shawl fabrics, with strips of another colour and fringe for the trimming. Also for Winter days we approve of the complete costume of waterproof tweed, consisting of skirt, tunic *à panier,* and loose jacket. There is a deep *plissé* upon the skirt, the fringed edge of which does not come quite down to the bottom of the skirt. The tunic and jacket are merely bordered with fringe.

Other waterproof suits are merely composed of an upper skirt, gored in front and falling in full folds behind, and cut out in deep scallops and neatly piped round the bottom; and of a loose jacket, also scalloped out in the same manner round the edge, and buttoned down the front. A turndown collar with revers, all piped with black silk, forms a nice finish to the jacket; the sleeves are loose and open. This suit is very nice to wear over any skirt, and may even be put on over a dress.

Even hats are made of waterproof tweed to match the costumes. They are perfectly simple and merely trimmed with *biais* and bow of the same material piped with black silk. It is so annoying to see the feathers of a hat completely spoiled by the vast amount of rain, that many ladies used to going out in almost any weather will gladly adopt the waterproof hat for decidedly wet days. On such occasions the less liable clothes are to get spoiled the more in really good taste they are – for nothing looks so wretched as a pretty but fragile toilette in the mud and rain – the prettier it is, indeed, the more wretched it appears – and who has not known the horrors of a white skirt when a shower has turned the roads to mire?

...

All evening dresses will certainly be train-shaped this winter, and made with the tunic *à panier,* with plain tablier in front.

Jacket bodices are very likely to supersede round waists even for ball toilets, the bodice to be made with points in front, and with a small basque at the back, which will lie over the pannier.

It was thought at one time jacket bodices would make panniers go out of fashion, but both basque *and* pannier adorn all the latest dressy toilets. Sashes, however, are very much given up, though bows are not by any means. In evening dresses the basque is always much trimmed with lace, or with flutings of crape or gauze.

...

The following is a handsome train dress composed by Worth. A long full flowing train of black faille, with French box-pleatings of the same alternating with white organdie pleatings. The "scarf tunic" has an apron front, is of pink *crêpe de chine,* and is edged with heavy silk fringe of the same colour: the ends are fastened behind and simulate a bow. *Crêpe de chine* bows loop the skirt. A low square sleeveless bodice *à la Paysanne* is worn over a pink silk bodice with sleeves having mousquetaire cuffs trimmed with black silk and pink organdie pleatings. ...

New corsets are made with decidedly longer waists. The introduction of the jacket bodice has hastened the increased length of waist.

Sleeveless jackets of velvet are made with deep basques, and are trimmed with Greek or Maltese lace; these are worn without waistbands, but the waistband without bow or trimming is allowable for young and slender figures.

Sleeves are all open, *demi-ouvert,* or *mousquetaire,* the sleeve *à coudre* with the flowers springing gracefully from the elbow, where it is confined by a bow and band of ribbon or velvet. ...

Down skirts are much used as jupons, both as under and over skirts. These skirts present a plain but handsome appearance and are covered in silk, satin, and printed cotton. The quilted satin jupon is less *à la mode* than that where the down is placed between runners.

Skirts of satin cloth are worn as jupons, and as short skirts. These are now made with rows of bouillons of the same material kept in position by doubly stitched bands. These bouillons are placed between rows of narrow loose flounces with covered hems stitched on the right side. These may be had in all colours and in mixtures of two, three, and four shades of the same colour.

Plain velvet jupons are also shown in great quantities in Brussels. These skirts are worn *ras de terre* under velvet or cashmere costumes.

It is observable that with black cashmere casaques coloured velvet jupons only are worn. The well-known fact that black velvet "kills" black cashmere is well understood the other side of the Channel; here, unfortunately, we see handsome cashmere suits absolutely trimmed with black velvet *en biais* and even with plain ribbon velvet.

Black velvet is a deep, satiny, shining black, with lights and effects of brilliant brightness: black cashmere, on the other hand, owes all its beauty to its deep, dull, soft blackness, and to the utter absence of silken shimmer and bright "high lights."

French cashmere is quite as costly as velvet, and is stylish *au plus haute degré;* it is little known and still less appreciated in this country, where it is confounded with French merino and other like fabrics. It is of all materials, whether in black or in colours, the fabric most suitable for home toilets and for everyday dress.

The Milliner and Dressmaker, December 1870

◤ The basque of gray cloth, of which we have engraved the both the front and back, is particularly stylish; it is trimmed with black velvet, and is very effective in consequence.

...

We also call attention to the basque of black velvet, of which we give front and back views; it is in an entirely different style from the gray-cloth basque, but will be liked better by many ladies. ↗

...

Fig. VIII. – High-Necked Evening-Dress, Made of White Muslin. – The skirt is trimmed with a deep flounce of open embroidery, put on over a flounce of blue silk; a quilling of blue ribbon heads this embroidery. The tunic, sleeves, and waist, correspond with the lower-skirt trimming, except that the ribbon is festooned above the flounce on the upper-skirt instead of quilled. A large bow at the waist, and double bows and ends at the bottom and back of the tunic, complete this beautiful costume.

...

Fringe is very much used, especially on upper-skirts; for cashmere this is very pretty and suitable, giving a richness to the dress, which makes it rival a silk costume. We must state, however, that handsome silk fringe is expensive.

...

Sashes are very much reduced in size; the new Grecian cestus promises to supersede them for evening wear. This newly-invented cestus is a richly-gilt ribbon, adapted to the figure with faultless accuracy, which, by means of an entirely novel fastening, enables the wearer to regulate the size to the greatest nicety.

Fig. VII. – Low-Necked Evening-Dress, Made of Maize-Colored Gauze, worn over a slip of the same color. The skirt is trimmed with three flounces, which pass all the way round, and by seven other flounces at the back, the front of the dress being made quite plain, and trimmed with five rows of narrow, black lace, separated by rows of black velvet; this trimming terminates in rosettes at the sides.

...

Under-skirts for short dresses touch the floor, except just in front, a pretty but untidy fashion, really less cleanly than a longer skirt, where the facing (which can be renewed) takes the soil. These under-skirts are between three yards and a half and three-quarters wide; the front width is but slightly gored, the side width much gored, and the two back widths not gored at all, but gathered as full as possible. The trimming of these skirts may, of course, suit the taste of the wearer. ...

The basque is so much newer than the sash and belt so long worn, that it is very popular; the basque may be either long or short, open at the sides, or the back, or not open at all. Some of the newest of Worth's dresses have points in the front, with a bow of the dress material at the back; others have a long, soft point at the back, with a belt going from the seams under the arms, fastened with a bow in front.

...

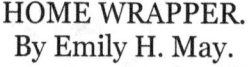

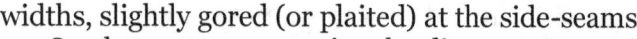

HOME WRAPPER.
By Emily H. May.

We give this pretty wrapper entire. For winter wear, we would suggest that it be made of colored flannel: either of one color, and trimmed with black velvet ribbon, or of plaid flannel. The one-colored flannel comes in single width, at from sixty to seventy-five cents per yard: the plaid flannel usually in double width, at from one dollar and twenty-five to one dollar and fifty cents per yards. Six yards of the double, or twelve yards of the single will be required for the wrapper. These flannels are easily washed, and look well until worn out, especially the plaid ones.

This Home Wrapper is so simple that it requires no particular description. The only essential thing is that the yoke should fit, and the length be right. For the fronts, on single width, with a small gore, will make enough fullness; for the back, three full widths, slightly gored (or plaited) at the side-seams.

On the next page we give the diagram. It consists of three pieces, viz:

No. 1. Half of Front.
No. 2. Half of Back.
No. 3. Sleeve.

We give, also, marked on each piece, the length. This, of course, is for a woman of ordinary size. It is hardly necessary, however, to have these length. All that is really required is to know the length of the person from the yoke. No two women, indeed, are of exactly the same height.

Peterson's Magazine, December 1870

1871

EVENING-DRESS. COLLAR AND SLEEVE.

Fig. VII. – Evening-Dress of White Striped Gauze Over a Yellow Silk Skirt. – This is trimmed with bias scalloped folds, bound with black velvet; the white gauze skirt is not very long, is trimmed with a full plaited ruffle, set on beneath a row of black velvet; and an upright row of blond lace; a puffing of the gauze is put on between this trimming and a narrower one of black velvet and blond; the white skirt is worn in the "court train" fashion over the silk skirt, not coming together in front. A slight pannier is formed at the back by drawing the skirt up with broad bands of black velvet, trimming with deep fringe. A short, plain tunic is also caught up by these bands of velvet. Waist high and plain, over a yellow silk under-waist; the half-long upper-sleeve is cut in points, and trimmed with velvet, beneath it is a deep plaited ruffle with a heading of black velvet, and beneath it is a deep plaited ruffle with a heading of black velvet, and finished by a fall of rich lace.

...

EVENING-DRESS. CHEMISETTE AND SLEEVE.

Fig. VIII. – Evening-Dress of Thin, White Muslin. – The skirt is short, and trimmed with one deep flounce, not very full, headed by a row of green ribbon, above which are two standing-up plaitings. A pannier of the muslin reaches to the top of the ruffle, and is caught up at the sides by a row of green ribbon, trimmed on either side with blond, and finished by a bow without ends; green ribbon around the waist, with bow at the back; low waist, trimmed with blond and green ribbon.

...

GRAY REPS COSTUME – FRONT AND BACK.

Figs. IX. and X. – Gray Reps Costume, (Front and Back Views.) – The round skirt is bordered with a twelve inch flounce, with a plaiting to match to form a heading, and measuring three inches. Tunic folded underneath in front; the skirt, full at the sides and forming at the back a point like a shawl. A plaiting loops up this tunic at the sides, is carried down the sides of the point to within six inches of the extremity, and is then carried up at each side to the waist. High bodice and basque, and black velvet revers to the waist. The bodice and basque are cut in a single piece; the latter forms two plaits at the sides, and terminates with a point in the center of the back. Two buttons mark the commencement of the plaits. Sleeves ornamented with a three-inch plaiting.

...

DRESS TRIMMING.

In the front of the number, we give an engraving of this pretty trimming for a dress. The scallops are of pinked silk, with stitched rouleaux running across. Under the scallops is a row of ribbon-velvet, and beneath this hangs a plain silk fringe.

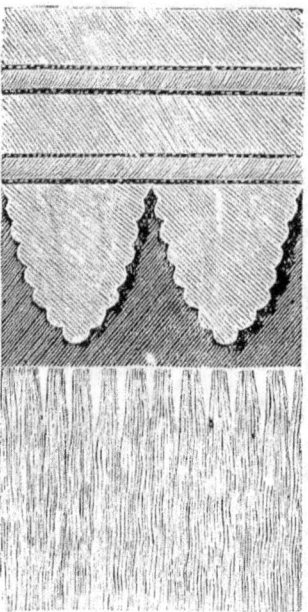

...

Our next illustration, this month, is a walking costume of woolen serge. We give it for its simplicity of make and graceful drapery. It will take fifteen yards of woolen serge, double fold, which can be bought at from seventy-five cents to a dollar and a quarter a yard. The under-skirt or petticoat is made with the front breadth gored – a gore on either side, two full widths in the back, simply bound with alpaca braid on the edge. The over-skirt is cut precisely like the under one, save length and width, and also simply bound with the braid. On the side gores sew rings or eyes six inches about (beginning six inches from the bottom) all the way up the side seams, through the eyes pass a tape to draw the skirt up. Then two tapes, tying together at the back, will keep the upper-skirt in position: add three tapes to the back widths about one-third of the length from the bottom of the skirt, with corresponding ones on the waistband, to form a puff at the back. The bodice has a rounded-off basque, back and front. Surplice at the throat, turned back with black velvet or silk, and worn over a linen plaited chemisette. Belt and butterfly bow at the back, only short ends. Coat-sleeves, trimmed to match the bodice. If preferred, the upper-skirt may be scalloped or pointed, and then bound either with the braid, or with the material, cut on the bias.

We give, next, a party-dress, very stylish, yet comparatively economical. The dress is made of very thin, white muslin: but French muslin is the best. This can be bought at from one to two dollars a yard, and as it is two yards wide, it is really not more expensive than a good Swiss muslin. Or two old muslin dresses can be made into a new one. The skirt has no train, but lies on the floor a few inches. The front of the dress is slightly gored; the side width a good deal more gored, and the back not at all, being left full enough to gather and fall gracefully. The skirt must be three yards and a quarter around the bottom; the flounce must be straight, *not* bias, and measure four yards and a quarter around, and thirteen inches deep when hemmed. Above the deep flounce is put a plain piece, about three inches deep, which has stripes of narrow, green satin ribbon run lengthwise at short distances apart. Above this is another flounce, about five inches in depth, headed by a second plain piece, striped with the green ribbon. This finishes the under-skirt. The tunic, or upper-skirt, must reach from the waist to the top of the upper ruffle on the under-skirt in front when finished. It should be three yards and a half around at the bottom before the flounce is put on; this flounce is slightly fulled, being only four yards in length and five inches deep, and is striped with the green satin ribbon: it is put on with an inch-deep heading. The skirt is cut with a slight slope at the back, making it shorter than it is in front, and is finished with a large green bow at the waist. The body is cut with a point in front, and the neck is square, both back and front. A narrow trimming, like that on the upper-skirt, finishes the neck of this exceedingly chaste costume. The short sleeves are trimmed with a plain hemmed ruffle an inch wide.

...

BORDER IN BRAID AND EMBROIDERY.
By Mrs. Jane Weaver.

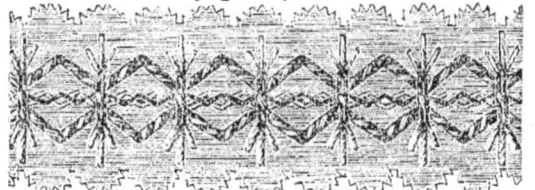

This is a very pretty Border in braid and point Russe embroidery, and is a trimming particularly suitable for a house-jacket, or sacque. If enlarged, it will make a very effective finish for a table-cover, if the table-cover is made of plain cloth. This border should be of some brilliant contrasting color. The diamond pattern is formed by laying on braid, over which the ornamental stitches are worked with purse-silk of the contrasting color.

The edges of the foundation are pinked.

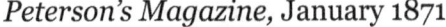

The long walking-skirts have generally usurped the short ones on the street; we do not mean by this, that skirts with trains are worn to walk in, but that what is termed the round skirt is made to touch the ground two or three inches. As we have before stated, cashmere, and, in fact, all soft, woolen materials, are very much used for walking-dresses; but the most elegant of these are worn over silk petticoats of the same color.

...

NEW STYLE OF HOUSE DRESS.

Fig. XIII. – House-Dress of Gray Silk, with a Blue Over-dress. – The skirt is "round" and rather long, and trimmed with one deep, scant flounce, which is headed by a row of black guipure lace. The waist is high and plain, and the sleeves wide and long, and trimmed with black guipure lace. The blue skirt is not very long, and is looped up high on the hips, and is without trimming; over this falls from the sides toward the back, a second skirt, cut in sharp points, and full enough behind to form a plait, and is trimmed with three rows of black velvet. The waist is high and plain, and has no side bodies, so that the gray waist shows under the arms; this waist is also trimmed with black velvet. Two half-worn dresses, of good contrasting colors, make a costume of this style admirably; or cashmere or poplin may readily be substituted for silk.

Peterson's Magazine, January 1871

HOUSE-DRESS.

Fig. VII. – In-door Dress of Violet Cashmere, with long train under-skirt; upper-skirt, forming tabs of different lengths, trimmed with a fluted flouncing and bands of satin. High bodice, with long, hanging sleeves, trimmed to match; waistband fastened with a double row of black velvet. Coiffure cap of *point d'Angleterre*, ornamented with velvet ribbon.

...

We give here an engraving of two charming new style costumes. ↓ The first is a walking-suit of Navy-blue sattine: a material made of worsted and silk. It consists of one skirt, cut after the usual manner; that is, the front breadth gored, one gore on the sides and two full breadths in the back. This skirt has a deep flounce, which should be twelve inches in depth if the lady is tall, or ten inches if she is a medium-sized person. Cut the flounce on the bias, and only allow one width extra for fullness. The edge of this flounce has two rows of very narrow back velvet ribbon, also a narrow quilling of the material. The flounce is headed by a bias puffing, with the quilling and one row of velvet top and bottom. The waist is cut in a deep basque, buttoning down in front, and rounded off as seen in the design.

Any lady, having a basque body that fits well, can easily cut this one from it by cutting it much longer, and then shaping it by the one in the engraving. The back of it comes down long enough, (as may be

seen,) almost to touch the top of the flounce, thus forming the upper-skirt: a small cape is worn over the basque, and the sleeves are half flowing. Cut a small, flowing sleeve, and then shape it. Trim all to match the skirt. This is decidedly the newest design out. It will require sixteen yards of material, and three pieces of quarter of an inch velvet ribbon. The sattine can be bought, very nice, for seventy-five cents per yard, or a better quality at one dollar, or one dollar and twenty-five cents per yard.

The next is a walking-suit, also of a new style. The under-skirt is entirely plain, and may be of either black silk, poplin, or alpaca, or velveteen. The over- dress is an ordinary house-dress, moderately long, and looped as seen in the engraving: bows of velvet, or a large button with tassels attached, are placed where the skirt is looped, which is done by sewing tapes upon the under-side on the seams. Any one-colored, or plaid skirt will look pretty over the black petticoat.

The basque is tight-fitting, and made of cloth, or velveteen, with a coat-sleeve. To make this, simply cut a long, tight basque, then slash it directly up the back seam to the waist, then cut it off the hips, as seen in our design. The fronts are long, like the back. Four yards of velveteen, from one dollar and twenty-five cents up to three dollars per yard, according to the quality you wish, will make the basque, or two yards of black cloth, at three dollars per yard. It is scarcely necessary to give the quantity for the petticoat and upper-dress, as this costume is intended to bring into use something on hand, as an old dress or dresses.

...

Our next engraving is of a walking-suit of gray serge, trimmed with plaid serge or poplin. It is to be made with two skirts. The lower one, or petticoat, has a bias fold of the plaid on the edge of the skirt, with a quilling of the same material as the dress above it. Nine inches above, on the same skirt, is a second fold, headed by a quilling: then comes the upper-skirt, which is cut with a very short apron-front, to the side-seams of which are placed the side-gores of the upper-skirt: one full breadth is added at the back, and the whole is trimmed to match.

The jacket is cut simply in the sacque form, about ten inches long, on the hips and front, from the waist; and just to the waist at the back. A half-loose sleeve. All are trimmed like the skirt. Under this jacket, a plain, round waist is worn, with a plaid sash at the back. This suit will require fifteen yards of plain serge and three yards of the plaid. These serges can be bought from fifty cents to one dollar per yard, according to the quality.

This suit could be copied, or, rather, made out of two old dresses: say a black, or gray, or dark-green merino or poplin for the foundation; and then trimmed with the best parts of an old plaid silk of gay colors, or a plaid poplin. Many varieties may suggest themselves, according to the material on hand.

...

For quite young people, the dresses are made to touch the floor two or three inches, about the length of the present fashion for walking-dresses; for older ladies, they are made half a yard longer than the ordinary dress.

The long walking-dress is still worn, notwithstanding the untidiness; its superior gracefulness has made it popular. With this style of costume the long-discarded shawl can be worn, if the pannier is not large.

Lace is most profusely employed on all kinds of elegant costumes, especially evening-dresses, but it should never be used on common materials, or for morning-dresses.

...

YOUNG LADY'S WINTER JACKET.
By Emily H. May.

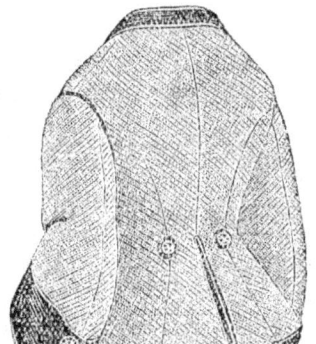

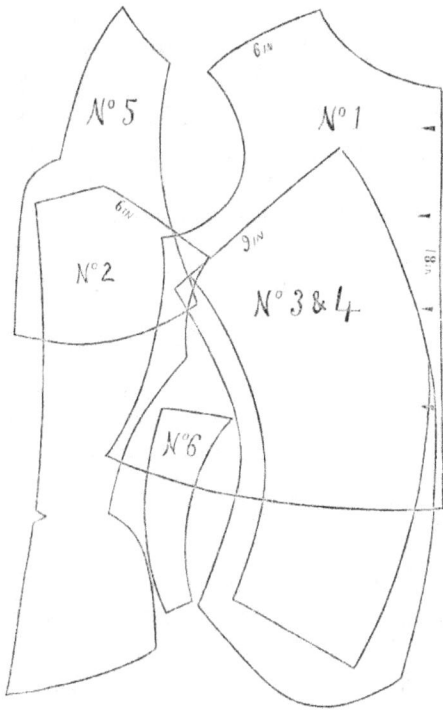

We give, this month, an illustration of a new-style Winter Jacket for a young lady, and also a diagram, by aid of which it can be cut out without calling in a dress-maker. The material is thick-ribbed cloth. The cuffs, collar, and binding, are of velvet. The cuff is cut to the shape of the sleeve. The jacket is left open at the back, as far as the notch in the pattern. There are six pieces to this jacket, as follows:

No. 1. Front.
No. 2. Back.
No. 3. Under-Side of Sleeve.
No. 4. Upper-Side of Sleeve.
No. 5. Side-Piece.
No. 6. Half of Collar.

It will be observed that the two sides of the sleeves are drawn one on top of the other: the upper and smaller representing the under-side of the sleeve.

To make this jacket will require a yard and a half of cloth, which must be a yard and a half wide; one yard of velvet, and fourteen buttons.

Peterson's Magazine, February 1871

Fig. 1. – Dress with Double Skirt and Basque- Waist.
Fig. 2. – Dress with Basque-Waist for Elderly Lady.
Fig. 3. – Dress with Swiss Muslin Over-Skirt and Blouse Waist.
Fig. 4. – Dress with Train and Heart-shaped Basque-Waist.
Fig. 5. – Suit for Boy from 4 to 6 Years old.
Fig. 6. – Evening Dress for Young Lady.

...

WHITE SUITS.

The furnishing houses show very pretty suits of white bishop's lawn. They are made with skirt of walking length, a simply constructed over-skirt, with short apron front and longer back, draped high on the sides, and a slightly loose basque, that may be worn with a belt or without. On the lower skirt are three rows of small side pleats, each row a finger deep, slightly separated from each other, and each headed by a ruche of lawn, scantily gathered in the centre. A single row of this trimming trims the upper skirt and basque. Ruche around the high neck; coat-sleeves, with the trimming outlining the duchesse shape; and a belt of lawn, with short sash ends trimmed like the skirt. Such suits, in very sheer but not fine bishop's lawn, are sold for $9. It is scarcely possible to make them a less expense, if a lady's time is at all valuable. Other suits have deep side pleating, headed by puffs and a row of diagonal tucks. If the figure is thin, a yoke of puffs and tucks is introduced in the basque. Nainsook and white organdy suits similarly made will be worn over colored silk slips for evening, and over white in the daytime. Embroidered Swiss muslins are also shown. A model of these had a French waist gathered into a belt, to which full rounded basques were added, and trimmed with an embroidered ruffle. The over-skirt had an embroidered pyramid in each breadth, and a needle-worked ruffle. This was to be draped over a white muslin, or else a colored silk skirt.

BUFF LINEN SUITS.

The first linen suits exhibited are of pale écru lawn, fashioned like the white suits just described, and trimmed with straight side pleatings not hemmed below, but edged with a fold of brown lawn stitched on. The bias bands, with brown folds at the edge, are above this. Some of these suits have the pretty over-skirt and jacket of the Half-fitting Jacket Suit illustrated in *Bazar* No. 50, Vol. III. A cut paper pattern is given of the suit. The over-skirt may be left open, but the newest fancy is to bring it together, and button it all the way down the front.

Suits of batiste – a linen-finished lawn, in gray grounds striped with white or black – are prettily trimmed with three straight flounces a finger deep, edged with tiny fluted ruffles, an inch wide, cut bias.

Harper's Bazar, March 25, 1871

SATINEE COSTUME – FRONT AND BACK.

Fig. VII. – Costume of Plum-Color Satin Cloth. – The skirt is bordered with velvet to match, and trimmed with two plaitings of satin cloth, each headed by rows of velvet. A narrow, upright plaiting terminates the trimming at the top. The tunic forms a *tablier* in front; and the back, which is gathered up in the center, is full and long. The trimmings correspond with those on the skirt, only they are in smaller dimensions, and terminate with a rich plum fringe. The jacket, with its square *basques* and pagoda sleeves, is trimmed like the tunic.

This useful morning-robe is made of gray serge, and is trimmed with black and white shepherd's plaid. The bodice is full both at the back and front, and the demi-train is bordered with a gathered flounce, edged at both sides with plaid. The trimmings down the front and round the sleeves are in the same style, and the round *basque* at the back is entirely of shepherd's plaid. From six to eight yards will be required of the serge, and two to three yards of shepherd's plaid.

SERGE COSTUME – FRONT AND BACK.

Fig. VI. – Green Serge Costume. – This costume consists of a skirt trimmed with three flounces, each edged with narrow woolen fringe. The tunic, which is full at the back, is bordered with a frill of the same; the second frill is continued on to the front breadth of the skirt, where it simulates a round apron. The bodice is plain and high and the double-breasted jacket with *revers* has *basques* in front. A band with sash ends and bow confines the jacket round the waist.

NEW STYLE BODICE
By Emily H. May.

This new and pretty style of Bodice forms a postilion basque behind, and a simulated waistcoat and jacket in front – as may be seen from our two engravings, one representing the front, and the other the back. It may be made of the same material as the dress, or merino, cashmere, or alpaca, or even of velvet if a more expensive material is desired. It should be trimmed with black velvet ribbon or braid. The simulated waistcoat may be made of silk, or velvet, or of the same material as the basque itself.

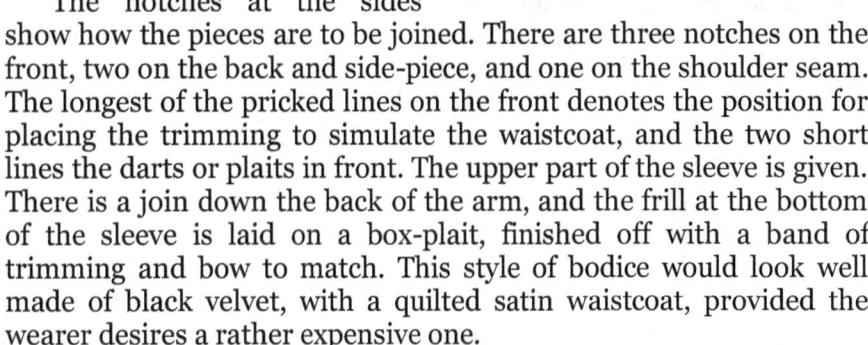

We also give a diagram by which to cut out this basque. It consists of four pieces, viz: –

No. 1. The Front.
No. 2. The Side-Piece.
No. 3. The Back.
No. 4. The Sleeve.

The notches at the sides show how the pieces are to be joined. There are three notches on the front, two on the back and side-piece, and one on the shoulder seam. The longest of the pricked lines on the front denotes the position for placing the trimming to simulate the waistcoat, and the two short lines the darts or plaits in front. The upper part of the sleeve is given. There is a join down the back of the arm, and the frill at the bottom of the sleeve is laid on a box-plait, finished off with a band of trimming and bow to match. This style of bodice would look well made of black velvet, with a quilted satin waistcoat, provided the wearer desires a rather expensive one.

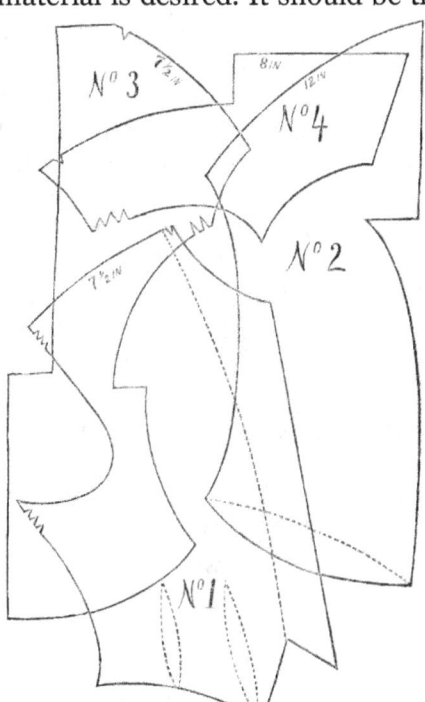

Peterson's Magazine, March 1871

Colors in Dress. – As most of the costumes now worn consist of a long tunic dress, looped up at the sides over an over-skirt, but train-shaped at the back, and as these two parts of the dress are frequently two different colors, of not of two materials, it may be as well to give our fair readers a few hints as how to choose these colors.

One reason why English women, as a class, are never well-dressed, is that they appear to be utterly deficient in the sense of color. French women, especially, get it, apparently, by intuition. Next to them, perhaps, American women have it in the greatest perfection. Still, there are thousands, and tens of thousands, of the sex, even in the United States, who spoil their costumes by illy-assorted colors. Half the money, if spent with an eye to the judicious arrangement of colors, would make such ladies look infinitely prettier.

Now it is a maxim of universal application, that, in every dress, there should be a predominant color, or character. If this ever seems contradicted, it will be found that the combination of colors is of a kind that produces and effect equivalent to that of a dominant character, and comes under the order of a predominant character. The co-existence and continuity of two colors of equal intensity and equal in quantity, is a barbarism repugnant to good taste, and opposed to every principle of art. But where there are more than two, the discordance, though equally real, does not seem to be so obvious – at least such an arrangement is more often seen. Only when the colors are somewhat numerous, and so arranged in small quantities in patterns, or otherwise, as to produce on the eye the general impression of blended and harmonized tints, can it be tolerated.

The next rule is of very general application, and is, that the secondary, or subsidiary colors, should be employed, not for their own sakes, but as subsidiary to the predominant color, and with a view to strengthening the impression intended to be produced by it. It is by no means meant by this to increase the brilliancy of the prevalent hue, or to attract attention; on the contrary, the purpose may be to increase the quiet purity of its aspect, or to lower its brilliancy. From these rules it naturally follows that the subordinate or subsidiary colors should be in well-considered proportions and proper relation to the principle color. Next, the prevalent color, or character, should be adapted to the person, season, and occasion. The rule reaches beyond glaring instances of inappropriateness, and applies equally to personal peculiarities and special places – to the conditions under which the dress will be seen, and the character of the surroundings.

The next rule, that where the predominant color is vivid in tone, subordinate colors may be larger in quantity in proportion as they are tender, neutral, or broken in character, does not accord with the rules laid down in works on color generally, and is not universal in its application, but it is in accordance with the practice of the great colorists, and will be found, we believe, to accord with the practice of the most successful cultivators of the art of dress. Another rule, that the contrasting colors should be larger or smaller in proportion to their intensity, may appear only another way of expressing what we have just laid down in the preceding paragraph. They are, in fact, corollaries from the same principle; but the former may apply either to extension by harmonious views, or to contrast; this applies to contrast only. The rule is given here because it is commonly said in works on color that the contrasting colors should be of equal intensity, and it is left to be implied that their masses may also be equal. But this would be absurd in a dress. The contiguity of two contrasting hues of equal intensity and nearly equal quantity would be felt at once to be crude and unpleasant, even by an uneducated eye. In small quantities the contrast, by its sharpness and force, may serve to give strength and clearness to the rest, just as a point or small quantity of a stronger color may serve to correct the excess of a color or hue. If, for instance, there is an excess of yellow, a small portion of a deeper yellow will probably cure the evil, or if the particular color be too much diffused, serve as a focus to it.

Should these ruled be attended to, there is no fear of any glaring contrasts or jarring of ill-matched colors offending the eye. Should they be neglected, you may spend money, even to extravagance, on your dress, and yet never look well.

...

IN-DOOR DRESS.

Fig. VI. – House-Dress of Gray Summer Poplin. – The long skirt is quite plain; the upper-skirt is cut short, and square in front, is open part way up the side, longer at the back, but not very full, and is pointed by a narrow bias band of the poplin, edged with blue silk cord. The waist and sleeves are high and plain; over the waist is worn a sleeveless basque of blue silk, open at the sides, with two plain, square flaps back and front. This basque is edged with a white Maltese lace, put on to turn up. Sash-bow, without ends, of gray ribbon.

New corsets are made with decidedly longer waists. The introduction of the jacket-waist has hastened the increased length of waist.

Sleeveless jackets of velvet are made with deep basques, and are trimmed with Greek or Maltese lace; these are worn without waistbands, but the waistband without bow or trimming is allowable for young and slender figures.

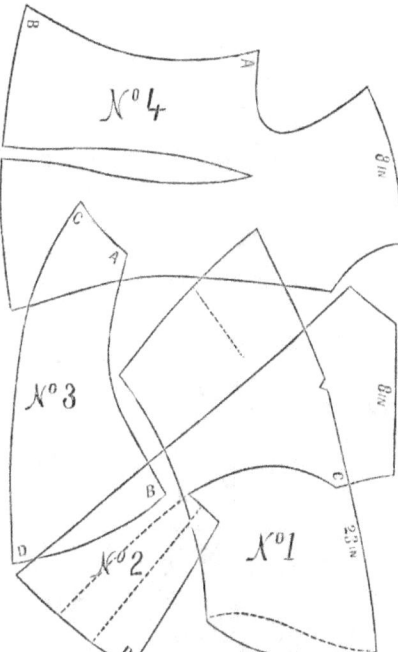

HIGH BODICE, WITH BASQUE.

In the front of the number we give an engraving of a walking dress, with a high bodice and basque, and we add here diagrams from which to cut it out. There are four pieces, viz:

1. Front.
2. Side-Piece.
3. Back.
4. Sleeve.

The materials for this dress may be satins or reps. The high bodice has basques in front and back, and is trimmed with silk buttons and Brandenbourgs. The puffed tunic and flounced skirt is trimmed to match. The sleeve is open and cut up at the place indicated by the notch on the sleeve. Bands of black velvet buttons may be introduced on this costume, and form a more economical trimming than that of the silk Brandenbourgs and buttons.

TRIMMING FOR DRESS.

←

SASH-BOW.

PLAITINGS FOR DRESS-TRIMMINGS.
By Mrs. Jane Weaver.

We give, here, two new and pretty patterns of plaitings for Dress-Trimmings. These plaitings are now very fashionable. By following the engravings, any lady can make these plaitings for herself. If anything, the one we give below is prettier than the one at the head of this article; but these are matters of taste; one plaiting would suit one style of dress best; and another would suit another. The choice ladies must decide for themselves.

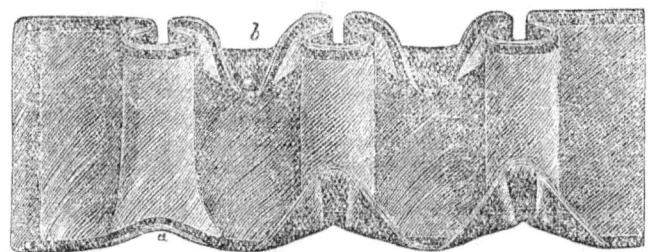

SLEEVE. ↘

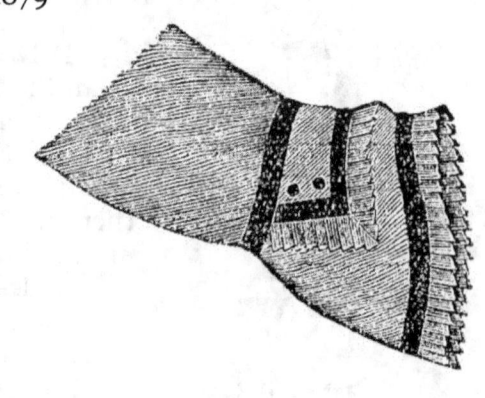

WALKING-DRESS.

Fig. VIII. – Walking Costume of Scotch Poplin. – Tartain [sic?] plaid skirt, with one deep flounce perfectly plain. Bodice and tunic of black silk, draped into a large puff at the back, and forming four flounces in front. Jacket with basques of poplin to match the dress, with silk collar and bow, and with deep, square-cut sleeves.

...

Since the engagement of the Princess Louisa, of England, to the young Scotch Marquis of Lorne, plaids have become wonderfully fashionable with her majesty's loving subjects. Of course, all this is out of complement to the bride elect; but plaids are not becoming, nor seasonable-looking at this time of the year, and we do not prophesy a "great run" for them in America.

Sleeves are all open or *mousquetaire*. The sleeve *a coudre*, with the flounce springing gracefully from the elbow, where it is confined by a bow and band of ribbon or velvet, is very pretty.

Peterson's Magazine, April 1871

Fig. I. – Walking-Dress of Fawn-Colored Silk, with a Crepe Over-Dress. – The silk skirt is made with three graduated ruffles, put on with a narrow bias band of silk. The crepe over-dress is trimmed with wide, knotted fringe, looped high up on the hip by a bow, with long ends of crepe of a darker shade than the dress. The crepe-basque is open at the sides, and also trimmed with fringe. Straw hat, trimmed with wheat and ribbon.

Fig. II. – Carriage-Dress of Pearl-Colored Pongee. – The skirt is trimmed with three scant flounces, put on beneath a plaited heading of the same material; plain waist and tight sleeves. Black grenadine tunic, trimmed with bows of black velvet; the waist of the tunic is trimmed with bretelles of velvet and lace, and the wide open sleeve is ornamented to match.

As to the Berlin fashions, which some of our contemporaries have been trying to introduce, they are unutterably ugly. Paris is, and must always remain, the fountain-head of fashion. Nobody, with any pretentions to style, will dress after any other mode. ...

Fig. IV. – Carriage dress of Venetian-Green Silk. – The skirt is trimmed with five plaited ruffles of white muslin, edged by a narrow imitation Valenciennes lace; at a little distance above each ruffle is a band of green velvet. The waist is low in the neck, with short sleeves; over this is worn a white muslin basque, with long sleeves, trimmed with a plaited ruffle and green velvet ribbon; a series of white ruffles and green velvet bows is placed at the back of the basque.

We give, this month, such dresses as will be suitable for this particular season, with suggestions, that, by a little variety of material, the dresses and walking-costumes may be applied to the different latitudes of this great and varied country.

The first is a home-dress for a young lady. It is made of white alpaca, serge, or mohair, either of these materials can be bought for from fifty to seventy-five cents per yard; and if made in white, the dress will be beautiful either for dinner or small evening-party, and not too dressy to be worn at home, after the first freshness is worn off. Make the under-skirt, or petticoat, just to touch the floor. This is cut after the usual way, and trimmed with a deep plaiting of the material all the way around. This plaiting must be three times as full as the width of the skirt, and cut straight; fold down the plaits, making them about one inch deep, and not quite to touch each other, then press with an iron; place the plaiting upon the skirt, tacking it at every plait at the bottom. Above the plaiting is a band of black velvet ribbon, one inch and a half wide, or a band of silk, or ribbon of any color. The over-skirt has the front width cut quite short, square across, as may be seen; then come the side-gores, which just fall as long on the sides as the petticoat; then two full breadths, only nine inches longer in the back; this is trimmed with a box-plaiting, five inches wide, of the material, headed, the same as the under-skirt; plain, round waist, trimmed to simulate a square yoke; coat-sleeves, belt, and no sash-ends; a small bow on the left side. Sixteen yards of double material will be required. This design, carried out in white muslin for warm weather, or if designed entirely for a home-dress, let it be some of the pretty gray mohairs or poplinettes. If made of gray, trim with brown, green, or black, and it can easily be converted into a walking-costume by looping the over-skirt in the back, so answering a double purpose, and one very desirable where economy is required.

WALKING DRESS.

We give also, but in the front of the number, a walking-dress of pearl-colored mohair. It has a pretty little jaunty sacque, it will be seen, that is especially desirable at the season. The lower-skirt of the dress has one plaited flounce six inches deep, cut on the straight: line this with crinoline, before plaiting. Three times the fullness of the skirt will be required. Four bands of black alpaca, cut bias and put on with the sewing-machine, completes the lower-skirt. The upper one is cut with an apron front, caught up at the sides, and longer in the back. Trim with a narrow plaiting, say three inches and a half or four inches, put on the edge. Five rows of the material, crossed with the black, up the front of the apron; one row of the black trimming to head the plaiting. The waist is perfectly plain and round, with coat-sleeves. The sacque is simply a loose one, and quite short; its beauty consists in the manner of putting on the trimming. Cut surplice at the throat, continue the plaiting one inch and a half down both sides of the bias band in front, and the trimming, which goes over the shoulders, is continued down the back. Open sleeves. Any black trimming may be substituted for the alpaca, say silk, velvet ribbon; but for cheapness, the alpaca is the thing, and the effect good. From sixteen to eighteen yards of the pearl-colored mohair, and three yards of black alpaca, or three and a half yards of silk, will be required. Plenty of those light colored summer mohairs add in the stores for fifty cents, and so up according to quality.

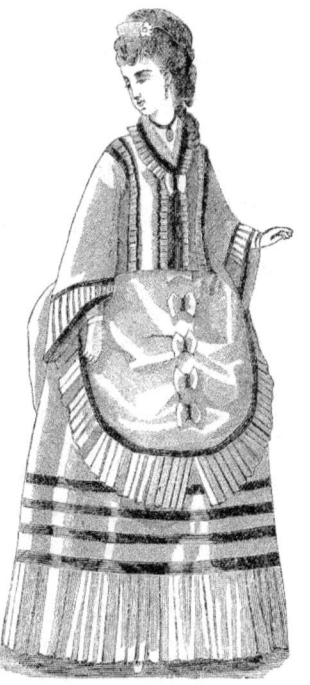

...

The passementerie trimmings for dresses and mantles are excessively rich and elegant. Many are made in very large detached patterns, and intended to cover the whole of the front breadth of a skirt. We lately saw a very rich black silk trimmed in this manner. It had two skirts; the under-one, merely touching the ground, was ornamented with a splendid pattern of fern-leaves and lilies, interspersed with jet, entirely covering the tablier. The train had a very handsome border of the same, seven inches all round, and running up each seam to the waist where it became so narrow as to be merely a delicate tracery. The postillion basque bodice and sleeves were also very profusely trimmed.

Plaitings of white tarlatan are again in great favor for trimming silk dresses, and exceedingly well they look when the dress is black. Sometimes black lace is added above the tarlatan, and sometimes black Duchess lace is to be seen over white blond. Tarlatan plaiting, although economical to commence with,

are not cheap in the end, for when once their freshness has departed they are useless. Embroidered muslin is, therefore, used in their stead, as it can be washed and come out as good as new; whereas tarlatan must be confined to the rag-bag. The white muslin plaitings are used on black silk dresses, and likewise on dresses of fancy materials, the in the latter case black lace is not added above them. If tarlatan is used, it is mounted as a plaiting; if white muslin, it is gathered into a flounce.

...

EVENING AND HOUSE-DRESS.

← We give, in the front of the number, a house, or evening toilet, for a young lady, made of white, dotted muslin. A gathered flounce, headed with two rows of black velvet ribbon, trims the bottom of the skirt, which is a trifle longer and fuller than the ordinary walking-dress. Waist with long, pointed basque, open behind, and trimmed with a flounce and two rows of velvet. Coat-sleeve with a deep frill falling on the wrist. Rosette of the velvet at the waist, both before and at the back. Nothing could be prettier than this for a young lady's evening toilet, and as it is so simple, any one can may it at home. It will require about fifteen yards of dotted muslin, or plain white Swiss, and two pieces of velvet ribbon, three-quarters of an inch in width.

MUSLIN BODIES.

Next we give, also in the front of the number, two patterns for French muslin bodices. The first has narrow bias bands of fine linen, stitched down with the sewing-machine, and edged with a narrow Cluny lace. The other is cut out to simulate an under chemisette. The lappets of the over-waist are ornamented with embroidery, and edged with Valenciennes lace. Coat-sleeves slightly gathered at the hand, with a cuff to turn back, and a frill to fall over the hand, trimmed to match.

...

A beautiful dress for a young lady has just been made in Paris. It is of milk-white gauze, made with three skirts, the under-one flounced, the two upper-ones looped-up with bunches of blush roses and lilies of the valley; the draperies of the waist were looped-up with sprigs of the same flowers, and edged with a soft fringe of floss silk; coiffure to correspond.

If the crinoline is going out, the *tournure* has increased more than ever. It is now quite a large panier, rising high above the waist, and altogether of vast dimensions. The skirts of dresses have to be made very full and ample of the back and sides, so as to fall gracefully over this panier.

...

HOUSEWIFE'S APRONS.

We also give, in the front of the number, two engravings of housewife's aprons, simple, cheap and useful articles. The material may be chintz or gingham. They require no description.

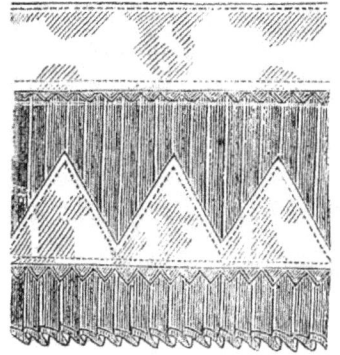

PETTICOAT TRIMMING.

UNDER-SLEEVE

Peterson's Magazine, May 1871

PLAID TRAVELING-DRESS.

Also, in the front of the number, is a traveling suit of black and white plaid. These goods can be bought in all qualities, from thirty-one cents up to one dollar twenty-cents per yard – those at thirty-one, thirty-seven, and forty cents, are very nice, and of wool and cotton mixtures, and will wear very well for a cheap summer trip. The design is a very pretty one, and the trimmings, which are of solid black, can be made either of silk or alpaca. Quillings of the latter look exceedingly well, and for a traveling suit, will last much better than silk. Sixteen yards of plaid, and four yards of alpaca, or four yards and a half of silk, will be required. The lower-skirt is made to match, and is trimmed with a flounce, cut on the bias, fourteen inches deep, put on with a heading, separated with one or two narrow bands of black, stitched with the machine. The upper-skirt is not very full, and is trimmed with the revers open on the sides, which are trimmed with a quilling two inches wide (cut straight and double) also extending across the front and round the back. Basque waist, surplice front, trimmed to match. Coat-sleeves, waistband, and short bows at the back. The suit would also be very pretty in linen, trimmed with white linen, or Nainsook for the quillings.

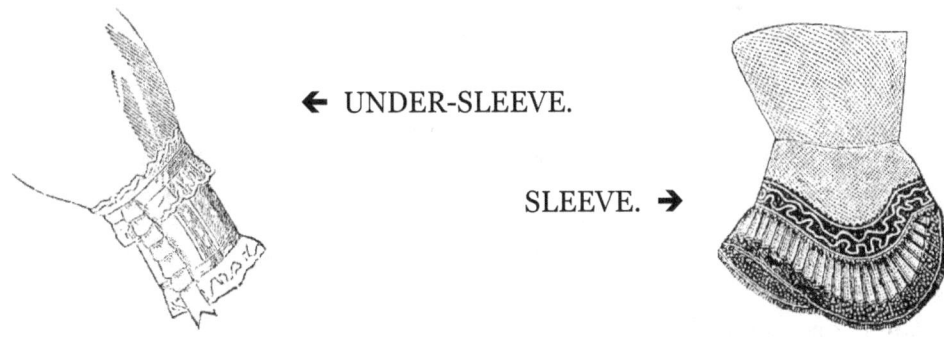

← UNDER-SLEEVE.

SLEEVE. →

Sashes are quite out of fashion, particularly sashes with long, flowing ends at the back. The new sashes are fastened at the side, and are rather scarfs than sashes. They are made either of China *crepe*, or of satin, and are tied as over the hunting costume of the seventeenth century.

Many home jackets are made of black *crepe de Chine*, with large hanging sleeves. The following is a novelty: The front fits tightly to the figure, in the waistcoat style, with a long basque at the back. It is composed of black *crepe de Chine*, worked in straw, the basque being edged with straw fringe.

Peterson's Magazine, June 1871

Swiss muslin flounces in pleats all turned one way appear in various ways on summer toilettes. In the broadest patterns, about six inches wide, they are used for freshening up last year's silks, two such flounces being placed around the trained skirt, and the evening toilette completed by a simple upper skirt of Swiss muslin and a basque, or else a polonaise trimmed to match. This is a stylish plan for black silks as well as light ones. The wide Swiss flounces made up admirably are sold for 60 cents a yard. Narrower pleatings two inches wide for necks and sleeves of dresses, for over-skirts, basques, and, above all, for edging the flounces of colored and black silks, cost from 25 cents upward. Ladies who desire to make their own flounces are advised that they are merely crossway strips of Swiss muslin hemmed on each edge, and laid in the kilt pleats so often described, not sewed in tucks, but ironed flatly after being pleated and held down by a band of the Swiss a quarter of an inch wide stitched on with two rows of stitching an inch below the top. On broad flounces the hem on the lower edge is an inch wide, the upper edge very narrow.

Harper's Bazar, June 3, 1871

Next, we give an illustration of a Dinner, or Evening Toilet, for Watering Places; a very pretty and seasonable costume. The under-skirt is perfectly plain, and made of blue silk, or blue mohair, of the color commonly called "French blue," which is a trifle deeper than sky-blue. This under-skirt will require six and a half yards of silk, or more, according to the height of the person. All skirts are made just to touch the ground. Over this blue is worn a plain skirt of white alpaca, trimmed with four rows of inch-wide velvet ribbon, without looping. The waist is cut in a long basque, slashed half way up the back, and open in front, trimmed with one row of velvet, as are the open sleeves and surplice-neck. The skirt of the basque is looped with bows of the black velvet ribbon. This design would look well, also, in white pique, or French muslin. If the latter, there would a waist of the blue be required. Fourteen yards of white alpaca, or ten yards of pique, is sufficient to cut this over-dress, and two pieces of inch-wide black velvet for trimming. The hood is of blue cashmere, trimmed with narrow velvet ribbon.

...

In Evening Dress ... As a change from the panier, of which one is getting very tired, the upper-skirt is sometimes made very long, and then just caught up at the back with a bow, or a branch of flowers.

...

Demi-trains are entirely superseding the awkward court trains of last year.

WAISTS.

Walking-dresses are made rather longer, and do not clear the ground. Flounces still maintain their sway, and a number of these cut bias are used for stylish dresses.

NEW STYLE OF DRESS APRONS.

Elegant aprons are now worn, generally with plain silk receiving-dresses. We give, in the present number, tow pretty engravings of these kinds of aprons. For afternoon callings, it is the fashion to receive in rich trimmed dresses of black moire antique, with elegant aprons, covered with rich lace, or embroidered with jet, with silk, and even with gold and silver, in imitation of mediæval embroidery. These dresses are closed at the neck, and Valenciennes lace is usually worn with these toilets.

Peterson's Magazine, July 1871

TRAVELING-DRESS. FRONT.

Fig. VIII. – Traveling-Dress of Dark-Gray Mohair. – The skirt is trimmed with five plain ruffles; the upper-skirt is of lighter-colored gray mohair, trimmed with a band of the darker shade, like the petticoat. The sacque, which fits into the figure partially, is of the color of the upper-skirt, and trimmed in the same way. There is a plain waist, like the under-skirt, with long, close sleeves, worn under the sacque.

...

TRAVELING-DRESS. BACK.
←

...

Fig. VI. – Walking-Dress of Gray Poplin, trimmed around the bottom with a deep, black tassel fringe, above which the skirt is ornamented with black velvet, put on in points, and black braid embroidery. The upper-skirt, which is deep in front, is cut up at the sides and at the back, and with the basque trimmed like the lower-skirt. →

...

← A Walking, or Traveling-Dress, of Linen, is our first pattern for this month. These linens now come in every variety of shade, from the lightest buff, or gray, to brown, lead, etc., at from twenty-five to fifty cents per yard. The costume which we give this month, is of light buff, the lower-skirt perfectly plain. The waist and upper-skirt are in one, in the form of a pellisse, with a basque set in at the back and sides. The trimming is simple, being only slashed at distances of six inches, and bound with brown alpaca braid; a narrower braid is sewn above the binding. Coat sleeves. The pellisse may either be buttoned down the front, or fastened with hooks and loops. Twelve yards of linen will be required for this dress.

IN-DOOR SACQUE.

There is no change in the width and length of skirts this spring – we allude to those belonging to costumes. They are flat and gored in front and at the sides, and full at the back. The length is a matter of taste; those who desire comfort and convenience, wear a skirt that just escapes the ground, while others order it to trail an inch or two on the ground; they measure from three and a half to four yards round the edge. All costumes are made either with an over-skirt or a Polonaise, which has the same effect.

Fig. VII. – Home-Dress of Green and White Striped Silk. – The petticoat is trimmed with eight rows of green velvet ribbon, put on in groups; the waist and tunic are of white muslin, spotted with green. The tunic is short, very much puffed, and trimmed with a ruffle of the material. A fichu of white organdy crosses the bosom.

...

The Polonaises are very popular for white and buff linen suits. They are made in many white materials, and worn over silk skirts. When bishop's lawn is selected, a cross band of the same, and a frill or ruche forms the trimming; embroidered frills and insertion decorate Nainsook muslin, and either Duchesse or Valenciennes lace is used on Swiss muslin Polonaises. These white over-dresses look exceedingly well over black silk skirts, and similar skirts are worn under Polonaises of buff linen and *ecru* linen; the trimmings for these are Flemish guipure, made of unbleached linen. There are several forms of Polonaises – this one with apron front, and the other with postillion basques, are the two favorites; the latter is the more becoming to stout figures.

Peterson's Magazine, August 1871

WALKING-DRESS.

Fig. VI. – Visiting-Dress of Gray Poplin, with one very deep, full, plaited flounce on the bottom, which is headed by a band of poplin, and a full, plaited quilling of the same. Tunic and over-dress of black cashmere, trimmed with a deep black and gray fringe, and a band of gray cashmere, embroidered in black. The long, hanging sleeves, and low jacket at the back, are trimmed like the rest of the tunic.

...

Women in Calico. – A correspondent of one of the leading New York journals says that the three most charming women he ever knew wore calico, and were, in the opinion of all the men acquainted with them, never so charming as when they were thus dressed. Certainly, any girl, in a clean, morning-dress of calico, looks prettier than a soiled, greasy old silk. One of the most intelligent and cultivated men we ever knew, fell in love with his present wife in a calico dress. It is not the money that a toilet costs, it is the appropriateness, that makes it irresistible. We wish our American girls would bear this in mind.

...

WALKING-DRESS.

Fig. VII. – Walking-Dress of Black and White Wool Plaid. – The skirt has three bias folds of the material, headed by bands of black velvet. The close-fitting waist is made with a coat-basque at the back, long, apron tabs in front, and with loose sleeves, cut up at the back, all trimmed with a band of black velvet, and white and black fringe.

...

Nearly all short dresses are made with two skirts, cut long. House, or evening-dresses, are often made with only one skirt, but long enough to be looped up gracefully. Trains are not so long as formerly. For walking-dresses of woolen material, and sometimes of silk, especially black silks, braiding is a favorite way of ornamentation; braid, however, of the same color as the material of the dress, is indispensable. Shaded trimmings are less popular than formerly, most of the handsomest French dresses being trimmed of the very material from which the dress is made. One deep flounce on walking-dresses, is the most popular, as in heavy fabrics this looks better than several narrow ruffles, which ought to be reserved for light materials.

← We give, this month, a walking toilet, made of light-brown serge. Under-skirt entirely plain, and long enough to touch; upper-skirt also plain. Basque waist, with an inside vest of the same color as the trimming, which is of a darker shade of brown. Cut the basque entire of the dress material, and after it is fitted, cut away from the front and insert the darker shade for the vest, and shape after the design. The trimming is simply two rows of piping. Long, flowing sleeves, with under-sleeve, made tight, of the darker shade. The trimming and vest may be either of silk or a darker shade of serge – the latter will be equally effective, and much less expensive. Serges cost from seventy-five cents to one dollar per yard. Fourteen yards of the lighter, and two and a half or three yards of the darker shade. If silk is used, three to three and a half yards will be required for the trimming.

...

Next is a walking toilet of black alpaca. ↘ The under-skirt has a deep flounce cut on the bias, and only slightly full, either bound on the bottom, or hemmed by the machine. At the head of this flounce are four bias folds, which are lined with crinoline, to have the effect of being double; the top fold is headed by a row of braid. The over-skirt is cut with an apron front, and open at the sides; the back sloped toward the back, where it is long enough to loop in a large box-plait. Basque waist, slashed to the hips and in the back, with bias folds put upon the body heart-shaped, back and front. Fringe all round the basque and upper-skirt. A bias ruffle may be substituted for the fringe, if the latter is too expensive, although mohair fringe looks very pretty upon these dresses, and cost from forty to fifty cents per yard for three inch; narrower less. Sixteen to eighteen yards of alpaca.

...

Dust-proofs, as they are called, are coming quite into fashion, and it is one of the most sensible fashions we can remember. These dust-proofs are made of light-gray, or stone-colored thin cloth, circular, and without sleeves; they do not crush the most fragile dress, and serve for a useful wrap also when returning home at night. ...

For evening wear, the prettiest style adopted at present is the toilette made with a train, which is looped up at one side only, passing through a bow of ribbon, a circle of flounces, or a twist of rich silk cord. ...

Very pretty Louis XVI. *redingotes* are now made of silk, and intended to be worn over dresses trimmed with several flounces. They only look well over this style of dress, because, being made almost plain at the back, they require frills beneath to keep them out and make them stylish. Striped silk is very popular for these *redingotes.*

For evening toilets *redingotes* are made to open squarely in front with two basques; the sleeves are pagoda in form, and at the back there are two long, pointed basques, slightly gathered at the waist; there is never any band whatever outside, and, though one is sewn inside, to keep the garment in place, it is, of course, not visible; two buttons mark the position of the waist. *Redingotes*, intended for wearing over morning and afternoon toilets, cross on the chest, and are fastened at the side; square basques in front simulate the waistcoat, and they have long, pointed basques at the back like the evening ones, but the sleeve is long, with a deep cuff.

Peterson's Magazine, September 1871

Sleeves are close-fitting coat shape, provided with broad, square cuffs, or else open up the outer seam nearly to the elbow, and trimmed up the opening. The half-flowing sleeve, with frill toward the wrist, is also retained. Wide flowing sleeves are only seen on outside garments.

Skirts are not changed in shape, but are now seldom lined, and are no longer finished with worsted braid around the bottom. They are faced to the knee with crinoline muslin, and the dress material is turned up at the edge for about two inches, and hemmed on the crinoline.

Beaver Mohair Walking Suit.

This suit consists of a double skirt and basque-waist, and is made of black beaver mohair. The trimming is composed of bias strips of black velvet and twisted silk fringe. The velvet strips are cut out in scallops at the upper edge. Black Neapolitan bonnet, trimmed with feathers and flowers. To make the waist, cut of the material and muslin lining two pieces each from Figs. 46-48, Supplement, allowing an inch and a quarter extra material at the front edge of Fig. 46, and one piece from Fig. 49. Cut the sleeves from Fig. 4 of No. I. of the present Supplement, but only to the straight line given on the pattern. Baste the material on the lining, sew up the darts on the fronts, hem down the extra material of the right front on the wrong side, and make the button-holes therein. The extra material on the left front is left for a fly, on which the buttons are sewed. When the waist has been joined according to the corresponding figures, cut a slit in the back from the bottom along the double line to *, and face the bottom of the waist, including the slit, with a bias strip of the material an inch and a quarter wide; the neck of the waist is corded. Sew on the trimming as shown by the illustration and partly indicated on the pattern. Sew up the sleeves, face the bottom with a strip of silk and inch and three-quarters wide, trim them as shown in the illustration, and sew them into the corded armholes.

...

Waists of French dresses are cut long, and are very high in the neck, a standing bias band half an inch wide being added to some, while others are merely corded. Shoulder seams are very short and high, defining the line of the shoulders. There is a seam down the centre of the back of all dresses, and two side bodies are seen in many, thus cutting the back in six separate pieces. The longest of the side forms goes into the armhole just below the elbow. Basques still prevail, though postilion pleating is not as universal as last year, many plain basques being fitted smoothly over the tournure. There is also a tendency to lengthen basques. Square and pointed vests are both worn, usually falling open below the waist. Many basques on which vests appear are not cut with separate vests, but the material of the trimming (of which vests are invariably made) is laid on the front of the basque to simulate a vest, and is bordered with trimming. For example, a rich Parisian suit is of peacock green and black silks combined. The skirt is of peacock silk, with diagonal pleatings of the same; the over-skirt of black silk is piped and faced with peacock silk, and edged with black passementerie and fringe; the black silk basque has a pointed vest of peacock silk laid on the front, and edged with passementerie. Buttons and button-holes finish the front of the vests; basques without vests are often fastened by hooks and eyes, and ornamented with bows.

...

Fringe will be the trimming of the season. It is shown in every conceivable design, and arranged on every part of the dress, two rows often passing straight around the skirt, taking the place of flounces, and being headed like flounces by bias bands and folds. These fringes are often made by hand at the modistes', being many strands of thick Italian silk caught in the edge of a bias band, and tied in separate tassels. Again, there are richly embroidered velvet bands, or bias pieces of the dress material braided, the lower edge cut in deep Gothic points, to which is added a wide fringe, with rich heading netted in points to fill up the spaces between the velvet points. Although ruffles and flounces are still greatly used, there is at last a probability that flat trimmings will be considered most stylish and distinguished. Indeed, fringe embroidery, braiding, passementerie, and folds represent the trimmings most seen on French garments. Folds are deprived of their stiffness and made very attractive by placing them of two shades alternately, or of two materials. A pretty gray poplin suit is trimmed to the knee by four bias folds of two alternating shades, the folds overlapping, and the cluster finished at the top by a wide passementerie and fringe; a brown delaine skirt has velvet folds alternating with others of delaine, each fold edged by Tom Thumb fringe; An ashes-of-roses poplin has two bias bands of black velvet corded on the upper edge with gray velvet, while a row of tassel fringe (black) falls from below each band. Royale, or uncut velvet, is much used for folds, bands, piping, cuffs, collars, and vests on silk and fine woolen dresses. Few crochet or other fancy buttons are used; the preference is for large button-moulds coved with the material with which the dress is trimmed.

...

Poult de Soie Evening Dress.

The suit consists of a skirt, over-skirt, and pointed waist of violet poult de soie. The under-skirt is trimmed with three box-pleated ruches of the material five inches wide. The back breadths of the over-skirt are cut straight. Arrange the shorter front breadths as shown by the illustration. The waist, which is heart-shaped and has a long point at the front, is cut from Figs. 1-3 of No. I. of the present Supplement, making the point somewhat longer. The small basque consists of a box-pleated strip of the material four inches wide, which is sloped off toward the front as shown in the illustration. Tight sleeves. Collar and cuffs of fine linen trimmed with lace.

...

Box-pleated blouses of woolen fabrics are shown at the furnishing houses. They are of gray, scarlet, or blue merino, or of fine flannel, or else of black cashmere, or even alpaca. They are for breakfast and house wear instead of jackets, and will serve a good purpose with double skirts of dresses whose bodies are worn out, or have gone out of fashion. Mothers will find them invaluable for growing girls. Three double box-pleats in front and back is the handsomest style; coat sleeve with square cuff and collar of black velvet. For stout figures a plain blouse is made, the pleats being simulated by bias bands piped at each edge with a color, such as tan, plum, or white. Plaid pipings enliven black waists worn by young girls with plaid skirts.

Harper's Bazar, October 7, 1871

HOUSE OR DINNER-DRESS.

Fig. VIII. – Dinner-Dress of Pearl-Gray Silk, cut with short train, and trimmed with violet gros grain silk, put on in bias folds, headed by a plaiting of the same. Three folds across the front breadth, the third one crossing the others, and continuing around the back. Plain waist, points in front, and long, square basque at the back, finished at the ends with wide, black lace, put on full. Trimming on the waist comes over the shoulders, down the back, forming a postillion, also trimmed with lace, and plaiting of the silk. ←

...

A short time ago the petticoat was made of one material, the bodice and tunic of another; now the bodice is made to match the petticoat, and the tunic, which is placed between them, is alone different.

...

HOUSE OR DINNER-DRESS.

Fig. IX. – Dinner-Dress of Amber Silk, trimmed with black velvet and white lace. The skirt has a short train, trimmed with a deep flounce, pinked out, and slightly full, headed by a quilling of black velvet between two rows of white lace, the same put on perpendicularly, at intervals, all round the skirt, finished with a bow of velvet. Over-skirt, apron front, crossing and caught up at the back of the waist over the full back breadth, which is looped up with a large bow of velvet, same as at the back of the waist, with the ends coming from under the puff. Sleeves puffed to the elbow, with a deep flounce at the bottom, trimmed to match the skirt.

...

A Walking-Costume is our first illustration this month. It is something quite new, as it is almost entirely untrimmed, which is a relief after so much ruffle and flounce. It is of chocolate-colored cashmere or merino, and the under-skirt is perfectly plain, and to touch. Then comes the second skirt, just below the knee, and only looped a very little at the sides. The waist is cut in a deep Polonaise, coming to a point in the back, which is then looped up entirely to the waist, and fastened with a large butterfly bow. This is simply scalloped and bound, as is also the little cape which is worn over it. The sleeve is slightly fulled into a band just below the elbow, terminating in a ruffle which is also scalloped to match. Fourteen yards of merino will be required.

...

Something of a Paradox. – The most celebrated dressmaker in the world, strange to say, is not a woman, but a man. Stranger still, he is not a Frenchman, but an Englishman, though he lives in Paris. We allude of course to the famous Worth. In the days of the Empire, he was the supreme arbiter of fashion, in France; and to be the arbiter of fashion in France, is to be its arbiter the world over. The Empress even had to bow to the fiat of Worth. She once quarreled with him, but soon after, wishing a peculiar costume, and finding no one who could satisfy her fastidious taste, had to go back to

Worth. The Empire has fallen, but Worth still reigns. We have lately seen some of his recent costumes, and they are, if possible, lovelier than ever. The rest from his labors, afforded by the two sieges of Paris, appears to have renewed and invigorated Worth's inventive faculties, so that he is now, perhaps, regarded, more unanimously than ever, as the supreme arbiter in fashion. To have a dress from Worth is a sort of patent of nobility in the fashionable world.

...

BRAIDED HOUSE JACKET. ↗

...

LOW WATTEAU-BODY.
By Emily H. May.

We give, here, an engraving of a Low Watteau-body for full evening-dress, and also a diagram of the pieces of which it is to be made. They are, as will be seen, three in number, viz: the front, the side-piece, and the back. This Watteau-body has a square opening both back and front, and is made without sleeves. That pattern is for a body a little above the usual or average size, say thirty-four and a half inches round the chest, and twenty-four inches round the waist. As we have often said before, these diagrams give the shape of each piece, and have their size marked on their sides. Before using them, they should be enlarged, that is, a piece of newspaper, or other paper, should be taken, and patterns cut out, according to the diagram, of the full size: these patterns should then be fitted to the person who is to wear the

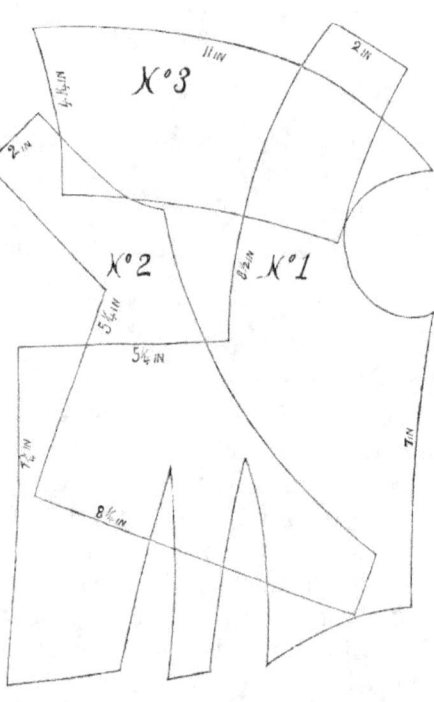

waist, and after they have been made perfect, then, and then only, should you cut into the stuff. In this way you will avoid all mistakes.

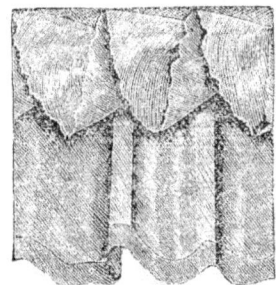 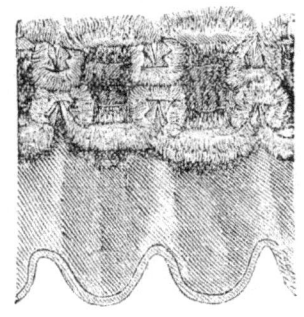

TRIMMINGS FOR DRESSES.

Tight-fitting tunics are buttoned in front like paletots, the trimmings to simulate basques; the long Louis XV. waistcoat is very fashionable at this moment; white muslin cravats and lace bows are worn this this waistcoat, or a lace fall is used, if the waist is open shawl shape.

...

POSTILLIONS, WITH BOWS FOR
BACK OF DRESS.

Peterson's Magazine, October 1871

We give next, a Walking Costume for a Young Lady. It is one of the new designs in two colors, say brown and soft-gray. For this month, we suggest the material be either of merino, or heavy corded poplin. Be careful to select shades of each color, so that they may harmonize. The under-skirt is made quite plain and round, but long enough to touch. It is trimmed with a scalloped-out band of the gray, put on about nine inches from the bottom; then a space of three inches; then another band of gray; and between these bands there is a box-plaiting of the brown. The gray upper-skirt is cut quite as long as the under-one in the back, but shorter in front, and is trimmed with two bias bands of brown. Our design has the addition of gray fringe, four inches deep; but this is optional. Loops at the sides and back, by means of tapes sewed underneath. The side tapes are tied back, after looping, to keep the fullness all in the back, leaving the front perfectly plain. Waist of the gray, cut in a basque, slashed at the sides, and trimmed with one bias band of brown. Bands of brown join the basque on the hips. Open sleeves, with tight ones underneath. Small, round cape of gray, lined with brown, which may be worn, or not, at pleasure. Seven and a half yards of brown poplin, six and a half of merino, for the under-skirt and trimming; nine yards of gray in poplin, eight yards in merino. Either of these materials can be bought from seventy-cents a yard up.

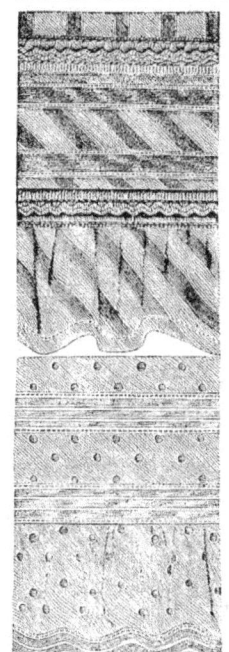

 ← PETTICOAT TRIM.

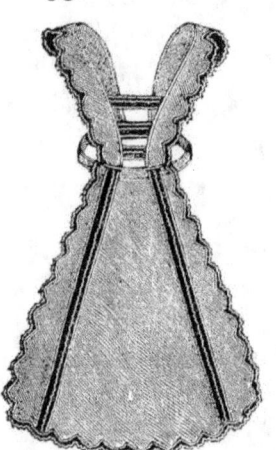
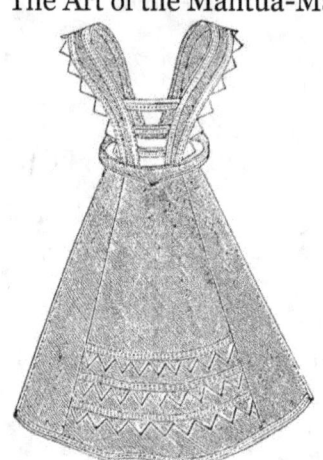

We give also, in the front of the number, illustrations of two aprons of fine corded pique, braided plaid, or plain linen, or of black silk. One, if of black silk or alpaca, is to have the material folded, as will be seen, into points, and to be stitched down with sewing-machine. The other is to be trimmed with velvet ribbon, and a narrow Tom Thumb fringe.

KEY POCKET.
By Mrs. Jane Weaver.

Our first cut (in the opposite column ➜) represents the front of the key pocket, which may be made in any size suitable for the key it is intended to hold. The cut below gives the border in the proper size.

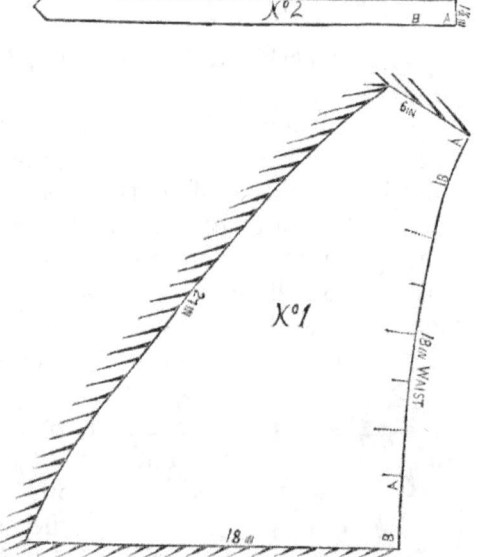

The pocket may be made of cloth, silk, or velvet. The border is fastened down with an open button-hole stitch of two colors. This is a neat and serviceable article, and an appropriate present for either a lady or gentleman.

...

PLAITED BASQUE ON A BELT.
By Emily H. May.

In the diagram No. 1 gives the half of the basque open. The dotted and straight lines from A to B, indicate where the plaits are to be put. After plaiting, the fullness, all comes into the space from A to B, and that is joined to the belt in the space A to B. Trim the whole with fringe, which is continued around the belt in front. This basque is to be worn over a simple round waist, and may be made of the materials of the dress, or of velvet, satin, or whatever the dress is trimmed with. Fringe or lace is only suitable to trim with, on account of the plaiting, which shows the wrong as well as the right side of the trimming.

No. 1. Half of Basque.
No. 2. Half of Belt.

...

Chintz patterns are also seen in silks, the prettiest being composed of the blue corn-flower with the field-poppy mixed with wheat ears. These silks are only suitable for evening-dresses, as they are on white or pearl-colored grounds, and are worn over pearl-colored or blue silk petticoats, a good deal puffed up. This it is seen that we are returning to the dresses of a century ago. And with these dresses, which are made open on the bust, either square or heart-shaped lace, tulle, or very thin muslin must be worn, such as the dames of the ancient regime wore; and it must be confessed that nothing is more becoming to a lady than the *bouffant* folds of their dainty fichus. ...

The old-fashioned tight-fitting sacque, which was so popular in Marie Antoinette's time, and which is now called a *Polonaise, Gabrielle*, etc., is exceedingly popular for an over-dress. The body and skirt is cut in one, and the latter is a good deal puffed up over a colored petticoat. This style of dress is wonderfully becoming to the figure.

WALKING-DRESS.

Fig. VI. – Walking-Dress of Chestnut-Brown Poplin, with an Over-Dress of much Lighter Brown. – The under-skirt is trimmed with rows of quilled silk; the upper dress of lighter brown, is trimmed with two rows of the darker shade of silk; it is looped high up on the hips, and cut open part way of the back, where it is fastened up with a dark-brown bow and ends. The close basque of the lighter brown poplin is trimmed like the upper-skirt.

Peterson's Magazine, November 1871

MODERN COSTUME.

There is no more harm in a woman being brightly dressed than in a flower being brightly dressed, no more wrong in an innocent woman's study of dress effects than in an orator's study of pose, or elocution, or poetic effects. Drab is not in itself holier than scarlet one whit, and the subdued colors are no more favorable to virtue than they are to artistic beauty. Nature hates them, and the notion that they are virtuous is an absurd effect of bad taste. Phryne dressed in spotless white, and among the really vicious races, like the Turks of Constantinople, female dress has as little brilliancy as grace. There is absolutely no reason for simplicity except economy, and no guild of fashion could settle what for any particular individual was economical or the reverse. The only real departure from simplicity now common is the rapidity with which a really pretty dress is laid aside, and that practice does not arise from any social pressure, but from the spirit of pecuniary ostentation which has infected society, and which is no worse in female dress than in any other department of life.

...

Evening Dress, Figs. 1 and 2.

This suit consists of an under dress of plain blue gros grain, and an over dress of blue and white chiné gros grain. Fig. 1 shows the under dress without the trimming, and Fig. 2 shows the same trimmed with ruffles and puffs of white organdy, and black velvet bows. Pleated Swiss muslin fichu, with ruffles of the same, which are edged on one side with lace half an inch wide. On the middle of the fichu in the back is a velvet bow with long ends; a bunch of flowers is fastened to the front of the corsage.

...

Evening Dresses.

The engraving on page 780, of which a cut paper pattern is given, presents the newest features in evening dresses. The low corsages sent over this season by Parisian modistes are simple round waists without points or postilion. It is said that Worth brought about this return to a fashion not long laid aside because of his admiration for the handsome sashes that accompany these waists. The top of the corsage is very low, and is prettily rounded in the shoulders, instead of being half high and square, in the style worn last winter. The trimming is a sort of bertha, or else Grecian folds. The sleeve is a mere epaulet or a tiny puff. Trained skirts with short over-skirts are not as fashionable at present as short under-skirts with trained over-skirts. The engraving represents an adjustable court train, that may be left flowing its graceful length, or shortened by tapes underneath to a trained or shorter bouffant over-skirt.

...

LOW-NECKED EVENING DRESS,
WITH ADJUSTABLE COURT TRAIN AND ROUND SKIRT.

This pattern compromises three articles – low-necked waist, adjustable court train, and round skirt. ...

Adjustable Court Train. – This pattern is in two pieces, side piece and back breath. ... The front edge of the side piece is laid in three small pleats, turning back, and covered with a lace bow. The side and back breadths are laid in three double box-pleats at the line of perforations in the back, about three-quarters of a yard from the bottom, and fastened with a lace bow. The back breadth is sewed on to the belt with large box-pleat in the middle, and side pleats on each side, and the side breadths are sewed on plain. The train is looped by means of three tapes, the middle one seventeen inches, and the others eleven inches long. Sew one end of each tape to the belt, one in the middle, and the others two inches on each side of it, and set buttons on the ends of the tapes. Sew a small loop at each of the perforations on the back and sides.

...

Silk and Organdy Evening Dress.

This evening toilette consists of an under dress and peasant waist of apricot silk and an organdy over-skirt draped with a silk scarf of the color of the dress. The under-skirt is cut with a demi-train, and is untrimmed; the over-skirt is cut considerably longer in the back than in front, and is edged on the bottom with a gathered ruffle seven inches and a quarter wide. The pleated waist is finished at the top with a fichu as show by the illustration; the seam made by setting on the fichu is covered by a ruche of white organdy; a yellow tea-rose is fastened on the front of the fichu. The half-long organdy sleeves are edged on the bottom with a ruffle and a ruche of the same material, and are trimmed with apricot silk tabs.

Harper's Bazar, December 9, 1871

Jackets cut up the back almost to the top, are very frequently made now to wear with buff cashmere dresses, and the opening is trimmed with two rows of either white or buff guipure. The sash, likewise of cashmere, is striped slantwise with guipure. The sleeves, both of muslin and cambric dresses, are made considerably wider than the sleeves of silk dresses. ...

Velvet jackets, without sleeves, called Parabere jackets, after the famous beauty of the last century, are very fashionable. One of the prettiest costumes that has appeared, lately, in Paris, was of white silk, with gold-colored stripes, worn over a black velvet petticoat. The Parabere jacket was of black velvet, and the sleeves striped gold and white silk.

Bodices different from the skirts are very popular for evening wear with low dresses, and for winter these bodices will be made of black velvet, the basques ornamented with appliques of white lace, or white silk embroidery. If either scabious, blue, or orange-velvet be used, it will be considered more dressy than black.

...

The Polonaise is the newest fashion and is most graceful of all garments. It is close-fitting, long, and can be easily and beautifully draped. Both stout and slender figures look well in this garment. For a full figure the skirt can be more gored below the waist, thus preserving the present style of dress, and for slight persons, more fullness can be added, and both ways be equally in the fashion. The Polonaise buttons all the way down from the neck to the bottom of the skirt, and may be worn to look well over a skirt of any color suitable with it. No belt is worn with this garment.

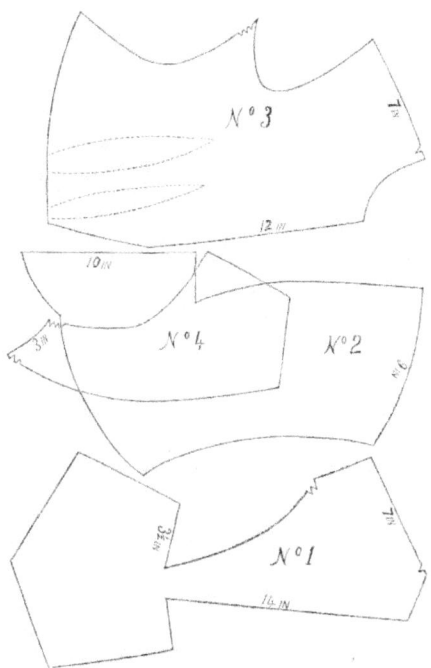

NEW BASQUE BODICE.

In the front of the number we give an engraving of a new and pretty Basque Bodice, and we add, here, a diagram, from which to cut it out. Winter bodices, both for in-door and out-door wear, will, for the most part, be made with basques. Our pattern is suited to silk or velvet or any other material. The pattern consists of four pieces, viz., front, back, side-piece, and sleeve; the basque, as will be seen, is cut in one piece with the bodice. There are two darts in front, marked by perforated lines. The front is joined to the back by one notch at the neck, the back and the side-piece by two notches, and the three notches indicate the seam under the arm. There is a seam

down the center of the back. The basque is plaited in a box-plait at the back; it will be found to form a double point at the back and one point on each hip. In front it fastens to the waist with buttons; from there it diverges at each side, and forms a point. The sleeve is pagoda in form; it is box-plaited at the elbow, and the frill falls with the point. It can be trimmed with fringe, gimp, or velvet. Our model is of black silk, ornamented with buff lace, headed by a full silk ruche.

...

CARRIAGE-DRESS.

Fig. VII. – Carriage Dress of Gray Silk. – The skirt is trimmed with five bias bands, and three rows of narrow plaiting of a shade of silk darker than the body of the dress. The tunic is round, and gathered up in front without any trimming, and has two, long wing-like ends at the side, and two long, straight tabs at the back, trimmed with one bias band of silk, and one row of narrow plaiting, like those on the skirt. The tight-fitting coat basque is short on the hips, and turned back with *revers* to the back, and is cut rather long and square in front; wide sleeves, with the trimming put on in points. Small, gray, velvet bonnet, trimmed with pink roses.

WALKING-DRESS.

Fig. IX. – Walking-Dress of Chestnut-Brown Poplin. – There is a row of embroidery about a row of fringe some distance up, on the under-skirt; the upper-skirt is also embroidered, and cut in deep scallops, edged with fringe; it is slightly puffed in the back. Tight-fitting basque, quite short in front, where it is edged with fringe, made with three Gothic ends at the back, embroidered and trimmed with fringe. Bonnet of chestnut-colored velvet, trimmed with pink roses.

Peterson's Magazine, December 1871

1872

WALKING-DRESS.

Fig. VI. – Carriage-Dress of Blue Silk. – The skirt has one deep, scant flounce, quite plain, with the exception of the narrow ruffle which heads it. The upper-skirt is puffed at the back, is cut in points at the side, and trimmed with very deep chenille fringe, put on below a bias band of satin of the color of the dress. The plain basque is also cut in deep points in front, but the waist is round behind. The coat sleeve is finished with a cuff, trimmed only with a bias fold of satin. Gray velvet bonnet, ornamented with blue ostrich tips. →

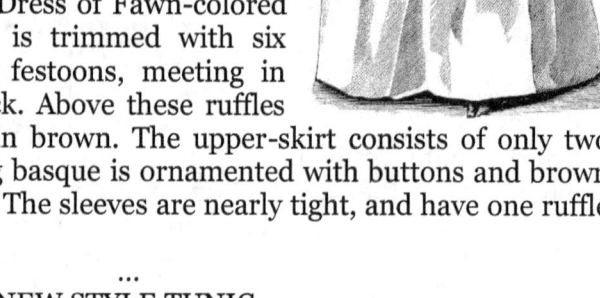

...

WALKING-DRESS.

← Fig. VII. – Walking Dress of Fawn-colored Poplin. – The lower-skirt is trimmed with six narrow ruffles, put on in festoons, meeting in front as they do at the back. Above these ruffles are four rows of braiding in brown. The upper-skirt consists of only two plain puffs. The tight-fitting basque is ornamented with buttons and brown braid, like that on the skirt. The sleeves are nearly tight, and have one ruffle with three rows of braiding.

...

NEW STYLE TUNIC.
By Emily H. May.

We give, here, an engraving of a new style of tunic, with a diagram, by aid of which it may be cut out. A paper pattern should be first made, by enlarging the diagrams, and to facilitate this, the size of each diagram is marked in inches on its side. Having made your paper patterns, fit them to the person who is to wear the tunic, enlarging, or diminishing, according to her height and figure. Then cut out your stuff from the paper pattern.

This tunic is of cashmere, and trimmed with a band of gross grain silk, cut on the bias, three inches wide on the skirt, and two inches on the basque and cape. Four sleeves. Bullion fringe, either worsted or silk, finishes the edge. We give a diagram of all parts.

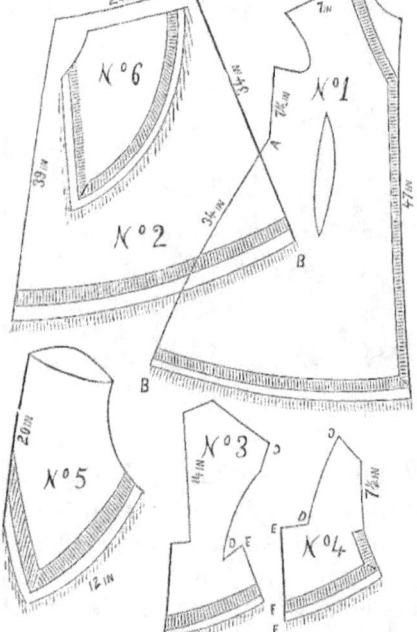

No. 1. Half of Tunic.
No. 2. Half of Back Skirt.
No. 3. Half of Back of Waist and Basque.
No. 4. Half of Side-Body of Same.
No. 5. Sleeve.
No. 6. Cape.

...

For house-dresses there seems to be less trimming used, though the suits for the street continue to be very much ornamented. It is no longer obligatory, however, to have skirt, tunic, sacque, and bonnet to

match; in fact, the bonnet is more frequently of some pretty contrasting color, and dark-green, mulberry, dark-blue or black cloth sacques, are worn with either black or colored suits. The new velvet casaques are made in the shape of long and ample tunics, draped and ornamented with headed gimp work and very handsome black silk guipure of Chantilly lace.

Peterson's Magazine, January 1872

WALKING-DRESS.

← Fig. VI. – Carriage-Dress of Rich Black Silk, Elaborately Trimmed. – The lower-skirt has three flounces, put on with a heading, and cut out at the bottom in a bag-shaped pattern, which is finished at the edge with a narrow black silk braid. Just above this bag-shaped pattern, on each flounce, is a piping of black satin. The tunic is rounded in front, square at the back and sides, and slightly caught up in the back. This tunic, as well as the jacket, is trimmed to correspond with the skirt.

...

WALKING-DRESS. →

Fig. VII. – Walking-Dress of Brown Poplin. – The skirt has but one scant flounce, headed by three rows of fur, the tunic is very deep in front, and quite short, and rather full at the back; that, as well as the small basque, with its very wide sleeves, is also trimmed with fur.

...

THE NILSSON SACQUE.
By Emily H. May.

We give, this month, an engraving and diagram of a new style sacque, which has been called the Nilsson Sacque, in compliment to the celebrated Swedish prima donna, whom many of our readers may have heard.

This sacque can be made of black cashmere, *Drap d'ete*, or fine habit-cloth. It is ornamented with embroidery in black silk, to which is added a simple pattern of braiding, with narrow, silk braid, forming the border. Heavy saddler-silk fringe completes this novel and handsome garment. We may add, that the entire ornamentation for this sacque may be done in braiding, if preferred. The heavier the design, the more elegant, of course. An inter-lining, slightly wadded with wool, should be added for winter wear; but it should also be made separate, so as to be easily removed as warmer weather approaches, or as may be otherwise convenient. We also give the diagram, from which it may be cut out.

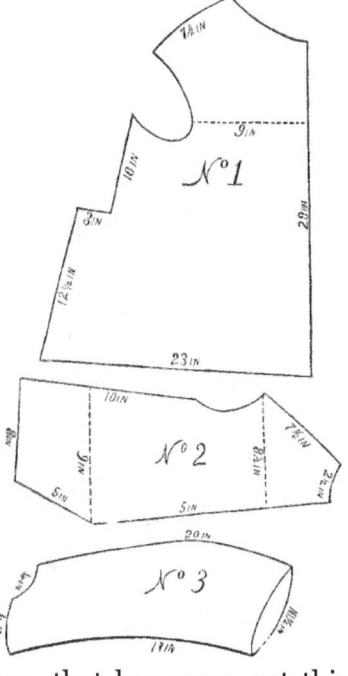

No. 1. Half of Front.
No. 2. Half of Back.
No. 3. Half of Sleeve.

Altogether, this is the most stylish, and will be the most popular, sacque, that has come out this winter.

...

What are called *costumes denteles* are much worn in Paris. These are trimmed neither with fur, lace, or fringe, but the edges are cut out in round scallops not very far apart. When the material of the costume is silk, these scallops area piped with velvet, and when it is velvet, silk is used for the piping, and the silk is often of a contrasting color. One exquisite dress (scarcely suitable for our working country, but which we describe, in order to show the style) was of prune velvet, scalloped out at the edges, and the scallops corded with pale-blue corded silk. The style was original, and it was in exquisite taste. The petticoat was bordered with a scalloped flounce, the open tunic was looped up at the sides, the bodice had deep basques, likewise scalloped out at the edges, and over it was worn a Chine *crepe* sash, fastened at the back. Very frequently a fringe is added below the scallops with good effect. An iron-gray poplin dress, scalloped out with black velvet, forms a very distinguished toilet.

Some of the newest dresses are made without tunics, and the skirts flounced up to the waist. In some cases the flounces are bias, trimmed at the bottom, and put on with a cord; in other cases they are box-plaited, and again they are scalloped, and corded with velvet, like the dress just described. Of course, these flounces must all be narrow, and there is but little difference between the width of the lower ruffle and the upper one. In these dresses the body has a deep basque, and is trimmed to correspond with the skirt. ...

Lace is much used for evening dress, put on in all the devices that fancy may suggest. It trims tunics, forms flounces, vandykes, spirals, side trimmings, etc., according to the quantity of lace, or the wish of the wearer.

Peterson's Magazine, February 1872

We give, first, a walking-suit of striped mohair. This dress is of striped mohair in two sizes. The narrow stripe is used for the foundation, and the wider one for the trimming. On the under-skirt, one deep flounce, slightly full and straight, headed by a band of the same, cut on the bias, stitched down by the machine. The over-skirt has the short apron front, which is now so popular, and the back trimmed up the back-seam, which seam is left open for ten inches, making the points as seen. The basque fits the figure; slashed, back and sides. Open sleeves. A narrow bias band trims the over-skirt and basque. Twelve yards of the narrow stripe, and four yards of the wide, will be required. These mohairs cost from thirty-seven up to seventy-five cents per yard.

...

Also, in the front of the number, is a walking-dress for a young lady, which, for simplicity of cut, style, and trimming, is unexceptionable. It is made of a light silk and wool material, called Poplinette, and comes in the shades of gray. This dress consists of an under-skirt rather longer than ordinary, and a trifle fuller in the back, perfectly plain, and provided with loops underneath, near the waist, in order to shorten it for walking, if desired. The over-skirt is cut exactly like the under-skirt, only shorter, being about nine inches shorter in front, then sloping off to the back, where it is looped, and slightly at the sides; this is ornamented with a band of black silk, cut on the bias, put on the edge, where it is finished with one row of bullion fringe. The waist is plain and round; over it is worn the jacket, for walking, which is cut with the figure, but not fitting tight; slashed at the waist. Open sleeves, all trimmed to match the over-skirt. The jacket may be cut surplice in front, with a rolling collar, if preferred. For the coming season, it would probably be more desirable.

...

Somebody to Teach Her to Dress. – The Princess Marguerite, who will be Queen of Italy some day, dresses as badly, it seems, as an Englishwoman. She appeared at the theatre in Rome, recently, in this absurd toilet. Pink *faille*, with a black velvet jacket, sleeveless, and around the edge of the pink, open sleeves, between the riche, white lace and pink sleeve, was a fall of chocolate-colored gauze; over the pink skirt was an over-skirt of the same chocolate gauze!

...

House-Dress of Black Silk. – The under-skirt is of black velvet and silk striped; the upper-skirt is of silk, quite short, with an apron front, edged with a black feather trimming. The back of the silk skirt is quite long, and is trimmed with a double ruffle. There is a short skirt above this long one, which is trimmed with two rows of feather trimming. The edge of this skirt is turned back at the side to from revers. The waist is round and high, and with the sleeves. In trimmed with a narrow feather trimming. ➜

Peterson's Magazine, March 1872

A Well-Dressed Woman is always more charming than one who is out of style, or carelessly dressed.

The costume we give next, is made of a very light shade of buff mohair, or summer poplin, and the trimming consists of pipings of a pretty contrasting shade of brown. These pipings may either be of silk or of the same material as the dress. Of course, the latter is much less expensive. The dresses still continue long for the under-skirt, but care must be taken not to make them too wide, as too much width produces the lapping-over, and that is when the skirt becomes worn-out. Seven rows of piping ornament the under-skirt. The upper one is cut, as may be seen, with quite short apron front, under which the sides of the back breadths are disposed. This upper-skirt is neither as long or full as those of the winter style, slightly looped at the back, and trimmed with five rows of piping. The waist is a close-fitting basque bodice, slashed up the back seams as far as the waist. Open sleeves, with passementerie button and tassels added to the trimming, which is, of course, like the rest of the costume. Clear muslin frills still continue to be worn for street costume, with sleeves to match. Sixteen yards of poplin, and five to six yards for trimming, will be required. These poplins cost from fifty cents up to one dollar per yard.

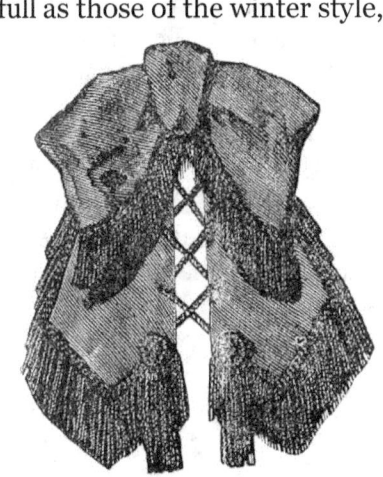

SASH.

TRIMMINGS FOR DRESSES.

JACKET BASQUE.

All the early spring poplins, poplinettes, pongees, percales, etc., etc., are now in the market, in every variety of color and shade, and at almost every conceivable price, from the percale, at twenty-five cents per yard, to the pongee, at a dollar and twenty-five cents. These latter, by-the-by, though expensive at first, are really not so in the end, for they both wear well and wash well.

Peterson's Magazine, April 1872

We give, this month, two beautiful evening dresses. The first is suitable for either a large or small party, and may be made of French muslin, tarlatan, gauze, or any of the light gossamer fabrics which are to be had at this season of the year. Perhaps the French muslin, Swiss, or tarlatan, should have the preference, both from their suitability for the style, and the inexpensiveness of the material. Ten yards of French muslin, two yards wide, at a cost of seventy-five cents per yard, will make the dress. Or a piece of tarlatan, which can be bought in white, pink, or blue, from six to eight dollars the piece.

The under-skirt of this dress is cut in a short demi-train, and ornamented with one flounce, twelve inches deep, trimmed at the bottom, and not too full, cut straight way of the muslin, of course. This is headed by another ruffle, hemmed on both sides, and gathered in the center, four inches wide. Inside of this is a second ruffle, three inches wide, and gathered with a fine cord. This double ruffle is duplicated, and arranged just above the first one, as seen in the engraving. This upper-skirt is perfectly plain, looped up quite short in front and at the sides, where it is drawn into the middle of the back, thus producing the puff. Plain, low-necked dress, with short sleeves, and round waist, fastened with a sash with short ends, completes this dress. Of course, the waist may be made high in the neck, and the sleeves open, if preferred, and still the style of the dress not materially altered.

The other is of the same kind of material, with the addition of black velvet ribbon, which makes a very effective dress. This skirt is cut also in demi-train, and has the bottom band with black velvet ribbon, two inches wide. This is ornamented with a plain-hemmed flounce, twelve inches deep, put on with a ruffle to stand up. Black velvet bows and ends are disposed at equal distances around the skirt. The velvet should be one and a half inches wide. The upper-skirt is rounded in front and open in the back, trimmed all round with a ruffle four inches deep, when made with the velvet between it and the heading. The skirt at the back is folded, as may be seen, and looped there at the sides with corresponding bows of the velvet ribbon. The waist is cut low in the neck, and with a short basque, which is open at the back, to display the trimming of the upper-skirt; this is trimmed at the neck, and around the basque, to correspond with the skirt. Bows at the shoulders and back, and front of the corsage, are added. Twelve yards of French muslin, and three pieces of velvet ribbon will be required.

EVENING POLONAISE.
By Emily H. May.

We give, this month, an engraving of one of the polonaise dresses so fashionable this season. Our pattern may be made up in either silk, gauze, grenadine, or figured tulle, and trimmed with lace, plaitings, or ruches. Our model is black figured net, edged with black lace, and rose-colored satin bands above; maize satin and black velvet also look well for trimmings.

The pattern consists of four pieces, viz:

No. 1. Front.
No. 2. Back.
No. 3. Sleeve.
No. 4. Ruffle of Sleeve.

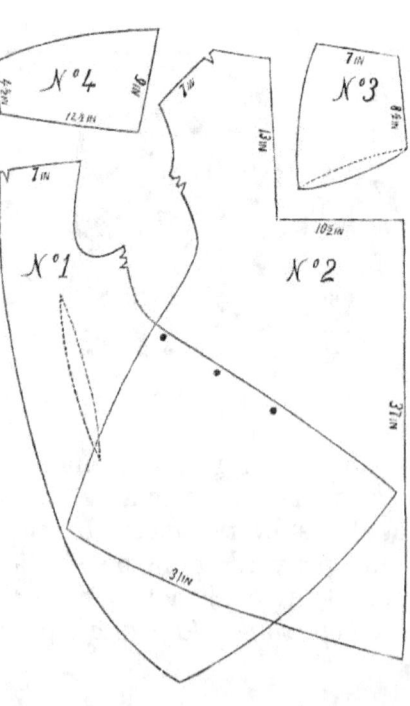

The joining of front and back is indicated with one notch on the shoulder and two notches under the arms, and these pieces must be joined before draping. Three punched holes will be found in the front; these show where the tunic is draped. The second hole is to be lifted to the first, and the third to the second. The piece that projects from the back is to be laid in double plaits at the waist. A bow is added on the waistband, both back and front. The sleeve can be plain or puffed to the elbow, and a ruffle is added. Half the ruffle only is given in our model. This polonaise also looks well in white *Algerienne*, edged with Thibet fringe. Nothing could be prettier for the coming season.

...

Fig. III. – Evening-Dress of White Silk. – The lower-skirt has two scant flounces, vandyked, and trimmed with a row of very narrow white ribbon, fringed with pink roses; the flounces are edged with narrow blonde lace, and headed by a row of the ribbon. The tunic is cut in points, and trimmed to correspond with the waist and skirt. Pink and white roses in the hair.

Fig. IV. – Evening-Dress of Rich Blue Silk. – The lower-skirt is trimmed with two flounces, the headings of which are lined with golden satin; bunches of yellow satin bows are placed at intervals on the flounces; the tunic is open in front, and cut out in a gothic pattern, edged with black lace; the back is lined with yellow satin. The trimming on the waist corresponds with the front of the tunic.

...

The graceful but untidy walking-dresses are still the fashion. These are especially uncomfortable to gather up in the hand, as they are made heavy and awkward by the depth and great amount of trimming which often reaches above the knee. Sometimes the upper-skirt is cut long in front, gathered high up on the hips, rather far back, and is comfortably short behind. Again the tunic will be rather short in front and very long behind, but always gathered up rather far back. Most of the walking-dresses are made with some kind of postillion basques, though many persons still cling to the comfortable sacque. The polonaise is exceedingly popular, but a good fit is indispensable to elegance.

BOWS.

SLEEVE.

PATTERNS FOR TUNICS.

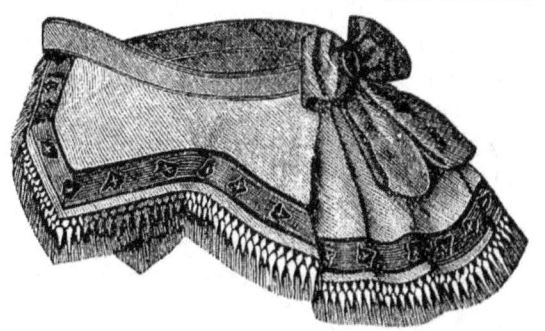
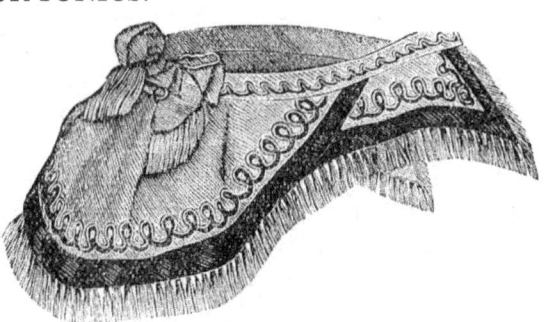

GARMENTS ORNAMENTED
WITH "STANDARD TRIMMINGS."

We give, in the front of the number, a lady's wrapper of white cambric, ornamented with "Standard" puffings, "Standard" bias tuckings, and "Standard" plaited flouncings. A very pretty house-dress of Swiss muslin can be made from this pattern. The "Standard Trimmings" supply the requisite ornamentation for all articles made of white goods. They can be bought at any drygoods store. The assortment comprises every variety of puffings, plaitings, tuckings, flutings, and flouncings, are for elegance and economy are unsurpassed.

...

The Secret to the Art of Dress is to wear only what is individually becoming in both style and color, and not to be tempted into unbecoming eccentricities, however fashionable they may be. Thus, for example, a blonde must never be led away into any dark and heavy colors, however popular they are. Nor should she wear, as is too commonly the case, washed-out and faded hues, but should choose bright, light tints, which assimilate with her complexion, and heighten its effect. She can, however, wear black, especially if her hair be one particular shade, with very good results; and, indeed, with regard to that color, people of all complexions look well in it, except brunettes without vivid complexions. Even a dark-haired person with a bright color can wear black with impunity, and in combination with white, it is at once effective and fashionable. A brunette should avoid, on the other hand, all pale colors, and can wear, according to the tone of complexion, dark-blues, reds, and the like, and a certain shade of dark violet. People with red hair, now so popular, owing to the artist mania for it, should be especially careful. Violet and purple should be eschewed. A medium shade of green is, perhaps, the most effective, and black, as a rule, is becoming, but inasmuch as this color of hair is of so many different tones, and allied to such very varied complexions, it is exceedingly difficult to lay down any strict rules.

No matter what the complexion or color of hair, there should always be one prevailing tint in a costume, and large masses of different colors should be avoided, except in the case of black and white, or where the tones are merely gradations of the same tint. Two or three bright colors, not assimilating, are far too commonly worn among us; a purple dress, with a pink or red rose in the bonnet, for instance, is a popular offence against taste, and so are curious mixtures of brown and gray, and analogous colors. Trimmings and similar accompaniments to a dress should, as a rule, be some gradation, preferentially a darker one of the prevalent tint, especially in costume dresses; or else a contrast, such as brown with blue or green, or gray with scarlet sparingly used. The choice of texture also is very important, and should be exercised with due discretion. Every part of a lady's dress should be chosen with reference to the other, and to her means and position in life. And yet we see women sacrifice large sums of money on some special part of their apparel – say a jacket – and then constantly wear a heavy and handsome one over a threadbare dress of some flimsy material. Thus, one part of the attire kills the other, and the beholder is impressed with a painful incongruity. Again, it would seem almost unnecessary to warn ladies to dress in a manner becoming their ages. This is the more to be deplored, as the older a woman gets the less she can afford to dress with carelessness or eccentricity.

Moreover, a lady should adopt the prevailing fashions only so far as they suit herself. Whatever is not suited, no matter how fashionable it may be, should be discarded, or, at all events, considerably modified; for surely it is the height of absurdity for ladies to disfigure themselves by adopting a fashion or style of costume that happens to be utterly unsuitable to them. Thus, for instance, there is at present a rage for elaborate horizontal trimming of all kinds. This, exceedingly effective on a tall and commanding figure, or even sparingly used on ladies of medium height, makes a short person look much shorter, and adds, moreover, very much to the breadth of the figure. And yet how few little people remember this, and how many of them pile on flounces and ruches till a figure, passable, though small, becomes what we can only stigmatize as "dumpy." How many, by wearing too large a panier, make themselves ridiculous.

It is that ladies may be able to select the style most suited to themselves, that we give so may costumes every month, and such various ones. Among our many patterns it is always easy to find the suitable one. Taste and refinement, we repeat again, may be exercised with only the humblest materials at hand.

Peterson's Magazine, May 1872

A house-dress for a young lady, back and front views, is given in the front of the number. Or it may be worn as a dinner-dress. It is made either of grenadine, berage, organdie, Swiss, or Victoria lawn; in fact, any of the summer tissues look well made after this design. The first, or skirt proper, is cut somewhat longer in the back than an ordinary walking-costume, but it may be provided with loops underneath, so that it can be shortened at pleasure. This skirt has three ruffles, slightly gathered, headed with a band of the material one inch in width, cut straight, sewed down by the machine. The last, or third ruffle, is continued up the back, as may be seen in No. 2, and caught together with bows made of the material; or if the dress is white, the bows may be of black velvet. The front is trimmed to simulate an apron, which has one ruffle, headed by the same width band; also further ornamented by like bands, arranged as seen. The tunic is composed of the pointed halves of a square, trimmed to match, and the front sewed back, as also may be seen. Basque bodice, with open sleeves, trimmed with bands like the skirt, finished by a narrow fringe or guipure lace. The manner of arranging the bands upon the body may be seen by the engraving. Eighteen yards of organdie or muslin, or twenty-two to twenty-five of grenadine will be required. English grenadine may be bought from thirty-seven cents up to one dollar per yard. Organdies from thirty-seven to fifty cents.

EVENING-DRESS.

Fig. VI. – Evening-Dress of White Muslin. – The trained skirt is trimmed with five plain flounces. The upper-skirt of white muslin is perfectly plain, and looped up with black velvet loops and ends, the low bodice, with short sleeves, is made of black velvet, and is worn with plaited fichu or collarette, edged with lace. ➜

↖ Fig. VII. – Evening-Dress of White Hernani. – The lower-skirt, which is not very long, has one deep flounce, headed by a loose puffing, fastened down at intervals by bows and ends of black velvet ribbon. The upper-skirt opens in front, is rounded at the sides and back, and is edged with broad guipure lace, headed by a narrower puffing than that on the lower-skirt. The high, square-necked basque is edged with lace, and like the sleeves, is trimmed with black velvet.

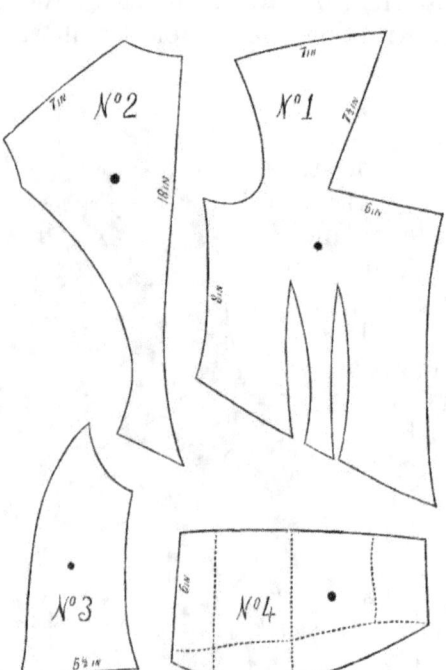

DRESS-BODY.
By Emily H. May.

We give, on the next page, a diagram for a dress-body, with sacque-opening in front, suitable either for a dinner-dress or an evening house-costume.

This stylish dress-body is high at the back, and is cut out to from an open square in front. The waist is a good deal lengthened all round, (*en basque,*) and forms points both at the back and the front.

The short sleeve is to be fulled along the straight pricked lines, so as to form rows of *bouillons* or puffings.

The pattern is given complete, and consists of four pieces, viz.,

No. 1. Front.
No. 2. Back.
No. 3. Side-Piece.
No. 4. Sleeve.

This is a pattern which is quite fashionable this season, and which has the advantage of being simple, so that it can be made at home, if more convenient.

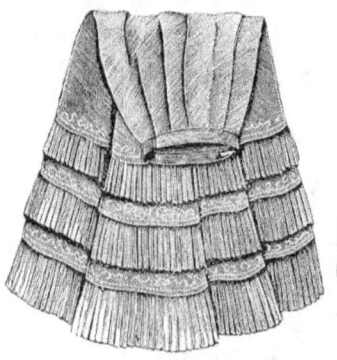
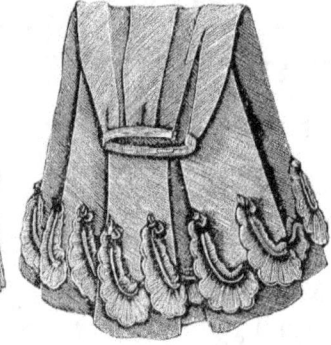

SKIRTS FOR TUNIC.

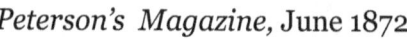

Peterson's Magazine, June 1872

Fig. 1. – Brown Silk Dress. – Back.
Fig. 2. – Brown Silk Dress. – Front.

This brown silk dress consists of a double skirt and basque-waist. The skirt is trimmed with kilt-pleated ruffles and with bias bands of the material seven-eighths of an inch wide.

...

Polonaises are the most important features of spring suits. They are of every design possible. The ample drapery of the Marguerite Dolly Varden is chosen by those who like very bouffant garments; while the more scant drapery of the plain Marguerite and the simple Dolly Varden polonaise is used by those who like more quiet dressing. Two large buttons now mark the taper of the waist in the back of

polonaises, instead of sash bows. Coat sleeves are very simply trimmed for stout ladies; those with long thin arms require more elaborate ruffles below the elbow.

In costumes composed of two shades of a color the height of the wearer determines the arrangement of the shades; for instance, tall ladies should have the lightest shade in the upper skirt, as the dark color below makes them look shorter; ladies who are under size should have the lightest color in the lower skirt. The sleeveless basques called vests enter into these costumes. The corsage is a simple basque of the darkest shade, with sleeves, and perhaps a vest, of the lightest tint.

The fancy for embroidery done on the costume increases. It is an expensive trimming, yet dealers say the prices they get for it scarcely pay the needle-women. Bias bands of silk for heading flounces are cut an inch wide, and sent to the fancy stores to be embroidered. A set of black bands had a vine wrought in lavender floss, and the charge for the needle-work was $3 50 a yard. A sage green faille costume had an elaborate pattern four inches wide bordering the polonaise. The work was as beautifully done as that seen on imported costumes, and the price was $9 a yard.

FASHIONS FOR SUMMER.

[ad for A. Burdette Smith patterns] DOLLY VARDEN Polonaise is the charming novelty of the season, and becomes the decided favorite of all who see it, when Dolly Varden goods – much in vogue – or any kind of wash material is used. By unbuttoning the lapels at the side and back, and by loosening the belt, it becomes a plain pelisse, without plait or gather; by readjusting it again it is transformed into an elegant, tight-fitting polonaise. As this change can be made in less than THREE MINUTES, and as it requires only six yards of yard-wide goods, it is easy to see why it is so highly honored. All sizes. Price of pattern, including a CLOTH MODEL, which shows exactly how to make and put it together, and how it will look when finished, $1.

...

The *Bazar* has said many times that side pleatings are cut straight across the goods from selvedge to selvedge. ...

The kilt pleating is left loose at the bottom of the skirt, but held in place by stitches on the wrong side.

Harper's Bazar, June 1, 1872

We give, above, a design for a summer walking-suit of Hernani, of a light shade of buff or gray. The one skirt has a side plaiting of the material, fourteen inches deep, which is finished, top and bottom, (also separating it in the center,) with a box-plaiting two inches wide, edged with a narrow Tom Thumb fringe in black. The waist is made high, and with a small pointed basque. Coat-sleeves. Over this is worn (for the street) a sacque, fitting slightly to the figure in the back, but loose in front. As may be seen, the fronts round up to the side seams, and under the back lappets of the under-waist, is a large, loose puff of the material, under which fall broad sash-ends of black ribbon or silk. This sacque is trimmed with a box-plaiting, the same width as that which ornaments the skirt. The sleeves are slightly flowing, with a plaited under-sleeve of clear muslin. This style would be very pretty in organdie, buff linen, lawn, or almost any thin material. Of Hernani, twenty yards would be required. In colored they can be bought for seventy-five cents per yard. Of yard-wide material, fifteen to sixteen yards would be sufficient. Three pieces of Tom Thumb fringe, at one dollar twenty-five cents per piece of twelve yards.

...

The Fashionable Materials, this summer, are muslins, jaconets, organdies, unbleached linen, and satin cottons – in a word, all washing materials. With all their air of simplicity, toilets of this kind have great elegance, especially where tastefully trimmed. They also possess the advantage of being economical.

CORSAGE A GILET.
BY EMILY H. MAY

This new and stylish affair, which is a dress-body with waistcoat front, call a Corsage a Gilet, consists of a front, side-piece, back, and sleeve. It was no seam at the waist, and the basques form deep points at the front, are narrow at the sides, and again deepen out to the back, where they are left open to the waist,

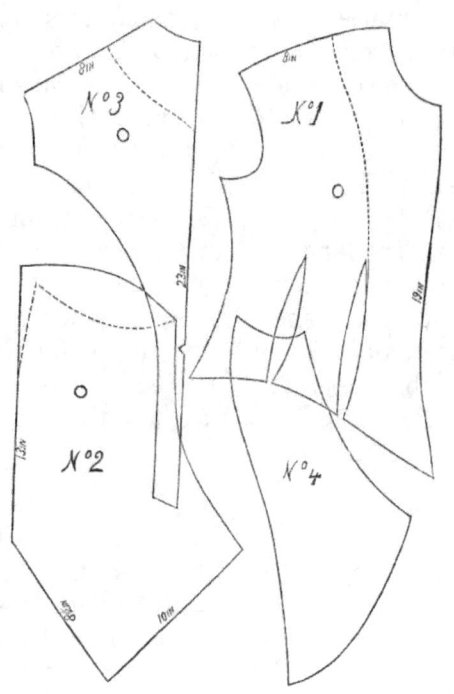

so as to display the *bouffant*, or group of bows, worn underneath. The sleeved is wide at the wrist, and is left open at back of arm as far as the elbow. The middle, or waistcoat portion of the fronts, should be covered with silk of another color, or a darker shade; and this waistcoat, or "Gilet," is carried over the shoulder, terminating in point at the back of the neck, as shown by the lines of picking on the patterns. We give, here, a diagram by which to cut out the corsage, which is for a lady of the ordinary size.

No. 1. Front.
No. 2. Sleeve.
No. 3. Back.
No. 4. Side-piece.

GARMENTS ORNAMENTED WITH "STANDARD TRIMMINGS."

We also give, in the front of the number, three illustrations of garments ornamented with the "Standard Trimmings." The first is a lady's lawn-suit, just the thing for this season of the year. The "Standard," box-plaited flouncing overlaps the straight-plaited, on the under-skirt, as will be observed, forming a heading of unequaled richness. These flouncings can be obtained in either cambric or Swiss, so that they can be adapted to any description of white suits. The second is a lady's polonaise, showing another style of the "Standard Trimmings" in the bias plait, which cannot be imitated by hand or machine. It is both elegant and graceful, and evidences the perfection of manufacture which the "Standard Trimmings" have attained. The third is a skirt for a lady's trained dress. The styles of "Standard Trimmings" – with which every lady should be familiar – are the straight-plait, box-plait, bias-plait, and fluted. These, each, can be obtained in any width from two to twelve inches, and of suitable materials. They can be used separately or in combination; and the "Standard" bias tucking, used in connection with either style of flouncing, as in this cut, is stylish and effective.

...

A Woman Should Dress Herself suitably to her age and style of beauty. Ladies of regular beauty require great simplicity in the lines and from of their dress and outer garments; those who are only graceful and pretty, require dresses smartly trussed up, dashing bows and saucy bonnets: in short, whatever is calculated to give piquant charm to their persons. ...

Many Ladies, who aspire to a reputation for elegance, do not hesitate to put a flower in their hair, even when they wear a high-necked dress. This is certainly wrong. A high-necked dress, however elegant it may be, down not harmonize with flowers, which should be worn only with low-necked dresses. A bow of ribbon, or an artistic comb, is admissible; that that is all that can be regarded as approved by good taste, in a high-necked dress.

...

Nothing but the coolest, softest materials are to be seen now, except at the sea-side, where soft, flexible woolen dresses and wraps are often found very comfortable; even the heavy cretonnas and chintzes, of which so many of the so called "Dolly Varden" costumes are composed, which are in reality warm, are intended to look cool. We think that the immense bouquets, tropical leaves, birds and birds-nests, swinging cupids, and love-lorn shepherdesses, which adorn these dresses, are in the very worst taste; they look as if the bed-room curtains had been made to do double duty. The true "Dolly Varden" dress is really picturesque and very becoming, except to persons over middle age; and even then the gay skirt, open in front, and puffed up a good deal behind, and the rather short petticoat can be very much modified, so as to be becoming. The low-crowned, broad-brimmed hats, looped up at the sides, are suitable to most faces, trimming them according to the age of the woman. Nearly all the foulards, chintzes, organdies, and lawns, are covered with bright, rather large bouquets, etc., which makes the modest, delicate striped, dotted and small-figured cotton goods of past years look both pale and plain beside them. The immense figures on some of these cretonnas, etc., have given the dresses so common a look, that some very fastidious ladies have gone to the other extreme, and wear their dresses quite long, and gracefully drooped, but not very much puffed out. These ladies select the quietest colors, some of those indescribable new tints which are so exquisite in themselves, though, as we have said before, not always effective nor becoming.

The Russian Plaiting, which is now so fashionable, takes an enormous amount of material; and even if this plaiting is not used, the innumerable ruffles or flounces, puffings, quillings, etc., help to make a dress cost a vast amount. We think a reaction must come, and that the plain redingote or polonaise, buttoning down the whole length of the front, with tight sleeves, will begin to creep slowly into favor. Some few dresses in this style have already been made in Paris, but they require good figures, and an aristocratic bearing to carry them off well. some few grenadines, with large checks or plaids, have appeared; but they are not popular.

White Muslin Dresses are much worn this summer; but persons inclined to stoutness must not be tempted to wear them for any other purpose than morning wrappers, under pain of appearing twice as thick as they really are.

Peterson's Magazine, July 1872

No. 1. – Toilet of black silk grenadine over black silk. The deep flounce is plaited, and divided quite near the top by a rouleau of silk. Just above it is another rouleau. This flounce is set on to simulate a rounded tunic, and a second tunic is outlined by the smaller flounce, which is met at each side by ribbon bows. The fronts of the loos-fitting casaque form two large scallops. At the back the basque is but slightly rounded, and finished with ribbon bows. Large sleeves. Trimming of plaited ruffles and rouleaux. Silk buttons fasten the corsage. Lace collar and undersleeves.

...

The present style of Dolly Varden, modified somewhat, of course, in its most extravagant features is extremely well adapted for a girl of any age from five upward. The Dolly Varden is simply an overdress cut skirt and waist together, and fitting to the waist, while the skirt is gored to considerable fullness. There is one back, two side pieces, and two fronts. To economize material, the waist and skirt may be cut separately and sewed together afterward without a cord, the top of the skirt being just wide enough to fit the body without plaiting or

gathering. The skirt is long behind than in front, and may or may not be puffed up. A small cape or loose sack may be worn of the same material as the overdress. To be strictly a Dolly Varden this overdress should be of some gayly-figured material, the pattern being in wreaths and sprays. The underskirt should be plain, of a color matching or harmonizing. Or the skirt may be striped and the overskirt plain. This same style of dress is pretty in plain contrasting colors.

...

JACKETS

Of clear white muslin trimmed with lace and velvet bows.

Arthur's Lady's Home Magazine, July 1872

HOME-DRESS.

Fig. VII. – House Dress of White Foulard. – The skirt has one deep flounce, made of white and blue striped foulard silk. This flounce is cut in sharp points, and falls over a plaited white muslin ruffle. The upper-skirt and wide cuffs of the sleeves, are faced with silk, like that of the flounce; and the back of the upper-skirt is composed of the blue and white striped silk. Above the half-high waist a white muslin heading, edged with lace and blue ribbon, is carelessly tied. A white guipure lace edges the upper skirt. →

← HOUSE-DRESS.

Fig. VIII. – House Dress of Black Silk. – The under-skirt quite plain; the upper-skirt round in front, looped up at the back, and draped in deep points at the sides, and trimmed with rich, black fringe.

...

↘ We give, first, a walking-suit for a young lady. This costume is composed of two shades of Victoria lawn: a light shade of brown and a lighter one of buff. The main part of the under-skirt is made of the brown, and it is trimmed with two flounces of the buff, pointed, top and bottom, and bound with brown. These are slightly full, and put on with a bias band of the brown to form a heading. The lower flounce measures nine inches, including the heading, and the upper one seven inches. The Polonaise has a vest front of the brown, buttoned all the way down. The back is of the buff, and is cut close to the figure, and is looped up to form the puff at the back, where it is ornamented with buttons of brown. This is pointed all round, and bound with brown to match the bottom of the skirt. Coat-sleeves, with a turned-back cuff of brown, also pointed complete this costume. Six and a half yards of brown, and seven yards of buff lawn, will be required. These plain-colored lawns or linens can be bought from thirty five-to forty cents per yard.

...

The next is a walking-suit of two shades of gray and black summer poplin, serge, batiste, or any of the light texture summer fabrics; or the style would be very suitable for an English barege in two shades of brown; or for a black Hernani. One skirt, very much trimmed, is the latest style, and will, no doubt, supersede the over-skirt, which has long been so fashionable. All skirts continue unaccountably long for walking. This one is ornamented by attenuated flounces of the two shades, first the darker, then a light; then dark, again a light one. These flounces are cut on the bias, if the material is poplin, but if barege, or any textured, of course, they are to be on the straight. All are scalloped with deep scallops, and bound, the dark ones with the light, and the light ones with the dark material. There is a bias band of the dark shade, separating the flounces from the quillings, which form the heading; of which there are two, a light and a dark one, corresponding with the flounces. A plain waist, with a short-pointed basque, close coat-sleeves, over which (for the street) is worn the outside jacket, which is fitted loosely to the figure, slashed up at the back, and trimmed to simulate the same at the sides. This jacket is of the same shade with the skirt of the dress, which is the lighter one, and is trimmed with a band of the darker, and the same width as that

upon the skirt. A mixed bullion, or sewing silk fringe; buttons also mixed. A turned-down, rolling collar, open in front; open sleeves, with turned back cuff. The cord and buttons, coming from the neck, and passing under the arms, are fastened in front. These are optional, and easily dispensed with, without injuring the style of the costume. Six yards of dark, and twelve yards of the lighter shade, will be required for this dress. Sixteen buttons. Five and a half yards of fringe. Bullion fringe, two inches deep, cost fifty cents per yard; sewing silk seventy-five cents. Any of these summer fabrics can be bought from fifty cents to one dollar per yard, according to the quality, at almost any good store. ...

The Dolly Vardens. – It is not at all necessary to spend large sums of money to wear those graceful Louis XV. costumes, generally called Dolly Vardens, which are as convenient as elegant. Chalis, alpacas, mousseline de laine, give us good and cheap imitations of foulard, the expensive material of this summer's costumes. For very warm weather, we have muslins, cambric, organdi. Trimmed all over with lace, ruches, delicately-tinted ribbon bows, and chiefly with black velvet ribbon "*de Saint Etienne*," what delightful toilets have been produced this season!

Never was Fashion so Fanciful as it is now. Every lady can modify it, according to the exigencies of her purse and figure, without being obliged, for that, to renounce being fashionable. We are no longer, as we used to be once, subjected to *one* fashion for each season, and whether fat or thin, tall or short, obliged to wear dresses all of the same shape, without daring to alter it. In short, we are making great advances in the civilization of dress.

Peterson's Magazine, August 1872

Those who still fancy the Dolly Varden style will probably like the brocaded and figured tunics, Polonaises, etc., to wear over plain petticoats; but fashion is so fickle, that even now, in Paris, the Dolly Varden is being discarded, and skirts will be worn, profusely trimmed to the waist. On the back breadths this is to be a succession of narrow flounces to the top, and in front a row of horizontal bars or stripes, and each stripe is to have a large bow in the center. These bows decrease in size as they ascend to the bodice, upon which they are continued. This style is quite Louis XIV. Our fifth figure in the color plate [*previous page*] is made in this style in the back, but with a different front. Woolen goods will not look well in this style, and for such materials a plain tunic or coat, with a cape, will be worn. These tunics can be belted in at the waist, if desired, and the depth of the cape is left to the taste of the wearer; some button close down in front, and some are left partly open, all reaching to the trimming of the under-skirt.

...

To Dress Out of Fashion is to make one's self the subject of remark, a contingency which every woman ought to avoid. How would even a man like to go down the street, in knee-breeches, and with powdered hair, as his great-grandfather did? For a woman to be behind the fashion is absurd. To make one's self conspicuous, in any way, is a mistake.

Fig. I. – Walking-Dress of Gray Alpaca. – The skirt is made with two scant flounces, each headed by three bias bands of silk of a darker shade than the alpaca. The waist is made with a plain, pointed basque at the back, and a deep apron in front, and is trimmed with a bias band of silk. The sleeves are half-wide, with a plaiting of alpaca inserted in the bottom, forming a ruffle. Gray straw hat, trimmed with a white and gray plume. Gray veil.

Fig. II. – Carriage-Dress of Peach-Colored Silk. – The skirt is trimmed with one plain ruffle, headed by a band of black velvet. The loose Polonaise has a finish of black velvet, and black ball fringe, and a large bow of black velvet at the waist behind. Straw bonnet, trimmed with blue and black feathers.

Fig. III. – House-Dress. – The lower-skirt of which is of dark claret-colored velvet, made quite plain; the upper-skirt is of rich crimson silk, very much puffed up at the back, and with the front trimmed with five ruffles; two long ends of the velvet fall from beneath the trimming of silk at the side. Sleeves rather loose, with lace under-sleeves, and a heavy fall of Valenciennes at the neck.

Fig. IV. – Walking-Dress of Olive-Brown Cashmere. – The skirt has one deep flounce, headed by a scant quilling of the material of the dress; a second quilling is placed some distance above. The Louis XV. basque has a deep vest, and is richly braided down the points and around the skirt; it is slightly looped up at the sides. Coat-sleeves, with deep cuffs. Felt hat, trimmed with white and blue plums, and bows of black velvet.

Fig. V. – House Dress of Steel-Colored Grenadine, Piqued with Claret-Colored Flounces Over a Gray silk Skirt. – The grenadine skirt is composed of four wide flounces at the back, and of five narrower flounces in the front, with a small apron above them, fastened back by a bow and ends of steel-colored ribbon. The high waist is round and open in front, with a deep basque at the back, the sleeves rather wide, and cut up on the back, and with the flounces are trimmed with quilling of steel-colored ribbon, headed by a row of claret-colored velvet.

HOUSE-DRESS.

Fig. VII. – House-Dress. – The skirt is of gray cashmere, trimmed with one deep flounce, put on in box-plaits, headed by a full quilling, bound with silk; the upper skirt is of de laine, striped in two shades of gray; it hangs long at the back, is very much rounded at the sides where it meets the back of the skirt, and is cut in shallow scallops, and bound with silk. The waist is made with shallow points, back and front, and the coat-sleeves have deep cuffs, scalloped. A fichu of white muslin, trimmed with black velvet, is worn over the body.

We give here a walking-costume. The material for this costume is plaid woolen serge, either, solid blocks of black and white, or the mixed plaids of blue and green. It is made with one skirt, just to touch, which is trimmed with two flounces, slightly full, cut on the bias, nine inches deep. These flounces are trimmed with worsted bullion fringe, two inches deep, mixed to match the material. There is a Polonaise waist, cut to the figure, buttoned from the throat all the way down the front. The edge of the Polonaise has a bias band of the material, two inches wide, and below that the fringe. As may be seen, this Polonaise is much shorter than those of last season. There is a box-plait, cut separate from the waist, and set on at the neck at the back, coming down about nine inches below the waist, the end of which is trimmed to match the bottom of the Polonaise. This is belted in at the waist, and may be dispensed with if preferred. A tight coat-sleeve, with a wide frill at the wrist, cut on the bias, and also trimmed with the fringe. These surges [sic] cost from seventy-five cents to one dollar per yard. Fifteen to sixteen yards will be required, and seventeen yards of worsted bullion fringe, from forty to sixty cents per yard. A lighter and cheaper material than serge can be bought in plaids, from thirty-seven to fifty cent per yard.

Peterson's Magazine, September 1872

Fashion has suddenly decided on a change of base. Fall dresses are being made after a new pattern, by which the over-skirt is abolished, while preserving its general aspect. For short dresses the skirt is cut very long, the back breadth being two yards in length; then the side breadths are pleated in precisely the same manner as for polonaises and over-skirts, and buttons are set on so as to drape the back breadth at pleasure, or leave it its whole length if a trained skirt is desired. In a word, the dress is composed of a single garment, instead of having an over-skirt or polonaise. The general effect is exactly the same as that of the present costume; the sole advantage rests in the possibility of using the same dress both for a walking suit and trained dress, and also, and above all, in the pleasure of change and of wearing something new, or at least something that is considered such.

Harper's Bazar, September 21, 1872

← Fig. VII. – Walking-Dress of Black Silk. – The lower-skirt is trimmed with a rather wide but scant flounce, headed by narrow bias bands. The tunic, which is long at the back, and a good deal puffed up, is trimmed with a deep black fringe, and a pointed gimp trimming. The jacket has a basque at the back, and wide-flowing sleeves, trimmed like the upper skirt.

...

We give this month a walking-costume for a young lady, something entirely new in design for a walking-costume. This material, for early fall wear, are cashmeres in black and dark colors; these will be very much worn. The first, or under-skirt, of this, as may be seen, is entirely plain, quite to touch in front and at the sides, and slightly trailing at the back. The over-skirt has a gored front, but no gores at the sides or back. The fullness is disposed in very large box-plaits, fitting to the waist; they must be laid very deep. This skirt is about twelve inches shorter than the under one, (that is, measuring from the front,) it is then cut evenly all round. After the box-plaits are laid, then they are cut away, as seen in the engraving. By folding a piece of paper in large box-plaits, with a few experiments, the shaping will prove successful. The trimming here used is simply a binding of silk, satin, or velvet, as the taste may suggest. The basque-bodice has a box-plaited skirt to correspond with the tunic. Wide, pagoda-shaped sleeves, are here given, but lose coat-sleeves we would consider an improvement. Costumes in black cost from one dollar fifty to one dollar seventy-five cents per yard. Ten to twelve yards will be required.

We give here a walking or house-costume. This costume is to be made of any of the numerous woolen fabrics suitable for the season – reps, poplin, cashmere, merino, etc. It would look best in poplin, one of the new shades of olive-greens. The trimmings are of the material of the dress. The under-skirt is made to touch all round, and has a box-plaited flounce, nine inches deep, upon the bottom, headed by a Vandyked piece, cut on the bias, and the points bound with the same material; this is sewn down at the top points, but the lower ones are loose, falling over the plaited flounce. As may be seen, the points are twice as large at the bottom as they are at the top. The Polonaise is somewhat shorter than the spring styles, buttoned down the front, and cut square in the bodice; however, this is optional. It is to be worn over a muslin chemisette, coming close up to the throat where it is finished with a stand-up ruffle. A box-plaiting, five to six inches deep, put on with a heading, is the sole trimming for the Polonaise. The sleeves are slightly open. Sixteen to eighteen yards of material will be required.

We also give, on the preceding page, another walking or house-costume, the design of which is entirely new. The side-plaiting on the under-skirt shows, in some places, a quarter of a yard in depth, and in others nearly one-third of a yard. This is managed by making the plaiting all one-third of a yard deep, and sewing it upon the lining of the skirt. The skirt is cut shorter, and in large and deep squares, turret-shape, which are trimmed with velvet ribbon, one inch wide. This falls over the plaiting. The effect is very stylish. The tunic is looped quite high at the sides, making an apron-front, and then in the center of the back with a velvet rosette. Fringe and one row of velvet forms the trimming for the tunic. The bias [sic: waist] is cut in a basque, extending a quarter of a yard in depth below the waist, in front, trimmed with two rows of fringe and velvet ribbon. At the back it comes just to the waist, where it is finished with a row of velvet and fringe falling from the waist. Tight-fitting coat-sleeves, with small cuff, edged with fringe. Twenty-two to twenty-four yards of silk will be required for this dress, or eighteen to twenty yards of double fall material. Two pieces of velvet ribbon. Five and three-quarters of a yard of fringe, three inches deep.

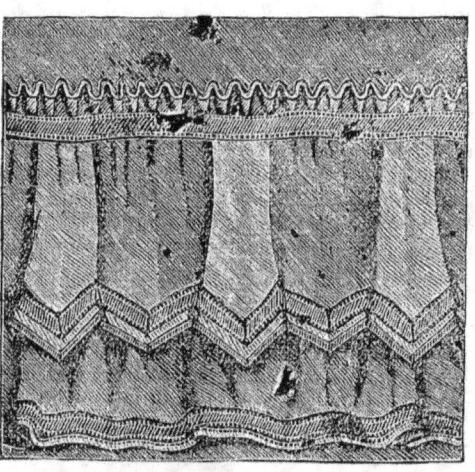

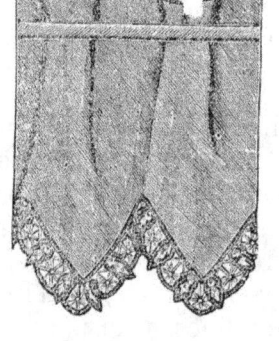

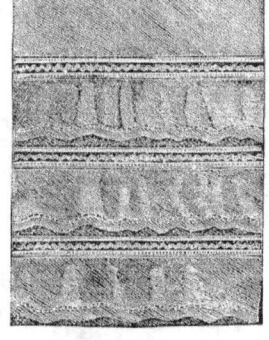

FLOUNCE FOR A DRESS.
←
...

→
FLOUNCE AND TRIMMINGS FOR DRESS.
By Mrs. Jane Weaver.

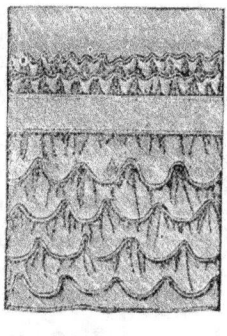

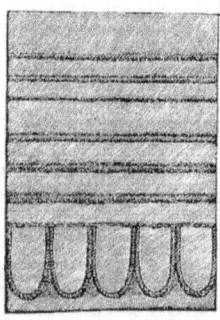

For ladies, who make their dresses at home, new styles of flounces and trimmings are always desirable. We give, accordingly, four such designs. One is for a flounce, (see above,) and the others are for trimmings. These are the prettiest of the new patterns that have come out this fall.

Peterson's Magazine, October 1872

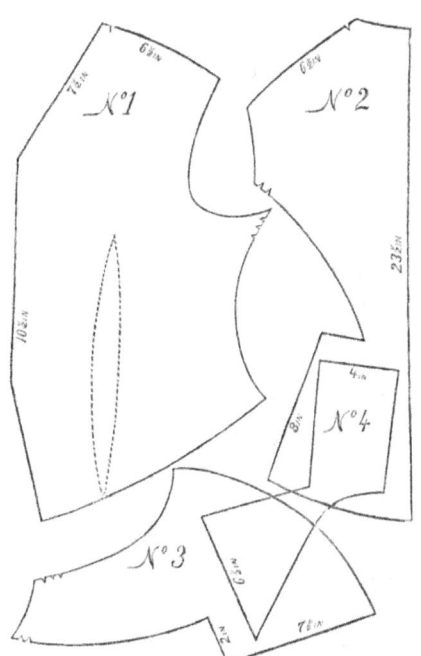

A SLEEVELESS JACKET.
By Emily H. May

These sleeveless jackets, which have been worn abroad for two years and more, and of which we have, from the first, given illustrations, are, at last, becoming very popular in this country also. Accordingly, we give an engraving of one, and also a diagram of it.

These jackets should be made either of the same material as the skirt, or that of the tunic; for unless they match some part of the dress, they look patchy, and are out of taste. Our pattern consists of four pieces, viz.

No. 1. Front.
No. 2. Side-piece.
No. 3. Half of Back.
No. 4. Half of Revers and Collar.

The jacket fits closely to the figure at the back, and is half-fitting in front. It has one small dart in front, which is marked on the diagram with perforated lines. The front is joined to the back at the neck, where there is one notch on the side of the diagram; two notches mark the back and side-piece, and three notches the seam under the arm. The basque at the back is full, the plaits being formed with the join. The collar is of the sailor form, and the pointed end is the revers. The sailor collar can be either simulated with trimming or made separate; in fact, its addition at all is a matter of taste. The pattern is added, as it will serve for Polonaises and boddices, on which it is frequently worn.

...

WALKING-DRESS.

Fig. VII. – Carriage-dress of Black Silk with only One Skirt, which is trimmed with three graduated flounces, scalloped and bound with black. A bias band and plaiting heads the top flounce. Gray cloth jacket, with very wide sleeves, edged with a pointed trimming of the cloth, and bound with black. Black straw hat, timed with a black plume and gray ribbon. ➔

...

Caring Nothing for Dress. – A New York editor said, the other day, that one of the merits of an Englishwoman way that she cared nothing for dress. This is on a par with a good deal of nonsense that comes from the pens of men, when the attempt to write about the sex. Any one who has been to England, knows than English women absolutely seem to have no taste at all for dress. They are, almost universally, dowdy-looking. In traveling, they wear old dinner-dresses and dirty white gloves, instead of the pretty and fresh costumes their American sisters do. They mix colors in the absurdest way even in a ball-dress. They spend quite as much money as others spend on dress, only they do not know how to spend it. If this New York writer has a wife, or sister, and she was to dress as most Englishwomen dress, he would be horrified. He would be too ignorant, probably, to tell what was the matter: but he would feel that his wife, or sister, had suddenly grown ugly. A becoming dress does wonders for a woman. As it is an affectation to pretend not to wish to look well, so it is folly not to wish for becoming dresses, provided they are within one's means. Just as a neat, prettily furnished parlor is a proof, that she, who presides there, is cultivated and refined, so a tasteful dress renders her who wears it greatly more attractive, and in the very highest sense. When a husband comes home at night, and his wife has on a fresh and becoming dress, it makes her seem prettier than ever in his eyes, even when he does not know the reason. It is not a merit, it is a fault, in a woman, to be indifferent to dress.

TRIMMINGS FOR UNDERSKIRTS.
By Mrs. Jane Weaver.

We give, here, several specimens of differ ways of trimming under-skirts, which can be varied as to material and color, according to the time of year and taste of the wearer.

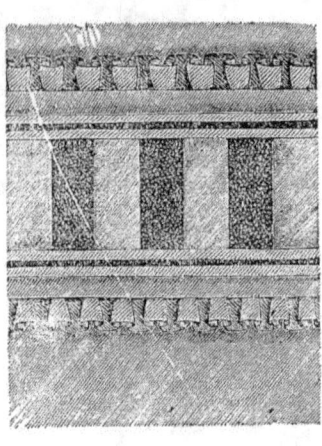

No. 1.

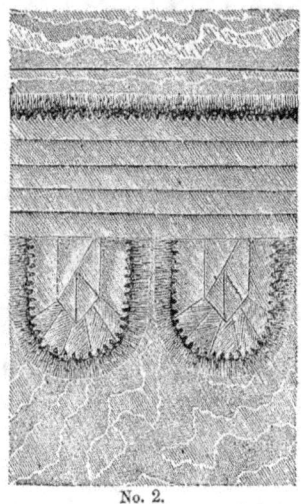

No. 2.

No. 1, is composed of a strip of the material, rather more than three inches wide, box-plaited at equal distances, with black velvet inserted between the plaits. Cross-way folds of the material sewn on with narrow black velvet ribbon, and edged with a small box-plaited frill, finish each side of the wider trimming.

No. 2, has five cross-way folds, under which straight strips of the material, an inch and a half in breadth, are arranged in flat plaits at the lower end, so as to form tabs. The center of them is filled up by a narrow double-piece of the material, first folded so that the edges meet in the center, thus forming a point; the sides are then again brought toward the center, and cross over each other. The outer edge of these tabs is trimmed round with fringe of a darker shade than the material, and a row of it is also placed above the cross-way folds.

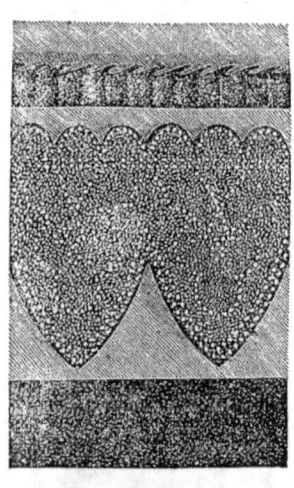

No. 3.

No. 4.

No. 3, has velvet three inches deep at the edge, above which a space of eight inches of the gray or other colored material appears, on which is applique a border of velvet, cut into the shape seen in the illustration, and enriched with white stitching, in the pattern there shown. A plaiting of velvet finishes the upper edge of the gray stripe.

No. 4, commences with a hem of two and a half inches in width of the material of the skirt, which is joined under a folded piping of the same to a strip of black velvet, five and a half inches wide; or, instead of velvet, a silk that contrasted well with the color of the skirt, might be substituted with good effect, although it would not be so durable. The upper part of the skirt is to be cut out at the edge, so as to form the shape seen in the illustration, No. 4, and laid down upon the velvet or silk with a folded piping of itself. Buttons, either of black velvet, or to match the silk, are placed between the points, and complete the trimming.

Peterson's Magazine, November 1872

Evening and house-dresses are made with skirts cut in the form of a peacock's tail. They are plain in front, with the smallest of tabliers, and at the back there is a quantity of narrow flounces, hemmed and corded. These cordings, or pipings, are always of a different color from the dress. For example, the shade of blue, called *bleu de lin*, is corded with prune color. When the flounces are cut out at the edge in leaf-like vandykes, and piped, they give the effect of a well-opened flower. Thus a pink silk toilet, with narrow vandyked flounces, is extremely pretty; the addition of a short tunic, either of black or white lace, renders it more dressy.

Basques, or rather waists, round or pointed in front with small coat-like plaiting at the back, are almost universal in all dresses not made with a Polonaise. These basques are not timed with fringe, ruffles, etc., only corded with a silk the color of the dress, or of some harmonizing color.

All sashes are tied at the side, and if not made of watered ribbon, are made with silk, lined with some color.

Fig. I. – Evening-Dress of Mauve Silk. – The skirt is trimmed with black lace, caught up here and there with rosettes of black velvet, surrounded with narrow, black lace. The tunic is composed of black net, edged with black lace, and looped up with rosettes of mauve silk. Berthe of black lace.

Fig. II. – Evening-Dress of Primrose-Colored Silk. – The skirt is trimmed with two rows of black lace, and bias folds of the silk, and festooned with bows of primrose-colored ribbon; the skirt is not very long, and is quite simply tucked up in back. The waist is half-tight, with a black lace cape over it; and the Maria Antoinette sleeves are trimmed with black and white lace.

Fig. III. – Carriage-Dress of Chestnut-Colored Poplin. – The lower-skirt has one very scant flounce, headed by a band of chinchilla fur. The upper-skirt has a deep, round, apron front, is very much puffed up behind, and finished by a band of fur. The waist has a round, apron-front, and is only a short, plain basque at the back, and with the neck and sleeves, is trimmed with a band of fur.

Fig. IV. – Carriage-Dress of Wine-Colored Silk. – The skirt has one deep, scant flounce. The black velvet Polonaise is deep at the back, and looped up at the sides, and is untrimmed. The wide, hanging sleeves, and long front, are trimmed with two rows of guipure lace. Bonnet of crimson velvet, with a long ostrich plume.

Fig. V. – Walking-Dress of Black Velvet and Blue-Gray Colored Silk. – The lower part of the skirt is of the silk, plain; above that is a row of black velvet, plaited; then a puffing of silk; than a straight flounce on the upper-skirt of velvet; than a puffed panier of the silk. The jacket is of black velvet, slashed in the back and at the sides; has wide sleeves, and is trimmed with a row of fur.

...

CASAQUE AND TUNIC.

The tunic is of a darker shade, and cut straight round the bottom, and ornamented with a braided pattern, done in the same shade as the under-skirt, either in silk, for fine, worsted, embroidery-braid, and edged with a knotted, or bullion fringe.

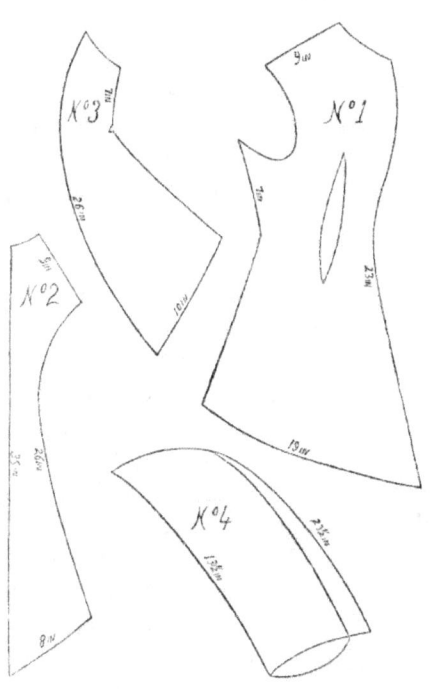

The diagram is in four pieces, viz: –

No. 1. Front of casaque.
No. 2. Half of Back.
No. 3. Side-Piece of back.
No. 4. Sleeve.

The casaque is made of the light shade of cashmere, and is braided to correspond with the tunic. There is an under-skirt to the casaque, made of the darker shade, and about four inches deeper all round than the casaque proper. The shoulders and sleeves are braided and fringed to match. A side-plaiting of the darker shade of cashmere may be substituted for the fringe, if preferred, or a bias-bound ruffle, four inches deep.

...

In France, every woman knows more or less of dress-making. Even the richest do not think it beneath them. There is, indeed, no more legitimate occupation for the sex. Women, as a class, have less money than men, and less than they would like to have. To be able, therefore, to make a dress, or trim a bonnet, or even to superintend these things, not only helps out one's income, but affords a pleasant and natural occupation. The knowledge of what is to be worn, and the cultivation of taste and economy in dress, are actually more useful to nine out of ten, than the learning of music, or the acquisition of half the accomplishments taught to girls. It is simply absurd to say that a dress is a matter of no importance to a woman. A good magazine, like "Peterson's ," which give styles for all varieties of income, and all descriptions of persons, is indispensable. Instead of stimulating extravagance, it shows how waste in dress may be avoided. A lady writes: "Not only have I saved money, by following your patterns and instructions, but everybody says I was never dressed so handsomely. It is a sort of patent of social superiority, in our neighborhood, to be dressed, *a la Peterson!*"

...

Coat Sleeves for dresses are almost universal. Most of the outside garments have wide sleeves. Ornamental buttons are much in vogue; alpine lapis-lazuli, agate, coral, malachite, silver, gilt, enameled buttons are all found on the new French costumes.

Peterson's Magazine, December 1872

Of morning-dresses or business-suits there should always be a good, though not a very large supply. No half-worn finery can, or ought to take the place of these. Every woman needs business dresses just as much as her husband, father, or brother need their business coats. And as a woman's employments usually vary more than a man's, she requires a greater number of the suits, which should vary to fit her temporary occupation. Thus, the "house-mothers," or daughters, who have frequently to assume some of the duties of housemaid, or of cook, should keep constantly in readiness dresses suitable for the performance of those duties.

The pretty calico, or delicate muslin morning dress, in which a lady would preside at the summer breakfast table; or the alpaca, or French flannel wrapper, which look so comfortable on a winter's morning, might present anything but an attractive appearance after having been worn while cooking the breakfast. It is true one may, by aid of good luck, a big apron, and rolled-up sleeves, escape soiling the dress; but the bottom of a spider that has just been lifted from the fire is apt to be black, and if, in moving it about, it comes in contact with the gown, the condition of the latter is not improved. Besides, tired hands are not always steady in their motions, and a coffee-pot may tip, or a gravy-boat may incline from a safe level with results disastrous. So it is safer, if one is occasionally obliged to play cook, to have two or three cooking-dresses. These should be of dark, and closely-figured calico – *not,* as the oft-quoted "old-woman" said of the delft-tea-set, that it may "not show dirt" but that iron rust, fatal to all light calicoes, – coming from no one knows where, – or equally fatal fruit stains – unremovable save by acids quite likely to remove bits of the fabric at the same time, – may not render it old and soiled-looking on the first day of its use. In fashion these cooking or housemaid dresses should be as simple as possible; flounces, tucks, folds or ruffles are all equally unendurable.

The usual morning dress admits of some ornamentation, but excess should be guarded against; much trimming is not "in keeping," either on the gown, or the apron, which old-fashioned dress-protector will never be despised by neat women; on the contrary they will always endeavor to be fully supplied with an abundance of them.

Every lady who lives in the country is, or should be, something of a gardener. For this employment she will need a special costume, and nothing is so comfortable and convenient as a dress of light woolen material, made with full trousers, loose waist, and skirt reaching a little below the knee, like the costumes worn in classes for calisthenics. The same style of dress is most appropriate for berrying expeditions and mountain-climbing, and for boating and fishing excursions.

But home duties and enjoyments do not form the sum of life's employments for all women, and in the lives of many they are supplanted by occupations more nearly resembling those of their fathers and brothers. Women thus situated will need regular business suits. These should be of strong, serviceable material, quiet in color and but slightly trimmed. Shabby finery – always detestable – is never more so than on the person of a self-supporting woman. But we do not necessarily mean that a dress of fine material may not be so remodelled as to be suitable for a business dress. If of dark color, neatly kept, and all expensive or "fussy" trimmings removed, a gown that has served its time as a "best dress," may be very becoming and suitable for daily use; or light colored all-wool materials may be dyed for this purpose. What we object to, is that when a dinner or an evening dress has become *passée,* its owner should don it "about house," or in her school-room, her office, her studio, or her shop, without fitting it for its new use. For, besides that the long skirt will speedily get frayed and soiled, and the flounces and ruchings, once so pretty, must soon share the same fate, and that the finery is now as out of date, as in its new surroundings it is out of taste, it is a very wasteful way. The dress re-made would last twice as long, and the trimmings, if of real lace, or handsome passementerie, or fringe, or velvet, might serve for another nice dress instead of being worn out in a service for which they are not adapted.

An old black silk, neatly remodelled, forms, perhaps, the most useful of all business dresses during cool weather. Next best are dark-colored silks, then the ever ready, long-suffering, black alpaca; or, for very cold weather, a dress of dark, fine English flannel or waterproof. For business use, in weather too warm for silks, we can recommend colored cambrics or linens, but only such as are so plainly made and trimmed that any Bridget can wash and iron them; for no one can enjoy wearing a dress that will show the slightest spot or stain, when it cannot be made up without calling into requisition the services of a French laundress and incurring an expense of nearly one-third its first cost.

In addition to business suits, one always needs one or two dresses that will answer for calls, for church, and for small evening gatherings.

We know we are shocking the notions of many when we say but one or two of these, for is it not considered essential that one shall never, or at least rarely, appear twice in the same dress, upon even the most informal occasions? This may be. There are a great many foolish fancies in our world, and surely this is not least among them. But we are glad to know that there is a very large class who recognize that they are of more consequence than their dress, and that if the latter is in good taste, not too far past the style, and in good preservation, it will bear being viewed many times in different or the same places.

...

Goods of startling patterns, or those which are "the rage," even though very pretty, are not safe purchases for persons with limited purses. The articles are marked, and as such, the eye of the wearer and of beholders soon becomes wearied, and the dress, though still in good condition, can only be worn under protest, or be laid aside for the next beggar. Plain goods are never out of date, and narrow perpendicular stripes, tiny checks, or "chênés," or small figures, though not always fashionable, are rarely out of taste. But the "robe," or "pattern dresses," however beautiful when in vogue, are *outré* when not "the rage" of the moment; "bayadere" or diagonal stripes, barely endurable when Fashion gives them her sweetest smiles, are positively ugly when viewed in the shade of her frown; and the exaggerated flowers twined about miniature towers, or decorating the brows of Liliputian Cupids, which excite smiles even in their palmiest days, will become grotesque to an unendurable degree when Fashion shall have decreed their doom.

Those ideas of taste which are formed simply upon "what is worn this season," are always unreliable, and are apt to lead those who suffer themselves to be so guided, into many needless expenses; while true taste, based upon the unvarying laws of color, form, and fitness, will preserve its followers from extravagance, and from that *whimsicalness* of attire which the devotees of mere Fashion are almost sure to exhibit. Even in plain colors, or narrow stripes, etc., Fashion decrees frequent changes, but Economy requires that Fashion's views shall not be strictly followed. If any particular shade is the approved novelty of the day, Economy knows that though pretty in itself, its very prevalence will, in another year, render it almost tiresome, and therefore that it will be better to purchase a dress of a shade that has been overlooked of late, not only because it is at present cheaper, but because it will not as soon fatigue the eye. But in the choice of ribbons, or other articles which are not expected to be worn more than one season, it is not necessary to regard this point.

Those goods which are alike on both sides – whether plain or figured – as they can be turned, are more economical than those with but "one face;" and those which have – in dressmaker's phrase – "no up nor down" to the figures, can be cut to better advantage than those in which the direction of the pattern must be considered. Indeed, it requires from one to three yards more material to cut a dress where care is necessary to match the figures, than when there is no such necessity.

Colors that readily spot or fade are undesirable, even if the material is one which can be dyed without injury, which can scarcely ever be said of any but thick and soft all-wool fabrics. Very light shades should rarely be chosen in any but washable goods, for though the wearer may be one of the neatest and most careful of beings, she cannot avoid all contact with dust and dirt; and she will feel decidedly more comfortable if her dress is one that can be washed or brushed into cleanliness, than if she is conscious that even a slight dinginess of hue must remain after her best efforts to remove the traces of a soiled car-seat, or the accidental touch of grimy fingers. In choosing trimmings, it is always best to select something that, like real lace, is ever in fashion, and can be used upon different dresses. A few yards of good lace may cost more in the first place, but in the end will be found to be more economical than the cheaper sorts of trimming, or than cutting up into endless ruffles and puffs, the stuff of which the dress is made, unless the latter is of some comparatively cheap material. ...

For expensive dresses we should prefer to buy the material and have it made up by a dressmaker in whom we have confidence, or by ourselves, if we possess the requisite skill, as we are then more certain of a perfect fit, and can also plan to have the stuff cut out to advantage; that is, so that it can be remodeled to suit the changes of style. But for business-suits, or any dresses made of the more serviceable, but comparatively inexpensive materials, as alpacas, linens, lawns, etc., it is usually more economical to buy the ready-made suits now offered at all our best dry-goods stores. These suits may frequently be purchased at but a slight advance of what would be the cost of the material alone to those who have not the privilege of buying at wholesale rates, if the purchaser has sufficient independence of character to by a dress made in a fashion three or four months old. Of course the dress should be examined to make sure it is well sewed, etc., but at a reliable dealer's – and we should patronize no other – this is always the case.

One silk dress during the year, made up first as a dress of ceremony, and the next year transformed into a suit, and its place taken by a new one, will keep a lady, who only does the average amount of visiting, very well supplied with silks, old and new; while one really useful suit for winter, and another for summer, with an incidental linen, and two or three house dresses, will comprise, as far as dresses are concerned, a sufficient wardrobe.

In respect to the manner of making dresses, the most important consideration is never to be led to the extreme of the *mode,* but rather to aim at the least expense of money, material, time, and *fuss,* which will enable us to pass without an appearance of singularity. And this will ensure that a dress can be worn a much longer time, without alteration, than if made in servile imitation of the fashion plates. Persons of taste – whether economically disposed or not – will avoid *tormenting* their dress with an over abundance of trimming, or with exaggerated outlines. Thus, if we must wear *paniers,* they need not be of extravagant proportions; if some trimming is essential to finish the skirt of a walking dress, it is not necessary that we indulge in fifteen scalloped flounces; if bonnets and hats are aspiring in tendency, it is not important that they resemble Towers of Babel; or, if they incline to breadth of outline, it is not necessary that the sides should emulate the wings of a condor. In short, *moderation* in following the vagaries of fashion is one of the most essential principles whether of economy or taste.

Hints on Dress, 1872

1873

HUSSAR JACKET. ➜

...

We finish with a white cashmere house-sacque for a young lady. This sacque is cut in, to fit the figure at the back, and is loose in front. Open pagoda sleeves. The trimming is one row of black velvet ribbon, one inch wide, headed by a narrow black silk embroidery braid, put on in loop pattern, seen in the design. One and a quarter to one and a half yards of merino, one piece of embroidery braid, and five yards of velvet ribbon will be required. Line, either with white flannel, or silk, as the merino is scarcely warm enough for a winter wrap, even for the house.

LOUISE CASAQUE.
By Emily H. May.

We give, here, an engraving of a new and stylish casaque, called "The Louise Casaque." No other article of wearing apparel for ladies is so fashionable this winter. It consist of four pieces, as will be seen from the annexed diagram, viz:

No. 1. Back.
No. 2. Side-Piece.
No. 3. Front.
No 4. Sleeve.

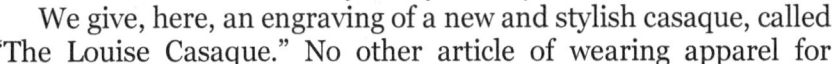

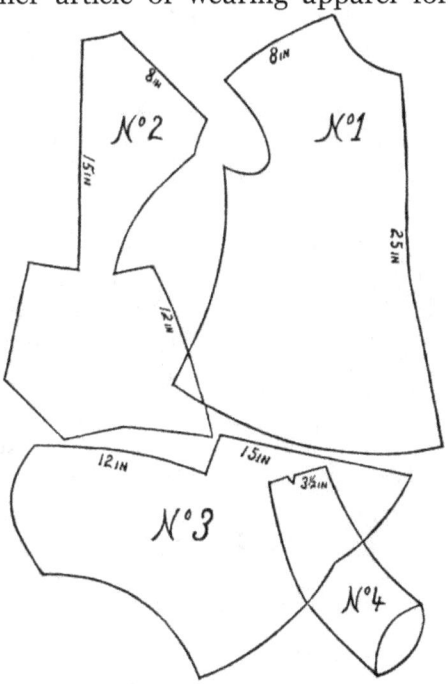

We may add that the back, when made up, will have a hollow plait in the middle, and one on each side, and these plaits are to be laid underneath: and there is a similar large plait at the back of the sleeve, but this plait is to the outside, (as shown in the engraving,) and to be headed by a ribbon or band of *passementerie*. This casaque forms a very elegant out-door garment for mild days in winter, especially if made of velvet, or cloth, and lined.

...

Dresses are now worn exceedingly flat in front, so much so that no starch is used in the petticoat itself; only the flounce that borders it is starched. At the back a dress improver is worn, with whalebone or steel in it, or else made entirely of horsehair; but the size of this tournure is decidedly less exaggerated than last year.

Large square pockets and vests, the latter often coming down low on the skirt of the dress, are very generally worn. Lace, gimp, fringe, quillings of silk and embroidery, are all much used as trimmings. ...

The Feather Trimmings are again exceedingly popular. In furs, that called in Paris the skunk, and the silver-fox, are as yet the most fashionably worn. Poplin Polonaises, trimmed with silver fox are exceedingly lady-like; but the cloth Polonaise is considered more suitable for walking wear.

Peterson's Magazine, January 1873

Fig. VII. – House-Dress of Dove-colored Silk Poplin. – The under-skirt is made with three ruffles in front, headed by a standing-up ruffle and bias band of poplin, and with seven deeper ruffles at the back, with the hem bound up on the right side, and finished with a piping. The over-skirt is made open in front, and trimmed with a narrow fringe. Close sleeves with a wide cuff. Over the body of this dress is worn a fichu, made of black velvet, or crepe, trimmed with fringe, which crosses in front, and is tied in a large bow, with long ends, which fall on the skirt at the back.

Fig. VIII. – Back of the Dress, No. VII, which shows how the over-skirt is finished at the back.

...

At this season of the year, but few changes are made in the style of dress; they only depend on the individual taste of the wearer. We notice, however, that lengthwise trimmings are creeping in; they have yet, by no means, taken the place of flounces and horizontal trimmings, but will probably be much more generally adopted by spring.

...

We give, here, something quite new in the shape and design of the Polonaise. The material is cashmere or merino. This costume is composed of two colors, or two shades of the same color. A darker or lighter shade of olive-green, or black and light gray; the latter combination is represented by our cut. The under-skirt is of gray, "kilted," after the fashion of the Highland kilt. It is cut perfectly straight, (no gores,) and very full. Five to six widths of merino will be required. There is a large box-plait laid down the front of the skirt, and then the side-plaiting are laid back from that on either side. Most dress-makers fasten these plaits down upon a lining of crinoline. The plaits may be continued entirely to the waist, or stop at about nine inches from it. A large figure would be improved by this arrangement, while a slight one should continue the fullness to the waist. The Polonaise is cut with a vest of black. The skirt and upper part of the sleeve is of black, while the over-jacket is gray, forming a basque at the back. The skirt and jacket are trimmed with a knotted silk fringe, as may be seen. The back part of the skirt of the Polonaise is cut square, and not looped up in any way, coming down to within twelve inches of the under-skirt, while the front is looped quite high at the sides. The sleeve has six small pieces down the arm, from the shoulder to the cuff, which is formed of a full plaiting of the gray merino. A small bow at the top of the shoulder, and at the cuff, completes the sleeve. Twelve yards of gray, and five yards of black material will be requisite. Colored merinos of all the new shades, can be bought in good qualities, "Lupin's" make, for $1.25 per yard.

...

SLEEVELESS JACKET.

We also give, in the front of the number, a jacket without sleeves. This gray cashmere jacket is lined with gray silk, and bound with silk along the scalloped edges. It is made to fit the figure, with buttons down the front, and a scalloped stand-up collar.

IN-DOOR JACKET.

Also a new and stylish pattern for an in-door jacket, with a sash tied about the waist. It is made of gray flannel, and the edge is festooned with blue. The cuffs and collar are quilted in blue satin, and the band likewise is blue, being finished off with tassels.

...

Too Much Extravagance. – Do not, for a moment, suppose that a costume is elegant in proportion to its cost. Beyond a certain point, on the contrary, expense becomes vulgarity. The luxury of a fine lady's toilet, in Paris, and among the more extravagant here, has now reached its utmost limit. Formerly, when Worth, Aurilley, or Roger asked, for an out-of door dress, a hundred, or a hundred and twenty dollars in gold, people said that their prices amounted almost to a swindle. Such dresses, by the time they reached America, and the duties and other expenses were paid, cost from two hundred and fifty to three hundred dollars in greenbacks. But now, even in Paris, it is a common thing to pay a hundred and fifty or two hundred dollars in gold for a walking-dress. Worth gets four hundred dollars in gold for a velvet dress, and from two to three hundred for a cashmere one. These dresses, by the time they arrive in Philadelphia, or New York, cost the fair wearer from five hundred to eight hundred dollars in currency. Others are even more expensive. An evening-dress, with lace, frequently represents a thousand or two dollars, the price of a small farm. We used to hear loud outcries about the extravagance of the French Empire, but the French Republic has put its predecessor quite to shame. In our opinion, extravagance in dress has gone too far, and a reform, and a speedy one, is needed. We shall do what we can to bring about such a reform. Of course, it is only very rich ladies, who buy the dresses we speak of; but even the wives and daughters of millionaires spend too much, when they spend thousands on a dress.

...

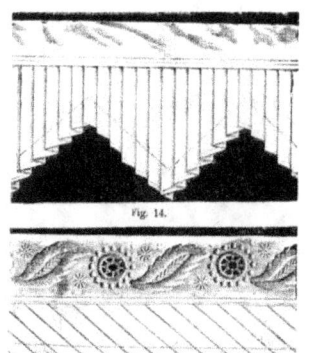

Standard Trimmings. – In the front of the number, we give a handsome extension sheet of the popular standard trimmings, of which we have often spoken. These trimmings can be bought at almost any store, and save a world of trouble to ladies, who, ordinarily, would have to make the trimmings for themselves.

12 ... and 14. – Standard Plaitings, made 1, 1 1/2, 2, 2 1/2 inches wide, Banded and Embroidered. ...

17. – Standard Plaited Flouncings, from 1 to 10 Inches wide. ...

The Standard Trimmings are made of Victoria Lawn, Jones' Cambric. Swiss Muslin. and Linen, and are all the fashionable widths.

...

Belts of very thick grosgrain silk are more fashionable than the leather belts, which are already getting common. These belts are fastened with agraffes of oxydized silver or of jeweled enamel, in the medieval style. The wide moire sash, looped at the side, is also fashionable for dressy toilets. ...

Buttons of oxydized metal are very fashionable, and for simple costumes the plain black mother-of-pearl button, which is not so black but that it lights up with a thousand tints of color in the sunshine. This button looks best for cloth and velveteen costumes.

Peterson's Magazine, February 1873

Many flounces, ruffles, puffings, and quillings, are still worn as a rule, though a simpler style is adopted by many who are tired of excessive trimming. Bodices are worn longer, and more trimmed, than they were; but, to a stout person, this is not a becoming mode. It is now the fashion to wear skirts clinging about the ankles as much as possible. There is still a puff at the back, but not an exaggerated one. Evening dresses, however, require more support underneath them than costumes. Long train muslin under-skirts are worn bordered with a deep flounce, which are edged with either embroidery or lace. These minor details are important, for, however skillfully a dress may be made, unless its wearer is well petticoated, the effect is frequently ridiculous.

The trimmings on evening dresses, such as puffs, ruches, laces, etc., are arranged mostly in perpendicular lines. The over-skirts are extremely long at the back, and much ornamented, but in front they are short and untrimmed. Light organdy muslin flounces and frills, notched out at the edge, are again coming into favor for trimming demi-toilets for evening wear. They are arranged in a variety of styles.

It is very much the fashion for trimmings, and also for cravats or bows for the hair, to use black or dark-colored velvet, lined with some light shade of grosgrain silk or moire. For instance, brown bronze velvet will be lined with pale-blue, and green bronze with flesh color; maroon with maze, and garnet-color with pale-rose; while all shades of red, pink, orange, mauve, and yellow, look well with black velvet. Crepe de chine and satin are also combined in the same manner, and make up very prettily into bows for the hair and throat, which give a nice finish to the most simple dress.

...

HOUSE-DRESS.

Fig. VI. – Home-Dress of Dark Sage-green Cashmere. – The under-skirt is laid in with plaits both back and front. The upper-skirt is of a lighter shade of cashmere, and has a deep apron-front, edged with fringe; at the back it forms a full, short puff, looped up by a sash of the darker shade of the cashmere. The body is made with a small basque, which opens at the back, and is made of the darker shade of the material.

...

On the preceding page is a walking-costume for a young lady, made of light-pearl cashmere, or alpaca, trimmed with black silk. It has simply one skirt, trimmed in front as far as the side gores, with a flounce, half a yard deep, put on in two large double box-plaits; top and bottom of this flounce is bound with black silk. The center of each of these plaits is ornamented with a bow, consisting of one loop and end made of black silk. Then there are two flounces half the width of these box-plaits, each bound and slightly full; those meet the plaiting at the gores, and extend around the back of the skirt; over these is a third flounce coming from within ten inches of the waist, also bound. The basque has a rest [sic: vest] in front of black silk, trimmed with a flat fold of the same, and flaps to simulate the pockets, as may be seen. The fronts of the basque are turned back, and trimmed with loops of black, fastened down with gray buttons. Small coat-sleeve, with pointed cuff, trimmed to match. The left side, the skirt of the basque is looped with a large sash, bow and ends of black grosgrain ribbon, or this may be made of the black silk, if more convenient. Sometimes the best parts of a partly worn black silk dress will cut up into very nice trimmings for a suit of this kind. Eighteen yards of mohair, or twelve of cashmere will be required; four or five yards of black silk, including sash; two dozen buttons.

Peterson's Magazine, March 1873

CLOTH MODELS.

Our Cloth models represent the garment completed of the pattern which they come with, showing every seam, pleat, gather, tuck, etc. They are *perfect guides*. Compare the pieces after they are cut by the pattern, with the pieces of the same shape in the model, and it will show you just where to sew them together, where gathered, where pleated, where tucked, etc., and how and where to loop. Besides the model we notch most of our patterns, though notching is of very little use, and of no use at all where the pattern is the least difficult, without the models. Competent dressmakers very often find it impossible to "get them together," even when the description and engraving are before them. Our Cloth Models overcome all of these difficulties, for they are the garment right before you. Any lady who can sew can put together and complete any garment, however difficult, without assistance or trouble, while she would be *totally* unable to put the plainest garment together with out the model. However, we charge no more for our patterns with the cloth model than we did before we invented them, although they cost us more than four times as much as the patterns; for the cost of the material in a pattern and the making of them is very small. But the cost of *importing*, making it into cloth to sketch, sketching, engraving and *sizing* is enormous.

We are the **Inventors** of these **Cloth Models,** and they cannot be obtained from any other house.

1570 – Evening Dress for a young lady – is far more appropriate and becoming than many of more costly materials. It is made of white tarlatan, trimmed with ruches of blue silk and box-pleatings of itself. It has a sash of blue watered silk, and should be worn with ornaments of blue, as the feather or flower for the hair. Slippers and jewelry of blue. It requires twenty-six yards of tarlatan, and ten yards of silk, costs, ready-made, from $40 to $50. Pattern, with cloth model to show trimming, $1.00.

WAISTS. – All the new waists have a plain, sensible tone that relieves and charms the eye, while it defines the perfect mold or form which has so long been hidden and disfigured. One of the most expensive model costumes is made from a French design known to us as number 1550. The front is cut in three deep points; the back has a graceful postillion, nearly square, while the side forms continue in two points, which are trimmed, and lay over the postillion. Notwithstanding its plainness, it is one of the richest designs for silk or camel's hair.

...

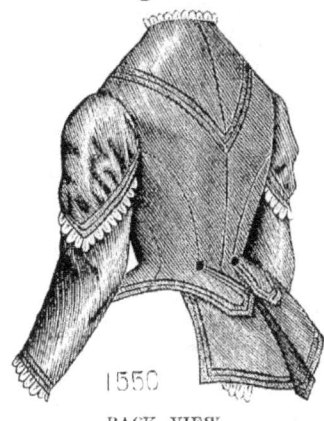

1550 – Waist – is particularly adapted to the new dress materials. The original is made in a reddish gray camel's hair cloth, trimmed with narrow black velvet. We recommend it highly to the stout figure as it is calculated to give extra length to the waist, both front and back. Though elaborate in appearance it is quite simple and neat. The sleeve has a pointed puff, which is far more becoming than the old style, which passed around the arm. Requires three yards of twenty-four-inch goods. Pattern, with cloth model, 50 cents.

BACK VIEW.

1550

FRONT VIEW.

928. – Waist – usually made in velvet, silk, or satin, sometimes in black cashmere studded with jet or bugles, is one of the most becoming for a stout figure as it causes the waist to look longer than it is. This garment will be popular for early spring suits; it transforms the plain, inexpensive material into a desirable costume. We furnish no cloth model with it, as the notches and perforations are perfect guides. Requires one and three-quarter yards of twenty-four-inch goods. All sizes. Pattern, 25 cents.

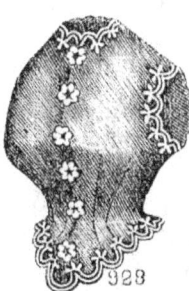
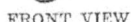

FRONT VIEW.   BACK VIEW.

...

The sleeveless waist is in great demand for early spring suits and is much appreciated when two shades are to be used. The one given in this number as 928, is very popular, ...

FRONT VIEW.

1517 – Waist – is one of the choicest selections for the coming season. It may be made in two shades or one; the vest is not separate but simply laid on. A superb suit has this style of waist made in pearl-color poplin; the fan vest and cuff are of blue silk and the points trimmed with blue velvet ribbon, lace and buttons. The fan is also finished with lace. If waist and vest are made of the same material they require tree and a half yards of twenty-four-inch silk. Pattern, in any size, with cloth model, 50 cents.

1518 – Is a basque waist that serves for either the house or street, and probably will give much more general satisfaction than some of the more novel designs. There is a deep box-pleat in the center of the back and at the side-form seams. The garment is open on the hips and the trimming is brought up the front to simulate a vest. Requires three yards of twenty-four-inch silk. Pattern, with cloth model, 50 cents.

FRONT VIEW.

1518
BACK VIEW.

SLEEVES. – Sleeves are fashionable in, we might say, every possible shape. We find the small open sleeve the most popular although some of the newest costumes have a tight coat sleeve; others a puffed sleeve; the large square or pointed or flowing, the elbow puff sleeve, the bishop or Louis 14th also appear in the most expensive materials.

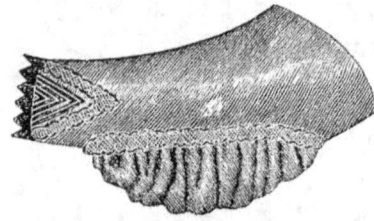

899. – Sleeve – is very desirable for thin goods; especially for the tall, slight figure. It is remarkably dressy for lawn or wash materials of any kind. Pattern, with cloth model, 25 cents.

Linen Costumes are always made with Redingote and skirt. Leather belts with the bag attached are quite indispensable to traveling or shopping suits. Linen lace and insertion or pleating are most used for these costumes. Muslin suits in white, ornamented with standard trimmings, are very popular.

Grenadine suits are more frequently made with the Redingote than the waist and overskirt; still we have seen some bodice waists which display the fine figure to a good advantage; when waists only are worn, the skirts are trimmed with endless ruffles, puffs and pleatings. More material will be required to make a thin dress this season than at any former time; six different designs are often put on one skirt. The most popular trimming for grenadine is Sicilienne, a material which may be procured in all the new shades.

...

VOYAGE COSTUME. – is made in either black, blue, or purple waterproof, and cut from the Magic Redingote. (See page 7.) [figure 1666]

The hood may be drawn over the head or used as an ornament. When the garment is draped as in No. 1 it serves as a dressy polonaise, and by simply unfastening one button it falls in a complete and unequaled waterproof dress; the straps that served to festoon it now appear as ornaments only.

No. 1. WALKING SUIT VIEW.   1666   No. 2. WATERPROOF SUIT VIEW.

1666
No. 1. WALKING SUIT VIEW.
No. 2. WATERPROOF SUIT VIEW.

The above engraving represents the MAGIC costume that surpasses all others for convenience and novelty.

The original is a French design, of summer waterproof – dark blue – trimmed with black Herculean braid. The back is slightly fitted to the figure by a gored seam under the arm, which removes the bulk at the waist, and produces sufficient width for the skirt. The front is loose, and double-breasted, with large pockets, belted and festooned; it is a bewitching polonaise. The skirt buttoned down forms a draped apron. When elevated and left open it forms two deep points at the side and a pointed puff in the back, and by the simple arrangement of unfastening one button, the beautiful polonaise falling into a waterproof cloak, complete, by the aid of cap and hood. (The cape may be carried in an inside pocket.) It is also a valuable pattern for wash materials, being without pleat or gather when unbuttoned.

The choicest batiste and cambric are in this design. The same pattern is used for white wrappers.

Voyagers cannot fail to appreciate it when made in flannel, ladies' cloth or waterproof. Ladies coming in town for a day's shopping, may be provided with necessary protection against inclement weather while enjoying a convenient promenade suit, without extra baggage.

The above garment of linen or waterproof may be purchased *only* of A. Burdette Smith, 914 Broadway. It requires 5 yards of 54-inch goods. Pattern, any size, with model showing how to drape, $1.00. Waterproof, ready made, any size, $9.00 to $25.00: Linen from $5.00 to $15.00.

...

BELTS AND POCKETS. – Are an important part of the walking costume. The pocket is not confined to leather but will be imported in all the new shades of silk, with belt to match. While they are a beautiful ornament to any suit they are of invaluable service.

...

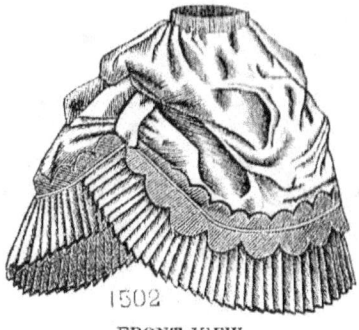

1502
FRONT VIEW.

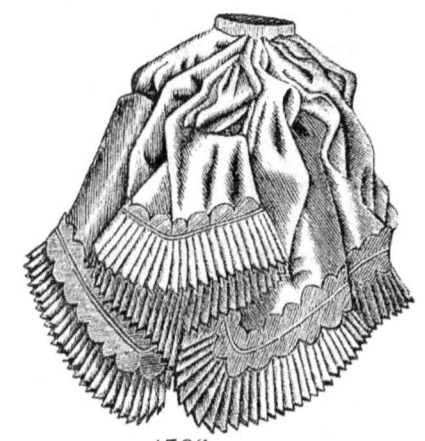

1502
BACK VIEW.

1502. Overskirt – achieves one of the greatest results. It requires simply three yards of twenty-four or twenty-seven-inch goods which are not cut; the effect represented being produced by the gathering, festooning, etc. When the garment is ripped the goods are as whole as purchased, which feature will gain it many admirers. The cloth model which accompanies this pattern together with the holes and niches, will make it readily understood. Pattern, with cloth model, 50 cents.

1507. – Apron – is a beautiful and useful article for house toilette. The original is made in black silk, each seam being finished with a large cord of the same, and finished round the bottom with a ruffle. It may be made of wash goods, with insertion between each gore. Requires one yard of twenty-four-inch goods. Pattern, with cloth model, 25 cents.

724 – Skirt – is a new design that will meet with great success, as it removes from the hips all fullness or bulk, so objectionable in starched skirts. The upper part in front and on the hips is of the corset shape, while the back is quite full. For long and wide train skirts it superiority over other styles is prominent. As the bottom is straight it can be trimmed and tucked very neatly. Requires six yards of muslin for a moderate train. Pattern, with cloth model, 50 cents.

No. 3 – Costume – is of white cambric, made from the French Redingote. It is something entirely new for wash-materials, and very desirable for any goods. The back is arranged by strings that may be loosened, leaving it a long sacque; by drawing it up again, a beautiful polonaise back is formed. It is gathered at the lower part of each shoulder, and when brought in at the waist, produces fullness for the skirt. We cannot speak with more pleasure of any style. The trimmings are embroidered tucks and puffing. Number of Redingote, 1573. Requires six yards of thirty-six inch goods. Pattern, with cloth model, $1.00. Requires for the entire suit fourteen yards. Number of skirt, 1572. Pattern, with cloth model showing trimming, 50 cents.

No. 8 – Is made of hair striped silk. An appropriate style for house or street. A basque waist, neatly fitted, left open in the back of skirt to display a sash. The trimmings of skirt is one of our choicest designs, and may be worn with or without the overskirt, which is two deep-pointed puffs in the back. Requires thirty yards of eighteen-inch silk. Number of the waist, 1586; with cloth model, 50 cents. Number of overskirt, 1587; pattern, with cloth model, 25 cents. Number of underskirt, 1586; pattern, with cloth model showing trimming, 50 cents. Entire suit, $1.25. It is also desirable in Grenadine.

No. 9 – Is commended by our Parisian correspondent to be exclusively adapted for any kind of wash material. The Redingote, when belted down and draped, is a beautiful polonaise. By unfastening the belt and unbuttoning the straps on the underside, it falls into a perfectly plain sacque, a most valuable novelty for laundring. The above illustration is made in gray battiste [sic], trimmed with a new point-plaiting. Requires thirteen yards of one yard wide material. Number of Redingote, 1555; pattern, with cloth model, any size, $1.00. Number of skirt, 1589; pattern, with cloth model showing trimming, 50 cents.

1500 – Wrapper – is a loose-fitting gabrielle, with pieces arranged in back and front to form a fancy jacket, which may be left loose (see cut) when worn by the slight figure. If laced from the bottom of the waist to three scallops, it is a most becoming style for the stout figure; it may be adjusted to the comfort of the wearer with little trouble. Requires twelve yards for medium train. All sizes for a lady. Pattern, with cloth model, $1.00.

Smith's Illustrated Pattern Bazaar, Spring 1873

No Female Suffrage Yet. – But something far better and more valuable, a Wilson Sewing-Machine for every wife and mother in the Union, and at the low price of $50 each for the full finished machine. People ask why the Wilson, a leading machine in all respects, can be sold for $50. The answer is easy and direct – because its proprietors do not belong to a great "ring," whose purpose it is to keep up the price of sewing-machines. They are the true friends of the people, and show their sincerity in a way that cannot be misunderstood. Salesroom at 1309 Chestnut Street, Philadelphia, Pa., and in all other cities in the United States. The company want agents in country towns.

BASQUE WAIST.
By Emily H. May.

We take pleasure in laying before our readers a very neat and tasty Basque Waist, as will be seen by the accompanying engraving. It is easily constructed, and we think will amply repay any one for making it up. It is appropriate for this season of the year.

We also give, here, a diagram for the Basque Waist, with vest front and postilion back. This will enable any lady to cut it out and make it herself.

No. 1. Half of Back.
No. 2. Half of Front.
No. 3. Half of Sleeve.
No. 4. Half of a Side Body of Back.

This basque is suitable for either a house-dress or walking-costume.

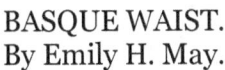

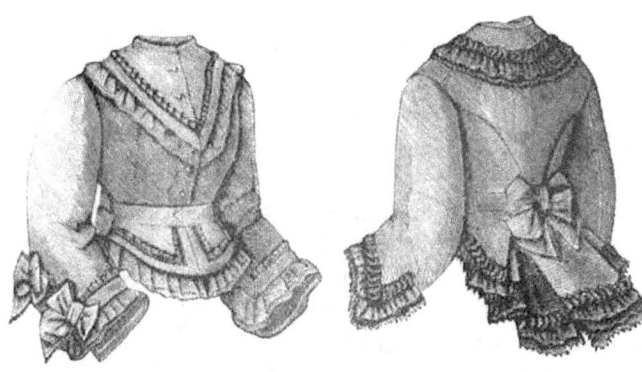

BASQUE – BACK AND FRONT.

HOUSE-DRESS.
→

April, of all the months in the year, may be termed *demi-saison*. It is too late for velvet and cloth, and too early for spring suits of light colors and materials. Old dresses may be altered and worn to great advantage, and some hints may be useful on this subject. We predict that dress-skirts, far both in and out-door wear, will be made perfectly plain; that is, without flounces, bands, or piping. Of course, this style of skirt will bring the basque again into vogue; also, the sleeveless jackets, called waistcoats. These waistcoats are of different material, or else a darker shade than the coat sleeves of the basque. They may be made as part of the garment, or else separate, and added, after for warmth. The latter plan is adapted for very slight figures. The only trimming admitted is one or two thick cords of silk as an edge. Colored silk jackets are much worn with black dresses. Black cashmere, over-dresses, basques, and Polonaises, have also colored jackets.

Peterson's Magazine, April 1873

Although the Princess dress is once more patronized by fashion, for walking out and at home, the skirt and Polonaise are still preferred, as both more elegant and more convenient. The newest style of Polonaise, however, which is known by the name of "Montespan," is cut princess fashion, and is, in fact, a short-gored dress, worn over a skirt. For demi-toilet this Polonaise is buttoned down the front, but for more dressy costumes it remains open, to show the richly-trimmed underskirt.

← WALKING-DRESS.

Polonaises, made of embroidered white China crepe shawls, are gaining ground in public favor. When they were first adapted to this use the trimming was not rightly understood. These shawls, when richly embroidered, sometimes terminate with a long, straggling fringe; when this is the case, the fringe should be cut off, and replaced either by a richer and thicker one, or with lace, as nothing looks in worse taste than a poor trimming upon an exceedingly rich fabric. Polonaises of blue cashmere are also much worn over black skirts for the house.

Sacks are cut in every style – with tight sleeves and with flowing ones, tight in the back, and then again without any seams. The Dolman does not seem to take as well as at first predicted.

We conclude with a muslin waistcoat and sleeve, to be worn under a jacket-bodice. The front is formed of tucked muslin, edged on the outside with a row of insertion. Valenciennes lace encircles the top, is continued down the front as a jabot, and then edges the basque. The waistcoat fastens down the front with three velvet bows. Sleeves in the same style. These waistcoats add very much to a dress made with an open jacket-bodice; very pretty and dressy for a small evening party; or the design will be just the thing for a Swiss muslin over-dress, for the waist and sleeves, only continue the trimming of the waist around the back, same as the front.

Peterson's Magazine, May 1873

◤ GUIPURE BODICE.

...

Change in fashion is simply the expression of an awakened intellect, groping in small things as in great for something better than it has known; and the use for a manual of fashion, such as we offer is, not to dictate to women any rule which they must blindly follow, but to afford such knowledge of varying costumes, and the manner of making them, that each may clothe herself appropriately, according to her appearance of age, or even mood.

Why should not a woman's purity of mind, her quick eye for color, her aesthetic sense of fitness, be disclosed in her attire as well as in the pictures on her walls or her garden? Very few of us will ever carve a great statue, or paint a great picture but we all have clothes to wear; and it is a duty we owe to ourselves and those around us, to so drape the bodies God has given us, as to make no discord in this beautiful, pleasant word. All of us have friends, or, it may be, children, with whom we would have a fair and tender memory. Carelessness and bad taste in dress, so far from being indicative of strength of mind, argues a certain vulgarity of feeling, just as vanity and foppery, on the other hand, prove a weak brain. Wise men or women make their dress so thoroughly in accordance with their person and character, that nobody notices it any more than the frame of a picture; but to be clothed shabbily, in the hopes that our inner perfections will overshadow our dress, is but the extreme of vanity.

We give first, this month, a pretty, stylish, and effective costume in percale. The under-skirt is perfectly plain, and the material is striped percale – our design calls for a buff and blue percale. The over-dress is of solid blue percale, and is made in a Polonaise, rounding off short in front, like a short basque, to the waist. The long apron-front is cut entirely separate, is put upon a waistband, and worn as an apron under the Polonaise. The whole is trimmed with a plaited ruffle, four inches wide, headed with a narrow bias band of the material, stitched down with the machine. Sleeves tight to the elbow, with a plaited ruffle, six inches wide, at the back of the sleeve, rounding off to three inches on the inside of the arm The bodice is cut heart-shaped in front, and a collaret of Swiss muslin, edged with Valencia lace, is worn with the dress. On the left side a sash, made of the blue percale, is worn, consisting of one long loop, and two ends. Six yards of striped material for the under-skirt, and nine yards of plain blue will be required. Percales can be bought from twenty-five to fifty cents per yard.

Next we give a breakfast-dress, also of striped percale, one of the narrow black and white, brown and white, or any other color. So numerous and pretty are they, that it is almost impossible to select one that will not make a charming breakfast-wrapper. The trimming is of a solid color, corresponding with the color of the stripe in the material, and is cut on the bias, and stitched on as seen in the cut. Coat-sleeves, with a deep cuff of the same, moulds covered for the buttons. The shape of the wrapper is gored in front, and fulled into the waist at the back. The pockets may either be entirely of the solid color or striped, as in the design, with the pointed lappet falling over. Ten yards of striped percale, and one and a half yards of solid color, will be required.

CAMBRIDGE JACKET.
By Emily H. May.

We give, here, a pretty jacket for out-door wear. It is very short, falls square, and is double-breasted. The sleeves are very wide at the wrists. This pattern consists of front, collar, a *revers,* back, and sleeve. The notch in front of the armhole, marks the place for the front seam of the sleeve. The back is to be cut open in the middle as far as the notch. The places for buttons and button-holes are all marked; and we have indicated the revers on the sleeve by a row of pricking. This is a very pretty pattern, and the diagram which accompanies the engraving, will enable a lady to cut it out and fit it herself.

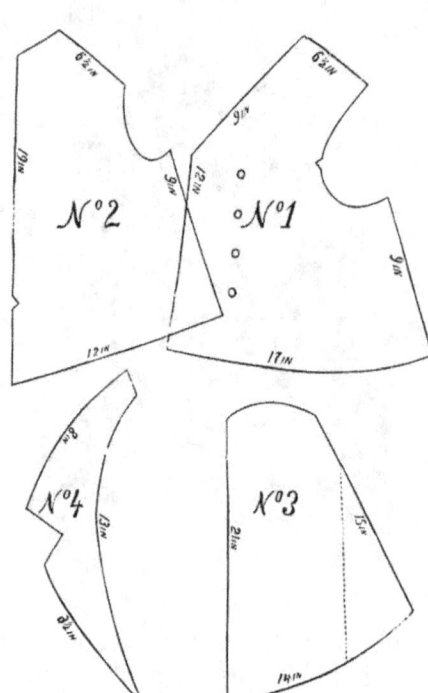

...

The toilets of the month are of polka dotted foulards or light summer silks for dressy occasions, but for morning and general wear, chintzes and wash goods. These appear in finer qualities than we have had for many years. The tissues called foulards, should be purchased at reliable houses, and the India foulards are always better than the French. The former are the most expensive, but repay first cost by their durability. ...

There is no absolute fashion at the present time; almost any style can be worn, providing it is becoming and in good taste; pale-blue, salmon, pale-green, and pink, are worn in the evening, but for the street, all the indescribable tints that have been worn all winter, are reproduced with startling effect.

Skirts are made about three and a half yards around, and are either trimmed very much, or not at all. The "soft finished" cambrics are usually untrimmed, made with a long Polonaise, as we have described. It is predicted white nansooks will be worn again this summer. For the mountains and inland resorts, there are lovely organdies in the loveliest shades of mauve, blue, green, and pink, but they will not wash, and require care to keep them looking well one season.

Peterson's Magazine, June 1873

BASQUINE OF WHITE MUSLIN.
By Emily H. May.

We give here a Basquine, to be made of white Swiss muslin. We also give a diagram, by which to cut it out. It is very neat and simple, and at the same time effective. No. 1 gives the half of the back, and the dotted lines show where the plait is turned back. This is to be trimmed with insertion, edged on both sides, and fastened down the back by bows of ribbon, which should correspond with the dress it is to be worn over. The edge of the basquine, sleeves, etc., are trimmed to match the other material.

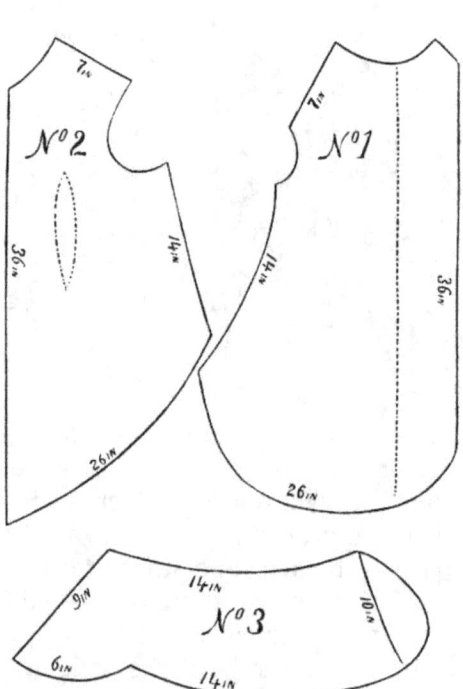

No. 1. Half of Back.
No. 2. Half of Front.
No. 3. Sleeve.
Price of pattern 50 cents.

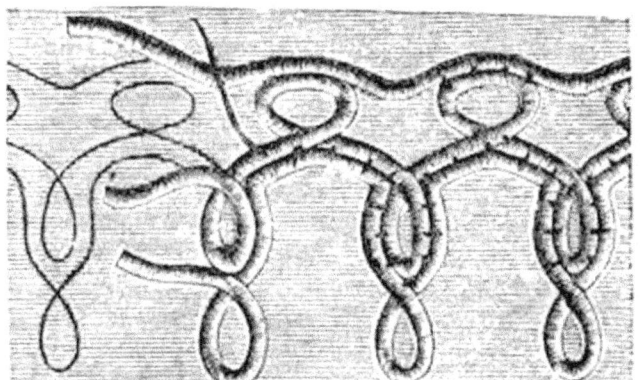

CORDING DESIGN, TO ORNAMENT PIQUE DRESSES, JACKETS, ETC.
By Mrs. Jane weaver.

The cord may be purchased. White cotton, if for pique, or of silk, if designed for cashmere or cloth jackets, should first be tacked upon the design, and then sewn together with ornamental stitches of the same color, or of a darker shade. See the design.

PATTERN IN EMBROIDERY FOR DRESS. →

Silver and steel buttons, that are worn on Polonaises and mantles, are greatly on the increase. The buttons are large and flat, and many are dull, like old silver.

Both jet and steel beads are largely introduced into passementerie, and lace and tassel-fringes are likewise made of a mixture of steel and jet.

For a length of time our fashions have been stationary, and the leading milliners and dressmakers are constantly declaring that a great change – in fact, a revolution – is about to take place in *la mode*. I cannot say that I see much change; the fact is, the middle classes, who represent the majority, desire that the prevailing styles shall continue, while the upper classes desire a transformation.

Peterson's Magazine, July 1873

Guipure lace, and jet fringes, are much used for Polonaises. A very elegant confection, useful for wearing on many occasions, is made of alternate stripes of black guipure, and Sicilienne, embroidered with jet; a heading of jet divides the stripes. The dress worn beneath is visible through the guipure stripe. In front the confection falls with square ends, and at the back it forms paniers. It is confined round the waist with a band passing through a large jet buckle; but instead of the buckle being in front, it is at the back. Guipure and jet fringe edge this Polonaise, and sometimes these are replaced with black and white Bruges lace, a novelty in laces, which produces a good effect.

Fig. V. – Dress of Batiste and Foulard. – The under-skirt is made of striped foulard, without trimming. The Polonaise is of Batiste, trimmed with a band of foulard, and large silk tassels placed at intervals on the edge, caught together in the front by large ribbon bows and ends. Leghorn hat with a wreath of ivy.

← TOILET FOR THE SEA-SHORE.

↘ Next on our list comes a pretty design for a sea-side costume, in light mohair goods. The under-skirt here, as in the first costume, is also perfectly plain, which seems to denote a decided change in the prevailing fashions, and to herald a much simpler style of dress, especially for very young ladies. The colors, too, are contrasting, the under-skirt being a lovely sea-green, and the upper one and coat-basque are of very light gray, simply ornamented with a narrow band of the green, put on bias. There is very little fullness to the over-skirt, and it is but slightly looped at the sides, and not at all in the back. The coat-basque has long postillion, beginning at the side-body, four inches shorter in the front. A deep sailor collar, back and front, of green entire, and coat-sleeves, very tight, completes this charming costume for a young lady of sixteen to eighteen years. ... Six to eight yards of green mohair, and eight yards of the gray, will be required. Much depends upon the height. of the person that is to wear it.

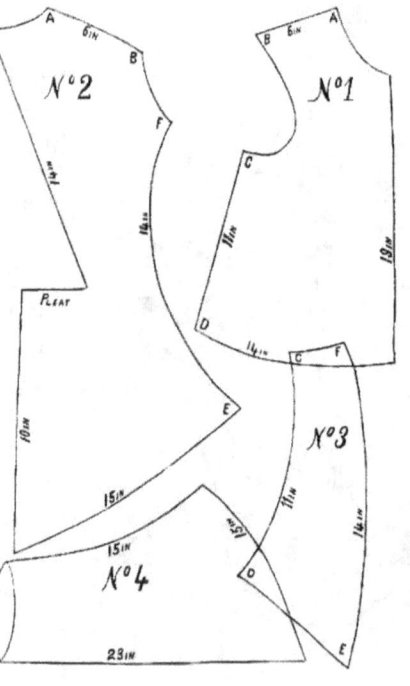

LADY'S SEA-SIDE JACKET – FRONT AND BACK VIEW.
By Emily H. May.

We give, here, the front and back view of a Lady's Sea-side Jacket. It is made of light cloth or flannel, and braided, as seen in the design. The diagram on the next page which represents the front and back, will enable any lady to cut it out, fit it correctly, and make it up at very little expense. It cannot fail to please.

No. 1. Half of Front.
No. 2. Half of Front.
No. 3. Side Piece
No. 4. Half of Sleeve.

↙ Above we give an effective and inexpensive design for trimming a white pique or nainsook. The front of the skirt has five very scant ruffles, scalloped and bowed, and put on "en tablieu," on the front breadths; one deep flounce is continued around the back of the skirt, twelve inches deep. The Polonaise is simply scalloped out on the edge.

...

Some skirts are cut with a train which spreads out at the back, but can be looped up at pleasure for an out-of-door costume – for this may be either an in-door toilet or walking dress. Short skirts, generally are trimmed with many narrow ruffles, rather than several deep ones. A pretty way of making up tarlatan dresses, is to train the back of the skirt with wide, plain flounces, taking care that it hangs well as a train. The tablier in front is covered with narrow flounces, pinked out and arranged *en spirales*. The effect is very light and pretty. The bodices have small, full, *Directoire* sleeves, confined around the arm with a ruche of pinked-out tarlatan. Other tarlatan skirts are trimmed with narrow flounces, arranged in zigzag, and with a tulle veil completely covering the skirt. This style is especially pretty in pale-pink. The veil is caught up at one side only with a tuft of flowers.

For country wear some new white piques have been made according to special orders, and turned out very successfully. In one costume the skirt is kilt-plaited, and between every plait there is an insertion of English embroidery. Casaque, with large Robespierre revers, with a double row of buttons. Basque trimmed with English embroidery. A dark-blue and a light-blue faille bow ornament the casaque. Another costume is made of slate-gray batiste; the flounces at the back are embroidered with white. The tablier is ornamented with a wide band, embroidered flat upon the skirt. Bodice embroidered on the basque and collar; waistcoat entirely of white English embroidery. The redingotes are, for the most part, cut either ordinary Polonaise, or Princess shape. The double-breasted Polonaise will also be much worn, for two reasons, viz., their novelty and extra warmth, the latter of which is a great consideration for the approaching season. When first introduced by some of our leading modistes, it was not successful, but at present is the favorite over-dress for all suits except those designed for full dress. It is a graceful and comfortable garment, is worn by young, middle-aged, and old, and is therefore popular on the score of availability, as well as beauty. To be *comme il faut* it must be very long, with ample fullness in the skirt, and abundant drapery. After the collar, cuffs, buttons, pockets, and sash, are added, all other trimming is superfluous, and detract from its style. It may be loose, like a morning-wrapper, or else belted down.

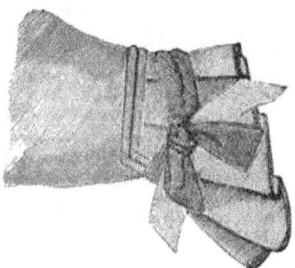

We also give two new patterns for dress sleeves.

Peterson's Magazine, August 1873

Skirts are worn much closer to the figure, and petticoats are cut so that there is not the least fullness about the hips. Flounces are worn at the back only with a pouf at the top, immediately below the waist. In order that the skirts may cling very closely to the figure in front, it is usual now to border them with a fringe, or lead them. The short dress, or costume, shows a portion of the boot in front, but at the back the skirt almost trains.

For day wear, the chatelaine dress, with plain, close-fitting bodice, buttoned considerably below the waist, is coming into vogue again. The skirt is entirely kilt-plaited from beneath this long basque. There is at the back a pouf, and at the side a wide sash to match the dress, either of watered of velvet ribbon.

Colored flowers applique on the materials are much worn on summer dresses. These flowers look as though lace, embroidery, and passementerie are all used in their composition, and yet there are none of these things; but they are very beautiful and costly. They are worn especially as Pompadour wreaths on tourquoise-blue China crepe. ...

What are known as Restoration sleeves are struggling hard to become fashionable. They have a small balloon at the top of the arm, and the rest of the sleeve fits closely to the wrist. I do not know if the attempt to popularize this unbecoming style will succeed; it should have no encouragement, as it will most certainly lead the way for the leg-of-mutton sleeve, which is equally frightful. ...

WALKING-DRESSES. →

↙ We give next a Polonaise of dotted foulard, delaine, or percale. It is worn over either a black silk skirt or one the same shade of the material. The under-skirt has a deep-plaited flounce at the back, and is kilted all the way to the waist in the front. This Polonaise is open in front, and also in the back. The flap in the back, which is the same as the binding, and forms the trimming, is ornamented with large, white pearl buttons, with simulated button-holes; the same upon the cuffs. This trimming is of plain material, and color the same as the dress, and is four inches wide. Belts are much worn over Polonaises, and is here the same. The waist is trimmed, as may be seen, with the addition of guipure edging on both sides of the hand. Foulards are yard-wide, and six yards will be enough for the Polonaise, one and a half of the plain for trimming. Delaines are much cheaper, and the percales of this pattern are very effective in dark-blue and chocolate, with white dots. Foulards cost from one dollar fifty cents to two dollars per yard; delaines fifty cents; percales, twenty to twenty-five cents.

...

All dresses are worn *bouffant* at the back, and are arranged to look very flat and slender at the sides. The skirt is tied back over the tournure, which should be long and narrow, and consist of twelve springs encased in muslin, and kept in place with elastic bands. This bustle should add nothing to the breadth of the hips, but is required to push the skirts far out backward, and is long enough to support them half their length, making them flow out gracefully instead of falling in below a projecting pouf at the waist as they have recently done.

Waistcoats, which are more often silk than any other material, are now worn of the same color as the costume. Those of startling colors, or contrasting with the dress, are beginning to be abandoned. With the exception of white pique, or black or white silk, waistcoats are, as a rule, of the same color as the dress; or if they differ, it is simply in being either a lighter or a darker shade.

Peterson's Magazine, September 1873

BLACK DRAP DE SOIE JACKET

Never do I remember fashion so independent; it is varied to an unprecedented extent; the selection of styles is so great as to be confusing. The fronts of costumes may be plain or covered with flounces and bows, the train opening to show off the ornaments. Polonaises and bodices with basques and tunics are both equally fashionable. The Polonaise is considered the more *neglige,* and

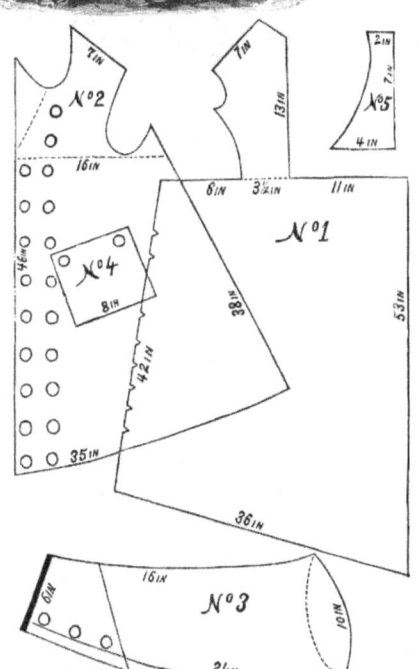

the more suitable for day and in-door wear. When the skirt is trained, then the Polonaise is no longer worn, except it differs in material from the skirt.

EVENING TOILET.

For Traveling Costumes, alpaca has come into great favor. Steel-gray is a favorite color, and it is usually trimmed either with black velvet, or with faille to match the material. These alpaca costumes are almost invariably made with a silk waistcoat, and often with a white pique one likewise, the latter being trimmed with a narrow quilting of muslin, festooned at the edge. These waistcoats make a convenient change when traveling, as they afford variety without adding considerably to the luggage.

...

DOUBLE-BREASTED POLONAISE, BELTED IN AT THE WAIST.
By Emily H. May.

In presenting this beautiful design to our fair readers we also, as usual, on the next page, give diagram which will enable them to cut it out and make it themselves.

No. 1. Half of Back.
No. 2. Half of Front.
No. 3. Sleeve and Cuff.
No. 4. Pocket.
No. 5. Collar.

The dotted line shows the collar turned back.

Sashes are always worn with white muslin dresses, whether they have high or low bodices; and, indeed, ribbons are now arranged in the most fantastic manner in front, at the back, at the side, on one shoulder, and on both shoulders; and they are manufactured in every imaginable variety. They are of all widths, too, and seem to have no wrong side. Some are watered on one side and satin on the other; half moire and half faille; or half faille and half gauze. Another variety is thick, with fine satin stripes that look like streaks of lightning traversing the color. Ribbons are also made of two shades, and worn on dresses of the same tints – dark-violet or dark-blue on one side, and light-violet or light blue on the other, of two different colors to suspend a locket or cross from the neck, black on one side, and the color of the dress on the other – that is gray, blue, or green; in fact, French ingenuity appears to have devoted itself specially to ribbons and laces this year.

TRIMMING FOR FALL DRESS.

We give here a stylish house or walking-costume of mohair in light-buff or gray. It is made with the lower-skirt just to touch, which is trimmed with a gathered flounce, eight inches deep, placed a little lower than half the skirt. Through the flounce two rows of velvet are placed, and form an insertion. This is done by cutting slits in the flounce at equal distances, and turning the square made in this way back on the wrong side, then run the velvet ribbon in and out. The velvet should be an inch wide, no more. The rounded tunic is trimmed to match, and is fastened on each side by a bow and ends of wider black velvet. Round-waisted bodice, open in front, with a narrow gathered flounce and velvet insertion, arranged to match the skirt, but of narrower width. Same trimming at the sleeves. This costume would be very effective for a dinner or evening-dress for a small party, say in this way. The under-skirt to be of silk of one color, and the flounce, tunic, and waist, of French Swiss muslin, with the black velvet insertion. An old dress could be thus re-trimmed to look quite fresh, and certainly very stylish and effective. An old pink or blue silk skirt, with the muslin and black velvet trimmings, could not be more effectually brought into use, and at very little expense. Fifteen or sixteen yards of mohair, two pieces of one-inch black velvet, four yards of two-inch, for bows, six yards of half-inch, for the waist and sleeves.

Above we give a walking-costume for a young lady, composed of two kinds of material, a plain silk for the under-skirt, of any solid color, or black, and the tunic and vest of bodice of striped poplin of lighter and darker shades. These striped poplins and mohairs come in blue and back, two shades of brown, two shades of green, and, in fact, so many nice combinations, that almost any half-worn silk dress can be matched in color, or else in a contrasting color for the tunic and vest. The under-skirt is trimmed with one deep flounce, slightly full, and put on with a frill to stand up, separated by a row of narrow, black velvet ribbon. The apron-front is simply trimmed to simulate an apron, with a narrower flounce, and a wider row of velvet. The tunic is faced in front with some of the silk, and the flounce with which it is trimmed, is the same as the under-skirt. The basque-bodice has a vest of the striped material, and the rest of the bodice and sleeves are the same as the under-skirt, trimmed with the same width velvet as upon the apron of the skirt. Seven yards of striped poplin or mohair, one piece of inch-wide velvet ribbon, and four yards of half-inch, will be all that is required to alter an old silk into a new and fashionable costume. A black silk, with a blue and black stripe, or black and white stripe tunic, makes a very pretty combination.

...

Dresses of rich material, such as faille, gros grain, etc., will be made generally without tunics, but often at the back with a bouffant, and that not a very voluminous one; but the lower part of the skirt will be trimmed with a heavy fringe, or one bouillonne, or with folds. The front will be made short enough to show the feet, and the back with a train. Costumes will be made shorter than last season, so that there will be no necessity to hold the skirt in the hand, or to risk its being soiled if allowed to hang its full length.

Costumes, all made of the same material, are even more in favor than last year. Polonaises that do not match the skirts are seldom seen.

The new braided costumes differ considerably from those worn last year. The dolman, or jacket, as the case may be, is braided all over, and the tunic is not braided all over, but all round only.

BRAIDED TUSSORE SILK COSTUME

Plain faille dresses, for early winter wear, will be much trimmed with revers made of damask velvet. The faille bodice will have a damask waistcoat, and this substitution can also be easily effected when remaking dresses. The damask velvet is gros grain silk, covered with detached designs, as are to be seen on silk damask, only the designs are in velvet, instead of being in satin, and the style of material is altogether first-rate.

Bodices are made at the present time either with waistcoats or as worn in Charles IX. reign, that is to say, very close-fitting, with a double coat basque rather long at the back, and frequently ornamented with pearl buttons. In front there is no basque, but a straight band of faille is carried round the neck and down each side the bodice to the waist. This ornament or band gives the stiffness to the upper part of the dress recognizable in all Velasquez's portraits. Round the throat there is a fraise of tulle or lace, and in front of the bodice there are large bows. The sleeves are made to simulate very high epaulettes, quite in Charles IX. style. The generality of the full-dress toilets are copied more from models of that epoch than of any other. The Louis XV. and Directoire costumes are considered the most appropriate for street wear. But, while adopting and remodeling these fashions, the modern Parisian, in order to give the effect of close-fitting drapery in front, ties her skirts back with such contrivances of strings and lacings, that she will soon find it impossible to walk. These extremes of styles always border on the ridiculous.

The low bodices for ball dresses are made to cover the shoulders, and are pointed very low both in the back and front. A plaited ruff is added all round the neck, but considerably higher behind than in front. The ruff is made of the dress silk with white silk lining, and a stiff muslin interlining to hold it erect. The plaits are small half-inch box-plaits, scanty enough to spread out like a fan at the top.

For traveling there is nothing more fashionable than either dark-blue violet, prune or chestnut-colored bege cashmere, fastened the entire length of the front with large, plain jet buttons. There are square pockets on the fronts, the back half fits the figure, and there is a waistband on the front only, which is confined with a large jet buckle.

The most elegant dinner-toilets at the present time are made of Chambery gauze, either striped or dotted, and trimmed with coquilles of the same. These coquilles commence in front, in the center of the skirt, widening as they descend so as to describe a tablier. At other times these coquilles are arranged at the sides, and piped with faille of a different color from the dress. The ornaments at the sides of the skirt, formerly called "quilles," are now in great favor, particularly when it is a train. ...

The English Walking-jacket again appears, made of warm, rough cloth, nearly half an inch thick. It retains its jaunty shape, fitting like a gentleman's coat, with high shoulder-seams, double-breasted fronts, coat collar, and three back seams, far apart at the waist, but no postillion plaits. Coat-sleeves and pockets, with flaps, complete this trim, tidy, and withal masculine-looking jacket. Children's and misses' jackets are shown in precisely the same shapes just noted.

Mantillas are used when greater warmth is needed than the jacket gives. They are heavily wadded, and have large scarf-like ends.

Peterson's Magazine, November 1873

WINTER WALKING-DRESS. ↘

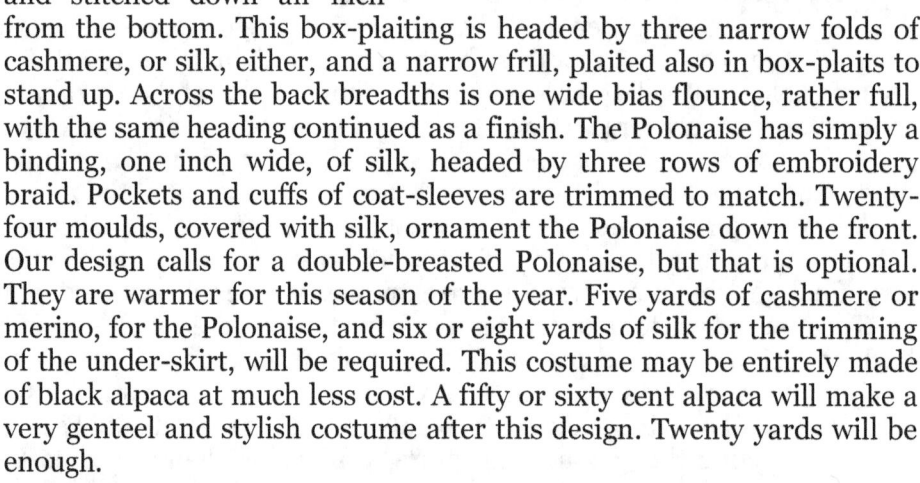

We give, first, this month, a walking-costume with Polonaise of black cashmere or merino. The under-skirt may be either of the same material as the dress or of black silk. An old silk, re-turned, will always look better, and make a more elegant costume, than to have the skirt of the same material. The skirt is made slightly to touch, and very narrow, not more than three and a half yards round. Across the front breadth and half of the side gore are two rows of narrow side plaiting, four inches deep each; above that is a bias flounce, put on in box-plaits, and stitched down an inch from the bottom. This box-plaiting is headed by three narrow folds of cashmere, or silk, either, and a narrow frill, plaited also in box-plaits to stand up. Across the back breadths is one wide bias flounce, rather full, with the same heading continued as a finish. The Polonaise has simply a binding, one inch wide, of silk, headed by three rows of embroidery braid. Pockets and cuffs of coat-sleeves are trimmed to match. Twenty-four moulds, covered with silk, ornament the Polonaise down the front. Our design calls for a double-breasted Polonaise, but that is optional. They are warmer for this season of the year. Five yards of cashmere or merino, for the Polonaise, and six or eight yards of silk for the trimming of the under-skirt, will be required. This costume may be entirely made of black alpaca at much less cost. A fifty or sixty cent alpaca will make a very genteel and stylish costume after this design. Twenty yards will be enough.

...

Skirts no longer bulge out, except just immediately below the back of the waist; all that clings is *de rigueur*. Under-skirts should be arranged thus: A short, narrow petticoat of either flannel or calico, trimmed with either embroidery or guipure; a tournure petticoat, or petticoat with bustle at the back, with flounces and whalebone as well as cords – the last to tie it, so that the petticoat falls flat in front, and keeps out well at the back. A second unstarched petticoat of cambric, with embroidered flounces, generally two narrow ones. Muslin petticoats are worn under trained evening skirts.

Polonaises will be worn, but not universally, as last year. Bodices with basques, skirts highly trimmed at the back, and plain and flat in front, tunics for demi rather than grand toilets, will be worn.

A new Polonaise, called "the Austria," has lately made its appearance, and is likely to grow in popularity, as it is exceedingly stylish. I will describe a toilet in which this Polonaise forms a conspicuous part. Dark-prune velvet skirt, bordered with a deep plaiting of pearl-gray faille, headed by a ruche which is studded at regular intervals with prune velvet bows; pearl-gray faille Polonaise, like a French coat in form, and with large square pockets. It is trimmed all round with bands of prune velvet and gray silk guipure. Prune silk frog-buttons fastening down straps of velvet with chased silver buttons at the opposite end, decorate the front of the Polonaise. Velvet sleeves, with faille cuffs and prune frog buttons.

LOUIS XV. WAISTCOAT. ⬂

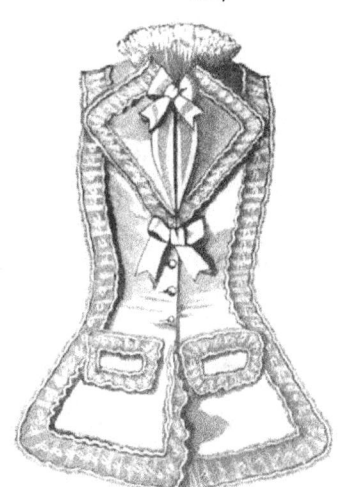

Waistcoats, either simulated or real, are more fashionable than ever. Cloth and cashmere costumes, for neglige wear, are made with velvet waistcoats fastened with gimp olives made of dead silk. Generally speaking, the waistcoat matches the dress in color, but we have seen the following exceptions look stylish. A steel-gray bege costume, with chestnut-brown velvet waistcoat, a coffee-colored cloth dress with a blue velvet waistcoat, a myrtle-green and marine-blue cashmere, each with black velvet waistcoat. The close-fitting, sleeveless jackets, with basques, are still in favor, although they have been worn for the two past years. The form of the basque is slightly altered, but a last year's jacket is still fashionable.

⬃ SILK WAIST.

The small, cloth jacket now worn, are very much in the style of gentlemen's garments; they cross over in front, often have pockets at the sides, and invariably a small one in front, in which the watch and a flower are placed. This fashion of flowers in the button-hole is so pleasing that we cannot criticise it. Some ladies wear artificial flowers in this way, but the real ones are far prettier. Those jackets, which are called "Sportsman," are made of gray, marine blue, or chine cloth, also of coarsely-twilled serge, and are trimmed with a quantity of buttons. If the handsome cut-steel ones are found too expensive, we should recommend our readers very dark, smoked pearl, or tortoise-shell, those which are sold in imitation of silver being very ugly.

Next we give a costume in two shades of any of the new winter colors – brown, green, plum, etc.; the variety is endless, and in all such fabrics as poplins, mohairs, merinoes, etc. Here the under-skirt barely touches, and is without any train-slope, trimmed with a kilted plaiting nearly half a yard deep. There is a short Polonaise with the waist, untrimmed. The skirt, from the waist down the front and around the bottom, is trimmed with a plaiting four inches deep, to match the under-skirt. Over this is a sleeveless jacket of the darker shade of the material; and the cuffs are of the same shade, but made entirely separate, and easily adjusted when the outside jacket is worn, which is not always desirable, as by omitting it sometimes, the advantage of two costumes is gained. The kilting and trimming for the Polonaise, of course, is of the darker shade of the material. Ten yards of each shade will be required. The outside jacket needs only a thick cord to finish it all round, and cover the cord with the light shade; let it be as thick as your little finger.

Blond is very fashionable at the present time for veils, dress trimmings, Marie Antoinette fichus, etc. Thick, black and white blond is lavishly used. Lace, embroidered with jet, is also used in vast quantities for trimming. Flounces can be worked with jet, and arranged on a black silk dress to great advantage.

Fraises and ruffs for the throat will continue to be worn, and many will be black, embroidered with jet beads, even out of mourning. Sufficient attention is not paid to the length and shortness of the throat, as the case may be. Every lady appears to wear huge ruffs indiscriminately, whether her throat be swan-like or the reverse. Where the figure suits, the ruff has a graceful effect when continued down the front of the open bodice.

Waistbands and sashes are universally worn, from those made of leather, and adorned with plaques or chased oxidized silver or cut steel to the finest lace ones, which may be seen in profusion.

Peterson's Magazine, December 1873

1874

The Swiss are said to be beating both the French and English manufacturers in the silk ribbon trade. A correspondent of the *London Times*, speaking of the decline of the London silk trade, says: –

"The broad black silk trade of this country is entirely gone. There are, comparatively speaking, no black silks for dresses now made in England, we being undersold by the manufacturers of Rhenish Prussia and the Lower Rhine. This has not been altogether an unmixed good to the consumer, who by free trade is enable to purchase the best article for her money, it being a common complaint with English

ladies that there is no getting a black silk dress to wear as they formerly used to do, as they now crack and wear out speedily. The real reason of this, especially in the case of the cheap black glace silks which are sold, is that the 'weft,' instead of consisting of honest silk, fairly dyed, is loaded with adulteration, or 'weighted' in various degrees, sometimes up to the extent of 300 per cent. The great art in doing this consists of the introduction of foreign materials into the silk, and giving it an extra substance or weight without being prejudicial to its brightness or lustre."

...

Fig. 7. – Visiting dress of blue silk and gray Cashmere. The front part of underskirt is made of gray Cashmere, trimmed with two ruffles bound with blue silk; the back breadths are entirely of blue silk covered with narrow blue ruffles. The redingote is cut with a basque back and vest front, is bound with blue silk, has blue vest and sash.

...

Flannel is an excellent material for winter morning costumes for house wear, and can be employed either as a polonaise or as a Princesse morning dress. We think this the most useful form, as the dress is complete with the trifling additional expense of a half yard flounce, which takes three yards of flannel in addition to the quantity required for a polonaise. It requires eleven yards of print to make a Princesse dress with a Watteau plait and flounce, with a double ruffle at the top, and ladies can from this judge of the quantity of flannel required.

BREAKFAST AND VISITING TOILETS.

Fig. 1 – Breakfast dress of light gray Cashmere, trimmed up the front on cuffs on the sleeves of satin quilted in diamonds.

Fig. 2. – Visiting dress of navy blue silk and camel's hair cloth. The underskirt is made of the silk, without any trimming. The polonaise is of the camel's hair cloth, the edge cut in small turrets, and bound with silk braid; a band of the material piped with silk and trimmed with buttons heads up the turrets. Bonnet of the same shade, trimmed with lace, ribbon, and feathers.

Fig. 19. – Sash bow of black velvet and silk, the ends embroidered and finished with fringe. ↖

We have been asked by several of our correspondents to give a design for a simple, inexpensive evening dress for a young lady. For young ladies making their *début* in society, tarlatan will be very fashionable this winter. The material itself is cheap enough for the most economical, the elegance of the dress depending upon its trimming and ornaments. Ruffles trim prettier than anything else. They are light and airy, a requisite in a tarlatan dress. An excellent substitute for a silk slip to be worn under a tarlatan is the yard-wide French cambric. Made wrong side out, it is very difficult to distinguish from silk, and by having several of these skirts of different colors, varying also the trimming, a variety of pretty toilets may be made from one dress. The sash, flowers, and gloves should be of the same shade, or lighter, as underskirt.

...

Fig. 9. – Bows made of black and blue ribbon to fasten on the left shoulder, and across the waist under the right arm; the blue ends are embroidered. ↗

...

MITTEN.

Mittens are much worn by ladies in the morning. The pattern shown in the engraving is of fine cloth, embroidered with silk of a contrasting shade.

Godey's Lady's Book and Magazine, January 1874

Walking-dresses do not quite touch the ground – a most rational fashion; and those dresses which are of a suitable material for both house and street wear, are made longer for the house, if wished, and looped up at the back, near the waist, with three buttons and loops, when worn in the street. All dresses lie close in front, tied back, if necessary, with long tapes. Skirts with or without over-skirts, are equally fashionable, and very much trimmed costumes, as well as those severely plain, are equally worn. Sometimes a great deal of lace, embroidery, buttons, cords, etc., are worn; sometimes only perfectly plain, or petticoat, with an over-dress, trimmed with two or three bands of the material of the petticoat. A black silk underskirt is useful, as it can be worn under an over-dress of any color or material.

An economical way of re-trimming black silk skirts, so as it to make them look new, is with cross-bands of color, and such ornaments as buttons, buckles, agrafes, etc., which are on a monster scale, and abound everywhere. Straw-colored , bands are fastened down with a gold buckle; bands of Ispahan blue, which is shot with green, are fastened down with smoked pearl buckles, and bands with steel buckles.

ENGLISH WALKING-JACKET. ↘

Paris is always famous for creating fantasies or accessories to the toilet, and the tradesmen have the art of rendering these fantasies almost indispensable. Take, for instance, the black velvet belt, mounted with silver clasps, which every élégante is now wearing with negligé costumes. A chatelaine bag is suspended from the belt, but for evening wear the bag is changed for a fan. With dressy toilets this belt is not worn, but the fan hangs from either a gold or silver hook. Some of the new belts are made of either black or maroon velvet, ornamented with Renaissance agrafes, made of chased silver, and lined with either pink or blue silk. These velvet belts and sashes are extremely elegant, and are quite in the style of the Italian ones of the sixteenth century. The small umbrellas, suspended from the belts, are invariably black, with ebony handle, incrusted with silver. The chatelaine-bag, always sold with these belts, is likewise velvet, incrusted with silver.

Several novelties are appearing in our shop. Among the most conspicuous is the pelerine collar, made of black velvet, and forming a fraise round the throat. The fraise is lined with such light-colored silks as pink and blue, and the pelerine is piped with silk of the same color. A wide tulle ruche encircles the throat. These new pelerine collars are excellent for smartening up a dull dress, and for wearing at either a small friendly dinner-party, or the lecture-room.

Peterson's Magazine, January 1874

Fig. 4. – Visiting dress of light gray silk poplin, made with one skirt, trimmed in the front with a plaiting going up in a point, finished at the sides by bows of narrow colored velvet. The back breadths are plain, looped up in a puff. Basque waist, with vest and revers of narrow colored velvet. Cuffs on sleeves and bows of the same. Hat of velvet, of the two shades, trimmed with lace and flowers.

Fig. 5. – Dress of two shades of brown silk and Cashmere. The dress is of dark brown silk, with a plaiting of the same around the bottom, headed with ruffles and bands of Cashmere of a lighter shade. The vest, revers, cuffs on sleeves, and ruffles around the underskirt, are all of the lighter Cashmere.

...

Rough grained fabrics are employed for *négligé* costumes, for walking, or for travelling. For the latter purpose, no costume can, however, rive the waterproof cloth, lined with red or small bright plaid flannel. These costumes are amply provided with pockets of all sizes and descriptions, the most novel of which is one upon the revers of the left hand sleeve, and especially meant for holding railway tickets. In some models there is a reversible hood added at the back, and lined with plain flannel or tarlatane. ...

There is a novel skirt that is intended for carriage wear, and for the dresses that are made partly of silk and partly of velvet. It consists of five breadths, namely, a wide gored front breadth, one narrow gore on each side, and two full straight back breadths. This brings a seam down the back, and this seam is left open three-eighths of a yard from the bottom. The flounce that borders the skirt is taken in this seam, and held there in deep triple plaits, adding an extra breadth, and giving a graceful fan or pigeon-tail slope to the slightly drooping skirt. These skirts are made of two colors, such as pink and brown. The front breadth would be pink, the flounce and the side and the back breadths brown.

For ordinary walking costumes, the skirts are now cut round, and measure about three yards and a quarter in width. They cling flatly in front, and are either tied back with strings attached to the second side seam, or they project over the new sloping tournures.

...

INSERTIONS OF TAPE WORK.

Our two designs are intended for insertions for children's linen, dresses, etc., and are excessively strong for the purpose. You require tape the width of the figures in the engraving; cut each piece double the length of each figure in the design, fold them, and sew them together with a needle and thread, joining them to each other as you proceed. The edge is made of fine braid, to which the tape is sewn, or it may be crocheted in chain stitch. The bars are worked with a needle and strong cotton, in the same manner as the lace bars.

...

Sashes of plain *gros grain*, watered, and velvet ribbon are worn very long and flat, without bouffant loops. The sash of ribbon, two yards and a half long, is doubled in the middle and strung over the belt, leaving one long flat loop and two streamers; it is placed immediately in the middle of the back, or else slightly on the

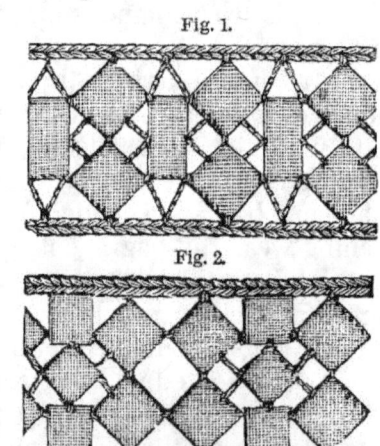

Fig. 1.

Fig. 2.

left. Sashes of the dress material have square ends, and sometimes pocket flaps are placed upon them. Black velvet sashes have pockets of lace, or of jet beads in network of trellis pattern.
Godey's Lady's Book and Magazine, February 1874

TRAVELING-DRESS.

Fig. VII. Traveling or Walking-Dress. – The under-skirt is of very dark gray silk, with one deep flounce, headed by two standing-up ruffles, piped with a light-gray silk of the color of the over-dress. The silk under-dress is made with one large puff at the back, the fullness of which takes the place of the back of a top dress. The over-dress is of light-gray camel's-hair, made long, and buttoned down the front; it only extends to the side, where it is finished with a piping of silk of the same color. The jacket is of gray camel's-hair, loose in front, with a silk vest of the color of the under-skirt, but partially fitting the figure at the back, and having a tolerably deep basque, which comes down over the dark-gray under-skirt. The pockets, basque, collar, revers, etc., are made of, or trimmed with, the dark silk. Velvet hat of dark-gray silk, trimmed with a light-gray feather.

...

As we have often before said, the greatest latitude is allowed to taste; skirts of costumes are to be cut short enough to escape the ground, or to be allowed to trail on the ground. Two different modes prevail at the present time. The *élégantes* are all wearing skirts which are short in front, cling very closely about the legs, and fall at the back with a small train. The manner of holding this train up gracefully is with them quite an art. When the train is left to trail, the outline is exactly that of a Chinese figure. It is very narrow; the gores being sewn to the waistband without any fullness.

It costs little to remodel last year's garments, so as to suit the present fashions; the short basques may be lengthened, by joining a square basque at the waist, concealing the join under the universally worn waistband. Coat sleeves can be cut narrower, a frill of silk to match the fraise can be added at the wrist so as to fall over the hand, and a revers with stiff lining turned upward toward the elbow. Pockets can be removed from the sides of Polonaises and redingotes to the back, where they remain half hidden among the folds; the châtelaine bag is added at the side, and a standing Rabagas collar turning outward round the throat. These are the principal alterations.

...

WALKING-DRESS.

Fig. VIII. – Walking-Dress. – The under-skirt is of dark-brown velveteen, and made quite plain; the upper-dress is of a lighter shade of brown vicugna cloth, open and rounded in front, trimmed with a band of brown velvet, the shade of the under-skirt, puffed and caught back, with a broad sash of ribbon of the darker shade of brown. The basque is close-fitting, cut very short just at the back, but with longer points at the sides, and square basques in front, the collar, etc., is trimmed with a narrow velvet of the darker shade of brown.

There is a new and pretty skirt made for house wear, and can be made of two different colored silks, or of silk and velvet. It consists of five breadths, namely, a wide gored front breadth, one narrow gore on each side, and two full straight back breadths. This brings a seam down the back, and this seam is left open three-eights of a yard from the bottom; the flounce which borders the skirt is taken in this seam, and held there in deep triple plaits, adding an extra, breadth, and giving a graceful fan or pigeon-tail slope to the slightly-drooping skirt. The front breadth would be pink, the flounce, and the side, and back breadths brown.

We give, first, this month, a walking-costume, with Polonaise, which is as much in vogue as ever, for out-door wear, made of woolen material, for which it is exclusively reserved. Our design calls for a myrtle-green cashmere. The skirt is made just to touch, and is kilted in front, and across the side gores, while at the back it is simply a slightly gathered flounce. This trimming is half a yard deep. The Polonaise is entirely closed down the front, and the back and side gores are cut very full, to allow the sides to be turned back, as seen in the design, which forms the trimming. A plaiting of silk, five inches wide, is laid on, and separated in the middle by a bias band of the cashmere. Narrow bands of silk, to emulate loops, ornament the front, where it is fastened with small mould buttons, covered with cashmere. The same trimming ornaments the side revers. The sleeves are slightly flowing, trimmed to match. A bow, with long ends of taffeta ribbon, is added at the back just under the ruff, which forms the collar. This Polonaise is only slightly looped on the side gores of the back, just enough to make a pouffe. Of cashmere, fifteen yards will be required, and four yards of silk for the plaiting. This Polonaise may be worn over a black silk skirt, and thus make variety.

...

Out-of-door garments, such as basques, sacques, Polonaises, etc., are now made with sleeves different from the rest of the garment. A half-fitting black velvet jacket, bordered with a band of black curled feathers, will have faille sleeves ,with velvet revers. It is by no means difficult to transform a Polonaise into the newer coat, especially if the Polonaise is closed in front. The basque of the Polonaise is turned back with two revers, and the revers are lined with either faille or velvet. A waistcoat is formed in the bodice, and the straight collar, which modernizes all dresses is added.

...

JACKET-WAIST WITH UNDER-VEST – FRONT AND BACK.
By Emily H. May.

We give; here, an illustration of a jacket-waist, with under-vest; and that our readers may understand it the better, engrave both the back and front. On the next page we give a diagram, by which to cut it out. In former numbers we have told how this is to be done.

No. 1. Half of Back of Jacket.
No. 2. Half of Side Back of Jacket.
No. 3. Half of Front of Jacket.
No. 4. Half of Sleeve of Jacket.
No. 5. Half of Back of Vest.
No. 6. Half of front of Vest.

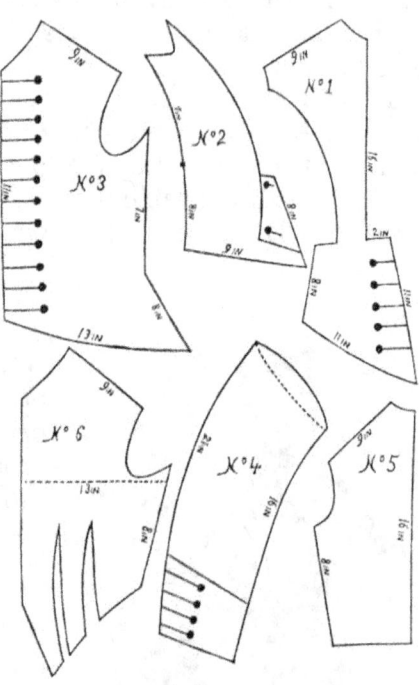

...

In the front rank are the English velveteens, with both cotton back and face, which are much worn for ordinary skirts; second, Roubaix velvet, with cotton back and silk face; third, Lyons cotton back velvet, with more silk and less cotton than the Roubaix production; fourthly, St. Etienne velvet, lighter, with silk, still with cotton back; and, lastly, the Lyons silk velvet, which is all made of silk. The best qualities are marvelously fine, but, of course, these are the most costly of them all. Besides plain velvets, there are brocaded velvets, and silken fabrics figured with velvet, both of which are used for Polonaises and tunics; they should be of a lighter shade than the skirt, albeit of the same color. The brocaded velvets look well as waistcoats with the black velvet coats that are coming into favor again, as we indicated. The gray brocaded velvet is particularly effective with a black coat; but these should be worn over either a gray or black skirt.

...

We next give a very stylish costume of gray merino. The skirt is trimmed with, first, one deep flounce, cut on the bias, simply hemmed top and bottom, and put on in box-plaits, stitched two inches from the top, thus forming the heading. The next flounce is six inches deep, put on in the same way, and the third one is five inches; of course, the heading is in proportion. The Polonaise is perfectly plain on the bottom, and very much puffed at the back. There is an extra sleeveless jacket, which is worn over the Polonaise and adds much to its stylish appearance, as well as to its comfort. The whole is trimmed only on the fronts, with bands of blue silk, one inch wide, doubled and turned to form a point. The sleeves are small, coat-shaped, with a deep mousquetaire cuff. Sixteen yards of merino, and one yard of silk, will be required. This costume would look well in black alpaca, trimmed with black velvet ribbon.

Peterson's Magazine, February 1874

Figs. 7 and 8. – Front and back view of house dress, made of steel-colored silk. The front is trimmed with bands of black velvet; the back with four ruffles bound with velvet, and a pouf, looped up with a black velvet sash. Jacket waist, coat sleeves trimmed to correspond with skirt.

...

Never have we seen such a variety of buttons to choose from, and they now from no small portion of a modern dress. Metal, steel, burnished brown or blue, engraved or cut diamond fashion; antique silver, oxidized metal, tortoise shell, jet, nacre, or shell buttons are equally in vogue. The most novel style is perhaps the coquillage button, made of beautiful shells, smooth, with pearl-like lustre, and fancifully spotted here and there; in fact, they are made of real sea shells. A set of these buttons is very expensive. Jet buttons are, however, very much employed, because they correspond with the handsome jet trimmings now so fashionable. The bands of threaded jet beads, called *rivieres de jais*, which look

so well on Cashmere or silk, looped jet fringes, and large jet agraffes, and buckles to hold up *retroussis*, and fasten large bows, gives great elegance to the modern costume.

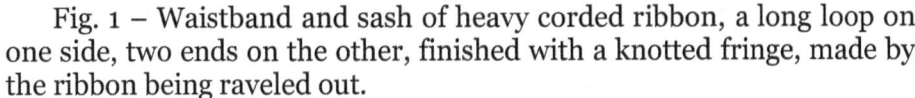

Fig. 1 – Waistband and sash of heavy corded ribbon, a long loop on one side, two ends on the other, finished with a knotted fringe, made by the ribbon being raveled out.

Some novel bodices have just appeared that can be worn with any dress, whether high or low. They are made of black tulle, are small, have basques, but not sleeves. They are completely covered with rows of very narrow lace embroidered with jet; the rows do not follow regularly, but two are sewn on close together, than a space and two more; a jet fringe covers half each row of lace. The bodice is partially open, and the opening is filled in with a faille bow and a jet buckle.

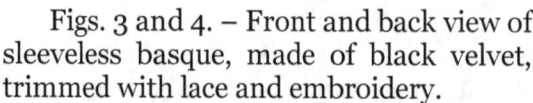

Figs. 3 and 4. – Front and back view of sleeveless basque, made of black velvet, trimmed with lace and embroidery.

We have been asked to give some directions and hints about dress for aged ladies. Gladly will we endeavor to do so, for, as a general thing, ladies do not seem to think there need be any difference in their dress, whether they are on this or that side of fifty. The costume of a lady who is no longer young must be simple in shape and dark in color; but the material should be as handsome as her means will permit. She will leave all flimsy, bright-colored stuffs to the young. A few rings, a handsome brooch, and a watch, are the only jewels she will wear. Her luxury, if her means permit, will lie chiefly in splendid lace, and rich velvet and silks. If, on the contrary, her means are moderate, the proverbial Quaker snowiness of cambric and muslin will gracefully harmonize with a dress of black or dark silk, or poplin, of modern but simple cut, with very long ample skirt and high bodice. If she wears an overdress, the *retroussis* should be of the most moderate proportions. A pretty, graceful, loose jacket is very becoming to an aged lady; at home it can be made elegant enough to be admissible in the drawing-room, even in the evening. Then for her mantles she will choose loose flowing ones, leaving jaunty little jackets to the young gay girls. For bonnets, however eccentric the fashions, she will accept none which do not really protect her head. Lace or ribbon strings are absolute requisites. It is evident that no showy colors will be accepted, that flowers will be superseded by feathers, and that the *tout ensemble* will have none of the fly-away look which characterizes the actual fashions. These are the general rules; we feel no more is needed. We were asked for hints. If we have spoken to plainly, pardon is asked; but we so rarely see what we consider growing old gracefully. Dressing becoming to our years, instead of detracting from our appearance, adds to it, when all is in harmony, and nothing is glaring.

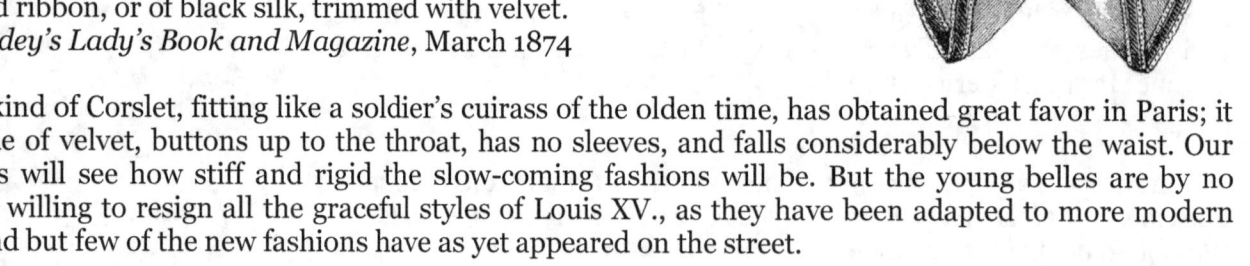

...

Fig. 21. – Apron, with bib and shoulder straps, going down to the waist in the back. The apron can be made of thin white muslin, trimmed with a colored ribbon, or of black silk, trimmed with velvet.

Godey's Lady's Book and Magazine, March 1874

A kind of Corslet, fitting like a soldier's cuirass of the olden time, has obtained great favor in Paris; it is made of velvet, buttons up to the throat, has no sleeves, and falls considerably below the waist. Our readers will see how stiff and rigid the slow-coming fashions will be. But the young belles are by no means willing to resign all the graceful styles of Louis XV., as they have been adapted to more modern use, and but few of the new fashions have as yet appeared on the street.

CASHMERE JACKET.
By Emily H. May.

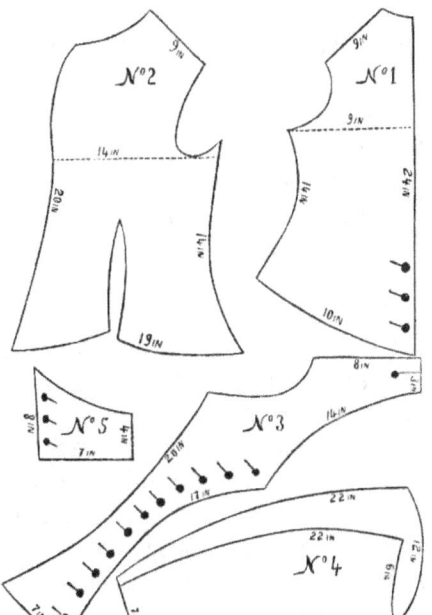

We give, here, an elegant jacket of black cashmere, or drap d'ete, with cuffs and revers of the same. Trimmings are fringe, ribbon, and lace. Handsome buttons are also introduced, and narrow piping are laid to simulate button-holes. The jacket is edged with a narrow binding of corded silk. Materials required, three yards of cashmere, four yards of silk, for lining, two and a half dozen buttons, three and a half yards of ribbon, five yards of lace, and two and a half yards of fringe. The buttons may be moulds, covered with the black silk, one yard of which will be required for binding and buttons. Pockets four inches deep by seven inches wide, also trimmed with buttons. On the next page we give a diagram by which to cut the jacket out.

In the diagram,
No. 1. Half of Back.
No. 2. Half of Front.
No. 3. Half of Rever.
No. 4. Whole of Sleeve.
No. 5. Half of Cuff.

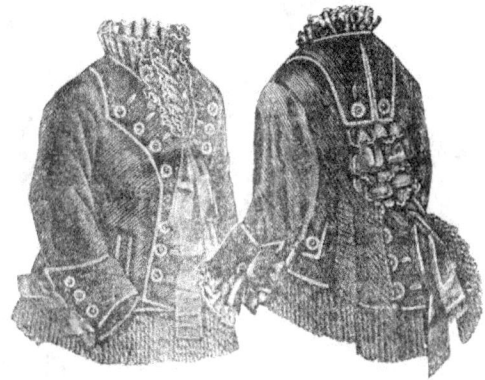

...

Those persons who have been fortunate enough to have seen Christine Nilsson as "Valentine," in the Huguenots, will have an excellent idea of what the newest and most fantastic style is for ordinary wear; and if a picture can be found of Marie de Medici, there will be an evening-dress of the latest fashion. It is quite impossible to explain these new dresses, and it is almost as impossible to understand them after a careful inspection. The lines are all straight and stiff, (an admirable style, however, for short people,) the front of the dress is all in one piece, like the Gabrielle dress of a few years ago, or it opens straight down the front, just showing the perfectly plain piece which may be underneath; the waist is extremely long; the bodies are laced down the back, and the lace around the neck is held upright with a collar of the same material as the dress, and lined with stiff net; even for ball-dresses the shoulders are surrounded with an upright fraise, or frill of lace. The sleeves are close at the hand, and puffed, some all the way up, some only from the elbow, and either round the arm or lengthwise. One of the dresses sent to Russia was in the Anne Boylen style, yet elegant and simple; it was made of turquoise-blue damask, without any ornament save a black velvet chatelaine bag. The front of the dress opened over a plain piece of black velvet; the upright collarette was of Venetian point, and the sleeves were black velvet. A ladder of blue satin bows decorated the outside of the sleeve.

Of course, these fashions are not yet by any means general, and can scarcely ever become so, except among very rich people. For such a style of dress as we have described, very rich material should be used, and these are by no means within the compass of people in general. But equally as a matter of course, the fashions will be so modified that they will come within the reach of all, and in a little while we will find brocades and damasks, and velvets, popular for those who can afford the expense, and figured silks, brocaded woolen materials, etc., for those whose purses are not so full.

Peterson's Magazine, March 1874

Overskirts are and are not worn; the overskirts of many of the dresses are so very odd as to entirely baffle description; one style still remains the same, the front and sides of the skirts still cling tightly to the figure; this effect is produced by cutting the gores very narrow at the top, not allowing any fulness at the band except in the single back breadth, which is gathered on. This clinging effect is further aided by tying the skirt back underneath with bands which are put on the second side seam, half a yard below the belt. Overskirts are fastened on the underskirts, in fact form part of the trimming of them. Many skirts are trimmed with lengthwise puffs over the entire skirt, others have merely the front breadths trimmed so. The shirred skirt is a novelty, these are entirely without flounces, but have the three front breadths formed of six lengthwise puffs separated by double shirred lines. The three back breadths are plain

Fig. 1.

Fig. 2.

below, slightly gored at the top, and are draped in irregular paniers, with a large sash bow in their midst. The shirred tablier fronts are very effective. The flounces of silk skirts are to be plentifully shirred or gathered at the top. Kilt plaiting still continues in vogue, but shirred flounces are lighter, and to not require much material.

Fig. 1. – Front and back view of a morning dress, made of pink Cashmere, trimmed with a plaited ruffle and puffs of pink silk; pink ribbon sash fastened at the side, and bow of pink ribbon in the back.

Fig. 2 – White muslin morning dresses can be made after this pattern, and trimmed with muslin; with colored ribbons and sash.

Fig. 13. – Black watered ribbon sash, with jet buckle in the centre, knotted fringe on the ends.

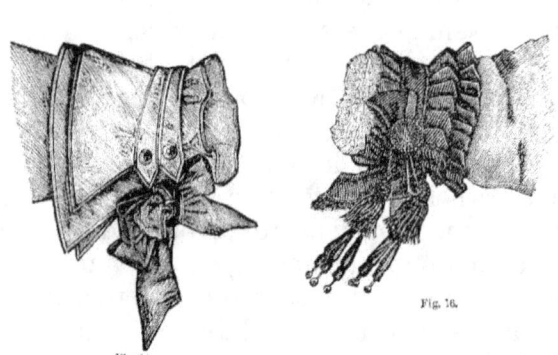

Fig. 14.

Fig. 14. – Fashionable sleeve. The upper part of the sleeve is quite plain. The trimming consists of a double open cuff, with a slightly fulled ruffle. The cuff is separated from the ruffle by a double strip pointed at the ends. All these separate parts are bound. A handsome ribbon finishes the sleeve.

...

Fig. 16. – The upper part of the sleeve is plain. The cuff is ornamented with two quillings going up, and one down; these are finished by a row of stitching at the edges. A crosswise band separates the plaiting; this is corded at the edge. A bow and handsome passementerie ornament finishes the sleeve.

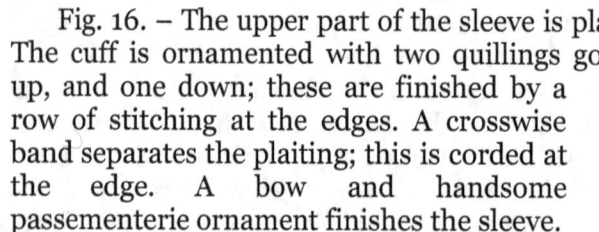

Fig. 16.

Figs. 21 and 22. – Front and back view of *paletôt*, made of black silk, bound around the bottom with a bias band, and a heavy passementerie gimp above it; the side and back breadths are scalloped where they are fastened on, bound with the band, and a silk button in each one. The front is cut with a deep vest finished with fringe around the bottom. Coat sleeves with cuff, trimmed to correspond.

Basques continue in favor, many are made entirely without postillon plaiting or vests, and have very high, flaring Medicis collars, with a double silk box-plaited ruff inside of this silk collar. Piping on the lower edge of the basque is gradually giving place to lace and fringe as formerly used. Many basque backs have tabs set in the seams below the waist like English walking jackets. ...

English jackets more closely fitting are worn; they are made of light quality cloth, and are slightly embroidered on the revers, pockets, cuffs, and on the flaps of the back. Many are now made single breasted with a rolling collar. The Mary Stuart ruff, very high, very full and flaring, will continue to be made of the dress material. The English collar, with turned-over points, will also be used as well at the rounded Medicis, already spoken of.

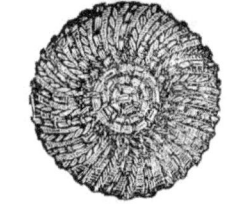

Fig. 1.

Fig. 2.

Fig. 24. – Bows, and cord, and tassels, to fasten on the right shoulder, and carry across to the waist under the left arm. They can be made of colored ribbon to wear with a white or black dress. Black ribbon ones can be worn with a colored dress.

DESIGNS FOR FANCY BUTTONS.

Fig. 1 gives a design in embroidery from which fancy buttons can easily be worked. Fig. 2 is ornamented with cord and bugles.

Fig. 1.

Fig. 2.

BUTTONS FOR DRESSES, ETC.

Fig. 1. – The mould is covered with velvet, a large jet button ornaments the centre, and smaller ones cover the button in a sort of net-work. Fig. 2 has a velvet covering, and, like Fig. 1, is ornamented with a large bead in the centre, surrounded by smaller ones, and finished with long stitches in purse-silk.

Godey's Lady's Book and Magazine, April 1874

BRIDEMAID'S EVENING DRESS.

Fig. VI. – Bridemaid's Evening-Dress of White Organdy, Spotted with Blue. – The under-dress is trimmed with a quilling of blue ribbon, festooned here and there with bows of black velvet and forget-me-nots. Over-dress with the skirt and body cut in one. The skirt is rounded in front, and square at the back, and trimmed like the under-dress. The waist is high on the shoulders, and square back and front. The trimming stands up over the shoulders, and a knot of black velvet and forget-me-knots is on the bosom in front. The same ornament in the hair.

TULLE EMBROIDERED.

By Mrs. Jane Weaver.

The above is a design for embroidering a white or black tulle dress. These are much worn, and when, worked in bright colors, have a very good effect, and save expense, as they are costly to purchase ready worked. This pattern looks remarkably well, worked in red silk on black net, with dots of blue, gold, and green, alternately.

A lady writes, "I have come across, lately, two or three friends who have established quite an artistic reputation for silk embroidery and applique work. Several yards of exquisite trimming have been produced, by working a bordering of flowers in floss silk, copied from nature, on tulle; the foundation, when complete, being cut away from round the pattern, and quite hidden in the flowers, both right and wrong side showing only silk. This is the kind of trimming which formed such a costly addition to the beautiful evening dresses worn by the Princess of Wales and her sister, during the visit of the Shah, last June. It may, of course, be advantageously applied to anything, and I saw it used as a bordering to light-blue silk curtains in a charming boudoir the other day.

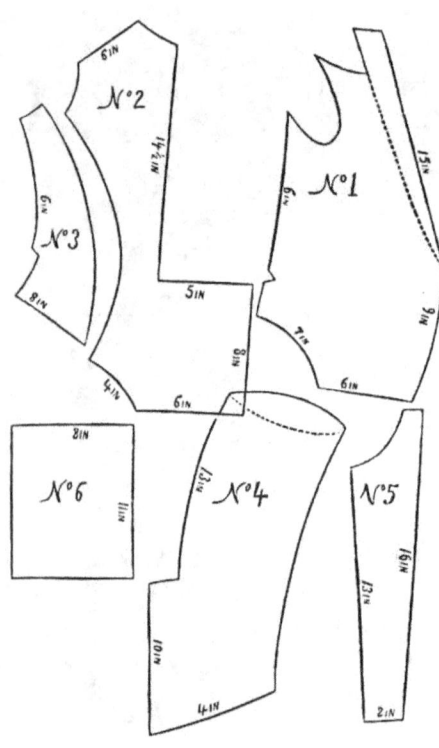

WAISTCOAT-BODICE FOR DEMI-TOILET.
By Emily H. May.

We give, on the preceding page, an engraving of a waistcoat-bodice for demi-toilet. It is a new and exceedingly pretty affair. It may be made of any material that is suitable for the skirt to be worn with it. We add, here, a diagram from which to cut it out. The inches marked in the sides of each pattern, show to what size to enlarge each.

No. 1. Half of Front.
No. 2. Half of Back.
No. 3. Half of Side Body.
No. 4. Half of Sleeve.
No. 5. Half of Waistcoat.
No. 6. Half of Box-Plait Back of Bodice.

The dotted lines on No. 1 shows where the bodice is turned back.

Fig. XI. – Cuirass Waist of Pink Silk, to be worn over a black silk skirt. Sleeves of pink silk, striped with black velvet. ...

The Cuirass Bodice, that fits the figure closely, is very high, with long basque, and has the effect of being moulded to the body, is always made of a different material from the dress. This cuirass bodice is frequently worn over the bodice of the dress. When the sleeves are of one material the bodice is of another. The sleeves match the trimming. When a ruff is not worn, a straight, upright collar, with a ruch [sic] of tulle or white crepé lisse around the throat, is worn. We give an engraving of one of these bodies.

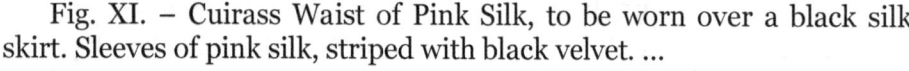

GABRIELLE WAIST.
Fig. VIII. – Gabrielle Waist of Black Silk, with high, full ruff; full, puffed sleeve at the hand. Black straw hat, trimmed with black ribbon and velvet and pink roses.
Peterson's Magazine, April 1874

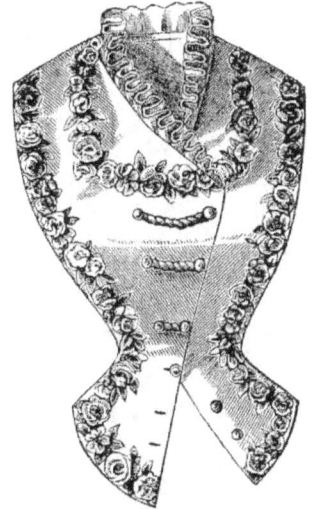

FIG. 8.

Fig. 8. – Vest to wear on the outside of dress waist, made of either white, black, or colored silk, with a border of flowers all around, embroidered in their natural colors.

Fig. 10. – Vest of black velvet, trimmed with pink *gros grain* ribbon, falling in loops and ends on right shoulder, and fastened at the waist on left side by a bouquet and sash ends.

Fig. 12. – Over vest made of pink silk, with revers of blue silk, small bouquet pm left revers. White muslin ruche, edged with lace inside.

FIG. 10.

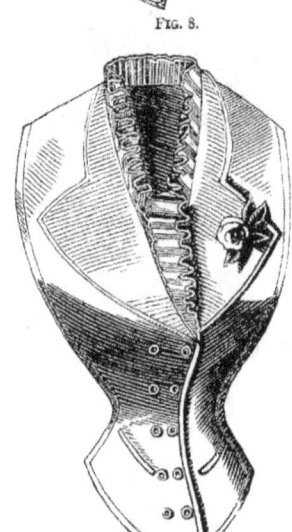

FIG. 12.

The open English embroidery before spoken of, becomes more popular as the new goods are daily opened. Black silk dresses have a deep border of it, for trimming to the overskirt, sleeves, and basque; this can be lined with a color or not, as the fancy of the wearer dictates. Polonaise are completely covered with it, made of white, gray, or cuir-colored batiste, camel's-hair, silk, or wool goods, and are to be made over silk of a darker or contrasting color.

The newest summer costumes that we have seen, have Nainsook waistcoats, and aprons for the overskirts entirely covered with open English embroidery, and are ornamented with black velvet bows, and with flounces of batist [sic]. This embroidery is composed of large wheels and eyelets, and is done by machinery. The blue batistes, which promise to still continue popular, are trimmed in the same style, with bands of white Nainsook embroidered in open work; the tabliers match the bands, being worked all over, and the sashes that drape the *poufs*, are blue velvet, embroidered with white silk. Embroidery of one kind or other is, where you can have it, decidedly the most fashionable trimming. Even the white woollen dresses which are being prepared for seaside wear, are being worked with white sadler's silk. But it is too early to speak of these dresses, we merely brought them forward to convince our readers of the extensive use of embroidery this season, so that even now it is not too late for a lady of leisure to commence embroidering a dress for herself.

Almost all the suits are either made of two shades of a color, or of contrasting colors; basques and overskirts or polonaises are both equally fashionable. Basques are made either the same depth all around, or else much shorter behind than before; they are both double and single breasted. The double breasted basques are made with a "plastron," or straight narrow vest piece set on the front, and fastened by two straight rows of buttons from the high throat down to the edge of the square basque. The flaring Medicis collar, of both the materials of which the dress is composed, finishes high necks; ruffs are also added to this collar, and are sometimes used without it, but are always voluminous. Indeed, the neck will be dressed more elaborately than ever; never has there been a time when there was such a variety of styles for arranging the necks of dresses.

Sleeves continue to be made of a different material from the waist; they usually match the underskirt, in color and material. The skirts still cling closely to the figure, which is produced by drawing the front breadths back by strings, as before mentioned; these strings also draw the back breadths up, forming a *pouf*, and shortening the dress for street wear.

Shirred flounced are going to be very much worn; these are made by running single threads through the upper part of the flounce one inch apart for a distance of an eighth of a yard; this, when drawn up, has the appearance of puffs; the flounce is about half a yard in depth, a narrow standing ruffle finishes the top. One of these flounces trims a skirt. Folds are put on to set up, not down, as they have been heretofore.

...

Figs. 19 and 20. – Sleeveless basque, made of black silk, trimmed with lace, insertion, passementerie, and ribbon. It has a vest which may, if desired, be made of colored silk.

...

When lace now forms the trimming of a dinner or evening dress, there must be an abundant supply. White lace is used on white dresses, and black lace upon black ones, and the material is so covered that the wearer has the effect of being clothed in lace. When it merely trims, and does not form a contrast, the effect is very stylish. The lace is arranged at the back, either flounces or a cascade; narrower lace is used

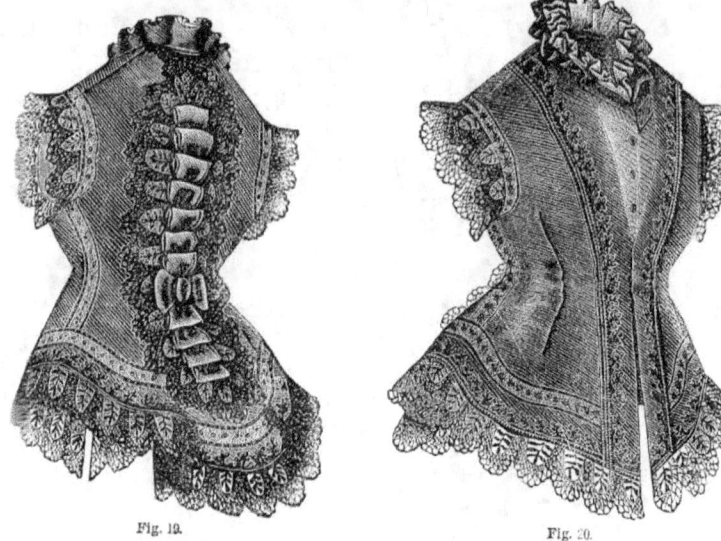

Fig. 19.   Fig. 20.

for the tablier. Old lace, arranged without fulness, is worn upon the bodice; white blonde embroidered with jet; and colored silk guipure, worked with gold or silver beads, are all worn; but we consider it a fashion much too glaring to be either ladylike or to become popular.

Ladies do not always pay sufficient attention to the manner in which the opening of their evening dresses is cut, and yet it is the most important part of the whole toilet. We have often seen ladies with horizontal shoulders of the kind we irreverently call *un porte manteau*, with low, round bodices, trimmed just upon the shoulders with bows; bouillions of flowers, which aggravate a hundredfold this defective outline; whilst others, with narrow, sugarloaf shaped shoulders, wear square bodices, thickly trimmed about the neck. Both, from contrary causes, look equally awkward, and devoid of grace and elegance. If they had exchanged dresses, the high shoulders hidden under the square bodice, and the low ones heightened by the round bodice, both would have gained immensely.

We have seen several dresses, made at a fashionable modists [sic], without trimming on the underskirt, one of which we will describe for the benefit of our readers. We very much fear it will be some time before the style becomes popular; but we hope the time is not very far distant when some of the superfluous trimming on dresses will be dispensed with. One, a walking costume, consisted of a skirt of very heavy black silk (for plain skirts require handsome material), made sufficiently long to form a moderate train, but provided with tirettes, which could convert it into a rasterre skirt, if convenient. Over this skirt, a very graceful tunic, with most *inédit* tucking up behind, and a little *paletôt*, close fitting behind, loose and double breasted in front; tunic and *paletôt* of pinkish gray silk; the whole simply edged with a bias band of gray silk. The revers and pockets of the *paletôt* are, of course, lined with the same.

Godey's Lady's Book and Magazine, May 1874

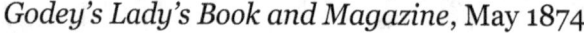

CORSLET.

Many still cling to the graceful over-skirt, with the puffed back, apron-front, and high looped sides. The style is old, but infinitely becoming to most persons. The Medici style is much more severe, and really requires a more elegant material, to look well, than the old, puffed, looped, airy fashion of the past few years. We gave two waists of the Medici style in our last number, and it will soon be seen how unbecoming they are to the figure. Almost all the skirts of Medici dresses have perpendicular trimmings down the front; sometimes a train, which is slightly puffed at the back, is added, and sometimes only a straight, side trimming is seen, and the back of the skirt is ruffled rather high. Some puffed sleeves are seen, sometimes puffed the whole length of the arm; sometimes there is only a puff at the shoulder, which is most unbecoming, giving a high-shouldered look to the prettiest slope of neck in the world. All dresses cling closely to the figure in front, and at the sides, so that the front widths of a dress much be very narrow at the top, then tapes are sewed on half-way down the seams, and tied back.

WALKING-DRESS.

Fig. VI. – Walking-Dress of Dark Gray Cashmere. – The skirt is quite plain, and made long enough to wear in the house; but with buttons at the back, by which it can be looped up for the street. A large black velvet bag is worn on the left side; it depends from the waist by two wide ribbons of the color of the dress, having two pearl buckles, which fasten the ribbon when it is attached to the dress; these ribbons extend below the bag, thus forming a very stylish trimming for this very stylish but plain dress. The basque fits closely, and the pockets, collar, and cuffs are of black ribbon.

...

EVENING-DRESS.

Fig. VII. – Evening-Dress of White Muslin. – The front of the dress has five puffings at the bottom, and a row of ruffles trims the sides; the train is puffed lengthwise, and the whole dress ornamented with wreaths and clusters of pink roses, and sashes, and looping of blue ribbon.

TULLE EMBROIDERY.
By Mrs. Jane Weaver.

This design is intended for a flounce to a black or white net dress. It is to be darned in colored silks. The work is very simple and effective. The scallop is worked in blue silk, with a line of red above and below; inside each scallop you introduce alternately stars of red, yellow, green, white, etc.

Peterson's Magazine, May 1874

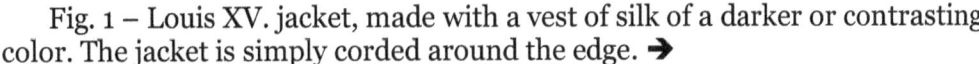

Fig. 1 – Louis XV. jacket, made with a vest of silk of a darker or contrasting color. The jacket is simply corded around the edge. ➜

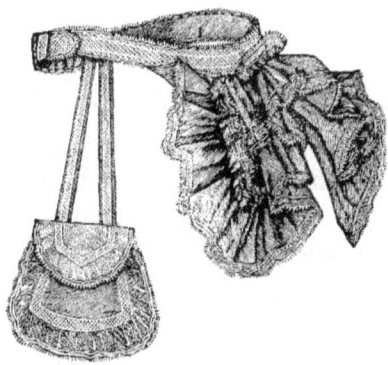

Fig. 5. – Basque, with sachet, for evening dress. This pretty basque will make a nice addition to a simple evening dress for a young lady. It is made of book-muslin, trimmed with lace and insertion. The flap and middle of the sachet, also the band of the basque, are of colored silk; the strap which holds the sachet is a piece of ribbon of the same color, covered with lace insertion.

Fig. 5.

Fig. 1.

The mixture of colors in some of the new dresses is most curious. Dark hues are most affected, and such strange contrasts as scabious and marine blue are to be seen. One of the newest colors is called *bois de rose*; it is made in three shades, which are constantly used in one costume. The lightest shade is an unhealthy salmon; the middle shade reminds us more of raspberry ice-cream than anything else; and the darker shade is a rich claret. These shades will, of course, not be worn for street dresses, but for carriage, dinner, or watering-place toilets. Crevette or shrimp promises to be very popular for evening silk dresses; *centre de Cedra*, an ashy gray, and various shades of *réséda* and moss are very much seen in silks.

If the silks are remarkable for their strange colorings, buttons are not less peculiar from their variety and size. French ingenuity displays itself in these buttons, which are made in bone or composition to match every imaginable hue. The large revers now worn at the sides of skirts are often fastened back with enormous buttons of ether green enamel, mother-of-pearl of all shades, steel, blue, jet, tortoise-shell, and a variety of other compositions, but always on a large scale.

What style is most popular for making dresses it is impossible to decide; Parisians seem to give the preference to overskirt, underskirt, and jacket or basque waist. Americans cling fondly to the polonaise; both are equally fashionable. There are so many goods this season that comes exclusively for polonaises that would not look well made into an overskirt and basque, and worn over a silk underskirt, judgment should be used in the choice as well as taste. One fashion which certainly cannot be recommended for its beauty is the clinging skirts; this fashion, like most fashions, is carried by our American sisters to such an excess as to in many appear ridiculous. With the present fashion of dresses it seems rather a difficult matter to sit or walk comfortably. The width of the skirt does not exceed three yards and a half, and this is made to cling to the figure so as to retard locomotion. Many odd devices are used to arrive at this end; tapes tied back, and latterly, we are told, a species of canvas corset set on the lower back seams and laced together so tight as in many cases to make it almost impossible for the wearer to walk. Where the beauty is we cannot see, and certainly they are not graceful. The street skirt has one full straight back breadth, two side gores, and one gored front; all of these are made to fit with perfect smoothness to the belt, umbrella shape.

The fancy for tablier fronts is continued, and the overskirts are made after a Greek model, falling straight on one side and being drawn up high on the other, hanging in diagonal folds on the front. Other shapes are made to fall back with revers, and others made like a drapery sash; another has a sort of pointed apron. Demi trained skirts are given a graceful effect by the new extension flounce, a kind of Spanish flounce set on the three back breadths, and which, by the way, offers a good plan for renewing skirts that are defaced by dragging. The flounce is merely five straight breadths of silk sewed on the skirt, or else attached to it, with the skirt beneath cut away. It is gauged in clusters (three rows of gauging and five clusters of gathers), leaving about five inches of space between; the upper edge is piped, and the gauging is three inches below the edge; the lower part of the flounce is finished with a piped bias fold three inches wide, and this fold extends all around the whole skirt. This style is very pretty for black silk or grenadine dresses. The front breadth is then a puffed tablier, or else it has an elaborate overskirt that is trimmed in apron fashion. Any pretty basque completes the suit.

...

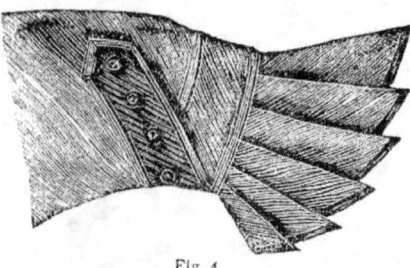

Fig. 4.

Fig. 4. – Fashionable sleeves, trimmed with a plaited ruffle, with a band of silk corded on each side above it.

We have been asked for styles to make ordinary print and percale dresses. These goods are made up into suits that will answer for home and street alike. For ordinary dresses the belted polonaise and short skirt are very useful. The polonaise has a French back with one seam; the front is shaped by a half seam, that extends from the armhole to the pockets. It is caught back to form an irregular *pouf* in the back. ... Calico ruffles wash better if cut straight, and are improved in appearance by having a bias band stitched on two inches above their lower edge.

← Fig. 14. – This sash may be made of the material of the dress, lined with a contrasting color, and piped at the edges. The buckles and beads may be of jet or pearl, according to the color of the material. A handsome fringe may be worked around one end of the sash.

→ Fig. 18. – Sash, intended solely for evening dress. It is fringed out at the ends, and the fringe is tied. Sprays of flowers are fastened on to one of the bows.
Godey's Lady's Book and Magazine, June 1874

Dresses for evening parties are now almost invariably made with tabliers in front; and these tabliers are entirely of either lace or tulle, or embroidered with jet. A beautiful evening-dress was made, lately, of pink satin; the train was draped in folds; the edge was cut in petal-like scallops and mounted over a very narrow plaiting; the front was entirely covered with a black tulle tunic, embroidered.

FIG. 14.

FIG. 13.

MEDICI VEST.

Whole Polonaise are made of the white English embroidery, as the muslin comes entirely covered with the embroidery, (which is all open work,) and the Polonaise is cut out of it as out of common white muslin. A Polonaise of this material should be worn over a colored silk waist and skirt.

The Medici costume is more difficult to produce in thin summer goods than in the heavy, stiff materials worn during the winter, so the Polonaise and apron-front, with loops, are still popular, if old.

...

Buttons are remarkable for their variety and size. French ingenuity displays itself in these buttons, which are made in bone or composition to match every imaginable hue. The large revers now worn at the sides of skirts are often fastened back with enormous buttons of either green enamel, mother-of-pearl of all shades, steel-blue, jet, and a variety of other compositions, but always on a large scale.
Peterson's Magazine, June 1874

Fig. 2. – Walking dress of gray *de bège*, made with one skirt and apron overskirt in front; the skirt is trimmed with narrow ruffles and gray silk bows; folds of gray silk on the overskirt, and sash in the back. Basque waist, trimmed to correspond.

...

As travelling forms a large part of the business and pleasure of this month and the next, and as we have received several inquiries for hints on travelling costumes from our readers, we will endeavor to fulfil their requests, which we thought had been attended to in former articles. Before commencing, however, we wish to make a remark in reference to the styles we mention, as we so often have requests for a description of articles of plain goods. Any of the models we quote can be made of plain goods as the taste of the wearer desires. It is the shape and harmonious contrast of color which are the only important items in tasteful dress. True elegance can be as well purchased with a small sum as a large, and does not at all exclusively belong to wealth. If the

FIG. 2.

dresses we describe are of costly material, it is because we have seen them made of such by first-class dressmakers for wealthy customers; but they are always, with very few exceptions, copied in the most modest goods for less fortunate sisters, who are none the less ladies on that account.

The choice of a nice and suitable fabric for a summer travelling suit is rather a difficult problem, as the material should combine a variety of qualities. It should be neither to warm nor too cool (in case of a sudden change in the temperature), sufficiently elegant, yet not too dressy, fits both for walking and driving if the occasion demands it. A dress that will stand a certain amount both of rain and dust. Such a material we have seen in the many new *beige* fabrics which have appeared this season. *Beige* is the name given to sheep's wool in its natural state, that is, of a brownish-gray color, and, by analogy, it is applied to materials of that shade, whether their color be a natural one or acquired by dyeing. The genuine article, the real *beige*, is a fabric of pure wool of various shades of the same color, brownish-gray spun together. It is a light, soft, and very durable tissue, indifferent to both sun and rain, and which we strongly recommend to our readers. The same shade is found in most of the fashionable fabrics of the season. Quiet shades of color, and more particularly every variety of gray, grow more in favor as the season advances. Fancy colors have been so much worn that persons have in a measure become tired of them, and gray has the double advantage of being becoming to all complexions, and of looking well with any other color, which is a great simplification of the bonnet question, and leaves personal fancy unlimited scope in the choice of bows, cravats, etc. We will give a description of a simple and tasteful travelling suit, made of the material spoken of, and then pass to other styles for the benefit of those who are not interested in the travelling question. The skirt of dress should be trimmed with one gathered flounce, a tight-fitting polonaise with jacket bodice, all made as plain as possible, and with no trimming beyond one or several rows of stitching, worked by machine, and a set of steel, nacre, or oxidized buttons; the sleeves coat-shaped with deep revers.

...

Figs. 6 and 7. – Front and back view of morning dress, made of gray percale. The bottom of skirt is trimmed with lengthwise bands of blue stitched on, as is also the front of polonaise; collar, sash, and sleeves.

...

Almost all the evening robes now made by first-class modists, whether high or low corsage, are made with a skirt perfectly flat in front and at the sides, every breadth being deeply gored. The back part of the skirt, trained and very ample, is all gathered or plaited within a space of eight inches. The front of the dress is fully trimmed, but the back remains quite plain, and flowing naturally.

Figs. 6 and 7.

Godey's Lady's Book and Magazine, July 1874

Paris Fashions. ... Traveling dresses are for the most part of batiste delaine, which is light, and does not rumple easily. Soft felt gray shades are the preferable colors, and are combined with black or bronze faille, judiciously used as trimmings; these are confined to the pipings of flounces, revers, and linings of basques. The prevailing style for traveling suits is the round skirt, without polonaise or over-skirt, trimmed in front with horizontal or perpendicular folds, piped with black or bronze. The rest of the skirt is covered with gathered flounces, also with black or bronze pipings. Black or bronze vest, with a morocco belt of the same color. Small jacket of the same material as the dress, closed only at the throat, and springing apart so as to show the vest completely. Black straw bonnet, trimmed with bronze or plum-colored ribbons. From the morocco belt is suspended on one side the watch, and on the other an oxidized silver hook and watered ribbon loop, from which are hung a number of little chains, which serve to hold the fan, Russia-leather pouch, and short parasol with a round and flattened head.

Harper's Bazar, July 25, 1874

PRINCESS BEATRICE CORSAGE
By Emily H. May.

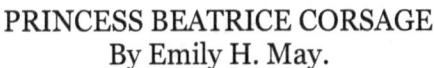

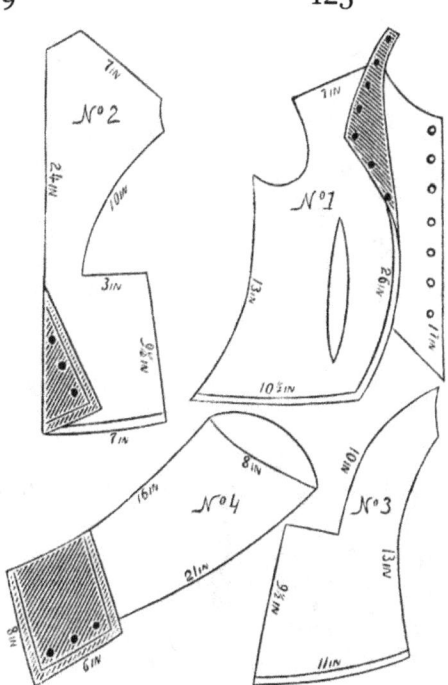

The corsage consists of No. 1, Front; No. 2, Back; No. 3, Half of Side-body; No. 4, Half of Sleeve. On the front we have fastened in the proper place, the vest and the revers. The vest may be either continued up to the neck, as in the diagram, or cut off across the chest, as seen in the engraving. If the open style is preferred, it is more usual only to have the vest imitated, by putting in the front piece, as we have given it; although some prefer to cut the vest entire, sewing it in at the shoulder-seams, and under the arms. The middle of the back is cut open, and ornamented by revere, as indicated in the design. The coat-sleeve has a deep cuff falling over the seam of the sleeve, and wider at the bottom.

...

Worth, the great Parisian dress-maker, is making many dresses trimmed with double and triple loops, arranged in longitudinal lines. These loops are of a different color from the dress, but are lined with the same color. Several of the newest dresses in his show-rooms have draperies arranged on the front of the skirt, and, although these draperies sometimes give the effect of three tunics, yet the plaits cling so closely to the skirt that it has the effect of being moulded to the figure. This is owing to the skillful manner in which the breadths are cut. Worth is also making costumes of shot or changeable silk. He made lately an exquisite pale-blue one, trimmed with insertions of steel gimp.

...

The fashions are quite fixed at this time of the year; nothing that is startlingly new is seen, only the established fashions are modified, as apron-fronts, Polonaise, coat-basques, will all be worn, as the fancy may dictate. Thin dresses do not look well without an over-skirt, if not a good deal ruffled, puffed, or trimmed in some way. One thing is obligatory, the two skirts, both upper and under, must be very much tied back, making walking very uncomfortable, and sitting very difficult. Many Polonaise are made with loose fronts, and outlined at the waist with sashes, not belts, the latter are no longer worn. Some Gabrielle or Princess dresses have been made by Worth. These are tight-fitting, long Polonaise, quite plain in front, if for the house, made with a train, but look well only in a material that is at least moderately heavy. Young ladies wear pale-blue, pink, buff, or mauve cashmere Polonaise over black, or any colored silk that may be suitable. One of the prettiest dresses we have seen was of plain pink batiste; the demi-trained skirt was edged with three ruches of the material, each five inches wide, separated by a space of an inch and a half; these ruches were platted, and fastened only on the upper edge. The Polonaise of the same material, without a lining, was adjusted in the back only; the trimming was composed of a ruche like that of the skirt; the same trimming simulated on the waist a jacket with pockets. The Polonaise was heart-shaped in front. Another pretty and less expensive dress was a dark-blue linen, trimmed with four or five flounces, each one edged with three rows of narrow, white braid. The Polonaise was hemmed and edged with three rows of white braid.

...

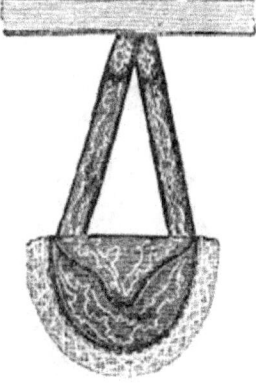

We also give a design for a "chatelain bag," now so universally worn. These bags are to be seen in the shops made of white Swiss, trimmed with valenciennes, and lined with colored silks; black silk and velvet, braided and beaded with jet; and they will be very pretty for morning dresses, made of the material, and braided, say in pique or percale. The design we give is black silk, braided and edged with guipure lace. They are fastened to the belt, and hang from the left side.

First, this month, we give a traveling-dress, in gray *de bége* – a soft, mottled, woollen fabric, particularly adapted to traveling purposes, as it neither rumples or catches the dust. Our design has the short rasterre skirt, which escapes the ground, and is made very scant, only three yards in width. The bottom of the skirt is ornamented by first a graduated flounce, cut on the bias, which is eleven inches deep in the back, sloping away to six inches in front. Above this, arranged *en tablier*, or apron, are six small ruffles, also cut on the bias, five inches deep. The Polonaise here is cut long and plain, buttoning over to the left side, and simply trimmed with a bias band of black silk, two inches wide, set above the hem. The looping of the front of the Polonaise is done by putting several button-holes over one button, in three places, perfectly simple, and the effect is, we think, charming. This would be particularly well suited to a white pique, worn over a black or colored-silk skirt; and where the band of black silk is put upon this Polonaise, trim the pique with a band of Hamburg insertion. Fifteen to sixteen yards of *de bége* will be required, and the cost of a good one is from forty to fifty cents per yard.

...

BALL FRINGE FOR POLONAISE.
By Mrs. Jane Weaver.

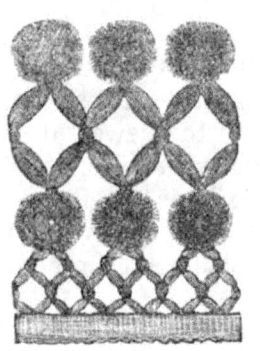 

Cut two rounds of cardboard alike, and a little larger than you wish the balls to be, and cut in the centre of each a circular hole, about the diameter of one-third of the whole round. Put the two card circles together, and with long needlefuls of wool sew through the centre hole and over the outer circle of the card, so as to cover it completely and evenly, and continue thus till the centre hole is quite filled up; then with a pen-knife or scissors cut quite through the wool all round, down to the edges of the card, and slip a piece of wool of sufficient length in between the two cards, and tie it tightly, leaving an end hanging; tear away the cards, draw the two sides of the ball together, and trim them with scissors. The good shape of the ball depends on the centre hole being quite the right size. If it be too large, the ball will be rather flat; if too small, it will be elongated. With the piece of wool left hanging from the balls, thread a Berlin needle,

and sew, at even distances, to a piece of narrow gimp, as show in No. 1, and knotted at equal distances; and in No. 2, the wool can be wound round a mesh, tied at the top close to the ball, and sewn at the upper part to a linen foundation.

Peterson's Magazine, July 1874

Fig. 3 – Evening dress of rose-colored silk; the skirt plain in the back, trimmed with two ruffles in front. Low corsage, with short basques, trimmed with silk and grenadine. Long apron overskirt, of white striped grenadine, trimmed with broad lace.

Fig. 4. – Evening dress of peach-colored silk, made with one skirt and low corsage, and trimmed with Valenciennes lace. Opera sacque of heavy white corded silk, embroidered and trimmed with fringe.

Fig. 5. – Walking dress of black silk. The front breadth is trimmed with one ruffle, with a band above it; the sides with three narrow ones, with bands above; the back breadths with one deep, and narrow ruffles to the waist. Walking jacket of silk, corded. Black chip bonnet, trimmed with lace, feathers, and black silk. ←

...

Fig. 6. – Walking dress of two shades of gray. The underskirt is of silk, the front breadth trimmed with kilt plaiting; the back breadths are trimmed with narrow ruffles. The polonaise is of summer camel's hair of the lighter shade, finished with a thick cord of silk. →

...

Dresses composed of a mixture of plain and fancy silks are in great demand. Black silk dresses are now much trimmed with cross-bands of fine black and white striped silk; the sleeves and waistcoat being striped like the bands. This style is capital also for renovating a black silk that has been otherwise trimmed. But the greatest novelty for this style of dress is the tunic made of plain silk, worn over a checked skirt. The bodice is made with the new violin back, the centre being of the checked silk. "Violin" is the name given to a bodice with a long waist, the back of which is in the form of a violin, and its rounded basque is also cut like that instrument.

...

Fig. 11.

Figs. 11 and 12. – Bow of black *gros grain* ribbon with slide of black beads, for ornamenting dresses, etc., made on a foundation of doubled leather or buckram, as shown in illustration, Fig. 11.

...

Fig. 12.

The question of skirts is not yet quite decided. Many ladies have adopted the clinging fourreau, bordered simply with a narrow plaiting. The fourreau has, as a matter of course, a train, and produces an ungraceful effect if the train be not very long. Other ladies, on the contrary, wear short skirts covered with trimmings, and very *bouffante* at the back. In the matter, therefore, of long and short and demi train skirts, individual taste can be consulted, for all lengths are fashionable. The only general rule observed is the clinging front, and that is universal. The fourreau is becoming; it is very *distingué* and in excellent taste; but then it is inconvenient for a costume intended for street wear. For such occasions a shorter skirt is preferable, covered with a profusion of plaitings, and a double or triple tunic with pouf.

The new tunics and bodices, made entirely of open gimp work and jet, are most admirable for new dresses and for furbishing up those that have lost their first freshness. The tablier, which is almost as long as the skirt, is cut in a very simple fashion, and consists of alternate stripes of open gimp work and jet. It is tied at the back, fitting to the figure both in front and at the sides. It can be worn over almost any variety of silk dress. The bodice, which matches the tablier, is worn over the silk bodice, and the gimp, being of an open pattern, the silk is plainly visible.

...

Fig. 4. – Vest of blue silk, with neck cut surplice, and finished with a plaiting of silk; muslin can be worn inside if desired. It is trimmed with ribbon bows, narrow bands of silk, and buttons; it is made double breasted.

...

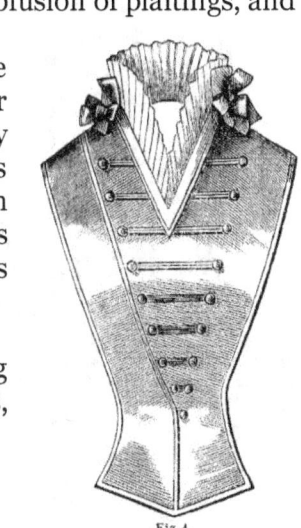

Fig. 4.

Fig. 16.

Fig. 16 – Vest made of lace and muslin insertion, and trimmed with lace and colored ribbon bows.
Godey's Lady's Book and Magazine, August 1874

Summer costumes continue to be made of lawn, with sleeveless jackets, and with basques which, if square, are invariably short, but if round, they are generally longer. Net mantelets, embroidered with jet, will be fashionable for summer wear; they are all tied round the waist with an inner band, the bow to which may be either visible or invisible, according to taste. There is no better investment at the present time than the tablier and sleeveless jacket of jet embroidery, for they can be worn over almost any dress. The tablier is long and round: it has no back, but is hooked behind the waist, and terminates with loops and sash-ends; the jacket is finished off with a rich jet fringe. Both are easily put on, and require no adjustment. Similar tabliers and sleeveless jackets are also made of black silk, which is covered with open embroidery; they are rich looking, but not so effective as the jet, which glistens in every light.

...

Light silk dresses that have lost their first freshness, and are otherwise out of date, can be made to look very elegant and fashionable in the following manner. Take, for example, a peacock-blue faille skirt, cover it with plaitings of grenadine, striped with a pencil line of black; the top only should remain plain. A wide sash of the blue faille commences on the hips at each side, and is tied under the pouf and plaits at the back. The sash-ends also are covered with grenadine, and edged with passementerie and front. Muslin plaitings are again used on silk dresses, but these are a costly trimming; they soon rumble and require renovating. ...

Over-skirts are not draped on the hips, but are merely long aprons hooked together at the back, under sashes made up with loops. When either cashmere or camel's-hair forms the tablier, it consists of two breadths, cut with a seam down the centre of the front and drawn upward on the dress improver, terminating at the back with straight frills and many loops and ends of ribbon. Bows of ribbon, or else a tuck are placed down the front seam. These deep tabliers are also successfully simulated with trimming. Plaitings and flounces are still plentifully used on lower skirts; the former are caught to the skirt twice, once at the upper edge and once in the centre, giving the effect of a flat plaiting, with a loose frill below. The front breadth is trimmed with one or two of these double-stitched plaitings, which are curved higher tat the back until five or seven or introduced, this curve serving to outline the tunic or upper-skirt.

For morning wear, linen and batiste costumes are now made in every variety. Dark-blue is still the favorite, and will share popularity with stones and grays. Embroidery in white cotton is preferred for ordinary linen or lawn costumes before any other ornamentation.
Peterson's Magazine, August 1874

Fig. 1.

⬃ Fig. 1. – Casaque of Cashmere, trimmed with silk, fringe, and yak lace. This garment can be made to match the dress or as an over garment.

Figs. 4 and 5. – Front and back view of a casaque, made of heavy black silk, trimmed with black velvet, lace, frog buttons, and cords. ➜

Figs. 4 and 5.

One of the most original styles of making up striped goods is to make it have the appearance of being three different fabrics in one dress. Take a fabric having exceedingly broad stripes, say blue and gray, the skirt is made without either overskirt or trimming; the back breadth is plaited almost from the top to the bottom, each plait being exactly the width of the dark blue stripe that comes to the top. The plaits are not fastened at the bottom, and consequently spread apart and widen as they descend. The side breadths are plaited in the same way, only in these it is the gray stripe which forms the top of each plait. Lastly, the front breadth is plain, and it is there alone, in the front of the dress, that the two stripes, light and dark, are apparent at the same time. The cuirass corsage is plain, like the front breadth. The sleeves are plaited like the side breadths, that is, from top to bottom, in such a manner that the light stripe forms the top of each plait. For a wrapping, or rather a pretty addition to this dress, a China crepe scarf, of the same shade as the blue, is thrown across the shoulders, with the left end falling straight, and the right end draped across the bust, and fastened on the left shoulder with a large oxidized silver brooch.

Godey's Lady's Book and Magazine, September 1874

During September and early October, summer dresses generally continue to be worn, with the addition of darker trimmings and warmer wraps. The change in fashion is so gradual, and such latitude is allowed to individual taste, that it will soon be most difficult to say that anything is the fashion. But we think that plain under-skirts are gradually creeping into favor. These skirts are made with trains, some quite long, others just defined. Of course, this fashion will be most inconvenient for walking. Yet we have seen a costume just from the hands of the renowned Worth, of Paris, where the under-skirt was very much trimmed, the upper-skirt rather short, and arranged at the back in the most complicated, indescribable style. But all skirts, whether long or short, are tied tightly back, a most troublesome arrangement, and producing a most ungraceful walk.

The new "Violin" back, is also another fashion not to be desired. We think "Violin" is the name given to a bodice with a long waist, the back of which is in the form of a violin, and its rounded basque is also cut like that instrument. The effect is produced by the centre of the back being of a different color, or material, from the sides.

Black velvet is very popular as a trimming as well as jet.

CASAQUE OF CLOTH.
By Emily H. May.

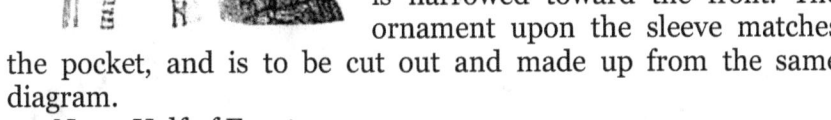

This casaque is for morning promenade wear, and should be made of the same material as the costume worn with it, or of ladies' cloth. The pattern consists of six pieces, representing one half the casaque – front, half the back, under-basque, pocket, collar, and sleeve. The fronts are buttoned from neck downward, and the basques, on the contrary, are left open to the waist, and trimmed. The front, under the arm, wraps over on to the under-basque, and has the effect of being buttoned there. The longest part of the under-basque is the centre of the back; it must, be sewn to a waistband, and tucked inside, under the upper-basque. The upright collar is narrowed toward the front. The ornament upon the sleeve matches the pocket, and is to be cut out and made up from the same diagram.

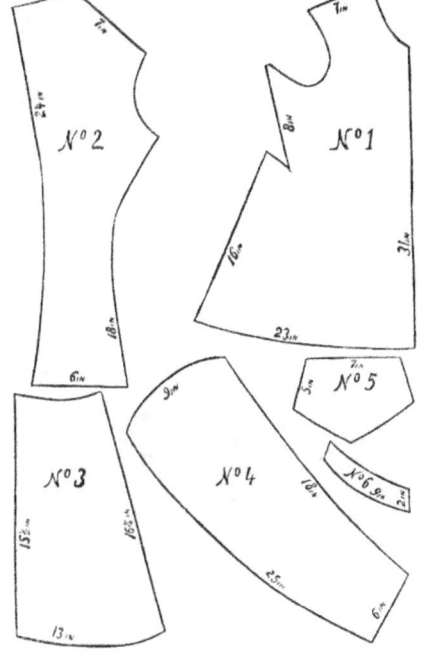

No. 1. Half of Front.
No. 2. Half of Back.
No. 3. Half of Under-Basque.
No. 4. Half of Sleeve.
No. 5. Half of Pocket.
No. 6. Half of Collar.

English embroidery continues to be, as it has been all summer, the popular trimming for all washing costumes. Very pretty are the Polonaises of écru batiste that are covered with those open wheels and compasses that compose the design. These Polonaises are looped up at the sides with sashes of light-colored ribbons, while bows to match are added down the centre. Blue and pink are the favorite colors for the sashes and bows.

Feather trimmings are becoming exceedingly popular again. They are made to match dresses of almost every color, and occasionally are varied with bands of cock's feathers and bands of peacock feathers. The small colibri pelerines, made of either coffee-color or gray vicugna, bordered with ostrich feathers, and with a gros grain ribbon bow at the back, are very suitable and tasteful.

...

HOUSE OR STREET COSTUME.

In the front of the number, we give a pretty costume for either the house or street. The combination is charming. and suggests an economical as well as effective way of disposing of two half-worn dresses. In our design, the skirt of the dress is of a light tan-colored cashmere, while the apron-front and basque is of black silk. There is ahead of the colored cashmere ornamenting the bottom of the apron, to which is added a black silk fringe, four inches deep. In front, the basque has a vest of the colored cashmere, and the front of the basque, as well as the postillion at the back, is trimmed with a band of the cashmere, two inches deep. The tight coat-sleeves have a double frill of the cashmere forming the cuff, separated by a band of black silk. The plaiting around the neck is also of the cashmere. Any of the light shades of gray or blue, would look equally well for this costume.

Black silk dresses are made with basque bodice, long apron, and skirt trimmed with Marguerite plaitings. These plaitings are cut straight across the silk, hemmed on the lower edge by hand, and turned-in at the top. The deep apron reaches almost to the top; it is rounded upward to the tournure, where it meets and fastens with long, wide loops and sash-ends. This apron is edged either with jet fringe or with jetted lace, and is often composed of alternate stripes of guipure insertion, or jet galoon with silk.

Peterson's Magazine, September 1874

One of Worth's novelties is the coachman's cape, and is quite popular for a simple dress. Imagine a Polonaise made of light cloth or iron-gray twilled woolen material, bordered with a deep hem of a darker shade. This Polonaise is but slightly open in front, and it forms at the back two immense points, which would fall as a long train if allowed to trail, only they are fastened up with buttons sewn at the waist. But what gives the effect of a coachman's coat to this Polonaise is the addition of two pelerines, the larger of which does not fall below the center of the back; one of these capes is light, the other dark.

...

Fig. 3. – Polonaise for lady, made of black Cashmere, trimmed with lace, passementerie ornaments, and gimp.

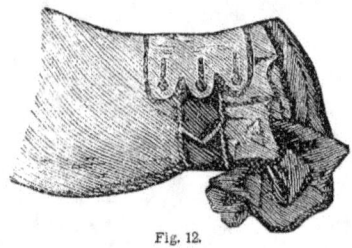

Figs. 12 and 13. – Fashionable modes of making dress sleeves.

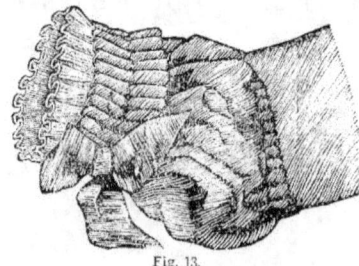

Fig. 12.

Fig. 13.

Fig. 3.

CASHMERE COSTUME.

Front and back view of costume of two shades of brown cashmere. The underskirt is of the lighter shade, trimmed with puffs; the overdress and waist is of the darker shade, trimmed with Yak lace. The sleeves are of the lighter shade, trimmed with the darker.

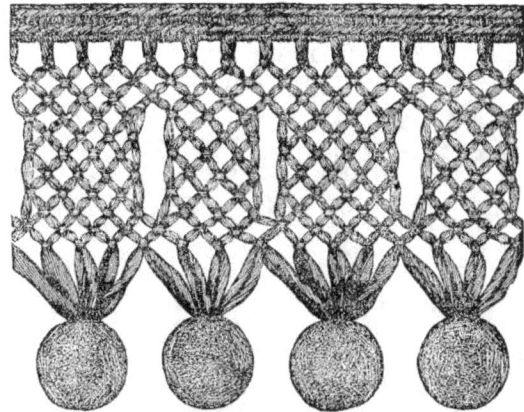

FRINGE.

Made of wool, with netted heading, and balls at the end. It is suitable for mantles or overdresses.

Godey's Lady's Book and Magazine, October 1874

Next, we give a back and front view of a pretty walking-costume of striped poplin, composed of narrow and wide stripes of black and white, producing a gray effect. The under-skirt is trimmed quite high, as may be seen, thus dispensing with the tunic. First, there is a plaited flounce, eleven inches deep, put on with a narrow puff, as a heading; the next flounce measures nine inches, the next only seven inches. The basque-jacket has a vest-front, cut pointed in front, and buttoning all the way down. Then the front of the over-jacket buttons only to the waist, and is finished with revers, forming a collar at the back. The back, as may be seen, is quite long, and cut open to the waist at the back. The whole is trimmed with a very narrow plaited trimming of the same. From twenty to twenty-three yards of single-width material will be required for this costume; and these striped poplins usually come in single widths only. Price ranges from fifty cents to one dollar per yard.

...

The Chatelaine Bag appears to have become and indispensable addition to all morning costumes. The most economical plan to adopt is to select a black velvet one, and to have your monogram embroidered on it. Such a chatelaine bag or "aumonière," as it is called, can be worn with almost any costume.

Peterson's Magazine, October 1874

One of the latest and most successful innovations in the fashion of full-dress toilets consists in this: the front and sides of the skirt, gored so that when standing it does not form one single crease, are covered with a multitude of narrow flounces overlapping each other from the waist to the bottom of the skirt. All the fulness of the skirt forms behind a large fold some eight or ten inches wide, three or four times plaited, and quite plain. It falls gracefully into a fan-shaped train, hiding on both sides the extremities of the fringe trimming. This fashion has the merit of being reasonable and practical, for, with

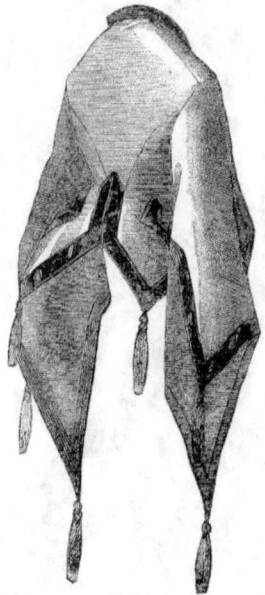

such a dress, one can sit down without crumpling and spoiling entirely the aspect of the toilet, as was too often the case when elaborate trimming occupied the back of the skirt. It adds much to the elegance of a woman, when she seems totally free from any thought of her dress, and can sit down without any of that pushing, twisting, tucking up of her skirt which we have all been obliged to practise for some years since puffs and *tuniques relevèes* have been in fashion. We saw last winter many evening dresses so covered behind with wreaths of flowers, that it was literally impossible to sit down in them. Standing or kneeling were the only alternatives. How comfortable! This was a case for the saying: *"Il faut souffeir pour être belle."* But it seems as if the sufferers had had enough of this absurdity, and the present good sense they show must be the teaching of experience.

...

↖ Fig. 17. – Jacket sacque of black Cashmere; it is trimmed with a band of heavy corded silk. Long open sleeves, trimmed to correspond.

Fig. 3. – Visiting dress of two shades of gray silk. The under skirt is made of alternated side plaitings of the two shades, with ruffles up each side. Pouf in the back, apron front formed of sideways puffs, ending in scallops around the edge, finished by tassels. Jacket bodice, of the darker shade, trimmed with the lighter. Bonnet of the two shades, trimmed with blue flowers and pink roses.

Fig. 4. – House dress of two shades of brown silk, the front breadth made and entirely trimmed with the lighter, as is also the revers and facing around the bottom of the skirt. The upper part of the skirt is trimmed with lace of the lighter shade and bands of silk, as is also the deep basque bodice and sleeves.

Fig. 5. – Walking dress of purple silk, made with two skirts, the lower one trimmed with a kilt plaiting, the upper one with a quilling and lace. Black velvet sleeveless jacket and sash embroidered with purple. Silk sleeves to match. Black velvet hat, trimmed with jet and feathers.

Fig. 7. – Casaque of heavy black corded silk, finished with a heavy cord of black velvet and guipure lace. →

Figs. 11 and 12. – Front and back view of black Cashmere casaque, embroidered with beads, and trimmed all round with fringe. ←

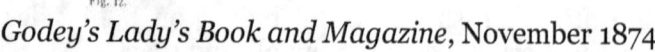

Godey's Lady's Book and Magazine, November 1874

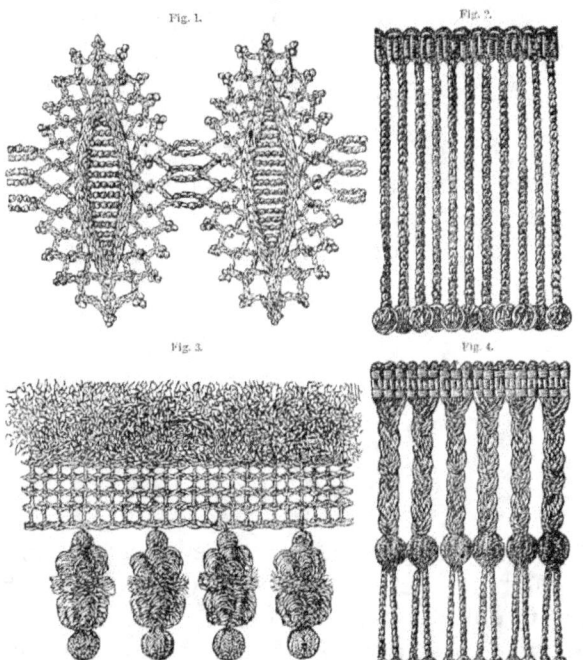

CARRIAGE-DRESS.

Fig. VII. – Carriage-Dress of Green Silk. – The back is made in longitudinal puffs, separated by bands of cypress-green velvet; the lower part of the skirt in front is also of green velvet; and the same material is used for the vest, the rolling collar, and the cuffs. The front of the skirt is of green silk, also puffed lengthwise, but in much long puffs than the back; it and the basque at the back are trimmed with cypress-green chenille fringe. ←

...

The Laveuse Tunic. – Among the very newest things is a tunic by this name. It is gathered up at the sides and tied under the pouf exactly as peasant girls tuck up their skirts when they are going to work, or as washerwomen before a tub. In order to make it, you must cut the front breadths as for an ordinary skirt, and almost as long as the petticoat. The front and side breadths are joined, gathered up, and secured at the back, where it is ornamented with a very large bow. The top of the tunic, at the back, is a pouf cut in the form of a hood, and gathered; the bow that fastens or draws the sides of the tunic together is placed under this pouf. This "laveuse" tunic is usually trimmed with a velvet band, and then the bow, as a matter of course, is velvet. When made of silk it is trimmed with guipure, with English embroidery, with gimp, and with jetted lace; but in every case the heading of the trimming is arranged to face upward. The effect of this "laveuse" tunic is graceful and original, but always *negligé*. It could not be worn with an evening toilet except by quite a young girl, and in very light materials, such as white muslin, trimmed with Valenciennes lace, crepe de Chine, or foulard.

Peterson's Magazine, November 1874

MORNING COSTUMES. →

Fig. 1. – White Cashmere morning robe, made with a broad box-plait and pouf in the back, and trimmed with blue or cherry-colored ribbon bows.

Fig. 2. – Morning robe of blue and gray striped reps, made plain, with cuffs, collar, and pockets of silk darker shade; blue silk buttons up the front.

FASHIONABLE TRIMMINGS
FOR MANTLES, ETC.

Beads and bugles from a prominent portion of the popular trimmings on both mantles and dresses. Not only are black and white jet seen, but blue beads and steel beads are both mixed with the finest makes of passementerie. These engravings will serve as a guide for the style of pattern most in vogue in Paris from trimming garments of all sorts.

All these passementeries are intended for trimming dresses, etc. Fig. 1 is entirely composed of gimp and beads; Fig. 2 is jet fringes, with a fancy satin galoon heading; Fig. 3 consists of floss silk tassels with a satin heading; Fig. 4 is a fringe with satin heading – every strand is a plait, terminating with a ball from which jet drops escape.

Godey's Lady's Book and Magazine, December 1874

We give, this month, first, a house, or walking-costume, composed of plain and striped reps, or mohair. The skirt, which is made of the plain material, is kilted all the way from the waist with a large box-plait down the front. The basque is pointed from the waist, in front, to the sides, forming a diamond shape on the sides, and at the hack the postillion is simply open up the middle seam to the waist. The whole is trimmed with a side-plaiting of the striped material cut on the bias, headed by a broad band, one and a half inches wide, of black velvet ribbon. This same trimming forms the collaret around the neck, and the cuffs and frills for the sleeves. The scarf trimming the skirt is of the striped materials, out on the bias and join, three yards long, and half a yard wide, edged all round with a narrow plaiting. same as the bodice. Twelve yards of double-fold material in the solid color, and six to eight, according to the width, of the striped. These striped materials come in all colors, with black, or two shades of one color – and the combination makes a very stylish costume. It also suggests the possibility of making a new costume out of two half-worn dresses. Fringes of worsted may be used for trimming the scarf, if preferred – either ball or bullion fringe. These fringes can be bought from fifty cents up to one dollar twenty-five cents per yard.

THE "VIOLIN BODICE."
By Emily H. May.

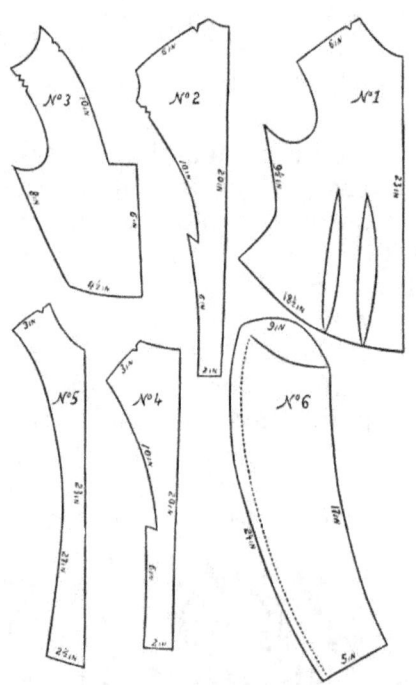

As bodices of either two shades of the same color, or two contrasting colors, are now fashionable, we give the latest style, namely, the "Violin Bodice," so called, because the back assumes the shape: and on the next page we give a diagram by which to cut it out. The parts marked No. 1, 2, and 3, form the outside of the bodice, while Nos. 4 and 5 are the underneath parts, forming the vest in front, and the centre-piece of the back. In making a bodice after this design, the parts 4 and 5 should be the same color or shade of the solid part of the dress, while Nos. 2 and 3 should be of the lighter or contrasting shade, as are also the trimmings of the tunic and under-skirt.

No. 1. Half of Front.
No. 2. Half of Back.
No. 3. Half of Side-Body.
No. 4. Half of Back (Inside Part.)
No. 5. Half of Vest.
No. 6. Half of Sleeve.

Worth, as a rule, makes his new black silk dresses with large revers on the skirt; they cross in front, and then separate as they descend to the feet. The train at the back is either plaited or draped, it rarely falls in long, unbroken folds. The revers are ornamented in different ways, sometimes with wide insertion embroidered with jet, sometimes with loops of faille, mixed with laces arranged ca cascade, etc. A very elegant black dress has bands of jet arranged diagonally on the front breadth, and at the sides black faille loops lined with pale pink faille; these loops descend *en cascade*, and are accompanied by coquilles of black grenadine. The bodice is made with a waistcoat, striped on the cross with jet bands. Another black faille dress has bands of black velvet upon the revers, and loops of very narrow black ribbon velvet following the line of those bands; the loops are lined with violet. The train is entirely velvet; the bodice is faille, with velvet sleeves.

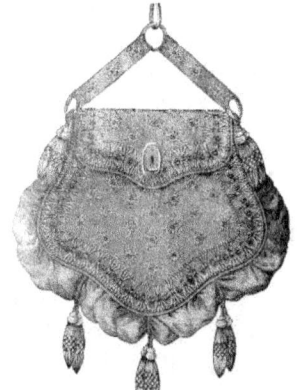

EMBROIDERED POCKET, TO BE SUSPENDED FROM BELT.
By Mrs. Jane Weaver.

We give, here, one of those embroidered pockets, now so fashionable, to be worn at the waist.

This pocket is made of brown cloth, lined with lutestring and embroidered with two shades of brown purse-silk and steel beads. The front and back are joined together by puffings of brown silk. At the top of the pocket are metal rings, to which are attached strips of embroidery; these strips are joined to another ring, as shown in the illustration, and fastened to the waistband by means of a metal hook. The pocket is also ornamented with brown silk pendants.

WALKING-DRESS.

Fig. VII. – Walking-dress. – The under-skirt is of black velveteen, made quite plain. The upper-dress is of very dark-blue poplin, bordered with a wide band of blue velvet, lighter than the dress. The deep basques, sleeves, and waist are also trimmed with the velvet.

The bodices are almost all made in the same style. The basque is sometimes continued all round the waist; sometimes it stops in front, when it is replaced by a waistband. The Joan of Arc bodice has been very popular, but it is a mistake to adopt it absolutely. To look well it requires magnificent materials, and a very pretty figure – neither too stout nor too thin – otherwise it has a ridiculous and an ungraceful effect. Ostrich feathers, made into a trimming and put on with bands of fur, are very elegant.

Poufs are gradually disappearing from the back breadths of skirts. Sometimes the top of the breadths are gathered, and look like drawn silk, so close is the stitching; but the most general style is to plait the back breadths in wide folds, extending the entire length of the skirt. It is difficult to keep these plaits in place, so either cords or tapes are sewn on the wrong side of the skirt, at intervals of about four inches apart, and each plait is fastened to these cords at the intersecting points.

With the disappearance of puffs and drapery, cloth dresses for the street will gradually creep in; though we do not think them very warm, they will be very stylish.

Peterson's Magazine, December 1874

I fancy I hear my readers, should any be found to open my little book, altering the text and asking, "How can a lady dress on fifteen pounds a year?" Well, this question vexed me much, as no doubt it has vexed and is vexing many others to whom, may be, it is of the greatest moment. Of course any one *can* dress on this sum, this is not questioned; but the gist of the matter lies in three words, "like a lady." To this some may urge, and with truth, that dress as she may, a "lady" will always look like one. So she will, I do not deny it for an instant; but still, that is no reason why she should not also dress like one if possible. It sounds as if it must be a hard task to do this on such a little sum, almost a hopeless one, you think to yourself; and you are perhaps inclined to throw aside my poor little book, exclaiming, "What a scrubby notion! Fifteen pounds a year! Why, one's gloves and odds and ends alone come to more than that! Whoever wrote this cannot have an idea of the heaps and heaps of things one is always wanting. What horribly scrubby ideas she must have – for the author, of course, is a woman." But stay! If you look again, you will see that it is written by a *lady* – a poor lady, I grant you, but possibly not such a scrubby one after all; at any rate, the little manual may be less objectionable than its title leads you to expect: it cannot do you any harm to peruse it; you will not catch scrubdom or beggarly ideas in half an hour. But, no! on second thoughts I agree with you: you had better throw it aside; it was not written for such as you, who, in all probability, will only read it out of curiosity and in hopes of finding some amusement in its petty economies, at which no doubt you can well afford to smile; therefore leave my unpretending pages for those who might profit by them, and to whom I earnestly hope they may be of use, – namely, women of slender means, possibly more straitened now than in days gone by, to whom the saving or spending of a few shillings is of more importance than were as many pounds in past and more prosperous times. Girls whose allowance is necessarily of the smallest; young married women who have left their maid and other luxuries in their old home, and who have now, as they express it, "awfully" little to spend on even the necessaries of life – it is for these, and such as these, that this pamphlet is written, in the hope – nay (if, without conceit, I may say it), the certainty that it will prove a help to them in the economical management of this, their purely personal expenditure. Nor is it for the young only that I am writing: I trust that my elder readers may find some suggestions, new to them, with which to supplement their own experience.

No remark is truer – and, as a consequence, more hackneyed – than that a woman is more or less judged by the style of her dress; and further, that half her influence for good or bad depends on it also. Few deny this in theory, and if they only could or would put it into practice, what a marvellous increase of pleasantness and comfort there would be for the remainder of the world – to say nothing of what would accrue to themselves. It makes one quite sad to think of the husbands, brothers, and male relatives in general, who are daily rubbed up the wrong way by their womankind on limited incomes, the said limitation being continually made the excuse for shortcomings and shabbiness.

...

DRESS AND MANTUA MAKING.
Cutting out, &c. – Seams – Button-holes – Shapes and Patterns – Cheap Dressmakers – Shopping on a cheap method.

Of course so much depends on the size of the person and the pattern chosen, that it is impossible to lay down any definite rule for quantity, especially as some people are more economical in cutting out than others, though really any one with average sense can teach herself to cut out with economy. It only requires thought, and not to be in a hurry about it. Let us suppose, for instance, that you want to make yourself a jacket; and before buying the stuff, you wish to know exactly how much it will take. The material is to be serge, which is thirty-two inches wide. You fancy that it will take three yards – from that to four. Clear a strip of the floor, about four yards by thirty-two inches; mark it out distinctly on the carpet with white chalk, and then lay the different parts of your pattern on it; turn and twist them till you are satisfied that they lie in the smallest compass, and before taking them up make a little sketch on paper of the way in which they are arranged, lest you should forget; then measure exactly the length taken by them on the carpet; and, lastly, give two minutes to thinking it all over, and satisfying yourself that there is no mistake, such as forgetting a sleeve, or having arranged the two fronts for the same side. By doing this a few times you will soon get into the habit, as it were mechanically, of knowing where each little piece will fit in, and then you will cut out to advantage without all this preliminary trouble. Another thing to be mindful of is to be sure to allow for a right and a wrong side, should there be a difference, and that the grain or nap of the stuff is the same up and down. By careful attention to all these little things a reduction of two or three yards can frequently be gained, for an inch or two here and there soon mounts up to yards in cutting out a costume.

I need hardly remind you that it is quite against all dressmaking rules to cut anything against or across the selvage. Backs, fronts, and skirts must all, as a decided rule, run up and down with it. The only instance in which this rule may be evaded is in regard to cutting out sleeves. Here, if very hard pressed for material, the under part may be cut as is most convenient, sideways even, if no better plan can be devised; but that can only be done in a plain material, or it would look very bad. The part of the sleeve under the arm may also be carefully pieced, if necessary.

In making up cloth materials, the seams should be carefully stitched, first tacking each piece together to insure against puckering, and also, when all is tacked together, you can judge of the fit. When you have satisfied yourself on this point, and stitched it permanently, take the tacking out, and press the seams on the wrong side with a heavy iron. If you can borrow a tailor's goose for the purpose, it will be all the better; you can buy a second-hand one for half a crown. After the seams are pressed, trim the raw edges neatly, and lay over them narrow galloon; hem it down slightly, so as not to show the stitches on the right side. Every seam must be treated in this manner to be durable, excepting for waterproof materials, which must be stitched and felled in the ordinary manner, again taking pains not to allow the felling stitches to show, or, if you prefer it, stitch on the right side, so as to look as if intended to be seen. For this, one part must be laid over the other, tacked down, and afterwards stitched very evenly. This seam is also the most convenient for thick, stubborn materials. The seams of cotton, linen, and silk it is sufficient to run closely, taking a backstitch now and then; but for the bodies, especially tight ones, close stitching becomes necessary. For all materials of a fraying nature, a mantuamaker's seam is needful; or a still better and neater plan is to run the parts together on the right side, then turn them, and run them again on the other. This, for thin materials, is better than the ordinary running and felling. Washing silks and grenadines should also be treated in this manner. In a very thick woollen material – such, for instance, as frieze – the seams should either be stitched or run closely, and then covered with galloon; or else (which will save the expense of galloon) run and felled in a wide hem. When pressed it will set quite flat, and the looseness and thickness of the material will prevent the stitches being perceived.

All dark materials should be made up either with black thread – not cotton, which wears rusty – or very dark grey silk; tailor's silk twist, which is sold by the yard, is best for stitching seams which are intended to be seen, and must also be used in making button-holes: these last are a great stumbling-block to some people, but they would soon learn to make them if they set about it in a business-like manner. Suppose, now, that you wish to make the button-holes of a tweed jacket: the front must be lined with silk or the same stuff as the jacket; if the tweed be thin, then put a stout piece of calico between it and the lining, so as to make it three-fold, and thus you will have a firm substance on which to work; mark the exact size in chalk before cutting the hole, and tack it round carefully about half an inch from the chalk-mark. Be sure before beginning to work that the needle is large enough to allow of the thread passing through the treble thickness without an effort; any jerking or pulling will fray the edge, and get you into trouble; also take care that your thread be sufficiently long to work all round the hole without requiring to be renewed; pass the thread several times between your finger and thumb to free it from kinks – if with a little wax, all the better. In button-hole stitch you work from right to left, and keep one or two loose strands of thread against the raw edge, taking each stitch over it. When you have gone all round and back to the place from which you started, fasten off the thread with which you have been working, and thread the loose strand on your needle; pull it slightly to bring the edge of the hole even, and then overcast about six stitches straight across the button-hole, and fasten off tightly. Button-holes in thick cloth must be cut in the shape of an elongated – the wide end to the edge; this is to allow of its lying flat when buttoned, if otherwise, the hank of the button would get in the way. In sewing on the buttons take very loose stitches, and then twist the thread several times round before fastening off. If you wish to be very neat, cut a little round of cloth, and fell it over the stitches at the back. Some of my readers may think me unnecessarily fussy about these comparatively small matters; but there is a wrong and a right method of doing everything, and in the long-run it is true economy – besides being satisfactory in other ways – to do everything as neatly as possible, especially in the matter of clothes, for they will last in consequence ever so much longer; and this being the case, surely it is worth while to spend a few extra hours in the making of a gown or jacket – for, not only are we spared the annoyance of seeing things untidy or ill-made, but the garment itself will set better, and, consequently, will look ladylike and nice, even when worn threadbare. It is a good plan – and one which you will find most economical and useful on all occasions – to keep in your pocket-book or purse a little table of the widths of different materials and the respective quantities required. Thus, fourteen yards of serge, at thirty-two inches wide, is equal to eight yards of tweed at fifty-two inches; sixteen yards of a twenty-four inch silk equals fourteen yards at twenty-seven inches – and so on; for it is difficult, when in a shop, and the shopman worrying you with his own ideas, to calculate at once and to a nicety the quantity you will want, and it is in this nicety that the economy lies. How provoking it is to find, on your return home, when you begin to measure, that you might have managed with half a yard or so less; or, still more annoying, to discover that you have not enough! It is astonishing to what a sum all these little carelessnesses mount up by the end of the year.

How to Dress on £15 a Year, 1874

1875

CARRIAGE-DRESS.

Fig. VIII. – Carriage Costume. – The dress is of gray silk, and is trimmed with bands of black velvet. The upper-skirt is untrimmed in front, and is looped back by a full lasode of black velvet, which is tied in a bow low down. Jacket of black velvet, trimmed with gray ostrich feathers, and loops and buttons.

We give, first, this month, something quite new for a walking-costume. The material is either of cashmere, merino, or reps. Here the lower skirt is cut three and a quarter yards in width, and very slightly trained at the back, and is provided with loops underneath by which to raise it for walking. The front breath and the side gores, are ornamented by a deep kilted flounce, put on straightway of the material, and this is headed by two kilted plaitings, turned-up each three inches deep, which is separated from the lower kilting by a narrower one, turned down two inches deep, finished by a narrow bias band of silk of the same color as the dress. The Polonaise opens from the waist down, finished by buttons and button-holes. The bottom of the Polonaise has a kilted plaiting, four inches deep, headed by a bias band of silk, two inched in width. At the back the Polonaise is looped , so as to form a double pannier. It will be seen that the trimming on the back of the under-skirt is bound, top and bottom, with the silk, and that the band just below the heading is much wider than the band which finishes the front. This band is not less than three inches

wide. There is an open, pointed collar at the back of the neck, forming lapels in front. The sleeves are tight coat, with cuff to match the collar, as may be seen, ending at the hand with a double puff. At the neck and wrists are worn frills of clear muslin. For this costume fourteen yards of cashmere or merino will be required. ...

Nearly all walking-dresses are made short enough just to escape the ground, and are of some woolen material, the coarser the more fashionable and stylish looking. Almost any cut seems fashionable, provided that it falls very flat in front and at the sides, and is tied back so uncomfortably, that a long step is difficult, and sitting down almost an impossibility. Strings are now put on under-skirts to tie them back to within a quarter of a yard of the bottom. Polonaise are still worn; but jackets are more popular, especially for young people – a modification of the old-fashioned round basque being one of the prettiest for a good figure. The very thin persons should eschew them, and more especially very fat ones. This basques are called *cuirass* waists, jackets, etc. ...

For House-Dresses, skirts box-plaited at the back are superseding the poufs entirely. It is a deeply-folded triple plait, with the centre box-plait about an eighth of a yard wide. The plaiting occupies the space hitherto given to a plain back breath, which, for this make of skirt, should measure a yard in width. The material should be lined, and the plait is kept in place with rows of tape sewn underneath, the lowest row being half a yard from the edge. When properly arranged, the plait is well defined to the edge of the skirt, and spreads out in a fan-like train below the last tape. This dispenses with all flounces at the back, and is newer than the rows of horizontal plaitings recently worn from the waist downward. Two large bows of long loops of doubled silk are placed upon the plait, and an ample tournure – not abruptly projecting, as in the days of the Grecian bend, but sloping, is worn under these plaited skirts to give them a graceful effect. ...

As Rows of braid are now so fashionable, they can be used with advantage in modernizing last winter's costumes. Narrow silk braid is sewn in rows upon sleeves, collars, and jackets, while upon the rest of the costume there is no braid at all. The rows go round the sleeves, not down them; and if braid be used on the tunic, it is arranged in short rows, falling like a fringe above the hem. There are several new galloons introduced, all woven with beads – blue, steel, green, violet and black.

Jet Trimming is still much used on black; but some of the newest black silk dresses made by Worth are piped, and have flounced lined with pale maize, light blue, or cardinal red. These colors light up a black silk very much, and make it quite "dressy."

...

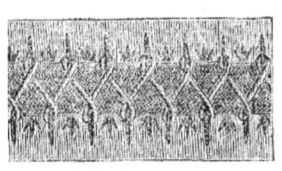 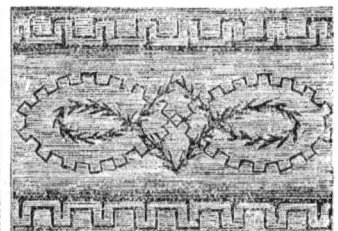

BORDERS FOR SACQUES, ETC.

These borders are worked in coral and long stitch, with silks of different colors, on black. They are now very fashionable, and they are very pretty, two important considerations, for to be merely fashionable, without being beautiful, is not always a recommendation, especially for ornamental work like this.

Peterson's Magazine, January 1875

Dresses of vigogne, cashmere, and other woollen fabrics are much trimmed with velvet, but this trimming is no longer put on in plain rows as it used to be. It is placed round the edge as a piping (without cord), and turned back about two inches deep inside, so that the trimming is really more on the wrong side of the material than on the right.

The Young Englishwoman, January 1875

We give, first, this month, a walking-costume of brown woolen serge, trimmed with velvet, either brown or black. The under-skirt is made to touch all round, a trifle longer at the back, with buttons and loops at the waist, for raising the skirt in wet weather. This skirt is ornamented with one deep plaited flounce, nine inches deep, and the plaits are laid in half inches; this is headed by a puff of the material, cut on the bias. We give the front and back view, so the looping of the tunic can easily be managed from the illustration. As may be seen, it has not much fullness. The basque has a postillion at the back trimmed with velvet, and there is a vest of velvet, over which the fronts are buttoned, double-breasted. Collar, cuff, and revers, are all of velvet. It is not necessary to make the whole vest of velvet, only the part which is seen. Three-quarters of a yard of velvet, and sixteen yards of serge will be required. The latter can be bought at any price from fifty cents up. For the cheap material we would suggest the vest and trimming of the same material, only a darker shade. Pieces of black velvet, which have been in use, can by dyed, or steamed, to look equal to new.

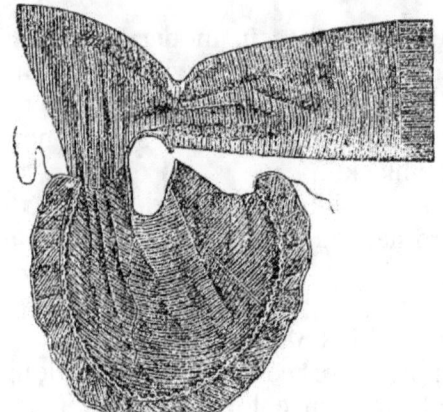

We add the latest design for an apron-tunic, showing how it is cut and made, and where the plaits are put, and how the buttons and strings are adjusted.

A WINTER COSTUME.
By Emily H. May.

We give, here, a very pretty, yet inexpensive costume, to be made of any of the warm, yet cheap cloths, so much in fashion now. Costumes of this kind are, this season, trimmed with several rows of machine stitching, and are made as plainly as possible. The skirt is narrow and round. The engraving, above, ➜ illustrates it as too long if worn as a walking-costume. The tunic is buttoned down the front, and the jacket is close-fitting and double-breasted. The indoor bodice is in the habit style, with short basques. We give, on the next page, a diagram of the tunic, which consists of two pieces – half of front and half of back. The tablier has five notches on the side seam; the lowest notch must be joined to the one corresponding notch on the back of the tunic. The four remaining notches on the tablier must be formed in to plaits. The piece at the back that remains from the first notch to these two plaits must be gathered into the tablier, and forms the drapery. Inner strings must be sewn on the seams to tie the tunic close to the figure. The back of the tunic must be draped according to the illustration, as well as the figure of the wearer. This really is the prettiest costume of the season.

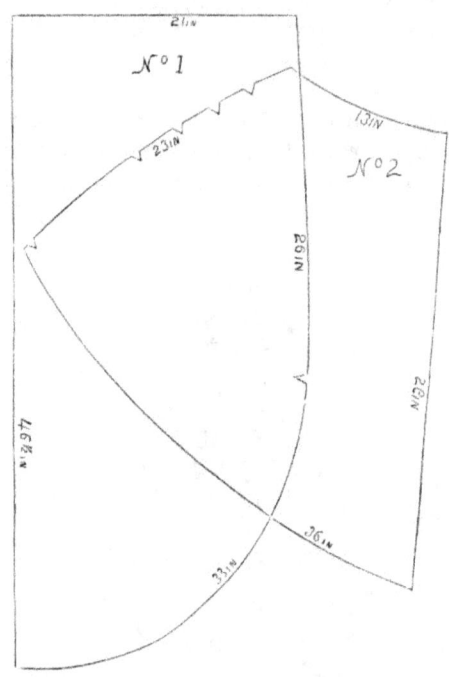

...

Perpendicular stripes cause the figure to look more slender, and should, therefore, be worn by stout ladies, but eschewed by thin ones. Over-skirts that are long in front and short at the back, increase the figure.

...

The celebrated Worth uses, for trimming purposes, a considerable quantity of a peculiar variety of gimp, somewhat in the Chinese style, with small silk tassels, and which produces the happiest effects. He places at the sides of skirts immense square pockets, made of this gimp, ornamenting them with small tassels; and the gimp always matches the dress in color.

We give also an illustration of a white cashmere basque, prettily braided in white, and having a blue silk collar and cuffs, and ornamented with blue bows. The collar and cuffs are trimmed with white guipure lace.

Peterson's Magazine, February 1875

BLACK SILK COSTUME, WITH OPEN WAISTCOAT.

↙ Fig. VI. – House-Dress of Black Silk. – The front has three deep cross-tucks, edged with fringe, and ornamented with a jet gimp. The sides are trimmed with a ladder of jet fringe. The bodice is open to the waist, where it fastens with a single strap, and, like the sleeves, is trimmed with jet gimp. The plastron is of pink silk, covered with tulle, embroidered in white jet.

...

Next is another walking-costume, also of woolen serge, either of a little dotted pattern or plain, for the Polonaise, over a skirt either of black silk or cashmere. A black silk skirt, that has been worn, may be retrimmed, either with silk or with the same material as the Polonaise, put on as here designed. For the front width there is, first, a scant bias ruffle, four inches deep, then a plaiting, cut straightway of the material, and plaited very fine, each plait being carefully basted, and when all is plaited, then ironed on the wrong side. This is repeated three

times, the last time the plaited is made to stand up, forming a heading. For the back there is a kilted plaiting, as deep as the front trimming. The Polonaise is simply faced on the edge, forming a hem; and there is a design in vine and leaves, done in worsted or silk embroidery; but this is entirely optional, as a trimming of plain mohair braid, sewed on flat, or a pattern braided with worsted braid; either will make a pretty finish. But quite as many of the Polonaise we now see worn have no trimming at all, just finished either with a cord of the same, or else a hem. Coat-sleeves, and a rolling collar completes this costume. The amount of material for the Polonaise, if of double-width cloth, will be three to four yards; if single, six to eight yards.

...

LOW BODICE FOR EVENING-DRESS.
By Emily H. May.

Low bodices are now chiefly worn at balls; but at dinner-parties they may be seen when the wearer intends being present at some large evening party afterward. Our model is among the newest from Paris; it is white silk, and the folds, or bretelles, are of colored crepe. The pattern consists of five pieces: 1. Front; 2. Half of Back; 3. Side-piece;

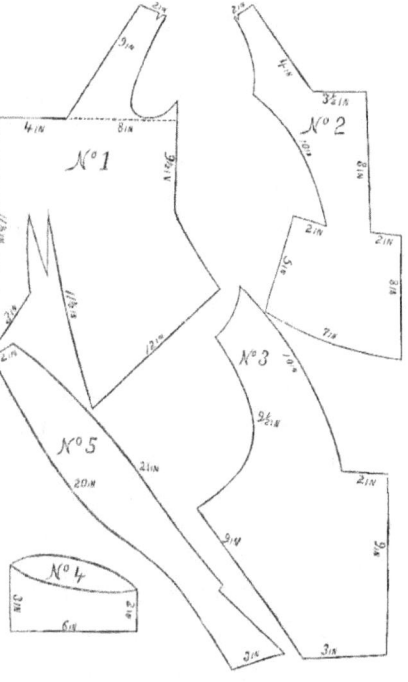

4. Sleeve; and 5. Half of bretelle. The bretelle is laid on the front of the bodice, so as to simulate a waistcoat. Half the bretelle is only given, as the back and front are the same as far as the waist. The basque on the side-piece is laid in a single plait, and that of the back is laid in a box-plait, and not joined on the side-piece. The perforated

lined marked on the front point out the two darts. The bodice fastens on front with buttons and button-holes. The buttons should be either sill or satin, and should match the dress in color. The first toilet is a combination of embroidered gauze and satin; the second is made of tulle over white silk, and ornamented with flowers and faille ribbon.

For the benefit of our readers who do not know how to cut from a diagram, we give the following directions. Take a piece of paper and cut, say the front of the bodice; then use the tape-measure, and compare with the number of inches on the diagram; next cut across the top of the bust – measure; then slope up for the shoulder, then across the shoulder-seam; then cut out the arm-hole, down the seam under the arm, then the skirt of the basque. Compare each cutting with the number of inches given. Proceed in this way with each separate piece.

...

Demi-Trains and Aprons. – There is no fashion more popular at the present time, than the deep, round apron, to be seen on so many dresses. When wide cashmere, or camel's-hair, or Sicilienne is used, the apron is cut in a single piece, without seams. It should reach almost to the edge of the skirt, and should curve gracefully up to the waistband at the back, where it is hooked or tied across the tournure. The front is sewn plainly to the belt, and its entire fullness consists of four plaits sewn into each side of the belt at the back. The sash-bow consists of two long loops, a strap, and two ends, and conceals the joining of the tablier over the tournure. If the skirt is velvet, the sash is velvet; if not it is of lined faille. Demi-train skirts have now narrow sloped side and front breadths, but the back widths are full and straight; the clinging effect is given by tying the back seams of the second side breadths with tapes on the wrong side. This masses the fullness, and gives a fan-shaped demi-train.

...

The tunic has had its day, as it is seldom seen now *on the back of a dress*; but the apron front, tied with a sash just below the basque at the back, is very much used, especially the shawl pattern, which is pointed and long in front. All dresses cling closely to the figure in front. Sashes are tied in every conceivable style, except in the simplest, manner, sometimes passing from the right hip to just over the left foot, where they are tied in large bows, sometimes passed in and out of drapery and puffs in a most extreme manner.

...

The colors of the new goods are no brighter, but more decided than they were a year ago, and quite violent contrasts are used for more expensive dresses. ...

Much of the success of the present style of dress depends on the petticoats and bustle; the latter should be small and at the back only, and the petticoats should be cut so that they spread out in what is called the peacock's tail train.

Peterson's Magazine, March 1875

We give, this month, a walking-costume of black and white striped material; it may either be of silk, poplin, or mohair. These fine striped silks are now selling in the stores for seventy-five cents and one dollar; mohair and poplins, in half wool, at from thirty-seven and a half to seventy-five cents. Our design has but one skirt, made just to touch, and trimmed all round with one flounce, nine inches deep, without the heading; cut on the bias; made very scant in front, where the skirt is additionally ornamented with three smaller flounces each, put on with a heading, each five inches deep. These trim the front breadth, and are finished with a stylish bow, made of black and white taffetas ribbon, as may be seen in the engraving. Another bow of the same description is placed further around upon the main flounce. The tunic is composed of two widths of silk, fifty inches in length, finished with a narrow bias binding, gracefully made into puffs, and looped at the sides, where it is caught up with another bow and ends of the same description as those used upon the bottom of the skirt. A basque bodice, simply bowed, for a finish. Coat-sleeves, with deep cuff, nearly to the elbow, where it also terminates with another bow. The rolling collar is lined with black silk, which turns over on the bodice. Twenty yards of silk, or sixteen years of mohair, will be required.

...

We give, this month, a walking-dress, especially suitable for this season of the year, and to be made of any material, not too high-priced for every-day wear. The merit of this particular costume is that it is both stylish and economical. On the next page we give a diagram, from which to cut out the bodice. This bodice is what is called a habit bodice, and consists of four pieces, one front, half of back, side-piece, and sleeve. The various pieces join with the corresponding notches, all of which are marked on the engraving. The basque projecting from the side-piece is flat, plaited into the bottom of the back, and a button is added at the waist. The basque is extremely short beneath the arms, and it is not joined, but is left open, the joining commencing at the waist. Several rows of machine-stitching are the only trimmings. The coat-shaped sleeve is joined as far as the projecting cuff, from whence to the wrist it is fastened with three buttons.

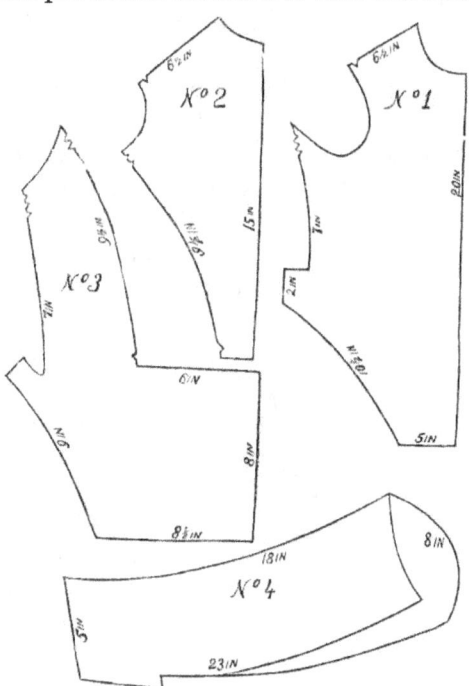

NEW SPRING STYLE FOR WALKING-DRESS.

Fig. VII. – Walking-Dress of White Mohair. – Skirt and tunic trimmed with black velvet. Black velvet bretelles, and sailor collar and cuffs, and Marguerite bag in black velvet.

The Magnificence of Dress has reached a point, in Paris, under the so-called Republic, that was never surpassed under the Empire. The new brocades, that are so much the fashion, and that are made in imitation of those worn during the sixteenth century, and the Genoa velvets, cost twenty dollars a yard. For a train and bodice at least one dozen yards are required; therefore the robe is not a cheap one. But if these splendid materials are only used for the plastron and tablier, about three yards are required. The striped and checked velvets used for Polonaise, tabliers, and cuirass bodices, are also rich fabrics. They consist of alternate stripes of velvet and gros grain, varying from half an inch to nearly two inches in width. They are only used as parts of costumes in conjunction with plain gros grain or velvet of the same color. Of course, it would be absurd to wear such dresses in America; they are fit only for duchesses, princesses, and others of fabulous wealth; but we allude the them in order that our fair readers may see how extravagant some of their European sisters are. ...

Lace Trimmings are very much worn at evening parties, by those, at least, who are fortunate enough to have old lace, or can afford to buy new. It is generally sewn as a flat border, without fullness round the tunic, and square ends of a low pink satin ridingote, with a bouillonné skirt of white tulle under the ridingote. Brussels application is one of the few laces never worn flat; it is always gathered.

...

The *cuirass*, or armor, or corset-waist, as it is indiscriminately called, is very much worn; but it shares popular favor with many other styles, for it, above all other corsages, should fit perfectly to look well. Round points in front, with basques turned up at the back, finished with large bows, are made by Worth;

one of the most beautiful dresses we have seen this season was made by him in this style. For house-dresses, either the high, close waist, or the heart-shaped or spun Raffael neck, are all worn, only the trimming still continues very high around the throat, or at the back of the neck.
Peterson's Magazine, April 1875

There is a great furore at present for combining checks, plaids, and stripes with a plain stuff, and checks seem to have the preference; but the style is by no means in good taste, for even when cleverly arranged it gives the idea of two or three old dresses having been made into one, and as this is sure to be the practical result of so economical a fashion these secondhand looking costumes will probably have but a short reign. When only one material though different shades of the color are used, this patchwork effect is lost, and the combination most elegant.
The Bazaar, The Exchange and Mart, April 21, 1875

↙ We give, this month, a morning-dress for a middle-aged lady, and the material may be either a striped mohair, cambric, percale, or calico. The form is Princesse. The skirt terminates with a deep gathered flounce, cut on the bias, and headed by a cross-band, put on with the machine-stitching. The flounce is a part of the dress, there being no skirt under it. The pockets have a cross-band at each end of them, and a button in the centre. The bodice is plain, with a deep ruffle collaret, cut on the bias. The robe buttons the entire length of the front, in the centre of a wide band, which is added on to the breadth. The material of our model is a striped percale, in chocolate-brown and white. Twelve yards will be required. Percales can be bought at from eighteen to twenty-five cents.

TUNIC AND BASQUE OF EMBROIDERED MUSLIN
We also give a beautiful open-worked tunic and jacket of écru muslin, heavy with English embroidery, to be worn either over a black or brown silk skirt.

→

Peterson's Magazine, May 1875

Skirts are to be trained for fête and all full-dress occasions, demi trained for morning and walking wear, the treble pleat, called the Bulgare, being the only fulness, and that used entirely for the train. Tabliers are on the wane, though by no means extinct or likely to be, but the Parisian houses of most note are reducing toilettes in the Princesse form, body and skirt all in one, or with the fronts and sides trimmed longitudinally, diagonally, or half and half, indeed, many of the newest differ completely on each side of the dress. When the loose tablier is adopted, it is either long and hangs quite in a sharp point in the centre, or is short and square, bearing really more resemblance to large aprons than any of the shapes we have been using; in both cases they must be very high at the back. Bodices remain of the cuirasse style whether for morning or dinner wear; even low dresses, which are again in favour for balls, are the same out. Sleeves are invariably made to resemble the style of trimming used elsewhere. Checks are introduced even into the various cottons, muslins, foulards, and light stuffs, but dresses are never made of these alone. Silk and cashmere united is still the rule for reception and visiting costume, or if a dress is made wholly of silk the patterns, make, or colours are varied. The polonaise is supposed to have died out, but in reality it is resuscitated with slight alterations (longer in front and shorter at the back), under the name of the "Princesse tunique" or is sleeveless and draped peculiarly at the back when it becomes "Russian blouse."
The Bazaar, The Exchange and Mart, May 8, 1875

The newest tabliers are square, almost meeting at the back; in fact, hanging like a milkwoman's apron, though dispensing with the fulness at the waist. The jacket tails must set close to the figure, quite encasing the hips; indeed the so-called cuirass bodice is only a plain jacket, with the tails meeting in front, out long, but of an equal depth all round and without the least fulness. The armholes of sleeveless dresses are now trimmed by epaulettes, puffs, or other ornamentation made from the same as the bodice; they greatly detract from the hard appearance of some of the present garments and makes the waist appear smaller. Black and white washing silk of a very small size check is the most effective for mixing with old black silks; it is astonishing what a stylish costume can be produced with these two. If the check is small it does not give the effect of patchiness, no matter where or how it is used; but I recommend that, whether flounces or bands be selected, the check shall be cut on the cross, and for flounces, gathered, not plaited. On a trained black skirt have a deep flounce headed with two bouillonnés and an upright frill, but carry this trimming only as far as the bulgare (the bulgare is the train formed by the treble box-plait), letting it terminate under the fold of this. Trim down the centre of the bulgare either with a bouillonné edged with a frill or bows of the check. The bodice should have a trimming down the back, narrow at the waist, and widening at the neck, where it seems to divide, go round the throat, and continue down the front, matching the back. All this trimming to be cut on the cross. Sleeves of the check in puffs from the shoulder to the waist, tight to the arm (white cuffs to be worn outside), pocket of the check to be placed on the left of the skirt. Make the pocket in the shape of a horn by joining a strip into a circle, running cords at intervals, and then drawing all up so as to graduate from a point to the mouth, lay this on the dress in a curve, cornucopia fashion. These pockets are very pretty on all dresses. The tops are left as a frill, made by the last cord, and the point is often finished by a bow and ends. The box-plaited skirts are universal, whether as an under one to the various over dresses, or entire trains and demi trains. The front breadth is narrow and has two gores, also narrow, each side, all of which must fit to the waist without a plait; the back is two whole widths, and all of it put into a wide treble box-plait, measuring 10 in. at the top. This plait must a kept in place for at least half its length, by having tape bars on the underneath and tacking the folds of the plait to them. For a demi train the straight back breadths need not be two whole ones, but one and a half, the bottom of the skirt measuring but 4 yds. when made. The bulgare must only widen very gradually, and even at the edge not spread out much. The two back breadths should be a few inches longer than the gore to which they are joined, and the difference sloped off to the middle, so that the centre may be the longest part, and make the plait lie on the ground rather rounding instead of in a straight line.

Young ladies who affect masculine apparel will have their taste gratified in the redingotes or capotes, which are exact copies of the greatcoats worn by powdered footmen; they reach within a quarter of a yard of the feet, are cut up to the waist at the back, with large buttons are the opening and two at the waist, are double breasted, closing right up to the throat with two rows of large buttons, and have an upright deep collar (no white one is shown) of the same material (which is tweed, vicugna, or cloth), two wide pockets with flaps, and coat sleeves buttoning at the outside seam. These are used as indoor garments over a perfectly plain dark skirt, and for walking the fast appearance is increased by adding a little cape of the same, just falling over the shoulders, sometimes double or treble, as though a cabman's wraprascal had been the model. A little modification would render them sensible and convenient for travelling.

The Bazaar, The Exchange and Mart, May 26, 1875

PATENT GEM SKIRT SUPPORTER.

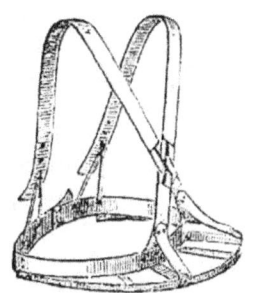

Health and comfort secured by wearing the new Patent Gem Skirt Supporter, an article introduced this season, and pronounced by experts to be the most perfect Supporter ever invented. It can be worn without a corset, or with any kind of corset made. It takes the weight and pressure of the clothing from the waist and hips, gives perfect freedom and ease to the wearer. *Every Lady and Miss should wear one.* Recommended by all who have used them. Sold by all first class Dealers. Price, 50 cents.

1 and 2. Dinner Dress of Chestnut-Brown Silk and Con-Can Tissue.

Page 397. Nos. 1 and 2 are illustrations showing the front and back of a dinner toilet. The long, untrimmed skirt and sleeves are of chestnut-brown faille, the sleeves composed of lengthwise puffs, laid on to a coat-shaped lining. The overdress is of a lighter shade of the same color of con-can tissue – an East Indian fabric. It is cut in the princess style, and is rendered perfectly tight-fitting by darts, and a seam in the center of the front, sloped out to fit the figure. It is closed down the centre of the back by lacing with a silk cord of the same exact shade, and is trimmed round the lower circular edge with a gathered flounce – deep at the centre front, and narrowing off to almost nothing at the back, where the draping is arranged to rest on the tournure, and from which depends a tied-bow sash of watered ribbon, matching in color. The neck is decorated with a ruffle of the two materials, cut quite deep behind, and terminating very narrow on the bust under a small ribbon bow, and has an inside frill of Malines lace, with cuffs of the same ornamenting the sleeves. The amount of material required is thirteen yards of faille and fine yards of con-can for the overdress.

1 and 2. Dress of Gray Cretonne, Trimmed with Indigo-Blue Silk.

Page 399. – Nos. 1 and 2 are illustrations of the front and back of a dress composed of gray cretonne,

trimmed with wide indigo-blue silk. The front of the skirt is shirred on each side of the breadth, from waist to foot, framed in narrow plaited ruffles, having a heading formed by a fine piping of the blue silk. The side-gores, shirred in like manner, are crossed at regular intervals with pointed straps of the blue silk piped around the edges, and the points confined by a small button of crocheted silk. The back-breadths are also disposed in a quadruple box-plait, the outlines of which are preserved to the bottom of the skirt. The corsage has basques, pointed in front, and the back plaited *en postillon*, with the sides turned over *en revers*. It is bordered with a wide band of the silk, and on the coat-shaped sleeves are two cuffs of the silk, divided by a puff of the cretonne. The fronts of the closed corsage are trimmed with lapels of silk, which depend below the waist in short tab-ends, and the neck is completed with a small standing collar. The amount of material required is nineteen yards of cretonne and two yards of silk.

...

MORNING ROBES.

Page 401, No. 1. Wrapper of striped blue-and-white cashmere. It is cut with a close-fitting back and side-forms, which have each an extra width allowed at the waist, to be disposed in triple plaits, allowing the skirt to descend in ample folds. The fronts are designed in a short jacket, belted to the waist, under which the front widths of the skirt, cut bias, are sewed into a belt, and fastened with hooks and loops.

Around the lower edge of the skirt is a bias-cut flounce, sewed on with a piping, and down the centre of the fronts, both of the jacket and the skirt, is a double ruffle formed by a shirred piping through the centre. On each side of front is a small circular pocket with a ruffle heading, and the lower edge of the straight sleeves are finished with a ruffle and bias band. Eleven yards of single-width cashmere are required for the making of this garment. Cap of white lace, trimmed with blue ribbons and a large tea-rose.

No. 2. – Wrapper of striped percale, deep rose color and gray. The design is a long loose-fitting sack, the length perfected by a deep Spanish flounce, cut bias, with a heading formed by a bias band confined on either edge by machine-stitching, and allowing a small standing ruffle. The fronts are closed with buttons of pearl, the button-holes being made through a bias fold laid down the right side, and small ornamental pockets are placed a little distance below the waist. A small cuff, trimmed with machine-stitched bands, finishes the close sleeve, and an embroidered cambric ruffle completes the

neck. The amount of material required for this wrapper is ten yards of twenty-four-inch wide goods. White lace cap, trimmed with deep rose-colored ribbons.

No. 3 is a morning wrapper made of fine Scotch gingham, with a white ground, checkered with bright colors, and trimmed with ruffles of cambric embroidery. It is designed in a long gored sack, merely outlining the figure, and has coat-shaped sleeves with a ruffled cuff, with a pocket finished in the same style, laid on each side of front immediately below the waist. Down the centre of front is a fold of the gingham, formed in cambric ruffles, and closed with pearl buttons and button-holes; a ruffle of the cambric completes the neck. Nine yards of gingham are required for the making of this wrapper. Cap of Swiss muslin, trimmed with lace and pink ribbons.

No. 4. – Morning wrapper of striped de laine – brown and écru. In design it is very similar to No. 2, before described, trimmed around the neck and down each side of the front with a ruffle of écru silk, set on under a narrow band of brown silk of the same shade as the stripe. The straight sleeves are gathered at the wrist into a brown silk band, edged with an écru ruffle, and a small ruffle of the same completes the neck. Ten yards of de laine will make the wrapper, and three-quarters of a yard of the écru silk and a quarter of a yard of brown silk – the two cut bias – will be needed for trimming. A ribbon rosette of the two colors decorates the hair.

...

The general appearance of modern fashions tends more and more toward those of the period of the Directoire: dresses fitting more and more tightly, with scanty drapery; bodices with revers, gilets, cravats of white muslin, which are daily becoming more voluminous, so that very soon the upper part of a lady's body – we mean the bust – will become much more fully developed than the under part of her clothing – that is, the skirt. The latter is, generally speaking, very long, and possesses a train, long but scanty-looking, in spite of the quantity of material it contains; it is, in fact, at once narrow and trailing. There is no great beauty in this, after all, if we may be permitted thus to speak of so important a personage a Madame la Mode. There is no longer any crinoline – none whatever. Only a tournure which supports the dress at the back of the waist, but none at all over the hips.

And then, on the other hand, besides these characteristic traits, Fashion shows others in perfect contrast to them; it favors costumes – costumes for ever, and tunics and polonaise, draped, looped-up still, but all in very reduced proportions; that is, the costume is tending more and more to be circumscribed to *négligé* toilets for walking on foot, and consequently gets smaller and has fewer trimmings; it becomes, in fact, modest in the extreme, so as to pass as much as possible unnoticed.

...

Plate 1223.

Fig. 1. – *Promenade Costume* of fine twilled silk. The skirt has a long full train, disposed in the Watteau plait, sewed into the waistband, and the upper fold of this plait is clasped at even distances by short scarfs, attached under the sides of the plait, and the ends loosely looped in the centre. The remainder of the skirt is composed of lengthwise shirred puffs, shaping a tablier on the lower edge, to which is attached a gathered flounce with a ruffle heading. Over the puffs falls an apron, clinging closely to the figure. It is almost covered with one inch wide overlapping folds turning upwards, and trimmed around the edge with deep silk fringe, matching in color, having a handsome net-work heading. The sleeves, which are coat-shaped, are also trimmed with fine folds, describing a point down the centre of the arm, and finished around the wrist with a flounce, while the cuirass-shaped bodice has the Watteau plait laid down the centre of the back, proportioned to come on an even line with the folds of the skirt plait. Ruff and under-sleeves of embroidered muslin. Chip hat, trimmed with flowers and ostrich tips. The amount of material required for this costume is twenty-eight yards of twenty-four-inch wide goods.

Fig. 2. – *Costume* of soft repped faille and fine linen batiste. The train-skirt is of the former material, the train-breadths disposed in the triple or Balgare plait, and the front of the skirt is trimmed *en tablier* with wide folded bands, the border formed by doubling the edges over on to the plaits, and confining them with a blind stitch, allowing it to open in a fluting. A deep flounce trims the lower portion, describing a semi-circle, with the heading formed in a similar manner. The overdress is a polonaise jacket – meaning that the back is of the Marguerite-shaped polonaise, with the fronts are designed as a jacket and draped tablier; the drapings confined with those of the polonaise back, and ornamented with a wide tied sash ribbon. A flounce of embroidery trims the lower edges, and also the V-shaped neck and sleeves, while the lower edges of the jacket-fronts have a neatly made piping. Hat of French chip, trimmed both under the brim and on the outside with a profusion of flowers. The amount of material required for tis costume is fifteen yards of faille for the skirt and five yards of batiste for the polonaise jacket.

Frank Leslie's Lady's Magazine, June 1875

USE FOR BEETLE'S WINGS.

The effect of beetles' wings on evening dresses is extremely pretty; they are coming into fashion again in these fantastic days when every lady may wear anything she pleases, the more fanciful and peculiar the better. Beetles' wings have generally been arranged on black net, but they are equally effective on white. A net tunic, worn over a flounced or bouillonné net skirt, with beetles' wings sewn on in the form of stars and arranged at some little distance from each other all over, looks very beautiful. The stars should not be very large nor the wings placed very close together, and the tunic should merely be caught up very high on the hips, with no other trimming; the body, whether low, square, or V-shaped, must have some trimming to correspond, and the sleeves also; and the plan is to arrange the net skirt with flounces (either two or three), deep full ones, and sew on the beetles' wings as a heading above each. If the flounces are only to be in front, and the back of the skirt is puffed or otherwise differently trimmed, the wings should be carried up the side. It is best, for this style of trimming, to sew the beetles' wings first on to a strip of net, either black or white, according to the colour of the dress, and then tack the strips on to the skirt. In this way they can be removed easily and altered from one dress to another if necessary. A tunic edged with beetles' wings arranged in stars or in some simple design is very pretty. Primrose net or tarlatan is a good colour to show up this kind of trimming. It must be very pale and the beetles' wings put on lightly. I have seen a white silk dress trimmed with tulle, small white feathers, delicate gold sprays, and beetles' wings, and it was quite beautiful.

The Bazaar, The Exchange and Mart, June 9, 1875

On the preceding page is a house-dress of light cashmere. The front and sides of this dress are trimmed, "en tablier," by light, small puffings, finished, top and bottom, with a narrow frill. Below these puffs are three flounces, two in front and three at the sides. The back of the skirt is arranged in fixed plaits, falling from the waist. These plaits are taped at regular intervals underneath, to keep them in position. The corsage is slightly open in front, heart-shaped, and finished by an upright frill. Sleeves, coat-shaped, with a puff put in lengthwise; cuff slightly loose, finished by two buttons. Twelve to fourteen yards of cashmere will be required. ➜

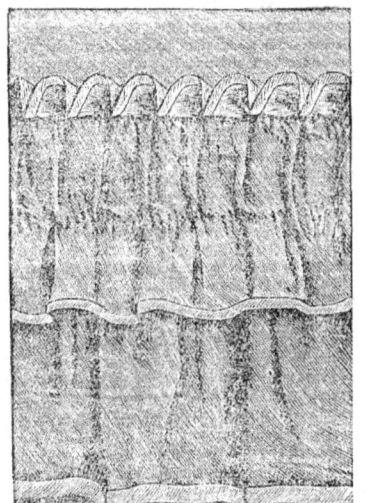

...

DESIGN FOR TRIMMING A DRESS-SKIRT.
By Mrs. Jane Weaver.

This is a very simple and pretty way of making a trimming for the bottom of either a dress or under-skirt. It consists of two frills of the material of the dress. The lower frill is bound with silk at the bottom edge. The upper frill is bound at each edge with a narrow binding of silk. It is gathered about half an inch from the top, and plaits are caught down the frill at regular distances. The frill is gathered in the middle between the heading and edge.

...

To Join Lace. – The edges of the lace to be joined must be carefully placed over each other, pattern on pattern, and mesh upon mesh, exactly. It sometimes happens a small piece of the lace must be sacrificed to thus enable the pattern to be continuous and perfect, but this cannot be avoided. With colored cotton, tack this firmly in the direction you intend this join to go, for a join is seldom made straight across the lace, generally in a zigzag form, as it shows less, and also with the purpose of avoiding or taking in part of the pattern, as the case may be. Now with very fine lace thread, such as is used for Honiton lace, take two plain and one buttonhole stitch in each mesh of the ground, on each side of the line decided on. When finished, cut away the edges of the lace that were placed over each other, close up to the join, and you will find it almost imperceptible and the pattern continuous. ...

All the varieties of grenadines and other thin goods are made as elaborately as the silk, foulards, mohairs, etc., of the early spring. In fact, what is usually termed "wash goods," cannot be washed at all, in many instances, the many gores making ironing straight an impossibility, and the ruffling is so elaborate. But we have often seen lawns, cambrics, etc., do duty a second season without washing, an occasional "pressing out" being all that is necessary. The make of dresses has changed in no respect. All skirts are drawn as far back as possible, giving an ugly wriggle to the walk, and making sitting down most uncomfortable and often inelegant. It is rumored the crinoline is to be again worn, but it is only a rumor, for in no respect have we seen any indication of it. The best French dresses are not drawn back as tightly as those made in this country, and are not so very uncomfortable to wear.

Bright colors will be worn this summer at watering places, the Madras colors being particularly popular. These colors are like those of the plaid bandana handkerchiefs, and make most showy suits, and if not too common will be very elegant, especially for brunettes. Two of these suits, just from the hands of Worth in Paris, are exceedingly admired. These Madras plaids come in ginghams, elegant grenadines, twilled silks, etc. Batiste is delightful for summer wear, it is so cool, and keeps clean a long time. Fringes and knife-plaitings are much used for trimmings. Ginghams and the old-fashioned seer-sucker have been revived for more inexpensive dresses. ...

Since dresses are made to cling so closely, the white petticoat, after a few hours' wear, becomes so soiled that a lady who is at all neat with regard to her under-clothing, is unwilling to put it on a second time. To obviate this, the white petticoat is now made shorter than the dress, but a white muslin ruffle flounce, a quarter of a yard to three-eighths of a yard in depth, is basted around the bottom of the skirt, inside, and so falls with the dress, which a petticoat does not. The ruffle can be made of any kind of cambric, not very full, and sewed on a tape. Strange to say, the ruffle does not seem to catch the dust as much as the longer petticoat did. We can speak from experience on this subject.

Peterson's Magazine, June 1875

It is surprising how quickly fashions, even for a special kind of material, appear and disappear. A few summers since every one possessed an assortment of Organdie muslins, with coloured patterns, the season's novelty being shown in the design alone; but 1875 seems to ignore this fresh and cheerful fabric, and richer ones find greater patronage. When muslins are assumed they are white (and this is very popular even with those past early youth), or are of a sober self colour, a delicate lead grey being perhaps most approved. These self-coloured muslins are trimmed with Valenciennes lace. Grey batiste is chosen in preference to the écru linen for morning wear, and all thick or semi-thick costumes are lavishly trimmed with broderie Anglais, either worked on white cambric or coloured linens. Pink gingham washes so well that it is greatly used in Paris for embroidering on, sometimes whole tabliers and jackets being made of it, and worn over white skirts. Trains are still on the increase, and are worn very long, even for demi-toilette. The bulgare plait, which forms the train, proves very stiff-looking when an excessive length, and consequently is much ornamented with bows, scarves, cascades of lace, and various devices.

...

Sleeves are simple no longer, being made to match the rest of the dress altogether or in part. Outside pockets, or, rather, a pocket, is indispensable. It is made in any and every shape, and placed on the left of the tablier, high up, so that the mouth of it reaches almost to the edge of the cuirass bodice basque.
The Bazaar, The Exchange and Mart, June 16, 1875

TRIMMINGS FOR SKIRTS, AND METHODS OF HOLDING THEM.

More and more are dress skirts made to differ back and front; none of the new ones have the same style of trimming on the train which is used to border the middle breadth and side gores. The peacock tail is almost as separate a feature of the dress as the bodice or tablier; for instance, the front may have narrow flounces, and the train be a series of bouillonnés terminating in one deep flounce; or the bulgare plait can be apparently tied by scarves nine inches apart, and the edge of the skirt have the single flounce, which is only half the depth in the centre to what it is at the sides where it joins the train, or rather where the latter hangs over it. This make of flounce is quite the newest, and certainly the slope gives a graceful effect. The lower edge is straight, the difference of width being made from the top; of course it is necessary to waste some material, though not much in cutting this, as, supposing four breadths were to be in it, the two middle ones could be cut narrower than the others, and the sloping done after joining them. At present they are gathered on either side with a cord on the inside, and leaving a heading of 2 in., or a small puff laid over the gathering string. They are not very full; half as much again as the space they are to occupy is the proper allowance. Narrow flounces may surmount this, all following the same curve. If a dress is of two shades, the flounces should not be the same as the skirt itself (which ought to be the lighter of the two), and the outside plait of the train also be like the flounce. This is not a law, but it shows the outline of the sweep, and it is only the grace of the flow which redeems the inconvenience of the present fashion.

Flounces of all kinds are quite the order of the day, and they are mounted in various ways even on the same dress; one of kilting will alternate with a scantily gathered one, or one of single box plaits, made on the straight of the material, be overlaid by one out on the cross and plaited diagonally, the edge of each plait thus being on the straight. Numberless skirts, notably those for out door wear with a mantle, have no tablier, the trimmings I have described being quite as high as the knees, and all finished under the train. Some, especially for young ladies, are kilted as far as the tunics hang, and it is the prettiest style for tops of the Swiss embroidery or Hamburgh net. As I have said before, practical people – and it is to them I address myself – will find it far best to complete the two halves of the skirt, and then unite them.

All clinging stuffs should have the two back breadths lined; it makes it so much easier to arrange the bulgare properly. Some dressmakers keep the train in place by tape bars underneath, and others stitch them down to a plain strip of muslin; this is the most effectual, but it is a matter of difficulty to creep in and out of these cocoons; one is chrysalis-like enough when the dress is fastened back with elastic bands. Elastic is better than tape, at any rate for the top straps, as they give when sitting down.

Sleeves that are puffed longitudinally should be roughly cut to shape, almost as wide again as the lining, and quite half as much again in length, gathered down the centre, then each side; every running being a trifle nearer the middle puff, afterwards laid on the lining, drawn up, and tacked in lines following the bend of the sleeve. Many have only the top half puffed, the under side plain. Cuffs on coat sleeves are very deep, generally double, one up and one down.

Ruffles are still worn, but they turn outwards, and a flat, upright, graduated band is inside them, with lisse, lace, or other lingerie inside that again. The standing band or collar is of very stiff muslin, and the inner part should be different to the outer if two shades are used elsewhere on the dress. This style is for some of the throat and neck to show. For morning dresses the double white collar gains ground. I suppose gorget is the proper name, as we already have corslets, cuirasses, and plastons. The wide turned-down piece is of single cambric, with a 1/2 in. hem; the upright is of two thicknesses, either close round the throat like a soldier's stock, or with corners higher than the back, and bent outwards.

Rumours are rife that the next bodice pattern will be copied from the old hunting and hawking jackets, open over waistcoats, with much lace frill and very deep tails with pockets. Several of the cuirasse bodies at Ascot were laced up the back, but, though it is said to insure a more perfect fit, it is not really becoming for day wear; and now that all dresses have a centre seam, it is very easy to make the proper hollow at the small of the back and between the shoulder blades.

Holding the train in the full of one hand is elegant, but most cumbersome to those whom fate compels to do much walking, perhaps carrying a waterproof, parcel, and umbrella. Patent hooks answer if sewn low down; but, as it is impossible to reach eyes if put on the skirt, it being so tight, they should be attached to tapes fastened to the inside of the waistband and hanging loose. Another plan is to have a scarf of the dress material, and hook one end under the jacket basque on the left-hand side (front), the other connected in the same way to eyes put under the folds of the train about half yard from the edge, so as to bring the latter forward as when held in the hand. Do not imagine that one pocket looks crooked, and so put on two; the width thus defined is most detrimental to the figure.

The Bazaar, The Exchange and Mart, June 23, 1875

Fig. VI. – Walking-Dress of Gray Camel's-Hair. – The under-skirt is of gray silk, the back widths laid in deep box-plaits, the front ornamented at the bottom with a bias band of gray silk, striped with brown. Pocket of plain gray silk, ornamented with a brown bow. Brown sash and collar, and trimming on the sleeve. Worsted fringe of brown and gray.

...

Worth makes many new faille dresses with skirts that are plain and clinging in front, bordering them with a heavy fringe, which keeps the breadths in place. The front is cut in one piece, bodice and skirt having no join, while at the back there are pointed basques in the form of tulip-leaves. Beneath these basques there are sash-ends, which fall considerably lower on the skirt. This habit-bodice and the train are always different from the front of the skirt. For example, the front will be striped pink and white, the train and the bodice damask pink. The bodice is cut square, and a small bouquet of flowers is added on the left side of it. This style of toilet is only fit for in-doors.

...

MADRAS PLAID OVER-DRESS.
Fig. VIII. – Madras Plaid Over-Dress of Blue and Gray. – The sash and trimming down the front, and of the cuirass, is of blue silk.

Summer always brings out charming toilets in thin, vapory materials, which, though they look so inexpensive, sadly belie their appearance. White muslins, organdies, lawns, batistes, besides innumerable grenadines, and other thin, silky materials are only simple at the first glance. The ruffling and the puffings, and the silk under-dresses, all make the summer toilet a somewhat costly affair.

Many ladies now use the delicate pink, blue, or violet lawns (plain ones, of course) in the place of silk, for slips under their dresses.

Plaitings, and especially marguerite plaitings, which are as fine and as closely laid as the petals of a flower, and look like crimping, are decidedly the favorite trimmings at present. The long tablier reaching to the foot, has abolished wide flounces on the skirt, it being found that two narrow plaitings on the front and side breadths, and several rows on the back breadths, form a more effective trimming. These plaitings are sometimes sewn by machine, but they are better with flat hems held by blind stitches. Sometimes the raw edge of the silk is merely turned up once and secured by what is called "cut stitching;" but, at any rate, the plaits should be always pressed flatly and left to flare open; if they are deeper than the eighth of a yard, they should be caught by a thread in the centre on the wrong side. Plaitings are also intermixed with froncés – or, as these are called sometimes, drawings, gatherings, or shirrings; but, with all this multiplicity of names, they are nothing more nor less than the material drawn up into a wrinkle by means of threads run through it, each from half to three-quarters of an inch apart. A strip of the material, from four to eight inches wide, is used for these gatherings.

The bodices that are made with five seams at the back, and without curved side-pieces, are gaining ground with the public. The seams each side of the one in the centre of the back commence, as a matter of course, on the top of the shoulder; they are held in position by slender whalebones, which are carried to the end of the three centre seams. The difference between the Joan of Arc bodice and the cuirass (both of which are popular,) is that the former is slightly hollowed out, or describes something of a curve, whilst the latter is straight all round.

Black silk guipure is again in fashion. Those who possess deep guipure flounces can utilize them advantageously by mounting them on stiff net, and without any fullness, in rows one close to the other. This makes a charming Spanish tunic or tablier, which can be worn over a variety of dresses; the sleeveless bodice is also cut out in net and covered with piece-guipure. Guipure is used in the same manner over white silk, and can be worn thus over light silk dresses.

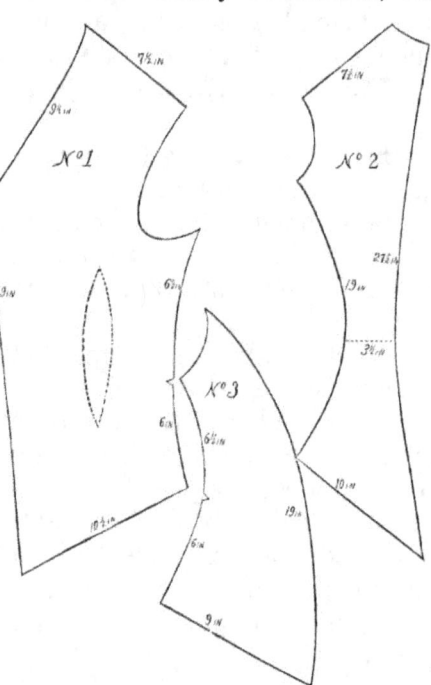

THE GEORGIAN VEST.

No. 1. Half of Front.
No. 2. Half of Back.
No. 3. Side Piece.
Make of blue silk or cashmere; edge with guipure lace, or embroidered Swiss flouncings, and finish with back ribbon velvet, two inches wide, for the heading, and three inches for the bows and ends.

Straw fringes are in vogue for trimming light dresses, and several stylish ball toilets are ornamented with black ribbon velvet embroidered with straw.

Skirts are now bordered inside with narrow flounces of Swiss or Madeira work, and with cambric plaitings, edged with Valenciennes lace. These additions to the lining of a skirt are called *balais* or sweeping-brooms. Formerly they were only to be seen on ball-dresses, but now they are added to most skirts with trains and demi-trains.
Peterson's Magazine, July 1875

Ladies Dresses are made every month more and more close-fitting, and the ingenuity that was brought to bear only a few years ago on expanding skirts is now employed in contrivances to cause them to cling tightly to the figure. Bands of elastic and strings are now fastened inside the skirt, in order to reduce its expansive tendency as much as possible. Sitting down in a dress of the latest fashion is almost an impossibility – that is, if sitting down means placing yourself straight and in the centre of a chair – and walking is not always easy of accomplishment. Perching sideways on the edge of a chair or sofa seems the nearest approach to sitting in these days of tightly tied-back drapery; and yet, uncomfortable as they are, the long, narrow trains, confined with elastic, have a very graceful appearance.

Opposite is a peignoir of white nainsook, made in the Princess shape. The bottom of the skirt has a deep-plaited flounce, twelve inches deep, including the heading, which is one and a half inches deep. This flounce is stitched on at the heading, and the plaits are tacked down to a narrow bobbin, on the under side, hold the plaits in position half way down. The coat-sleeves are trimmed to match, with a plaiting five inches wide, arranged to form a cuff. Pockets shell-shaped, finished with a bow of ribbon, or muslin, edged with Valenciennes lace. Their [sic] is a plaiting for the finish of the neck, and down the front of the peignoir. For a home breakfast-dress, this will be both comfortable and pretty for these hot summer days. The same model will look well in percale, or for cooler days. Soft cashmere, such as light-gray, piped with blue or crimson. Twelve yards of nainsook or percale, or ten yards of cashmere, will be required.

...

Madras is a copy of Indian cotton handkerchiefs, and is consequently always checked; it is trimmed with silk ruches, selected to match the darkest color in the check. All dresses of light materials, such as linen, batiste, fine cambric, colored muslin, and light foulards, are made in the Watteau style. They are looped, and gathered up in intricate, irregular folds, and profusely ornamented with bows, which renders them very elegant. The style of make called "the soubrette" is one of the prettiest. The material is striped pink and black linen. The under-skirt is covered with plaitings. The second skirt is round, forms a pouf at the back, and is bordered with a pink and black silk ruche, with notched-out edges, in the centre of which there is a ruche of Valenciennes lace. The bodice has a cascade of Valenciennes lace, studded with bows in front; the pockets in the skirt are ruched round, and there is a black and pink silk bow in the centre of each pocket.

...

IN-DOOR COSTUME, WITH TABLIER AND BASQUE.
By Emily H. May.

Our diagram for this month consists of four pieces – two for the tablier, one for the basque, and one for the chatelain-bag. The first named three are joined by the corresponding notches on the diagram. The piece with two notches is plaited into the basque, which has also

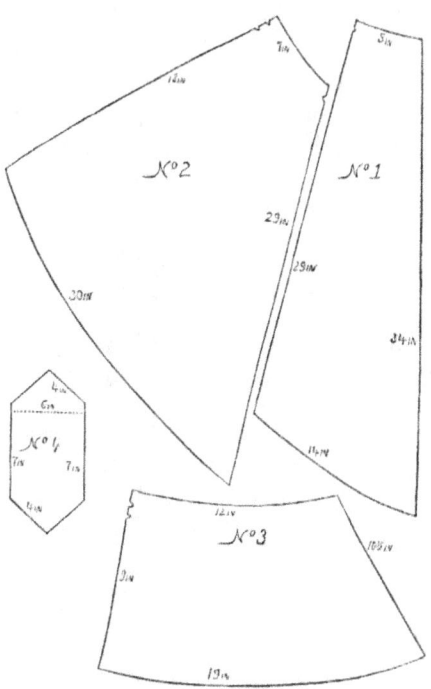

two notches, and these pieces represent one half of the pattern. The dotted line on No. 4, shows the form of the flap that is buttoned over on the bag. A bow is added at each side of the bag suspenders. The bodice has a deep-pointed basque in front, and a short, round one at the back. Coat-sleeve, either puffed or plain. This is suitable for soft, woolen fabrics, or washing material.

No. 1. Half of Front of Tablier.
No. 2. Half of Side of Tablier.
No. 3. Half of Plaited Basque.
No. 4. Chatelain Bag.

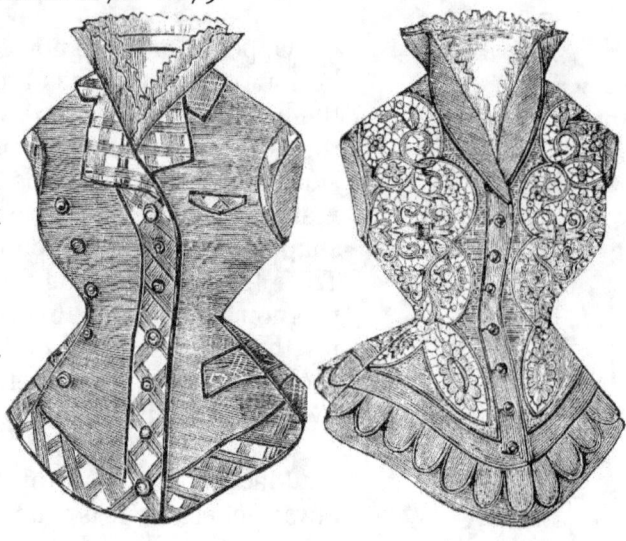

One of the jackets is of light-blue silk with blue silk applique on white, and the other is of black silk, trimmed with a bias band of blue and green silk plaid.

FASHIONABLE BASQUES.
Peterson's Magazine, August 1875

On the preceding page we give a Watteau wrapper, made of cashmere, either gray, trimmed with blue or crimson, or a pretty solid blue, with trimmings of the same color. This wrapper is cut all in one from the neck. Princess shape, cut into the figure, but not quite tight. At the bottom there is a plaited flounce, nine inches deep, just in front, widening to twelve at the sides and back, where it meets the Watteau-plait. If trimmed with a contrasting color, edge and line the top frill of the flounce with the color, and put it on with a narrow band of the same. Cord and trim the pockets, cuffs, and collar to match, and the bows upon the Watteau, cuffs, and front of wrapper, make entirely of the color. From nine to ten yards of cashmere (according to the height of the lady) will be required. Two yards of silk to trim. This design is only suitable for soft, woolen material. Merino would be less expensive than cashmere; and we have seen a very pretty wrapper made in gray de bege, and trimmed with the same material, several shades darker.

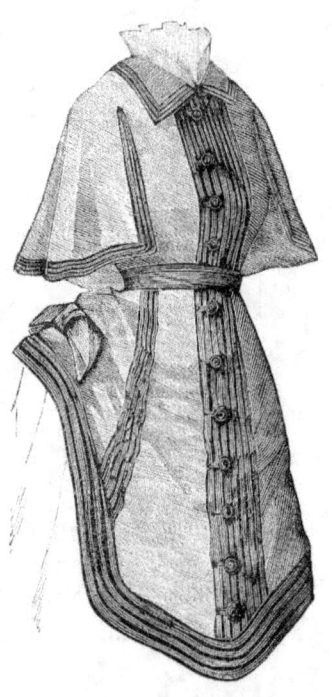

CAMEL'S-HAIR OVER-DRESS.
Fig. IX. – Over-Dress of Gray Camel's-Hair, trimmed with many rows of black braid, fastened down the front with large button, and looped high upon the hips. In the front the waist and cape are cut in one. Deep, square collar. This is a very nice traveling dress, especially if made of water-proof, and worn over a water-proof skirt.

PLAID OVER-DRESS.
Fig. X. – Over-Dress of Plain Colors and White Plaid Foulard, trimmed at the bottom with ruffles of the silk. The waist is trimmed with two folds of the plain plum-colored silk.

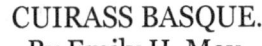

CUIRASS BASQUE.
By Emily H. May.

Make of cashmere or cloth, and braid all over with mohair braid. Our design is sleeveless, but we give on the diagram a sleeve for those who may prefer it.

Bust measures thirty-four inches; waist twenty-four inches.

No. 1. Half of Front.

No. 2. Half of Back.

No. 3. Half of Sleeve.

The dotted line shows the under-side of the sleeve, which may be used by those who wish it.

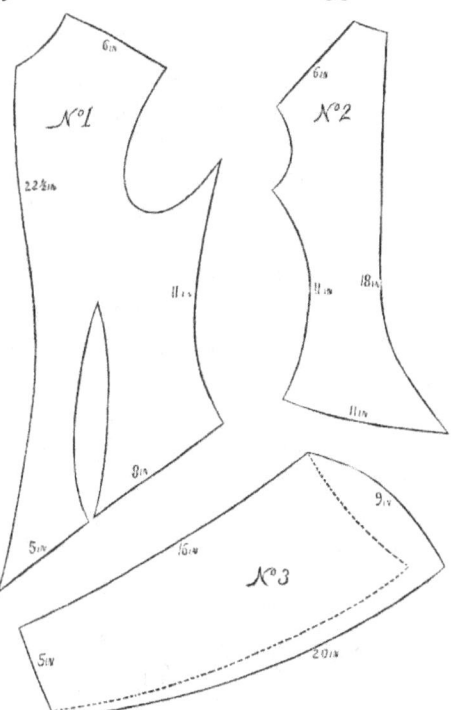

...

Economical Party Dress. – Young ladies find no expense so great as that of party dresses. For this season of the year, however, one not too expensive may be made by taking a white silk gored petticoat, with a train not more than three inches on the ground, and wearing over this, a white net, grenadine, or clear muslin skirt with three graduated flounces, headed with open-worked insertion, which may be lined either with white or colored satin, the front breadth trimmed *à la bébé*, that is to say, with alternate goffered frills and insertion, revers to correspond, Grecian bodice and sleeves, wreath of natural flowers from the left shoulder across the bodice. This costume may be varied by wearing a colored slip under it and trimmings to match; its chief merit consists in the fact it may be got up by a clear-starcher, to look as good as new, again and again.

Peterson's Magazine, September 1875

On the preceding page, is another costume, simple and suitable for either house or street. It is of brown bege, a pretty, soft, and inexpensive woolen material, suitable for the season. The skirt has a quadruple plait forming the back breadth; the sides and front breadths being kilt plaited. The tunic forms a square tablier, and is draped at the back, under a brown silk or ribbon sash. This square tablier is quite new, and a pleasant variation on the inevitable pointed apron-shape, so universal. The trimming consists of a knife-plaiting of brown silk, but it would look very well made of the same material as the dress, and much more economical, unless one has an old silk dress, the best part of which to utilize for this kind of trimming. The casaque is loose in front and is cut into the figure at the back, but does not fit closely. It is trimmed with the knife plaiting, like the tunic. The coat-sleeves terminate with a similar plaiting, headed by a band of ribbon, tied in a bow, with ends, at the back of the sleeve. A plaited frill forms the collar, and the buttons are of brown silk. This will require from sixteen to eighteen yards of single-width material; and bege can be bought from thirty-seven and a half cents, single-width, up to one dollar and fifty cents, double-width – a very serviceable material for every-day wear.

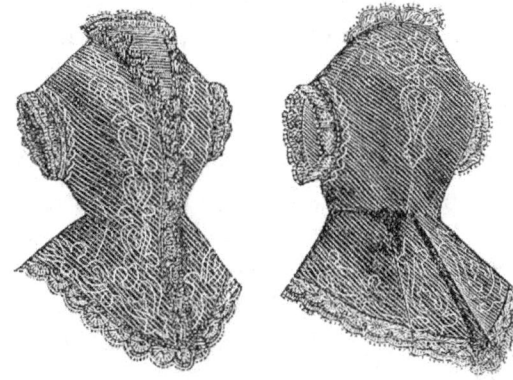

A sleeveless jacket, of black cashmere or silk, braided and trimmed with guipure lace. This any lady can make for herself, and worn over an old dress, quite freshens up an otherwise somewhat shabby toilet. Black worsted or silk braid may be used, and jet beads sewed on, if desired. We give the front and back of this jacket in the accompanying designs.

Artistic Fashions, So Called! – An attempt was made recently in London, to introduce what were called artistic fashions. A popular landscape and figure painter gave a reception, at which the various ladies who were guests, ignoring the fashions of the day, appeared in historical costumes, that they considered beautiful, or in fancy costumes, which they had "evoked," as the Germans say, "out of their own consciousness". This attempt to dethrone fashion, however, was a signal failure. We have never heard of anybody wearing any of these costumes since.

The reason is not far to seek. A well-bred woman avoids, above everything else, making herself conspicuous, and to wear a costume, that deviates too much from the prevailing mode, is to do this. Taste in dress should, therefore, be exercised within certain limits. The fashions of the day may be modified to suit the wearer's individual style; but they cannot be entirely ignored. A woman, who should walk down Walnut Street in Philadelphia, or the Fifth Avenue in New York, or Beacon Street in Boston, wearing the towering head-dress of a century ago, would draw a crowd after her as great as follows an Indian chief in his paint and feathers. This is, of course, an ordeal from which every modest woman shrinks.

We have seen several attempts, in this country, to get up so-called artistic dresses, but they have invariably made even pretty women look like *guys*. The style of one century cannot, safely, be imported into another: manners have changed; the costume becomes incongruous. Think of an auctioneer crying his wares, or a lawyer addressing a jury, in the velvet doublet and feathered hat of a cavalier of the time of Charles the First! It is just as absurd for a woman to dress like Henrietta Maria, or Marie Antoinette. Nay! it is an offence against true taste. The truth is that modern fashions, on the whole, are as graceful as any that have gone before. Of course, horrid things are sent out by third-rate designers here; but as a whole, the real Paris fashions are invariably in good taste. Worth never turned out a really ugly costume. We think *we* never engraved one.

A lady, unless she wishes to be eccentric, *must* follow the fashions, at least in a modified degree. The first requisite to dressing well yourself, is to know what is going to be worn. You may then adapt the style to suit your complexion, etc. But you cannot entirely ignore it.

BLACK VELVET SPENCER AND POCKET.

The black velvet spencer is finished with a black guipure lace, and is fastened across the front with rows of black beads. A white *crépe lisse*, in quilling, goes round the neck and front. The pocket is of black velvet, with white net over it, and a rose with buds ornaments it.

Peterson's Magazine, October 1875

We give, first, this month, the back and front of a walking-costume for a young lady, composed of plaid and self-colored material. Plaids! plaids! either alone or in combination, and so much of them in the shops, and on the street, that, as a natural consequence, there will soon be no more to see; but such are the present fashions, and so we say, "hasten to wear them while fashion bids us declare them pretty." This costume is of plaid gray and black camel's-hair cloth, with plain gray for the tablier, jacket, and trimmings. The under-skirt is ornamented with one deep flounce, cut straight, with a narrow plaiting upon the edge. A puff of the plaid is put on for a heading. The over-skirt forms a pointed tablier in front, and one long tab in the back, all edged with a narrow plaiting. The tablier is gathered up at the back, under a large bow of black taffetas ribbon. The jacket-bodice is of the self-colored material, with collar, sleeves, and trimmings for the edge and pockets, of the plaid, as may be seen from the design. To cut this jacket, any lady who has a good-fitting, simple basque pattern, can, by adding to the length of the skirt of the basque and shaping on the sides and at the back, cut this jacket for herself. The coat-sleeves have a deep-pointed cuff of the plain material, also a narrow plaiting of the same down the outside seam of the sleeve. Of double-width material, eight yards of the plaid, and six yards of the plain will be required.

ALEXANDRA CORSAGE BASQUE.
By Emily H. May.
No. 1. Half of Front.
No. 2. Half of Back.
No. 3. Half of Sleeve.
No. 4. Half of Collar.
The dotted lines show where the plaits are to be laid – a double box-plait.

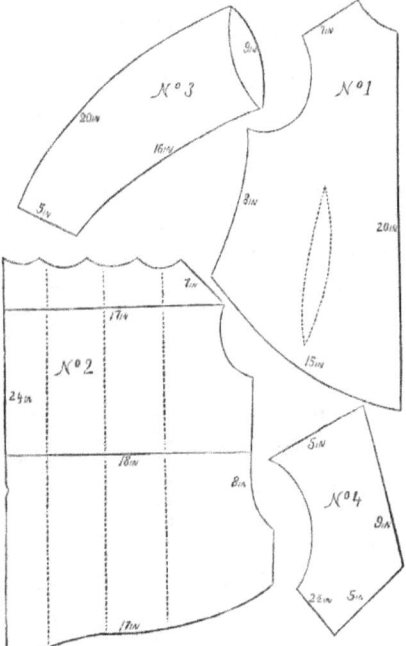

Waistcoat bodices are again much worn; but the waistcoat must be made to fasten to the bodice, because it is so large – in many cases it descends almost to the knees. It is made of velvet when the dress is faille with velvet sleeves; and of faille with the dress is woolen.

...

The autumn dresses are draped more closely to the figure than the summer ones, if that is possible. At the back the trains are very narrow, and very long; the form is to be compared to that adopted by abbesses. There is a single wide plait upon the skirt in the centre, and this plait is frequently ornamented with either a ladder of bows or a cascade of lace. Another variety of the abbess train consists of kilt plaits arranged the entire length of the back of the skirt.

DRESS FOR THE HOUSE.
Fig. VI. – House-Dress. – The under-skirt is of black silk. The over-dress is of gray plaid silk, with black sashes; waist of the plaid silk, with black silk sleeves, with plaid cuffs.

The Princess or Gabrielle dress (which as all our readers know, is a dress with the skirt and the waist cut in one) is being worn in the house in Paris, but the bottom of the skirt is usually elaborately trimmed.

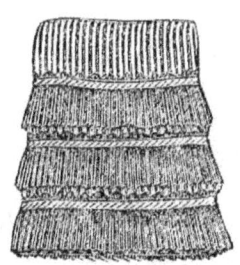

Two designs for making up striped black and white, or black and gray skirting, we give for the benefit of those who desire colored skirts for walking or winter wear. The one with three ruffles is cut in large, or rather long, scallops, before plaitings. Thee [sic] plaitings are put on with a narrow bias band of the material. Do not make the foundation of the skirt over two and a half yards in width.

On the preceding page, we give another dress in black silk or cashmere, suitable for house or street. It has but a narrow flounce of six inches upon the under-skirt, headed by three rows of gathering, terminating in a frill at the top. The long Princess Polonaise reaches almost to the bottom of the skirt, and is trimmed with guipure lace, or left perfectly plain, being faced with silk, fastened all the way down the front with bows of black velvet or silk. A square pocket, with the lower edge trimmed with lace, and also ornamented with a bow, is the only trimming on the Polonaise. Where it is draped at the back, a larger bow and ends is placed. Coat-sleeve, with cuff, on the back of which is a smaller bow is placed. High, standing collar. This Polonaise would be very elegant, made of cashmere, worn over black silk. As it is very long, an old silk skirt could be retrimmed at very little expense. A silk, trimmed with cashmere, looks very well. Eight to ten yards of cashmere for the Polonaise, will be required, as it is so long. Very dark green, it is said, will be the fashionable color for this winter; and this would be very elegant in that color.

...

For Evening Dresses, two or three colors, as well as two or three materials, are used; for instance, gray and pink, blue and maize, or cream color, or salmon, light-green and pink, or light-green and straw, mauve and primrose, etc.

For evening wear, the skirts of dresses are now frequently plaited entirely from waist downward, like the trains worn by abbesses; they open on one side over a simulated under-skirt, which is a complete contrast to the upper one. For example, a jade-colored silk dress (a whitish green, or sea-foam shade) will open over a breadth of muslin and white faille – a faille plaiting and muslin plaiting arranged alternately – and the opening, which is at one side only, will be barred across with black velvet. The jade faille bodice will be a cuirass with a plastron, half of white faille and half of muslin, inserted in the front, and edged with Valenciennes lace; black velvet bars likewise cross the bodice. The sleeves may be either black velvet trimmed with a white muslin plaiting and a bow of jade ribbon, or entirely of white muslin and Valenciennes lace, with a black velvet bow. The style of dress is quite novel, and the effect is most stylish; it is repeated in all colors, and in many different materials. When white muslin is used for this dress, the order is reversed. The Abbess train is muslin, and the simulated under-skirt, over which it opens, is flame-colored silk, the breadth being plaited its entire length. The muslin bodice is lined with flame-colored silk, and at the end of the sleeves there is a plaiting of flame silk.

WINTER BASQUE.

Fig. VII. – Basque and Over-Dress of Myrtle-Green Camel's Hair. – The apron-front is short, and reaches to puff at the back. The back is rounded at the ends, and looped up in one puff. The basque is close-fitting. Coat-sleeves, with under-cuffs. Trimming of myrtle-green worsted fringe.

Pockets Outside. – As it is no longer possible to get the hands into the pockets inserted in the tied-back skirts, large pockets of all shapes and styles are worn, usually on one side only, sometimes on both sides. We give an illustration of one in the "Every-day" department. ↘

...

We give next a design of the newest style for a dress pocket for dresses, tabliers, and Polonaises. It is formed with a gathered frill, top and bottom, with the pocket put on in a box-plait in the middle, and almost plain at the sides; a bow of ribbon crosses the top of the pocket just under the frill, and is stitched under the pocket at the sides.

1876

WINTER POLONAISE, FOR A YOUNG LADY.
By Emily H. May

We give, here, a Winter Polonaise, the very latest in style: with a diagram, on the next page, by which to cut it out. The skirt is of navy-blue French merino. The Polonaise is of black cashmere, ornamented with rows of black mohair braid. The edge is finished with a heavy silk fringe. Navy-blue ribbon is used for the bows and sash-ends, or black, if preferred. This design will look well also in any of the striped goods now so fashionable.

No. 1. Half of Front.
No. 2. Half of Side-Piece.
No. 3. Half of Back.
No. 4. Sleeve.
No. 5. Band to Lift Plaits.
Notches on No. 2, where plaits are laid.

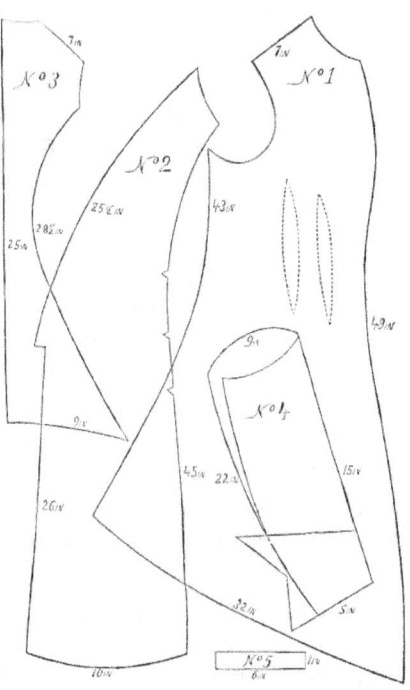

We give first, this month, a promenade costume of black silk and checked woolen material: in either camel's-hair, vicugna bege, or checked poplin. The skirt of this costume is perfectly plain, and made with a demi train, which is furnished with loops at the back, to lift for the street. The tunic, which is a combination of neutral tints, is pointed in front, and fastened at the side with black silk buttons. The trimming for the edge of the tunic is black silk, and consists of two knife-plaitings, one overlapping the other, and the upper one stitched on, forming a heading a half inch deep. These plaitings are three inches deep, when finished. They should be laid quite small, and just to touch, carefully basted, and then pressed with an iron, to look nice. The back of the tunic is looped, and forms a pouf, which is ornamented with bows of black silk or ribbon. The cuirass bodice is double-breasted, and fastens on the right side, to correspond with the tunic. It is cut square, back and front, and shorter on the hip, as may be seen. There is a high, standing collar, piped with silk. Coat-sleeves, with cuff also piped to match. Pocket on the right side. All dresses, now, have the pocket either put on the outside garment, whether Polonaise or tunic, or else depending as a chatelaine-pocket from the waist. The tightness with which the over-dress is draped makes this necessary. Five yards of double-width material, in check, will be required; or double the quantity of single. I need only say, these plaid suitings can be had from fifty cents to three dollars per yard.

MODE OF WORKING HEM-STITCH.
By Mrs. Jane Weaver.

This stitch is useful for the borders of handkerchiefs, and also for cravats and puffs of lawn or cambric. No. 1 shows the mode of raising and separating the threads, also the stitch of the first worked side; No. 2, the stitch of finishing side. The working will be more easily followed from the engraving than from any description. This mode will be found less tedious, and stronger than the ordinary mode of drawing threads.

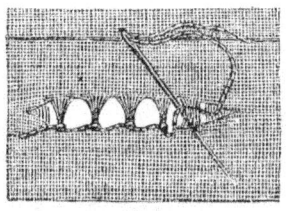

No. 1.

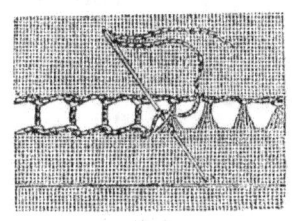

No. 2.

Always dress according to your complexion, figure, and style. It is the duty of every woman to look as pretty as she can; and this is a chief way to look pretty. ...

Most of the costumes seen on what is considered the best-dressed women in the streets, are quite simple in appearance, no matter how intricate the make really is, nor of how many materials they may be composed. Silk, velvet, and metalisse, are often seen in one dress; on others, are fur or rich braid; but we think the tendency is to trim the over-skirts less than they were last year. ...

There is a change in flounces. The new styles are not flowing, but are attached to the skirt almost as closely near the lower edge, as at the top. They are made full and bunchy, with double and even treble box-plaits. Various netted tabliers have come into vogue. Some are made of soft silk braid, either colored or black, tied in diamond shape, and richly fringed; others are of chenille, netted in diamonds, and fringed with chenille. They are very rich looking.

Braid, up to the present, is decidedly the most fashionable trimming for day-dresses. There are mohair braids in loosely-woven tresses, either to match the dress, or of silk, mixed with gold, silver, or steel. There are also braids made entirely of metal, but then they are very narrow; while, on the contrary, the wider a mohair braid is, the more stylish it is considered. There are many new galoons for silk and cashmere dresses. They are loose, basket-woven tresses, ornamented at intervals with tufts of crimped braid. As for the fringes, their name is legion. They are crimped, netted, tufted, tasseled, made of crimped braid, of chenille, of loops of galoon, with strings of buttons here and there, and are of all widths, from two to six inches. These new cashmere fringes are full of color, and are used effectively on plain colors. Cloth bands, intended for trimming cloth dresses, look well embroidered, and then bound with the new cashmere galoons of soft, rich silk. Feather trimmings are also much worn, the newest design being a ruche of feathers for the heading, below which there is a fringe of feathers. This is made in finely-curled ostrich-feathers, and in greenish-black cocks' feathers. Another novelty, but rather a costly one, is a row of pheasants' feathers, placed in the midst of a band of ostrich feathers.

Peterson's Magazine, January 1876

Next is something more elaborate, suitable for a visiting costume, of which we give a front and back view. The under-skirt is of black cashmere. First there is a knife-plaiting, four inches deep; then a puffing; another knife-plaiting; and then another puffing. This is again repeated, bringing the trimming quite high on the skirt. The tablier is round in front, and looped in the back to form a pouf. It and the cuirass bodice are of plaid black and gray camel's-hair. The edge of the tunic is trimmed with a narrow knife-plaiting of the black cashmere. Sleeves, piece down the back of the bodice, scarf, and bow and ends, are all of the black cashmere. This design may be carried out in any of the dark colors. Very dark blue and green are the most fashionable. Twelve yards of plain cashmere, and four yards of plaid camel's-hair serge.

A rival power is already rising to dispute the supremacy of plaids. We mean stripes, either alone, or combined with self-colored materials, and arranged in various ways. Thus plain skirt, with flounces, puffings, or ruches of some fabric to match, but self-colored, also; tunic of the same fabric, but striped; self-colored bodice, striped sleeves; in fact, every combination, so that it is done with taste, and a certain harmony. ...

The Polonaise Dress, that is, skirt and waist cut in one, which is so becoming to most figures, that it has never gone quite out of fashion, though for awhile the separate skirt and jacket generally replaced it, has come again in favor. They are not as full and puffed in the back as formerly, but are straight, simply-shaped garments. There are always three long seams down the centre of the back and these continue over the tournure. Instead of the side seams commencing in the shoulder-seam, they start like the centre one, from the back of the neck. Worth calls this revival the "pelisse Polonaise." It somewhat resembles a gentleman's double-breasted frock coat in shape. It is open plainly from the waist down the back, has pocket-flaps on the sides, and is fastened with buttons in front. Some are made of black brocaded silk, with facings on the collar, and cuffs of cardinal red silk, slight lines of the same on the seams of the back; others are of black, basket-woven natté silk, draped with a sash on the tournure. There is no decided shape yet popularized, but there is a strong attempt to bring Polonaises again into fashion.

Peterson's Magazine, February 1876

We give, first, this month, a walking-costume for a young lady. The material is a very dark brown, (what is called an invisible shade,) cashmere, and the costume is composed of two skirts; the under one is cut very narrow, measuring not over three yards, and tightly gored on the front and side breadths. It is ornamented by a deep, gathered flounce, cut on the bias, headed by a narrow knife-plaited frill. For this knife-plaiting, cut straight way of the cloth, and allow three times the fullness; fold in quarter-inch plaits; baste each plait carefully, and iron on the wrong side before removing the bastings. The upper-skirt forms a tablier quite deep in front, and edged with a narrow knife-plaited frill. The back is caught up, *en draperie*, and fastened by bows of silk, with fringed ends. From under the sides of the tablier appear pointed pieces, edged by pointed frills, same width as that upon the tablier. Sleeves trimmed to match. Sixteen yards, double-width material, will be required. Buttons for the corsage of dresses are now quite small; and the basque buttons all the way from the throat to the end of the basque.

◤ WALKING-DRESS OF CAMEL'S-HAIR.
Fig. VIII. – Walking-Dress of Plaid Camel's-Hair, over a dark brown silk skirt. The sleeves and the back of the jacket are of dark-brown. The over-skirt is of a plaid, of two shades of brown, the lighter being almost an ecru color. It is edged with a ruffle of silk, of the lighter color, and has a large bow at the back, of the same color. Hat of ecru-colored felt, trimmed with brown leaves.

Skirts are made still more clinging, those for full dress elaborately trimmed, whilst all street costume seems to be growing plainer. One large pocket is almost always put on the left side, the very tight skirt making it impossible to use a pocket inserted in the dress. All trains are cut narrow, and pointed in the middle; and when there is a looped-up tunic, it is so complicated that it is utterly impossible to describe. The cuirass bodices are still the favorites; they are made much longer than they were three months ago, and waists are elongated in such a manner, that all arrangements of petticoats are entirely altered. The art of the dressmaker lies in making the basque fit smoothly, but not too tightly. The figure is not compressed, but the outlines are clearly defined. Very often the cuirass extends at least two-eighths of a yard below the waist all round, and it should lie without any fullness over the hips and tournure.

Sleeves are made to match the skirt, and contrasting with the bodice; but the sleeves that are made of two materials are the newest. For morning wear, sleeves are cut exceedingly narrow; and for demi-toilet they rarely reach below the elbow. They are then turned up with lace, and a flower is added at the bend of the arm.

The close-fitting Polonaise, with waist and skirt cut in one, is the newest style sent out by the best French dressmakers. It has more the effect of a gentleman's overcoat than anything we can compare it to. There is no drapery, and no trimming but a binding, or a cord and buttons. ... The sleeves of the Polonaise habits are often without cuffs, the lower part of the sleeve only flaring over the hand.

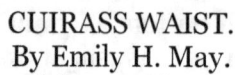

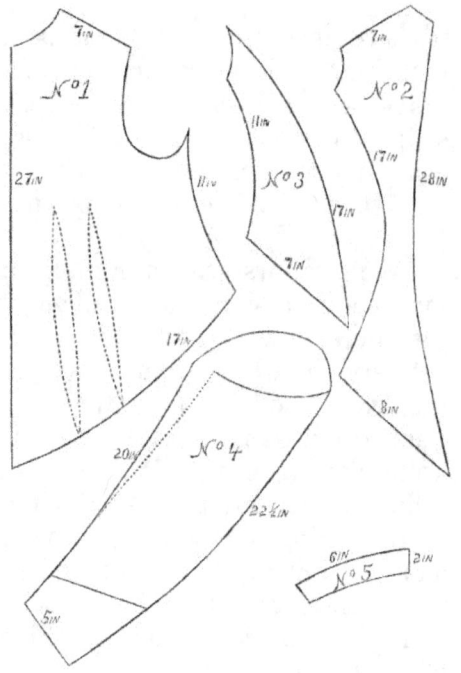

CUIRASS WAIST.
By Emily H. May.

We give, this month, one of the fashionable Cuirass Waists, but with long, pointed basques; a new fashion. We give also, on the next page, a diagram by which to cut it out.

No. 1. Half of Front.
No. 2. Half of. Back
No. 3. Half of Side-Piece.
No. 4. Half of Sleeve.
No. 4. [*sic*] Half of Standing Collar.

Peterson's Magazine, March 1876

We give, first, this month, a pretty toilet for a young lady, suitable either for home or walking. It is made of a very light-gray mohair, serge, or cashmere for the foundation, and the trimmings are of plaid, either black and white, or any other combination that the taste my suggest. There is but one skirt, made very plain in front, the fullness all being arranged in the back breadths, where it terminates in a demi-train. The trimming is arranged to form a square tablier, and is placed directly upon the skirt. The folds are cut on the bias, and graduated. The bottom one, which goes all round the skirt, is six inches wide; the next five, next four, next three inches. It will be seen from the engraving hos they are arranged. On the left side the skirt is held back by bows and ends of the material, trimmed to match. The bodice is cuirass, (Jeanne d'Arc,) cut very long in front and short in the back, where the fastening is. This, however, is optional; it would look quite well fastened in front, and be much more convenient. Our design calls for a square cut at the throat, to be worn over a muslin habit-skirt. This is also optional. A small fichu is worn over the shoulders, and knotted in front. The sleeves are cut coat-shape, ruffled at the hand, and finished with a band two inches wide, as a heading, terminating with bows and ends. The edge of the bodice is also trimmed with a ruffle, with a narrow band as finish. The sleeves should be made of the plain material, also the ruffles. Eight yards of single-width material for the foundation, and eight yards of the plaid will be required.

...

On the preceding page is a simple walking-costume made of tamise, or alpaca. It has two skirts, the lower one made just to touch and only three yards wide. It is trimmed on the bottom with a broad-plaited flounce, headed by a bias band. The tunic is simply hemmed or faced, and is caught up at the back, and fastened by two groups of large bows and floating ends, the lower group finished by a sort of fan-shaped piece placed under the lower bow. Corsage "cuirasse," finished on the edge like the tunic. Sleeves coat-shape, finished at the hand by double-plaited frills, with a bias band between. Standing collar. Buttoned in front all the way down to the bottom of the corsage. Sixteen to eighteen yards of material required. ➔

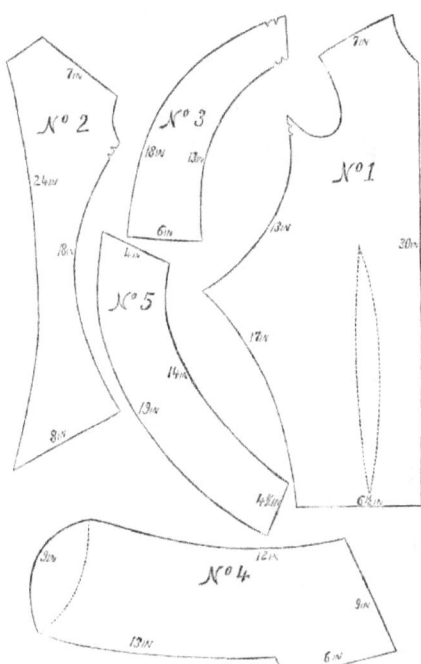

PROMENADE JACKET.
By Emily H. May.

We give, here, a new style of promenade jacket, to be made of cashmere. On the next page we give a diagram, by which our lady subscribers can cut it out.

No. 1. Half of Front.

No. 2. Half of Back.

No. 3. Half of Side-Back.

No. 4. Half of Sleeve.

No. 5. Half of Collar.

Trim with braid, three rows all round; one row down the front to simulate a waistcoat. Fringe and buttons.

...

Dressmaking at Home. – To make "Auld claithes look amaist as weel as new," is an important part of dressmaking in families where economy is a necessary institution. To remodel an old dress, to make it a success, is sometimes a difficult matter, and a few hints may be acceptable to some of our lady readers. Take, for instance, a half-worn black silk and cashmere. The first thing to be done is to carefully rip up both skirts. The black silk, brush and shake very carefully; then take a basin of water, and squeeze the blue-bag into it until it is almost black; and a tablespoonful of spirits of ammonia. Spread the breadths, one at a time, upon a table, and sponge it thoroughly on both sides, then fold it carefully, and lay it on a clean towel. Proceed until you have all the breadths sponged; then roll them up tightly, and on the following day, iron them on what is to be the wrong side. By doing this you will avoid the stiffness which is so disagreeable in a cleaned silk. Do the cashmeres in the same way, only hang them up in the sun until they are nearly dry, then take them in and iron out the creases. It is always advisable to line an old silk skirt; nice crinoline should be selected, and each breadth lined separately; then sew them together. Face with a narrow facing of alpaca, and bind neatly with skirt-braid; the alpaca facing will throw off the dust, and from it mud can easily be brushed, whereas a muslin facing can never be nicely cleaned.

For our next step, making the over-dress out of the old cashmere, our supposed home dressmaker must be guided, as regards style, in a great measure by the amount of material she possesses, and the good condition of it. Having chosen the style of tablier, lay the pattern down on the material, and cut it out of the best parts. Some piecing will, no doubt, be necessary; but a little judgment and care will make this a success.

Now for the trimming. Nothing so well uses up bits of old material as the fashionable side plaitings, now so much in use. Cut these always straight, and no matter how many joins, they will not show, if you are careful in laying and basting your plaits. Make them either a quarter or half an inch deep. Baste carefully, having previously hemmed them, and allow three times fullness; then iron on the wrong side. Catch the plait to a narrow black braid upon the under side, each plait so as not to show the stitches on the right side. Now your trimming is ready for disposing of; and here taste and the quantity must determine how and where it is to be put. If the old basque or Polonaise is much worn, freshen it up by adding a vest-like piece (made of some of the silks) down the fronts, and folds neatly, and tastefully arrange down the back seam, continuing below the waist, and ending in a postilion over the basque. The sleeves may be of silk entirely, with a cuff of cashmere. In these days, when all fashionable dresses are made of two materials, it is not so difficult a matter as it at first seems to be, to make a new costume out of an old one. Contrivance and ingenuity will do a great deal, if to these are added industry and determination to succeed.

The Corset Bodice. – The richest costumes for out-door wear are now made with the corset bodice, which has six seams in the back, every seam extending the entire length of the bodice, and furnished with bones to the end of the basque. These bones are very light and supple, in order that they may taper in at the waist and expand over the hips. This bodice gives the elongated waist, which is now the fashion, and displays a good figure to advantage; the danger, however, is, that it will bring about a return to tight lacing, and compression of the waist, so injurious to health. The back of this new bodice is quite as long as that of a basque bodice; but as it has none of the fullness given to basques below the waist, two or three long-looped bows, made of the same material as the dress, are placed there. A jabot of lace is carried down the front, covering the buttons, and, by concealing all means of fastening, causes the bodice to appear as though moulded to the figure.

Peterson's Magazine, April 1876

No. 345. – Lady's Suit. – The great novelty just now in suits is illustrated in the above overdress. It is worn by both young and middle-aged ladies, and is usually intended for a costume of two shades of color. It is appropriate for either house or street wear, and will be much appreciated in freshening or making over the last season's dress. It will be worn in lace, also thin wash materials over colored silk, and is the preferred style for making the new damask goods, débege, pongee, etc. No. of Overdress, 4546; pattern, with cloth model, $1.00. No. of Skirt, 4401; pattern, with cloth model, 50 cents.

...

There is no longer any exaggeration of style or cut adopted by either the best *modistes* or their customers; striking colors in juxtaposition and caricatures of shape and trimming are things of the past. Skirts, though still worn without any drapery at the front and sides, no longer cling so closely to the figure as to render movement on the part of the wearer awkward and ungraceful. They are gored to the waist, and the fulness thrown to the back; but instead of being tied back in one place, a gored breadth is placed underneath at each side; these are laced together more or less closely, in the manner used to keep *crinolettes* and *tournures* in place, or casings and draw-strings are used for holding the fulness of the back breadths in the proper shape for forming the fan or peacock tail effect. These methods are found more convenient and infinitely more elegant than the old way of tying back in one place, which produced a very sudden and ungainly effect.

The draperies at the back are more flowing, standing farther from the figure in a graceful slope from the waist, and the *tournures* decidedly more *bouffantes*, though by no means exaggerated or sudden in outline. The leading Parisian *modistes* are highly recommending a new *tournure*, made of cane-seating; it is very light, though strong, and produces exactly the desired effect.

The trains are of medium length, or very long, according to the class of *toilette*; some are sloped gradually from the length of the sides; others, the extra length is left on, forming a decided train, the corner being left square or cut round, according to taste. The really short dress – that is, clearing the ground all round – has totally disappeared from the horizon of Fashion; but there is a probability that it will be revived for the autumn traveling and winter walking dresses. Let us hope so, at least.

Polonaise No. 4216, with a basque front, is easily fitted to the figure, and a suitable pattern for wash material.

...

No. 4216
Ladies' Polonaise. All sizes. Pattern,
with cloth model, 50c.

...

4216   4216

HOME DRESSES.

Fashion articles, as a rule, deal almost entirely with expensive goods – silks, laces, and velvets. Feeling sure that amongst our numerous readers there are many who prefer to know how ordinary dresses are made, we propose right here to give some hints on washing-dresses, by which is meant, cambric, percale, lawn, and print, all of which are actually very *fashionable* at present. All washing-dresses should be made up simply, have few seams cut on the cross, and the draping managed with tapes and drawing-strings, so that they are easily straightened and present no difficulty to the laundry-maid. Dark prune will be a favorite color for print dresses; the skirt plain, and the polonaise plaid prune and white. Stripes, plaids, and even dashes of color are preferred to figures and plain grounds; but stripes of two widths, cut on the cross to produce variety, find the greatest favor. The manner of arrangement is thus: Jacket, sleeve, tablier, bands, and binding are bias or cut on the cross, while the basque-bodice, skirt, and flounces are straight. The basque has no lining, and fits the hips smoothly and yet not tightly, so that the bodice may be worn with or without a belt, as preferred. The skirts are often draped at the back with three lengthwise tapes hanging from the belt, and these are buttoned to the skirt at intervals, two or more button-holes being made to each tape; the belt of both upper and lower skirts is now made quite large, and tape drawing-strings are run in the top to make them the size the wearer prefers; this is the best plan for washing-costumes. Navy-blue will still be worn, likewise plaided ginghams, mixtures of blue and gray, but most frequently with two different patterns in each costume; the polonaise being plaid, and the skirt of the predominant color of the plaid, or else with dashes, waves, or curves, imparting a mottled effect.

...

A good model of trimming washing-dresses is as follows: Two or three rows of fine side-plaiting round the skirt; one row round the overskirt and basque, headed by a bias fold stitched on. Skirts of wash-dresses are cut quite plain in front and at the sides.

No. 346. – Lady's Costume. – We need only to illustrate the accompanying beautiful design, and our friends will readily see its desirable features. It promises to find great favor this season in both silk and camels'-hair suiting. The waist may be used open in the back, or in front, as preferred. It is one of the latest designs, and may be selected for any style of figure. The overskirt is entirely new and will do justice to any kind of goods. The entire effect is one of grace and neatness. It is especially appropriate and convenient for wash-goods, as the shirr strings can be so arranged as to let out, leaving it a plain flat skirt for laundrying, and in a moment of time can be readjusted. For grenadine it is the great favorite, and is also appropriate for silk, débege, etc. No. of Basque, 4544; pattern, with cloth model, 50 cents. No. of Overskirt, 4555; pattern, with cloth model, 75 cents.

...

FASHIONS FOR ELDERLY LADIES.

While it is certainly true that dress has become elaborate, and trimmings endless, it is also a fact that those who prefer simplicity and quietness in attire can find in the present fashions, models displaying these characteristics; and need we add, their greatest charm lies in this very simplicity?

The polonaise, always a favorite garment with middle-aged and elderly ladies, is destined to obtain new triumphs, have been perfected to the last degree, and, in form, plain enough to suit the most uncompromising advocate for the severely simple in dress. While there are several designs, and the shapes are certainly most varied, the prevailing idea appears to be to do away with the elaborate and bouffant drapery at the back, and to make them straight and simply shaped garments.

As some figures do not look well, and can not be perfectly fitted, with the plain fronts cut whole, the basque front pattern 4216 is chosen. [*See illustration above*] Although this pattern is represented in the illustration as having the skirt caught up quite high at the centre of the back, it may with good effect be allowed to fall quite plain at this portion. In this number of the World of Fashion, on the pages showing illustrations in reduced size, are several different designs for polonaise, from which selections can be made to suit any style of figure and for making up any material.

No. 344. – Young Lady's Costume. – We can not give a more popular or desirable design for a young lady's costume than the illustration. It is intended for either house or street wear, and will become the slight as well as the stout figure. It is buttoned in the back, and has a French gabrielle front, with extra side-fronts, the seams of which extend to the shoulder, giving it a new and graceful effect than can not be secured by the old style of darts. It may be buttoned in front if preferred and seamed up the back. It is suitable in any material. No. of Polonaise, 4540; pattern with cloth model, $1.00. No. of Skirt, 4401; pattern with cloth model, 50 cents.

...

Trimmings. – The fashionable fringe is very elaborate and of exceeding richness; the netted headings are deep and very finely wrought. Tassel, marabout, sewing-silk, and crimped braid are found forming fringes, either separately or in combination. Prices range from 50 cents to $20 a yard. Moss ruching, made of crimped braid, is a stylish and rich heading for fringe or lace, and costs from $2 to $4 a yard. Basket-woven braid continues to be fashionably used from narrow to very wide; those with gold or silver interwoven cost as high as $4 a yard. Titan braids in silk, mohair, and worsted, from half an inch to several inches wide, in solid colors or plaided diagonally, while others have a design in relief of the same color as the braid; the last named is exceedingly pretty, and the newest in style.

In trimmings, the most charming novelty is of English manufacture, known as the new lace ribbon and ribbon lace – both in silk, and of various widths, from one to several inches. These are made in all the new and beautiful shades of blue, pink, brown, and cream-color. The ribbon is made to match the lace in color, width, and design; they will be very fashionable during the late spring and summer season as trimmings on dresses, bonnets, fichus, caps, and pockets, being equally suitable, and making a charming finish for all. It is deeper in tint than écru, and mixes charmingly with either very pale or very dark colors.

← No. 4542. – Lady's Breakfast Sack. – The fashion now of wearing a loose sack of white with different skirts for the morning toilet, makes it quite necessary for every lady to have a large number of them prettily trimmed. The style given here is the very best fitting one now in use. The new shape of the side form in the front gives it an easy and graceful effect that could not be gained by any other shape. It is also very desirable for cambric suits. Requires of 27 inches material 3 yards. Pattern, with cloth model, 50 cents.

Silk Mits. – Our readers will doubtless be surprised and amused at the same time, to hear of the "revival" of the silk mits or mittens, worn so long ago, many of our *élégantes* having resumed the fashion. Some of them we see in black silk, others again in cream-color, and the beauty of a pretty arm loses nothing by being seen through the charming open-work displayed on these mits, which are worn with elbow-sleeves and for demi-toilet.

Belts. – A novelty that will be largely adopted with summer dresses is the lace belt. This consists of a strip of insertion edged with narrow lace laid over silk, like the dress or in contrast with it, and fastened on the left side by a knot and long loops of ribbon and two flowing ends. Made of Italian lace, over cream, rose, cardinal-red, or pale-blue silk,

4549

4549

this belt is sold for $2. Ladies can make for themselves similar belts to match their écru collarettes, fichus, etc., that now brighten all dark toilets. Leather belts, with several silver links, will also be fashionable the coming season.

No. 4549. – Lady's Overskirt. – This style of overskirt is intended for different materials. It is entirely new, and very stylish, each side is a design in itself and quite unlike each other, though cut the same, the difference being made by the draping. It will be appreciated because it does not cut up the goods as many of the other styles. Requires of twenty seven inches wide material, four and one half yards. Pattern, with cloth model, 50 cents.

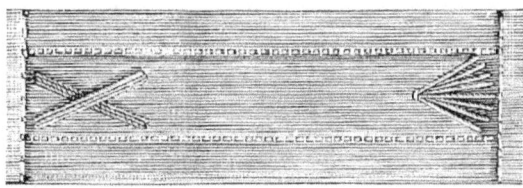

No. 6. – Mode of putting in Whalebone.

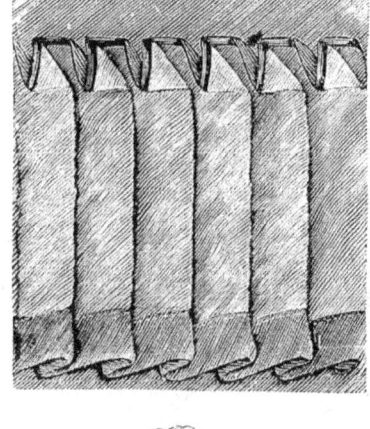

No. 9. – Trimming for Dress-Skirt.

No. 13. – Trimming for Dress-Skirt.

World of Fashion, May 1876

Above is an evening-costume of white tarletane. It is trimmed with plaintings [*sic*] and puffs. The under-skirt is demi-train, and has, first a plaited flounce, six inches deep, with the heading; then a puff four inches wide; above that another plaited flounce, five inches deep; another puff. The tablier is made long, and gathered up the entire front, forming a puff lengthwise. The edge is trimmed with a plaiting. At the back it is gathered quite full to the waist; and the ends are also trimmed with the plaiting, so disposed to fall, as seen in the design. The bodice is low, and trimmed with a puffing around the neck. Bows of ribbon or flowers may be arranged in the cascade at the back. The cost of such a dress would be about twelve dollars, without the ribbon or flowers.

Next is a handsome dress of black silk net or grenadine barrage. It has but one skirt, which is trimmed with puffing and ruching of the material. The tablier is simulated upon the front of the skirt, formed of folds of the material, and ruches. It has two diagonal bands of silk crossing the front, and finishing at the sides and back in loops forming large bows. Low-necked cuirass waist, trimmed to correspond. The cost of such a dress in black silk net, would be around sixty dollars; in black grenadine, twenty-five or thirty dollars, if made at home and worn over a half-worn black silk under-skirt. All black, thin goods should be made over silk slips.

CUTTING OUT YOUR OWN DRESSES.
By Emily H. May

It is a fact that some persons are more difficult to fit than others. This difficulty of fitting figures would not exist if dressmakers had only as excellent a system of measurement as tailors have. The diagrams above will assist our readers to understand the mode to be pursued: –

Take a good tape-yard measure with the figures plainly marked upon it. The first measurement to be taken, as will be seen from diagram No. 1, is the width of the chest. This measurement is a very important one, and is taken round the body under the arms. Make a note of the number of inches. The second is the size of the waist, of which also make a note. Proceed in the same way with No. 3, which will give the width of the fronts; No. 4, the size of the neck; No. 7, the length of the fronts; No. 8, the length of the same measured from the top of the shoulder; No. 10, which will afford the length of the sides, under the arms, completes the measurement of the front of the body. The sleeves must then be considered, and No. 11 gives the length; No. 13 the width round the elbow, and No. 14 that round the wrist. The only remaining measurement for the front portion is the length of the skirt, which is a very important one. The "set" of a skirt often proclaims a homemade dress in its failure of grace; but if the measurement of length be carefully taken, and our instructions carefully followed, there can be little doubt of success.

Having carefully taken down all these measurements, and numbered them as in diagram No. 1, we next turn to the measurements for the back, which will be found in diagram No. 2.

No. 1 gives the continuation of the important

DIAGRAM No. 1.   DIAGRAM No. 2.

measurement indicated by the same number on the first diagram. No. 5 gives the width of half the back. (It has been found that bodices sit much better with a seam up the back, and consequently they are almost universally made with a seam now, thus allowing the back to be cut to the figure, as it could not be in the absence of a seam. This method also makes it easier to fit the body. No. 6 gives the length of the back; No. 9 the measurement from the lower part of the shoulder to the waist. We now come to the skirt measurements, which, as we said above, are all-important. No. 15 gives the length at the back, and No. 16 the length at the side.

We will now suppose that you have all the measurements noted down, and that you have made yourself mistress of the details. If they seem complicated at first, a little study of the diagram and various parts of any tissue-paper bodice you have before you, will soon render them simple.

And now to use all these numbers, and to put in practice all this theory. (You must make, or get a paper pattern of a bodice to assist you in obtaining the outlines.) Take a piece of calico, which shall last you as a pattern as long as your refrain from growing stouter, or guard yourself from becoming thinner.

Lay this calico on a rather large table. With the selvage of the calico lying toward you, take the yard-measure in your hand, look at your note of the number of inches opposite No. 7 on your notes, and measure off a corresponding number of inches down the selvage of the calico, beginning your measurement three inches from the end, to allow for the extra height of the shoulder. Mark off this length with a pencil, and proceed to get measurement No. 8, studying the diagram that you may judge of the direction in which this line runs. Mark this measurement also with a pencil. Then get No. 9, which you will mark in the same way. No. 3 must now be measured off and then marked, and after having done this, you may begin to cut out. Laying your paper front on the calico, draw a line from the upper part of No. 8 to the upper part of No. 9, continuing it an inch and a half beyond it in the same direction. Cut the calico over this line. This gives you the shoulder. Now cut the calico *straight down* from the end of the shoulder. Proceed to cut the arm-hole, which is done by drawing a curved line from the end of the shoulder to No. 3, and thence to the top of No. 10, a measurement which must be got by measuring from the waist-line of the calico – the number of inches marked on your notes after No. 10. The paper pattern will help you to get the outline of the arm-hole, but you must, in addition, be carful [sic] to observe your own measurement. Having cut away the calico strait [sic] at the waist, you have now the front completed, with the exception of the plaits to fit it to the figure, and these must be arranged on the person, taking care not to make them too high. Now proceed to get the back. Line No. 6 on diagram 2 is the first to be measured. It gives the length, and if you have a seam down the back, this line comes close to the selvage. Mark it off, and then get measurement No. 9, after which you cut the shoulder in the same way as you did for the front, laying the paper pattern on the calico. Next measure No. 5, cut the arm-hole round to it by your paper pattern. Cut the calico away straight at the waist, and you have the half of the back.

Now take this back and the front, pin or lightly sew them together under the arm-holes and on the shoulders. Then put them on, and arrange the plaits, pin tighter under the arm till they fit quite closely, and cut away at the neck. If you are very careful in performing this part of the operation, you will find yourself supplied with an excellent pattern for your dresses.

It is well to have a good paper pattern of a sleeve, but you must be careful in cutting your own pattern to observe your private measurements of length and width, only using the paper model as a guide to the outline. With an accurate measurement of your own you will find that you can readily use any paper model, however new and original, by simply laying the latter over your own pattern and taking care only to modify, not alter, the details of the former.

Peterson's Magazine, May 1876

LADIES' BREAKFAST COSTUME.

The charming dress illustrated by the engraving is in wrapper style and is made of foulard cambric. It has box-plaits at the front and back of its waist-portion, and as they terminate just below the waist-line a ribbon passes about the waist to regulate the fullness. It also has an under-arm gore, which is shaped to fit the figure and adds fullness enough to the skirt to allow the train to fall flatly on the floor. The bottom is decorated with rows of braid of a shade or two lighter than the goods, or of the same tint as the ribbon at the waist and throat. The latter is surrounded by a Bryon collar, edged with braid and turned down over the ribbon cravat just mentioned. The front closes with button holes and buttons. The sleeve is wide and short, and is gathered at the bottom, where a cuff is added to lengthen it and then turned up far enough to conceal the seam. Collar and cuffs of linen, together with a jaunty little cap, complete the toilet. The pattern by which the wrapper was cut is No 4250, price 40 cents. It is in 13 sizes for ladies from 23 to 46 inches, bust measure, and to make a garment like it for a lady of medium size, 11 1/2 yards of goods, 27 inches wide, will be required.

LADIES' PRINCESS POLONAISE.

No. 4369. – The stylish garment represented by these engravings is made of cashmere, and on account of its peculiar drapery requires no decoration except the sashes which are part of the pattern. The latter is in 13 sizes for ladies from 23 to 46 inches, bust measure; and costs 35 cents. To make this garment for a lady of medium size, 9 3/8 yards of goods, 27 inches wide, will be required.

...

Damask silks, introduced last year, will be much used for overdresses; while light taffeta silks are very fashionable for spring suits. Gros-grain silks are nearly in all solid colors, and the new brands have a particularly rich and lustrous finish. In cheaper grades of silks, checks and fine hair-line stripes are equally in favor.

4369   4369

4375   4375
Back View.   Front View.

LADIES' SIDE-PLAITED BLOUSE.

No. 4375. – Garments of this description are very stylish to wear with skirts of another material, and may be decorated to suit the taste. The pattern is in 13 sizes for ladies from 23 to 46 inches, bust measure; and costs 25 cents. To make the garment for a lady of medium size, 4 yards of goods, 27 inches wide, will be required. Linen, percale, merino, print or any suit goods are appropriate for such a waist.

Combination suits have plaid or striped overdresses, with plain under-skirt and trimming, or a contrary arrangement. ...

Speaking of trimmings, many fabrics will be self-trimmed, in plaitings, shirrings, puffings, etc. Others – the lawns and organdies mentioned – have a border of trimmings upon the goods. Ecru and cashmere lace will be largely used upon grenadines, tissues and like fabrics. For black silks, handsome grenadines, etc., fringes and elegant passementeries will take the lead. Fringes from an eighth to a quarter of a yard, and even more, in depth, are composed of silk arranged in fanciful balls, pendants and tassels, and sometimes mingled with crimped tape in tassels or plain strips. Jets are no longer purchased, though those who have them will probably continue to wear them for some time to come. Wool fringe and self-trimming are alike suitable for evening wear, together with cashmere, French and Spanish laces.

4356

4356

LADIES' WRAP OVER-SKIRT.

No. 4356. – In making the garment represented, for a lady of medium size, 5 1/4 yards of goods, 27 inches wide, will be required. The pattern is in 9 sizes for ladies from 20 to 36 inches, waist measure; and its price is 35 cents. Cambric is the material represented, and the trimmings are made of chambrey of a corresponding shade, similar material being use for the bows.

Arthur's Illustrated Home Magazine, May 1876

Fig. VI. – Dress for the Country, of Toile d'Alsace. – This material is of cotton, but has a feeling of a silk finish; it is of blue and white plaid, with delicate lines of pink intermixed. The over-skirt is finished with a bias band, edged with a row of white embroidery. The basque and sleeves correspond.

...

Trimmings for Home-Made Dresses. – In our April issue we gave a few directions out to make dresses at home. We now add some remarks on the subject of trimmings.

There is this advantage in making one's dresses; each lady is enabled to exercise her own taste and ingenuity in getting up a costume which can be fashionable, and yet have an individuality about it. Dresses bought ready made, and even those made by the dress-maker, unless she is a first-rate "artiste," are apt to be of distressing similarity.

A woman of taste and cultivation, ought to have some idea of the fitness of things, and if possessed of leisure, although not of a well-lined purse, she may arrange and make toilets, more ladylike and artistic than ever could emanate from the hands of a second-class modeste. Of course, when dressmaking is undertaken at home, it involves considerable trouble at first, and a good deal of heavy thinking; but after two or three trials, the formidable intricacies become easy possibilities, and the occupation is both pleasant and agreeable; and, as a matter of economy, the cost of having a dress made, out of the house, is oftentimes greater than the cost of the material.

But let us proceed to the practical part of our lesson. In April we gave some hints for renovating and remodeling an old black silk; this month we propose to give a few directions about cutting out and putting on trimmings. If bias flounces are desired, the first point is to get them cut evenly and exactly on the bias. To do this, a beginner had better cut a long strip of newspaper the exact width of the flounce or band to be cut; then fold over the material cornerwise, so as to obtain a perfect bias. Lay the paper upon the bias so obtained; pin it securely, and then cut with confidence. Adopt the same plan with narrower frills, or you will be apt to waist the material; and if your frills or flounces are not cut evenly and due bias, they will never set well.

With bias fold, even greater care must be taken, and each fold must be lined with crinoline, also carefully cut on the bias, and pasted. In lining bias folds, hold the lining next the hand in sewing, and be careful not to stretch the edges. In sewing on the skirt, put a white basting-thread where the fold is to be sewn, so that it may be put upon the skirt evenly, and at equal distances, when several are arranged.

Flounces should lap over each other about an inch. Now that we are approaching the season for wash-goods, plaiting must be abandoned, and ruffles substituted; and for washing materials, these must always be cut straight. For simply gathered flounces, as full again will be enough; if to be goffered, three times fullness must be allowed.

For percales, calicoes, and cheviot shirting, bias-bands, stitched down by the sewing machine, look very well, either as the whole trimming, or made narrow, to head a flounce. These should always be stretched before sewing on, or else, when washed, will be apt to iron in wrinkles, caused by the extra fullness. A little care, and neat work, add greatly to the finish of a dress.

...

BLACK-SILK SLEEVELESS JACKET.

We give, first, this month, the back and front of an afternoon toilet. It is of two materials, a plain self-colored silk, or alpaca, for the under-skirt, and a delicate checked material for the over-dress. The under-skirt is ornamented on the front with three small ruffles, cut on the bias, bound and gathered; the back widths are trimmed with deep plaiting, ten inches deep. The tunic is cut square at the sides, trimmed with four rows of worsted braid, or piping of silk. The edge of the tunic is bordered with a long silk tasseled fringe. The drapery at the back is lined with the plain material of the under-skirt, and trimmed with the braid also. The basque, (cuirass) with five seams in the back, the front perfectly plain. Small collar and sleeves of the same material as the under-skirt. Body sash, tied low below the waist, with two long loops and one end, completes this costume. Buttons are all very small. Ten yards of twenty-seven inch material for the over-dress; ten to twelve yards of silk or alpaca for the skirt. This would be a good design for percale: for the under-skirt, navy-blue, or brown, solid colors, and any of the pretty checked Cheviots, for the over-skirt. This combination would make a charming country costume.

To Transfer Patterns. – For those of our readers who desire to transfer patterns for embroidery or braiding, we give a few simple directions. First trace the pattern upon a sheet of white paper – this tracing to be done by placing the design to the window, and following it with a pencil, or place a piece of tracing paper on a sheet of white paper, then the design, now with a stencil, or a knitting-needle, if nothing better is to be had; follow the design, bearing firmly, but not heard enough to mutilate the design. After it has been carefully gone over, raise the design and the tracing paper, and the pattern will be clearly traced upon the sheet of paper beneath. Now prick this pattern quite closely with pin-pricks clear through, then lay it upon the article desired to be stamped, and with a stamping pad, rubbed with stamping powder, rub hard, and the pattern will be clearly stamped upon the material. For those who cannot supply themselves with the stamping-powder and pad, use indigo, and make a pad by rolling some pieces of flannel into a hard pad.

The dress with the waist and skirt cut in one, known under the various titles of Polonaise, Princess, and Gabrielle, is very popular. But the cuirass waist divides the public favor. Still, the Princess is just now the rage in Paris. The dress is variously trimmed and draped, and assumes as many forms as the old tunic skirt. It is most becoming to a fine figure.

Peterson's Magazine, June 1876

BACK AND FRONT OF TUNIC.

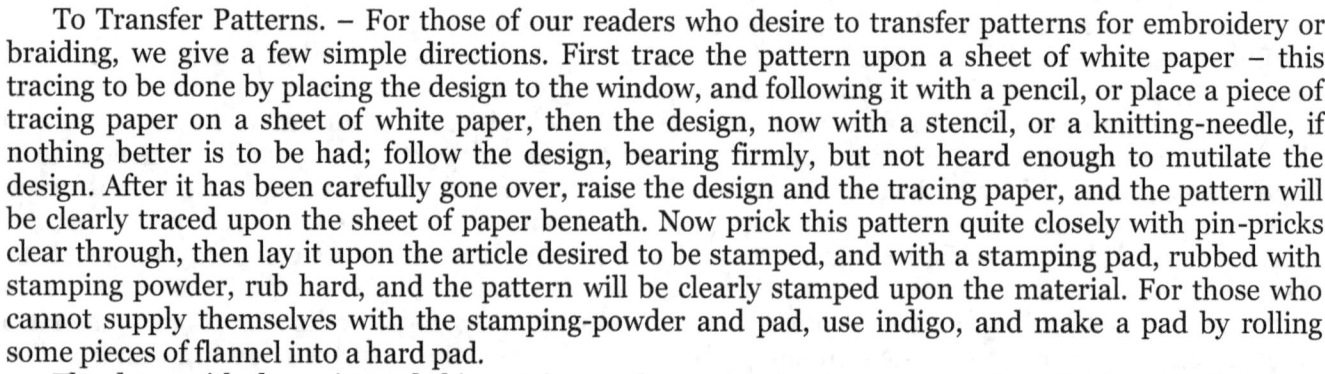

Basques are again made with postilion plaits at the back; in fact, Worth has never abandoned them.

Narrow fringe is again used on bias folds of dresses, and buttons are put on silk and other dresses of rich material.

It is now quite impossible to describe dresses with exactitude; the skirts are draped so mysteriously, the arrangement of trimmings is usually one-sided, and the fastenings are so cunningly contrived, that, after studying any particular toilet for even a quarter of an hour, the task of writing down how it is all made remains hopeless. The style of dress known as the Princess is universally adopted, and skirts are cut so to fit the figure about the hips, that much of the tying back erewhile adopted is now found to be useless.

CORSAGE A BASQUE.
By Emily H. May.

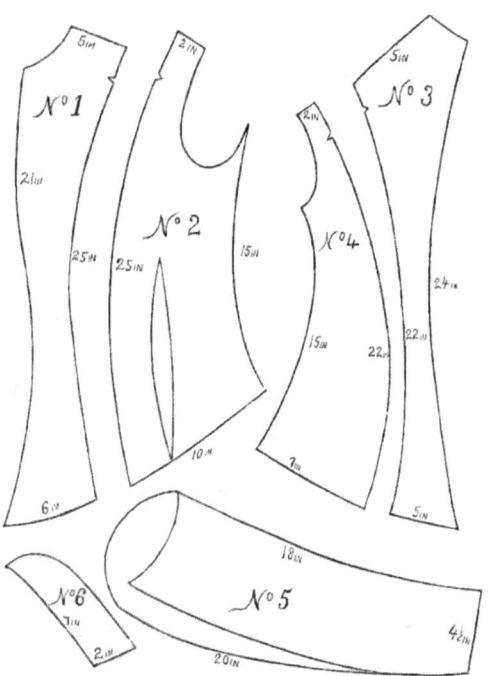

We give, this month, a pattern for a new and fashionable corsage, called a Corsage a Basque; and we add, on the next page, a diagram, by aid of which to cut it out.

In former numbers we have given directions how to enlarge these patterns. It is best to cut them out, full size, in paper, and fit them on, before proceeding to cut into the stuff. A little attention, in this way, will enable every lady to be her own dress-maker.

No. 1. Half of Front.
No. 2. Half of Side of Front.
No. 3. Half of Back.
No. 4. Half of Side of Back.
No. 5. Sleeve.
No. 6. Collar.

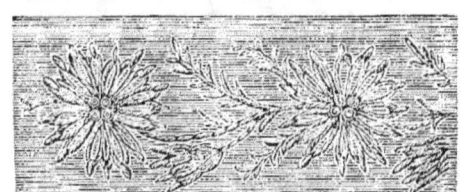

BORDERS IN RUSSIAN EMBROIDERY.
By Mrs. Jane Weaver.

Dresses trimmed with embroidery are so fashionable, that we give here two borders suitable for pique or washing dresses, in designs that are quickly worked. The first is worked in one shade of color only, the stitches used are a long stitch, as short back stitch, and a feather-stitch; the second requires a braid in addition. These borders are very pretty.

Peterson's Magazine, July 1876

We give, first, this month, a pretty design for making-up in calico. This is one of those pin stripes in two shades of brown, gray, or blue. The under-skirt is trimmed with two bias bands of the calico, stitched down with a narrow strip, lengthwise, of the material, for a heading, top and bottom, of the bias band. These bands are three or four inches wide, as may be preferred. The over-skirt is cut precisely like the under one, and finished on the edge with a bias band, one and a half inches wide, stitched by the machine. Loop at the sides and back. This band is of a solid-colored calico, or (cambric it is called when in a solid color) to correspond with the rest of the dress. The close-fitting basque has one narrow bias band, one inch wide, directly down the back seam; one the same width finishes the edge; and a second one is placed on both sides of centre of the back, and is continued around the basque, and up the fronts, forming a trimming there to correspond with the back. Coat-sleeves, with three bias bands at the wrist, edged with a bias ruffle to fall over the hand. A narrow standing-collar is added at the neck. This design is particularly fitted for wash goods, as it is easily ironed. Two yards of the solid-colored calico will trim this dress, but it will look very nicely with all the trimming like that upon the under-skirt, if the plain calico cannot be had to match. Even a calico dress can be made to look stylish; and one made after this model cannot fail to be so.

CERRISE BODICE FOR A MISS OF SIXTEEN.
By Emily H. May.

We give, this month, a charming new-style bodice, called the "Cerisse," for a young of sixteen, or thereabouts. We also give a diagram by which to cut it out.

No. 1. Half of Front.
No. 2. Half of Back.
No. 3. Half of Side of Back.
No. 4. Sleeve.
No. 5. Cuff.

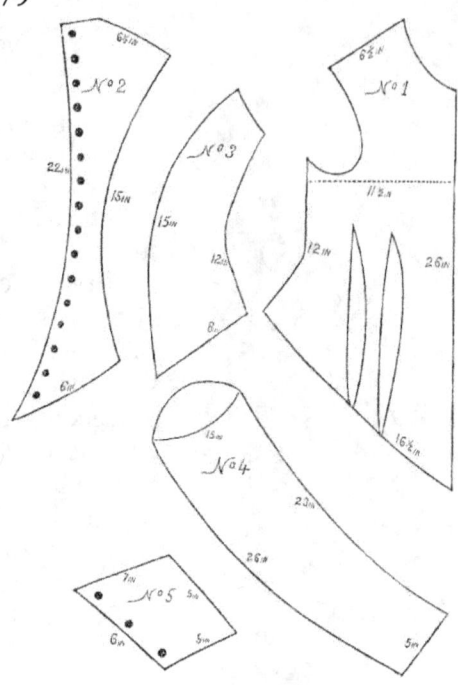

Some of the new summer silks have the back cut in the Polonaise style, with an elongated waist and train; and the front, on the contrary, is a bodice with a basque. The front of the skirt is, of course, separated from the bodice.

Batiste dresses are often made quite plain and round, and looped up at the back with wide bows and sash-ends of ribbon, which harmonizes with the color of the dress.

Jackets, half-tight fitting and cuirass waist, are both popular for batiste and chintz dresses. Worth, who has never quite abandoned the postillion basque, is making more than usual now.

Fig. VI. – Morning Costume of Checked Bege. – The skirt is bordered with a gathered flounce, headed with two cross-bands placed at a short distance one above the other. Tunic arranged entablier, round in front, and having the effect of being tied at the back, and falling on the skirt in two wide pointed ends. A ribbon bow is placed at the commencement of these two scarf draperies. Cuirass bodice, with pointed back. Pocket on the left side, with casings inside, through which elastic is run. The basque, sleeves, and tunic, are all trimmed with a cross-band of bege.

Peterson's Magazine, August 1876

We give, first, a morning costume of prune cambric, trimmed with striped prune and white cambric; but any solid or fine-checked or striped chintz, bordered with a wider stripe or check to correspond in color, will do well for this design. The skirt is cut only three and a quarter yards wide, and slightly trained at the back; but for every-day or country wear, we would prefer the skirt short enough for walking, without the necessity of holding up. The skirt is trimmed with a gathered flounce six or seven inches deep, edged with a cross-band of the striped chintz; this is headed with two narrower cross-bands of the same, a puff of the plain, and a third cross-band of the stripe. The tunic is cut with an apron front, gathered at the sides, and the back consists of two breadths, pointed at the bottom; these breadths, not over half a yard wide, open up the back seam a third of a yard, and the rest gathered into a pouf, under which a bow and ends is placed, made of the striped material. The edge of the tunic is bordered with a cross-band to match the bottom of the skirt. On the left side is placed one of the large plaited pockets, now seen on all costumes. The cuirass-waist is trimmed to match. The closely-fitted coat-sleeve has a triple cuff, likewise edged with the striped band, cut on the cross. Ten yards of plain, and four yards of striped chintz will be required.

Next is a pretty design for a muslin apron, to be worn over a nice house-dress when serving the tea, for protection, and at the same time a pretty addition to the home toilet. The pattern can easily be cut from the design. Make of Swiss muslin, and trim with insertion and ruffles, edged with imitation Valenciennes lace. The pockets are formed of double box-plaits, edged with a narrow frill. The same edges the pointed bodice, and the sash ends. ➜

The clinging fashion of drapery, we are glad to see, begins to show signs of going out of fashion. This style has always been very inconvenient. It necessitates first an exquisite figure, and then a first-rate dress-maker, for is displays every curve, and when badly cut, these dresses are frightful; then there is so little scope for variety. ...

Long, slender waists, like those of Louis XVII. reign, are decidedly the fashion of the day. Bodices are lined at the back, and all the details of make are contrived in order to compress the wearer as much as possible.

One of the newest dresses just come from Worth is of the "Incroyable" style. It is a dress with a small "collet de conspirateur," a long-waisted bodice, with a close-fitting skirt, and a narrow train, that can be looped up and made demi-long at pleasure. The incroyable is generally made of striped silk. The collet de conspirateur is often composed of several capes; at other times there is one cape, and that is continued in front as a long fichu.

We give the back and front of a bodice, which may be made of two shades of silk, or of silk and cashmere. The revers, collar, and side pieces of the back are of cashmere. The front of the basque, which is pointed, is edged with a crimped fringe. The back has five seams, which is new, and seems likely to become the popular cut. Thee loops and ends are of silk, also the cuffs. This design will be most useful in renovating a half-worn dress.

Some few gay plaid or Scotch tartan dresses have made their appearance, but they are not much in favor; stripes are much more popular. The new evening silks are all of pale, soft colors. As we have just said, stripes preponderate over plain materials and checks, and the habit or coat made of brocade, China silk, damask, lampas, Sicilienne, or crepe de Chine is the favorite over-dress; and it always differs in materials from the skirt. The waist of this coat or habit is long; the sleeves are narrow; there is a turned-down collar. The front has pockets, and there is a tail at the back; and over the coat there is a sash as wide as a baby would wear, forming plaits in front, and being tied at the back. Sometimes there is a jabot in front of the coat, and sometimes a row of old-fashioned buttons. This habit is at times fastened with a straight row of buttons, while others open over a waistcoat embroidered all over in the style of coats worn at the court of Versailles, the foundation being a dull, dusky shade, and the embroidery or brocade showing the bright, brilliant shades; a jabot invariably accompanies the waistcoat. The sash about the coat is always of a bright contrasting color. This style is called the "Revolution Costume," and the head-gear accompanying it is generally a hat with the brim turned up on one side, and a feather escaping from a large bow on the same side, then twisting around the crown.

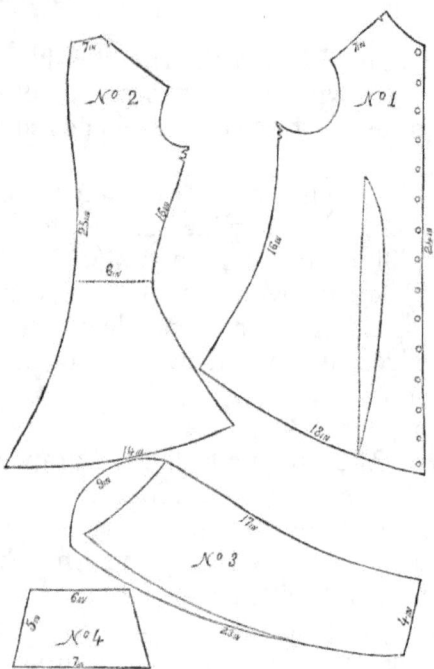

COSTUME OF CHINTZ.
By Emily H. May.

We give, this month, a very stylish, yet economical, costume, which will be very suitable for vistors [sic] to the country, or for a walking-dress any-where. We annex a diagram for the costume.

No. 1. Half of Front.
No. 2. Half of Back.
No. 3. Sleeve.
No. 4. Pocket.

TRIMMING FOR DRESSES.
By Mrs. Jane Weaver.

This trimming is suitable for cashmeres, prints, and summer materials, and would be pretty for trimming print dresses for children. Either the fashionable mixed braid or plaid material may be laid on and stitched down.

The trimming is of two shades of the material of the dress. The lower frill is gathered and finished at the edge with a stitched band of the lighter shade. The upper part is plaited and finished at the heading with a stitched band of the lighter shade, and at the lower edge with two rows of stitching.

Peterson's Magazine, September 1876

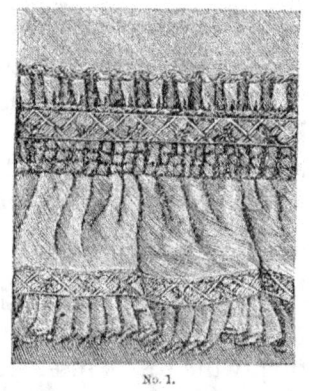

No. 1.

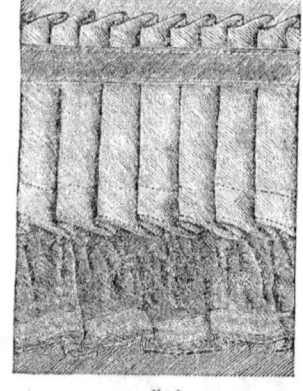

No. 2.

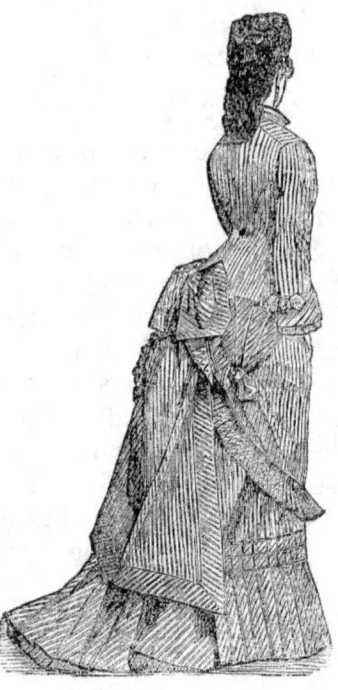

We give, this month, a walking-costume for a young lady, of a very light-gray camel's-hair material, striped with dark-blue in pin stripes. The skirt is bordered in front with a deep bias plaiting, sewn on with a double heading, and two rows of stitching. At the back there is a deep gathered flounce. Princess tunic, buttoned the entire length of the front, and bordered with a plaiting cut on the bias, and three inches deep; it is looped up at the back, under a large bow of the material, or silk, if preferred, edged with a plain bias band. From beneath this bow falls a wide breadth of the material, reaching almost to the edge of the skirt; this is similarly trimmed with a plain bias band. Pointed pocket, formed of plaits, and placed far back, with a bow at the point. Close coat-sleeves, open at the back seam for three inches, forming a cuff, which terminates also with a small bow of the material. This design will look well in any of the fine striped mohair or woolen materials now so much worn, and which may be bought from twenty-five cents up to one dollar per yard. Eighteen yards will be required.

A new fashion that promises to create a furor is to trim dresses from the throat to the hem of the skirt, together with the sleeves, pockets, revers, etc., with very small, round, flat metal buttons; these are set on in a series of four, five, or six rows. When they are selected of gilt or silver, they make the wearer look quite Oriental, and everything Oriental is now the rage.

POCKETS FOR DRESSES.

We also give two of the newest of the many styles of pockets. The first hangs straight, by a steel chain, or a cord from the side. The second has a large rosette at the top, made of the material of the dress, and is trimmed with ribbon bows, and is put on the skirt of the dress rather low down and far back, in a slanting direction.

For fall wear, many of the Polonaise have one small cape, or two or three capes, one smaller than the other, the largest of which does not reach so low as the waist. This makes a pretty finish to a dress for a tall, thin person. If the dress is made with a basque, rather than with a Polonaise, the basque is long and close-fitting, and usually finished at the bottom with a cord only.
Peterson's Magazine, October 1876

No. 352. – Lady's Evening Costume. – This graceful design is an exponent of the fashionable, close-fitting dress, the drapery being scant. The requisite fullness at the back portion, is supplied by the immense double box-pleat, which gives a graceful effect. The polonaise is a highly desirable style for a combination costume, and suggests numberless varieties of material, which may serve to illustrate its beauty of form and general acceptability, while both slender and stout figures may venture upon its proportions with equal security. The absence of trimming upon the skirt, indicates the use of rich material; but, if preferred, a skirt trimming may be added. No. of Polonaise 4575; pattern, with cloth model, $1.00. No. of Skirt 4555; pattern, with cloth model, 75 cents. ...

No. 4575. – Lady's Polonaise. – This design is a most elegant and practical design for an evening costume, displaying a fine figure to best advantage, also giving the short or stout-waisted figure more length and taper. The Marguerite back, is a very prominent feature in this most elegant, imported costume. Sometimes the polonaise is of velvet or silk, and worn over a high-neck and long-sleeve dress, with train of a different shade, this making it very practical when desiring to repair or make over.

A bizarre effect is given to dresses by trimming them down the front, on the collar, sleeves, and pockets, with numerous rows of small round metal buttons; but this is a "loud" fashion which we do not recommend, and which, like others of a similar nature, will soon wear itself out, being more like an exhibition of coins than aught we could compare it. Glittering trimmings are reappearing; back and white laces are interwoven with gold and silver with marvelously beautiful effect. ...

Fringes are now made to match almost every material, and many have distinguishing names; the fringe "Almee," about thirty inches deep, for scarf tabliers, being one of the most artistic in design. No less numerous and varied are braids; the mohair "Coat-of-mail" braid is now made in all the new shades. Black and colored diagonal braids form the most suitable trimmings for cloth jackets; others again with a thread or design in threads of silver interwoven are extremely pretty. ...

Raveled ruches of same material is a pretty trimming for silk dresses. These produce the appearance of the softest feathers, the effect being better, with fringe or lace added.

COMBINATION TOILETS.

The fashion of composing toilets with two materials is still in great favor; most elegant effects are produced by this means, allowing, as it does of so much artistic taste and variety. Cashmere and silk, cashmere and velvet or velveteen, silk and velvet, plain velvet and figured, plain silk and damask, are the favorite materials to arrange together. When these are of the same color, the difference of fabric gives different shades, and produces a very quiet, but elegant appearance.

Two materials employed in two shades of the same color should always have the lighter hue reserved for the upper part of the dress. When two colors are worn, one should be what is known as neutral – viz., gray, stone, drab or brown, with brilliant colors, such as claret, ruby, blue, green, or violet. There are exceptions to this rule, and some contrasting colors blend together very artistically; a few of the favorite combinations are black and white, cream and garnet, ivory and ruby or cardinal, cream and brown, bronze and pale blue, moss green and pink. Toilets arranged thus are only suited for dinner or carriage wear; for walking-dress, infinitely quieter hues are adopted, those preferred at the present moment being marine blue, scabieuse, maroon sealskin, Russian gray, French blue, or amiral, a new violet blue, very dark shade, which blends admirably with electric blue, and for evening wear, cardinal red, cream, flesh pink, turquoise blue, and amber.

No. 354. – Lady's Walking Costume. – The two charming models here presented, of overskirt and basque, serve to form an elegant costume. The overskirt is exceedingly long, and has the drapery arranged in deep folds across the front; these folds are carried well to the back, forming a drapery which is held in position by means of tapes. The basque, which is buttoned in front, is furnished at the back with eyelets and cord, a style, by many, greatly preferred to a closed front and buttoned back. The twelve lengthwise parts of the waist, produce the genuine corset effect, and is wonderfully becoming to most figures. The edge of the basque is finished in a novel and most effective manner. This costume may be effectively produced in any dress material, and is especially handsome in a combination suit of silk and cashmere. No. of Waist 4581; pattern, with cloth model, 50 cents. No. of Overskirt 4582; pattern, with cloth model, 50 cents.

Smith's Illustrated Pattern Bazaar, Fall 1876

Next is a peignoir, or morning robe of either cashmere or flannel. The front is trimmed at each side with a plaiting of the material, or silk, having a quilting of embroidered or plain muslin in the centre; it is fastened down the front, with rows of ribbon to match. The sleeves, which are slightly open and rounded, are trimmed to match the front. There is a pocket at the left side, also ornamented with plaiting, and rows to match. There are three tucks ornamenting the back breadths, which are piped with silk, to match the rows; this is entirely optional. Ten to twelve yards of flannel, or seven yards of cashmere will be required; eight yards of ribbon for bows. An old evening silk skirt might be utilized or plaitings, bows, etc.; purchasing the flannel or cashmere to correspond.

...

Waistbands and sashes, made of gros-grain, again are coming into favor, and they are always fastened with a buckle; the bands, which are very narrow, are worn above the basque bodice, and fastened with a Louis XV. buckle in Rhine crystal. ...

Old-fashioned aprons, with braces, are becoming popular. They give quite a *piquant* air to the wearer, if she is young, and especially if she is pretty. ...

Skirts are still ridiculously close-clinging; the ultra-fashionable people wear only one petticoat, buttoned on to a tight-fitting yoke. Under-skirts are still a good deal trimmed; cuirass waists are very much worn, and the whole appearance of the figure is to be made as slender as possible.
Peterson's Magazine, November 1876

The Redingote, which is made after the model of a man's overcoat, is very popular, also. It does not fit the figure close, and it is slightly wadded. It is double-breasted, has two square tails at the back, pockets on the hips, and velvet revers. It is made in bottle-green cloth, or slate-gray cloth: the revers are of velvet, to match. These redingotes are not made uniformly, for they fasten in three different ways. Sometimes they are buttoned high in the neck, and then they have a velvet collar; others open partially at the throat, with two large shawl-shaped revers, while a third style is to fasten them slantwise, with a wide velvet band crossing the figure. The basques which button down the back are only worn by quite young people.

The under-skirts are necessarily but little trimmed when the over-dresses are made so long, and the large tournure or bustle is not at all worn. All kinds of woolen goods are popular; in fact, they are more worn than entire suits of silk. The silk and woolen goods, combined to together, are very fashionable.

We give first, this month, a Polonaise costume, suitable for either the house or street. It is made of striped camel's-hair cloth, of two shades of gray, or two shades of brown. The under-skirt is scarcely three yards wide, and is cut with a demi-train, and furnished with buttons and loops, to raise it for the street. The bottom is trimmed with a gathered flounce six inches deep, cut on the bias. This is headed by a pouff also six inches, including the frill top and bottom, likewise cut on the bias; the Polonaise buttons up the back, as seen in the engraving. The edge is ornamented with a plaited frill four inches deep, of plain material, of the lighter shade. This is headed by a plaid braid of mohair. The looping of the skirt is quite low, and ornamented by long loops of ribbon or silk, to match. The coat-sleeves are trimmed up the outside of the arm with buttons, with simulated button-holes; cuffs to correspond. A standing collar finishes the neck. The front may or may not be ornamented with three rows, at pleasure. These striped cloths can be bought at almost any price, from twenty-five cents for mohair ones, up to $1.50 for good camel's-hair – sixteen to eighteen yards; three dozen buttons for sleeves and back, two yds. of wide ribbon, two and a half yards of plain materials for the plaited frill. Fringe may be substituted, if preferred; three and a half yards of plain mohair braid, which may be dispensed with, and a bias band of the material used instead.

Next is a Watteau Robe de Chambre, which is made of light blue or gray merino; and the wide Watteau plait, which commences at the top of the back of the neck, is embroidered in a flowing Pompadour design; but this may be left perfectly plain, or, at intervals down the plait, ornamented with rows of blue ribbon; the sleeves and pockets trim to match, and edge with a fringe two to three inches deep. We have seen a Watteau wrapper in light blue flannel, trimmed with coarse, white Cluny lace, and the effect was charming. Such trimming is inexpensive.

We close with something new, in the way of plaiting material, for the bottom flounce of a dress. As may be seen, there are four foldings, for a plait, and then the bottom is lifted, and tacked several inches to the left, forming a fan-shaped trimming. Very pretty.
Peterson's Magazine, December 1876

1877

We give, first, a half-trained skirt of all-wool black and white shepherd's plaid, made with a flounce and puffing, above a fine knife-plaiting of black cashmere. The tunic is cut very long, and almost straight round, plaited very much at the sides, as may be seen in the back view, which we give, as well as the front. Two broad bands of black cashmere trim the front, between which are three bows of gros-grain ribbon, with fringed ends; full pocket on the left side, ornamented likewise with bows of ribbon. The front edge of the tunic has a plaited trimming, and the back a band of black cashmere. The fullness of the back breadth is left unsewed in at the waist, trimmed with a like band of cashmere, and folded in the Arab style, making a very pretty drape at the back. Cuirass waist, with five seams at the back, edged and trimmed down the back with the cashmere, which is also used for the sleeves; cuffs of the plaid box-plaited on the outside of the arm, and ornamented with four buttons and simulated button-holes. A plaiting of the plaid, over a plaiting of the cashmere, is introduced at the back of the jacket. Eight to nine yards of double-width goods, with two and a half yards of cashmere for trimming. will be required. Shepherds' plaid cost from 50 cents to $1.50 per yard, according to quality.

...

Dresses, entirely of flowers, are the fashion, in Paris, for evening parties and balls. Poetical, isn't it? These dresses, or rather overskirts, are composed of a light foundation of ribbon or gauze, which is covered either with flowers of one kind, or else with a mixture of every variety. For the under edge, drooping flowers, such as fuchsias, are selected to form a fringe. Ribbons are the only trimming used on such toilets, neither jewels nor any other ornament being permissible.

...

The Princess Style, with the entire dress in one piece, is quite popular, because it is new; so many are tired of "over-dresses" and "under-dresses." All dresses cling as closely as possible to the figure, and some of the very newest are as plain in the back as in front, but these are not very popular as yet. High standing collars are still worn; and when the dress is not made all in one, in the Princess style, the cuirass waist is the most liked. The fashion is so liberal now, that provided a dress is sufficiently clinging, and tied back, anything else may be worn. There is very little luxury, and no elegance in the costumes for morning walking-dresses; the most fashionable Parisians are wearing costumes of thick cloth, the same as their husbands and brothers wear for morning coats – dark, almond-colored cloths, either checked or striped, or dark-brown, with yellow lines. The make is very simple – a habit bodice, fastened with mother-of-pearl buttons. Short, close-fitting jackets, made of mastic cloth, and cut exactly like a man's jacket, are also considered stylish wear at this season of the year.

...

Brocades and damasks, for those who can afford them, will form the prominent features of all winter costumes and Worth, the great Parisian *modiste*, is artist enough to suit the cut and make of the dress to the material composing it. He adapts the Renaissance and Marie Stuart styles to brocades; for striped fabrics he returns to the Louis XVI. style, and for thick, plain foulards, or ribbed material, he copies the dresses of the Revolution. The Watteau make he applies to flowered satins and velvets, and to embroideries.

Peterson's Magazine, January 1877

LADIES' COSTUME.

The costume represented in the engraving is made of cashmere and camel's-hair, and is composed of a skirt and a polonaise. The skirt is four-gored and in demi-train shape. It was cut by pattern No. 3904, price 30 cents, and is trimmed with a scolloped side-plaiting edged with braid, below a straight strip laid in alternate clusters of side-plaits and single box-plaits. No braid is used upon the skirt, its lower edge being turned up on the under side for about two inches, and hemmed to position.

The polonaise is diagonally draped and closed in front, the real closing extending from the neck to the point where the front skirt is sewed in with the under-arm seam; the clusters of buttons and buttonholes illustrated making a simulated closing. The side-back skirts are joined beneath the back skirt, which on one side forms a *revers,* and on the other is caught to the adjoining side-back under a ribbon bow. A stylish pocket is on the right side, and the neck is completed by a rounding collar with tab-like ends. The wrists are finished with cashmere plaiting, and the polonaise is trimmed with a narrow velvet band. The pattern is No. 4673, price 50 cents, and may be used for any suit material.

...

NOTICE. – We are Agents for the Sale of E. BUTTERICK & CO.'S PATTERNS, and will send any kind or size of them to any address post-paid on receipt of price and order.

...

Speaking of the prevailing mode of dress for the winter, an authority in fashion matters says: "The princess dress gains steadily upon the public taste, but it will receive many additions of various sorts to make it seem to be half a dozen different dresses, for wear upon half a dozen different occasions. A wide belt will be added, and the dress will appear like a Josephine waist with a plain gored skirt. Wear an overskirt and belt, and it is the same waist again, and has the effect of a full street toilet. Put on a peplum, and it is a belted cuirass with either a single or double skirt, as the wearer chooses to arrange it. This is considered a grand combination toilet. The deep polonaise, whether buttoned or laced behind, or closed in front, is still the beloved of the lady possessing fine proportions. She omits all *tournure* if she possibly can. A few overlapping breadths of crinoline may be placed permanently down the centre of the back of the princess or polonaise, but the close, clinging style is nearly as severe at the back as it is at the sides and front of the figure. No bustle is required, except for tall and slender ladies."

Lacings with silk cords, wherever they can be effectively arranged, are among the popular likings of the season, and, of course, garments are designed with a view to the adoption of this attractive decoration. Buttons in groups, lines, etc., are also popular, and are added to them.

One of the prettiest novelties of the season is the scarf overskirt. It reaches no higher than the hips, and is constructed to wrap the figure in wavy folds, whose arrangement, while apparently careless, is really the acme of studied grace. The great difficulty which the amateur dressmaker will experience in attempting to drape this overskirt with its proper negligent grace, will prevent its coming into common use.

Arthur's Home Magazine, January 1877

There is a Rumor that the cuirass is going out, to make way for the peplum bodice, which has very long basques at the sides, (pointed or square, according to taste,) a square postillon at the back, and are short in front. Other bodices have wide waistbands in front, which commence at the seams beneath the arms, and do not cross the back. Worth makes many woollen dresses with blouse bodices, that are held in place with a wide belt of either velvet ribbon or leather. ...

Skirts are worn so closely clinging to the figure, that invention is put to the test how to dispense with all under-drapery that bulges out or creates the smallest suspicion of fullness of material. Drawers and petticoats are now made of flannel; the petticoats are very short, but a deep white flounce, trimmed with edging, and called the "Balayeuse," is now always tacked in the wrong side of short costumes.

Next is a demi-toilet, also in striped and self-colored material. This is two shades of gray, combined either with a darker shade of gray for the plain parts of the dress, or it may be of black. The under-skirt is of the self-color, and trimmed with a flounce cut on the bias, of the striped material; this flounce is edged with a narrow plaiting of the plain, and is out eighteen inches deep, to allow for the two puffs and heading, as may be seen in the design. A Polonaise, cut of the stripes, has the front, from neck to edge of the skirt, made of the self-color, a bias land of which finished the edge of the Polonaise. A narrow plaiting trims the front, where the seam joins the front and outside. The looping is all low, and the skirt of the Polonaise is narrow. A suspended pocket ornaments the left side. Coat-sleeves, trimmed to match, and standing collar, complete this costume. Eight yards of double-width striped material, and four yards of plain will be required. Two dozen buttons. ...

We have given so many illustrations, this month, with the descriptions, as above, that but little remains to be said, in general. We may, however, state that square, low bodices are much more popular than round ones; the sleeve, or rather the apology for one, comes high on the shoulder, and the bodice is cut square at the back as well as in front. To slender figures this style is very becoming, but it should not be adopted by any others.

Although the Polonaise is probably the newest style of walking-dresses, it is by no means the only one worn, as a great many ladies still cling to the under-skirt, the tunic, cuirass waist, and long jacket, for out-of-door wear.

The costumes that include skirt, tunic, and bodice, are made in many different styles, but they are almost all, without exception, ornamented at the side. Oblique lines are the fashion, for we see them described with buttons, bows, fur, gimp, and feathers, on all the newest costumes. There are also a great many cut trimmings to be seen; the French term for them is "garnitures coupes;" they consist of a plaiting of some woolen material, interrupted at regular intervals by plaitings of silk, or of silk flounces crossed at intervals with satin plaitings.

The jackets that are worn over costumes, and made of the same material, are almost all one shape – close-fitting at the back, and double-breasted in front. These jackets are mostly trimmed with galloons made of black velvet, embroidered with either white or moss-green silk. The quantity and variety of these galloons is indescribable. Those made of canvas, with the design in chenille, woven in the Jacquard loom, are much liked.

Peterson's Magazine, February 1877

LADIES' EVENING COSTUME.

For evening wear, ruby, garnet, cardinal red and wine colors are again in favor. The costume illustrated is a ruddy garnet silk, and though the garments composing it are not elaborate, the richness of color and texture, together with the dainty trimmings, establishes it firmly as one of the season's favorites.

The polonaise has a deep front, closed only about halfway down the skirt, and fitted at each side by a single dart and a gore seam extending to the shoulder. The back is fancifully draped, and is also fitted by gores whose back edges are gathered up under the central portion of the back, the latter falling in sash ends nearly to the bottom of the dress skirt. Though there are sleeves to the pattern, which is No. 4683, price 35 cents, they are omitted in making this polonaise, and the arms'-eyes are bordered with lace frills. A *lisse* ruching encircles the heart-shaped neck, and cashmere lace falling from under a plaiting of the goods trims the edges of the front and the sash end. Bouquets of artificial flowers arc caught here and there over the closing, and also at the ends of the strip of plaiting simulating a pocket.

The skirt is a long full train and has a front gore, two gores at each side and two long back-breadths. It is trimmed with two rows of knife-plaiting, stitched near the upper edge of each, the lower one being quite wide, and the other very narrow. The pattern is No. 4226, price 40 cents.

Fashion decrees such closely-fitting and severe outlines in ladies' outer garments, that there has been necessitated a revolution in under garments. The change which is taking place in regard to them is in many respects for the better, since the old styles have been disadvantageous to health in many ways. Many ladies are making under garments that combine in one piece both chemise and drawers, and our fashion magazines give patterns for such combined garments. In addition to this, there are several establishments in our larger cities which make it a specialty to supply garments of this peculiar style, modeled on strictly healthful and convenient plans. The skirt is also remodeled by having a plain yoke over the hips, which does away with the extra fullness, which was heating and frequently oppressive. The move is certainly in the right direction.

Those who would be ultra fashionable go to an extreme of plainness in the trimming of their outer garments, only balanced by the extreme of trimming in vogue a few seasons ago. Still, trimmings are not utterly discarded by those who follow modestly in the wake of fashion.

Ladies' dresses are made with a sheath-like perfection of outline which causes them to seem moulded to the form; while for the street many beautiful half-fitting cloaks are offered, which conceal the imperfections at the same time that they reveal the perfections of the form. Among other outer garments are several models, under the general name of "waterproof" patterns, which are called "storm cloaks." No lady can afford to be without a "storm cloak," and if she dresses richly and goes out during the morning, she will acquire elegance of appearance, and practice economy at the same time, by the use of a handsomely outlined garment, protecting her dress, and announcing to her friends that she is occupied in other than merely social pursuits. The cut of these garments is quite as elegant as those of handsomer materials, the only difference being that they are of more serviceable fabrics. The hood and cape may be adjusted by hooks and loops beneath the collar, so as to be removed for a warm day, and replaced when required. They are made with extreme plainness, but the curves and seams are all perfectly arranged.

Arthur's Home Magazine, February 1877

The princesse dresses illustrated on our first page, and of which cut paper are published, are in high favor for home and carriage dresses, and promise with the advent of spring to be popular for general wear, being made suitable for the street by the addition of a Dolman, shawl, or other light wrap. The dresses from which our illustrations are taken are of silk, but the designs are also appropriate for fine woolen stuffs or for simpler fabrics for the house; and when spring and summer comes, we shall see them made of de bège, grenadine, and of light silk for best dresses, and of cambrics, lawn, or percale for summer wear. Readers who have already asked advice about preparing their wardrobes for next season will find these patterns of especial service.

...

THE PLASTRON PRINCESSE DRESS.

The Plastron Princesse Dress is one of the most elegant importations of the season. As it is illustrated in the picture it is a suitable design for full-dress occasions, and similar dresses are prepared for the Charity Ball, dinner parties, and receptions; moreover, some of the handsomest wedding dresses are made by this pattern, as it gives an opportunity for displaying rich lace, is of the stylish shape, and dispenses with the over-skirt and drapery that seldom dispose themselves gracefully beneath the lace bridal veil. When worn for full dress, the square neck is filled in with tulle, pleated or gathered, and the elbow sleeves are finished with a lace jabot. Other evening dresses are made of two shades of blue silk, or of cream or rose, or else silk is combined with satin, or velvet, or the rich damassée silk like that in the picture. But this pattern is by no means confined to dressy toilettes; when a dress for general wear is designed, the tulle square is omitted, and a plastron buttoned close up to the throat is made of the silk of the trimming, or else the material of the dress, and the sleeves are lengthened to the wrists. The general directions for making the plain princesse dress apply to this. This pattern will also be used for summer silks, woolens, grenadines, and wash dresses.

THE PLAIN PRINCESSE DRESS.

The Plain Princesse Dress from which our picture and pattern are taken is of seal brown silk, trimmed with pleatings and facings of lighter brown or ashes-of-roses silk. This is an excellent model for the black silk dresses which are now brightened by cardinal silk, or else trimmed with pleatings and facings of black velvet. In this dress the lower part of the skirt and sleeves is cut in squares – Madame Raymond advises scallops – and for this reason the skirt is cut shorter than the wearer needs it, and a facing is placed beneath, extending to the proper length, and on this facing is laid the pleated flounce. Sometimes this flounce is only on the front breadths, and the square train has merely the cut-out squares or scallops. Only the waist and hips of these dresses should be lined. If the skirt were lined, it would interfere with the clinging effect. The front and sides of the skirt must hang absolutely plain and straight, and for this reason only one dart is employed; two darts would give too much fullness across the stomach. The buttons and button-holes down the front should not be more than an inch apart, hence from three to four dozen are required. Another important thing in this dress is that the slight draping of the back be placed very low, leaving that part over the tournure as smoothly fitted as the waist of the dress. There should be whalebones in most of the corsage seams, and those in the back and front should extend far below the waist.

This model is excellent for the fine woolen stuffs yet to be noted in this article as new spring goods. These dresses will be trimmed with silk of self-color in the way just described, and in some cases scarf drapery will be added for tabliers and sashes, to give more fullness to slight figures, and also to have more dressy effect. For the hair-striped and small-checked summer silks this will be an appropriate pattern, and the only trimming needed is silk of solid color, fringe, or lace. House dresses of cambric and percale, and the pretty white muslins and lawns worn during the summer in the country, will be fashioned in this way, and trimmed with long-looped bows of ribbon. As these dresses are to be washed, it is well to make them slightly large, to allow for possible shrinking.

...

Lace shawls, or points, as they are called, are still worn as over-skirts. They are draped irregularly, with the back point falling low on the left side, and the fronts are caught up on the right, making a diagonal apron, and instead of being allowed to meet on the right, the space is filling in with ribbon clusters of loops, or else bouquets of flowers, or perhaps a jabot of lace to match is set on the dress skirt to fill the open space. Guipure lace and gimp are not fashionable this winter.

Harper's Bazar, February 17, 1877

... but the Princess robe is the newest, though it is, after all, but a return to the old Gabrielle, made narrower, and sometimes worn over another skirt. All skirts are very much too tight-clinging, both for comfort and real grace, but this fashion is the distinguishing feature of the present style. In order to add to the extreme attenuation of the a figure, the white muslin petticoats are not starched, and are put on a deep yoke, which fits perfectly around the hips. Many ladies, in fact, only wear a long flannel one, trimmed with white embroidery under-costumes, while for evening wear the flannel petticoat is short, and an over one made of white cambric is added – the latter being long, narrow, and terminating either with rich embroidery or deep imitation-lace. Batiste and fine muslin petticoats have only a flat trimming in front, and a finance gathered with a drawing string at the back; the strings, when drawn, cause the petticoat to be moulded exactly to the figure, and all the fullness of the petticoat to be gathered to the centre of the back. The same plan is now adopted with regard to the skirts of dresses. On the back breadths there are either two drawing-strings, or one in the centre, which are tied, so that the front and sides of the skirt hang perfectly plain, and the back flows in folds. All these details are contrived with a view to obviate all bunchiness and fullness about the hips, and to render the figure as slim as possible.

It is still so cold and blustering, that only dark costumes are seen on the street, but these are often brightened with a cording of cardinal-red, or corded red bows. Evening-dresses of dark material are also brightened up with cardinal-red or linden-green, which is the color of the flower of the linden or lime-tree, a most delicate light-green with a creamy tint.

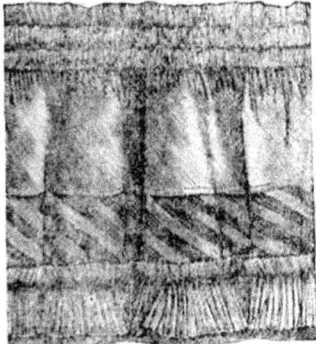 

TRIMMINGS FOR DRESS SKIRTS.
By Mrs. Jane Weaver.

First, is for a dress of two materials, striped and plain. The lower part is of the striped material, cut on the bias, and edged with a kilt-pleating. The heading consists of a kilt-pleating, stitched down thrice. Next is a box-pleated, flounce, trimmed with a wide band of braid, heading with five puffings, and a kilt-pleating to stand up.

Peterson's Magazine, March 1877

LADIES' WALKING COSTUME.

Plain costumes are among the modes of the day, and are receiving a large share of popular favor. The one illustrated made of fine serge suiting. The skirt is six-gored, and was cut by No. 4413. price 35 cents. It is of walking length, and the bottom is trimmed with two gathered ruffles of the goods, the upper one being a trifle the narrower, and set on under a bias fold of the material. If preferred, other methods of trimming may be adopted.

The over-skirt is composed of a plain wide front-gore, fitted to the bell, by darts, and slashed for a short distance through the center from the bottom, so that when the draping is performed and the skirt properly adjusted, the slash is drawn apart and joins a stylish Vandyke opening. The back-breadth is also long and plain, and with the front-gore is draped by upward-turning folds laid in each side. A broad bias band of the material is stitched on like a facing to form the finish of the over-skirt.

The jacket has only under-arm darts, side-seams, and a seam at the center of the back. A double collar is about the neck, and tasseled braids are disposed as illustrated. The pattern to the over-skirt is No. 4765, price 25 cents, while that of the jacket is No. 4780, price 30 cents. A basque is worn beneath the jacket, and is illustrated and further mentioned upon one of the succeeding pages of this Department. It is No. 4782, price 30 cents. The hat is of fine chip, trimmed with gros-grain ribbon and ostrich tips.

LADIES' COAT BASQUE.

 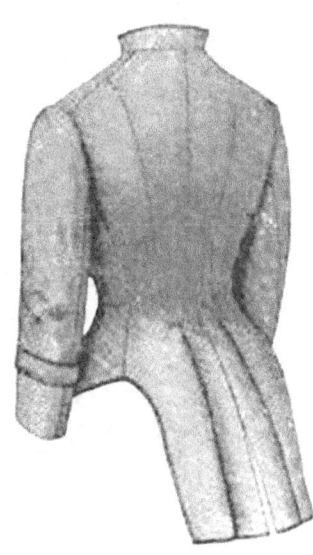

No. 4782. – This charming basque is one of the latest exponents of fashion, and is so gracefully shaped that it may be selected for any style of material, whether it be expensive or otherwise. The front is fitted in the ordinary manner at each side by two darts and a cross-basque seam: the darts shaping it handsomely to the bust, and the cross-basque seam giving a pretty length to the waist. The skirt of the front is deep and round, but that of the back is much longer, and in coat style. The waist of the back is fitted by side-seams and a seam at the center, the latter terminating at about half the depth of the skirt. The sleeves are in coat shape, and a military collar completes the neck. The pattern is in 13 sizes for ladies from 28 to 46 inches, bust measure, and calls for 2 7/8 yards of goods, 27 inches wide, in making the basque for a lady of medium size. Price of pattern, 30 cents.

LADIES' PLAIN, PRINCESS DRESS, WITH MEDIUM TRAIN.

No. 4761. – A charming dress, susceptible of many changes in its methods of draping, is illustrated by these engravings. Scarfs of the same or a contrasting material may be draped upon it for a dressy toilette, or it may, by an arrangement of tapes underneath, be transformed into a polonaise, the only inconvenience being the necessity of undoing the waistline button-hole and button, so as to tie or untie the tapes. The pattern is in 13 sizes for ladies from 28 to 46 inches, bust measure, and costs 50 cents. To make the garment for a lady of medium size, 7 yards of goods, 27 inches wide, are needed.

Easter is the period ordained by long usage, when winter garments may be laid aside, and garments more suitable for the spring take their place. There are no indications of marked changes in the fashions for this season. The tendency is only toward a greater simplicity and severity in general style.

"The most prominent example of the present statuesque modes is the princess dress," says an authority in fashions; "which, with its sweeping train, accurately fitted body and close coat-sleeve, approaches the nearest to the fashionable ideal of anything yet introduced. And when made of some dark rich goods, with only a cord of bright color edging the wrists, the military collar about the neck, and the pocket, if one is used, and a binding of the same finishing the buttonholes, the effect is most refined and elegant, and illustrates the latest climax in dress." A favorite way of decorating a princess dross is to border the bottom with a finely-plaited flounce, not more than four inches deep in front, and nearly twice that width at the back, with a gradual increase in from the narrowest to the widest point. This may be headed with a wide bias strip of the goods, in which several tiny folds are laid and invisibly basted into place. For evening wear the princess may be trimmed with different disposals of trimming, outlining an overskirt, or even a court train. With the neck dressed in pompadour style, and the sleeves cut off at the elbows or a little below, and finished with frills of *lisse*, blonde, net or whatever lace may be desired, the effect of the princess is antique, graceful and stylish in the extreme.

LADIES' POLONAISE, FITTED LOW AT THE BACK.

No. 4775. – In selecting material for this charming model, almost any style will be found appropriate, and especially those draping easily. Cashmere was chosen for the one illustrated, together with a band of silk for the trimming about the skirt, and silk-piped bands of the goods about the plain coat sleeves. The front is elegantly fitted by two darts at each side, and by an under-arm dart extending down over the hip. The back has a center seam, with side-seam extending to the shoulders, and at the termination of each is an extra width closed at its upper edges and allowed to fall loosely, the one at the center being drawn to the outside. The pattern is in 13 sizes for ladies from 28 to 46 inches, bust measure, and calls for 7 1/4 yards of goods, 27 inches wide, in making the garment for a lady of medium size. Price of pattern, 35 cents.

The latest model for a princess dress is fitted by upright under-arm and front darts, and seams to the arms'-eyes and centre of the back, and all the seams are divided by equal distances, so that the figure of the wearer, whether it really is thus beautiful or not, appears to be exquisitely proportioned. It has a demi-train, which, by flaring four inches or so at the back, may be lengthened to any desired extent for bridal or full-dress toilet. This dress may be shortened for a polonaise for street wear by a peculiar adjustment of tapes crossing from side to side at the back, and tied in front of the waist.

Overskirts are not wholly discarded. To many they are becoming, and to most they afford an acceptable variation of the toilet. They are made long and plain, and are draped low down in the back. Plain hems or corded bands are the usual finish of these overskirts. Sometimes a fringe is added. Some overskirts have a parted slash in front; others are deeper at one side than at the other. The underskirt need not be of fine material more than a quarter of a yard deep, or at most no higher than the knee. They are scantily trimmed, and never to a depth of more than ten or twelve inches. A narrow trimming may be placed on the front and back of the skirt, increasing in width toward the sides, so as to make its highest point where the polonaise or overskirt is draped highest.

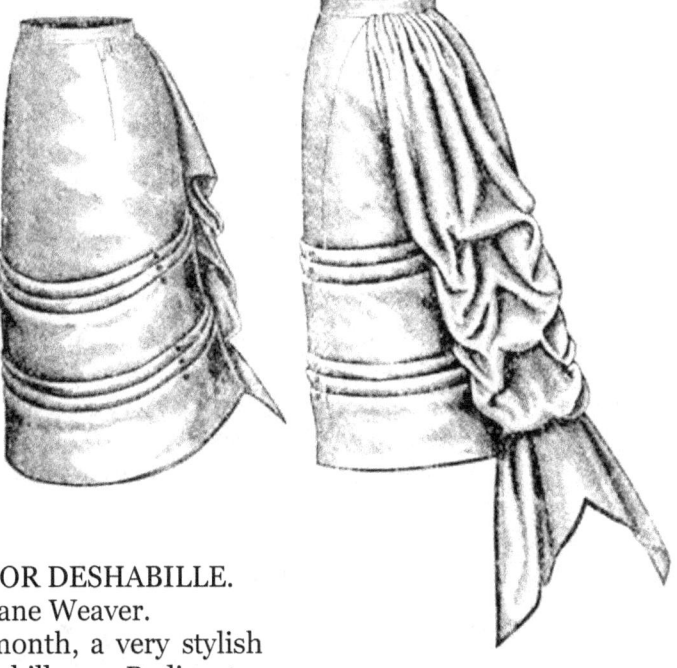

LADIES' OVER-SKIRT.

No. 4781. – This stylish over-skirt has a straight front-breadth fitted to the belt by darts, and widened sufficiently by triangular gores, to permit a handsome draping. The latter is accomplished by two clusters of three plaits each, the plaits being fastened under tiny buttons just in front of the side-front seam. The back-breadth is notched at its lower edge, so that points are formed at the sides. The pattern is in 9 sizes for ladies from 20 to 36 inches, waist measure. To make the garment for a lady of medium size, 4 1/2 yards of goods, 27 inches wide, will be needed. Price of pattern, 30 cents.

Arthur's Home Magazine, April 1877

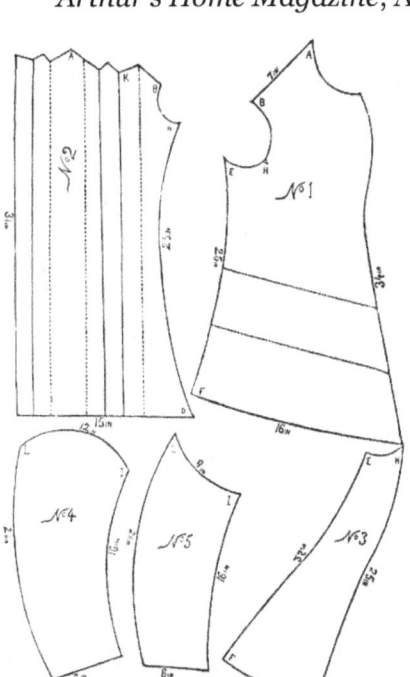

REDINGOTE FOR DESHABILLE.
Mrs. Jane Weaver.

We give, this month, a very stylish costume for deshabille, a Redingote, and the very newest pattern. On the next page we give a diagram, from which to cut it out. A full description is given in our "Every-Day" department."

The dotted lines on No. 2 show where the plaits are laid – on No. 1, where the trimming is placed across the front. (Plaited ruffles like the skirt.) As we have already said, this is the very newest thing in this way. ...

It is made of pale-blue cashmere, trimmed with cashmere lace, and plaitings of the same, if a very dressy robe-de-chambre be desired; or it may be made of flannel, and will be charming for the warm weather, if

made of Nainsook and Hamburg embroidery. In our diagram, we give only the long, loose Redingote, and it may be worn over a skirt of the same material, or over a black silk. If of Nainsook, of course the skirt of the same will be the prettiest. Price of pattern, fifty cents.

A word about collars. The standing bias collar, sloped off in front, is the popular one for dresses. It must be a trifle over an inch wide when finished, and is sewed on without cording at the bottom. It has an interlining of thin crinoline, to keep it erect and shapely. To make it fit neatly in front, and meet without lapping, the end on the left side, where the buttons are, should stop an inch from the edge of the dress-front, while the end on the right side goes to the edge of the garment. It should be lined with silk if the dress is of woolen. The cravat is placed between the linen collar and the dress collar, and tied in a bow at the front.

...

The long Princess-dress is adroitly gaining ground, for most persons are heartily tired of the elaborate trimmings so much worn; but when it comes to out-of doors wear, many prefer some looping or drapery to the dress, as one is apt to feel conspicuous in the long, straight, tight-clinging Princess-dress. Buttons of all kinds are very much used to fasten dresses, and for very slender persons, the waist buttoned diagonally is very becoming. The long waist is still popular, and when basques are worn, they are very long and plain. Waists open, heart shaped, or square on the neck, are, of course, not worn on the street, except with a wrap over it, but are cool and pretty for the house.

Peterson's Magazine, April 1877

LADIES' STREET TOILETTE.

Figure No. 1. – This stylish costume is made of striped percale and prettily trimmed with plain material corded with white. The skirt has a Spanish flounce, and was cut by pattern No. 4408, price 35 cents. It hangs neatly, and two piped bands finish its lower edge effectively. The over-skirt was cut by pattern No. 4805, which costs 25 cents and like the skirt model is in 9 sized for ladies from 20 to 36 inches, waist measure. On the right side of the garment is a full pocket cut bias of the material and additionally trimmed with a piped band. The basque is loose-fitting and very graceful in its outlines. It is trimmed to correspond with the remainder of the suit, and was cut by pattern No. 4798, price 30 cents. This model is in 13 sizes for ladies from 28 to 46 inches, bust measure.

LADIES' LOOSE-FITTING HOUSE DRESS.

4797

No. 4897. – This charming dress is designed for house wear and may be made of any soft clinging material, or of silk or velvet if expense be no consideration. The front is in Princess style, but the back has a basque portion falling over a long plaited skirt. A full pocket is at the right side, and like the basque and skirt is finished with a cording of the material. The sleeves are in coat shape, and each is completed with a narrow plaiting at the wrist, while the neck is encircled by a military collar. The pattern is in 13 sizes for ladies from 28 to 46 inches, bust measure, and requires 7 3/8 yards of goods, 27 inches wide, to make the garment for a lady of medium size. Price of pattern, 40 cents.

...

... dress is an important factor of the dance. At a fashionable gathering in the ball-room, the greatest extremes in dress are to be seen. To be in style is the all-important question, and that means that the latest fashions must be observed. The leaders of fashion who originate the styles have no regard whatever for physiological laws, and therefore do not aim to adapt the dress to the body on hygienic principles. If a new invention suits their fancy, they are satisfied, knowing that they will receive the support of fashionable people. Thus woman goes into the dance with her arms, neck and shoulders bare, while her limbs are encumbered with heavy skirts that are embellished by a train of respectable proportions. Under her load she is expected to be all smiles, dimples and affectation, and ready to bestow her favors upon any "lord of creation" who may solict [sic: solicit] her hand in the giddy whirl of the dance. The disproportion in her dress is an impropriety in many respects, but is unhygienic because of an undue exposure of some parts of the person, while other portions of the body are unnecessarily burdened. A long, heavy dress, with the waist tightly laced, is bad enough at any time; but under no circumstances is it more injurious than in the act of dancing, where the utmost freedom of movement is required. Dancing is performed with double difficulty where the dress interferes with the free action of the limbs, and the elasticity of the trunk is limited by staves and cords. By the latter the heart and lungs are oppressed, so that they cannot properly perform their functions of circulation and aerating the blood as rapidly as the demands of the system under its violent exercise requires. The result is congestion and displacement of internal organs, which create weakness and disease. Sometimes the oppression is so great that the forces of nature are completely overpowered, and the woman faints away. Why women will persist in heaping upon themselves such self-imposed burdens is a mystery past finding out. It is one of those strange anomalies in nature that is inexplicable.

Arthur's Home Magazine, May 1877

Breton Jackets, of which we give illustrations this month, are much worn with foulard chemisettes. The foulard it plaited length wise, and a jabot of valenciennes, or old lace, is added. A cuff is worn on the Breton jacket, composed of foulard like the chemisette, and also of lace; and when the foulard is bright and light, great variety may be given to the toilet through its means. The same may be said of bodices that are made with waistcoats. A black silk dress, with an ivory-white waistcoat ornamented with lace, or a waistcoat embroidered with delicate flowers, renders a toilet very dressy, with but slight trouble. Even when there is not sufficient embroidery for a large waistcoat, it looks effective when utilized for pockets and cuffs only.

...

Figs. VI. and VII. – Back and Front of Breton Jacket of Black Cloth, For Out-Door Wear. – The broad galloon that trims it is embroidered, and is held down by black velvet straps, on which is placed large crochet buttons. The vest in front is of cloth, or can be made of black silk; the plastron, or upper part of this vest, is trimmed with throe bands of the galloon, sewn close to each other, and two straps of black velvet are placed below the velvet collar.

Breton jackets are very fashionable for house-wear, and they are often trimmed with valuable old lace, which is mounted on a faille band of some bright color. Bretons are also made entirely of cashmere or Sicilienne, in such bright colors, as turquoise-blue, Sevres-pink, and coral-red; the lace is then placed on the material, and without any bright lining; and the skirt usually accompanying these gay vests is either black faille or black velvet. The real Breton jacket, which is imported from Rennes, is covered with embroidery, worked by the peasants with considerable skill; and there is no doubt but that it possesses a certain originality of style.

When the Princess form of dress is not adopted, the more the bodice dress resembles a habit with a postilion or a jockey basque, the more fashionable is it considered. This habit bodice is short in front, slopes longer toward the side, and extends down in the back, to a broad square. Pingat, of Paris, makes dresses in this style. One was of Holbein green velvet brocade, and tilleul faille, trimmed with white Smyrna lace of the finest thread, and applique chenille passementerie, representing leaves. The introduction of Smyrna lace for evening dresses is one of Worth's latest caprices.

Figs. VIII. and IX – Back and Front or House-Dress, of almond-colored and white-striped debege. – The under-skirt has a knife-plaiting of the malarial; the long Polonaise buttons on the right side diagonally; a band of bege heads the deep ball-worsted fringe; the skirt is but slightly looped at the back. Close, plain sleeves.

...

Worth has been paying great attention lately to the cut of dresses, with a view to imitating, as closely as possible, the drapery adopted In the time of the renaissance in the portraits painted by great masters, and in which slimness of form is conspicuously aimed at; and in this ho has succeeded. He has learned the secret of cutting materials so that when they are draped on the figure, its size is considerably diminished to all appearance.
Peterson's Magazine, May 1877

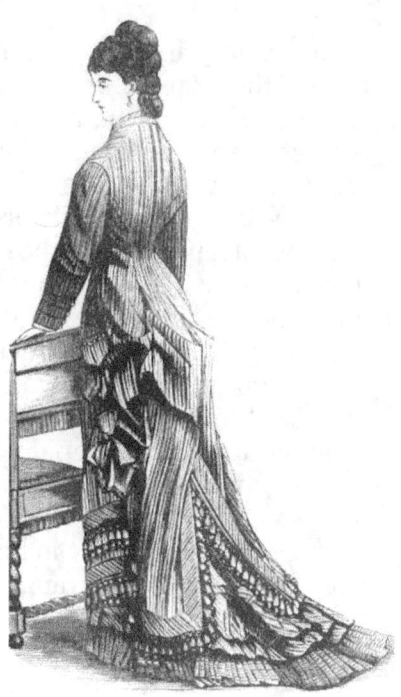

LADIES' POLONAISE, BUTTONED AT THE BACK.

No. 4848. – The Princess style of fitting is varied to a considerable extent, but each method seems to arrive at the same glove-like adjustment. The polonaise illustrated is made of *de bége,* and the shaping is perfected by an underarm dart, which, effectually removes all fullness, leaving the front smooth and plain. The skirt portion of the back is cut on a fold of the goods, and an extra width is allowed at the termination of the closing. The width is folded under in box-plaits to give sufficient skirt fullness, and is caught up at the center by a strap. Side-backs complete the adjustment of the back, and their skirt portions are draped quite high at the sides. By the latter process a slash made at the center of the front is drawn into a Vandyke opening. The sleeves are in coat shape, with wide rolling tops and narrow wrists, while the collar is in military style. The wrists and the bottom of the polonaise are trimmed with a piped fold of the goods. The pattern is in 13 sizes for ladies from 28 to 46 inches, bust measure, and calls for 6 3/4 yards of goods, 27 inches wide, in making the garment for a lady of medium size. Price of pattern, 35 cents.

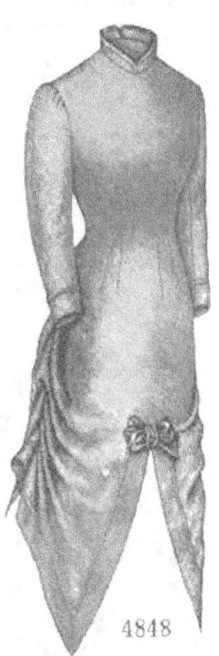

4848

LADIES' WALKING-SKIRT, WITH YOKE.

No. 4858. – This model may be made up as represented, with jean for the yoke, and suit goods for skirt portion, or the entire skirt may be of suit material. The pattern is in 9 sizes for ladies from 20 to 36 inches, waist measure, and requires 3 5/8 yards of goods, 27 inches wide, for the gores, and a yard of satin jean for the yoke, in making the skirt for a lady of medium size. Price of pattern, 35 cents.

LADIES' BASQUE, WITH DOUBLE SIDE-FORMS.

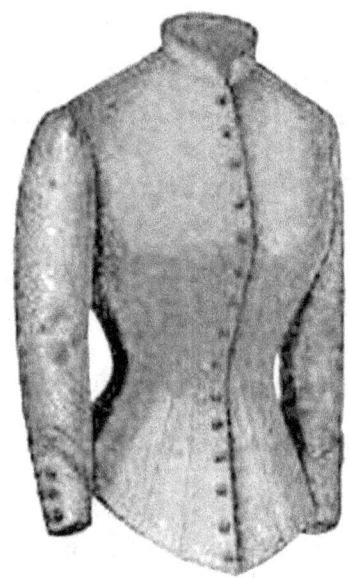

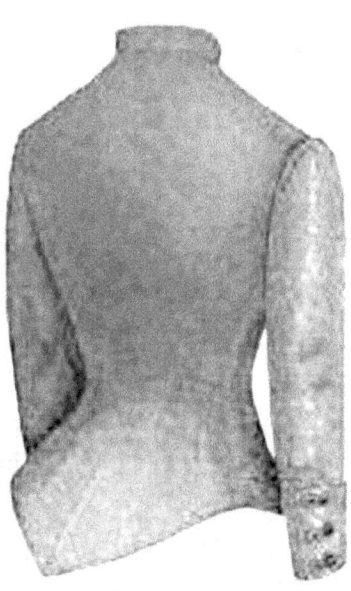

No. 4833. – A peculiar but very commendable style of fitting is illustrated by these engravings, and divides favor with basques fitted by seams extending to the shoulders. The front is fitted at each side by two curving bust darts, and an under-arm dart, which renders a cross-basque seam quite unnecessary. The double side-forms are shaped like ordinary side-backs, except that they are narrower, and together with a center seam complete the fitting of the garment. The pattern is in 13 sizes for ladies from 23 to 46 inches, bust measure, and requires 3 yards of goods, 27 inches wide, in making the garment for a lady of medium size. Price of pattern, 30 cents.

...

LADIES' BRETON JACKET.

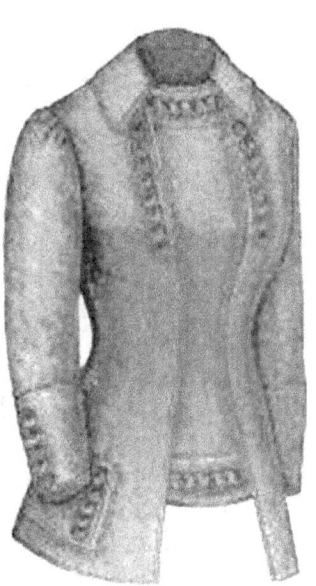

No. 4853. – The Breton jacket is a novelty of the season and is made up in a variety of materials, either as an independent garment or as a completion to a suit. The material represented is a light camel's-hair suiting, and the trimmings consist of pipings of silk and shank pearl buttons arranged in imitation of Breton buttons. The latter have eyes at their edges and are sewed on to overlap each other like fish-scales. The vest is shorter than the sides and is fitted by a dart at the center, while a single dart at each side side-backs and a center seam adjust the half-fitting jacket portion. The neck of the jacket is encircled by a deep rolling collar with square ends. The sleeves are in wide coat shape, and have cuffs simulated with piping and buttons. The pattern is in 13 sizes for ladies from 28 to 46 inches, bust measure. To make the garment for a lady of medium size, 3 1/2 yards of goods, 27 inches wide, will be required. Price of pattern, 30 cents.

Arthur's Home Magazine, June 1877

Natural flowers are now all the rage for ball-dresses. It is the fashion in Paris, and it might be imitated here, to wear cordons of marshals of France, which commence on the left shoulder, cross the bodice, and terminate on the right side of the waist. These are always composed of a variety of flowers: for example, a double row of shaded rose-buds, a cordon of Parma violets, a fringe of white lilac with tea-roses, a garland of convolvuli and white hyacinths, or of white azaleas and scarlet geraniums, can be seen across many of the newest low bodices. The flowers are mounted on wire, and a few leaves are interspersed with them.

There are many novelties in costumes. Worth has introduced, among others, a new dress with two waistcoats, which is pronounced a great success. An example in his show-rooms consisted of a skirt of moss-green Sicilienne. The Polonaise of a lighter shade was trimmed with a single fine silver braid. The first of the two waistcoats was dark-green velvet; the second, and longer one, was Sicilienne, striped with silver braid.

Next, we have a black grenadine Princess Polonaise, over a black silk Princess dress, simply ornamented with one row of box-plaiting on the bottom of the skirt. The grenadine is also cut Princess shape, with the front breadth cut long enough to gather upon the right side, into the side seam, as may be seen. When the right side of the back width of the skirt of Polonaise is somewhat longer and wider than the left half, and is caught up, forming two poufs box-plaited at the top, as seen in illustration, bows of black ribbon, lined with cardinal, ornament the back, sleeves, and throat. The whole of the garment is edged, and trimmed with a narrow knife plaiting of the grenadine. The same finishes the neck. Fourteen to sixteen yards of grenadine will be required. A half-worn black silk may be brought into requisition for the under-dress. Put no lining in the grenadine, even for the waist, but make a loose fit, so the goods may not stretch and tear, being careful to allow large seams, and finish inside by binding them with a narrow black ribbon, to prevent fraying. Price of pattern of Polonaise, fifty cents and stamp.

Notwithstanding the prediction that simpler dresses were to be fashionable this summer, all the newest importations are still a good deal looped, and have long, close-clinging trains. The looping seems necessary for the fine materials of which summer dresses are made, the straight lines looking better in the heavier stuffs of winter. But the present styles are most inconvenient for those who walk, and a few of the very fashionable women of Paris have had quite short dresses made for country wear. As yet none of those costumes have made their appearance on this side of the water. There are three popular styles now, the Princesse polonaise, basque bodices, with upper and lower skirts, and Princesse dresses. The prominent points in the best polonaises are the long seams of the back, the plainness over the tournure, and sufficient length to give a slender effect. Fringes and wide galloons are the trimmings universally used, and the galloon is very generally arranged in sloping lines, or in a long V down the back, from shoulders to waist; small fichus, or mantles of the same material, complete the costume. The aim appears to be to give the costume the effect of a Princesse dress; and in most cases the merest glimpse of the under-skirt is all that is visible; therefore, it is made both narrow and clinging, and is usually trimmed all round alike. The drawing-string across the back breadths is always added, no matter how closely the skirt is cut to the figure.

In these new dresses the shoulder-seams are very short, the neck is cut very high at the back, and the tight sleeves have the upper half slightly gathered on the elbows, to fit the arm more perfectly.

Some of the white trailing dresses are among the very prettiest of those imported, for young ladies, or for morning-dresses for married women, at the sea-side. These dresses are usually made in the Princesse or Polonaise style, but look equally well with a Breton jacket or a basque. They are trimmed with blue, pink, cardinal-red, coral, or buttercup colored ribbons; sometimes a continuation of colors is used – as cardinal-red and yellow, and black, blue and pink, and linden color, etc.

...

Economy In Dress is one of the things which this magazine has always favored. We do not mean, however, that economy which makes a woman a "fright." On the contrary, our purpose is to show that stylish and beautiful costumes cost no more than vulgar-looking ones, and that it is taste, not money, that makes the well-dressed lady. Hence we give the latest Parisian fashions, not only In all their entirety, in our colored plates, but adapted, in our "Everyday" department, to the cheapest and most ordinary materials. But whatever we give, whether the dress to be be silk or calico, velvet or debege, it is always the latest style. The pre-eminence of the French, in dress, is attributable entirely to their taste. We seek to enable American women, in this particular, to rival the French. We have no interest in any dry-goods, mantua-making, or millinery establishment; no articles of our own to dispose of; and therefore no temptation to recommend anything but the very latest and very prettiest fashions. In this respect we stand alone. No other magazine can say exactly the same. It is in consequence of this that "Peterson" has become indispensable, as a guide to fashion, in every refined household in the land. And through it all we study economy. Whoever will copy our patterns, and follow our instructions, will save, and save considerably; and will be always the best dressed of any of the ladles of their neighborhood. "I have long ceased to use the fashions in other American magazines," writes a professional dress-maker to us; "for I find that they are every way inferior to those of Peterson,' " We claim, in this particular, to have been a public benefactor, by elevating the taste of American ladies, especially in dress.

THE "DIRECTOIRE" HABIT BODICE.
By Emily H. May.

In the front of the number, we give the front and back of a House-Dress, the very last thing "out" in Paris, called the "Directoire." It is the most stylish costume, perhaps, that has appeared for years. We also describe it in our fashion department. Here we give a diagram by which to cut it out. Directions for enlarging diagrams were given in our last number.

No. I. Half or Front, with two pleats.
No. II. One Side-piece.
No. III. Half Of Back
No. IV. Sleeve.

The corsage, it will be seen, is cuirass-shaped, with very long habit ends at the back. These ends, as well as the cuirass, are finished off with pipings, one in faille, the other in the material of which the habit-cuirasse is composed. The two ends are fastened together by bows of ribbon placed down the centre. A row of buttons, covered with silk, is placed down each side, and the ends are finished off with plisses of faille.

Mode of Cutting Out. – Each figure is cut double, and all are joined together by placing the letters together. The front, with long rounded basque cut away a little on the hip, is cut with two pleats and a join. The side is joined to the back, by a seam made in the inside from F to the dots. From these dots to G, the seam forms a fold as in a man's coat, and on this fold the row of buttons is placed.

The size is given, in inches, for the front, back, and side-piece. The size is that for an ordinary woman. We do not give the size for the sleeve; that will vary according to the person for whom the bodice is made. From the dots, to the end, may be longer or shorter than our pattern, according as the lady is tall, or the reverse. Remember, that the pattern, when enlarged, should be fitted on before the stuff is cut into.

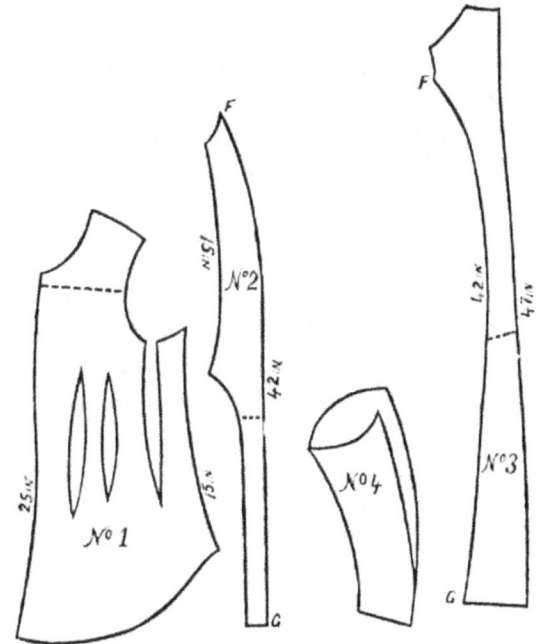

...

Cuffs and Collars are now being ornamented with strings of flat mother-of-pearl buttons, the same, but smaller, as those employed for Breton jackets, under-vests, and round pockets. Breton work is a perfect mania. It is executed on cloth, velvet, and ecru canvas cloth. It is a kind of herring-bone stitch, and very easy. All its beauty consists in the selection of the silks. As many as four and five jackets are worn by the rich peasantry, one over the other. The top one is the shortest. As this fashion would not suit in Paris, the succession of jackets is simulated by strips of cloth being placed on one only, but so as to appear four or five of different lengths. Some of this fashionable Breton work is so closely stitched as to have the aspect of incrustations on cloth. We gave illustrations of Breton jackets in our May number.

Peterson's Magazine, June 1877

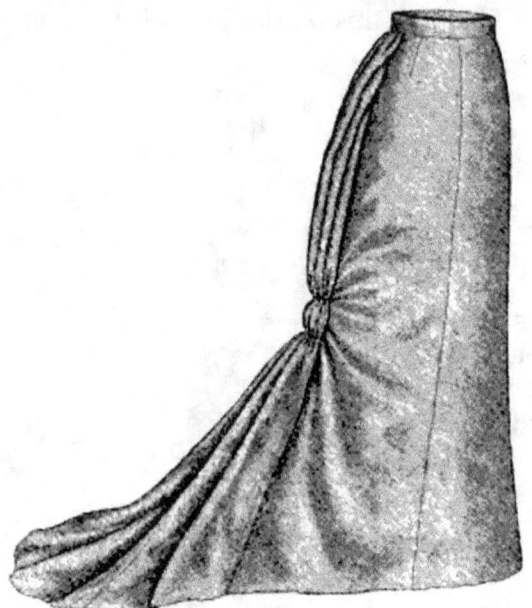

LADIES' SKIRT, WITH FAN GORES AT THE BACK.

No. 4886. – This skirt has a front gore, a gore at each side fitted by a dart, and a back-breadth slashed through the center of its lower half and widened by the insertion of a fan-shaped gore composed of two wedge-shaped pieces. A double shirr crosses the back-breadth at the top of the gore, and confines all the fullness in a narrow space, but may if desired be replaced by a box-plait. The pattern is in 9 sizes for ladies from 20 to 36 inches, waist measure. To make the skirt for a lady of medium size, 4 5/8 yards of goods, 27 inches wide, will be required. Price of pattern, 35 cents.

...

At this season of the year all who can afford it, if they have not already gone, are making preparations to leave their homes, and go to the seaside, the country or the mountains, for a few days or weeks of rest and recreation. "What shall I wear?" is, of course, the first question a woman asks in such circumstances. Wisdom will dictate to her to leave all expensive dresses – all rich and showy silks, and delicate flimsy muslins – at home, and to take with her only such costumes as shall prove seasonable, and, receiving all manner of rough usage, shall preserve their good looks to the last. Among the very best, for both service and appearance, are dresses made of bunting. It is inexpensive, it is suitable for all occasions, and it will preserve its good looks under rough treatment. A princess of bunting makes a charming breakfast dress or evening toilet, and when draped over a black or a bunting petticoat, is stylish enough for a fashionable promenade, and not too costly to wear upon a business errand, or for shopping or walking, or at croquet, or a picnic. Blue bunting is one of the most fashionable textures, and dark blue is a color which almost any lady can use, even though pale blue be an enemy to her complexion. Very handsome dresses are made of bunting of a creamy white. These, when lined with a dark color, and richly trimmed with pipings and plaited flounces, look very stylish indeed.

Arthur's Home Magazine, July 1877

Relative to changing the clothing, we consider it hazardous to lessen its amount after dressing in the morning, unless active exercise is taken immediately. No under-garments should be changed for lighter ones during the day ordinarily. The best, safest, and most convenient time for lessening the clothing is in the morning, when we first dress for the day.

The thin fabrics for summer dresses are innumerable. They are of all qualities and colors, figured, striped, and plain, and are usually made in a Polonaise or Princesse dress, draped over a silk skirt, or combined in some way with silk in scarf style, etc. The organdies are unusually beautiful, and can be made up over silk, or over chintz or percale, of the color of the dress.

Pockets are still worn, but are suppressed in many of the new dresses, as they got to be so exaggerated in size and style, and have become so common. Belts or waistbands are very much worn, but sewed on at the seam under the arm, not reaching all the way around the back. These belts are made of the same material as the waist of the dress usually, though sometimes the skirt material is used. They are fastened with any large, old-fashioned looking buckle.

EMBROIDERED GALOON.

This embroidered galoon is for dress-trimmings, and is in feather-stitch, in colored silks.

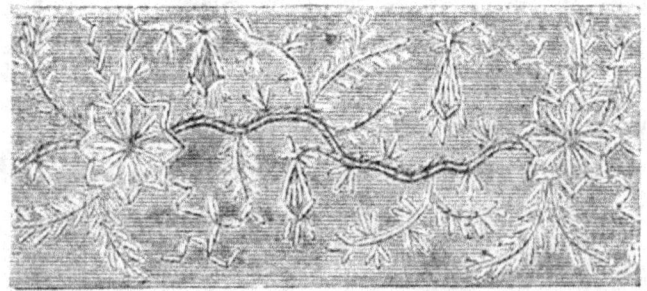

We give, in the front of the number, the front and back of a striped cambric costume, suitable for the season. The material is pink and white striped cambric, but any neat design, in calico or percale, may be used. The skirt is trimmed with ruffles cut on the straight and edged top and bottom with patent Valenciennes edging. These ruffles are put on with a cord, forming a heading an inch and a half deep. Cut the ruffles six inches, including the heading. The Polonaise is trimmed to correspond with the skirt; it is Princess in form, and is slightly draped at the back, where it is caught up by a bow of ribbon to match; two-inch wide ribbon, made into a long looped bow with ends. The sleeves terminate in two deep ruffles, to match. A corresponding ruffle, gathered in the centre, ornaments the front, from the throat down. The waist belt is of ribbon, same as bows. Sixteen yards of cambric, or percale, which is a yard wide, or eighteen yards of ordinary calico. We would not advise the lace edging, if calico is used; simple hem or bind the ruffles, in that case, with Lonsdale cambric, (white.) Price of pattern, fifty cents.

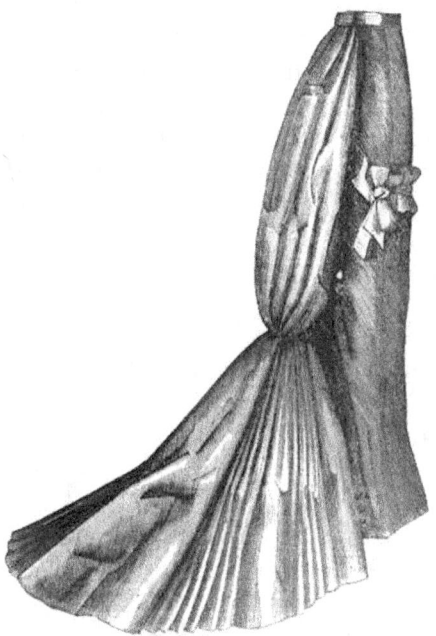

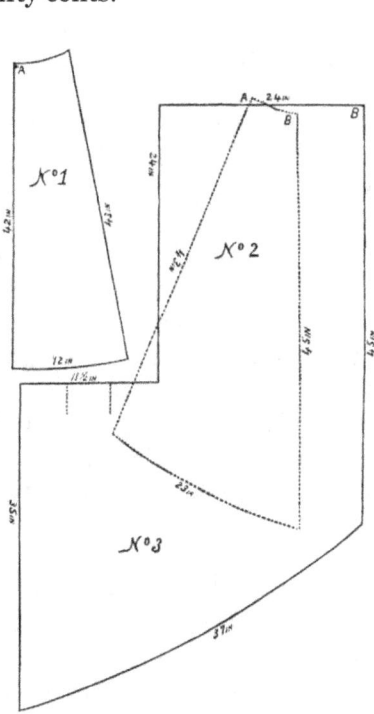

SKIRT, WITH TRAIN BALAYEUSE.
By Emily H. May.

We give, here, a very useful skirt, with a train, and also a diagram, showing how it is to be made. ...

No. 1. Half of Front.

No. 2. Half of Side Gore. (See dotted lines.)

No. 3. Half of Back. Dotted lines at the back show where the box-plait is put.

Begin to sew at the top – the letters, A to A – B to B.

Peterson's Magazine, July 1877

We must not forget to mention a new wash goods, which has become very popular for summer dresses; we mean linen brocade, which shows the exact patterns of finest brocaded silks, and is meant to be used in combination with plain linen batiste, matched in color. There are a great variety of very pretty Madras ginghams in patterns of vivid colors upon pale, neutral-gray, and *écru* grounds, which make up charmingly for children's and young girls' summer costumes. Beautiful costumes for summer are made of batistes and other lawns in very delicate colors, all of one shade, or else in stripes with white. They have polonaises, basques, and scarf draperies, as elaborately made as those of the richest materials, and are trimmed with narrow plaited ruffles, edged with Valenciennes lace. Zephyr ginghams, partly checked and partly plain, are also very popular. These are admired in blue and white check, made in Breton style, and trimmed with navy-blue bands wrought with white cotton in Breton designs. Strings of pearl buttons, with eyes near the top, are chosen in shades to match, and are set about on the fronts of the waist, the collar, cuffs, pocket, etc. ...

Fashion has a tendency to going back to the period of two reigns. From the time of Louis XVI., it retrogrades to that of Louis XIV., so that now we see once more berthas of ancient lace, bodices with long peaks, dresses with the front of some self-colored material, and the train of stamped velvet or brocaded satin.

Figs. 1 and 18. – Front and back view of house dress of navy blue silk and figured grenadine: the underskirt and sleeves of the silk; the polonaise of the grenadine, trimmed with fringe and ribbon bows; the front is cut as a basque, the back draped like Fig. 18.

...

Formerly fashion was absolute and exclusive; there was *one* pattern, and one pattern only, for all dresses, mantles, bonnets, etc.; now there are different patterns for all dresses to be worn on different occasions. Thus there is the *robe de chambre,* the home dress, the walking costume for the morning, the dress for calling and driving out in the afternoon, the toilet for the theatre or concert, and lastly for small or large parties. The Princess dress is excessively long; when it is high necked, it is suitable for dresses to drive out in, and for calling, and also for receptions at home. With an open bodice, square or heart-shaped, it becomes a fitting toilet for dinner or small evening parties, and with a low corsage for full dress evening costume. On account of its length, it is quite out of the question to wear it for walking in the streets; but it has long been worn on such occasions, however, under the name of polonaise, and it will continue to be worn thus from present indications for some time to come. The polonaise is, in fact, nothing but a *short* Princess dress, worn over a skirt more or less long, the one peculiarity of the Princess dress being that it is cut all in one piece – that is, with the bodice undivided from the skirt. Some changes have been attempted in the make and cut of dresses, but without success; almost as soon as introduced, innovations are given up.

...

Fig. 6. – House dress for lady, made of black silk and striped grenadine. The underskirt and sleeves are of the silk, the skirt trimmed with knife plaitings and ruffles. The polonaise is of the grenadine, trimmed with fringe, and wide ribbon sash in the back. ➔
Godey's Lady's Book, July 1877

Never before has fashion been so fantastic, ornate, beribboned, and beflowered as at present, and never has such a consumption of flowers and ribbons, the latter being employed even for *wrappings*. For this purpose take very wide ribbon (as wide as possible), ravel it out so as to form a fringe almost as wide as the ribbon in the middle, and becoming narrower toward the ends; fasten the middle of the ribbon on the middle of the back, cross it in front on the bust, and carry it again to the back, where it is fastened toward the bottom of the skirt under a large bow of the same ribbon raveled out. This scarf is considered a sufficient wrapping for the present season, when fashion dictates the wrapping which the heat interdicts. Such wrappings are of all kinds, but of the same nature – small fichus of black or white lace, small crêpe de Chine scarfs, small muslin mantelets, all as light as possible, and flung rather than fastened on the shoulders. Belts are beginning to reappear; then are fastened under the left or right arm with a buckle, a bow, or a metal clasp. These belts are not worn on belted waists, but rather with cuirass basques of all kinds; I purposely say all kinds, for cuirass basques are not by any means all of one shape. There are some which are laid in flat pleats in the back and front; others are made with a Breton or Swiss plastron (the Swiss plastron is pleated perpendicularly), and still others have a *Mousquetaire* or Louis XIV. vest.

WATERING-PLACE TOILETTE.

This handsome suit has a skirt of dark brown gros grain, trimmed on the bottom with two gathered flounces. The Breton polonaise of cream wool is trimmed with variegated galloon, with a red, blue, yellow, and white Persian pattern, and fringe of the same colors. The rolling collar is formed of the same galloon, which likewise trims the cuffs and the seams of the sleeves. The polonaise is slashed at the sides, and finished with bows of brown ribbon. Three rows of pearl buttons are set in front; the back is also ornamented with buttons. Tuscan straw hat, trimmed with brown ribbon, with a ruche inside the brim.

...

WALKING SUIT.

This pretty suit consists of a skirt, polonaise, and long close-fitting jacket. The skirt is of claret faille, trimmed on the bottom with a. deep side-pleated flounce, surmounted by a wide puff and narrow

side-pleating. The polonaise of gray foulard is closed diagonally on the left side, and slightly looped at the bottom. The polonaise is trimmed on the bottom and up the side seams with a side-pleating, surmounted by a bias fold of claret faille. The gray foulard jacket is bordered with claret faille; the cuffs, collar, and pockets are of the same material. Tuscan straw bonnet, with scarf of claret faille wound around the crown, and bunches of thistles on the side and in front under the brim.

...

The favorite trimming for dark dresses at present is *clair de lune* jet, which is used for embroidering bands of black tulle or gauze more or less deep; these bands are employed in the guise of galloons,

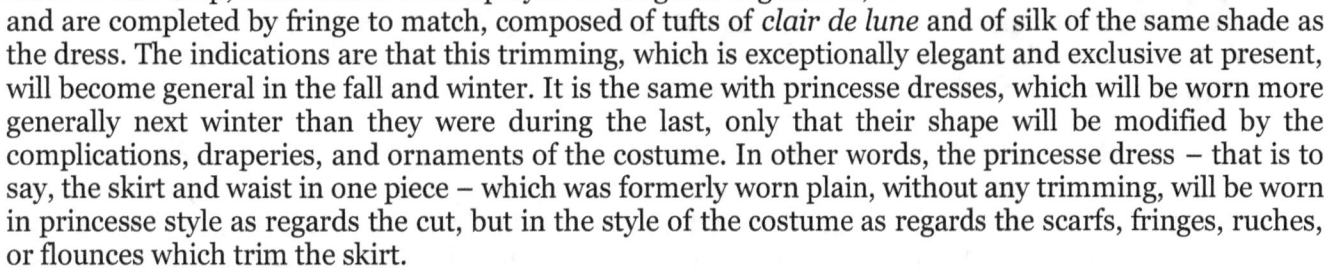

and are completed by fringe to match, composed of tufts of *clair de lune* and of silk of the same shade as the dress. The indications are that this trimming, which is exceptionally elegant and exclusive at present, will become general in the fall and winter. It is the same with princesse dresses, which will be worn more generally next winter than they were during the last, only that their shape will be modified by the complications, draperies, and ornaments of the costume. In other words, the princesse dress – that is to say, the skirt and waist in one piece – which was formerly worn plain, without any trimming, will be worn in princesse style as regards the cut, but in the style of the costume as regards the scarfs, fringes, ruches, or flounces which trim the skirt.

For the fall, pipings will take a leading place among the trimmings for dresses. Single pipings are no longer used, but, double pipings of two colors are employed for a dress of a different shade or color. For instance, a gray dress has two pipings, one bronze and the other red; a brown dress has pipings of a lighter shade of brown and golden yellow or mandarin; a prune dress is piped with straw-color of two different shades. For such toilettes a well-known trimming has been revived, which, however, is always pretty, and admits of many ingenious combinations. The under edge of the skirt and polonaise is cut in square tabs and edged with pipings, under which is set a pleated flounce of the same color as the dress trimmings. ...

All the corsages in preparation with a view to fall dinner parties in the country, that is to say, at the châteaux both large and small, are in the Breton or Swiss style; in other words, with a rounded plastron, and passing below the belt in the former case. In the Swiss corsage, the plastron, pleated perpendicularly, and made of the same material as the skirt and the sleeves, merely takes the place of the white linen chemisette which the Swiss peasants wear with their velvet bodice, which serves as a corsage with them. Sometimes, also, this Swiss plastron is made of black or white lace, according as the color of the dress is light or dark, and the sleeves are like the plastron.

BACK BREADTHS.

All ingenuity must be lacking this season if half-worn house dresses of silk, or wool, or cashmere cannot be converted by means of some new material into something novel and stylish. The over-skirt being no longer a necessity, much wider caprices in trimming may be indulged in. Some rules, however, have become fixed laws in fashion, one of which is that every skirt must at least have a demi-train, and present a sweeping or full appearance in the lower half of the back breadths, although the front be drawn back almost plainly. The back breadths at present used by fashionable modistes serve admirably in remodeling a half-worn garment; any old silk of solid color may be used to make back breadths, trimmings, and sleeves, a new or different material being employed for the front breadths and waist. There are several ways of making these combination dresses; one of the simplest, a house dress of dull brown silk and cream-colored cygnet cloth, will serve as the best illustration. The back of the skirt was composed of three widths of silk sloped to make a demi-train, and gored slightly at the sides. These were put on to the belt in six wide pleats facing inward, three each way. Midway down each side seam a pleat was taken, turned downward, which gave a certain fullness when tied back; about three-quarters of a yard from the bottom, the pleats were caught loosely together, then sweeping out in a half-closed fan. The front breadths of this costume were of the cygnet cloth, cut in princesse shape, three-quarters of a yard extra length being allowed for front draping, the pleats beginning eight or nine inches below the belt, and being laid across firmly, the side seams being finished with a bias band of silk, with colored galloon in the centre. A similar band extended each side of the front seam from the neck to the edge of the dress, and had the same strip of shaded galloon in the centre. A knife-pleating of cygnet headed by a double quill of Silk finished the edge of the front breadths; sleeves of silk, with pleating of cygnet and a frill of black lace; high collar of silk, with similar lace frill inside; the back of the waist was of course of cygnet, cut coat-shaped, with pipings of brown silk and two clusters of brown buttons.

This arrangement of back breadths, as will be readily seen, may be varied in many ways: by laying on one wide middle pleat, with two small ones each side; by leaving the train sweeping, with a row of buttons down the centre seam, or by looping it slightly with a diagonal scarf and bow of unhemmed loops of silk. They serve also in making wrappers or morning costumes of soft wool fabrics, percales, or nansook. Polonaises of the cheap all-wool materials are still worn over black and dark-colored silk skirts, but simply for convenience, not full dress.

Harper's Bazar, August 11, 1877

The Breton costume is very popular, even for wash-dresses, as a plain colored material can to made to look very pretty, by trimming it with bands of gay-striped chintz, instead of embroidery.

For other styles of bodies, the wide belt is frequently worn, starts from the seam under the arms. Of course this would be quite inappropriate for the Breton jacket.

We give first, this month, a costume suitable for ether house or street, the material of which may be either striped beige, percale, or any of the pretty madras cloths; these latter are mostly in plaids, but some stripes are to be found. Select some plain foulard cambric for the trimming, to correspond with the prevailing color of the material. If the dress material is of beige, or any other summer woolen fabric, the plain trimming may be of either silk or cashmere to correspond. The lower skirt has simply two narrow-plaited ruffles, two and a half inches deep – headed by a band cut on the bias, three inches wide, piped on the edges with the plain material. The tunic is cut very long and round in front, and gathered, as may be seen, into the plain piece forming the front trimming, which is cut straight-wise of the plain material, and ornamented by a row of buttons (white or smoke pearl) on either side. For a percale dress, linen buttons may be used, if preferred. The edge of the tunic is trimmed with a bias band of the material, two inches wide, piped to correspond with the one on the skirt. Two breadths of the material, if narrow, are put into the back of the tunic, and the looping is quite low. The jacket bodice is long and evenly shaped all round – finished on the edge like the tunic: cuffs and collar of the plain material ornamented by buttons. Three rows finish the front of the bodice. Eighteen to twenty yards of beige –

fourteen to fifteen of yard-wide percale will be required, one and a-half yards of plain for trimming. Price of pattern, tunic and jacket, sixty cents.

...

BRETON JACKET AND DIAGRAM.
By Emily H. May.

The material used is Vicuna cloth, the foundation of the embroidered band is white Indian cashmere. For ordinary wear mohair braid is used for ornamenting these bands, but for dressy occasions they are embroidered with color. The sequins are mother-of-pearl, and they are sewn on the jacket so as to overlap each other. The jacket fastens at the side upon the waistcoat.

A perforated line on this waistcoat (see the diagram) shews where the jacket is to fasten; an inside flap, with button holes, is added to the inside of the jacket, buttons being sewn to the waistcoat. The top of the waistcoat is square, and the widest part of the collar is the front; it is sewn on so as to meet the waistcoat. On the next page we give a diagram, by which to cut this jacket out.

No. 1. Half of Front.
No. 2. Half of Simulated Waistcoat.
No. 3. Half of Back.
No. 4. Half of Side Back.
No. 5. Half of Sleeve.
No. 6. Half of Collar.

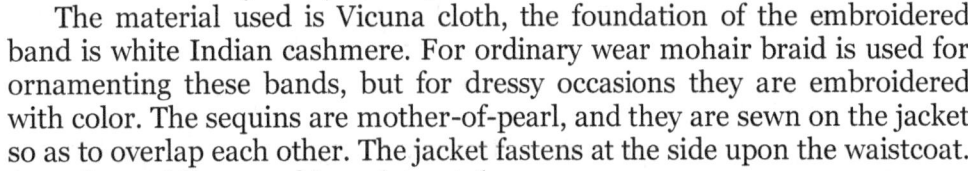

...

We are most happy to state that short dresses are being worn again, though as yet they have, by no means, become universal; the long, demi-train is certainly more elegant, but is very inconvenient and untidy for walking, but sensible people have adopted the "round-skirt" for its utility, and the ultra-fashionable wear it because it is a change from that so long in fashion.

Other costumes are made rather short in front and at the aides, and with extremely narrow trains at the back, which are looped up at the side with buttons, when it is desired to shorten the dress.

All dresses are still made as narrow and clinging as possible, and the under-shirts, which are now made narrow also and sewed on to deep yokes, tend to give more slimness to the figure.

An immense quantity of ruffling and plaiting is still put on the skirts of dresses, though its abolition has so often been predicted.

...

BORDERS FOR TRAVELING DRESS, TABLE DOYLEYS, LUNCH CLOTHS, Etc.
By Mrs. Jane Weaver.

We give two of these new designs in cross-stitch, now so popular, for embroidering lunch cloths, and the napkin to match; also, suitable for linen or pique washing dresses. For the lunch cloth and napkin, use coarse, unbleached linen, fringe out the edges, four to five inches deep for the cloth, two inches for the napkin; then work the border in red and dark blue working, cotton or black silk with red cotton. Two shades or colors are needed for each pattern.

The stitches are so clearly shown in the design, that further description is needless. For apron or dresses, the same material for embroidery may be used.

...

Square collars are also seen at the back of some of the new dresses, but these only look well on rather tall and slender persons. Still it is predicted that larger collars and cuffs, worn *outside* the sleeves, will be worn. Beads are still popular as trimmings; but they make the dress very heavy, if used in any quantity; embroidered bands, galloons, etc., are still extensively employed.

Peterson's Magazine, August 1877

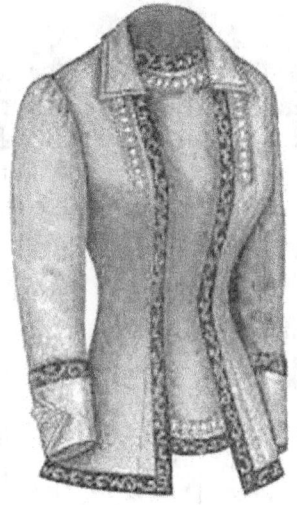

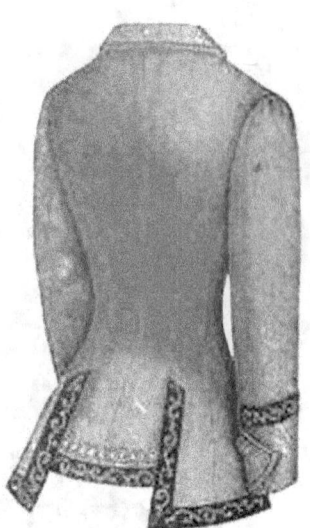

LADIES' BRETON BASQUE.

No. 4896. – The basque here illustrated is made of cashmere and trimmed in a manner considered most appropriate for the style. The vest sews to the side-front underneath at the right side, but is connected to the opposite side by buttons, buttonholes and a fly. Each side-front is fitted by a bust dart and an under-arm dart, while the back is adjusted by side-backs of the length of the side-fronts, and short central portions joined by a hollowing seam. The neck of the back and side-fronts is finished by a rolling collar, while the neck of the vest portion is perfectly plain along the edge. The sleeves are trimmed to represent deep cuffs. The pattern to the basque may be used for any goods, and is in 13 sizes for ladies from 28 to 46 inches, bust measure. To make the basque for a lady of medium size, 2 7/8 yards of goods, 27 inches wide, will be required. Price of pattern, 30 cents.

...

The latest fancy in dress is the introduction of adaptations of the picturesque costumes seen in Brittany. We have Breton overskirts, Breton jackets and Breton basques. The lady, the miss and the little girl, each delight in the Breton dress. These Breton costumes are made in every sort of material – in prints, in dainty cambrics, *de beiges,* summer camel's hairs and buntings. The late decided liking for buntings has led to the making of travelling, boating, mountain and evening dresses of it, and these are oftener fashioned in Breton style than in any other. White, pale blue, cream, fawn, pearl, canary, amber and other colors for evening wear, are made brilliant by glittering buttons and oriental galloons. The deep blues are often trimmed with gold-colored braids for the mountain and the sea, with black for travelling, and with white for useful morning and shopping dresses. This fabric, although just selected in America for ladies' costumes, is a fashion that has been cordially adopted in Europe, where the same material is used for the display of their national emblems and standards.

LADIES' BRETON COSTUME.

Prominent among the popular costumes of the season is the one illustrated by this engraving. It is composed of *de beige* and trimmed with embroidered galloon and "sequins," or Breton buttons. These buttons have eyes at the edges and are sewed on like scales; or else the eyes are situated in the usual places, with grooves crossing the buttons to direct and continue the fastening thread.

The skirt is four-gored and in demi-train style, enough width being produced for the formation of a fan outline by the introduction of a fan-gore in the lower half of the back-breadth at the center. The bottom of the skirt is trimmed with a straight flounce, plaited and gathered, and intermingled with short bands of the galloon. The pattern is No. 4886, price 35 cents, and may be used for any kind of goods.

The over-skirt has a square *tablier,* and a straight back-breadth crossed by a band after being gathered and draped. The pattern is No. 4872, price 30 cents.

The basque has long side-fronts fitted by darts, and a short under-lapping vest or *plastron,* while the back has similar side-backs and a short central portion. The sleeves have lapping points at the wrists, while a stylish collar completes the neck. The pattern is No. 4896, price 30 cents. Galloon borders the edges of both the basque and over-skirt.

THE "FISH-WIFE'S" COSTUME, FOR A LADY.

No. 4901. – The costume of this description, which was designed for girls a month or two ago, met with such decided success that it has been deemed advisable to introduce a similar style for ladies. The engravings represent it made of blue and white bunting, with trimmings of white braid. The skirt is four-gored and short, and is faced up with blue bunting. The over-skirt is reversed in kirtle style, and the reversed portion is faced with blue, edged with braid, and caught to position at the seams. The sleeves and waist are in a familiar style, and the collar is in sailor shape. The pattern is in 10 sizes for ladies from 28 to 40 inches, bust measure. In 27-inch-wide goods, 10 1/8 yards of white, with 5 1/4 yards of blue, are needed in making the costume for a lady of medium size. Price of pattern, 40 cents.

Arthur's Home Magazine, August 1877

A singular but very tasteful morning dress is in the Breton style of nainsook and *torchon* lace; the front part is drawn into small puffs, and trimmed with lace insertion and edging; this comes down like a sort of Breton kilt, to the middle of the skirt, and is buttoned at the side with a lace flounce all around. It is trimmed around the bottom with a deep flounce of nainsook edged with lace. Very narrow sleeves, with puffings and lace insertion up to the elbow, and lace frilling falling over the hand. We must congratulate our Parisian needlewomen for the charming lingerie lately introduced, which is trimmed with Clovis lace in shades of delicate pink and blue. The parures which we see displayed in this style are perfect. We will mention one from amongst the number. Collarette and undersleeves or *plissés* of white linen, bordered with Clovis lace in *écru* and blue; flat plaits, kept in their places by rows of stitching, the edges form a frill, which has a most coquettish effect. We also admire the *plissés* of white linen, with a hem of colored linen, in dark blue, red, black, etc., and made up in the same style as the preceding. Very light and elegant are the ruches in all the different shades of *crêpe*. Mix these with lace, and add a rosette of narrow ribbon or gauze, and you will have an exquisite novelty.

Fig. 1. – Visiting dress of two shades of gray silk; the underskirt trimmed with a plaiting, the polonaise with an embroidered band, fringe, and cord and tassels. White chip bonnet, trimmed with pale blue silk and colored flowers. ←

Fig. 2. – Fan suspender, made of colored silk braid, with ribbon bow at top, and the end where fan is fastened on a hook.

Fig. 3. – House dress of navy blue silk and grenadine. The underskirt is trimmed with ruffles and plaiting; the polonaise is cut very short in front, long and narrow in the back, trimmed with bows, fringe, and buttons. →

...

Wash goods are the principal ones that are made up into dresses for the extreme heat of this month, and the materials are shown in such endless variety that a great revolution has taken place in cambric and cotton dresses. The newest ones are called

"Indiennes," and are copies of those worn by Marie Antoinette and her maids of honor at Trianon. There are some that have a dark-blue ground, covered with palms of Cashmere design; some are studded with Cashmere flowers; others have blue and white stripes, with flowers on the white stripes that closely resemble the garlands painted on Sevres tea-cups; others have a blue ground, studded with pale blue palms; but the most stylish are the poppy red Indiennes, covered with Persian patterns. Another style of cambric dresses are those of dark plain colors so very popular last season; many of these are being made with a Louis XVI. bodice, the back being plaited, and the folds so closely laid that they touch each other; there is a small square collar of the same cambric, and the front opens to the waist over a white muslin chemisette, fastened with three bows of ribbon. These bows are of two colors, cleverly combined; for instance, pink and straw-colored ribbons will be used on plain brown cambric, red and turquoise blue on navy blue, and prune and salmon colored on prune color. Bows are placed on the sleeves and on one side of the tunic, as well as in front of the bodice, and the skirts are bordered with very deep plaiting. Other washing dresses are made very *collant,* which means as close to the figure as possible. One of navy blue cambric is trimmed with fine cream mohair braid; another of *écru* cambric is trimmed with washing galloon, embroidered with red. A pink and white striped batiste is ornamented in a lavish way with pink Clovis lace. All these dresses are enlivened with bows of two colors, or rather clusters of loops, for the prevailing manner of making bows is two upright loops, and three or more downward ones with a traverse in the centre; the loops are always lined with a contrasting color, and are sometimes piped with a third contrast. The batiste and lawn dresses now so popular follow very much the same devices as those of silk or woollen material; they are formed of a combination of striped or figured, with plain fabrics; the former being used for the polonaise or tunic, the latter for the underskirt. The prettiest stripes are the fancy or floral stripes in several shades of one color, such as blue, pink, violet, or maroon, upon a light gray, buff, putty or stone colored ground. Another style much in favor is the self-colored batiste, with openwork patterns. It looks extremely well in light colors, and, if worn over a silk skirt, makes up quite a dressy toilet. The style is either a long Princess polonaise over a silk skirt, or else a Princess dress, very much trimmed in the lower part, and with a scarf drapery arranged above this trimming upon the skirt. Another scarf, of the same material, is worn by way of mantle, sometimes quite plain, sometimes fastened in the middle of the back by a cluster of loops of ribbon. The openwork batiste also looks very pretty in black, making up a useful summer toilet over a black silk skirt. It is invaluable for ladies in mourning, making such a nice cool summer dress, and out of mourning it may be relieved by pipings and bows of maize, blue, or rose-colored silk, a very fashionable style. The bonnet to match may be of black chip, with flowers of the color of the trimmings.

Figs. 15 and 18. – Front and back view of ladies' dress, made of black silk; the back of skirt is laid in large plaits, the front part tightly gored, and trimmed with braid, crossed in diamonds, fastened at the sides with buttons; the front of waist is cut like a polonaise, trimmed with a plaiting, braid, buttons, and ribbon bows. This polonaise front forms a drapery in the back of skirt.

...

The favorite bodice of the season is that called Louis XIV., the front being of striped material, the train either plain or of small checks; the waistcoat matching the front of the dress, the bodice matching the train. For example, take a dress of the fashionable moss color and pale blue. By moss green is meant that peculiar shade of yellow green belonging to moss that grows on the bark of trees. The front part of the dress would be striped moss green and pale blue silk; the train is damask Lyons foulard, also moss green; the revers are blue faille; the waistcoat is striped moss and blue; and the bodice damask foulard. The mixture of materials is most general, even in thin dresses. The new cambric dresses are frequently mixed with silk, and striped linen dresses are made over silk skirts. The new underskirts are made gored and very narrow with one deep flounce coming about half way up, and itself trimmed with two or three narrower ruffles. These are more or less trimmed with embroidery and lace, and as fashion requires that a lady should be dressed with the least possible fulness, excepting quite at the back in the lower part, this style of skirt is useful as sufficing for all but evening toilets, with only a short skirt under it.

Godey's Lady's Book, August 1877

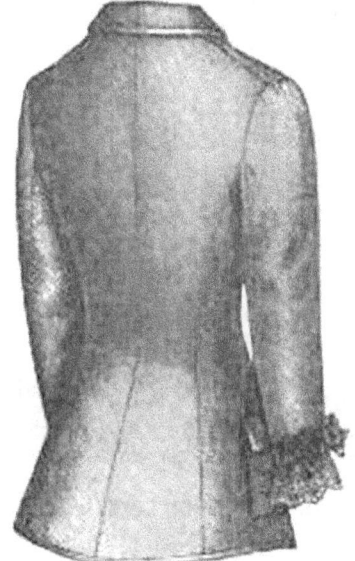

LADIES' CUTAWAY JACKET, WITH ADJUSTABLE VEST.

No. 4917. – In making a garment of this description the vest and pipings may be of a darker shade of goods than the remainder of the garment, or they may be formed of silk or velvet. While the vest produces a very jaunty effect, it may be entirely omitted and the garment worn over a tight basque, with the same appearance as here represented. The jacket is fitted by darts and the seams required by its peculiar form. The sleeves are in coat shape, and each is completed by a frill of lace set on under a band of ribbon tying at the top of the wrist The pattern is in 13 sizes for ladies from 28 to 46 inches, bust measure. To make the garment for a lady of medium size, 3 1/4 yards of goods, 27 inches wide, will be required. Price of pattern, 30 cents.

...

The most striking novelty of the present season is the "fish-wife's" costume. It was first introduced as a child's dress, upon the children of the Prince of Wales. But it was so picturesque and novel in its effects, that it was not long before it was adopted for adults, and is now a recognized and an almost indispensable costume. It is, properly speaking, a walking costume, being made short enough to clear the ground. It is made of two contrasting colors, the lighter being used for the body of the dress. The bottom is faced upon the outside nearly half a yard with the dark material, and the upper edge of the facing is confined by a row of wide braid, with two rows of narrow at each side of it. The skirt, which is four-gored, is joined to the belt in the ordinary manner, with no fullness except the gathering across the back breadth. The waist and overskirt are sewed together, the waist being in Spencer style, having a plain front and back gathered to a wide belt. The under part of the overskirt being faced with the dark material, it is reversed and caught together at the back, much in the same manner as an industrious and tidy housekeeper pins up her skirt when employed in performing her daily duties. The idea is quaint, the effect attractive and the process easily accomplished. Bunting and serge are favorite materials for such costumes, and Hercules braid trims them prettily. Linen and cambric may also be made up in this style, but not so effectively as worsted goods, and bands of the goods may be used for trimming, instead of braid.

Arthur's Home Magazine, September 1877

In fact, beads are very much used for trimming dresses now, as well as chenille and other embroidery. The beads are of all colors – black, bronze, sparkling blue, green, etc., etc.; they are very expensive, make a dress very heavy to wear, but are a stylish trimming.

Embroidery by hand on the dress is rare, as it occupies so much time. It is more elegant than the bands of embroidery that are purchased and sewed on. These embroidered bands and galloons come in all colors for the Breton suits. Ivory white berège bunting and foulard silks look charmingly made up with these embroidered bands, or with pinked out ruchings quilled, very full of silk, in two colors, such as delicate blue and pink, dark blue and dark red, black and orange, moss green and pink, blue and linden or tilleul, violet and primrose, etc.

The waistband or belt is worn even over the long vest fronts that appear with so many jackets, and coat basques; these belts are usually wide, and are especially becoming to slim figures, the unbroken line of the polonaise and cuirass waist is more becoming to stouter persons.

Next, we give a costume for the street, of Armure plaided woolen goods in two shades of the same color. The underskirt is simply trimmed with eight rows of worsted braid, sewed on flat. The tunic, which is a combination of Breton trimming with the Princesse form, is very elegant. Notice, it is cut without any seam in the middle of the back – something quite new, and going to be very popular. Three rows of braid finish the edge. Nine inches above, across the back, there are eight rows of the braid, edged with a tied fringe. Flaps are put in at the side seams, and ornamented with four buttons; this is repeated just below the waist. Two long loops of silk are added. The front is simply buttoned from the throat down. Eight rows of the braid trims the garment around the neck. Tight coat sleeves – trimmed to match – ten yards of double width material, or fifteen of single; two pieces of mohair braid, twenty-four yards long; three-fourths to one yard of fringe; four dozen buttons will be required. This style will be very fashionable for the early autumn. Price of pattern, fifty cents and stamp.

...

Fruit is as much the fashion for trimming ball-dresses as flowers. Pale blue, ornamented with crab apples; white, covered with cherries; tea-rose tulle, with garlands of black currants, etc., etc., are among the costumes at a recent ball, given by Mme. Rothschilds, in Paris.

Wearing real flowers is becoming, more and more, the rage in Paris. Wealthy ladies there, whose visiting list is large, contract with a nurseryman for a supply of flowers; and as much as fifty dollars a month is often paid for three small bouquets daily.

BRETON TUNIC TO MATCH JACKET IN FORMER NUMBER.
By Emily H. May.

In August number we gave a diagram for the Breton jacket, and this month we give the tunic to match. Many of the new self-colored cambric costumes are made up in this style, but the material used in our model is vicugna cloth; the foundation of the embroidered bands is white Indian cashmere. For ordinary wear mohair braid is used for ornamenting this bands, but for dressy occasions they are embroidered with color. The sequins are mother-of-pearl buttons, and they are sewn or the jacket so as to overlap each other.

No. 1. Half of Tablier.
No. 2. Half of Square Tunic for the Back.
No. 3. Pocket.

To enlarge this diagram, take a newspaper, and cut out No. 2 in a parallelogram, sixty-four inches long and fifteen inches wide. Then, cut out No. 1 in the same way, following the angles and curves, and making the several sides thirteen inches, thirty inches, thirty-four inches, and thirty-six inches. The same with No. 3. With a little patience, you can enlarge any of our diagrams.

...

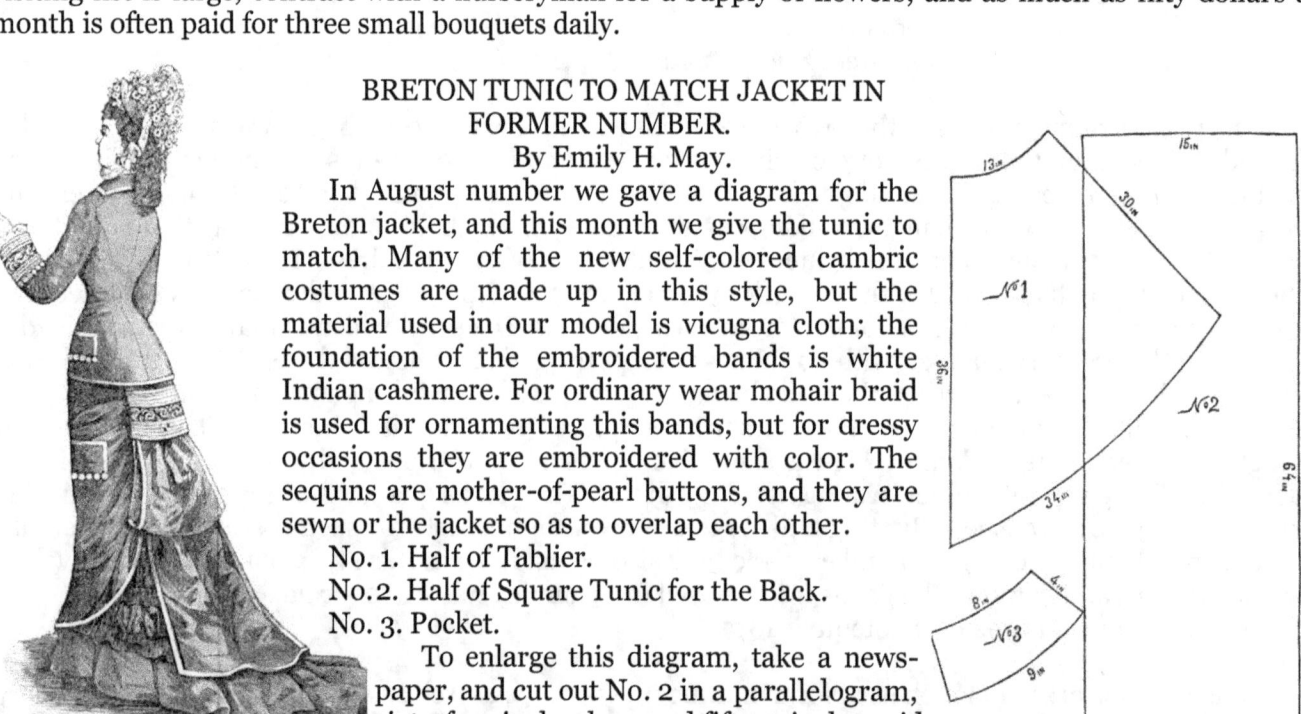

Figs. VII and VIII. – Front and back of a Breton Jacket. – This jacket is intended for house wear, but can be worn by young girls out of doors. It is original in style; is of dark blue cloth, and it is trimmed with braid embroidered with silks of bright and various colors, and with mother-of-pearl buttons. The jacket has a plastron, and fastens at the side; the square revers and the pocket at the back are in the same style.

...

Peterson's Magazine, September 1877

Fashion, taste, and style – these are the elements of a successful toilet. Fashion decrees the general form of the garments: taste protests and frequently attempts to obtain amendments; and style – the rarest of all personal gifts – applies the decrees with perhaps a little exaggeration, when beauty and fortune are the possessors of it. Fashion now decides that dresses, or rather sheaths (for skirts are nothing more), should be unprecedently narrow. How their wearers are to get into them is apparently a matter of no import, the inventive genius of dressmakers being employed rather in calculations for rendering all undergarments as scanty in proportion, and as few in number, as possible. There is quite a revolution in underwear. Not only has there been introduced a combination of chemise and drawers in one, but a high petticoat bodice is now added to the chemise, and thus makes three garments in one. It is a most impractical invention, and one we cannot even give the name of; but we regret to say many of our fair belles have adopted it so as to give to their drapery the extreme clinging effect fashion decrees as necessary. It is true, the Princess dress has in a slight degree done away with this scanty apparel, as some slight under-drapery is required to support the train.

As yet it is almost too early in the season to speak definitely about autumn fashions. Polonaises, very long, and caught up considerably at the back, will, with the Princess shape, prove (as far as we can now judge) prevailing fashions. Jackets of the same material as the dress are also seen; several different shapes are admissible. The "veste," long in front and shorter at the back, will be still to some extent worn. We have also the half tight fitting jacket, made very long both back and front. This is not as a general rule as popular as the former shape, as it does not have as jaunty an appearance.

Fig. 1. – House dress of myrtle green silk and striped camel's hair; the underskirt and basque waist are of the silk, trimmed with the striped goods; the overskirt of the striped, trimmed with a plaited ruffle to match those on underskirt. Silk cuffs and buttons on the sleeves.

...

Let us leave for a while the dominion of novelty, and see if for this present intermediate season some of last season's fashions may not be made available for present wear. By showing this to be feasible, we shall confer a boon on those amongst our readers who prudently wish to practise economy, and are ever seeking for means to accomplish this end. To find in an old costume the combinations requisite for a new dress, may seem perhaps an almost impossible achievement to those who have not given the subject consideration. If you have time, taste, and dexterity, the matter will not present any great difficulty. We will now suppose a costume composed of skirt, overdress, and cuirass, well recognized by all your acquaintances, and of which you are heartily tired. You would, we presume, prefer a Princess dress. We will endeavor to furnish you with a fairly accurate idea of the means by which this desired change may be brought about. Out of the skirt it will be easy to manage a plaited flounce, also a *gilet,* or waistcoat, to renovate the front of the original corsage. If you unpick the breadths of the overskirt, and join them judiciously to sides and back of bodice, you will find you have added sufficient length to the dress. The front breadth taken out of overskirt may be gathered at the sides, in order to make some sort of puffing, to relieve the monotony of general effect. Galloon forms a suitable trimming for the corsage, and must be so disposed as to conceal the seams, which serve to join the basque to the bodice. The flounce held in reserve is placed at the edge of the dress,

which must be rendered complete by an "added train," with a bow of galloon similar to that used for the bodice; sleeves with plaitings, and trimming to correspond with the rest. The width of the overdress, and the difference of materials employed in the original costume, will suggest modifications which must be skilfully turned to use. In most cases we confidently believe that the result obtained and the sum saved will prove adequate compensation for the time and trouble expended on the work.

...

Fig. 13. – Silk and Cashmere toilet. The color is the peculiar green bronze called Florentine. The faille skirt, which is of the darker shade, is bordered with a plaiting in front; this plaiting is headed with a crossband and a diagonal kilting. The Cashmere overdress consists of a tablier, bordered with crewel embroidery worked on the Cashmere. The plaited waistcoat matches the skirt, and is cut low in front, a white damask chemisette being worn beneath. The back of the skirt is plain, being mounted to the waistband with a Bulgare plait; the overdress is laced with silk cord that matches the skirt in color; the embroidery borders the edge of the overdress, and is carried up each side, forming an angle midway. The upper part describes a long vest, and the coat-shaped sleeves have cuffs that are laced, the lacing terminating beneath the arm with tassels; the dog collar necklet is likewise embroidered.

...

The toilets made entirely of chenille are new and very pretty, they are somewhat heavy for the present month, but will be particularly appropriate for later in the autumn: for example, the toad-green sicilienne, or *crêpe de Lyon* toilet embroidered all over with moss-green chenille, so worked that it forms the vermicelli pattern all over the foundation. There are also tunics and cuirasses, and polonaises made of an open net-work of chenille and fringed at the edge; they are usually in dark colors or in black, so they are useful over almost any variety of skirt.

Godey's Lady's Book, September 1877

LADIES' POLONAISE.

No. 4969. – Suit goods, with pipings of contrasting color and pearl Breton buttons, are illustrated in this model. The polonaise is double -breasted in front and in coat style at the back, and is handsomely fitted by darts, under -arm gores, side-backs and a seam at the center of the back. The pipings may be of silk, velvet or the material in the same shade. The pattern is in 13 sizes for ladies from 28 to 46 inches, bust measure. Of material 27 inches wide, 6 3/8 yards are needed in making the garment for a lady of medium size. Price of pattern, 35 cents.

...

The Breton styles of dress are just now in favor; but anything so pronounced as they are, which acquires such sudden and wide-spread popularity, is almost certain to be discarded early. The popular taste wearies of that which becomes too common.

In basques there are various styles, double and single breasted, closing perpendicularly and diagonally, long and short. Overskirts show a tendency toward a gradual but a sure decrease of drapery, and many of the newest patterns fall in entirely plain folds down the back of the dress. Some of those which are plain at the back are disposed in either straight or diagonal folds across the front. ...

Dresses of very rich fabrics have lace added to the wrists, sometimes extending over the hand as far as the knuckles. Light trained dresses have a delicate plaiting of muslin edged with lace around the bottom of the skirt, just showing beneath it, and serving as a protection against dust and dirt.

...

In trimmings, satin will be recognized the coming season as holding an important place. It will be used in either folds, pipings or plaitings. A well-finished quality of linen-back satin is more durable, and in every way more desirable, than a light grade of manufacture wrought entirely of silk. Fringes still hold their own, though it is whispered that laces are shortly to supercede them. One of the novelties of the season in the way of trimming will be a galloon of variable width, embossed with bright and positive tints, representing arabesques, leaves, vines, and even insects. Some of these galloons are in silk, and others in worsted.

Arthur's Home Magazine, October 1877

We give, first, this month, a dress which will be found convenient for both the promenade and the house, and which is one of the very prettiest costumes that has come out for a year. We give, it will be seen, both a front and back view. This dress may be made of fine woollen bège and striped foulard, but could also be made of striped and plain cambric, such as the fashionable green and tilleul. The form of the robe is Princesse; the back is continued as a demi-train, which is looped up behind with two buttons, and thus showing the striped lining of foulard similar to the underskirt. This skirt is bordered with a deep flounce, having a plaited heading. The bodice, which has revers, is cut with a square opening, and shows a guimpe of striped foulard: sleeve lined with a foulard plaiting. Price of pattern fifty cents.

FAN-GIRDLE.
By Mrs. Jane Weaver.

The Princesse dress and polonaise, which are now so fashionable, render the fan-girdle indispensable. The design we give is of blue silk cord, ornamented with a bow of blue ribbon, and tassel of silver and blue silk. This is more especially designed for evening wear, but made of black, mixed with silver, it could be worn on any dress.

DINNER, OR EVENING DRESS. VELASQUEZ COLLAR AND SLEEVE.

Fig. IX. – Dinner or Evening-Dress of Pink Silk; the skirt, which is plain in front, is ornamented at the back with a very deep flounce, mounted with a heading, and which is wider in the centre than at the sides, thus accentuating the train. Upon this skirt there is a sort of tablier, cut out at the edge in scollops, which are piped with silk, and edged with a fringe, which has a netted heading and tassels; this tablier falls squarely. Plain bodice, with double collar, one upright, and the other falling flat on the dress as revers. Elbow sleeves, with under-sleeves of crêpe lisse.

The looped up over-skirt is gradually being dispensed with, though the back of the drapery is slightly caught up here and there, when the Breton jacket is worn, but the over-dress is so long that it frequently only looks like one, and the lower-dress is really only a deep ruffle, attached to the long polonaise. Among the newest fall dresses is the redingote, which looks more like a gentleman's tight-fitting frock coat than anything else; this is worn over a plain skirt, and is sometimes made so long that it is worn without the under-dress. This style suits admirably for a fine figure, but a very slender person should be careful not to dispense with too many petticoats. The habit-basque is also popular for more dress occasions, and in-door wear; the costume is made more like a "dress-coat," or what is usually called a "swallow-tail" coat. ... The redingote is always simply trimmed with either a piping, heavy cord, or a narrow galloon; the habit-basque, especially for more dressy occasions, may be trimmed with lace, or narrow frilling. But for out-of-door wear, especially, the Breton jacket is still very popular, and is eminently suitable for young persons, and has a more youthful look for any age than the redingote. Basques of all varieties are still worn by those who do not like the pronounced style of the habit-basque; ... Piping is popular as a finish to many dresses, and when there are two colors in the dress, the pipings are of those colors.

...

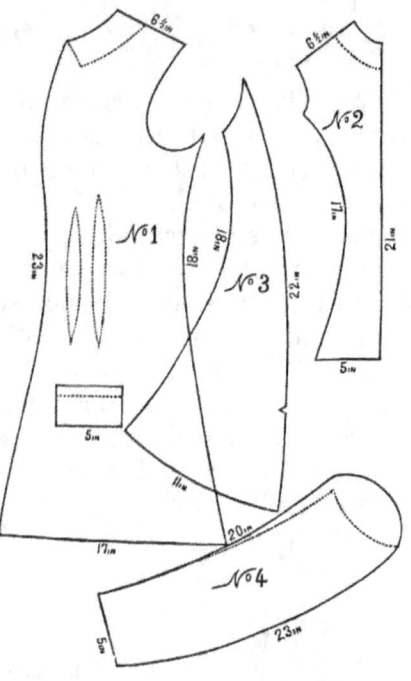

White costumes are beginning to be fashionable again. White is becoming to both blondes and brunettes, and for young girls is always elegant and appropriate. After the eccentric colors so generally worn, lately, it is a relief to see white once more.

We give, this month, a new and stylish pelisse, called the Windsor, particularly suitable for the season. It may be made of any kind of striped material desired; our engraving represents a striped camel's hair.

No. 1. Half of Front.
No. 2. Half of Back.
No. 3. Half of Side Back.
No. 4. Sleeve.

Peterson's Magazine, October 1877

At this season, when all sorts of plans are being made for the pleasant spending of the autumnal holiday, by so many taken and preferred to that of the heated summer, a few words respecting travelling dresses and other necessaries will hardly be out of place. The first object is to take as little baggage as possible when the case is one of a mere tour; that is, if there are no possible visits to make, the matter, with a little forethought, should be very simple.

The travelling dress is the first consideration, and its texture must of course depend upon the nature of the journey. If this is to be performed entirely by rail, a material that repels the dust is the first consideration. Alpaca is perhaps the best, but there are many other wool goods with smooth surface that will answer. If much walking is contemplated, a waterproof material becomes almost a necessity, for walks are chiefly undertaken in picturesque, mountainous districts, where heavy showers are of constant occurrence. And again, if there is a probability that much boating will be undertaken, it should be borne in mind that there is no material tint shows the stains of salt water so little as navy blue serge. There is nothing that looks so bad for a travelling dress as what is often seen in that capacity, namely, a dress never originally intended for that purpose, which is half worn out and shabby. Some ladies go on the principle that "anything will do to travel in," oblivious of the fact that they see more people on a journey than they probably do at almost any other time, and that nothing looks so bad as a dress inappropriate to its purpose. A travelling dress should be of strong material, neither light nor showy in color, nor overburthened with trimming, which only catches the dust. Above all things, it should be made of walking length, without a train, as it is of the greatest importance to leave the hands free for the conveyance of small packages, though these should be avoided as much as possible. Any outer garment should be made with sleeves, as loose flowing raiment is dreadfully in the way. An ulster is an excellent wrap, ugly as it is, but it can only be adopted by ladies of slight figure. The most comfortable hat is of felt, small, and to fit closely to the head. With respect to collars and cuffs, ladies cannot be too particular; their freshness or the reverse frequently makes or mars the whole appearance of the toilet. The old objection that it is so frequently "impossible to get them properly laundried" need no longer be urged, as they can be procured so well made of paper as to be absolutely undistinguishable from linen, and can be thrown away when done with, thus obviating much of the annoyance inseparable from strange laundresses. Gloves are another important item in appearance. Some people appear to save up all their soiled light gloves for travelling in, and nothing can by any possibility look worse. Dark gloves not very tight, but capable of being removed without vast effort, are the most appropriate – dog skin, *gats du Suêde,* anything, in short, in preference to soiled light kid. It is needless to say that boots should be neat, a lady's always should be; but a sensible woman will always travel in thick boots to avoid the danger of wet feet, if, as must often be the case, she has to get out at an uncovered station in the rain, and will also realize that high heels, dangerous under any circumstances, are absolutely perilous when brought in contact with carriage steps, rough platforms, and railway crossings. The travelling dress having been settled, the next point is what luggage is absolutely necessary. It is scarcely possible to do with less than two dresses besides the one worn, one somewhat similar to the travelling dress, either warmer or lighter according to the texture adopted at starting, and one handsome dress for wear at hotels; the latter can be black silk. Of course, as many more dresses can be taken as the wishes of the party consider necessary. The quantity of linen taken, of course, depends upon the length of the tour, and the anticipated opportunities of getting it washed. Colored skirts of linsey of a dark color are worn; colored flannel skirts will also be found much better than white ones. Some sort of neck-handkerchief should always be worn as a protection from the sun, as the skin of the throat is very delicate, and is very apt to quickly burn to a brick-dust red, which is not always easy to eradicate. There are now many contrivances for relieving ladies of their impediments, and leaving them the free use of their hands; one of the greatest boons is the power of slinging the umbrella from the waist-belt; and, by a like arrangement, the ever necessary waterproof, carefully rolled up in its leather straps, can be suspended on the other side.

...

Figs. 1 and 2. – Front and back of Princess polonaise. Olive-green Cashmere over a faille skirt of the same color, and trimmed with tilleul faille and olive and tilleul fringe. The faille skirt is trimmed with a flounce flat in front and plaited at the back; this is headed with a narrower flounce, and both are bordered with faille of the lighter color: the long Princess polonaise is fastened with buttons the entire length of the front, and is bordered with two rows of fringe, one with a netting and the other with a plain heading; the narrow coat-shaped sleeves terminate with a cuff of the same material. The back, which has an elongated waist, terminates with a full tunic, and the sides turn back with revers. The polonaise is trimmed with a double row of fringe. This costume also looks well made in violet gray faille and Cashmere to match, the fringe being red, and of the sort known as Spanish fringe. The crossbands on the back of the skirt should in this case be red faille; the cuffs and buttons also red.

We must now endeavor to give some hints to our readers who have done their summer travelling, and have returned with wardrobes sadly in need of replenishing. The fall goods look particularly bright and pretty, the warm tints giving just the necessary amount of color to the costumes needed. Percales, French chintzes, and ordinary calicoes all are shown in the navy-blue, brown, myrtle-green, and different shades of plum, with white figures upon them; the finish of all these goods is exquisite, so fine that they closely resemble foulard silk. These make up in pretty morning dresses, which can, by having a heavy lining, be worn all through the autumn and winter. The now so popular Cashmere again appears in all the new shades of color and also in black; these are usually made up with silk, but if a more economical dress is required, the Cashmere alone makes a neat and tasteful dress.

Silks are shown in endless variety, both plain and figured of all styles being equally fashionable; a dress is rarely composed of one kind; the two are generally mixed in a costume. If plain silk alone is used, a wool overdress is generally used with it. Numerous wool goods are shown; some of these have a plain, others a rough surface. Cloth is also much used for ladies' suits. Moss and sage promise now to be the favorite shades for the autumn, but it is rather early to speak positively.

Upper draperies or overskirts in wool fabrics are now cut the length of the cloth, thus draping in a softer, prettier fashion, and cutting without seams, and to much better advantage.

Fig. 13. – Walking dress of two shades of brown wool *damasée* and brown silk; the underskirt is of the silk, trimmed with a plaited ruffle. The overskirt and cuirass jacket are of the *damaseé,* trimmed with wool fringe and fancy buttons. Brown felt bonnet, trimmed with silk and flowers.

...

Great alterations are now being attempted in the fashions. The cuirass, it is rumored, is gradually disappearing; and, if so, we cannot regret it, as it was most often trying to the figure, lengthening the waist out of all graceful proportions. The ladies of fashion in Paris now wear the dress bodice full, either plaited or gathered, or arranged in three large plaits, and fastened with a round waistband and buckle at one side. Round waists are, therefore, once more hailed as a novelty; though it is only that a turn of the wheel of fashion has once again brought to light that which had fallen into oblivion. However, in spite of this new whim of fashion, the Princess dress still continues in great favor, and is most stylish; as are also the Louis XVI. coats, *à la Française,* of brocade or silk. The last transformation of the polonaise is the Directoire, with high, open collar and *paletôt*-shaped back. Belts are not only worn with round waists, they are also worn with polonaises; but, as yet, it is too early to decide whether this fashion of belts will be a popular one or not.

For early fall wear a pretty and inexpensive material is called albatross. It is like a finely-finished ladies' cloth or flannel; it combines beautifully with silk, or in two shades of the same. A pretty and inexpensive costume is of French gray and dark-green albatross, with knife plaitings of alternate shades and plaited train; the folds alternately gray and green, finished down the centre with green buttons. Jacket of gray and green, trimmed with two shades of green embroidered galloon, and with a deep frill of torchon lace on the neck and sleeves, the collar opening low in front and to be finished with a loose bow of green silk. Another plain and inexpensive dress is an overskirt and jacket of dark-blue or black ladies' cloth, being worn over an underskirt of silk. The overdress crosses diagonally in front, and is draped in two puffs in the back, with a band drawn across. The trimming is a wide galloon and wool fringe. The jacket has large side-pockets and cuffs trimmed with the galloon.

...

A novelty is polonaises plaited all over; these were introduced late in the season, and gain in popularity. They are made of some soft woollen material. The kilted polonaise is usually fastened at the side with large fancy buttons. Some *élégantes* amuse themselves with painting Louis XV. porcelain buttons, which they wear on these plaited dresses; and when there is a long row down the front they have all the effect of miniature plates. The studs on the cuffs, and the ear-rings worn at the same time all match, although the latter are composed of enamel, not porcelain. When the buttons are skilfully painted, they are eccentric but not ugly. The subjects are small flowers, dogs' heads, horses' heads, butterflies, etc. This costume would, of course, be only appropriate for home wear.

...

Figs. 17 and 19. – Front and back view of sacque for lady, made of heavy black silk, and trimmed with an embroidered band and buttons; it can be made either surplice or high in the neck as fancy may dictate.

Black silk dresses re-trimmed for house wear have received quite a new aspect by the addition of white waistcoats, and for evening wear of plastrons of flowers. The waistcoats are made of white Marseilles, and are embroidered all over with colored wools; the plastrons are covered entirely with roses.

Godey's Lady's Book, October 1877

LADIES' BRETON COSTUME.

Figure No. 1. – This costume includes a skirt cut by pattern No. 4886, which is in 9 sizes for ladies from 20 to 36 inches, waist measure, and costs 35 cents. The polonaise is cut by pattern No. 4998, which is in 13 sizes for ladies from 28 to 46 inches, bust measure, and also costs 35 cents. The skirt hangs very gracefully, having fan-gores inserted in the back, which fall easily into the outlines required by fashion. The polonaise is one of the latest and most elegant designs, and unites the most charming features of the Breton style with the plain drapery at present so fashionable. The material made up is a brocaded woolen. The trimming consists of wide and narrow galloon or Titan braid, though embroidered or Breton bands are considered very popular for such garments as require flat decorations. Bands may be embroidered by hand in any favorite design. In making the costume for a lady of medium size, 4 5/8 yards of goods 27 inches wide are needed for the skirt, and 8 1/4 yards 22 inches wide, or 4 1/4 yards 48 inches wide, for the polonaise.

...

The novelties in dress goods for the coming season have fairly made their appearance. We see in our shop-windows brilliant fabrics, differing from anything heretofore introduced for wear in this western world, and reminding us strongly of the rich gold and silver cloths displayed in the Oriental Department of the Centennial Exhibition a year ago. These fabrics have for their groundwork some dark tint; but over this is knotted and woven, in an indescribable manner, points of bright color. Some of these fabrics are of a deep gray tint, dashed with silver; others are brown with a ruddy glow; still others are bright with tiny dashes of gold. There has nothing so rich in appearance, or so likely to come into general favor, as these goods, been introduced for a long time. The plainness in style, which fashion now dictates, is peculiarly suited for these materials. They are so rich in themselves, they need no garniture of ruffles or plaitings to set them off.

The Princess and the Breton styles of dress vie with each other in popular favor, where they are not made to fraternize. We have not only Breton jackets, but Breton polonaises, and last, but not least, a very pretty and desirable Breton blouse, which gives, the plain sides of the Breton jacket, added to a full plaited front and back, and which will prove very accessible to ladies of too slender proportions.

Arthur's Home Magazine, November 1877

Dresses for dinner, evening, or house wear, still retain, as they should do, the graceful train. The general make of costumes is a long basque bodice in front, and a Princess back falling low on the skirt; the contour of the figure is little changed – clinging draperies, elongated waists, short shoulder seams, and no stint of seams in the bodice, consequently no excuse for misfits. Princess dresses much modified, and very much trimmed, will appear in the majority of toilets. It seems to us this composite style of dress continues to be called the Princess because one does not know how else to designate it. The Princess dress, properly so called, is cut all in one piece, from top to bottom, both in front and at the back, from the neck to the feet: it is plain, and void of all ornaments and trimmings. The present Princess dress is very far from such grand simplicity; it is far more elaborate and fanciful. It is now, indeed, very frequently made with a plaited back, and the plaits are continued, spreading out over the whole length of an immeasurable train: it is much trimmed in front with draperies and lace, passementerie braid and fringe, beads, and metallic buckles. Only one color is used in a costume; the effects of light and shade are attained by intermixing with self-colored silks, brochés, neigeuses, bourettes, etc. These decked, tufted, knopped, snow-flaked fabrics, known under so many different names, and made of so many colors, but still remaining subdued, are used as overdresses, with trimmings to match: they are difficult to handle,

and yet these French models are marvels of ingenuity: the fringes, the bows, the buttons, the galons match to perfection: not a shade too bright, not a color too obtrusive.

...

Figs. 1 and 2. – Front and back view of house dress made of two shades of bronze silk. The underskirt is cut in turrets, with a narrow knife plaiting of a darker shade below it. Polonaise cut in turrets, which extend up the front with a fringe below them. The waist is trimmed with a piece of plaited silk and small buttons up the front; the skirt part with a plaited sash, which extends across the back and down the light side of polonaise.

...

The newest galons are velvet and chenille, and some of the handsomest new fringes are wool and silk chenille mixed. Waistbands of silk elastic, leather, morocco, and silk are worn over some dresses and costumes. Ladies who like wearing these may wear them on almost any dress, without its being in the least obligatory to those who do not care for them to do so.

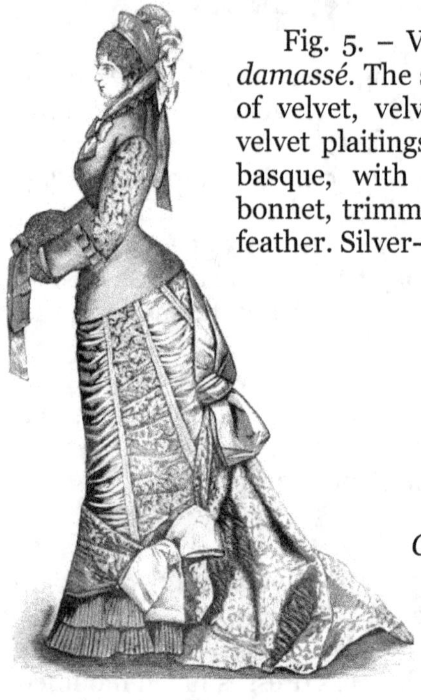

Fig. 5. – Visiting dress of black velvet and *damassé*. The skirt is of the *damassé* with puffs of velvet, velvet sash and bows, and narrow velvet plaitings on front of skirt Velvet cuirass basque, with *damassé* sleeves. Black velvet bonnet, trimmed with yellow-green ribbon and feather. Silver-fox muff.

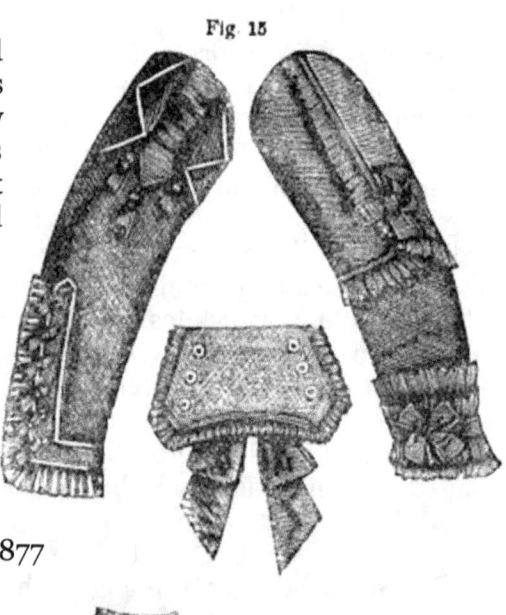

Fig. 15. – Fashionable styles of trimming sleeves and pocket for dresses.

Godey's Lady's Book, November 1877

Next we give the now universal mode of making the under-skirt to all costumes. There is first, the front breadth gored, then on either side a narrow gore, then one plain width, half length, for the back, to which is gathered, or plaited, the fan-shaped train, which consists of two or more breadths, according to the length of the train; these widths must be sloped at the bottom to form a graceful train. We are happy to hear that the round skirt, without any train, will be the most fashionable-for walking costumes, (and it certainly is the most sensible,) the coming season. It is already being adopted by the most fashionable ladies of Paris.

Next we have a very pretty street costume for early autumn, also suitable for later winter wear, by adding wadding to the paletot. This costume has first a cashmere skirt, with a row of knife-plaiting five inches deep – headed by a puffing, with the fullness put in groups. The over-skirt, basque and paletot are made of camel's hair cloth, of small diamond-shaped pattern, woven in, all of one color – dark green, blue, or prune will be the most fashionable. The tunic is cut very long, and is looped on the right side, in three deep plaits, fastened with a button on each plait. The opposite side is not looped so high, and the back forms a point. Trim with worsted ball fringe. The basque is a short one, with coat-tail back, and closely-fitting coat sleeve with turned-back cuff. The paletot is cut with five seams at the back, and is half-fitting, no darts in the front. This is simply corded on the edge, with a thick cord, covered with silk to match. The edge of the tunic and basque the same. A double row of buttons ornaments the front of the paletot. For winter wear, add a wadded lining, or, what is better, make it large enough to wear something under it, as the cold season advances. Six to eight yards of plain cashmere for the skirt, and eight to twelve yards camel's, hair cloth, according to the width.

Styles are gradually changing to something more severe, as was noted in our October number; drapery is still clinging when there is any; the '"habit basque," or redingote is very popular with those who are the quickest to adopt the newest fashions, and looks remarkably well on fine figures.

For very dressy occasions an embroidered satin vest, in the Louis XV. style, is worn, and this vest is then always of a lighter color than the basque, is very deep, has side pockets, etc., all of which are hand embroidered. One of the prettiest of these habit basques was of rich brocaded chestnut-colored velvet, with a delicate, creamy satin vest, embroidered in pink rose-buds and green vines. The skirt worn with this was plain chestnut-colored silk. Another, equally pretty, was of plain myrtle preen silk, with a silver gray satin vest, embroidered in forget-me-nots and green leaves. The skirt of this beautiful costume was of the myrtle green silk. For house-dresses the Princess or polonaise, slightly draped at the back, is still the most popular, though its reign is somewhat disputed by the cuirass waist, which is so becoming to many figures; these cuirass waists have often coat backs, which are cut long and are looped up in various styles to suit the fancy of the wearer, and which give a variety to the toilette.

...

Fig. VI and VII. – Front and back of walking dress made of light grey cashmere; the under-skirt is of black silk, trimmed with two knife-plaited ruffles' the grey over skirt and half-tight fitting sacque are trimmed with a band of fur; the pockets at the back, and the collar and muff are of the same fur.

...

Plain silk and figured silk, silk and velvet, brocaded silk and velvet, are all used now in combination, for all kinds of dresses. This is an admirable fashion, as it enables those who study economy, to make beautiful dresses, and of the newest fashion, out of old ones. Shorter walking-dresses are getting more popular, though many still cling to the untidy demi-train. These shorter costumes, will necessitate great care in the selection of boots and shoes. We are glad that the excessive high heels are no longer fashionable; they produced a most ungraceful walk, and ruined the feet.

Peterson's Magazine, November 1877

Fig. 9. – House dress of navy blue silk and mixed wool goods. The underskirt is of the silk, trimmed with ruffles of the silk and wool. Overdress of wool, trimmed in front with silk hand embroidered, the back merely piped with silk. It is fastened across the back with embroidered bands. Cuirass basque; sleeves flaring at the wrist, trimmed to correspond with overskirt

...

An elegant toilet strikes you at once by its general appearance, afterwards you are charmed by the minute details. Your first glance at a well-dressed lady rarely leaves a lasting impression, whatever that impression may be; a second or third inspection is required, either to confirm or rectify it. In a word, down from the coquettish grace of the hat to the whole agreeable outline of the costume, you see that which must be attributed to the skill of dressmaker or milliner; but the innumerable little things of the costume, these are due to the originality and the particular taste of each lady herself. Fashion still favors slight figures, for the more dresses we see prepared for the cold weather, the more convinced we feel that the simple Princess dress predominates over every other style. It is pretty because it is simple and unpretentious; but clinging, as it is now made, indeed so tight that it is difficult to get into it, there is no disputing the fact that it only suits very slight women. Another disadvantage about the Princess or Gabrielle dress is, that to look graceful it must have a train; so as yet it is principally devoted to indoor wear, while, as stated last month, the polonaise or tunic, with all round skirt is the style most generally adopted for walking and ordinary occasions. Basques are being added at the back or front of Princess dresses, also coat lapels; draperies and long, lengthwise plaitings give almost unlimited scope to individual taste and fancy; so that it seems to be certain that its first simplicity will be lost in the many new elaborations. The polonaise is undergoing the same change. It still holds a large place in favor, both for elegant and simple toilets; its shape lends itself to all combinations. Long ones drape slightly over the train; short ones open in front and fall straight at the back like a short skirt; in that case, the train escapes from underneath, very ample and very much trimmed. Others, still, are looped up on one side only, which simulates slanting folds in front, and others again are very simply draped with bows of faille. Taste and fancy have unlimited scope. Everything that looks stylish is accepted.

For elegant evening toilets the long polonaises are made of a number of yards of bands of white silk open-work embroidery, alternating with bands of mauve, blue, or pink *crêpe de Chine*. The polonaise is worn over a long, plain dress of silk, with trained skirt, low bodice, and short sleeves. This makes up a very graceful and elegant-looking dress, for the polonaise is looped up very low down, with bows or very handsome silk to match, or else of the color of the skirt. It allows of making use of silk dresses, which have already done duty some time, and the trimmings, and, perhaps, bodice and sleeves, of which have become rather faded or old fashioned.

A new kind of Princess dress, very much in vogue at present in Paris, has its outlines simple and elegant, all of black Cashmere, soft and clinging. It is trimmed in front with a wide band of multicolored embroidery. The same band forms a square pattern in the back; it is edged with a thick piping of the prevailing color of the embroidery. The dress fastens at the side and upon the shoulder. At the bottom, very handsome embroidery patterns upon cloth join the front part of the skirt to the train. On the opposite side the embroidery is different, and there is an embroidered pocket. Behind, plaits, proceeding from the waist, form a long train. When silk is used for a Princess dress, the front piece is either embossed or plain velvet; sometimes these plastrons or wide bands, that commence at the throat and are continued to the feet, are studded with blue jet beads; steel and silver beads are likewise used in the same manner, but the handsomest tabliers are composed of embroideries of dead silks mixed with chenille, after the fashion of antique work. Princess cloth dresses are frequently laced at the back, the band down the front is either silk or velvet, and the lacing is continued to the end of the elongated waist. If the plastron and tablier are cloth, rows of galon are added in front, and the lines running perpendicularly. When striped velvet or plush is used in front, then the cuffs match the band. The Princess dress made of cloth is in very good taste, but it is heavy to wear; a balareuse [*sic*: balayeuse] is tacked inside the skirt.

Fig. 25. – House dress of purple silk, the underskirt is of plain silk cut in turrets, with knife plaiting below them. The polonaise has a *damassé* front, with a facing of plain silk buttoned up at the bottom; bows and pipings of the plain. The back is of the plain, gathered from the shoulders to the waist, with revers on skirt of the *damassé*. Plain silk sleeves. ➔

...

Some of the new trimmings are very original. Fringes are now made to imitate flowers and fruit, and for evening dresses the effect is charming. For example, moss admirably imitated as silk fringe, also wild roses; and there are fringes of jessamine, lilies of the valley, daisies, and corn flowers, mixed with poppies. Among fruit fringes, strawberries, cherries, and currants are the favorites. For day wear, chestnut fringes are the most popular: sometimes they are made of wool, and at other times they are a mixture of silk and wool. There are two varieties of chestnuts, the Indian chestnuts in their green, prickly husks, suitable for trimming myrtle-green dresses, and the ordinary chestnuts in brown covering, as they are served roasted.

...

Pockets for the front of the dress begin to disappear. Some ladies have adopted the fashion of slipping the handkerchief through the belt, but this plan is neither safe nor pretty; little bags seem a more rational system to adopt; they may be made of silk to correspond with the garniture of the costume, and drawn in with suitable cordings passed over the arm. Some censorious people pretend to think that this fashion will be generally adopted, with the object of having one's bag carried for one; time will tell; and even should these would-be sages prove inspired, the burden inflicted on some devoted cavalier will not be likely to assume colossal proportions.

Figs. 29 and 32. – Front and back view of ladies' polonaise made of black Cashmere and trimmed with silver braid and small buttons; it is edged with a narrow fringe.

Figs. 30 and 31. – Front and back view of long cloth sacque for very young lady; it is bound with galon, and trimmed with small buttons up the front and back.

A very pretty finish to an out-of-door jacket or mantle is the boa ruche; it is not fur; but, as many ladies object to fur for the neck; it is to those more desirable. It is a quilling of lace sewn on to a piece of ribbon, folded double, and left wide at the ends to tie in a bow, thus forming at once a collarette and cravat: a very pretty device, and one which a lady can easily make up herself. It will be especially useful now with the turned-down collars, which do not show outside a jacket or mantle, so that a little lace makes a graceful finish around the neck. It can be made black or white at pleasure, or merely of tulle illusion.

Godey's Lady's Book, December 1877

The fall and winter models for overskirts show little or no draping at the back. Many of these overskirts show modifications of the Breton patterns, in having cross-straps at either front or back, and sometimes at both.

Walking-skirts are equally fashionable and elegant, whether trimmed or untrimmed. One of the new models is made perfectly plain, with a full, slightly-trained back, which is shirred across about half-way down, so that its fullness is held in permanent gracefulness.

Arthur's Home Magazine, December 1877

HOUSE-DRESS.

Fig. VI. – House Dress of Dark Brown Cashmere; the tunic is turned up with a deep crossband of the same material, and the skirt is plain. The tunic is draped at the back under a pouf, and the long cuirass bodice is ornamented with brandebourgs and wood buttons; it is laced at the back.

...

Sleeves for ordinary dresses are made closer-fitting, and some wear the cuff outside the sleeve in the Anne of Austria style. These cuffs fit closely around the wrist, are deep, and flare at the upper edge, but we warn our readers that they are unbecoming, except to the prettiest shaped, and whitest of hands, without they are made of lace. The stiff dried white linen cuff, turned back over the sleeve, is one of the ugliest fashions possible, but deep lace cuffs, which soften the hands, and form shadows, are not so objectionable. The same may be said of the large Anne of Austria collars, which accompany the cuffs – eschew the linen, and use the lace, if you have it. For home wear, the elbow sleeve with its softening ruffles, is very popular, and very pretty.

TRIMMING FOR JACKETS, Etc.: IN RUSSIAN EMBROIDERY.
By Mrs. Jane Weaver.

This pattern is to be copied in Russian embroidery, with an application of braid. The foundation may be either cashmere or cloth; the braid should be either a lighter shade than the ground, although if a very effective trimming were required, it should contrast strongly with it. The braid is then worked with feather stitch, and barred down at each edge with silk.

EMBROIDERED GALLOON.

These embroidered galloons are very fashionable, and are much used for trimming dresses, blouses, jackets, and children's aprons, etc. They may be worked on either cashmere or holland.

This pretty design is done in Russian embroidery. The large rosettes are copied alternately with three shades of pink, and the leaves with two shades of green; the sprays are brown. The ray and hearts are golden silk.

Peterson's Magazine, December 1877

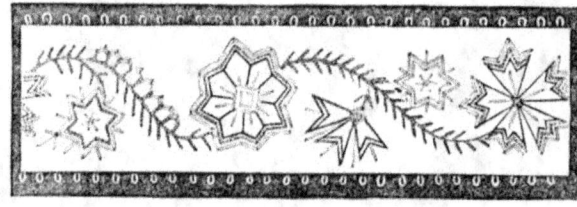

DRESSMAKING.

I take it for granted that you have at school solved the mysteries of '"sewing" (overhand), hemming, running, stitching, and back-stitching; that you are a tolerable proficient in plain work, and that you know at least a little of machine work. If you do not, it is utterly impossible for you to make a dress. If you do, the next mystery you have to unravel is to cut out by a pattern. Have you ever tried this? It is a little difficult at first, but comes to be simple enough after you have had a little practice. The cutting-out of underclothes is a good introduction to dressmaking, for then you learn to be exact in measurement, and how to lay your stuff with the pattern on it, and to follow that guide minutely. If you have not had even this experience, do your best to secure one or two good lessons in cutting-out. They are not difficult to be had, but, of course, require both money and time, of which, perhaps, you have little to spare. The next best thing is to get advice from an experienced friend, for in dressmaking to be *shown* how to do it is worth a whole bookful of written or printed instructions, and most people are ready enough to help their neighbours in such matters if they see that they are desirous to learn and put their hearts and minds to it.

But as there are positions in which even this kind of instruction is not to be had, I shall do my best to help you to make a dress unassisted.

Suppose you have chosen your material, and have got the quantity considered necessary for a plain dress, and that the material is printed calico, with a spot, star, or stripe – what else do you require before you set to work?

Of course, needles, thimble, and good, strong, sharp "cutting-out" scissors; but you want also–

1st. 2 yards of body-lining (if you want a jacket-shaped body, otherwise 1 1/2 yard will suffice).

2nd. 1 1/2 yard thin twilled lining for sleeves.

3rd. 1 1/2 yard thin calico for a false hem – unless you make the hem of the print, which is best for a washing dress; but your material may not suffice, in which case you must line the hem with white calico.

4th. A dozen buttons or hooks and eyes.

5th. A reel of coarse, soft sewing cotton for tacking, and two of better and different sited sewing cotton for the work itself.

6th. 1 1/2 yard of band tape for the skirt and jacket.

7th. Some narrow tape for bone-casings.

8th. A length or two of whalebone.

9th. A knot or two of "piping" cord.

10th. 4 1/2 yards of mohair braid to keep the lower edge of the dress from chafing; and remember that the braid must be shrunk in hot water before being sewed on, or the first time it is wetted it will draw in the bottom of the dress in unsightly puckers.

11th. A paper of pins.

12th. A tape measure.

13th. A large pincushion – *leaded,* if possible.

14th. A large deal table on which to do your cutting-out. If this is not to be had, you must manage as well as you can by making a table of your bed or of the floor. The latter, when well swept, is the best table you can have.

So much for necessary tools.

Fashion even in print dresses varies constantly; thus the best advice I can give you is to take a dress that fits you, and, if it is past wear, pick it to pieces, both skirt and body, and cut out your new one exactly like it, pinning each breadth together as it was in the old dress. If you cannot afford this, then you must measure and pin and *re*pin till you have got what you want.

Of course a printed calico dress must be made plainly, and, for the present, let us make ours only with a simple plain skirt, for that is the foundation of all others – flounces, puffings, tunics, &c. &c., being simply trimmings added to the original dress.

First clear your table, and on it lay the material on which you are to work. Make a rough calculation of the quantity required for body and sleeves; pin this together without cutting it off, and then measure whether enough of print remains to cut out your skirt generously, or whether you must give it a false hem. If the first, you must allow a full eighth of a yard for hem and turnings to each breadth you cut off. If you have to line the bottom hem, an inch longer than the pattern will suffice for turnings. Having cut off the back and front breadths (which are the full width of the print), lay aside the back one, fold the front one down the middle lengthways, lay it on the table, and pin it here and there to your pattern. You will then perceive that either side is sloped from *top* to *bottom;* fold this slope by the pattern, cut it off, and lay it aside for cuffs, pipings, &c.

Next come the gores, and, to the uninstructed, gores are very troublesome things. They are in form a little like the pieces you have sloped off the front breadth, but the way to cut them is to fold the side breadths of your dress (which must be cut almost as long as the back breadth) in a slope that leaves two-thirds of the width at one end and one-third at the other. Cut along by this slope, and you will find that the two portions are exactly alike, only that one has the pattern *up* and the other *down* (that, however, does not signify with a stripe, star, spot, or little sprig), and also that both slope the same way; and as you must put the selvedge side of the front gore to the sloped side of the front breadth, you must take your second gore and place its selvedge to the sloped side of the first on the same side. Then take a second breadth the same length, cut it in the *opposite* direction, and you will get two gores for the other side of the dress, they also sloping the same way, only that way is the contrary to the first two you cut.

You will now see the reason why the gores were cut so long. If you had made them shorter, one would have been long enough for the front breadth, but the second, sloping the same way, too short for the back.

You have now a front and back breadth, and four gores of equal length. Pin them carefully together, taking care that the selvedge or straight side of the gore is pinned to the sloped side of the front, and so on, and see that you neither pucker nor stretch the sloped side, for on that depends the "hang" of your skirt. *Machine* or run up all the six widths, and smooth them with a flat iron. Next lay up the hem. If of the print itself, this only requires to be laid back straight all round, and machined or run. But if you have to hem it with calico, to make what is called a false hem, it is a little troublesome.

Take the yard and a half of calico you have provided, and tear into three equal strips lengthways; join them together, and fold down half an inch of either edge all round. Lay your skirt smoothly on the table with the printed side outwards; take your lining, and tack or pin it closely all round (the folded edges outward), allowing a quarter of an inch to overlap the edge of the print. Do not spare your pins or tacking. Machine or run this all round through the folded lining, about a quarter of an inch from the edge. Turn the skirt inside out, and fold it along the edge, so that a quarter of an inch of the print is on the inner side of the hem. Smooth it with a smoothing iron, and tack through the four plies – the folded lining and the outer and inner fold of print – roughly, just enough to keep all nicely together.

Lay the skirt, still inside out, on the table, and with plenty of pins pin the upper edge of the hem to the print, making little plaits in it here and there where the slope of the gore requires it, and be sure that you keep the straight thread of the lining to that of the print, and only make the plaits where they are needed by the gores. Tack it lightly along; next machine or run it very closely; then put the braid round the edge of the dress, being very careful neither to make it too tight – a very common fault – nor to allow the stitches by which it is sewn on to show on the right side. It ought to overlap the edge of the dress about a straw breadth. If you put a pocket in your dress, it ought to be in the seam between the two gores, and to be lined a little way inside by a strip of print.

Now your skirt is complete except the plaiting it up and sewing it on to the band. How this is done depends upon the fashion of the day, but whatever that may be, let me strongly impress upon you that it is both unbecoming and uncomfortable to be girded as tightly as many people now are. While the present fashion of tight dresses continues, you must of course yield to it in moderation, but neither good taste nor anything else obliges one to wear what to most people is actually unsightly, and a very little fulness – scarcely perceptible when in the band – makes a dress hang closely enough to be in the fashion, and yet avoid the too common display of the figure according to the unsightly custom now prevalent.

To prepare the skirt for being sewed on the band, you must measure it and slope off all unnecessary length at the top of the gores. The easiest way to do this is to measure the middle of the back and front breadths, and each of the six seams, by your pattern dress. Put in pins at each of these eight points, and fold the skirt in an even slope from one to the other, carefully observing that the two sides of the dress are of equal length. Run round the top of the skirt finely as far as the gores and front breadths are concerned, but with large even stitches in the back breadth where the great fulness is. Your band – a bit of broad tape of the necessary length, covered with a strip of print – must then be carefully pinned to the skirt, so as to give as little fulness to the front and as much to the back breadths as possible. Sew the band and skirt strongly together, put on hooks and eyes, and it is complete.

For an unwashing dress the quadruple plait is so much used that the opening of the skirt is generally a little to the left side, but this is unnecessary for a washing dress. I have omitted to say that, when there is a whole breadth at the back, as is generally the case in a print dress, you must tear down the middle two finger lengths and a half for the "spare," hemming or machining it on either side; the right hem must be quite an inch wide; stitch it neatly at the bottom, to prevent it tearing further when put over your head.

As with the skirt so with the body, the easiest way is to take an old bodice to pieces from which to cut your pattern. If you can spare one, let me advise you to unpick only half of it, and keep the rest as a guide how to put it together again.

Lay the pieces you have unpicked (or a paper pattern taken from the dress) on thickish paper, piece by piece, and cut out all round, inlays inclusive. Pin the two lightly together, while with a coarse pin or needle you prick through the seam-marks, so that you have a pattern which not only gives you the lays, but also shows you where to tack the seams together. Mark legibly with pencil or ink where the several pieces join A A, B B, and so on; draw a line here and there, to show the *lie* of the stuff. Fold your lining, and repeat what you have done with the paper, pricking it along the seams after you have cut out the pieces, and being especially careful of those at the bosom, technically called "darts." See too that you have a good double fold in front for the buttons and button-holes, and there is no harm in leaving a little extra width for the seams under the arms. As you have cut through two folds of lining, you have got both sides of the bodice. Tack it together by the pinpricks and try it on, if possible getting some one to help you. If alterations are required, make them before cutting out your print, and see that they are made in the paper pattern as well, for to it you have to trust for all future dresses.

Cut the print as you have done the lining, and if you do it by folding it up the middle, you will get the two sides of the dress and sleeves to correspond exactly. Unpick your lining and retack it, bit by bit, to the print with large stitches. Then more closely tack the two together by the pinpricks along all the seams. Do the same to the sleeves, which *pin* into the sleeve-holes, for ten to one you will have to shift their position more than once at first, for one of the greatest difficulties in making the body of a dress to fit is the position of the sleeves as regards the body. Most ignorant people put the upper side of the sleeve undermost, for oddly enough it looks in the hand as if the circular side should be at the back instead of being in front. This is of importance. The sleeve seam is generally placed just beyond the shoulder seam, but people's figures vary so much that a straw breadth here or there makes all the difference in one's comfort. Remember, therefore, that the back seam of the sleeve is the longest portion of it, and must therefore correspond to the point where the pull of the elbow is greatest, and this varies with different people.

If your second trial of the body is satisfactory you have now to machine or stitch all the seams, lay them back with a smoothing iron, put in bone-cases below the arms and in the "darts," which must be split open for the purpose. Smooth and overcast the seams – make the button-holes and put on the buttons, and pipe round the whole bodice at skirt, neck, and sleeves; sew in the sleeves, cut and overcast the rough edges, fasten a narrow tape band to the back at the waist, and the bodice is finished.

General Remarks. – When cutting the gores of a dress of a marked pattern, it is necessary to do each separately, so as to avoid the bad effect of turning the pattern upside down in the alternate gores. The only plan is to cut one, and lay it face down on the material, so that each bit of pattern corresponds with its fellow. Of course this wastes a good deal of stuff, and makes a small unmarked pattern more economical.

The trimmings of the body of a dress must, according to the French phrase, *recal* those on the skirt. Thus if you have flounces, puffings, or crossway folds on the skirt, those on the body must be similar, though on a smaller scale.

Flounces may either be cross or plain. For the first the same number of cross-cut widths as the straight ones of the skirt are sufficient; for the latter a half more. They are made generally with rolled or machined hems, and frequently with "headings" – that is, the flounce is drawn up and sewn on about an inch below the upper edge.

Kiltings require three times the width of that on which they are sewn.

Puffings, the same as cross-cut flounces, and *crossway folds* the exact width.

All these trimmings, together with braid, gimp, fringe, &c., depend on the fashion of the day; but to be in good taste, it is better to have too little trimming than too much. A good material does not require it, a bad cannot stand it without looking vulgar.

You will perceive, from all that I have written, how much easier it must be to learn dressmaking practically than by description. Still, it is *possible* to do the latter, if you have patience, exactness, and neatness to aid you. Your greatest helps are pins and paper – but, above all, you must not allow yourself to be put out by one or two failures, for if you set to work with a ruffled temper you are sure to come to grief.

Mending. – In the present day, when "costumes" are to be bought ready made for little more than the value of the material, it is often better for those who have little leisure to get their dresses ready made. Thus it happens that to such, to be able to *mend* is even of more importance than to *make* a dress. And this requires no more skill than ninety girls out of a hundred may easily acquire. Nothing looks more untidy than a dress with frayed edges or torn-off braid, entangling the wearer's feet and catching in everything she passes. Yet a few minutes' labour would remedy both evils. Half an inch of the cut edges laid back and retrimmed makes a skirt comparatively fresh; or, if too short to allow of that, a broadish braid stitched over the cut edge "saddle-wise" looks quite neat and tidy.

It is a good plan, when you can contrive it, to get a yard and a quarter of extra stuff when you buy a dress; as generally speaking the front breadth gets shabby before the rest of the dress, and by substituting a fresh one, and using the old one for new sidepieces or cuffs (both of which wear fast when one has active employment) your dress may be made to last almost double the usual time. Otherwise you must "piece" them with any little scraps of your dress you happen to have. If it has a pattern, this can, with a little attention to the joins, be done with scarcely any perceptible "patch." A plain stuff is more difficult; but even that, if neatly joined by the straight thread, passes muster wonderfully; and even if you have to make your join the crossway of the cloth, it is – if neatly sewn and the cross lie the same way as the dress – infinitely better than a hole. I have seen dresses worn with dozens of joins in them, so managed that only the initiated were aware of their existence.

But sometimes, both in dresses and underclothing, a neat darn is less perceptible than a patch; but it must be very neat, almost invisible on the outside, and as close as the stuff it means to represent; the thread used must be of equal fineness, and the texture as regular. Abroad, the art of darning is an art indeed. In England, as far as I have seen, it is a botch and nothing more.

I wonder if girls are taught nowadays *how* to darn, or run stockings at the heels and toes, making them sightly to the eye and comfortable to the foot by the smoothness and regularity of the work? Or does it ever occur to them to catch up a dropped loop with a crochet needle, or to mend a slit across the loops with stocking stitch?

If they have not learned these things the sooner they begin the better, for ugly darns on their stockings or ill-mended gloves, whether the gloves are kid or thread, give an impression that the wearer has no natural taste for order or refinement; and why any girl should not be particular in these little things, that cost only trouble, I cannot understand. There must be some want in her if she can endure to be untidy, when "needles and thread" could so easily make her the reverse. However simple – nay, poor – a girl's wardrobe may be, if it fit neatly, and her stockings, shoes, and gloves are in good condition, she will look like the lady she may always be in feeling and appearance, in whatever social position it may have pleased God to place her.

To Turn a Dress and Refresh it.

To turn a dress is the best way of learning how to make one. And not only so, but it allows you when you have picked it to pieces to take the pattern which – you will see in "How to Make a Dress" – is the greatest difficulty in dressmaking.

And if the dress is not too much worn the turning it is easy enough, only requiring neatness and attention. Of course, the first step is to take it to pieces, and brush and wipe off the dust most carefully. The next is in most cases to wash the lining. Let us suppose your dress to be black silk – then you take a sponge or square of flannel, and dipping it into a basin in which you have dissolved a bit of ammonia about the size of a walnut, you sponge the silk all over, especially those places which are glazed or streaked.

Should you wish to stiffen the silk, use stale beer instead of ammonia and water, or, if the dress have turned brown, dip it in weak green tea. When almost dry, iron it on the wrong side, by which I mean the side that has hitherto been outside.

Tack the dress together exactly by the seam marks (of course turning them the opposite way to what they have been), and try on. If it fit, all you have to do is to sew them as they were before, and the dress is made, requiring only fresh buttons and trimmings.

But unfortunately most turned dresses are *worn* as well as soiled before they are turned, and, if you have no extra silk laid by, or if the fashion of the day will not allow you to use one of the breadths of the skirt to replace the worn side pieces and under parts of the sleeve – (the parts that invariably wear first) – you must use your ingenuity and manage in some other way. Should you have only *weak* places instead of worn ones, you may contrive by slipping a little bit of black ribbon beneath them, and darning them neatly – so that the stitches are almost invisible on the right side – to render the dress serviceable for some time. But the better plan is to avail yourself of the present fashion of using two materials in the composition of your dress.

The Young Woman's Book, 1877

1878

Figure No. 1. – This elegant dress is composed of very dark, soft wool goods, and its trimming consists of handsome silk bows at the side. The dress is fitted in the usual manner by bust darts, under-arm darts and long side-backs. The model is represented with a scarf drapery, which is unnecessary except upon full dress occasions. The pattern is No. 6036, price 40 cents, and is in 13 sizes for ladies from 28 to 46 inches, bust measure. To make the dress as described for a lady of medium size, will require 9 1/2 yards of goods 22 inches wide, or 4 3/8 yards 48 inches wide.

Arthur's Illustrated Home Magazine, January 1878

Skirt trains are of great importance in the world of dress. Several trains is the mode for one toilet, that is, a costume designed for evening wear has a train above a train. At first this style has the appearance of overskirts, but upon examination the most careless observer will perceive that they are only double trains. This mode of skirt is intended exclusively for full-dress wear. A graceful sweep to the skirt is imparted, and the artistic disposal of the draperies are fully appreciated. The hoopskirt worn with the double train is adjusted to suit the occasion, hence the new forms of hoopskirts now exhibited. All clasps and tied-back drapery are done away with. The hoopskirt does it all, giving the required graceful flow to the skirt, and a statue-like effect to the toilet. The move in the direction of hoopskirt improvement is one that will he received with joy by every society lady, since every fashion of crinoline for the last two years has been just so many annoyances to the *beau monde* dressers.

...

Fig. 2. – Walking dress for lady, made of myrtle-green striped bourrette in the Princess shape. The skirt is cut in square turrets around the bottom, with a knife plaiting of plain green silk coming below the turrets. The skirt is buttoned up the back, trimmed with bands and rovers of silk. Green plush and satin bonnet, trimmed with feather and flowers.

...

This winter all the most expensive evening dresses will be trimmed with lace. Crêpe de chine dresses, with point lace garniture, will be among the most beautiful and *distingué* toilets of the season. We shall also see lace tunics and deep lace flounces and scarves over satin dresses, for old-time fashions are constantly cropping up again nowadays.

Godey's Lady's Book and Magazine, January 1878

Fashion is getting practical, we are glad to say. We have short skirts, petticoats guileless of starch, woolen stockings, shoes, and a net for the hair; all of which are comfortable and consequently conducive to health, because, the toilette being no longer cumbersome, the exercise of walking is more readily undertaken. ...

The coat or redingote shape is the newest for basques; these admit of but little trimming on the skirt, especially at the back; sometimes only one or two plaited ruffles are used. The broad belt, made of the material of the dress (if it is not to thick and clumsy), is very becoming to slender figures; these belts only reach across the front, and are sewed in at the seams under the arms. The polonaise or Princess dress is still very much worn, but the palm is disputed by the cuirass or coat basque, and simple over-skirt. The rich heavy looking materials worn this winter suit admirably for the rather stately looking coat basque, and the slight drapery, for even the lower priced goods are heavy and coarse looking, though they fall in

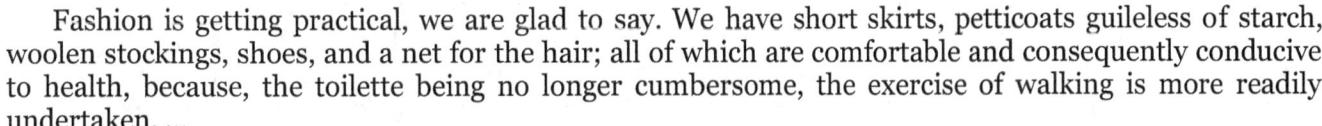

soft enough folds. The old-fashioned corduroy has been used in Paris for dresses; many winters ago, it was much worn here for jackets, and will, no doubt, soon reappear in that form in this country.

Some ladies add the Garrick or coachman's capes to their house-dresses, but only slender figures should do this, and the trimming on the cape should be flat like a galloon.

...

Figs. VIII & IX. – Back and front of House-Dress of Moss Green Camel's Hair; this style of dress, if made a little shorter, is equally appropriate for street wear, as the jacket makes a most suitable wrap, and should only be worn as a morning-dress if used in the house. The under-skirt is of moss-green silk, trimmed with plaitings of silk and camel's hair, and is trimmed with a band of rich colored galloon. The upper-skirt and jacket are also trimmed with this galloon.

...

ETIQUETTE.

Etiquette for Morning-dress. – For a lady, dress is so important, that, even as a matter of etiquette, it must be given the first place. In other words, there is an etiquette of dress as well as of manners. Certain dresses should be worn, at certain times, and in certain ways: one is fit for the house in the morning, another for promenade, another for an evening party; and one who dresses differently, in cultivated society, is apt to be thought underbred.

We would premise that we do not encourage extravagance, when we say there should be this variety of dress; for if a lady uses one dress, she cannot be wearing out another; and one suitable dress for each occasion will not only last for one season, but for two or three, if the material is good, and it is well made, and is not cut, or trimmed, in too pronounced a style. For, be it remembered, a very showy dress is one that will date itself; in other words persons will say, "She has lived in that dress for years; it was made at such and such a time." With this preliminary observation, we proceed to speak, this month, of the etiquette for the dress a lady should wear at home, and for morning callers.

For the morning, at home, a dress ought to be longer than one for out-of-doors. The demi-train is much more graceful than the short skirt; and with a ruffle, from a quarter to half a yard deep basted on the inside of the skirt, the train is kept clean; and the ruffle can be taken out, and washed, and replaced, as often as is necessary: this ruffle need only start from the side gores. One of the prettiest fashions for morning dress is the Princess, straight down the front and almost close-fitting there, but quite so at the back, with a train that is untrimmed: the front is usually trimmed all the way from the shoulders down, and buttoned the full length. This dress can be made of camel's hair, cashmere, merino, or any of the hundreds of varieties of woolen goods, that now come, varying in price from twenty cents up to two dollars a yard, and therefore can be brought within the means of all. Silk can be used, but it is not so soft and pretty. For those whose occupations are no more arduous than making point laces, embroidering in crewels, or reading the last new book, light blues, or pinks, or delicate buffs, even whites, or soft grays, or fawn colors, trimmed with knots of pretty gay ribbons, are suitable. In such a case, frills of lace, zigzagged down the front, with bows or knots of ribbon, add very much to the effect. For those who are older, and require a more sober style of dress, darker shades of blue, violet, crimson, deeper grays and fawns are in keeping.

The busy housewife should have the train of her morning dress made shorter than that of the woman of leisure. It should be without the lace, the many bows of ribbon, buttons alone being the only ornaments down the front, with ribbons at the throat and pockets only. Pretty flannels, in small plaids, or some simple-figured goods, will stand the wear of much use better than a plain material. Of course, for summer, the simplest chintz, or pique, or any white goods, may be worn, trimmed with braids, or ruffles: a belt or sash would add greatly to the summer morning drees. To protect the dress, while busy, a neat white apron should be worn; it may be full of pretty, suggestive pockets, if liked, or it may be made of one of the towels, that are now embroidered in red at the ends (for which embroidery we have given patterns), and pinned on. In our next number we will give an engraving of a morning dress with one of these towel aprons. When the breakfast cups have been washed, the room dusted, and the flowers watered, the apron may be laid aside.

Neatness, above all things, is necessary to the true lady. One woman will look perfectly thorough-bred in a shilling dress, while another may have on the most expensive toilet that Paris can produce and yet look – vulgar. No crimping pins, or curl papers are allowed after a lady leaves her chamber: the hair should be simply, but becomingly adjusted; the collars and cuffs should be spotlessly fresh; the shoes and stockings neat; and above all no jewelry is to be worn in the morning; rattling bracelets and dangling chains are utterly out of place then. If the ears are pierced, only the simplest ear-rings should be worn, and the fingers should be divested of all rings, except the wedding or engagement ring, or a seal-ring. By following those hints, any lady can be prepared for either the privacy of her own home, or for early morning callers. But no matter what the material of the "breakfast dress" may be, nor how pretty made, is it allowable to be worn during the whole day; the half tight fitting dress that looks so comfortable and appropriate in the morning, looks slovenly when morning occupations are over.

In large towns, where calls are so usual from one to four o'clock, the morning-dress, which we have described, is not appropriate after one o'clock: that is if the lady is "At Home" to any except her intimate friends. Then, a dress, with a demi-train skirt, made of silk, cashmere, or any other material that is preferred, should be worn. In winter, the tint should be rather dark for ordinary occasions; but it may be of some rich color. Plain linen cuffs and collars, with a little lace edging, or embroidery; a locket, suspended around the neck, by a velvet; a bow of bright, or light-colored ribbon; a bow of ribbon in the hair, suitable to be worn with the dress; neatly arranged hair, and well-fitting shoes. If the throat is pretty, a dress cut open at the neck, with a plain frilling, is admissible. A dress of this kind is suitable for a house-dress all day, let the material be what it will; and if the stuff of which the dress is made is not too cheap, the ruffling, etc., etc., may be rather elaborate, otherwise such ruffling would be out of place.

For more ceremonious occasions, such as a "Reception," or a formal "At Home," the dress should be of lighter tints, brighter colors, and more elaborate in make. It will be quite appropriate to have more trimmings on skirt and waist; and the hair may be a little more showily dressed. A small bouquet of artificial flowers may be worn on the breast, or in the belt: or if the window garden will afford it, a few geranium leaves, with a cluster of the rich flower, or a rosebud, may be substituted and will be much better. The sleeves, for a ceremonious morning-dress, may, if desired, only reach to the elbow; but in that case the gloves should have four, or five buttons; and for those ceremonious occasions gloves are indispensable. Or the long mitts, which have been introduced within the last year, may take the place of the gloves. A fan will often be found necessary, in the heat and excitement of such a reception; but it should never be of lace in the daytime. All morning-dresses, it must be remembered, should be high at the back and on the shoulders; but, if preferred, they can be cut open, square, or heart-shaped, in front. A good deal of lace may be worn about the neck, or tulle can be crossed over the bosom. The neck should not be too open, however; or, if the dress is very dark, a soft, white fichu, or one made of soft, light-blue silk, or crepe, pink, buff, or scarlet, will add very much to the "dressy" look of the costume. Very little jewelry should be worn, even with a "reception-dress;" but more is allowable than with other day-dresses.

Peterson's Magazine, January 1878

YOUNG LADIES' DEPARTMENT.
Dress Making.

The new fashion of combining chemise and drawers is gaining ground in Paris. The drawers are gathered scantily to a plain bodice of percale or cambric muslin, which is embroidered, or tucked like a chemise. Buttons are added to the belt, and on these the flannel, or underskirt, may be fastened.

The princesse dress and the princesse polonaise, so often described, remain leading fashions, and are seen in the richest as well as the plainest materials. For combination purposes, as well as for full dress evening service, these designs are without rivals, and the same may be said of their appropriateness for the flat garnitures which are at present supreme in favor. Readers are assured that nothing more desirable than these models will appear this winter, as the princesse in construction meets the requirements of every figure, and is more suggestive of trimming effects than any design that has yet been introduced. This form of dress has lost none of its fascinations for the tasteful lady of fashion. It is varied in decorations by oblique or horizontal folds across the fronts, or with plaitings or fringes added to the lower edges of three of the folds. Or it may have brocaded or embroidered galloons following the same outlines. A pinked edge of bright silk, cloth or cashmere peeping out from beneath folds of duller colors, produces a charming effect. Princesse house dress, gored to the shoulders, and not quite tight-fitting, is made of the most luxurious goods, and also of the least expensive. The lady who looks after her family may use it for untrimmed prints, and look as fresh, dainty and graceful as possible, and the woman of fortune and idleness may enrich her house princesse by carved buttons, embroideries, galloons and laces, and make it fit for the lady after whom it is named.

Just as the winter settles into place many ladies rebel against the burthen of trailing dresses for the street, and skirts are shortened quite perceptibly. This modification applies only to shopping and walking costumes, however, and it would even seem that as a compromise full dress toilets are exaggerated in length. A new design for a skirt which may be lengthened or shortened as required consists of the usual sections, viz.: front side-gore and back-breadth, with an extra flounce, which is to supply the length desired. Upon this well-proportioned skirts, draperies and trimmings which simulate the overskirts are permanently fastened. There are devices for raising the skirt by cords run through rings; and Paris dressmakers ingeniously set a ribbon loop above the train, which the wearer pasess [sic] over her arm when walking, and thereby elevates her skirt, while it serves as an ornamental trimming when not thus in use. All of which make-shifts cause thinking women to sigh for the return of the convenient short walking dresses which were in vogue a few years since, and which were obviously so neat and sensible that one wonders why they were abandoned.

The Christian Monitor, January 1878

We give, first, this month, a house toilette, with a tunic train, suitable for dinner, or for evening wear. The under-skirt, vest and trimmings are of plain silk: the tunic and basque are one of those pretty matelassé woolen fabrics, now so much worn. The under-skirt is cut with a demi-train, and trimmed with three narrow knife- plaitings, which style of trimming is still the most popular. The tunic is cut with one straight width at the back, slightly sloped, as may be seen. The front fits the figure as closely as possible, and all the looping is done quite at the bottom of the skirt. When the front meets the back train, it is plaited and finished with a large bow of the silk. The edge of the tunic has a narrower plaiting of the silk, as a finish. The pocket is underneath, and only the narrow flap is to be seen. Long jacket, fastening at the side, over a vest – a modification of the Breton jacket. Rolling collar. Coat sleeves, very tight, with pointed cuff to match. The chemisette and cuffs are of muslin and lace, and the cuffs are worn over the sleeve. The basque may be heart shape at the throat, or closed, as may be preferred. The surplice, of course, is the most dressy. Of these double width woolen goods, four and a-half to five yards is an ample pattern for any sort of a polonaise. Twelve to fourteen yards of silk will make a skirt, vest, and trimming of knife-plaiting. The plaitings three inches deep each, when finished.

...

Short skirts are decidedly gaining the victory over long ones. They progress in popularity daily; and not only are they to be seen in woolen materials, but in silk and velvet. It is now considered probable that the train, be it either of the peacock or foxbrush form, will be renounced for all walking-dresses, and that the embarrassingly long skirts will be reserved exclusively for reception and evening wear. And this is common sense; for anything more absurd than a long walking-dress, would be impossible to imagine.

For house-dresses, the polonaise front has been abandoned (except for morning-dress), but the back is cut in Princess or polonaise style, with either a fan or empress train; the front has the corsage and basque only, and a separate apron skirt or petticoat. For more dressy wear, nearly all dresses are made open on the bust, either square or heart-shaped. Many persons dispense with the basque front, and have the waist round in front, and wear a wide belt, which fastens with a buckle on the left side. If a basque is preferred at the back, instead of the polonaise, it will be of the newest style, if it is made with each form made long, and turned up, and simply corded; some basques have four loops, some only two. The bodies plaited from the neck to the waist, and confined by a belt, are very suitable for young girls, but not so appropriate for older persons, though very slender women look well in them; they will soon grow common.

A simple toilet for an evening at home, a fair, or a church tea-party, is of pale blue cashmere. A Princess polonaise, cut heart shape at the throat, and with elbow sleeves, with plaiting of fine French muslin, or crêpe lisse, for the neck and sleeve trimming. The bottom of the polonaise has a box-plaiting of the cashmere, four inches deep in front, and eight inches deep across the back breadth, which is cut en train. This is worn over a plain skirt of blue silk, or black silk, faced with velvet, or, if preferred, the under-skirt may be of the blue cashmere. These cashmeres can be bought for a dollar per yard, double width, and nine to ten yards will make whole dress. The Neapolitan apron worn with this costume, is both pretty and useful for the occasion mentioned. Any lady can make it for herself. It is of coarse white linen, embroidered in cross-stitch (many designs for such embroidery will be found in the work-table), with red and blue working cotton. Fringe out the ends. Cut the linen in shape of a long towel, one and one-eighth yards in length, twenty-three inches wide at the bottom, and sixteen inches at the top. Two pieces like this will be required. Embroider the bottom of one piece, and the top of the other. Sew both together. The top is turned over about nine inches, as may be seen. This is fastened to a narrow ribbon band or belt passing around the waist, to which the apron is attached only in the front, as may be seen.

...

ETIQUETTE.

Etiquette for Street-dress, Dinner, Etc. – Having, in the January number, spoken of the etiquette in regard to morning-dresses, we now proceed to that for promenade, for driving, making calls, dinners, etc., etc.

The dress for the street, or for the dusty and muddy country road, ought always to be made with a skirt that will just escape the ground. This very sensible fashion is slowly gaining favor, though most people are very loth to dispense with the more graceful, half-trained, walking-dress, which gathers up so much dirt.

For the ordinary morning walk, for shopping, and all the many occasions, in which the mother, or the useful daughter of the house, is required to be out of doors, the quietest of dresses should be worn, unobtrusive in color, and plain in make. This, we say, without reference to the money the wearer may possess. Good taste calls for the sober tones, and few trimmings for this kind of dress, in the woman who spends thousands on her toilette, as in the one who goes out early in the morning to gain her daily bread, and comes home late at night. Dark greys, browns, greens, or blues are appropriate, or a black cashmere, which always looks lady-like. If it is objected that this has too much the appearance of mourning, that can be remedied by a bow of some bright ribbon, at the neck. Silk, at the early morning hour, is not suitable, unless it is a plain black silk. From the myriads of woolen goods that come now, a cheap and pretty dress can always be made.

The hat or bonnet should have but few flowers or feathers; and felt is more appropriate than velvet; if a hat is worn it should be of some shape not too pronounced. But the middle-aged woman should be chary of wearing this style of head gear. The face, that has lost its youthful roundness and bloom, often looks hard and grey, under the severe lines of a hat. When large shade-hats were worn in summer, they had common sense on their side for usefulness; but the hat of the present day does no more than the bonnet to protect the face.

The outside wrap should correspond with the dress, in quietness. A deep plain sacque, like the dress, is the prettiest; but many persons wish to utilize an old garment, and cannot always afford to have the new wrap. In that case, take off all superfluous trimmings from the old one, and make it look as neat as possible. The colored street petticoats are more appropriate, for morning than white ones; they should be a little trimmed, but not gaudily so. The boots should always be neatly laced, or buttoned, so that the wearer need not fear a puff of wind. Plain linen collars and cuffs, always fresh looking, and carefully mended gloves, if new ones cannot be afforded, are very important. No jewelry, except a watch and chain (which latter ought not to be conspicuous), and small ear-rings. These remarks apply, in all respects, to women of all stations; the rich woman will have more latitude in the *quality* of her dress, not more in the quantity of ornament, or in color.

For the woman of leisure, who passes her morning on the promenade, or in calling on her friends informally, more richness of dress is quite allowable, but not much more ornament. Silks for out-of-door wear are now used much less than the rich, woolen materials; but if the silk is considered more desirable, it can be worn for visiting. We must admit that the fashion here is for the slightly trained skirt; we wish it was otherwise, pretty as it is; and some ladies have boldly taken up the cause of the "round" skirt, and had their nicest out-of-door dresses made in this way.

The dresses for the promenade and visiting in winter should not be of light or showy colors; but they may be more dressy-looking then than those worn earlier in the season, or worn for business. More trimming is allowed; but both color and trimming should be unobtrusive. Either a felt, or velvet hat or bonnet, may be worn, with feathers or flowers; the hat has greater latitude in shape also. A velvet sacque, or cloak, should never be worn with a woolen dress; a cloth one is much more stylish, as well as appropriate, for such a dress. The cloth sacque or cloak, however, may be worn over silk; a velvet wrap is, of course, appropriate for silk. Dark gloves to match the dress are very suitable; but those of a medium shade are a little more dressy.

For a carriage-dress, or for more formal visiting, the skirt can be longer, the colors of the dress a little lighter, or brighter, if it is desired (though the rich dark ones are in quite as good taste), the mantle or sacque more trimmed, the bonnet or hat gayer, the whole toilette with a more holiday look. Yet the costume for the promenade, or visiting, of which we have just spoken, is quite suitable for a carriage-dress.

For "Receptions," weddings, calls, etc., even more latitude is allowed; the dress may be dark, if it is wished (*never* very light), but the bonnet or hat may be much brighter, and the gloves light. But little jewelry is admissible with out of door dress, even in a carriage.

It is only in our large cities, as a rule, that dinner parties are given late in the day, or by gaslight, which is the universal custom abroad. Even at Newport the dinner is at three or four o'clock, as a rule: this is, that people may drive afterwards. In the country, or even in the city, where the dinner is early in the day, the hostess should wear some pretty, quiet dress, brightened up by ribbons and jewelry, if she likes; but she should always endeavor to be less dressed than her guests. This is a rule for a hostess, under all circumstances. The guests at a dinner, at this time, should never wear silks that are too light; but otherwise may make their dress as festive-looking as will be suitable by daylight. For small dinners, later in the day, the kind of dress, which we suggested, in the last number, for a lady to wear at a formal "Reception" in her own house, is quite appropriate for either hostess or guest. Even for small evening companies such a dress is suitable. Of course, the lightest shades of blue, pink, etc., are not to be worn at home, when a lady has a "Reception;" neither, as a rule, should they be worn at a small dinner at her own house, though, if she is sure that her guests will be much dressed, she may do so. But those light colors can be worn most suitably, when the lady is a guest at a small dinner, having the dress made as we suggested for the "Reception," in our last number. A few artificial flowers in the hair, and on the dress, can be worn; the hair may be more elaborately done up; jewelry is very appropriate; gloves are indispensable; and these are not to be removed till the seat is taken at the table. The dress open in front is very pretty, and cooler at a hot dinner table; but if that is not liked, the dress can be high in the neck, with a pretty lace fichu over it. Shoes and stockings must be neat, and ought to match the dress. If silks are too expensive, very right shades of cashmere make beautiful dinner, or small evening party dresses, especially for young ladies; in fact, are more appropriate for them than silk ones are.

For large, and very formal dinners (by gaslight), the dress may be still more elaborate. Rich silks or satins trimmed with velvet, or lace, or a few rich flowers, are suitable. For many years, nearly all dresses for formal dinners were cut low on the shoulders; now, dresses high at the back, and on the shoulders, are the rule. Elderly ladies may wear ostrich tips in the hair, or caps trimmed with flowers, lace, and ribbons. No dress is now considered too rich for a large dinner table. But as a true woman should never exceed her means, let her, if she has not the bright, rich dress, wear the best and prettiest she has, brightening it up as well as she can; and with a determination to be amiable and agreeable, she will hold her own with the best-dressed at the table.

...

Bows of narrow satin ribbon are a favorite trimming at present. There are three sorts of bows – the "butterfly," which is flat, and with ends of the same length as the loop, and so called because it recalls the form of the butterfly; the "flot," which consists of a quantity of falling loops, all made of narrow ribbon; and thirdly, the "trèfle bow," which consists of three loops and two falling ends. The flot bow is always made of a single color, but which must contrast with the shade of the dress; for instance, ruby flots trim black velvet dresses, pale blue tints trim brown dresses. The butterfly bow is composed of two colors, and the trèfle bow of three. The mixture of colors is most varied; myrtle-green and sulphur, to which ruby is added, if three are desired; réséda, pale blue and pale pink is another mixture; dark red, vert de gris, and pale yellow a third.

Peterson's Magazine, February 1878

The now universal mode of making the under-skirt to all costumes is, first, the front breadth gored, then on either side a narrow gore, then one plain width, half length, for the back, to which is gathered, or plaited, the fan-shaped train, which consists of two or more breadths, according to the length of the train; these widths must be sloped at the bottom to form a graceful train. We are happy to hear that the round skirt, without any train, will be the most fashionable for walking costumes, (and it certainly is the most sensible,) the coming season. It is already being adopted by the most fashionable ladies of Paris.

There is one garment, even now, which we can take off at night with a pretty fair assurance that it will be fashionable in the morning – the good, sensible, serviceable princess or gabrielle pattern – one a modification of the other. The scarf overskirt is the ruling queen in its realm – a shawl-like article of the material, suitably trimmed, and twined round a little higher than the knees. It is quite graceful.

Trimmings. – The chenilles or plushes that are cut in bias bands are used for borderings to jackets, cloaks, and polonaises, and in two strips they trim muffs which are made of the costume goods. Upon black velvet or velveteen they are as effective as chinchilla furs, without a tenth of the cost, or suggesting an attempt to imitate furs. There are also galloons with uncut plush centers, in both silk and woolen, and they are handsome to use in just the same way as the brocaded and embroidered galloons.

There is much improvement still, in the way of under garments. The chemise is gored to the figure. Many ladies adopt the combination which unites chemise and drawers. Of course every dealer has his own pet brand to advertise. One of the, to us, indispensable innovations, is the gem skirt supporter. They are especially valuable to ladies and girls who wear no corsets and desire loose clothing.

Combination dresses of plain surfaces, united with tufted, brocaded, honey-combed or basket cloths, should have but little ornaments.

Satin in pipings, bands and plaitings, and in narrow folds that are intermingled with silk and woolen dress goods is fashionable. The three combinations produce a picturesque effect.

Buttons are larger and fewer.

The Christian Monitor, February 1878

Fig. 4. – Fancy apron made of white muslin, trimmed with muslin ruffles embroidered down the sides and across the bottom; it has lapels fastening on the shoulders.

Fig. 5. – Apron of white cambric, with small bodice *à la gorgerette.* The trimming consists of white lace arranged in a ribbon pattern, insertion, and slantwise band of blue ribbon edged with lace.

Fig. 6. – Apron of striped muslin, with small waist in front, trimmed with Torchon lace insertion and edging, pocket at one side.

Fig. 7. – New apron of open-worked material, with centre of white cambric, laced with silver cord. Outside pocket trimmed to correspond.

...

The embroidered plastrons, reaching from the neck to the feet, already described, have led to the embroidered bodice, which can be worn with almost every variety of skirt. It is made of either black: silk or velvet, and is embroidered all over in either *clair de lune* or lophophore beads. It is low and square; above it are braces, and beneath it a plaited guimpe of *crêpe lisse,* or of guipure lace or tulle. The sleeves are of the same material likewise plaited. These guimpes are called "Bernois;" they have a narrow ruche round the throat, and below the ruche a close-fitting gold or silver necklet with locket is worn. They resemble the chemisettes worn by the Bernese women, with the exception of the inevitable black velvet ribbon round the throat.

Fig. 17. – House dress of seal-brown silk, made with one skirt; the edge of the shirt in back is out in turrets, with a knife plaiting below. The plaiting extends around in the front; the front breadth is trimmed with plaitings, slanting bands of velvet and galloon, and small tassels. The sides are also trimmed with plaiting; Cuirass basque, trimmed to correspond, made to button over to the left side. Surplice neck; open sleeves.

...

We are very happy to see that short round skirts are gradually making their way into popularity. They are cut quite narrow, and are short enough to escape the ground behind, thus relieving the wearer of the burden of lifting a long walking skirt out of the mud or dust. A single scantily-plaited flounce or else two narrow knife plaitings form the plain border round the edge. These skirts are used with heavy woollen goods, as they help to give the effect of a kilt skirt, which is always round, and would be destroyed if allowed to sweep. As woollen materials are so heavy, sham lower skirts of cambric or of alpaca are being made for heavy woollen suits, merely trimming them with flounces of the wool, or else facing them with woollen goods from the knee down. These sham skirts were formerly objected to, as they wore apt to be displayed when the overskirt was lifted or blown about.

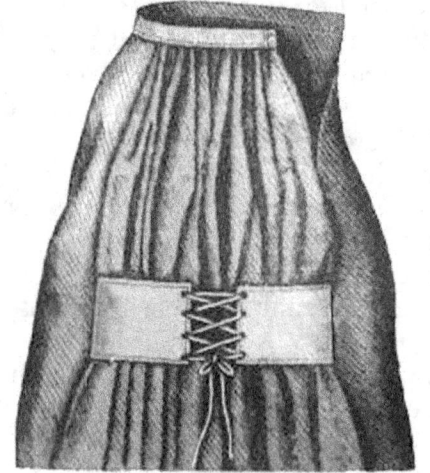

Now the polonaise or over-dress is made to cling so closely that it is never lifted, and the expense and weight of heavy woollen stuffs beneath it are dispensed with. This has become so general that suits of black silk now seldom have the lower skirt made of silk of the good quality used for the basque, overskirt, and flounces, as lower priced silk will answer the same purpose. In fact some of the most elegant dresses of the season are made in this manner.

Fig. 31. – Wrong side of underskirt. This engraving illustrates the manner of drawing to the back any fulness in front of the skirt. A strap is sewn at each side of the skirt, and the opposite ends are laced.

Godey's Lady's Book and Magazine, February 1878

LADIES' POLONAISE, WITH SIMULATED VEST.

No. 6093. – This novel and stylish polonaise is made of suit goods trimmed with silk of a harmonizing shade. The right front and the entire front skirt are in one piece, the left front extending only a little below the waist-line. The back is fitted by a center seam, together with a side-back gore. The vest is simulated with silk, the back facing and the sleeves being of the same material. The pattern is in 13 sizes for ladies from 28 to 46 inches, bust measure. For a lady of medium size, 8 yards of material 22 inches wide, with 2 1/4 yards of a contrasting shade in the same width, will be needed. If 48-inch-wide goods are used, 4 1/2 yards will be necessary, with 1 1/8 yard of the contrasting shade. Price of pattern, 35 cents.

6093

6093

...

Fashion presents us with three new designs for overdresses this season.

One of these designs has a deep yoke, which is slightly pointed at the back, where there is a cluster of plaits that extend half the depth of the back, to be supplemented by still other plaits arranged beneath to complete its length. In the front the plaits extend across the bust, and are narrowed at the waist, where they are crossed by another fold. This is a style suitable alike to the thin and the stout lady, as it rounds out the figure of the one and gives the effect of slenderness to the other.

The second overdress or polonaise is double-breasted, with double points in the lower front edges, and has cross-folds laid in the side gores to suggest the "panel" effect, and the deep back is gracefully draped by under-tapes. A rolling-collar and deep cuff-facings complete the dress, which may or may not be trimmed otherwise than with handsome buttons.

The third design has a triplet of plaits laid across quite high up in front, so that they conceal the termination of the front closing buttons, and the end of the simulated vest which overlies the bust.

Arthur's Illustrated Home Magazine, February 1878

Taking the vicar's wife [Vicar of Wakefield] for an example, it is far better economy to buy a really good article of wearing apparel than a poor one. We find an all-wool fabric, double-faced, to be the best investment for dresses – not a dead, no-colored, mousey drab, but one of the deep shades of brown, anywhere, from seal, all the way down through the reddish, wiry tints to the hue of glossy, withered oak or chestnut leaves. They wear so long and well, too; can be turned and made over at least twice, then dyed any of the darker colors, until you culminate in good, honest, respectable, abiding black. And even then, when it grows rusty, it can be made to look quite as well as new by freshening it up with diluted ammonia spirits, or chloroform, and trimming it anew with lustrous, shiny black silk. The contrast renders it really beautiful.

Now, how much better for any girl to get a fine all-wool cashmere or merino, instead of this stiff, wiry, glossy material, that fairly bristles, instead of falling into soft, graceful, clinging folds. Cashmere is so cheap, now, that a girl's wedding-dress, made after the approved style, need not cost more than six dollars, unless she hires it made. Our last dresses, cashmere, all-wool, double-faced, and thirty-eight inches wide, cost only fifty cents a yard, in New York. A single pattern could go as a mail matter, too.

...

Figure No. 1. – The costume illustrated on the previous page is composed of two shades of cashmere. The skirt is of the darker material, which is only about a quarter of a yard deep, as the polonaise comes nearly to the bottom of the skirt and makes a wider trimming unnecessary. Sometimes a velvet or silk flounce is used instead of one of the material. The pattern to the skirt is in 9 sizes for ladies from 20 to 36 inches, waist measure, and is No. 6065, price 35 cents.

The polonaise has a diagonal closing, is long and plain, and is fitted by the usual seams and darts. Extra widths at the side-back seams below the waist-line are folded in a box-plait at each side, one-half of which is under the gore and the other is on the outside of the back. Broad braid, buttons and simulated button-holes are used in decorating the lower edges, the sleeve and a portion of the back seam. The garment is called the "Carrick" polonaise, taking its name from the three overlapping capes about the neck. The pattern is No. 6120, price 35 cents and is in 13 sizes for ladies from 28 to 46 inches, bust measure. The hat is of velvet, trimmed with ribbon and an ostrich tip.

...

The first letter ... contains a piece of dress-goods – mohair, I think – of a light gray color, stiff and wiry, and substantial. ... the goods inclosed is a sample of her daughter's wedding-dress, worn ten years ago. After it was soiled and shabby, it fell into the mother's hands, as of no use, ... but she, like all prudent women, hoped to render the old dress into something serviceable. ... No cotton and wool fabric can be made to take a beautiful color, not even black; if silk and wool, it will shrink, and crease, and lose its lustre. All time spent in endeavoring to dye such a fabric is a trial to one's patience, and a loss of time and strength. It will dye in streaks and spots, and never be fit to wear. But this heavy, wiry stuff can be made into something useful, provided you are willing to take the time and trouble. It can be bleached out white, by the usual methods, such as soaking in sour milk, scalding in strong suds, scalding with lye; and, lastly, if you do not succeed satisfactorily, by putting it in a warm solution of oxalic acid, say six or eight cents' worth of the acid, dissolved in enough hot water to wet the goods thoroughly, then rinse in clean warm water. This liquid will be as hard on one's hands as moderately strong lye, so a clean stick must be used. Try and manage it without wringing; drain instead, for wringing breaks and creases it. Then, when white, make a skirt out of it, to wear next the dress. Cut bias flounces of the same, bind the edges to give them stiffness, and sew them on, the fullest behind. This will make a pretty skirt, and will give the dress worn over it a graceful, airy "hang." If you bleach it into to an *ecru* white, it will look better if the bindings on the flounces are pearl-white alpaca braid, or goods of the same quality and texture. The upper edge of the flounces can be bound, too, if you desire it; and, if the old wedding-dress was made long ago, or the pattern was scant, the upper part of the skirt can be made of another fabric entirely.

Arthur's Illustrated Home Magazine, March 1878

BACK AND FRONT OF WALKING DRESS. ↘

...

← Another walking costume is of myrtle green woolen broche, trimmed with pipings and buttons of mazarine blue. The skirt is made with a demi-train, bordered by a box-plaiting, and a double knife-plaiting of silk or plain cashmere to match. The tunic is draped in front by being gathered on the front seam. The back is slightly draped, forming shawl ends, as in our first design. Tight-fitting jacket, with a double collar (called a Garrick collar), finished off with an upright silk band, and a crêpe lisse frilling. Cuffs, collars, edges of tunic, jacket, etc., are bound with the plain material, either silk or cashmere, to match the knife-plaiting. Fourteen buttons, fifteen yards of single width goods, and two and a-half yards of cashmere, or five yards of silk for knife-plaiting and bindings.

Peterson's Magazine, March 1878

Fig. 1. – Home dress. Navy-blue *gros grain* and checked Indian cashmere of the *gris cendré* shade. Round skirt edged with plaited flounces; the tunic falls in a square train, and is draped under a bow, which terminates the torsade, concealing the coulisse; at each end of this is sewn a button on the wrong side, that, when attached to loops, secured at the height of the pocket, will shorten the train into a walking costume. The bodice opens upon a faille plastron, to match the turned-down collar. This waistcoat will also look effective in either velvet or plush when the skirt corresponds with it.

...

There is but little new to chronicle in the way of making dresses this month, the polonaise still being worn, as are also basques and overskirts. Worth has made one change from the cuirass basque, which has so long been popular, that is, of finishing the back of basques with loops made by turning up the end of each form separately. These loops are very effective, are easily made, and take the place of more expensive trimmings; some basques have but two loops, others have four. The round bodices are also destined to be popular, if Worth can make them so, as they are seen on many of his handsomest dresses; some of those, made of plain silk, have brocade set upon them, so as to outline a square neck bodice, like that formerly called a peasant's bodice. Plaited bodices grow constantly in favor; to make them very dressy the plaits are piped with satin, giving the appearance of an inner fold of satin. The fashion of coat basques is also becoming very general, and forms another pleasing variety. ...

For morning dresses, the blouse bodice, gathered both in front and at the back, is worn with a leather or *gros grain* belt and fancy buckle round the waist. Thus, a pretty breakfast dress of gray neigeuse, speckled with tiny spots of a variety of brilliant colors, is made with a blouse bodice, fastened with slides and clasps of old silver. This bodice is finished with a large square collar, trimmed with fancy galloon, as well as the cuffs upon the sleeves, and the deep, round basque of the bodice. A long skirt trimmed with similar galloon is draped over an underskirt of the same material, trimmed all round with a deep-plaited flounce. This style of dress is also very suitable for Cashmere, which can be made up for this intermediate season. As black silk dresses are also made up this month, to be worn until the new goods are seen and decided upon, we will give a good style to be used.

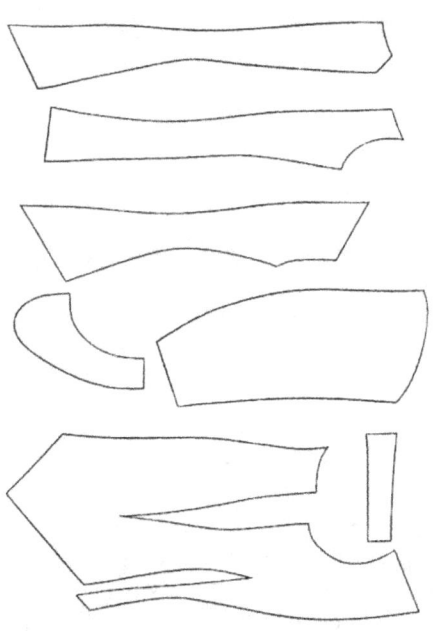

Fig. 4. – Striped grenadine dress. Evening dress of olive-green striped grenadine, over silk to match. The silk skirt is bordered with plaitings, and the tablier is covered with grenadine scarfs, each scarf being edged with tassel fringe. Long round tunic at the back, bordered with a similar fringe, headed with a silk ruche to match the skirt. The cuirass bodice is made over silk, and is fastened with silk buttons. Sleeves trimmed with plaitings and ruches. The bodice is cut out slightly heart-shaped in front, and the sleeves terminate with frills. *Crêpe lisse* under sleeves and tucker. The lisse should be double.

...

For evening toilettes, with long trains, the petticoat is always of stiff muslin trimmed with narrow lace around the edge. It is made extremely flat on the hips, and without any trimming in front and on the sides; but at the back, four inches from the belt, begins a succession of flounces, the first measuring only four inches in length, the second two inches and a half more, and so on to the under edge, in such a way as to support and spread the back breadths of the dress. Frequently these flounces are mounted on a separate breadth of muslin, which is buttoned on the back breadth on each side. This is for the sake of convenience in washing and ironing the flattened flounces.

Fig. 26. – Walking dress, the underskirt is of black silk, trimmed with narrow ruffles, headed with an embroidered band. The overskirt and basque are of cashmere, trimmed with fringe and embroidered band. Velvet bonnet, trimmed with silk and flowers.

DESCRIPTION OF PIECES IN FULL-SIZE DIAGRAM
Consists of half of vest, half of front, side piece for back, half of back, sleeve, standing-collar, and lying-down collar. The pattern is shown made up in Fig. 26, Fashion Department.

Godey's Lady's Book and Magazine, March 1878

Waistbands for the front of dresses that have Princesse backs are so popular that they are now added to Princesse polonaises. Some of the latter have a belt of the same material, set in at the first dart, and this belt is so wide that three or four large buttons are required to fasten it. In other polonaises the belt commences under the arms.

HOUSE-DRESS. →

...

EMBROIDERY ON BLACK GRENADINE.
By Mrs. Jane Weaver.

This design can be repeated to any length, and forms a pretty trimming for a black dress. Tilleul and mandarine silk are used – the mandarine for the chain stitch, and the tilleul for the cross stitches. As summer is approaching, we give this design, now, so that there may be time to work the grenadine.

Peterson's Magazine, April 1878

LADIES' OVER-SKIRT.

No. 6144. – A very handsomely outlined model for an over-skirt of any material used for suits, is illustrated by these engravings. It is here made of bourette cloth and trimmed with silk and buttons. The pattern is in 9 sizes for ladies from 20 to 36 inches, waist measure. To make the garment for a lady of medium size, 4 3/4 yards of goods 22 inches width, or 2 3/8 yards 48 inches wide, will be required. Price of pattern, 30 cents. ...

There are two new styles for over-skirts. One model has an apron front, that is fitted to the belt by darts, and is capriciously and effectively slashed at the bottom. It has a pretty pocket, and the back is full and draped at one side with buttons to ornament it. Slashed edges, or any fashionable trimmings, will be added to the sides and front, while the back will be trimmed, if at all, in a contrasting style.

The other over-skirt model is long, and also fitted by darts. It has four deep, upturned, cross-plaits in front, that terminate in the side seams, and a very handsome pocket is upon one side. The back is long, and attached to the front under buttons and simulated button-holes. It is draped by under-tapes, and is cross-gauged or shirred at the top to the depth of several inches. The front and back generally contrast in their decorations, provided any trimmings at all are added. This skirts may be worn with full waists or basques, and will be very popular.

6144

...

LADIES' SHIRRED POLONAISE.

No. 6145. – This very stylish pattern is in 13 sizes for ladies from 28 to 46 inches, bust measure. To make the garment for a lady of medium size will require 10 yards of goods 22 inches wide, or 5 yards 48 inches wide, together with 3 1/8 yards of silk for the *revers*, sleeves and laps, and 1 5/8 yard of goods 27 inches wide for lining the vest and back. Frequently silk, or goods of a contrasting shade, is chosen for the front or vest portion, and in this event the *revers* are faced with the goods and piped with the contrasting material. Price of pattern, 35 cents.

Arthur's Illustrated Home Magazine, April 1878

6145   6145

The Laveuse, or washerwoman's tunic, so fashionable at present in Paris, promises to be popular for summer fabrics. It has a short, wrinkled apron, with the lower edge turned up on the right side in a careless fashion, and the back hanging in two ends nearly straight or else slightly bunched up.

Godey's Lady's Book and Magazine, April 1878

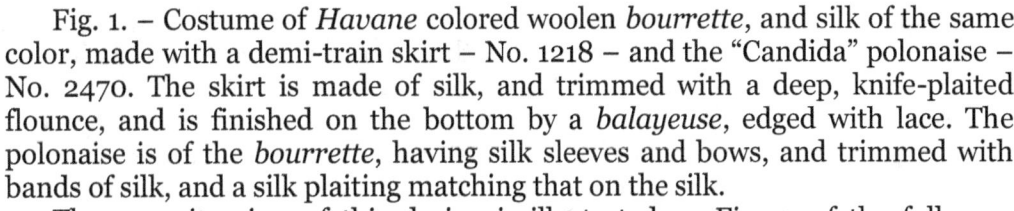

Fig. 1. – Costume of *Havane* colored woolen *bourrette*, and silk of the same color, made with a demi-train skirt – No. 1218 – and the "Candida" polonaise – No. 2470. The skirt is made of silk, and trimmed with a deep, knife-plaited flounce, and is finished on the bottom by a *balayeuse*, edged with lace. The polonaise is of the *bourrette*, having silk sleeves and bows, and trimmed with bands of silk, and a silk plaiting matching that on the silk.

The opposite view of this design is illustrated on Fig. 3. of the full-page engraving. Patterns of skirt and polonaise, each thirty cents a size.

...

The "Candida" is a polonaise of simple princess design suitable for the stylish mixed serges, the plain and figured camel's hair, the handsome tufted cloths, and other popular spring materials. It is very long, leaving but little of the skirt visible, and the drapery is arranged with grace, low down upon the skirt. The buttoned sides keep the whole in position, besides supplying a neat finish, and the bows impart a dressy appearance which corresponds with the silk folds, now used almost invariably as a trimming upon woolen costumes.

...

House and Street Dresses. ...

Fig. 3. – Costume in plaid debege, dark slate-color, trimmed with plaitings and bands of plain debege a shade darker. The skirt is a demi-train – No. 1218 – trimmed with knife-plaitings and bands. The polonaise – the "Candida" No. 2470 – is trimmed to match the skirt. Over this is worn a fichu cape – No. 2477 – which is crossed in front and fastened at the belt.

...

CANDIDA POLONAISE.

Simple and stylish, this polonaise is in "Princess" style, tight-fitting, with the usual number of darts in each front, a seam down the middle of the back, and side-forms extending to the shoulders. Deep darts or gores, extending part way down the skirt, are taken out under the arms, to avoid the necessity for cross seams at the waist

CANDIDA POLONAISE.

line. The drapery is similar on the back and front, and very low down. All classes of goods are adapted to the design, and the trimming may be chosen and arranged to correspond. This design is illustrated in Fig. 2 of the full-page engraving. Pattern No. 2470, price thirty cents each size.

...

The Essentials of Being Well Dressed.

It is a pity that the majority of ladies, many of them, too, women of taste and intelligence, do not understand that the foundation of elegance in dressing is laid in the fit and completeness with which the undergarments are adapted to the form. A perfect corset is not only indispensable to a perfectly fitting dress of the present style, but it is equally valuable from a sanitary point of view, no one part pressing unduly, no motion being impeded, and the perfect flexibility giving to the figure a grace which is finished and united to well-defined beauty of form.

A lady who has once worn a corset of this description will never willingly threaten her comfort or her personal appearance by adopting any other; and, when to the corset she has added the admirable suspenders for stockings, which have received the indorsement and approval of the best physicians, male and female, she can dress with a sense of security and satisfaction, which must be felt to be appreciated.

...

Fig. 2. – The "Carina" wrapper – No. 1423 – made in pale blue cashmere, and trimmed with pipings of cherry-colored silk, and embroidered bands, in which white, pale blue, and cherry-color are combined. The double illustration, showing the arrangement of the front, is given elsewhere. Cap of white organdy, trimmed with Valenciennes lace, and pale blue and cherry-colored ribbons. Price of wrapper pattern, thirty cents each size.

...

CARINA WRAPPER.

CARINA WRAPPER.

Novel and stylish in design, the "Carina" is about half-fitting, cut in "gabrielle" style, with side-forms back and front carried to the shoulder seams. It has a "Spanish" flounce added to the back, headed by two small flounces, and the trimming on the front is arranged to simulate a square jacket. The design can be suitably made up in all the materials usually employed for the purpose. The most appropriate trimming for washing goods is bias bands, and for woolen materials, flat trimming, or folds of silk, and bows. This design is shown on the steel plate. Pattern No. 1423, price thirty cents each size.

...

The "tie-back" no longer restricts the motions, though it is true the shape and size of the trained skirts, or dressy polonaise, afford as yet but little freedom. It must be remembered, however, that fashion and elegance are never in a hurry, and prefer sufficient restraint to impose a certain deliberation upon the movements, because this is necessary to dignity and grace.

The new style of walking-skirts however, is open to no objection on the score of ease or convenience. It is, as will be seen, a simple "Kilt-plaited" skirt (1220), with which can be worn a deep blouse waist, also plaited, and belted in, or the "Diana" basque (2641), which gives the effect of a vest and coat slightly cut away, and completes a very jaunty suit, particularly for a young lady.

Kilt-Plaited Skirt.

A fashionable style of walking-skirt, having a yoke at the top, to which the skirt is attached in kilt-plaits all the way round. A sash, about half a yard wide, tied loosely around the figure and fastened at one side with a loop and ends, may be worn with it, if desired. The design is an appropriate one for a great variety of materials, excepting, perhaps, the heaviest; and no trimming required. Pattern No. 1220, price thirty cents.

White aprons are worn in fine batiste or lawn, handsomely trimmed with lace, or plaitings. Bows of bright ribbon have a pretty effect.

Kilt-Plaited Skirt.

DIANA BASQUE.

DIANA BASQUE.

Simple and *distingué*, this basque is tight-fitting, with cut-away fronts strapped together over a vest that is fitted with a single dart in each side. It has double side-forms in the back, two extending to the shoulder seams and two rounded up to the armholes, and side-gores under the arms. It is suitably made up in a great variety of dress goods. The vest may be made of the same material, or may be made in plain or figured white *piqué*, to suit the taste. Pattern No. 2641, price, twenty-five cents each size.

...

Pipings of contrasting colors will be much worn, but they will not be round as formerly, but flat.

Scarfs are draped round the Princess dresses, and knotted behind with the ends falling over the train.

THERESA PRINCESS DRESS.

A short, tight-fitting "Princess" dress, with the front opened at the left side in "Breton" style, side-forms front and back extending to the shoulders, and side gores under the arms. A wide sash is draped across the front, and tied loosely in knot at the left side, and the edge of the skirt is finished by a side plaiting. The back piece is full, being crossed by three clusters of shirred tucks, and is finished by a deep flounce that is, in its turn, ornamented with three side plaitings. Two back pieces are given with the pattern, the full outer piece extending the entire length, and a shorter plain piece to which the shirred tucks are to be secured. The sleeves are trimmed to match the back. The collar may be of the same material as the dress, or be of lace, to suit the taste. The design can be suitably made up in a variety of dress goods, excepting perhaps the heaviest, and is especially desirable for thin fabrics, and a combination of colors or materials. The trimming can be chosen to suit the material used. Pattern No. 1422, price thirty cents each size.

House and Street Dresses.

Fig. 1. – The "Theresa" princess dress – No. 1422 – made in plum-colored silk, and silk and wool *bourrette*, in which white and gold are combined with the plum-color. This dress is short – walking length – the middle of the front and back, the sleeves, and trimming on the bottom made of the plain silk, and the remainder of the *bourrette*. A separate illustration, with description, is given in another portion of the Magazine. Deep collar and cuffs of Irish lace. Pattern of dress, thirty cents each size.

...

THERESA PRINCESS DRESS.

This design represents the back view of a costume in the same style as the one illustrated on Fig. 1. of the full-page engraving. This one is made in black *gros-grain* and *damassé* silks, trimmed with handsome *laminée* and chenille fringe, and embroidered galloon. Pattern No. 1422. Price, thirty cents each size.

"Voyager." – On board ship, even in May, you will need two good large thick shawls (woolen), one to fold round your shoulders, the other over your feet, when sitting or reclining on deck. Or in addition to your coat you may take an Ulster, which is useful afterward for traveling, one thick shawl, and a knitted one or warm scarf for your head and shoulders. A close felt hat simply trimmed is best for steamer wear, but you will need also a good gauze veil, and you will find several of the knitted zephyr things which are so common now, very convenient and comforting.

Take what you want with you in the way of dress, to wear while you are away. It is not so easy to buy costumes and garments ready-made, either in London or Paris, as it is here, and the prices are fully as high, often higher. You can economize in buying goods before you return, and in having them made up abroad, should you be able to find a good dressmaker at a reasonable price. Small articles and lingerie can also be purchased much cheaper in Paris than in New York.

The heavy camel's hair and silk dress, and black Italian cloth, would both be serviceable and possibly not too warm: it is considerably cooler in England and Scotland than in this country, in the summer months. But what you want most of all for comfort in traveling, is a costume walking length, not too heavy, dark in color, simple but lady-like in style, with a jacket that completes it, and to which a shawl or Ulster can be added at a moment's notice.

In addition to this, we would advise you to carry along a half-worn black silk skirt, and a couple of blouse waists to wear with it, either linen or foulard, for wear in July and August, with a linen or cloth Ulster as the necessity of the case may demand, and a black straw hat trimmed with black, red, and white currants, and a wreath of leaves.

Add to these a dark, plain silk, prune, navy blue, or myrtle green, one pretty suit of dark cambric, and a dressing-room sacque, or wrapper, and you are armed for a five months' stay, so far as dresses are concerned.

Have good shoes shaped to your foot, but a size too large, made before you go, and worn a little while; then put them aside, and wear old ones, but thick ones on the steamer. Do not expect to wear your traveling dress on the ship; use an old one for the purpose, but have it warm, and easy to take on and off. A dark flannel skirt is also indispensable, and a lighter colored skirt for traveling abroad, as white ones spoil so easily. On board you will also require to wear winter flannels, but these with the steamer dress, petticoat, shoes, etc., may be packed in the steamer chair, which is also indispensable, and left at the office of the steamer, in Liverpool, or elsewhere if desired, and it is very desirable. Properly marked, stamped, and addressed, the package will await your return, and will be found transferred without trouble on your own part, to your stateroom, if you return by the same line.

Demorest's Monthly Magazine, April, 1878

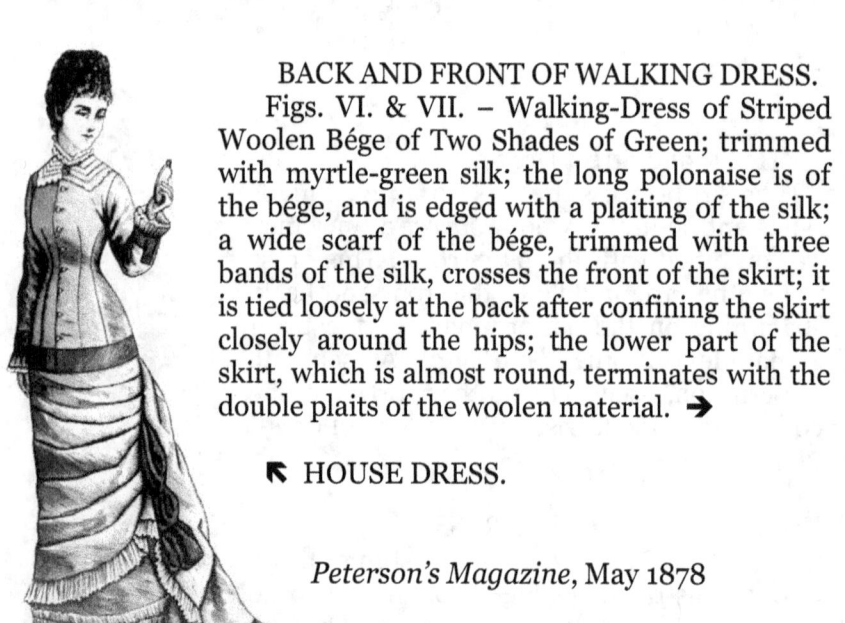

BACK AND FRONT OF WALKING DRESS.
Figs. VI. & VII. – Walking-Dress of Striped Woolen Bége of Two Shades of Green; trimmed with myrtle-green silk; the long polonaise is of the bége, and is edged with a plaiting of the silk; a wide scarf of the bége, trimmed with three bands of the silk, crosses the front of the skirt; it is tied loosely at the back after confining the skirt closely around the hips; the lower part of the skirt, which is almost round, terminates with the double plaits of the woolen material. ➔

↖ HOUSE DRESS.

Peterson's Magazine, May 1878

The basques are in square habit shapes, lined with thick silk, but most of them have no lining in the sleeves, leaving these transparent, like the lace sleeves worn during the winter.

Neat and pretty dresses for young ladies are made of the hair-striped summer silks that are now sold for from fifty cents to one dollar and twenty-five cents a yard. If two shades of blue are chosen, or two blue-gray stripes, or else plum-color, or, it may be, old gold and brown, they have a very nice effect when trimmed with solid-colored silk like the darker shade of the two striped. For instance, for a blonde of sixteen has just been made a cheap silk of dark navy-blue alternating with pale blue stripes. The demi-trained skirt has a single pleating seven inches deep as a flounce; the pleats are an inch broad, and are bordered near the lower edge with a bias blue silk band an inch wide. The over-skirt has an apron made of two breadths of the silk passed straight across the figure like a scarf, and cut on the edge in leaf-points that are bound with solid blue; the back drapery is two lapped breadths finished with narrow knife-pleating. The basque has a square back and belted front, and is trimmed on the breast with leaf-points to form a Pompadour square. Blue pearl buttons. ...

Waists are long, and fashionable garments fit symmetrically over the hips. A favorite sleeve is a tight coat shape, at the material must be smoothly lined, with the lining and fabric straight at the top of the arm and curving bias at the lower part. Cuffs and collars, whether standing or turned-over, are frequently corded along their unattached edges.

Arthur's Illustrated Home Magazine, May 1878

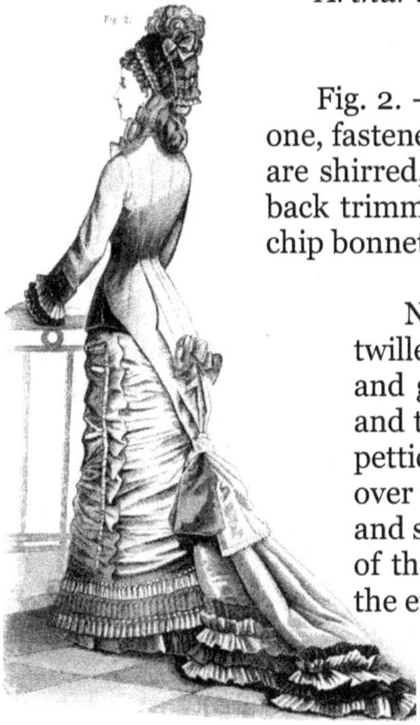

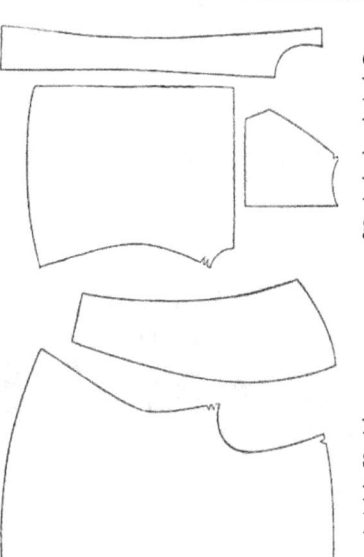

Fig. 2. – Walking dress of black silk. The coat bodice and back of skirt are cut in one, fastened by bows; the front of bodice is a basque. The front breadths of overskirt are shirred, as are also the sides, into the back. The front of underskirt is plain; the back trimmed with box plaitings. The apron overskirt is trimmed with fringe. Black chip bonnet, trimmed with black and old-gold-colored ribbon and feather.

...

New balmoral skirts for spring are made of light-gray, brown, or écru-twilled flannel, and trimmed with bias bands of plaid goods in the popular blue and green mixture, or in subdued colors. The top of the skirt is a deep yoke, and the flounces are gathered and trimmed with the plaid bands. The Princess petticoat is made of white muslin cut in a clinging shape that makes them plain over the hips. They have a yoke at least a fourth of a yard deep across the front and side gore, and this yoke extends plainly down the back to within half a yard of the bottom, where the fulness of the back breadth is gathered in and gives the effect of a fan balayeuse that supports the skirt nicely.

Figs. 10 and 11. – Front and back view of dress made of *beige*, suitable for either the house or street. It is made with but one skirt, trimmed to simulate a second skirt in front; the waist is plaited into a yoke in the back, and has a vest in front. The full-size pattern is given for cutting it upon diagram.

DESCRIPTION OF PIECES CONTAINED IN FULL-SIZE DIAGRAM OF YOKE BODICE.

It consists of five pieces, two for front, two for the back, and one for sleeve. The pattern is shown made up in Figs. 10 and 11 of our Fashion Department.

Godey's Lady's Book and Magazine, May 1878

White muslin dresses for afternoon wear are made with long princess polonaises, with embroideries down every seam, and trimmed with satin-faced moire ribbons in several tones of color. ...

Steel springs are used in the place of whalebones in the latest imported dresses. ...

The favorite buttons for wash goods are of porcelain.

...

MISSES' OVER-SKIRT.

No. 6200. – This over-skirt can be made of any suit material and trimmed in any tasteful manner. The pattern is in 8 sizes for misses from 8 to 15 years of age. It will require 3 1/4 yards of goods 22 inches wide, or 1 5/8 yard 48 inches wide, to make the over-skirt for a miss of 12 years. Price of pattern, 25 cents.

LADIES' OVER-SKIRT.

No. 6203. – To make the over-skirt illustrated for a lady of medium size, 6 5/8 yards of goods 22 inches wide, or 2 5/8 yards 48 inches wide, will be required. The pattern is in 9 sizes for ladies from 20 to 36 inches, waist

6200
Front View.

6200
Back View.

MISSES' OVER-SKIRT.

6203
Front View.

6203

measure, and its cost is 30 cents. The model is especially convenient for garments made of washable fabrics, as it can be let out smooth and plain for laundering with but little trouble.

Arthur's Illustrated Home Magazine, June 1878

The Polonaise. – As for the polonaise, nobody need endeavor to make it unpopular this season, because it cannot be abolished. There are several new models for it, and among them one that has some of the novel features just mentioned in connection with the latest Princesse model. It is gauged or shirred at the center of the back, and beautifully draped in cross folds at the sides, with button-trimmed laps above these plaits, and the center-front is shirred by clusters of drawing threads, with long button-trimmed *revers* at the sides descending from shoulder to hem. A standing ruffle finishes the throat, and the sleeves are trimmed to harmonize with the gathered front. The lower part of the polonaise will be variously, but always simply, finished. For dress goods of two sorts, or for woolens and silks combined, this new model will be in large demand.

The Christian Monitor, June 1878

Figs. XII. & XIII. – Afternoon-Dress for the Country of either Striped Batiste, Fine Wool, or Mohair. The skirt is bordered with two flounces, each one with a heading taken on the cross; long Princess tunic edged with a flounce matching those on the skirt; a double plaiting is carried down the front and round the neck, the front being slightly open. The polonaise is looped up at the back; sleeves with frills at the cuffs. →

...

Figs. VIII. & IX. – Front and back of Louis XV. Morning-Jacket, which is made of gray crêpe de chène lined with blue-colored foulard. In front there is a large simulated waist of blue silk, plaited slantwise, and fastened with a ruffle of Mechlin lace. A plaiting of blue silk, with a double heading and a row of white lace, borders the waistcoat, and trims the entire jacket. The pockets and cuffs terminate with bows. ↖

DRESS FOR SUMMER: FRONT AND BACK.

Figs. X. & XI. – Dinner-Dress for the Country of Delicate Buff Lawn; the front of the skirt is laid in deep plaits; the back has one long plain width, which is plaited lengthwise, and forms a train, and the whole is trimmed with knife-plaitings of lawn; blouse basque waist with a cape, which is also trimmed with narrow knife-plaitings; sash of rather narrow satin ribbon tied in long ends and loops at the side.

Peterson's Magazine, June 1878

The kilted skirt, with the washerwoman tunic before spoken of, is the style most generally adopted as yet. But in any case, no matter what the eventual decision will be, good sense has so far triumphed that the trained Princess dress is not generally adopted as a walking costume this summer. Simple costumes, meant for walking on foot in the streets or in the country, are made with an over-skirt and basque bodice. This tunic is very nearly as long as the underskirt, and is draped over it very low down at the back, the underskirt only showing its fluted or plaited trimming round the bottom. The bodice is long-waisted, with plain, round basque; it is, in fact, a cuirass, only one is so sick of the word that one prefers going back to the *corsage à basque*, though that also is anything but a novelty.

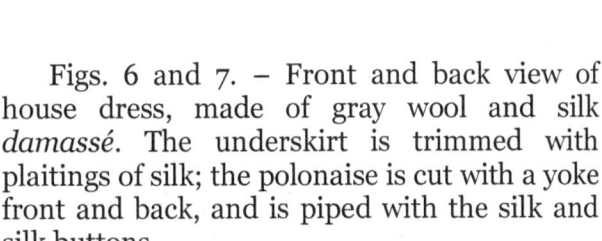

Figs. 6 and 7. – Front and back view of house dress, made of gray wool and silk *damassé*. The underskirt is trimmed with plaitings of silk; the polonaise is cut with a yoke front and back, and is piped with the silk and silk buttons.

Godey's Lady's Book, June 1878

"The fashion of half-long sleeves, coming just below the elbow," say the Paris correspondent of the *Bazar*, "will become more general during the summer. But it should immediately be added that such sleeves will only be worn at home, or in the country, and for dinners and reunions in the summer. In other words, a lady of taste and refinement will never wear half-long sleeves for walking-costume. With

such sleeves, very long mitts, which cover the arms, are indispensable. These are netted of silk in black, white and all other colors, in designs imitating lace. These mitts are also made of undressed kid. In summer neither gloves nor mitts are worn of dressed kid in Paris."

LADIES' PLAITED BLOUSE, WITH A "STOLE" COLLAR.

No. 6246. – This model is in 13 sizes for ladies from 28 to 46 inches, bust measure, and costs 30 cents. To make the blouse for a lady of medium size, 5 1/8 yards of goods 22 inches wide, or 3 3/8 yards 36 inches wide, or 2 3/8 yards 48 inches wide, will be needed. It is suitable for any material adapted to Summer wear.

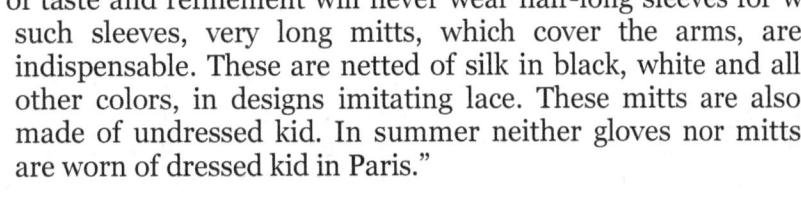

LADIES' BELTED POLONAISE.

6237

No. 6237. – This style of polonaise is particularly desirable for washable fabrics, and being decidedly plain is very easily laundered. Lawn polonaises made by this model will be trimmed with ruffles or plaitings of the material, edged with white or tinted lace, or with printed borders of the same. The bow, belt, and bands about the sleeve trimming will be of velvet or ribbon to made the color of the embroidery. Batiste polonaises of this description may be handsomely finished by using *écru* lace on the bottom and heading it by a row of *écru* insertion, from under which the material may be cut away after the edges are stitched. The pattern is in 13 sizes for ladies from 28 to 46 inches, bust measure, and costs 35 cents. In making the polonaise for a lady of medium size, 5 1/8 yards of goods 36 inches wide, or 4 yards 48 inches wide, will be needed.

Arthur's Illustrated Home Magazine, July 1878

The polonaise is still worn, but so very long that in many cases no underskirt is put on with it, but only a *bas de jupe*, or deep band of some kind of material, covered with flounces or flutings, which is tacked on inside the edge of the polonaise.

In fact, the polonaise is now but a short Princess dress, more convenient for out-of-door costume than the real Princess dress, which requires a long train to be really graceful. The plaited or gathered bodice is the most novel, although only from being so very ancient that the present generation ignores it; as we have before stated, it is particularly well adapted to summer dress fabrics.

We will describe a costume in which it is used: Plaited bodice of fancy *crêpeline*, with deep shoulder piece scalloped out and piped round the edge; round waistband. Short skirt of plain *crêpeline*, or of silk to match; deep scarf of the fancy *crêpeline* plaited and draped in front, and gathered up very low down behind. This scarf is scalloped out, and piped top and bottom. It covers all the skirt except a few inches from the waist and the hem at the bottom. The sleeves are also scalloped out and piped round the lower edge, showing a revers of the plain *crêpeline* which should be of a darker shade of the color. This pattern can also be employed for dresses with long skirts. It is suitable for thin figures, but stout ones should beware of the plaited bodice.

Another favorite style of costume this season is the skirt of white and light-colored striped Pekin, with very deep basque coat bodice, slightly draped at the back, and of a shade of self color matched to the stripes. This is worn both in silk and fancy woollen materials. To suit the lighter styles of fabrics employed, dresses are now made much less plain and narrow than during the winter; more plaited, especially at the back, and less long, because this season is that of travelling, and that it is, if not impossible, at least inconvenient, to walk about in at railway stations, or when getting into a carriage or car. Trained dresses have certainly a charm of their own; they look grand and dignified, but on condition of being exhibited only in large rooms and spacious galleries. In the streets or in apartments of small dimensions, the long train becomes, it must be confessed, not only uncomfortable, but absurd and altogether unbecoming.

...

For dressy toilets white muslin is very much worn this summer, laid plain over an underdress of silk, or, which answers the purpose almost as well, with colored satinette. The plain muslin is trimmed with bands of English embroidery, or with Mirecourt lace, which is a finer style of dentelle torchon. Even in the daytime for summer *fêtes*, croquet parties, etc., the white muslin dress over pink, blue, or mauve silk will form a very elegant and tasteful toilet. It is made in the Princess shape with moderate train looped up with flowing loops of ribbon. A peculiarity of trimming is the simulated style. Frequently the skirt of a handsome toilet has the front breadth made extremely long and gathered upon a cambric underpiece, so as to represent a shirred apron; lengthwise or crosswise bands of lace or embroidery are placed upon the side-gores, in the panel fashion, and the back is plaited or left plain. For cambric, Scotch gingham, and other inexpensive summer fabrics, bands of solid colors, with ruffle of machine embroidery, are as effective as anything; and these, with Smyrna or torchon laces, are the leading garnitures. Delicate

batistes are trimmed with colored needlework, done upon grenadine bands with silk. Such trimmings are also used to trim grenadine dresses. The new linen batistes are extremely delicate and in the most attractive colors, and are made up like grenadines and worn on dressy occasions.

...

Figs. 28 and 29. – Front and back view of house dress for lady. The dress is made of black grenadine with low waist and shoulder strap; the sleeves and high waist, ruffles on skirt, and scarf drapery, are of pale blue silk. Belt is of blue, fastened from the side seams across the front.

Godey's Lady's Book and Magazine, July 1878

The chief beauty of dress consists in not making yourself conspicuous, and in not distorting the body nor concealing it with unnatural additions. Your personal appearance is a subject for due consideration, for it is a duty for every lady to look just as pretty and pleasing as possible, and for every gentleman to present as good an appearance as is compatible with his employments and position in society. A business man's dress should be suitable to his occupations; and a lady's dress should always conform to the work her hands find to do. While attending to her household duties she will always look better in a plain, well-fitting morning dress, clean, and neatly made, than a furbelowed, flounced afternoon dress, which has seen much service and is now considered by her only fit for a morning toilette. Yet, in my opinion, it is utterly unfit for either the table or the kitchen. Long-trained skirts are doubtless very becoming in an elegant parlor, but when they are worn in the streets and dragged with mire, they are decidedly inappropriote [sic] and unbecoming. There should always be harmony between your dress and circumstances, and your toiletts should accord with the length of your purse, and the appearance of your home. A little more independence of character, and a little more self-respect, would make the women of the United States less the slaves of fashion, and better able to resist its absurd demands. There is a law of fitness in dress as well as in all things else, and the old and the young should never adopt the same style; neither should the tall and the short, the brunette and the blonde, the pale and the rosy, but each should have its own appropriate colors and fashions. Length-wise strips are suited to a short figure, and longitudinal trimmings will increase the appearance of height. Many flounces are not becoming to short or stout persons, while they harmonize well with a tall and slender figure. In these days of cheap cotton it is inexcusable not to have a good supply of underclothing, and the sewing-machine can make them with such rapidity that every man and woman should possess an abundance; while in our changeful climate warm flannels are a decided necessity.

White lawn wrappers are being prettily made with a flounce of embroidery around the skirt, while the princess waist is trimmed to outline a sacque. To brighten them knots of ribbon will be used upon all available points.

The Christian Monitor, July 1878

6262

LADIES' PROMENADE COAT, WITH A FRENCH BACK.

No. 6262. – This graceful and fashionable coat for a lady to wear upon the promenade is composed of two shades of suit goods, trimmed with satin pipings. The pattern is in 13 sizes for ladies from 28 to 46 inches, bust measure. It will require 4 5/8 yards of light goods 22 inches wide, with 1 1/4 yard if dark material in the same width, to make the coat for a lady of medium size. If material 48 inches wide be selected, 2 1/8 yards of the light, with 7/8 yard of the dark, will suffice for the purpose. Price of pattern, 25 cents.

The fancy for vests enables economists to remodel basques and sacques that have become soiled in front or are too tight across the bust. A separate vest of silk, or pique, or damask, striped or checked mohair, gray corduroy, or any appropriate material, is made, and the front of the partly-worn basque is turned back *en revers* to disclose the vest. The part turned back as a revers begins at the throat, and slopes gradually wider to the end. As it is defaced by buttons and holes, the revers is covered with the material of the vest to conceal these. For plain woolen dresses buntings and *de beige* are most used.

...

LADIES' SHORT, ROUND SKIRT, WITH DEEP YOKE AND ATTACHED OVER-SKIRT.

No. 6264. – This model includes a plaited skirt and round over-skirt. The pattern is in 9 sizes for ladies from 20 to 36 inches, waist measure. To make the garment for a lady of medium size, 12 7/8 yards of goods 22 inches wide, or 5 7/8 yards 48 inches wide, will be required. Price of pattern, 35 cents.

...

A pretty new model for a short walking skirt has a very deep yoke, to which is sewed the kilt so fashionable this season. Over the back of it fall two widths that are plaited to the belt and trimmed down the overlapping part of the centre and also about their ends, so as to hang like draped sashes upon the kilt. The front of the yoke is fitted by darts and overlaid by a similarly adjusted *tablier* that, like the lately popular "fish-wife's costume," has an upturned drapery, which may also have upturned ruffles or plaitings upon it or flat bands of ornament. This arrangement of yoke, overskirt and kilt requires much less material and is much lighter to carry than overskirts and long kilts, and by many will be considered prettier.

Arthur's Illustrated Home Magazine, August 1878

The sacque wrapper is one of the most comfortable, and, at the same time, graceful models for the easy-fitting robes worn early in the morning or during illness. The fronts are not closely fitted, but are merely adjusted to the figure by a single short dart for the bust and a long dart under each arm. This long dart under the arm does away with the necessity of a cross basque seam, and also widens the fronts, throwing the first long seam in the back edge of the side body, instead of cutting the wrapper in many long breadths. The sides hang smoothly, and the skirt is sufficiently narrow to give a slender appearance. The only additional fulness is in the three middle back seams several inches below the waist. The bordered calicoes and percales with bourette designs, or polka dots and striped borders, make up prettily by this design. A white cord and tassel of linen is sometimes worn around the waist, and Smyrna lace is added for trimming.

Figs. 14 and 16. – Front and back views of ladies' house dress, made of silk bourette navy-blue, divided by stripes composed of threads of gay colors. The sashes, knife plaiting, and back of basque and sides are composed of plain navy-blue silk.

...

The plain Princess polonaise suit has gained rapidly in favor, and is appropriate for various materials, grenadine, bourette, cashmere, *de bege*, or any soft fabric; it is used also for wash goods, but many consider it too elaborate for this purpose; for many wash goods, however, we consider it perfectly appropriate, as the dark colors admit of their being worn one season without being taken apart to wash. The back is very richly draped, yet so softly that nothing is added to the size of the wearer. The lining of the waist extends low over the hips to where the fulness of the drapery begins. The end of the plain part of the back forms is trimmed straight across with fringe, making it appear to be cut off just there, but all the breadths are intact, composing part of the waist and skirt also. The square pocket placed far back represents the most stylish way of arranging outside pockets. The front is closed, partly by a seam in the apron, and the upper part by buttons and buttonholes. Long looped bows are sometimes placed on the front seams below where the buttons leave off.

Godey's Lady's Book and Magazine, August 1878

Dresses of calico, percale, lawn, cambric or linen, are made in such simple styles that they are suitable alike for in-door or street dresses. They are almost invariably short in the skirt, and unless of very expensive materials they have none of the shirring and fluting that make them too elaborate for ordinary laundresses. The substantial torchon laces and the thick machine embroidery in colors are the trimmings for *very* handsome dresses that require to be frequently washed, while still plainer dresses have pleatings of the material, bias piped bands, or narrow Hamburg edgings.

The favorite style for making is that of a pleated basque with yoke and close sleeves that are quite short, reaching only just below the elbows; the overskirt is either the sheath shape or else the washer-woman, with the edges turned up plainly all around, and the top edge of the turned up part finished with a standing pleated frill that may, in its turn, be finished with narrow Valenciennes lace. The pleated yoke basque should be made over a smoothly-fitted, high-necked lining of the dress material cut in basque shape; the sleeves are not lined. The skirt is short, usually, may be demi-trained, and is always trimmed with one or two kilt-pleatings of the lawn. Such dresses are found at all the furnishing houses, but are so easily made up at home that they have become the favorite model of the season.

To complete such toilets are broad belts of black velvet, with wristlets of velvet, and bows on the overskirt. Polonaises, princesses, and basques, and overskirts hold their own. The cut-away jacket is also popular.

The fancy for vests enables economists to remodel basques and sacques that have become soiled in front, or are too tight across the bust. A separate vest of silk, or pique, or damask, striped or checked mohair, gray corduroy, or any appropriate material, is made, and the front of the partly-worn basque is turned back *en revers* to disclose the vest. The part turned back as a revers begins at the throat, and slopes gradually wider to the end. As it is defaced by buttons and holes, the revers is covered with the material of the vest to conceal these. For plain woolen dresses buntings and *de beige* are most used.

Ordinary street or house suits, uniting two shades of the same material, may have both tints represented in the bows; but street suits, except for little girls, are not trimmed with bows of a widely different color, although sets of bows are often provided, which aid in transforming a street suit into festive attire, or in varying the appearance of those specially prepared for extra occasions. Bows of silk and woolen goods, or of silk or wool in two shades, are made by first cutting the requisite number of strips of a desirable width, running the corresponding ones together with a loose stitch, turning them, and then fastening them in loops and ends.

Gold and silver tinsel is not worn in the day time.

Tinsel is a feature this summer in evening toilets.

Mantelets are cut short and square in the back, but have long fronts.

Victoria lawn suits will be trimmed with scarlet or navy-blue embroidery.

The Christian Monitor, August 1878

Basques are becoming quite short in front, extending not more than five or six inches below the waist-line. They, however, remain very long behind. Soft facings of barred crinoline muslin are used in silk skirts instead of stiff wigging. Very small buttons are being used again on dress-waists. They are both jet and crocheted. Sleeves are still made to fit to the arm closely, and have very small cuffs, if any. More often they are merely left open on the outer seam, buttoned by two or three buttons and button-holes, and are worn with lace cuffs, or a frill of crêpe lisse, or lace. English turned-over collars are made very high. They should not be corded or thickly interlined.

LADIES' PRINCESS TOILETTE.

No. 1. – This handsome costume consists of a six-gored skirt and an elegantly-fitted Princess polonaise. The skirt is made of cashmere, and is of stylish walking length. The pattern is No. 6053, price 35 cents, and is in 9 sizes for ladies from 20 to 36 inches, waist measure. The polonaise is of bourette and cashmere, and is very modish in appearance, though exceedingly simple in structure. Deep, lace-edged collar and cuffs complete the neck and wrists of the sleeves. The pattern is No. 6285, price 30 dents, and is in 13 sizes for ladies from 28 to 46 inches, bust measure. To make the costume for a lady of medium size will require 15 1/4 yards of material 22 inches wide; the skirt calling for 6 3/8 yards, and the polonaise for 8 7/8 yards. Or, if 48-inch-wide goods are selected, 7 1/4 yards are needed; the polonaise requiring 4 5/8 yards, and the skirt 2 5/8 yards.

Arthur's Illustrated Home Magazine, September 1878

The dress-holder is useful but not pretty. ... Those ladies who cannot reconcile themselves to a short dress carry their trains in a variety of ways – some over their arm, like a riding-habit, others sport a silver dress-holder, but the most practical have a loop of ribbon sewn to the back of their skirt, and through this they pass a hand when walking. Some of these short suits have become quite popular for the street, and for walking dresses at the fashionable summer resorts; they are called *trottoir* (sidewalk) dresses, and are made short enough to escape the ground.

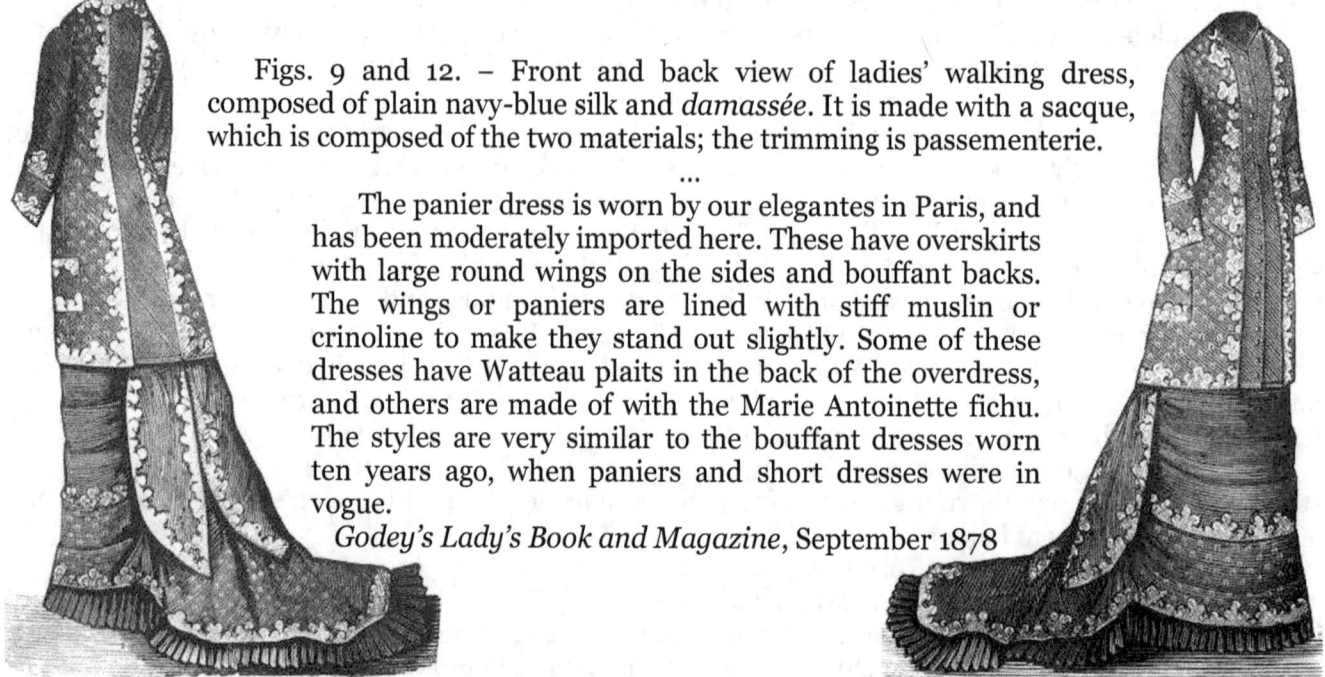

Figs. 9 and 12. – Front and back view of ladies' walking dress, composed of plain navy-blue silk and *damassée*. It is made with a sacque, which is composed of the two materials; the trimming is passementerie.

...

The panier dress is worn by our elegantes in Paris, and has been moderately imported here. These have overskirts with large round wings on the sides and bouffant backs. The wings or paniers are lined with stiff muslin or crinoline to make they stand out slightly. Some of these dresses have Watteau plaits in the back of the overdress, and others are made of with the Marie Antoinette fichu. The styles are very similar to the bouffant dresses worn ten years ago, when paniers and short dresses were in vogue.

Godey's Lady's Book and Magazine, September 1878

Dotted muslins will be very fashionable this summer.

From the back of basques and polonaises nearly all seams have vanished. This is not so much of an improvement as a change.

With square necked dresses a collarette or small narrow fichu of folded silk is used. Every variety of dress is onset with a vest of some kind.

The Princess polonaise and overskirt will be worn as generally by our leading fashionables as they have been, but many of them will have a pretty fullness added to them in lines of gathers and side or box-pleatings.

Many ladies who suppose that their figures are too thin will welcome the insertion of shirred or gauged centers to their garments, because they round their persons out to handsomer proportions. The fullness, being narrow and deep under all circumstances, is still further narrowed at the belt-line, so that no lady is so stout that she will not appear to be slighter when she adopts this novel arrangement of her dress material.

A wrapper, with a loose sack front and a clinging, shapely back, with a center seam, and also side-back seams extending to the shoulders, will form a very pretty and comfortable morning dress. The body of the wrapper extends in plain outline for some distance below the waist, and to its lower edge is attached a Spanish flounce to make the garment of an appropriate depth. The wrapper may be made of lawn, print, cambric, gingham, or any other fabric mamma may prefer, and trimmed with folds, plaitings, Smyrna lace, Hamburg embroidery, or narrow ruffles of the material edged with narrow Valenciennes lace. ...

It is an easy matter to dress a family neatly and comfortably when one can buy all the ready-made clothing necessary, call in the aid of the hatter, the shoemaker, the seamstress, the dry goods merchant; and yet there are hundreds and thousands of mothers who contrive to make a trim appearance for themselves and their families with very little outlay. Garments are turned inside out, up side down, back side before, washed, dyed, pressed; and from this mill of renovation come out almost as good as new.

The Christian Monitor, September 1878

LADIES' KILT-PLAITED SKIRT.

No. 6298. – This pattern is in 9 sizes for ladies from 20 to 36 inches, waist measure. To make the garment as pictured for a lady of medium size, will require 11 1/4 yards of goods 22 inches wide, or 6 3/8 yards 48 inches wide. Price of pattern, 30 cents.

LADIES' POLONAISE.

No. 6341. – Two shades of suit goods were selected for this polonaise, whose model is in 13 sizes for ladies from 28 to 46 inches, bust measure. To make the costume for a lady of medium size will require 10 1/4 yards of material 22 inches wide, or 5 yards 48 inches wide. Price of pattern, 30 cents.

Arthur's Illustrated Home Magazine, October 1878

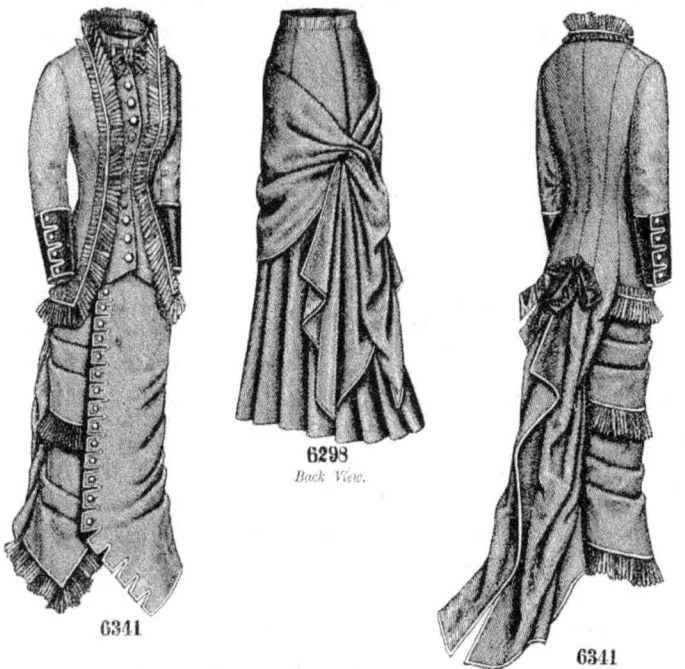

6298
Back View.

6341

6341

Very small buttons are being used again on dress waists. The leading French modistes use small jet buttons shaped like a shoe button, but cut in facets, for black dresses. These are held only by a shank, but there are other stylish jet buttons, quite flat, yet cut in facets round the edges, and sewed on through eyes in the middle. The newest crocheted buttons are bullet shape, and have tiny raised specks not larger than a pin's point.

The English turned-over collars of dresses are made very high, and do not flare behind as the Medicis collars did. They should not be corded on the edges, nor thickly interlined; thin lawn is sufficient stay for them.

A jabot of narrow ribbon is set down one side of the apron-front of dresses. Sometimes these loops, if for house dresses, are many colored. On black silk or grenadine dresses the ribbon is black satin on one side and *gros grain* on the other. This ribbon is an inch wide; the loops are about three inches long; they are in rows of three or four, and should be very thickly clustered. Soft facings of barred crinoline muslin are used in silk skirts instead of stiff wigging.

Narrow satin ribbons of dark Agrippina-red are worn with black silk or grenadine dresses. Those at the throat have long loops hanging, and the two ends are then carried down to the left hip, and fastened on the back of the basque, from whence hang loops and ends.

...

Scarfs. – The scarfs which, it is said, will constitute a great feature in fall drapings on out-door costumes, and will form the finish of the Princess dress about the knees and in the close folds at the back of the skirt, are now much used for reception dresses that are not low-necked and for dinner dresses, and are, in these cases, draped about the shoulders, bust, and back, as follows: You either take the centre of the scarf by doubling its length, and attach that at the middle of the bust with a bunch of flowers or of ribbon loops, and, carrying it round the shoulders, attach it in the centre of the back with another similar bunch, and let the ends float off from the figure, or you set the centre of the scarf to the centre of the back, and, after crossing it in from beneath the flowers, carry the ends back and attach them under a third cluster of ribbon or flowers. This constitutes a beautiful trimming to a dress. Lace, gauze, tulle, and very light knit silk scarfs, with a deep fringe of beads and silk, or of beads alone, are worn.

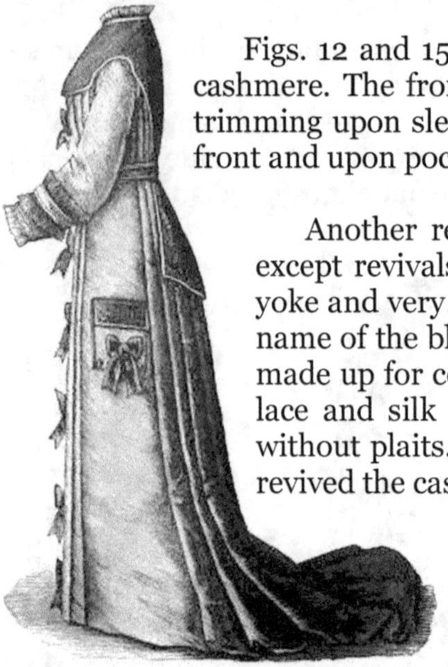

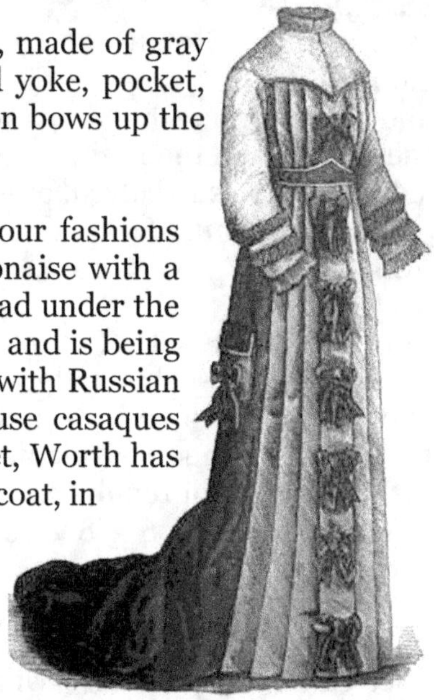

Figs. 12 and 15. Front and back view of ladies' wrapper, made of gray cashmere. The front and back are plaited into a yoke; said yoke, pocket, trimming upon sleeves, and belt are of blue silk; blue ribbon bows up the front and upon pocket.

...

Another revival for the autumn (for what are all our fashions except revivals of old ones?) is that of the plaited polonaise with a yoke and very wide belt. This has been introduced abroad under the name of the blouse casaque. It is a loose, easy garment, and is being made up for cool weather in India cashmere, trimmed with Russian lace and silk embroidery. There are also shirred blouse casaques without plaits. For fanciful short costumes for the street, Worth has revived the casaque. This casaque is a long close-fitting coat, in Louis Quinze style, with large pockets, large pearl buttons, and a lace jabot. The casaque falls so low on the skirt that an overskirt is not required. The newest short dresses have three kilt-plaited flounces crossing the back and covering the back breadths from belt to foot. In front there is an apron wrinkled across, and one wide knife-plaited flounce at the foot. Sometimes this short apron takes the washerwomen shape, and sometimes it is merely a plaited scarf. A great deal of shirring is used on the latest imported dresses. In the first place large round collars and deep cuffs are made up entirely of finely shirred rows. Yokes are shirred either across or perpendicularly. Plastron squares are shirred, and there are shirred vests.

...

Basques are becoming quite short in front, extending not more than five or six inches below the waist line. They remain very long behind, and when fulness is added, it does not begin at the waist line, but more than a finger length below it. It is more customary, however, to have the back forms flat, and to have each form end in a loop, made by lining the end of the form with stiff interlining, facing it with silk, and turning it up underneath. Two long looped bows of double-faced ribbon are set low down on the tails of the basque. Belts added to the front of basques and not to the back are intended to shorten the appearance of the waist. They must, therefore, be set rather above than below the line of the waist, and sewed in an under-arm seam that does not extend too far back. Those two and a half inches wide are not sloped narrower towards the middle, but when made three inches broad under the arm, they would shorten the front of the waist too suddenly; hence, they are sloped to two inches in the centre. We give a design of one of these basques with belt in Figs. 13 and 14 of our fashions. Sleeves are still made to fit the arm closely, and have very small cuffs, if any. More often they are merely left open on the outer seam, buttoned by two or three buttons and button-holes, and are worn with lace ends or a frill of crêpe lisse or lace.

Figs. 13. And 14. – Front and back of ladies' basque, with waistband from the sides (mentioned in the Chitchat); it is of silk. The side, back seams, vest at the throat, cuffs upon sleeves, and lower part of front are of velvet.

Polonaises of cashmere have close Princess backs with belted fronts, and these full fronts are drawn into shape by clusters of shirring done at intervals across the front breadths. Overskirts with deep aprons have rows of shirring down each seam, and it is probable that the shined flounces will also be revived.
Godey's Lady's Book and Magazine, October 1878

Skirts have become fresh objects of interest this fall, and while the kilt-pleated design is still admired for a variety of materials, ladies require another shape for fabrics which are too heavy after they are pleated. A new design of this kind gives the usual proportions of a walking-skirt, but the back, in which all the fullness is gathered, is cut off at a proper distance above the hem, and an extra width, cut much like a Spanish flounce, is added here to supply the shape desired at the bottom of the skirt. Above this gathered width, the back-breadth is kept in compass by bands and buckles, which are made to hold the fulness just as it may be desired for the time. For dresses which are made on the economical plan, with a foundation of cambric, this model is the best that has yet appeared, and is equally appropriate for a trimmed skirt or for a separate skirt upon which the overskirt is permanently draped. There is no variation in the shapes of trained skirts as yet this season, the square outline at the back being still preferred to the pointed, while the fan effect produced by pleatings has not given way to anything more admired. Overskirts are not so much changed in shape as in the appearances produced by trimmings. The most precise dispositions of drapery are in favor; the pleats which take up the sides are as accurate as it is possible to make them, although they are extremely simple.
The Christian Monitor, October 1878

No American woman who has hands and brains, and can use them, even in the most humble service, need fail of being handsomely, honestly, and properly clad. Fine cloth suitings in dark cloth shades, one yard and a half wide, are among the regular manufactures of A. T. Stewart & Co., at one dollar per yard; and as seven will make a complete suit, and trimming save stitching, is not required, eight dollars (one being allowed for lining and buttons), is sufficient for a warm comfortable dress, which will clean, make over, and always look neat and serviceable, not calculating of course for making, but taking it for granted that it will be made at home and by the thrifty fingers of the wearer.

The camel's hair and *damassé* cloths are still more attractive, though somewhat more expensive, and only suitable for parts of costumes, such as the overdress, not for the costume complete. All the difficulties in regard to color in these fabrics have been met and overcome, and the shades are now as fine in the American manufactures at $1.24 and $1.50 per yard, as they were in French goods at $2.50 and $3 per yard.

...

A complete short dress, of pretty and stylish design, will be found in the "Princess" walking costume. It is a combination style, the front forming a polonaise, and jacket over the short gored skirt, and the back saved from the unbecoming plainness by the insertion of a kilt plaiting surmounted by a bow, and ends. The design is one of the most fashionable of the season, and a good one for the Scotch checks now so much worn, or it may be suitably applied to any combination of figured and plain fabrics.

...

PRINCESS WALKING COSTUME.

Very novel and stylish, this dress escapes the ground all around, and is cut with a polonaise front over a gored skirt, and has cut-away jacket fronts over the others. It is tight-fitting, with the usual number of darts in front, side gores under the arms, side-forms in the back carried to the shoulders, and extending the entire length of the skirt, and short back pieces, to which a gathered skirt is attached. The design is appropriate for all kinds of dress goods, and is very desirable for a combination of colors or materials. The trimming can be chosen to suit the material used.

Fig. 1. – Walking costume, made in plume-colored India cashmere. The skirt is the design known as the "Mathilde," cut short enough to escape the ground all the way around, bordered with a deep, kilt-plaited flounce, haven a band of plum-colored silk near the edge. The front of the skirt is covered with a succession of broad folds, and the back has a graceful drapery, ornamented with a large bow made of plum-colored silk and velvet combined. The jacket is a simple design, the "Octavia," made in the same material as the skirt, and trimmed with a very heavy twist fringe, and bands of plum-colored velvet edged with a narrow gilt braid. Polished gilt buttons. Hat of plum-colored felt, trimmed with velvet to match, a skin plum, and gilt cordings. Blue veil. Skirt pattern thirty cents each size. Pattern of sacque, twenty-five cents each size.

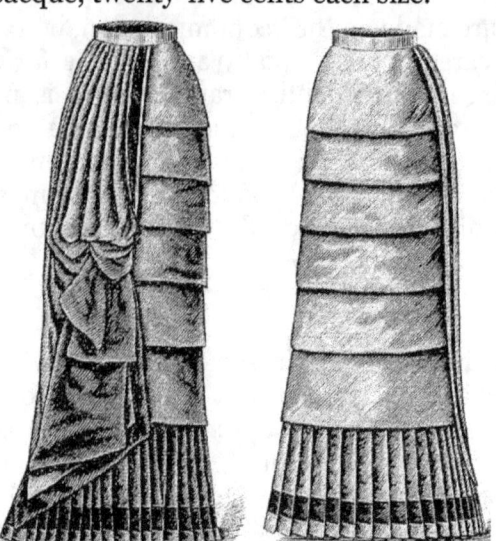

...
MATHILDE WALKING SKIRT
Quite short enough to escape the ground, and nearly equal in length all the way around, this simple and stylish skirt has the bottom finished with a deep kilt-plaiting, the front trimmed with broad, bias folds, and a narrow overskirt oat the back, gracefully draped. It is an appropriate design for a great variety of dress goods, and requires only the simplest trimming. The front view of this skirt is illustrated *en costume* on the full-page engraving. Price of pattern, thirty cents.

...
OCTAVIA SACQUE
A graceful, practical design, long, with loose fronts, and a partially fitting back, having side-forms rounded to the armholes. The trimming on the fronts imparts the effect of a vest, and the *revers* on the back and the long cuffs add greatly to the general stylish effect. The design can be suitably made up in suit goods, silk, and most of the that are usually selected for out-door wear. The trimming can be simple or elaborate, to suit the taste and the material used. This garment is illustrated on the full-page illustration, in combination with the "Mathilde" walking skirt. Price of pattern, twenty-five cents each size.

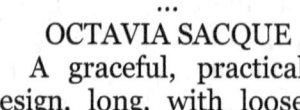

...
The Artistic Dress.
It is perhaps easier to comprehend what the "artistic" dress is not than what it is. It is not stiffness, or starch, or a multiplicity of trimming. Three qualifications are indispensable: the fabric must be soft and pure, the design must not be broken up into many pieces, but but be continuous and harmonious, and the ornamentation must be made an integral part of the dress, and not made up in unmeaning forms, and veneered upon it. The Princesse forms in some fine woolen material are usually chosen, and the decoration obtained from hand-embroidery upon the stuff itself. The designs area from nature, and consist of grassy and fibrous patterns, with a tiny fly, or bug, or beetle settling on a stem, or expanding its wings. Any flower patterns are in order, or leaf or vine, and they may be used as a border or in upright or pyramidal forms.

The body is always cut high, the sleeves long, unless the costume is a copy from antique art, or the authorized design of some great artist. It may be half high, and square, but it is always long and always cut in few pieces. The embroidery of such simple styles for indoor wear is now a rage with young ladies. It has taken the place of all the more trivial forms of fancy-work, but the *furore* is not confined to dresses alone; stand-covers, chair-covers, toilet-covers, toweling, all share in the passion for enriching pure and simple textures with hand-work, and certainly fancy could not take a more practical form.

An elegant polonaise in one of the new Panier designs, is given in the "Panier" polonaise. The drapery forms a series of scant puffs, between which large bows are placed. The side-trimming are very effective, and the pattern most suitable for black striped gauze, or some rich, thin, black material to be worn over black satin. It is also adapted to faille, fine camel's-hair, and any soft material. The amount of stuff required is less than nine yards.

...

PANIER POLONAISE.

Peculiar in cut and arrangement, but not difficult to adjust, this design is tight-fitting, with a single dart in each side in front, side gores under the arms, and side-forms in the back extending to the shoulders. The fronts are short and very fully draped, and fall in points on each side, and the short side gores and side-forms are very much trimmed, and fall loosely, giving a panier effect at the sides. The back is very *bouffant*. It can be appropriately made up in all dress goods but the heaviest, and the trimming can be chosen to suit the material used.

...

The Combination Street Costume.

This is cut walking length, of plain cloth suiting, or the richer camel's-hair in any dark "cloth" shade. It consists of trimmed skirt, vest, and jacket, made entirely of the woolen material, and only faced upon the cuffs and collar with a thick silk brocade or embroidered stuff, in mixed Persian or "cashmere" colors.

This is all the trimming, but there are ways of making them more dressy. For example, by making the vest of brocade, or of velvet, and adding to the trimming buttons of silver or gilt. A mixed silk and gold cord is also sometimes sewn upon the edge of the vest and jacket, but this finish is only suitable for young ladies.

The "Empress" Dress-Lifter.

Ladies are always inquiring more or less for a good, handsome, and reliable dress-lifter, and we think we have at last found one that we can safely and certainly recommend. The only way to raise a train securely is by a loop affixed to the lower part of the skirt. With the "Empress" lifter, or "Supporter," as it is called, are given six loops made of silver wire, which can be sewn to different dresses, and then with the Supporter suspended by its hook from the belt, it can be attached to the loop by a smaller hook at the other end, and the arrangement is complete, secure, and thoroughly satisfactory. In going out in the evening to theatre, concert, or opera, where it is sometimes necessary to wear a trailed dress, at the immediate risk of having it spoiled, and the certainty of fatigue from the endeavor to keep it well held up, the "Empress Supporter" is invaluable, for it as a stylish ornament as well as a reliable safeguard.

...

The "Empress" Dress Train Supporter.

The most perfect Train Supporter ever offered.

It is warranted to carry the train securely, is light, and highly ornamental. Finished with Ebony or Tortoise Shell handle, $1.00; Ivory handle, $1.25; Pearl handle, $1.50.

Address, Mm. Demorest, 17 East 14th St., N.Y.

...

Costumes for Stout Ladies.

This is a season when no one need wear what is not adapted to their particular style and figure. Stout ladies, for example, wear basques, or polonaises, cut perfectly plain, and no trimming excepting flat folds, or lengthwise bands, excepting round the bottom of the skirt, which for a large person should never be very short. Stout women, and especially those who are short also, should – must indeed – avoid plaids and broad stripes, and as far as possible restrict their use of fabrics to dark self colors, and narrow stripes or armure patterns. Short jackets and fichus increase apparent size, but collars long in front, and cascades extending the entire length of the garment decrease it. Made up laces are also unbecoming; the collar and cuffs should be deep, and of tatting or real lace; the drapery slight, and arranged low on the skirt.

...

Hints for Home Dressmaking.

In using patterns, it must be remembered that the general design and form are everything. The special details of cut and style may be changed and modified to suit individual tastes. For example, some persons require more fullness upon the hips than others. Some ladies like a very high cut upon the shoulder, while others prefer that the sleeves should be set just in the bend of the arm. This minutia cannot be graded to suit each person, but they can very easily take in a little larger seam, or set the sleeve up higher to suit themselves.

The fashion of bringing the sleeves high up on the shoulders was introduced by the Princess of Wales, and it is still retained. In fact, the "tailor cut," as it is called, is now adopted, more or less, for jackets, and all garments that have sleeves. It is much easier to fit a dress with a short seam upon the shoulder than when brought down low. It also increases the appearance of height – a very important matter now-a-days, when a tall, slender form is considered essential to a distinguished appearance.

An excellent plan, in making dresses at home is to cut a plain, close form out in lining, and mount the material upon it. This method is especially suitable for dresses consisting of trimmed skirts and basques. Cut your skirt lining after the pattern of the "Walking Skirt" or the "Demi-Train," and then add flounces of the dress material, a draped tablier, or folds across the front, as preferred, and a back draped or kilt-plaited, and either made in two parts, or divided by a strap, so as to from a slight panier at the top, which falls over the smallest possible *tournure*.

Basques are made very plain, but the require a very perfect fit, and as they are cut long, well-shaped underclothing and a good flexible corset are indispensable. The basque may be the plain "Cuirass," or it may be buttoned over at the back like the "Balsamo," or turned back like the "Pamela," or made double-breasted like the "Cecilia." All these are stylish, well-fitting models, and with the clear directions given with each pattern, few can go wrong.

More youthful designs will be found in the "Mélanie," and "Marjolaine," the first of which is belted in, the other cut away from a very pretty vest. The distinction which the basque obtains, it derives almost wholly from the neatness and grace of its form, the picturesque variety which is given to the falling collar, the addition of the vest, and the frequently quaint, and the charming, individualization of the sleeve.

Pipings, or what are more properly called "cordings," are not now used at all.

Sleeves are put in with a narrow strip of soft linen braid or tape, and the rough edges, after being trimmed, are covered by French dressmakers, with soft narrow silk ribbon.

In the selection of a style, it is important to know exactly to what purpose it will be put. If the dress is to be employed for many different occasions, for day as well as evening wear, for in and out of doors, it is necessary to select a quiet, close design, one that will be proper for the street, and relieve it, when needed for occasions of more ceremony, by the addition of handsome collar and cuffs, or a pretty fichu of lace. If the dress is to be reserved for indoor wear, the cut of the sleeves, and the bodice should be more dressy, the former half-short, reaching only just below the elbow, the latter open or square as the "Camille," the "Annette," and the "Toinette."

The "Balsamo," previously alluded to, is a good example of a new style of costume, made of plain satin or faille, combined with a rich brocade or embroidered stuff in India colors. These Oriental-looking fabrics are purchased in very small quantities, and are only used for the little simulated vest, the cuffs, and a broad strap here and there upon the skirt. One yard, at from three to nine dollars, is sufficient for the purpose.

No other trimmings are necessary than the conjunction of the two fabrics, and fringe or lace is now rarely put on as a border. Lengthwise bands, cascades, ladders composed of loops and ribbon, broad bands, and straps are all employed to complete, or give effect to the design. But independent trimmings are very sparingly used, and should therefore be rich, and as much as possible made to seem an essential part of the dress. Ladies who cannot afford a great variety in their wardrobe, and yet have to go considerably into society often make up their one handsome dress with two basques, and two pairs of sleeves. The elbow sleeves may be of lace, gathered full upon the arm, and finished with a double ruffle below the elbow. This ruffle is important. If the sleeves are lace, the outside ruffle will be of lace also, and the interior one of finely quilled tulle or *crêpe lisse*. If the sleeves are silk, or of the fabric of the dress, the exterior ruffle may correspond, and two interior ones will be required, one of *crêpe lisse*, or finely-plaited muslin with lace edge.

Dresses high to the throat are always finished with a narrow standing as well as a falling collar. Some of the latter are round at the back, and cut in square tabs across the front, while others round off almost to a point in front. Very becoming collars are made of round, deep plaitings with a narrow standing ruffle, which surrounds the throat, and inside which the narrow rim of linen collar or crimped ruffle is placed. The skirts of silk dresses are no longer bound with braid. They are simply turned over upon the lining, and finished with a handsome balayeuse, which consists of a deep muslin plaiting with lace edge.

Walking dresses are no longer bound upon the edge of the skirt, but they are completed with an inferior plaiting composed of a dark resisting fabric, which is patented, and protects the lining as well as the edge of the fabric.

All woolen materials are made as much as possible with what is called the "cloth finish," that is, without trimmings or bindings of any kind, except buttons, and these are rarely used for fastening. A cloth suit may have facings of velvet, or silk, or brocade. It may have cuffs, collar, and straps of either of these fabrics, which, like the facing to a coat may form a very handsome trimming. But the edges of the suit will be plain, or only finished with stitching.

...

A Traveling Wardrobe

has been invented and patented by an English lady, who, indulging in an unusual number of rich dresses, found this method of carrying them the only way to secure their freshness without constant unpacking. Like many others, she had to move from place to place, and this invention supplied her with a wardrobe, go where she would. When closed they resemble an ordinary trunk, but are made strong and light, weighing less than any luggage of the same size. They are intended to be put up on end. The dresses are hung to wooden rods, set in a frame, and there are partitions for bonnets and for various other portions of dress, so that without unpacking the things are always ready to hand.

...

Button Eyelets.

For setting shank buttons without sewing. The cloth may be slightly pierced, if heavy, the shank pressed through, the smooth flat plate or eyelet laid over and secured by any lacer large enough to prevent the shank pulling through the eyelet. For white vests or wash dresses whole rows may be removed by drawing the lacer at one end, and a child can replace them. They prevent the drooping of the button, or dragging out of the cloth. One dollar per gross, or twelve cents per dozen, post-free, in sizes corresponding to the button used.

Orders received at Scott's Fashions, 615 B'way.

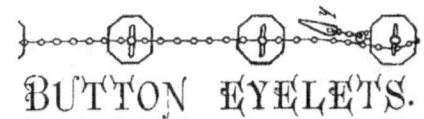

BUTTON EYELETS.

For setting shank buttons without sewing. The cloth may be slightly pierced, if heavy, the shank pressed through, the smooth flat plate or eyelet laid over and secured by any lacer large enough to prevent the shank pulling through the eyelet. For white vests or wash dresses whole rows may be removed by drawing the lacer at one end, and a child can replace them. They prevent drooping of the button, or dragging out of the cloth. One dollar per gross, or twelve cents per dozen, post-free, in sizes corresponding to button used.

Orders received at Scott's Fashions, 615 B'way.

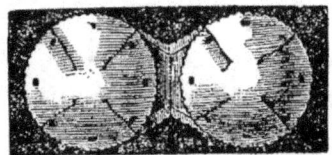

Among the models for street costumes is the Trocadero, or Exposition suit. This is similar to the kilt suit, lately so popular, but differs in this, that it is a complete garment. The upper part is closely fitted, like a polonaise, down to a considerable distance below the waist line; the back, made with five seams, ends like a coat. The deep kilting is sewed to the front, and is attached to a belt in the back, to pass under the jacket part. The join is concealed by a broad scarf, which is attached at one of its ends to the left side, passing around the front under the jacket gathered into a large puff, the other end meeting the starting-place, and falling gracefully at the side or back. Buttons, pockets, folds, etc., may be arranged according to individual fancy. This exceedingly pretty suit may easily be made by any lady of taste and ingenuity.

Overskirts and polonaises are frequently made up in what is called the "washerwoman style;" that is, with a wide piece turned up at the bottom of the front and side breadths. In a combination suit, with a short skirt, this is very effective when of a contrasting color. If of the same material as the rest of the dress, with the two sided of the goods are unlike, the right side is turned outward and joined by a hidden seam near the lower edge. Overskirts generally are more bouffant.

Arthur's Illustrated Home Magazine, November 1878

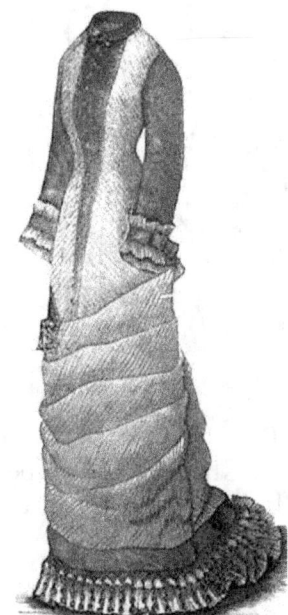

Figs. 1 and 4. – Front and back view of lady's dress, made of olive green cashmere and silk. The underskirt is of silk, trimmed with a plaiting. The polonaise is trimmed in the back to simulate a basque with fringe, and band of silk, the sleeves, trimming for bodice, skirt and bows are also of silk, fringe around the edge of overskirt.

...

Old dresses can be made in the present style with but little alteration; and combination of material still being as much worn, makes the combining of two old dresses in one a great advantage. It is curious to trace how completely one mode springs from another.

To begin with, "La Matinée," or morning robe, so much in vogue at present, is simply the result of the *paletôt* or cuirasse (long jacket), which was for a long time reigning favorite. Then again, the decided and prolonged success of the Princess robe proved to be the plastron and gilet, a slight variety being considered advisable. These trimmings, from at first playing a comparatively unimportant role, took by degrees a prominent place in every stylish toilet; consequently, when the waistcoat had obtained its highest degree of success, the vest and basquine made their appearance on the horizon of fashion. The latter is in reality a reminiscence of the modes of 1850, though supposed to be a recent invention. In fact, this garment was in existence as far back as 1786, under the title "Casaquine." Two or three basquines of the recent mode deserve a word of notice. One is of satin, *à la reine* (a material of the old times revived); the back, front, and sleeves are striped with rich gold embroidery. A second is of gauze, embroidered in several shades of color, *à la pompadour*, and trimmed with lace. There may likewise be seen some of cardinal silk, with gilet of brocaded texture; they are tight-fitting, and look well over black or dark-colored skirt. The question now is, whether this renovated fancy will take; we cannot say positively, although we think it probable, that modern taste may not altogether reject the "old new" style. The adoption of the basquine will create almost a revolution in dress, for the upper part of this latter will be completely distinct from the rest. We could readily understand the basquine worn as a black confection, or out-of-door jacket; but as the model is at present conceived, it cannot possibly be utilized in this manner. There are several shapes, one we saw called the Sultane will, perhaps, prove the most popular. It is made quite tight-fitting in the back, and loose in front. It reached only to the waist, and from thence fell two long, wide sash-ends, fringed, which were tied together about half-way down the skirt. The material was a rich ruby velvet, lined with silk to match, and embroidered in flowers with white and pale pink silk.

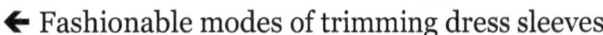

...

← Fashionable modes of trimming dress sleeves.

...

It will be the fashion this autumn and winter to have the bodices of evening dresses made of a different material to that of which the skirt is composed (this, we believe, is another very old fashion lately revived). Thus, for example, a pale blue silk skirt may have a bodice of the some color in plush, and a pink brocade one of pink velvet.

Short dresses are made without tunics, in kiltings, to within about eight inches of the waist, where they are met by the plaited jacket bodice, which is drawn into the waist with a belt. These dresses have usually sleeveless jackets without trimming. Short skirts are still the exception to many. Economy has a good deal to do with the matter, as along dress furnished with a shortening apparatus contrives a "double debt to pay," being useful both for the house and for out door wear.

As regards dress-holders, their name is legion, but we do not think any we have seen are as satisfactory, considering the subject from every point of view, as the plan of cordons (or strings) and rings adopted by the French. These strings are attached to seams of skirt, pull with the greatest facility, and tie round the waist. A button fastened at the end of each cord, where it is brought out at the top of the side-seam, prevents the extremity of string from slipping when the dress is let down. It is a grave mistake to suppose that a dress shortened produces the effect of a short skirt; by adopting this plan one follows "the letter" of the fashion, but not "the spirit" thereof. For the correct form of short dress, the lower portion is plaited, and the back has a certain amount of fulness or drapery. The bodice is separate from skirt. A simple polonaise of the ordinary length combined with a short skirt, would fail to give proper effect. In fact, short costumes constitute their own particular style, and require special treatment; glad are we, however, to see them so generally adopted, as they make walking a much more easy and healthy exorcise, being free from the burden of the weight of the long trailing skirts so long worn.

We regret to observe that very small waists are once more forcing themselves on our notice. This fashion will tend to fill doctors' pockets with considerable rapidity, and help to people cemeteries in an ever-increasing ratio. It is all very well that medical men and undertakers should earn their living, but unavoidable diseases gives them ample opportunities of doing so, as far as we can judge. The motto, "Charity begins at home," might fairly be put in practice in the case of tight lacing; and no one with an ounce of common sense can dispute the point that to this evil habit are due many of the maladies so difficult (in some cases impossible) to cure.

...

First, as to color. The new shade that is associated with every hue in the prism is called "Thiers red;" it is a rich, dark garnet, darker than the cardinal red we have recently been wearing. It is especially handsome in satin and velvet; and as a foundation for brocade, for belts, for ribbons, and bonnet trimmings, it is also a success. We are going to look gay this winter, for the sombre greys and yellow browns are to be replaced by clearer hues, and by rich colors softly blended. In one material that came under our notice we counted four shades of olive, pale blue, garnet, and deep yellow, all so subdued and happily amalgamated that the eye was not even startled.

Silks in velvet and satin stripes are both elegant and stylish made up over a plain silk or plain velvet underskirt. Watered silks have been revived; we saw an exquisitely beautiful black one composed of alternate stripes of watered and brocade; this would be elegant made up with satin or velvet. Silk *damassé* is even more fashionable than it has been heretofore. The patterns are in raised velvet or satin on a plain silk surface.

Many of the new fabrics have Eastern names, and are oriental in coloring and design. There is the "Palmyra *broché*" of fine wool, closely ribbed with a satin-like surface thrown up in small brocaded flowers. There are new loosely woven Indian cashmeres; there are chudder cloths, with tiny woven stripes in herring-bone pattern; and there are camel's-hair fabrics in olive, hazel brown, and blue gray. These last, made up with satin, are already greatly in favor.

Coatings is the name given to a material resembling homespun. They have a comparatively smooth surface, and are a mixture of three or four dark, rich colors perfectly blended, so that they produce, at a short distance, the effect of one color. Olive green and *réséda* prevail in these coatings, and in nearly all there are threads of orange, Thiers red, or sulphur. Coatings are to be made up as short costumes. Another material for substantial winter walking dresses is *drap de soldat*, a very heavy gray-blue cloth, of which is made a short skirt, a corsage, and a wrapping, which is rather long, and in modified habit shape.

...

The English coat of homespun cloths, with velvet collar, cuffs, and pockets, is the jaunty and comfortable-looking wrap for autumn wear. It is of medium length, not too long to wear with short skirts, nor too short for carriage costumes. The front is double-breasted, and the back is in coat shape, with short side-forms that are very broad at the waist-line. Buttons define the waist, and there are plaits or revers in the seams below. Their shape and whole appearance are very much like a gentleman's English morning coat. Gray and brown are stylish colors.

Godey's Lady's Book and Magazine, November 1878

LADIES' RECEPTION TOILETTE.

Figure No. 1. – This charming costume is made of grosgrain and watered silk or *moire antique*; two materials combining handsomely and often to be found in the "laid-aside" wardrobes of many ladies, the cost of the costume in this event being but a trifle. Even in buying new the amount is comparatively economical.

This skirt was cut by pattern No. 6330, which is in 9 sizes for ladies from 20 to 36 inches, waist measure, and costs 30 cents. The front and side gores have a narrow plaiting at the bottom of their lining, over which falls the bottom of the outside, the latter being cut in deep, pointed scollops. The outside of the back-breadth, however, extends to the edge of the lining under a double row of plaiting, the upper row of which forms the heading.

The polonaise is closely fitted and has a diagonal drapery front and a coat-tail back with long back drapery falling from under it. Vest and cuff facings and a back central facing of watered silk are used, together with facings on the reversed portion of the scarf and the back drapery. The reversed portion of the front drapery may be left to fall in the usual manner if desired, and faced to represent a *revers*. The pattern is No. 6372, and is in 13 sizes for ladies from 28 to 46 inches, bust measure. Its price is 35 cents.

To make the costume for a lady of medium size will require 17 7/8 yards of goods 22 inches wide; the skirt calling for 7 5/8 yards, and the polonaise for 10 1/4 yards. Of 48-inch-wide goods, 8 1/2 yards will be needed; the skirt requiring 4 yards, and the polonaise 4 1/2 yards.

Arthur's Illustrated Home Magazine, December 1878

Short dresses having so rapidly gained in favor, and as we are receiving so many inquiries in reference to the proper models for making them, we feel we cannot better please the majority of our lady readers than by giving them good models for making up these popular walking dresses. To those who want an inexpensive and easily made walking dress, we will describe one we saw lately made of all wool navy-blue serge. The skirt was a rounded short one, with a deep, broad, kilted flounce, reaching to within sixteen inches of the waist. This flounce was only stitched down where it was put on to the skirt, the lower part of the plaiting being only confined by being tacked to a tape on the inside; and the folds fell naturally and gracefully. At the top it was headed with a crossway band of silk of the same color as the serge, about two inches wide, finished behind with a sash of the same, with falling bows, and ends lined with the serge. The bodice was a simple one, quite plain in front, and with a little gathered fulness in the two centre-pieces to tally with the fulness of the back of the skirt, and was worn with a leather belt with a silver buckle. The dress had the effect of a Princess one, as the bodice and skirt buttoned in a line down the front as far as the flounce, and small plaits were made in the skirt to correspond with those in the front of the bodice; but the bodies and skirt were really made separate, and joined together with a band at the waist. We think ladies who make their own dresses would find this an easy way of making one, it being much easier to fit. The sleeve was quite plain and rather tight, with a narrow kilting held down by a band and bow of silk to match the skirt. Over this was worn a sleeveless jacket of the serge, made just long enough to reach to and show the band of silk round the skirt. This was quite untrimmed, with the exception of a turned-back collar, lined with silk, fastened with a bow of ribbon with long ends.

Figs. 1 and 2. – Front and back view of ladies' short costume. It is made of navy-blue cashmere; the bottom of the skirt is trimmed with a plaited ruffle, trimmed with three bands of silk. The waist is plaited into a yoke, extending into a long basque plaited. Scarf drapery forming an overdress; it can be plain or trimmed with a narrow embroidery as shown in Fig. 2.

Plaids have become quite popular. Blue and green are the usual combinations, although red also appears, and all the Scotch clans are in requisition. This, then, forms a fresh variety in the already multitudinous choice of materials which are offered for winter costumes. The pretty blouse jackets, which are in vogue just now, and are so be, coming to youthful figures, remind us of a time when fashions were simpler and less elaborate. Our grandmothers and mothers were no less charming for that, and had their hours of beauty and fashion, much as any lady of fashion of the present day. Simpler toilets seem all the prettier and more becoming now because they are more rare. Figured and brocaded staffs are not required to be much trimmed; but this is a fact that modern fashion takes no account of. All fancy materials are new combined and trimmed with self-colored ones. so that no place is left for sweet simplicity. There are lappets of every shape and length, waistcoats of one color and tablier of another, flutings of cashmere and draperies of brocade, ruches of silk and bias bands of striped satin. Most of the new costumes we see, if of an elegant style at all, are made with the coat, jacket, and waistcoat. Nor does this necessarily imply a toilet of silks and brocade. Equally pretty costumes of this style are made with fancy woollen material, plain cashmere, merino, or beige. A pretty suit of Rob Roy plaid tartan is made with the first skirt cut round, just clearing the ground; it is trimmed round the bottom with a deep kilting; the second skirt wrapped close round the body, and fastened, being in small, neat folds. Long jacket bodice, double-breasted, fastened slantways across with tiny steel-ball buttons, and forming deep revers at the top. Leather belt and steel buckle round the waist, from which hangs a small leather *aumônière*. Tight sleeves, with bias facings and steel buttons. Plain linen collar and cuffs, and dark-blue cravat. Hat of black felt, bell-shaped, with a plaid scarf round it, and small bird's wing at the side.

Godey's Lady's Book and Magazine, December 1878

1879

CAUTION.

If you have had no experience in cutting or making dresses, or if you are not accustomed to the use of paper patterns, the following simple directions will help you: Take the measure carefully as directed, then select the pattern according to the measure. If the material to be used is expensive, first cut the garment out of common but firm bleached muslin. Baste it up and fit it as you desire the garment to fit. If alterations are required, make them on the muslin. In this way, if you are careful in fitting, you will have no difficulty. Basting is the most important part in the making of a garment. A good authority on dressmaking has said that "more than half of all the ill-fitting dresses is the result of bad basting."

...

Ladies' Patterns, such as Basques, Polonaise, Cloaks, Mantles, Capes, Chemises, etc., should be selected according to the bust measure. Pass a tape measure around the breast, just under the arms, and above the bust, as seen above, draw it *one inch tighter than the dress is to fit*; the number of inches then ascertained is the size of the bust. Overskirts, Drawers, etc., should be selected according to the waist measure. The waist measure should be taken tight under the belt.

Bazar Glove-Fitting Patterns, No. 1-8, 1879

We give, first, this month, a house or dinner-dress, of plain and brocatelle material, in either silk or woolen fabric. The color is a very dark, almost invisible green. For woolen material, use dark green cashmere, or camel's hair cloth, with a bourette, or brocaded material, in the same color, with a dash of mixed colors running through. This to be used for the vest and trimmings. We give the front and back views.

The dress is cut with a skirt, in the Princess shape. First, a lining for the front and side gores; on to this is draped the cashmere, for the apron – the bottom of the front being trimmed with a box plaiting five inches deep, with the heading when finished. A band of the mixed material, one inch wide, separates the box-plaiting, as seen. The train has, first, a narrow, knife plaiting of the plain material; then the edge of the train is faced four inches deep with the mixed material, and caught up at intervals, and fastened with a button. The long, coat-tail basque has a long vest of the brocade, and it is turned back, and the revers faced with the same. The revers form the trimmings for the back of the basque, and are finished with a tiny bow, as may be seen from the engraving of the back view. Tight coat sleeves, with cuffs of the brocade. This dress is cut V shape in front, but if preferred, it will look equally stylish cut high in the throat, and finished with a standing collar. Six yards of double width goods. Handsome India cashmere, or camel's hair cloth can be bought for $1.50 per yard; inferior qualities, from 50 cents, up to 75 for single width, $1.00 for double. Four yards of brocaded, or bourette material for vest and trimming. One dozen buttons.

BORDERS: RUSSIAN EMBROIDERY
By Mrs. Jane Weaver.

We give, here, two very pretty borders in the Russian Embroidery, now so popular. Work in colored silks, or wool, or braids, for sacque and dress trimmings.

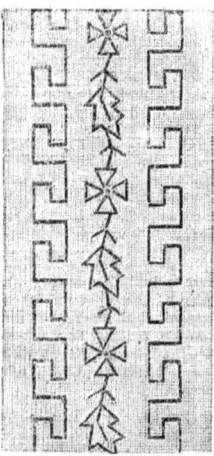

CLOTH COSTUME FOR WINTER: BACK AND FRONT

Figs. VI and VII. – Back and Front of Cloth Costume of Gray Cloth, Trimmed with Dark Green Cloth and Dark Green Velvet; the skirt is kilt-plaited; the gray tunic is turned back with the dark green cloth, and falls at the back as a puffed square end; green cloth jacket, fastened at the sides; it has *revers* collar, and pockets of the dark green velvet; the buttons are all mother-of-pearl. ...

An old light silk dress may be made to do service as a new one, by flouncing it at the bottom with thin, soft white muslin, (but the *yellower* the white muslin is, the better), and draping it with scarfs of muslin over the front, and at the back.

Peterson's Magazine, January 1879

To sum up fashion as it is and will remain throughout the winter, it may be said that the toilette varies according to the hours of the day. In Paris morning is confined to the hours between rising and four o'clock. Toilettes for the morning are simple, sombre, almost masculine. Black or dark cloth, cashmere, vigogne, and all woolen goods are employed for these dresses. The dress is short, the wrapping nearly tight-fitting, and in the shape of a long sacque with vest, and very large revers, which are fastened near the shoulders. Linen lingerie, and an enormous white muslin cravat, or else a lace jabot. Sleeves almost tight-fitting. Fur toque. This (with many variations) is the uniform for morning wear.

The evening, on the contrary, is devoted to historic or individual fancy. Velvet, satin, brocade, damask, plush, pékin – all these contribute to the magnificence of the toilette, which, according to fancy, copies the costume of the Middle Ages, of the days of Louis XIV., Louis XV., or Louis XVI. There is no curb nor rule. Every woman dresses to suit her fancy, and modern reunions, by reason of this unlimited liberty, present the appearance of fancy-dress balls. Like every thing else here below, the independence of the toilette has its inconveniences as well as advantages. In order to dress at present one must exercise one's judgment above all things, and show good taste, which is not given to all women. On the other hand, this independence favors individual taste, and permits extreme simplicity to mingle in the *salons* with the greatest luxury and most audacious fancy. ...

SHORT DANCING DRESSES.

Short dresses for dancing are being worn in Paris, and a few have been made here. These have panier over-dresses, and herald probably the prevailing fashion of a future season. These short dresses are confined to very young ladies, and are usually the white dresses so suitable for débutantes. The skirt is quite short in front and on the sides, but the back, while it has no train, is sloped away to a point that touches the floor, or perhaps it is long enough for two or three inches of the point to rest on the floor. These are so convenient in dancing, more especially now that it is becoming the fashion to take steps instead of merely walking through the figures of a quadrille, that they will doubtless grow in favor. A short white satin skirt of this kind was made plain, with only a pleated satin frill sewed to the bottom for trimming. Over this was a plain white India muslin basque and panier over-skirt trimmed with many yards of Breton lace. Another pure white dress for a young lady who is enjoying her first winter in society has a short white satin skirt with three or four narrow satin pleatings around the bottom as a border. The over-skirt of white gauze with diamond-shaped bars is disposed like a deep apron in front, and forms bouffant yet soft panier puffs behind. This over-skirt is edged with very filmy gauze lace, and is large enough to cover all of the satin lower skirt except the flounces. Three garlands of white violets are curved on the apron from the right side downward to the foot on the left, where a scarf drapery and a single garland meet them. Two waists, one high and the other low, are usually made to such dresses.

MANNER OF MAKING.

Three kinds of low corsages are used this season, viz., the waist with long points, the belted Josephine corsage, and the corset basque. The pointed waist has very sharp points in front and back, while the sides define the waist line; this is much liked for satin waists, and is always laced behind. The Josephine corsage is round, with very low darts, and a wide belt of silk or satin folds. The corset basque fits precisely like a corset over the hips, and merely outlines a fine figure. It has but few seams, and may be laced behind or buttoned in front. It has no regular darts, but there is a seam down the middle of the front, and what is usually a dart is carried on up to the neck, making two middle forms; there is than an under-arm gore and a short side form in the back; the middle forms of the back support the eyelets for lacing. The lower edge is finished by two silk cords. The low neck is round, and is finished by the becoming Grecian drapery made of folds of tulle edged with lace, and caught together in the middle of the front by a knot or cluster of soft folds of the dress satin or silk. The sleeves are the merest band or frill. Square necks are also much used on low corsages, and not a few are V-shaped; the preference, however, is for the round low neck. A rosette of satin ribbon is worn high on the left side of Grecian berthas, and a bow of many loops is on the top of the right sleeve.

When high corsages are used the waist has always a basque back, but may be short and round, with a belt in front. This basque is made dressy by full jabots of lace from the throat down, or else it is cut out square. The sleeves are transparent, of lace or of thin silk muslin, and may be long in coat shape, or else only half-long, to the elbow. A youthful dress of white grenadine with half-inch stripes of satin has the silk foundation skirt entirely covered with the grenadine, which is sewed upon it in shirred breadths down the front, while the back is straight and flowing. The three shirred clusters of the front are covered with rosettes and loops of satin ribbon. The grenadine basque is lined throughout, then cut down square in the neck, and has elbow sleeves made of very thin silk muslin, without lining, and finished with pleated frills of the satin-striped grenadine. Tulle dresses have three-cornered revers of satin on the skirt, or else long narrow panels of satin enriched with pearl passementerie and embroidery on tulle; the back has billowy puffs that are supported underneath by crinoline flounces, to make them remain bouffant. The pearl trimmings and satin are especially effective with tulle. One pretty fashion is that of making a satin apron, wrinkled and fringed with pearls, to cover the three front breadths, while the back breadths are flounced from the belt to the end of the train with pleatings of doubled tulle. Sometimes there are only five wide pleatings across the back, while others have from ten to fifteen narrow pleated flounces. The basque may then have a satin vest, and if the arms are not fine, the sleeves may be of satin. If the neck is handsome, the waist may be a low peasant bodice of satin, with merely tulle extending upward to the throat. As in the dress of white gauze trimmed with white violets, just described, the preference is for an all-white dress, yet many tulle dresses are trimmed with clusters of dark Jacqueminot roses, and sometimes the bright yellow Marshal Neil roses are mingled with them. Velvet leaves, mosses, grasses, and foliage are massed in panels on the side, or are placed low down on the train, or else outline the apron.

White satin dresses worn by more elderly ladies are trimmed with a great deal of creamy old lace in jabots down the waist and sides, mingled with pearl trimmings, while the sleeves are entirely of pearls or of lace. Dresses of the princesse shape are retained by stout ladies. The back is left quite plain, with waist and skirt in one, while to the front is added a short round wrinkled apron of embroidered tulle or of crape richly fringed. This apron begins below the waist line just where a basque would leave off. Another plan is to add two revers of brocaded satin in three-cornered shape, forming a sort of apron, and extending to the middle of the back. ...

THE STRAIGHT SKIRTS WITH FLOWING TRAINS.

Some of the most distinguished-looking evening dresses have skirts with straight fronts in panels and flowing trains, and are without over-skirt or drapery. This style is effective in combinations of two materials, as in a beautiful dress of pale pink brocade and pink silk. The front gore – which is divided in two narrow panels by a seam straight down the middle – is of brocade, while the side gores are of plain silk turned back in four-inch panels from the brocade; at the foot of the front gores is some fly fringe, and there are rosettes of satin ribbon in the panels. Back of the side gores a brocaded revers begins very narrow at the foot and widens at the top, where it meets in the back and holds down the fullness of the straight flowing train; a knife-pleating edges the train and the side gores. A low round basque for this dress will have the two middle forms of the front of brocade to match those of the skirt. Greek tulle bertha with pearl fringe and satin rosettes.

PANIER BUSTLES.

The furnishing houses are selling regular bustles of dimity or brilliantine with flexible steel springs in them to support short or demi-trained dancing dresses. For the long trains modistes prepare for each dress a support of its own, consisting of voluminous flounces of stiffly starched muslin on a foundation of barred crinoline that is cut to fit the three back breadths of the skirt.

Harper's Bazar, January 25, 1879

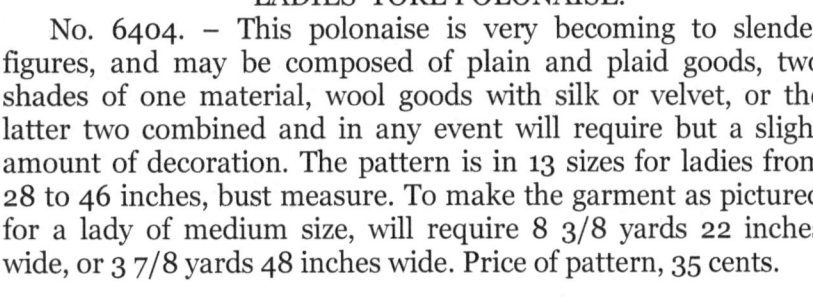

LADIES' YOKE POLONAISE.

No. 6404. – This polonaise is very becoming to slender figures, and may be composed of plain and plaid goods, two shades of one material, wool goods with silk or velvet, or the latter two combined and in any event will require but a slight amount of decoration. The pattern is in 13 sizes for ladies from 28 to 46 inches, bust measure. To make the garment as pictured for a lady of medium size, will require 8 3/8 yards 22 inches wide, or 3 7/8 yards 48 inches wide. Price of pattern, 35 cents.

...

Winter fashions have now assumed a definite form. An abundance of bright color is the most striking characteristic. ...

In place of the dark, subdued shades worn within the last few years, we have garnet, plum, olive and myrtle green. Satin is once more a fashionable material for trimming, and in pipings and facings it is often used upon elaborate costumes.

...

LADIES' PLAIN, ROUND SKIRT.

No. 6410. – Plain, round skirts with flat trimmings are quite popular, and one of the prettiest models for them is here represented. The pattern, which is in 9 sizes for ladies from 20 to 36 inches, waist measure, calls for 4 1/2 yards of 22-inch-wide goods, or 2 1/4 yards 48 inches wide, in making the skirt for a lady of medium size. The price of the pattern is 35 cents. ↘

...

Speaking of dressmaking, we may here remark on a modification or two of old habits. Dress-sleeves are not corded now, but are stitched directly into the armholes. The cross-seam from the dart to the side-form no longer appears, the waist being fitted by a third dart running up and down, directly under the arm.

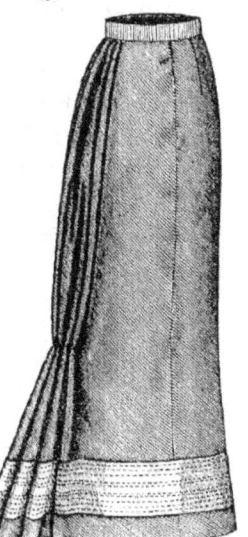

Bretonne lace is the style now for trimmings, and ruchings and jabots of itself and loops of ribbon. This is simply white net, with the pattern darned in. The latest neckties are broad scarfs of white crape or muslin, embroidered with pale silk, or finished at the ends with plaitings of the lace.

Arthur's Illustrated Home Magazine, January 1879

EVENING-DRESS. DINNER-DRESS.

Fig. IX. – Evening Dress of Silk, of the greenish-white tint called crystal; the front is covered with alternate bands of dragon-green velvet and silk embroidered galloon, ornamented on either side by scalloped embroidery. The back falls in easy folds, and has narrow box-plaiting, surmounted by the galloon. Embroidered flounces and triple folds of velvet trim the Marquise sleeves. A lace ruching edges the square opening, and composes the necklet.

Fig. X. – Evening and Reception-Dress of Dark Blue Velvet; long skirt, bordered with a blue satin plaiting. Narrow tablier of pale blue satin, laid in a triple plait. The sides are full, and terminate with a blue sash at the back. Bodice with short basque, double collar at the back; light blue satin laid in folds on the waist; large blue bow of the satin, with a bunch of red roses above it; illusion in the neck.

...

Paniers are, as yet, seldom seen, though some of the imported dresses are strewn with them; but they will certainly be *the* fashion, before long, as crinoline, or *tournures*, or "bustles," (the thing is known by all three names,) are already appearing, though very modest in size, at first.

We give, first, this month, a walking costume. It consists of a long paletot, in gray camel's hair cloth, which is worn over any short walking-suit. This paletot is cut in a long close-fitting sacque, fastened down the front with cords and large passementerie buttons. These buttons and cords are the chief ornaments to the garments, and to those of our readers who are not in a place where such ornaments can be procured, a little care with the following direction, will make a very good imitation: take a piece of letter paper two thickness, cut size of a twenty-five cent piece; lay over it a piece of black silk, large enough to meet in the centre, or under the under side after the button is completed. Take some narrow, worsted embroidery braid; punch a hole in the centre of the foundation, and bring the braid through; then begin, and sew the braid down flat, passing the silk over the braid, at equal distances; continue this, round and round, until you have the size of the paper covered. Have ready a piece of cardboard, same size; place this under, and then cover with the edge of the black silk, drawing it up to the centre, just as you would cover a mould button. If desired, these can be ornamented with jet beads, sewed on. Knot the cords in the centre, and sew the double on the left side; covering it with the button; leaving the loop to fasten over on the opposite button. It is advisable to have the first five buttons and cords sewed on to the paletot on both sides, leaving only enough open to make it comfortable to get into. The buttons slightly graduate, as they approach the waist. The same trims the flaps at the sides, and in the middle of the back; also the cuffs. Two collars, bound with braid, same as the edge of the paletot, finishes the garment at the throat. A waist-band made of the same material, and bound on both sides with the same braid, fastens with a jet buckle in front. This is optional. Three yards of double-width goods will be required, six pieces of narrow braid, and twelve yards of cord.

...

Next, is a design for trimming for bottom of dress skirt. It is combination of cashmere and silk. The box-plaiting is seven inches deep, and is of cashmere; above that is a bias ruffle of cashmere, edged with a narrow knife-plaiting of silk. This is put on full enough to allow it to be tacked in the form shown in the engraving. Two and a-half inch ruffle, with two inch knife-plaiting, will be in good proportion.

Peterson's Magazine, February 1879

Fig. 11. – Front and back view of house dress for lady made of navy blue silk. It is made in the

princess form half-way down the skirt, below which in front the skirt is kilted, divided by bands of velvet; a piece of the silk is put down the back which is laid in fine plaits, crossed by bands of velvet. It is finished off by a double piece laid in large box plaits, the front is laid in three plaits, and fastened under this. A vest is outlined with the velvet bands, and the sleeves are striped with them.

...

Very pretty dresses are made of dark shades of cashmere trimmed with moss cloth. This is a lovely soft, rich mixture of silk and wool, and has a mossy texture from which it takes its name. A dress of olive green cashmere we saw was trimmed with this material in the same shade, with a great deal of silk in it, gold color, pearl white, and green. The skirt had at the bottom a kilted

flounce headed by another, in the centre of which was a band of the moss cloth. The over-dress, which was a long one, was lined with the cloth and turned up in front to show about eighteen inches of the lining, and fastened behind over the back of the overskirt, which was untrimmed, with about six pearl and gold buttons. The bodice was made with a yoke, and the pleated part below was of alternate folds of the cashmere and the moss cloth. The sleeves were as tight-fitting as possible, and had pointed cuffs of the cloth reaching to the elbow, fastened with buttons like those upon the overskirt.

...

Fig. 22. – Polonaise for street wear, made of black velvet, trimmed with damask and plain satin, fringe ribbon, and passementerie.

...

There seems to be quite a revival of the fashion of having the sleeves of jackets, or bodices, of a different material. This fashion had lost favor in the past few months; we are however glad to see it revived, as it gives a *distingue* air to a dress. ...

A great many dresses are made entirely of the one material, with no other trimming than a quantity of bows of ribbon, generally the fashionable kind, with a reversible side. For instance, a bronze dress has bows of bronze satin ribbon, of which the other side is a pale shade of blue, and a dark blue dress has ribbons of the same color, the other side of which is a dark red. These bows are arranged to show the inner side as well as the outer, and make a very pretty and effective trimming.

As before stated, the jacket bodice and double skirt is preferred in general for winter dresses to the long polonaise, but the latter is by no means forsaken. Many ladies consider it more becoming, and wear it with a simulated second skirt, which is merely a kilting sewn on to a false hem under the edge of the polonaise. Polonaise are very much too economical to be quickly discarded, for with one really stylish polonaise, any number of half-worn skirts can be made to look presentable. Embroidery and old lace, both of which are conspicuous in present fashions, contribute to make our modern toilets resemble those of a century ago. With the casaquin and waistcoat, Rembrandt hat and lace ruffles of fashionable costumes, a lady needs but a cloud of powder upon her coiffure to make her look like a portrait of the time of Louis XVI.

Godey's Lady's Book, February 1879

Breton lace will not lose its favor with the present season, but will be employed for trimming summer dresses of batiste and printed jaconet. This lace, being inexpensive, can be used lavishly in ornamenting a dress without involving a ruinous cost. Meanwhile it serves for all purposes – bonnets, coiffures, fichus, cravats, bows, etc. ...

A fashion unjustly abandoned, but which seems about to regain its former favor, is that of fine laces; they are much worn now, especially white. Black lace is used only on black satin, while white lace is worn with every thing and on all colors, both dark and light. Lace is much employed for trimming the front of skirts in flounces, one above the other, the lace being turned back on each side so as not to cut it. When used, on the contrary, for trimming the back of trained dresses, it is put on flat, with a pinked silk ruche or a tulle puffing headed with satin stars between the flounces. Satin is employed every where and on every thing, for morning dresses as well as ball toilettes. This beautiful fabric seems determined to make up for lost time, and to avenge its undeserved banishment. ...

Many evening corsages are pointed in the front and back, and are laced behind. One of the ornaments most used for the trimming of evening dresses is beaded cord. Imagine a round silk cord wound spirally with a shining metal thread; this produces exactly the effect of a row of beads, and is capable of striking combinations.

A favorite arrangement both for evening and walking dresses is that of looping the skirt after the fashion in which our soldiers loop their capotes when on the march. Each front is turned back and fastened on the hip, or even at the bottom of the back of the waist, by an ornament, the whole disclosing another skirt front covered with lace and embroidery, and almost always of a different color from the upper dress.

The revival of lace permits sundry combinations at once elegant and economical for the fortunate possessors of black lace flounces. On a perfectly plain dress, without over-skirt or trimmings, are set *quilles* formed of a cascade of black lace mixed with long loops of black or old gold satin ribbons. Over these trimmings fall cords and tassels of the beaded cord described above. Old gold beaded cord forms a tasteful accompaniment to black dresses as well as laces.

Harper's Bazar, February 22, 1879

LADIES' *PANIER* POLONAISE.

No. 6433. – This very novel and elegant polonaise may be made of any of the suitings in vogue, and trimmed as the taste dictates. The pattern is in 13 sizes for ladies from 28 to 46 inches, bust measure. To make the garment as pictured for a lady of medium size, will require 11 1/8 yards 22 inches wide, or 4 5/8 yards 48 inches wide, each with 2 1/2 yards of brocade 22 inches wide. Price of pattern, 35 cents.

...

For the street, short shirts have triumphed, and there is good reason to suppose that their reign here will be long continued. They are even encroaching upon the acknowledged domain of trains, being seen in some of the latest evening dresses. But fashion says now that they shall be used for morning and out-door wear, while flowing robes shall hold sway, as heretofore, for the dinner, the reception, and to ball costume.

Polonaises are beginning to diminish in popularity. Very long, closely-fitting basques and panier over-skirts are taking their place, dividing favor with the princess dress, which follows the universal fancy for more elaborate drapery, and appears with greater fullness in the back. We mentioned in our last the Trianon polonaise, which was noticeable for its contrasting revers caught together at the corners over the bouffant back, and spoke of it as a good model for renovating an old garment. Another way in which this can be done is to leave the back breadths for a train, cut off the front to the length of a basque, and attach three short, petticoat breadths of a contrasting color – as, for instance, the former part may be of black silk, and latter [sic] of pale blue. In this manner a fancy dress may be made even more elegant than the original, substantial one. In nearly all fashionable dresses, there is a combination of materials and colors, and a basque made newly often has the back terminating in a long train, to be worn over a different kind of a skirt. ...

A very pretty novelty for evening wear is long, lace sleeves. Dark, high-necked dresses of heavy silk or velvet, have them of black or white net, cut in coat-shape, and finished off by ruches of Bretonne lace and bright bows of ribbon. The same lace is used to fill in the neck and edge the bottom of the vest, while a jabot of it, mingled with ribbon loops, completes the costume.

Arthur's Illustrated Home Magazine, February 1879

We give, first, this month, one of the newest pannier dresses, of which we have lately spoken, in the fashion department. It will be seen that, as yet, the pannier has not arrived at the enormous size that was worn some years ago, but no doubt it will soon do so. The dress here given, is intended for home wear; the under-skirt is of brown and old gold striped satin, and a piece set on near the bottom, which has only the very slightest more fulness than the skirt itself; just above this piece is a scalloped bias flounce made of the silk like the over-dress, and with but very little fulness also. The over-dress is of greenish-blue summer silk, with a brown chêne figure on it; it is made in the Princess form, with an elongated waist at the back, and the full skirt which falls from the buttons, is puffed out by a crinoline of either horsehair or steel hoops run through muslin; the front is cut open and square on the neck, where it is filled in with lace and is also cut off square some distance below the waist, near the striped petticoat; it is fastened across the front by three brown satin bands with pearl buckles. A second and lower skirt is only simulated, and apparently fastened on to the upper skirt on each side, by three satin-covered buttons; a large brown satin bow loops up the lower skirt beneath the puffing of the upper one. The sleeves are three-quarters long, bound with brown satin, and have a strap of the satin and a pearl buckle just above the elbow. There are two large, brown buttons on either side of the body, and the collar is partly of plain brown satin, and of the brown and old gold striped satin.

...

As will be seen in our various fashions, this month, the pannier is gradually creeping in; just now, especially for street-dresses, it consists only of a mere puffed appearance at the *back*, and rather low down, but many of the imported dresses have a decided fulness on the hips, especially the evening-dresses. Still it must not be supposed that the close-clinging dress is by any means thrown aside; so far from it, the pannier is the great exception. For very slender people the pannier will be advantageous, but stout ladies should beware how they adopt the new style. The *very* tight-clinging dress, however, is becoming to none, except the figure is one that can scarcely be found once in a thousand times – the perfect figure; and neither the very thin nor the very stout look well in a robe that is so tight-fitting. The *fronts* of dresses still fall quite close. Short dresses are *almost* universal for walking; they are much too comfortable not to be adopted, but long dresses are still worn in the house, being so much more elegant and graceful. For dancing, however, young ladies have the trains made much shorter than heretofore, and some have even gone so far as to dance in quite short dresses, that is, made only to walking length; these should fall close about the ankles, however, as in dancing the feet would be too much exposed otherwise.

...

Colors for Evening Dresses. – In selecting a dress to be worn in the evening, by gas-light, it should be remembered that colors present a different tint in the daytime to that shown in artificial light. The color of a texture gains or loses by the latter, according to the amount of yellow contained in it. Violet, which is a complementary color to yellow, is decomposed in gas-light; the blue disappears, and it becomes red. Blue, if pure, thus borders on green; if dark, it appears harsh and black; and if pale, loses color, and becomes gray. Turquoise silk, which, by sunlight, is beautiful, loses it brilliancy, and appears faded. In ascending the scale of cold colors, yellow greens are among the prettiest for evening wear. Thus, apple-green is not far from emerald, and emerald, without changing tint, gains in richness; straw-color slightly reddens in the folds; sulphur does not change. There is nothing, perhaps, more charming than maize; for, without losing its peculiar qualities, it gains an indefinable warmth of tint. The same effect is produced in red shades; for the yellow glare of evening lights, which is so fatal to blue, augments their splendor. Ruby is heightened in its beauty, particularly in plush materials; orange-red brightens, and pure orange takes a flame color. Black and white do not escape the action of artificial light. Those beautiful blacks, so well named after the raven's wing, become dull and heavy, by not retaining the blue shade which gives them life and depth. White, on the contrary, improves at night, and, if faded, revives. A color which retains its charm is silver-gray. It even gains a slightly rose-color hue; but, should the gray contain a suspicion of blue, like pearl-gray, the blue tint is lost, and the distinctive characteristic of pearl-gray disappears.

Peterson's Magazine, March 1879

LADIES' HOUSE COSTUME.

Figure No. 1. – Princess dresses continue to meet with favor from most ladies, and are draped and trimmed with a variety of pretty ways. The one forming this costume is handsomely fitted in the close style peculiar to Princess dresses, by bust darts, under-arm and side-back seams through the whole length of the garment, and a center-seam extending from the neck to a little below the waist-line, where it terminates in an extra width that is folded in an under box-plait. Upon the front edge of the back a *revers* extension is allowed, and is faced with brocaded silk, which material also forms a broad outside facing across the bottom of the skirt, back of the *revers*. The lower edge of the front and side-back is bordered with a double box-plaiting of the dress goods, which is cashmere; and the plaiting is set on so as to form its own heading. From under the *revers* at each side, two sash portions, placed a short distance apart, extend to the center of the front, where they meet in a handsome double bow-knot with ends. The front closes from the neck to the upper sash with button-holes and buttons, and below that the hems are tacked together with invisible stitches. A collar of the brocade passes about the neck and extends quite low on the breast, where the ends meet under a bow of the same. A tiny plaiting of the cashmere edges the collar, and the front inside the collar is covered with cashmere laid in wide bias folds, that meet in points at the center. A military collar completes the neck edge, and is encircled by a ribbon cravat. The sleeves are close and are finished with a plaiting of cashmere, set on under an upward-turning cuff-facing of the brocade; the facing slanting at the ends so as to leave the outside seam exposed by a V-outline.

The whole costume is charming as represented, but silk, velvet, or the material in a contrasting color or of the same color with bright pipings, may be used in place of the brocade; and if desired, the ends of the large sash bows may be fringed out and knotted for a self-finish, or ready-made fringe may be added as an ornamental completion. The sashes, being simply decorative additions in this case, are not given in the pattern. There is no material in vogue for any style of dress that does not conform readily and gracefully to this model. Elaborate trimmings are not called for, but simple, tasteful decorations of any kind are appropriate. One broad sash may take the place of two narrow ones, if preferred to them, or, if the dress is intended for ordinary wear, it may be entirely untrimmed.

An exquisite robe for elegant morning wear may be fashioned by this model from white cashmere or alpaca, with sashes, *revers*, and bows of a delicate tint, with additional decorations of Smyrna or Breton lace.

The model is No. 6437, and is in 13 sizes for ladies from 28 to 46 inches, bust measure. To make the untrained garment for a lady of medium size, will require 9 1/2 yards 22 inches wide, or 4 5/8 yards 48 inches wide. Price of pattern, 40 cents.

...

LADIES' SHORT PRINCESS DRESS.

No. 6437. – A great deal of taste and ingenuity will be called into play in diversifying the decoration of this garment. It is graceful, convenient and stylish just as it is, but may be elaborated to any extent desired, or rendered more simple even than in this instance. The model is in 13 sizes for ladies from 28 to 46 inches, bust measure. To make the garment for a lady of medium size, will require 9 1/2 yards 22 inches wide, or 4 5/8 yards 48 inches wide. Price of pattern, 40 cents.

...

Various little modifications in the methods employed in dressmaking creep in from time to time. Ladies who do their own sewing should always bear in mind the fact that if we double the stuff before cutting, so as to be able to shape two sides at once, we will make no mistake, such as getting the right and wrong faces, or the grain, or the pattern, or the nap transposed. The linings should be cut first, and then basted upon the uncut material. The best dressmakers at present make the button-holes and sew on the buttons before trying on and adapting a waist for the last time, as it is difficult to pin a hem so as to insure a perfect fit. In preparing a front for the buttons and button-holes, the button-hole side only is turned back, and the button side is left open, the buttons being place on the line of the reversed edge, if it *were* reversed, so as to form a facing and a background for the button-holes. A tape is put inside a body exactly at the waist-line, caught fast at the seams, and furnished with a hook and eye, so that it may pass round the form, and, being adjusted, keep the garment in place. The two edges of seams are no longer overcast together, nor are whalebones placed between them, as these practices have been found to make the dress draw; the former are completed separately, and pressed flat, and then a casing for the latter is placed directly upon them.

Arthur's Illustrated Home Magazine, March 1879

Whilst fashion is in a transition state, we will see the two extremes meeting often. The Louis XVI style, with coat, and vest, will be adapted to the Marie Antoinette style of panniers and fuller skirts; in other words, on some toilettes, the vest remains, and the coat basque is lengthened on the hip, and gathered up in a *pouf* at the back, forming small panniers. The tight-clinging skirt is already giving way to slightly fuller drapery, and, as we have said before, long dresses are now but seldom seen on the street.

But our fashion plates are so varied, and so full of all the latest styles, that it is unnecessary to write more fully as to the prevailing fashions; a study of the plates is the best guide.

YOUNG LADY'S EVENING DRESS.

Fig. XI. – Young Lady's Evening-Dress of White Striped Algerine; the short skirt has fine, narrow knife-plaitings, with a much wider one above them, cut in points at the sides; the front of the dress is laid in small plaits the entire length of the skirt; the over-dress is of the Algerine, (which is a plain white striped material,) cut princess shape at the back, and with full *panniers* at the sides; white satin ribbon, with long loops, and ends meeting in front, come from beneath the *panniers* at the back; the princess body opens in front over a plaited waist, and a collar *berthé* is made of black velvet, edged with narrow, white lace, and has a large, pink rose on one side.

Peterson's Magazine, April 1879

Fresh importations of French dresses arrive daily, and the panier draperies upon them become more and more bouffant. The panier proper – which is a very full scarf passing around the hips and back in clusters of drapery – is especially used on evening dresses with long flowing trains. In Paris these scarfs are stiffened with crinoline lining, and in many instances an artificial panier support of wicker or of whalebone is introduced beneath them. But the skirts of short walking dresses retain their narrow dimensions – measuring about two and a half yards in breadth – hence bustles can not be used with them, and their bouffant appearance is given by the elaborate draping of the over-skirt. In some suits just received from Paris this draping is really voluminous; for instance, on a short suit of the new gendarme blue camel's-hair, after the front and sides of the lower skirt have been smoothly covered by two flat straight curtain breadths of olive and blue striped satin, there are two full breadths of double-width camel's-hair, cut very long, and draped in their entire length and breadth upon the back of the short lower skirt. These widths are nearly twice as long as the silk skirt beneath them; they have very large gilded pearl buttons down each side near the top that appear to fasten them there, and they are draped by three rows of thickly clustered pleats, one of which is on each side, and the other in the middle. With the very flat fronts of this over-skirt the bouffant back is very effective.

Another feature in these draperies is that they are gradually being made higher, with the fullness added just below the belt instead of quite low down on the skirt, as has been the fashion for several seasons. As an example of this a cashmere over-skirt will be made to part slightly down the middle in curtain fashion, and at the sides of this will be turned up a revers like that of the Trianon polonaise. Although this revers, which is quite full, would serve to enlarge the hips sufficiently, there is yet another drapery above it, passing like a scarf around the entire front and sides, and bordered behind to form two large shawl-like draperies that reach to the bottom of the lower skirt.

Still another stylish model of the new overskirts is so simple that it may be easily carried out from a description. It consists of four long straight breadths of wool goods, each nearly a yard wide. These are hemmed across the bottom and up each side within half a yard of the top, where they are sloped slightly, sewed together, and the seam concealed by broad shirring. This shirred part is sewed to the middle of the front breadth of the lower skirt, beginning at the belt; the upper part of the middle seam in the back is held in full pleats just below the belt, and the two side seams are taken up from the bottom and made to meet in the back just below these full pleats; this exposes the under side of the back breadths which hang down straight, and by way of garniture these are widely faced with plaid satin, or with striped satin, or brocaded silk. It will be seen that many of the new over-skirts retain the curtain fronts that have been in vogue during the winter, and a special object with French modistes seems to be some quaint arrangement of the space shown between the parted fronts of this curtain. In some skirts of plain wool there is simply a lapped seam down the middle of the front, on which are set very large buttons of the new gilded pearl that is speckled with all the colors used in the gay brocade or satin employed for the trimming of the dress. In other dresses the entire front is shirred in lengthwise clusters, and in some cases there is horizontal shirring, though this Bayadere effect is not very popular. Lengthwise pleats of silk may also cover the space between the curtain breadths, and sometimes it is entirely covered by regular rows of loops of satin ribbon.

A border from four to six inches wide is the trimming most used in these bunched-up overskirts, and this is sometimes edged with knife-pleating of the silk or wool goods. When made of plaid satin, this border is invariably straight, and the same is true of the very marked satin stripes of bright colors; only narrow stripes, that are not effective when straight, are cut bias. There are quaint Oriental brocades that are also best used straight, as, for instance, those with tiny palm leaves of old gold between bars of cardinal red on a blue or green ground. These gay trimmings serve to lighten the dark fabrics of the dresses, and illustrate precisely the same contrasts of light and dark colors already noted as a feature of the season in millinery. Thus a Panama tweed dress of écru shades has a plaid satin border with the écru ground barred with cardinal red, olive, old gold, and gendarme blue. The gay palm leaf brocaded silk just mentioned trims a dress of olive green cashmere. Gendarme blue camel's-hair has a vest, panels, and border of satin of the same blue shade, with stripes of old gold and pale olive green. Watered silks are also used for these trimmings, both in solid colors and in stripes alternating with solid stripes of satin,

To make black silk dresses look more spring-like there are vests, revers collars, and borders of white and black striped silk and satin, the stripes being about three-fourths of an inch wide. Others have white moiré stripes on black, or else old gold satin stripes for garniture. Black camel's-hair and the finest

French bunting dresses have facings, vests, and borders of plaid foulard in white with black. There are also very gay plaid foulard silks in which the new blue, red, old gold, and Olive colors are combined for trimming the plain woolen costumes.

...

Plain and Plaid Summer Cashmere Dress. – Back.
Figured Camel's-hair Dress. – Back.

...

DRESS WAISTS, ETC.

The waists for the bouffant skirts described above are very simply shaped basques and coats with vests like those so frequently described during the winter, but modified in each case with reference to the over-skirt and its draping. When the panier drapery is very high around the hips, the basque is short on the hips to prevent crushing this drapery, though the back is a longer habit square, and the front slightly pointed. The lapped double-breasted front may be given to any single-breasted basque left over from last season by adding a piece to lap on the left breast (sewing a seam down the middle), and fastening it by from three to six buttons. In many new basques the revers collar rolls almost to the waist line, disclosing the vest that far; the basque is then buttoned across by one, two, or three buttons in a space about as wide as a belt, below which it slopes away sharply, again showing the vest. The revers collar may be either of the figured fabric used for borders or of the plain silk of which the lower skirts of woolen dresses are now invariably made; but if loops and cravat bows are used with the pretty Breton lace jabots, they should be made of the trimming silk. The most stylish sleeves are those that are most simply finished at the wrists: an elaborate cuff detracts from style. Thus the wrists will be turned back two or three inches and covered with bias plaid, striped, brocaded, or watered trimming, and perhaps below this may fall a pleating of the plain silk; or else shirred satin or silk in very fine gathers will form the entire cuff. Two sizes of buttons are used in most of the imported suits, viz., those an inch in diameter for the basque-or coat, and twice this size for the over-skirt. The flat, round-tinted pearl buttons, with a good deal of gilt in them, are seen on most new French dresses. It is also true that elaborate flounces as well as large cuffs diminish the stylishness of the dress. In the lately imported suits a narrow pleated flounce is most often seen, as the long over-skirt drapery conceals the greater part of the lower skirt. A little shell-pleating is occasionally used for heading a knife-pleating or box-pleating, but so far this is the exception to the rule.

WASHING DRESSES.

Bandana plaids, handkerchief patterns, and chintz figures promise to be the summer caprice for washing dresses of gingham, satteen, and other cottons for ladies, misses, and children. Large plaided handkerchiefs of blue with white or yellow with red are being made up at the best furnishing houses in short suits for ladies to wear in the country. The square handkerchiefs are pieced together and made to trim themselves by being arranged with their most conspicuous stripes down the front and middle of the basque, through the sleeves, on the edge of curtain over-skirts, and at stated intervals in the pleated flounces. Two breadths of these handkerchiefs are draped to form a curtain over-skirt by lapping them slightly at the belt in front, drawing them back on each side, and tying the ends in large bunched-up drapery behind. Less conspicuous than these are dresses of navy blue handkerchiefs with white polka dots and striped border. These have the deep apron over-skirt formed of three handkerchiefs shirred down the middle, and three pleatings of the striped border across it representing three aprons; others have jabots down the entire front made of long-looped bows of the striped border sewed together double; the loops are then an inch wide and four inches deep; two loops and two ends cut off bias are tightly strapped together to form the bow, and these are put so tightly together that they form a cascade or jabot.

...

The Pompadour chintz-figured satteens are made up with the long sacques called matinées and demi-trained skirts. The only trimming is a wide edging of Hamburg-work on the sacque and flounce.

...

Fringes for Dresses, Wrappings, etc., Figs. 1 and 2.

The fringe Fig. 1 is four inches wide, and is made of fawn-colored saddler's silk. It is composed of thick and thin strands, which are knotted to the heading. On the thin strands are knotted tassels of crimped silk of the same color. The strands are joined a quarter of an inch from the top with double threads of silk.

The fringe Fig. 2 is made of crimped gray China grass and silk cord in a darker shade set on in scallops. To the middle of each scallop is fastened a tassel of China grass, which is tied with gray silk.

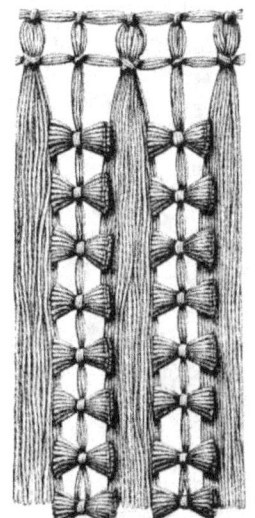 

Harper's Bazar, April 5, 1879

LADIES' WALKING COSTUME.

Figure No. 1. – Black velvet and a plain yet neat bourette suiting are used in the construction of this costume. The skirt is short and round, and was cut by pattern No. 6410, price 35 cents. [*see January*] It is decorated with two fine knife-plaitings of the plain material, and a *revers* or panel of black velvet scolloped at the back edge and held in place by buttons and imitation button-holes placed in the scollops. The over-skirt is charming and coquettish in effect, and is handsomely ornamented with heavy grass fringe. The model to the over-skirt is No. 6485, price 25 cents. The coat is jauntily cutaway in front to disclose a stylishly notched vest of velvet. Velvet overlaps are sewed in with its side-backs, and a jaunty velvet collar completes the neck. The sleeves are trimmed with a strip of velvet cut in three scollops, which are fastened in place by buttons and simulated button-holes. One material may be used for the suit throughout, or any two or even three seasonable textures may be combined in it. The style of the trimmings may be changed in favor of any other mode preferred, and their arrangement may be elaborated or simplified according to the preference of the wearer, the fancies of the individual taste always being acceptable. The coat model is No. 6482, price 30 cents. The skirt and over-skirt models are each in 9 sizes for ladies from 20 to 36 inches, waist measure; and the coat pattern is in 13 sizes for ladies from 28 to 46 inches, bust measure.

To make the costume for a lady of medium size, will require 13 7/8 yards 22 inches wide, the skirt calling for 4 1/2 yards, the over-skirt for 5 1/8 yards, and the coat for 4 1/4 yards. If 48-inch-wide goods are selected, then 6 3/8 yards will be sufficient; the skirt requiring only 2 1/4 yards, the over-skirt 2 1/8 yards, and the coat 2 yards.

…

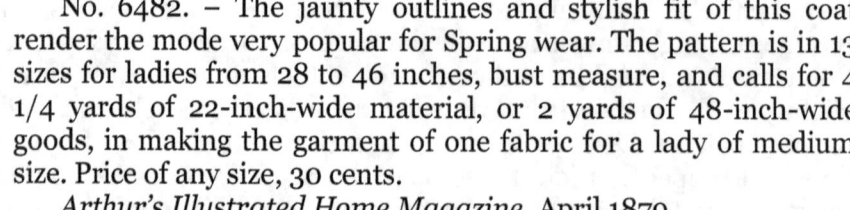

LADIES' COAT, WITH VEST.

No. 6482. – The jaunty outlines and stylish fit of this coat render the mode very popular for Spring wear. The pattern is in 13 sizes for ladies from 28 to 46 inches, bust measure, and calls for 4 1/4 yards of 22-inch-wide material, or 2 yards of 48-inch-wide goods, in making the garment of one fabric for a lady of medium size. Price of any size, 30 cents.

Arthur's Illustrated Home Magazine, April 1879

6482

We give, first, this month, a walking costume of navy blue Albatros cloth, a material resembling a fine, all wool delaine. It comes in white, light greys, pinks, and blues for evening wear; and the darker colors for street costumes. Its light texture will make it very popular for the coming season. This costume is made just to touch, but for real serviceable walking purposes, we would prefer it to be a trifle shorter. The skirt is kilt-plaited to a deep yoke from the waist, and the tunic, which is of the washerwoman or "laveuse" style, as it is called, is bordered with a cross-band of silk to match; quite short in the front, but the back is fuller and larger than those of last year, in this style, and draped in larger puffs. The bodice has a simulated waistband, and double, square collars. The buttons are of dead gold. Twenty to twenty-two yards of material will be required. Costs from 40 cents up to 60 cents per yard, according to width and quality.

…

The small *tournure* or pannier is gradually making its way, but it is very small on the hips, as a rule, and not very large at the back. Vests are so becoming that they will be worn for some time yet. Some of the new dresses, of soft materials, are gathered at the waist, just in the middle of the back; this is particularly pretty for a house or trained dress.

…

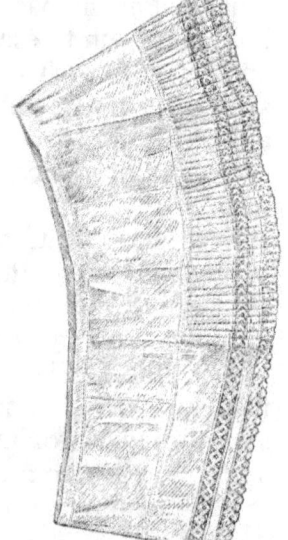

Next we have a new design for a Casaquin bodice. It is made of striped silk or velvet, in any dark shade; equally suitable for the jacket of the same material as the suit. It is worn over a waistcoat, either like the skirt, or else of a contrasting color, and different material. The revers are of satin of the same shade. The fronts are fastened with a double row of buttons the sleeves are trimmed simply with scalloped out tabs, coming from the outside seam, and ornamented with buttons. This would be a very suitable design for any of the pretty, light woolen fabrics, striped or plain, or both, as all costumes are made up of several designs of the same material; for instance, plain, striped, and figured may be seen in the same dress; therefore, we will have no trouble in remodeling old dresses, and can do it inexpensively, too, by adding some stripe, or figured, or both, to the old, plain, partly worn skirt. Four yards of striped silk or velvet will be required.

We also give a good design for a balayeuse; the upper part to be made of muslin, and the frill of nainsook, with a band of lace insertion and edging. Either Valenciennes or Torchon are best for this purpose, as they bear washing. This balayeuse can be button upon a short walking-skirt. Make the band to fit the skirt upon which it is to be buttoned. The fulness, and the length, must be determined by the dress with which it is to be worn.

Fig. XI. – Garden-Dress of White Albatross Cloth; the plain front is ornamented down each side with Torchon insertions and buttons, and a row of Torchon insertion heads the two rows of knife-plaitings the ornament the upper and lower skirt. The fulness at the sides is bunched together at the back, forming a small *pannier*, and is trimmed with pink ribbons; the lace mantilla has a pink rose in front, and the large, straw hat is trimmed with pink ribbons.

Peterson's Magazine, May 1879

As predicted, we see panier draperies in the newly-imported spring dresses. They are usually made by a full scarf passing around the hips and back in clusters of drapery. Some of these scarfs are stiffened by a lining of crinoline. Bustles are not used with short walking-dresses, which are still made narrow; but a very bouffant appearance is often given to them by the voluminous drapings of the overskirt. Sometimes the back breadths are fully twice the length of those immediately beneath them, and are draped throughout their entire length by rows of pleats caught at the sides and down the middle. Overskirts, too, are often divided half way up the front, the curtains so made turned back in revers and faced with some contrasting color or material, a scarf being brought around above the opening to pass over the bouffant back. A wide row of shirring down the middle and sides of another model makes a puffed appearance all around. One feature of the new draperies is that they are higher than of old, beginning directly beneath the belt instead of lower on the skirt.

...

Simple basques, and coats and vests, are still worn. When with a panier overskirt, they are made very short to prevent crushing the drapery. In many of the new coats, the revers roll back nearly to the waist-line, disclosing so much of the vests, and are fastened there by one or two buttons, beneath which they again show the vests. Woolen dresses are now always made with underskirts, vests and facings of plain silk. Elaborate cuffs on dress sleeves are no longer the style; they are simply finished by being turned back and faced, with a frill of lace beneath, or else a border of shirred silk or satin. For the bottom of underskirts, also, elaborate trimming is now out of place. A narrow-pleated flounce is all that is visible beneath a long overskirt.

...

LADIES' BASQUE.

No. 6522. – A very stylish combination of materials is illustrated in this basque. The pattern calls for 3 3/4 yards of plain goods and 2 yards of striped 22 inches wide, or 1 3/4 yard of plain material and 7/8 yard of striped 48 inches wide, in making the

basque for a lady of medium size. The model is adapted to all suiting in vogue and is in 13 sizes for ladies from 28 to 46 inches, bust measure, and costs 30 cents.

...

6522

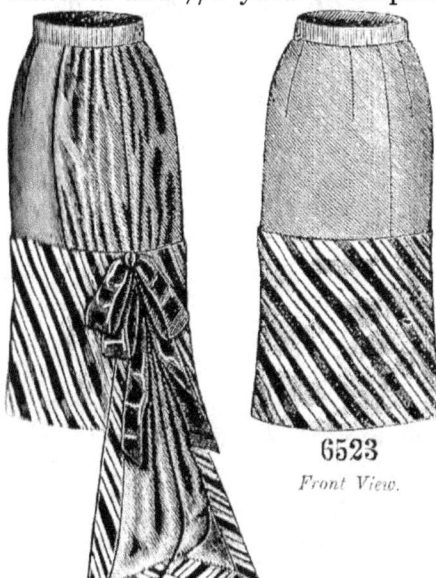

6523
Front View.

LADIES' OVER-SKIRT.

No. 6523. – Two materials are used in the composition of this garment. The shape before the drapery is accomplished is that of a plain skirt. The pattern is in 9 sizes for ladies from 20 to 36 inches, waist measure, and costs 25 cents. To make the garment as pictured in the present for a lady of medium size, will require 5 3/8 yards 22 inches wide, or 2 3/8 yards 48 inches wide.

...

LADIES' BASQUE.

No. 6541. – This model develops the combination of two varieties of washable goods very stylishly, and is also adapted to suit goods of any quality. The pattern is in 13 sizes for ladies from 28 to 46 inches, bust measure. For a lady of medium size it calls for 4 yards of plain and 1 yard of figured goods 22 inches wide, or 2 1/4 yards of plain and 7/8 yard of figured material 36 inches wide. Price of pattern, 25 cents.

...

6541

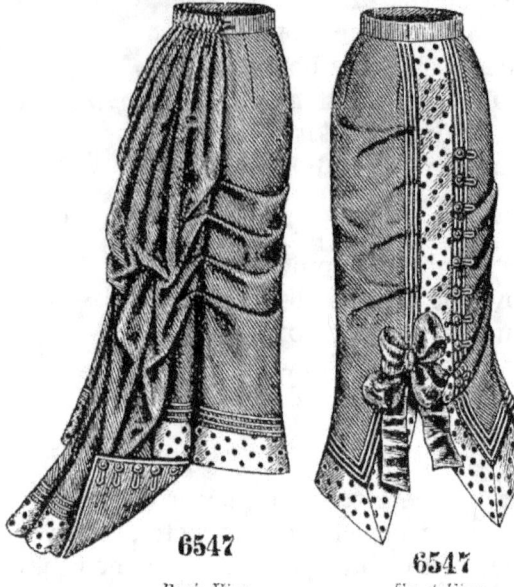

6547
Back View.

6547
Front View.

LADIES' OVER-SKIRT.

No. 6547. – This over-skirt unites very modishly with any style of basque. It is here displayed in a plain and polka dotted French cambric, but any of the new Spring suitings, including the dainty *momie* cloths, satinets, cotellines and *armures*, may be handsomely made up by the model, with lace, embroidery, fringe, etc., for the garniture. The pattern is in 9 sizes for ladies from 20 to 36 inches, waist measure, and calls for 4 1/8 yards of goods 22 inches wide, or 2 yards 48 inches wide, in making the over-skirt for a lady of medium size. Price of pattern, 30 cents.

...

No. 6543. – This skirt is of construction is nicely adapted to Plain, brocaded or striped silk, satin united in the model with plain texture, and the disposition of the dictates. The pattern may also be organdies, etc., and is in 9 sizes for It requires 6 yards of plain goods 3 1/2 yards of plain material and make the skirt for a lady of medium

...

LADIES' SHORT WALKING-

No. 6507. patterns for for any 20 to 36 for a lady of wide, or 3 1/4 cents.

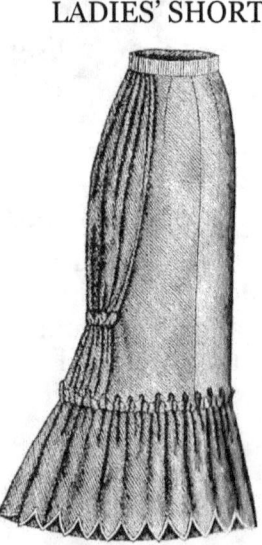

6543
Back View.

LADIES PRINCESS WALKING-SKIRT.

convenient walking length, and by its combinations of contrasting materials. or woolen goods may be handsomely material of the same or a contrasting trimming may be as novel as the taste used in making up cambrics, lawns, ladies from 20 to 36 inches, waist measure. and 1 7/8 yard of striped 22 inches wide, or one yard of striped 48 inches wide, to size. The price of the pattern is 35 cents.

SKIRT, WITH SPANISH FLOUNCE.

– This model is four-gored, and includes the flounce and its scollops. It is suitable material, and is in 9 sizes for ladies from inches, waist measure. To make the skirt medium size, will require 7 yards 22 inches yards 48 inches wide. Price of pattern, 35

...

Plain borders from four to six inches wide are generally used with elaborate drapery, sometimes edged with a narrow knife-pleating. Colored and plaid bands are cut now straight instead of on the bias, unless they are very narrow. Black dresses are sometimes trimmed up for spring with vests, collars, cuffs and borders of black and white, or old gold-striped silks and satins. In the same manner, gay foulard silks are used with camel's hair and bunting dresses. ...

One of the most striking novelties in wash dresses is the handkerchief costume. This is made by piecing together large handkerchiefs of blue and white or red and yellow plaid, so that their borders, down the front and middle of the basque, through the sleeves, on the edges of curtain overskirts, and at intervals in the pleated flounces will form the trimmings. Similar suits are made of navy-blue handkerchiefs, with while polka dots and striped borders. Slips of the same materials, laid in box-pleats in front down to a Spanish flounce, with a yoked and gathered back, the whole completed with a separate, gay, sailor collar, are made for little girls of three and four, to be used for morning-dresses in the country.

Arthur's Illustrated Home Magazine, May 1879

No. 4 is a linen costume, of prune-color, streaked with cowslip, yellow and red. Under-skirt bordered with a gathered flounce, crossed with a checked galloon, or else the bordering of the chintz or linen. Under this is a muslin balayeuse, princess polonaise, trimming to correspond; fastened in front, beneath a piped buttoned band, matching the one around the cuffs and sailor-collar. A muslin frilling finishes the slightly square neck. A waistband and buckle is used for the waist; from this the dress-holder is suspended by a prune silk cord. Twelve to fourteen yards.

...

Common Sense About the "Fashions." – An effort has been made, recently, in London, by certain artistic and literary persons, to revolutionize the "fashions," by substituting the ancient Greek costume for that worn at present. On this absurd proposition, Mrs. Oliphant, the popular novelist, has lately commented, with singular good sense. She shows, very clearly, that the change, for many reasons, is quite impossible. She also maintains, that, as there is no possibility of any revolution in dress, it is well to consider the possibilities of what we have. The fashion of close-fitting dresses, it is very plain, must have sprung first from special adaptation to the needs of the climate; and it as held sway through all secondary changes; while the long skirt falling to the feet, the original garment of all Northern women, is in itself one of the most reasonable and beautiful dresses that can be imagined. That it has been swelled out like a balloon, at one time, and more recently, tightened to "a single trouser," does not interfere with the general principle of the garment. The princess dress, the fashion of the day, could not be more agreeable and graceful in line. When made too tight, it is, of course, absurd; but this is the fault of the wearer, or of the maker, not of the design. The fashionable vagary of the day, the tightly tied-in skirt, which renders locomotion difficult, not only prevents the dress from being beautiful, but is objectionable on other accounts. But we must not be unjust; much uncomfortable appearance is appearance only, as Mrs. Oliphant affirms; and the sashes and drapery, tied in under the knees, seem to embarrass action much more than they do, and are really ugly rather than uncomfortable.

Now the true province of art in dress is to educate the eye to the full ugliness of all such seeming bonds, so that women may refrain from emphasizing those bonds, as many do, by outlines of what is called art-needlework, among other things. "As for the long skirt indoors, it is not a thing which ever will be abolished, in our opinion," say Mrs. Oliphant; "it is graceful and dignified in itself; it belongs to the fundamental idea of women's apparel, and possesses all the practical and symbolical qualities which are necessary to a noble and fine ideal of dress." Finally, she concludes, that, "it is far easier to rail at *la mode*, and accuse that capricious influence of all the insanities under the skies; easier, too, to talk of the Greek clyton, and imagine a causeless and impossible revolution. But neither of these heroic devices will at all meet the difficulty; whereas, here is a much humbler one that will do so, if we choose to try it. A little trouble, a little patience, and good sense, where needs must, perhaps; (for the moment,) a vigorous pair of scissors to cut the knot of a ligature, and it will be found that the thing is done – not with any flourish of trumpets, indeed, or in a heroic manner, but sufficiently and well."

In a word, the conclusion to which Mrs. Oliphant comes is that which has always been maintained in these pages; it is, that the art of dressing well consists in knowing the prevailing fashions, and adapting them to your particular style. What suits one will not always look beautiful on another. There should be discrimination, the result of a cultivated taste. To deviate from the prevailing *mode* entirely is, on the other hand, a grave blunder; for anything odd makes a lady a laughing-stock, and the dress quite out of the fashion is, therefore, to be avoided.

Fig. VIII. – Dinner-Dress of Light Violet Silk, made with a train and finished around the bottom with a knife-plaited ruffle; the over-dress, collar and cuffs are of a thick, violet grenadine of a much darker shade; the bottom of the grenadine dress is trimmed with two rows of silk fringe to match in color. ↗

...

The pannier is also growing larger on the hips, and is brought higher up at the back; this style is particularly handsome for tall, slender persons, on an evening or trained dress. Some of the imported French dresses have the *panniers* lined with thin crinoline to make them stand out more. The waist of dresses must, of course, follow the shape of the skirts somewhat, and with the pannier, the waist has only a small basque at the sides and back, if the pannier is worn high up. Some of the basque waists are cut very long and full, and are then caught back in plaits, rather high in the middle of the back, thus forming panniers.

...

No. 9. We give one of the new pannier dresses, a dinner toilet, the very latest from Paris. The basquine with pannier is of black silk, fastened with pearl buttons. The revers and collar are lined with pink silk. The ribbons fastening the sleeves are also watered. The skirt is piped with pink.

No. 10, a design for making trimmings for the skirts of dresses.

Peterson's Magazine, June 1879

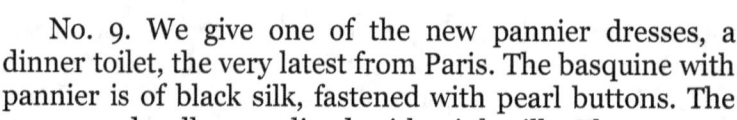

LADIES' WALKING COSTUME.

Figure No. 1. – One of the newest costumes of the season is here illustrated, and is composed of two novel garments in which two different materials appear. The skirt is formed of seal-brown camel's-hair of a heavy quality, and six straight breadths of goods are used in its construction. The back-breadth is allow to fall in the folds produced by gathering it at the top and shirring it by tapes at half its depth. In the other breadths, however, are arranged two double box-plaits at each side of the center, which extend from the top of the skirt to the bottom, being stayed underneath with tapes. A row of buttons, with soutache braid arranged *a la militaire*, extends down the center of the front-breadth between the first two plaits, and with the hem at the bottom completes the skirt. A full view of the skirt may be seen upon page 6 [*see illustration below*] of this issue. The model is No. 6582, price 35 cents. A skirt cut by it really requires no decoration, but ruffles laid in wide or narrow plaits may be added to the back-breadth as far up as the shirring.

The basque is known as the "zouave" fashion, and is composed of the skirt goods, with the exception of the front, which is formed of cream-colored cloth and is vest-like in effect. The front is fitted by two bust darts and an under-arm dart, and its lower edge is piped with silk of the color of its material. The closing is effected with button-holes and buttons like those on the skirt, while the arrangement of braid continues with them the whole length of the front. The zouave portion is of the familiar, long-ago popular jacket outline, and sews in with the shoulder and under-arm seams. Its edges are decorated with a flat line of braid, inside of which a line of soutache is arranged in a simple scroll. The back and side-back portions are extended in an extremely long coat-tail, with an extra width at the side-back folded in a backward plait and held down under a line of buttons and ornamental braid loops. The back edges of the back-skirt are turned under in wide

hems, and all the other edges are completed to accord with the zouave portion. The sleeve is close and has a cream-colored cuff-facing, military in shape and decoration, while a military collar stands about the neck. Upon page 7 [*see illustration below*] of this issue two views of this stylish basque may be seen, where it is made up of brocaded and striped fabrics. The front may be of any texture or color desired, and may have tiny pocket-welts upon it. The model is No. 6591, price 30 cents. Sometimes the skirt, between the plaits, will be faced with panels of the vest and cuff material, especially when silk and velvet or wool and velvet are used for the costume.

6591
Front View.

...

LADIES' ZOUAVE HABIT BASQUE.

No. 6591. – This pattern is in 13 sizes for ladies from 28 to 46 inches, bust measure. It calls for 3 yards of brocade 22 inches wide, with 2 3/8 yards of striped goods, in making the basque for a lady of medium size. If goods 48 inches wide are used, 1 1/4 yard of brocade and 1 1/8 yard of striped will suffice. Price of pattern, 35 cents.

...

LADIES' DEMI-TRAINED SKIRT.

No. 6567. – In making this beautifully trained skirt for a lady of medium size, 5 1/4 yards of goods 22 inches wide, or 2 5/8 yards 48 inches wide, will be required. The model is in 9 sizes for ladies from 20 to 36 inches, waist measure, and its price is 30 cents.

...

The two skirts of a dress are now frequently made as one complete garment. A skirt may be made long for the house and short for the street by means of a loop attached to the waistband and a button at the bottom of the placket. A very long skirt will need an additional button and loop on each side. The shirred apron front is revived especially for soft goods. Princess dresses, particularly of white, are often shirred entirely down the back breadths.

LADIES' WALKING SKIRT.

No. 6582. – This handsome model is in 9 sizes for ladies from 20 to 36 inches, waist measure. To construct the skirt for a lady of medium size, 7 7/8 yards 22 inches wide, or 3 1/2 yards 48 inches wide, will be required. Price of pattern, 35 cents.
Arthur's Illustrated Home Magazine, June 1879

EVENING-DRESS.

Fig.VI. – Evening-Dress of White Muslin, laid in kilt-plaitings the entire length of the front, with a short train at the back; the bottom of the front is edged with a knife-plaiting of the muslin, headed by a wide row of Breton lace; the bodice is round, and is laid in plaits, and from under the belt there falls a plaited piece of muslin, edged with Breton lace; the bodice is cut quite square in the neck, has a bunch of roses on the left side, and puffed, infant sleeves.

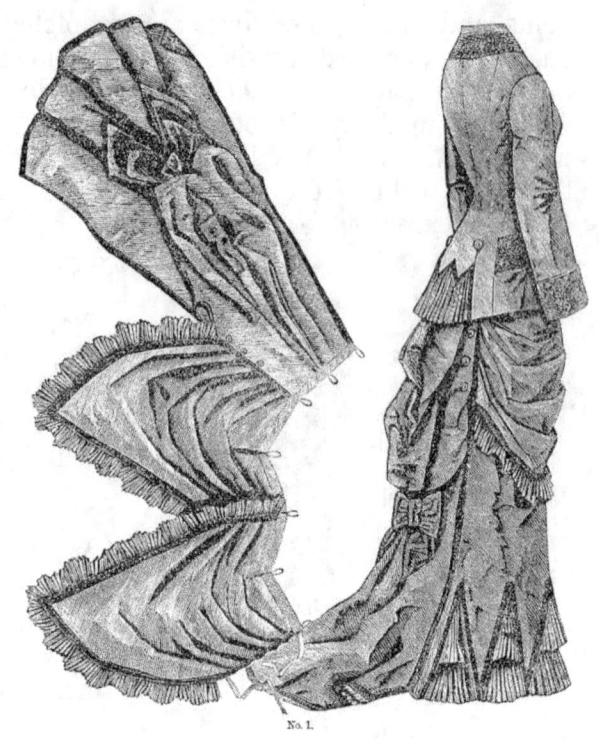

We give, (No. 1), this month, a costume of percale, made with tunic and paniers; the design for the latter we give in detail, showing how it is to be made and put together, which will be readily be understood. Our model has first a foundation for the front and side gores of the skirt, on to which two knife-plaitings are arranged. Over this the material is placed, cut out in deep vandykes. Then the tunic and paniers are made and adjusted to this under foundation; trimmed to correspond, with knife-plaitings on the front, and the back of the short demi-train is simply bound. The looping is arranged by strings underneath. The basque is cut strait in front, and the back is cut in two vandykes, half-way below the waist line, where it is filled in with fine knife-plaitings to correspond with the skirt. Cuffs, collars, pockets, bindings, are all in a solid colored cambric, to correspond with the other part of the dress, or else of a contrasting color. This costume may be made with a short, round skirt for walking, and the tunic adjusted all the same. For the latter, make the trimming for the bottom of the skirt, the same all around, and the back of the tunic shorter. Fourteen to fifteen yards of material.

...

No. 4 is a lawn dress, in a simple and effective style. There is first a skirt with a short demi-train; on this is a box-plaited, or gathered flounce, one-quarter yard deep, edged with Torchon or Breton lace. The tunic is cut like a princess polonaise, and opens in front, half-way down the skirt, where a fan-plaiting is inserted. The fulness at the back of the tunic is plaited in a fan at the bottom of the tunic, and sewed to a foundation piece which extends to the waist – which is from nine to twelve inches wide, according to the size of the wearer; on this foundation the back garniture is arranged, which consists of three plaited flounces, filling up the back to the basque. These flounces are all edged with the lace to correspond. A deep corsage basque, simply corded on the edge. The front is trimmed with rows of insertion and lace, forming a square. Collar and cuffs to match. This will be a very pretty design for a dotted muslin, over colored Silesia. Breton and Torchon laces are very much used for trimming all muslin dresses. Bobbinet footing two inches deep, put on in fine knife-plaiting, is also very effective, and a very inexpensive trimming for these dresses. Fifteen to sixteen yards of lawn; eighteen to twenty yards of lace; three yards of insertion.

Peterson's Magazine, July 1879

LADIES' SHORT WALKING-COSTUME.

No. 6606. – This model is suitable for both woolen and cotton fabrics, and will be much used for cashmere, camel's-hair, merino, silk and various kinds of suit materials. It is here shown as composed of suit goods handsomely trimmed with fringe, plaitings and ribbon bows, although any other stylish decorations are just as appropriate. The costume requires 15 1/2 yards 22 inches wide, or 7 yards 48 inches wide, in constructing it for a lady of medium size. The pattern is in 13 sizes for ladies from 28 to 46 inches, bust measure. Price of any size, 35 cents.

Surplice effects given by shirred pieces down the front are greatly in favor for dress waists. Striped, plaid or polka-dotted silk or satin is used for this purpose; thus, an almond-colored basque and overskirt is worn with a full-shirred front of Scotch plaid silk, and the kilt skirt is also of the gay plaid. Sometimes a broad belt passes over at the waist, and the part below the belt hangs in two loops, like a great Alsacian bow, or else forms a sash.

...

White flannel suits are made for ladies to wear at the seaside. They have kilt skirts suspended from a narrow yoke, and the pleats are bordered near the bottom with gay bandana plaid cut in a bias band. The overskirt has a very short, scarf-like apron, with a long, draped back, and is also bordered with plaid. The basque is caught up in the back to give full panier effect, and handkerchief pieces of the plaid are arranged like a sash bow in the back and around the neck.

Cheese-cloth suits are dresses made of unbleached muslin, and trimmed with rows of woolen skirt-braid, or else bias red and yellow plaids in the handkerchief.

...

LADIES' PRINCESS SKIRT.
(ADJUSTABLE TO DEMI-TRAIN OR WALKING LENGTH.)
No. 6621. – This stylish skirt is so planned that it may [be] changed from a demi-train into walking length and back again in a few moments' time. The pattern is in 9 sizes for ladies from 20 to 36 inches, waist measure. Of material 22 inches wide, 5 1/2 yards will make the skirt as represented in either of the pictures for a lady of medium size. If goods 48 inches wide are used, 2 1/2 yards will suffice for the purpose of construction. Price of any size, 35 cents.
Arthur's Illustrated Home Magazine, July 1879

How to Dress With Taste. – Very few persons possess an innate perception of the beautiful, while all may dress in taste by observance of certain laws of Nature. Thus, sky-blue is becoming to fair persons because it contrasts agreeably with the orange in their complexion. Light green is also becoming, particularly to fair complexions utterly devoid of color, because it adds the rose tint altogether wanting. Red and yellow are becoming to dark, fresh colored complexions, the yellow by contrast, the red by harmony. Violet, dark green, and pink are more limited in their adaptability, and require to be brought into juxtaposition with the complexion before decision can be arrived at, as there may be a tone in the complexion that will neither harmonize nor contrast favorably. Then, again, there are gradations in these – some that are not becoming, if placed in direct contrast with the skin, would, with a line of white or black intervening, had a most excellent effect.

...

BACK AND FRONT OF WALKING-DRESS.
Fig. VI and VII. – Front and Back of Walking-Dress; the under-skirt is kilt-plaited, and made of alternate stripes of watered silk and summer camel's hair; the over-dress is of the camel's hair, gathered in points on each side and at the back, where they are tied with bows of wide ribbon the color of the dress; a simulated vest is worn, made of the camel's hair and watered silk, which comes from beneath the pointed bodice on either side; the bodice is cut with a coat-basque, is double-breasted and has a wide, rolling collar.

...

Kilting Your Flounces. – A great many ladies send their flouncing to be kilted by machines, as it saves, they think, time and trouble. But for several reasons we would advise our readers to do it from themselves by hand; we regard, on the whole, the truest

economy, besides. In the first place, the heat used for the machine kilting is very often too great, and we have seen flouncing so scorched in places that it has been at the folds like tinder; and in the second place, in many materials it certainly takes from their beauty, silk especially looking poor from the heat and pressure used, as it does when dyed or cleaned.

To kilt silk, having cut and joined the breadths, next hem them with fine sewing silk, not putting the stitches too close, and drawing the silk as little as possible. Supposing the flounce be required to form its own heading, turn it down at the top, and tack it along on the wrong side, then, having decided upon the size of the pleats, fold two or three, pin them and crease them firmly, then take out the pins, and measure the width between the folds. You must now fold and crease your length of silk, or should it be a very long one a few breadths at a time, taking the width between the creases from the folds you have already arranged, so that when you begin to kilt you have very fold evenly and plainly marked. You will scarcely need to measure for creasing the folds if the flounce be a narrow one, but be careful to get them even and straight, and the work is then comparatively easy.

Begin kilting with the top of the flounce to your right hand, turning the pleats away from you and pinning them both at the top and bottom with silk-pins (fine long ones are sold for this purpose which do not mark the silk as ordinary ones would). This done – say about half a yard in length at a time – tack it in the centre on the right side, putting a stitch in each pleat, and again about half an inch from the edge, with a fine needle and thin white cotton. This done it is ready for stitching, which must always be done with *silk*, whether by hand or machine. If you do not want to stitch it upon the dress, tack a tape underneath and stitch it down upon that. For a flounce it is better always to put this tape about a third of the depth from the lower edge, and stitch it before putting it upon the skirt.

With the exception of satin and moiré other materials are not damaged by ironing, and after the hem is made it is better to press it, as also the fold at the top if it is not hemmed at each edge. Muslin, alpaca, and many other materials will crease as silk will, and that will be found the easiest plan, and the soft materials are not injured by being done by machinery.

← ... a new style of trimming for the skirt of a dress.

TRIMMING FOR WASHING DRESSES.

This trimming is composed of a band of blue linen, embroidered in long and chain-stitches with dark blue and white embroidery cottons. It is just in season for summer dresses.
Peterson's Magazine, August 1879

Grenadine suits are now made up with only one lining of silk, displacing entirely an inner lining of Silesia. ...

The substantial basque continues to hold its place, and is, perhaps, even more liked than ever. The latest style is the panier basque, to be worn with a skirt simply draped with a sash, or an overskirt having no bouffant effect, so that by its use an old costume may be made new. It has a long skirt, draped high all around, below the waist line, and is ornamented with ribbon bows.

LADIES' COSTUME.

FIGURE No. 1. – The costume illustrated consists of a combination of velvet and *écru* suit goods, with a trimming of lace of the same color as the material. The whole costume was cut by one model, which includes the blouse and skirts, and is very becoming to ladies of slender figure. The skirt and over-skirt are united in the making and are of very simple construction. The skirt is four-gored – that is, it has a front-gore, a gore at each side and a back breadth – and just escapes the ground. It is made of lining material, and then faced up on the outside as deep as the highest point of the over-skirt drapery with black velvet.

The over-skirt is all in one piece and like the skirt gores is fitted to the belt by darts. At the right side the lower portion of its back edge is gathered, and both the plain and gathered portions are sewed in with the seam of the back-breadth and side-gore at the right side of the skirt. At the opposite side of the over-skirt three straps of velvet are attached at intervals and have button-holes worked in their pointed ends, which pass over buttons sewed to the lower ends of the upper two straps, as well as over another button above the highest strap. The convenience of this arrangement for costumes of washable fabrics will be realized upon a moment's consideration. The bottom of the over-skirt is stylishly completed by a row of lace set on with just enough fullness to allow it to fall gracefully.

The blouse has a plaited center-front and center-back, each of which is attached to a yoke-portion extending from the shoulder to the middle of the bust and back. A side-front having a bust dart and an under-arm dart, and a side-back exhibiting elegant proportions, and both extending to the shoulders, complete the shaping of the waist, which is held in to the figure by a velvet belt that closes at the back with an oxidized clasp and accords fashionably with the decorations. The sleeves are shortened to three-quarter length and finished with a frill of the lace. The model to the costume is No. 6655, and costs 35 cents.

⬧ LADIES' CIRCULAR POLONAISE.

No. 6545. – This pattern is especially suitable for washable fabrics. The model is in 13 sizes for ladies from 28 to 46 inches, bust measure, and requires 7 3/4 yards 22 inches wide, or 4 3/8 yards 36 inches wide, or 3 1/2 yards 48 inches wide, in making the polonaise of one material for a lady of medium size. Price of pattern, 30 cents.

Arthur's Illustrated Home Magazine, August 1879

One of the prettiest of the new style of dresses is called the Parabère; it has three flounces in front, and paniers at the back; sometimes these paniers are one with the bodice, and sometimes they are fastened to the skirt. Black is very much worn in the evening, and black striped grenadine, trimmed with Breton lace, or jet or satin, with red or yellow roses make a most stylish dress.

...

No. 4 is a design for a coat-bodice, with vest. Suitable for a walking or house-costume. The vest is entirely separate, and made of striped silk and satin, corresponding with the color of the costume. The coat is cut to fit the figure to a nicety, and buttons on both sides to the vest, holding it in place. As it is very much cut away, this buttoning down is necessary to keep it in place. The collar turns over in front, and a jabot of lace is worn with this jacket. Coat-sleeves, with plain cuff. A good design for black cashmere, with striped silk and satin for vest, and a little of it upon the skirt to carry out the design in the whole costume.

We give (No. 1), this month, a front and back view of a dinner-dress of satin and cashmere, either in black or light colors. Both the front and back view is given. The robe is cut in the princess shape, and with a long train. The dress is of cashmere; around the bottom is a ruching of satin. Also, the entire plastroon [sic?] front is of satin. From under the lace the cashmere is very much wrinkled, for the sides, and the back is laid in a double box-plait, down which the lace is put on in a jabot, with loops of satin ribbon between, finishing with a flat bow just below the waistline. The front, which is cut square in the neck, is trimmed with lace laid on flat, turned in to shape the figure at the waist, and so carried around the neck. Large, flat-looped bows of the satin ribbon ornament the front. Elbow-sleeves, edged with lace, finished by band and bow of ribbon. Imitation Mechlin, Spanish, or Russian lace will trim well. Ten to twelve yards of cashmere, and four yards of satin will be required. Twelve yards lace, and twelve yards satin ribbon.

...

The waists with five seams in the back are exceedingly popular, as they are much more becoming to most persons than those with two or three seams, except to very slender people. The fronts of skirts still cling closely. Many colors are now seen in one costume, even on the street, for dress is nothing now if it is not effective, and great is the difficulty to keep within the line of good taste when handling these gay colors. Some years ago nothing but one color in all articles of dress was considered correct, and even now this severe style of coloring is allowed, if stylishly worn.

Peterson's Magazine, September 1879

LADIES' HOUSE COSTUME.

FIGURE No. 1. – The engraving represents a costume of plain gingham, trimmed with striped gingham and white linen buttons. The skirt is demi-trained, and has a bias flounce of the plain goods, bordered at the bottom by a bias striped band and set on under a narrow bias ruffle of the striped goods, for the lower trimming. The model to the skirt is No. 6567, price 30 dents, and is in 9 sizes for ladies from 20 to 36 inches, waist measure.

The over-skirt front has the shawl drapery effect, without the usual overlapping sides. Upon the right side is arranged a bias pocket-lap, with a row of buttons in front of it. The back-breadth is a straight width, draped by plaits laid in the edges before the seams are closed. The model to the over-skirt is No. 6660, price 25 cents. Like the skirt is in 9 sizes for ladies from 20 to 36 inches, waist measure.

The basque is in the new *panier* style, and is adjusted in a novel manner. Instead of being fitted by darts, the front is adjusted by a side-gore, that curves sharply out from the arm's-eye to give sufficient spring for the bust. An under-arm dart, under-arm, and side-back seams, and a center seam, adjust the remainder of the garment perfectly. A bow is over the end of the back, and a bias band of striped goods trims the edges. Lapel ornaments are upon the fronts of the model, but have in this case been omitted in favor of a Pompadour composed of narrow bias bands of the striped goods. The model to the basque is No. 6661, price 25 cents, and is in 13 sizes for ladies from 28 to 46 inches, bust measure.

...

Waists of wash dresses are usually made round with a belt attached, and are adorned with rows of shirring. Indeed, shirrings are seen in many forms and places. One of the caprices of the day is to have the waist one mass of shirred clusters, another, to have the vest part of a basque so made, and the middle form of the back gathered to correspond. Sides and fronts of overskirts and tops of flounces are similarly ornamented, whether the material be cotton or silk. For a deep silk flounce, headed with separate clusters of shirring, the material should be cut on the straight.

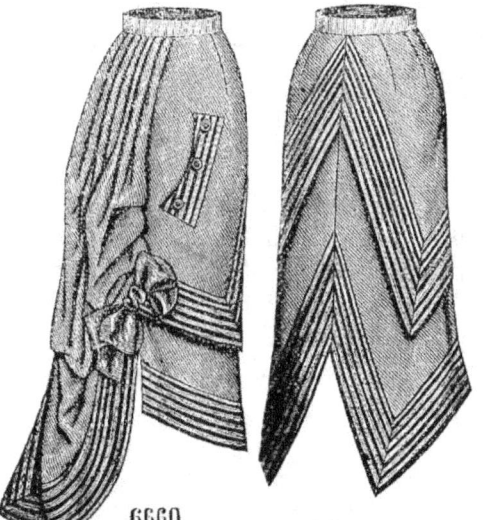

6660

LADIES' OVER-SKIRT.

No. 6660. – A very graceful model for an over-skirt of any material desired is here illustrated. By an arrangement of broad trimming-bands, a double effect is given to the front-gores. The pattern is in 9 sizes for ladies from 20 to 36 inches, waist measure. To make the over-skirt for a lady of medium size, requires 4 1/2 yards 22 inches wide, or 2 1/4 yards 48 inches wide. Price, 25 cents.

...

LADIES' PLAIN PRINCESS DRESS.
(MEDIUM TRAIN.)

No. 6664. – A plain Princess dress, suited to any kind of material, is pictured in these engravings. Ruffles, plaitings or any kind of trimming may be added on the skirt, and the front may be faced in vest or *plastron* style with any contrasting fabric. The pattern is in 13 sizes for ladies from 28 to 46 inches, bust measure. The pattern, for a lady of medium size, requires 9 yards 22 inches wide, or 4 yards that is 48 inches wide. Price, 40 cents.

...

New overskirts are short all around and puffed, not even reaching to the knees, reminding one of the styles worn about ten years ago. Another model has a seam down the front for about half its length, at which point it is cut away on each side, sloping gradually downward and backward, thence obliquely upward to join the long, separate, gracefully-draped breadths in the back. The bare look of the front seam is taken away by a row of deep folds (or any other trimming preferred) running diagonally from the waist in front paralleled to the lower edge from the, garment which should be similarly trimmed. ...

6664

New basques have the back breadths long, and trimmed to represent a panier effect. Skirts, intended to be worn with elaborately-trimmed overskirts or polonaises, are now frequently made perfectly plain around the hem.

Arthur's Illustrated Home Magazine, September 1879

No. 2 is a house-dress for an young lady, of plaid camel's hair, with peasant over-waist, and trimmings of black velvet, or silk. The skirt is demi-train, with three narrow, bias ruffles, each headed by a band of velvet ribbon, one inch wide. The drapery is arranged upon the foundation – which is of cambric, on and which the bias ruffles are placed. Three rows of velvet are disposed upon the apron front, which is very much wrinkled; and the fulness at the back is plaited under a large loop of velvet. A simple cuirass bodice, without trimming, and with tight coat-sleeves finished by collar and cuffs of velvet, completes the dress proper. Over this is worn a peasant's waist, which fastens in the front, and buttons on the shoulders. The form may be seen in the engraving. This costume may be carried out in plaid and plain camel's hair material, using bias bands of the plain for the trimming on the skirt, and the plain material for the bodice, cuffs, etc. Twelve to fourteen yards of double-fold, plaid material, two pieces of velvet ribbon, and two yards of velvet for bodice. The bodice and trimmings could be nicely managed out of some old velvet or silk garment, probably laid long aside as too old-fashioned for use.

...

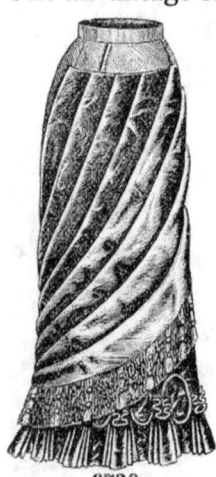

Fig. VII. – Louis XV. Coat Composed of Black Silk and Embroidery. The front of the dress is of black silk; the paniered over-skirt is of brocaded, cream-colored silk; the black silk coat has the revers, cuffs, and pockets of the cream-colored brocade. ✌

...

Figured and striped silks will be very much worn, this season; not very frequently as complete costumes, but as part of them. Thus vests, trimmings for collars, cuffs, fronts or side pieces of skirts, etc., in fact, in all the different styles that the fancy can devise. Figured and plain velvet, striped and figured satin, will also be used in the same way. Different colors will also be employed, as well as different materials, so those who are economically inclined can easily re-model two or three old dresses into a very stylish new one. But plain black dresses of silk, satin, cashmere or camel's hair, still hold their own; some persons find these too somber, and brighten them up with red, orange, old gold, or lemon-color. The newest shade of gray has a yellowish tint, and is not so gold as some of the other grays, and looks well with claret-color or dark green. The style of making dresses continues very varied, but paniers are decidedly gaining ground. They are usually small as yet, only the ultra-fashionable wearing the very large one.

...

DESIGN FOR TRIMMING BOTTOM OF DRESS-SKIRTS.
Peterson's Magazine, October 1879

In autumnal fabrics, and their making-up, the fashionable tendency still seems to be in favor of combining two materials. With very few variations, we still see plain goods trimmed with brocades, figured satins and velvets, and Pekins, appearing in vests, revers, collars, cuffs, pockets and facings. One suit usually displays two colors, such as purple and old gold, cream and garnet, black and cardinal, etc. One advantage of such a fancy is that it affords an opportunity for effective remodeling.

LADIES' WALKING-SKIRT.

No. 6730. – This stylish walking-skirt may be composed of any one or two materials, as it will make up very prettily in either. The pattern is in 9 sizes for ladies from 20 to 36 inches, waist measure, and calls for 7 1/8 yards of material 22 inches wide, or 3 5/8 yards of goods 48 inches wide, each with 1 7/8 yard of satin 22 inches wide, in making the skirt as here represented for a lady of medium size. Price any size, 35 cents.

6730
Front View.

6730
Back View.

The panier effect in drapery is with us again in its full force. We have overskirts and polonaises open in front, exceedingly *bouffant* at the back and sides, and very short all around. Garments of this description are usually worn with short, plain skirts. We noticed a quiet, elegant costume, made in this fashion, which we admired very much. The underskirt was of black striped satin, simply finished with a hem, and the polonaise was of black satin-striped grenadine, having a deep point on each side, and a third point in the back, deeper and wider, being made up of large puffs. The stripes in the lower skirt were about a quarter of an inch wide, those in the upper nearly an inch and a half. Belt, cuffs and bows were of plain black satin.

LADIES' OVER-SKIRT.

No. 6685. – This over-skirt model is adapted to any material in vogue for costumes, although it is here shown as composed of a pretty wool suiting of a deep *paon*-blue shade, with trimmings of darker bands and handsome tassel fringe. There are only three sections comprised in the formation, two of these uniting to form the sides and front, while the remainder constitutes the back drapery. It is in 9 sizes for ladies from 20 to 36 inches, waist measure. Of material 22 inches wide, 4 5/8 yards will be needed in making the garment for a lady of medium size. If goods 48 inches wide are selected, 2 1/2 yards will suffice for its construction. Price of any size, 30 cents.

...

Long overskirts and polonaises, as well as single-trimmed walking-skirts, are also very full in the back, abounding in elaborate drapery. Several new models of the two first-mentioned garments have short fronts – or long ones made so by being laid in deep, horizontal plaits – and long backs. Walking-skirts appear with deep flounces around the bottom, over which is a succession of puffs, sashes, bands and bows, or drapery arranged to simulate an overskirt. These are valuable, not only on account of their convenient adjustment and dressy appearance, but also because they admit of an equitable disposal of weight.

Arthur's Illustrated Home Magazine, October 1879

We give, first, this month, a promenade costume of silk and camel's hair cloth, in olive-green. The skirt, which is short and round, is made on an alpaca foundation of the same color. There is a narrow facing of the silk on this foundation, then it is trimmed with from six to eight two inch-wide knife-plaited ruffles of the silk. Over this is disposed the over-skirt, which is gathered quite full up the knee, where the trimming is put on, in a bias band of silk, extending all round. The over-skirt is made of the camel's hair cloth, and the fulness at the back is arranged in three large pouffs. For the basque, we have first a very deep basque, opening in front to match the over-skirt, this is made of the silk, over this a shorter one, cut as seen in the illustration, corresponding in length at the back; this is made of the camel's hair material. The coat-sleeves are made of the silk and camel's hair, in lengthwise stripes, with a double-pointed cuff of the silk. A turn-down collar completes this costume, which may be varied, in materials, by using cashmere in place of the silk, and some mixed material in place of the camel's hair cloth; and be less expensive, unless on old silk could be made to do service for the under-skirt and other trimmings. Fifteen yards of silk and four yards of camel's hair cloth will be required. If cashmere is used instead of silk, six to eight yards will be required.

No. 2. – Next, we have a walking-costume, for a very young lady, of a very dark maroon-colored woolen material, either cashmere, camel's hair, merino, or any solid-colored, twilled material; this is entirely trimmed with a two inch wide galon, embroidered in colors. There is, first, a very narrow, round skirt, not over two and a-half yards wide on this, which is of cambric to match, is put on outside facing one-eighth of a yard deep of the material. The kilt-plaited flounce, which is a half yard deep, is placed upon this foundation. There are three deep kilt-plaits, then a band of the embroidered galon, and this is repeated all round the skirt. The over-skirt is arranged permanently upon the foundation, in scarf fashion in front, and in pouf drapery at the back. This is done by taking three yards of the double-width material, and turning all of one side, lengthwise, across one end, and all of the other lengthwise side, except about one yard, which is arranged upon the front in scarf fashion, as seen by illustration. The jacket is a tight-fitting basque, trimmed in front with lengthwise rows of the galon, to simulate a waistcoat. The same trimming is arranged on the fronts, where the basque joins the waistcoat, and around the lower edge. Coat-sleeve, trimmed to match, with a narrow kilt-plaiting of silk, and ribbon bow to match. At the neck, it is finished with a rolling collar, or it may be closed at the throat, if preferred. Eighteen to twenty yards of

galon, ten to twelve yards of double-width material will be required. Plain bands of silk or velvet may be substituted for the embroidered galon, or bias bands of plaid cashmere, in blue and green, would look well upon a navy-blue, bottle-green, or black material.

...

POINT LACE: TRIMMING, INSERTION.

We give, here, patterns, in Modern Point Lace, one for trimming, the other for insertion.

The braid used is very fine, the edges being open, or *a jour*. The fillings, composed of various stitches, are made with *coleur de lin* thread. The bars that hold together the meshes are overcast.

The patterns make an effective trimming on a washing dress, if lined with red Turkey twill or silk.

Peterson's Magazine, November 1879

LADIES' PLAIN POLONAISE.

No. 6759. – This polonaise is especially adapted to soft, heavy goods, and is particularly admired by middle-aged and elderly ladies. It may be worn with a short or long skirt, either plain or trimmed, and may be decorated to accord with the taste of the wearer. The pattern is in 13 sizes for ladies from 28 to 46 inches, bust measure, and calls for 7 1/4 yards of material 22 inches wide, or 3 3/8 yards of goods 48 inches wide, in making up the polonaise for a lady of medium size. Price of any size, 35 cents.

...

The short, plain skirts now in vogue have necessitated a corresponding change in the length of polonaises. So, among the models represented by *La Mode* is one that closes in the front to the depth of a deep basque, and its skirt portion is shirred up in a graceful drapery of wrinkles at the termination of the closing, while below the plaits it falls apart triangularly to the bottom. The new styles generally are very short and bouffant, often scarce reaching to the knee. The back may or may not be also short – very frequently it shows the older curtain style, forming drapery at least three times the length of the front.

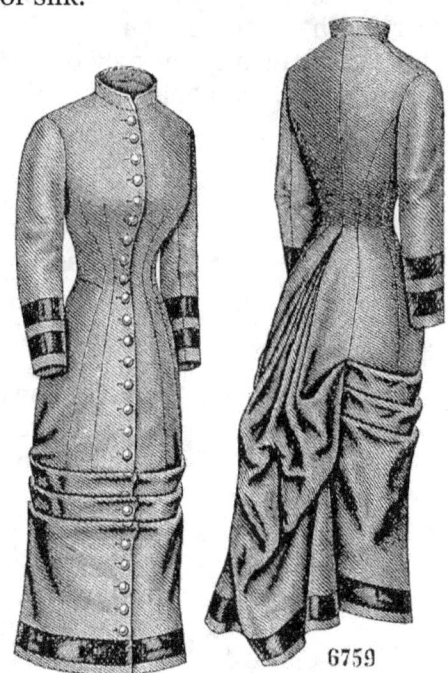

6759

LADIES' BASQUE.

No. 6736. – This stylish basque, which is one of the handsomest of the autumnal modes, is here composed of two materials, although the model may be still more effectively made up in three, as the construction permits the use of several fabrics in is [sic: its] formation. It is in this instance composed of a plain and striped suiting, and as the goods are very fashionably combined, the model presents a most attractive appearance when completed. The model is in 13 sizes for ladies from 28 to 46 inches, bust measure, and may be charmingly made of up any dress material in vogue. To make the basque as shown in the engravings for a lady of medium size, 5 1/8 yards of material 22 inches wide, or 2 1/2 yards of any suitable goods 48 inches wide, will be found necessary. Price of any size, 30 cents.

6736
Front View.

...

A new way of finishing off the hem of a skirt, is to turn about half an inch up over the facing and dispense with the braid.

Arthur's Illustrated Home Magazine, November 1879

No. 3. – For a young lady we give a short costume, either for house or street, with polonaise and panier. It is made of cashmere of a light fawn-color, with vest and trimmings of black velvet. The front of the skirt is kilted from just under the vest, where it is put on the foundation, the sides are kilted, only from the knee, where the trimming comes. This trimming is formed of a band of the cashmere embroidered in black, and edged with a very fine, narrow knife-plaiting, and edged with black velvet ribbon. The panier polonaise is trimmed to correspond. We give the front and back, showing two designs for trimming the sleeves. Twelve yards of cashmere and one yard of velvet for vest and cuffs, with several pieces of very narrow velvet ribbon for ruffles will be required.

...

Paniers are very popular for home dresses, and are even a great deal worn on the street, for anything is fashionable that is at all becoming or picturesque-looking. The fronts of dresses still cling closely, and the hoop that was predicted is only a small affair, want at the back by some ladies, as a "bustle."

...

EMBROIDERED DRESS TRIMMING.
By Mrs. Jane Weaver.

In the front of the number, we give a design for one of those embroidered dress-trimmings, now so fashionable. This band can be embroidered in either white or color, in white, using either jaconet or muslin, it is very suitable for children's frocks; if colored silks are used, the groundwork may be either flannel, satin, or cashmere, according to the destination of the trimming.

Peterson's Magazine, December 1879

LADIES' SHORT, HOUSE COSTUME.

Figure No. 1. – A very ingeniously constructed model was used in cutting the stylish costume illustrated by this engraving. It is made of suit goods and is neatly trimmed with silk facings, satin pipings, fringe and ribbon. The dress is a Princess having all the usual fitting seams, with the addition of two gores at each side so as to permit the side-back skirt and a portion of the front-skirt to be draped into the *panier* seen in the engraving. The section of the front-skirt between the first darts, and also the central portions of the back, extend in an unbroken length to the bottom of the costume; and the first dart is not fully taken up until its back edge below the waist has been shirred as seen in the picture. Then the under-arm seam is shirred to correspond, and after the back edges of the side-back extra-widths have been united, the seam is also shirred to produce a double *panier*. A number of gathering threads also shirr the top of this back-drapery, which is then attached to a wide belt encircling the waist. Stays are sewed to the shirred loose seams, and draping-straps and ties are added. The extra gores are arranged under the drapery and joined to the front and back, the belt at their tops being fastened at each end to the waist seams. The skirt is cut in deep slashes all about the bottom. The slashes are neatly piped at the edges with satin, and to the front edge of each is sewed a *revers* of silk. Three buttons are placed in front of each *revers* near the top; and plaiting may or may not be placed under the slashes; but if plaiting is not desired, the slashes may be seamed together. The side-drapery is trimmed with fringe headed by a fold of silk, while the heading alone continues about the back drapery. Sometimes, when the cascade is not desired, a facing of the material is placed over the hems from side to side of the drapery, so as to give the effect of a plain skirt. The sleeve is in coat shape and is completed with a fancy cuff of the two fabrics, which is composed of facings with piped edges and has a row of buttons on the middle section. A military collar and a bow of ribbon complete the neck neatly and effectively. The model is No. 6801, which is in 13 sizes for ladies from 28 to 46 inches, bust measure, and costs 35 cents. Rich or inexpensive goods in plain, striped, plaid, brocaded or fancy patterns, are both made up after this style in a most satisfactory manner, and may be trimmed with grass, jet, crimped tape or *laminee* fringe, lace, machine-stitching, *passementerie*, folds, braids or in any fashion suited to the fabric and design.

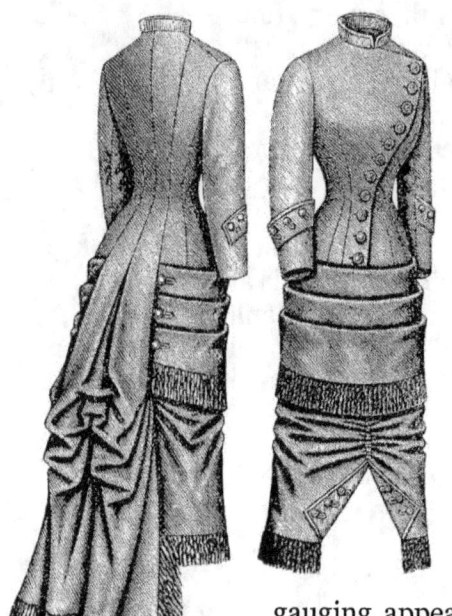

LADIES' DOUBLE-BREASTED POLONAISE.

No. 6776. – This stylish polonaise is made of cashmere, and though simple in its mode of formation, is exceedingly stylish. It is double-breasted; and its drapery is arranged in a most charming matter, being shirred through the center of the front, turned back in tiny *revers* below the shirring and over-draped by a plaited scarf; while the back is deep and fashionably *bouffant*. Any material makes up charmingly this way. The pattern is in 13 sizes for ladies from 28 to 46 inches, bust measure, and calls for 9 1/4 yard 22 inches wide, or 4 1/4 yards 48 inches wide, for the polonaise for a lady of medium size. Price of any size, 35 cents.

One of the newest ideas in dressmaking is to have across the back of bouffant overskirts, directly below the belt, a deep succession of French gathers, sometimes as many as seven or eight rows of gauging appearing about the panier, as indeed, is the case with several styles of costume, notably long, dressy wrappers.

LADIES' PANIER BASQUE.

No. 6775. – To make the handsome basque portrayed in these engravings for a lady of medium size, will require 3 yards of plain goods 22 inches wide, or 1 1/2 yard 48 inches wide, each with 7/8 yard of brocade 22 inches wide for elbow sleeves, and one yard of brocade extra for facings. The model is in 13 sizes for ladies from 28 to 46 inches, bust measure. Price of any size, 25 cents.

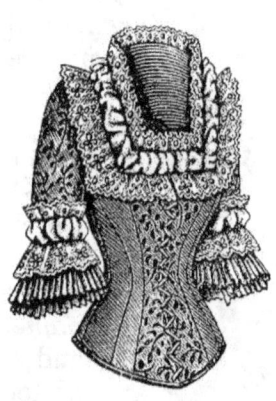

6775

Arthur's Illustrated Home Magazine, December 1879

Washing and Repair Advice

I do *not* recommend you try any of the cleaning recipes. Most of them look very harsh, and some of them appear to be poisonous. This section is to show you how clothing was cared for in the nineteenth century. It makes me very grateful for my washing machine and dryer.

1870

Chloroform will remove stains, but whether those caused by champagne we do not know. Try it. ...

How can I re-stiffen a nice black lace flounce? ... Dip your flounce in a solution of gum-arabic, fold smooth in a sheet, and iron damp with a moderate iron on the wrong side.

Demorest's Monthly Magazine, June 1870

1871

How to Wash Lace. – A fair correspondent asks us how lace ought to be washed. We have frequently answered this question before, but, as our correspondent is a new subscriber, we will reply to it again, especially as there may be other new subscribers who would like to know also. The first thing to remember is that lace, and all such fine materials, should be washed in hot, soft water. Well soap them and squeeze and shake them out, but on no account rub them. Repeat the squeezing and shaking out again till they are clean. Rinse them in some more clean, hot water, and well soap them again, and put them into a sauce-pan, with enough hot water to cover them. Soft water is best, but if that cannot be procured add a piece of soda – say a quarter of an ounce to half a gallon of water, or according to the hardness of the water. Boil for half an hour. Then wash them out again, and rinse in cold, blue water. Hang them on a clothes-horse till dry, when they can be starched. Lastly, roll them up in a dry cloth for two hours, by which time they will be fit to iron. ...

A bit of glue dissolved in skim-milk and water will restore old crape. ...

To Wash White Cashmere so that it will not Turn Yellow. – White soap must be used, and the cashmere must be washed with not too much of it and cold water. When quite clean, it should be well rinsed in cold water, with a little blue in it, then ironed while very damp with a not very hot iron, the ironing to be continued until the cashmere becomes perfectly smooth.

Peterson's Magazine, April 1871

1872

TOILET AND WARDROBE.

To Restore Colors Taken out by Acid, etc. – Hartshorn rubbed on a woolen garment, will restore the color without injuring it. Spirits of turpentine is good to take grease or drops of point out of cloth; apply it till the paint can be scraped off. Rub French chalk or magnesia on silk or ribbon that has been greased, and hold it near the fire; this will absorb the grease so that it may be brushed off.

Peterson's Magazine, May 1872

To Clean Black Lace. – Black lace looks well and nearly new if washed in skimmed milk. Of course, it is not to be rubbed, but constantly softly squeezed. When it seems clean take it out and put it into a little clean milk, also skimmed, then give it another soft squeeze and directly lay it out on sheets of stout paper, though a newspaper will do; touch it every here and there with the fingers to draw out the mitres or scollops, as the case may be; lay sheets of paper over the lace, and until dry a heavy weight over all. If laid on anything soft, the moisture is absorbed, and the lace is not so new-looking.

...

The "Novelty Clothes-Wringer." – We understand that this great labor-saving machine, with its many improvements over all others, not only saves labor and time, but will pay for itself in one year in the saving of clothing. This Wringer has long been before the public, and has steadily gained favor with the people. In purchasing a Clothes-Wringer, give the "Novelty" a trial, and you will be sure to give it the preference.

Peterson's Magazine, July 1872

To Remove Wax-stains from Cloth. – Lay over the stains two thicknesses of blotting-paper, and apply for a moment the pressure of a moderately-hot iron. The stains will be instantaneously and entirely removed. ...

To Prevent Flat Irons from Sticking. – Irons are apt to stick to starched articles. To prevent this, lay a little fine salt on a flat surface, and rub the iron well over it. This will make the iron smooth, and also remove smokiness.

To Prevent the Incursions of Mice. – Strew wild mint where you wish to keep the mice out, and they will never trouble you.

Peterson's Magazine, October 1872

1873

To Clean Old Silk. – A subscriber asks us if we can tell her how to clean old silk. The best way is to take the dress to pieces, then brush it well with a velvet brush on a dry towel, grate two large potatoes into a quart of water, strain off, and sponge the dress; iron each breadth or piece as it is sponged on the wrong side. Always, however, iron black silk on an old piece of the same, as the side not ironed is to be the right side. You must guard against lint from the ironing-cloth.

Peterson's Magazine, January 1873

Borax. – Borax is used in many large washing establishments as a washing-powder, instead of soda. It does not in the slightest degree injure the texture of the linen. Its effect is to soften the hardest water, and therefore is a pleasant and useful addition to the water for bathing. It is also recommended as excellent for cleansing the hair and teeth. ...

Glossy Starch. – Take two ounces of white gum-arabic powder, put into a pitcher, and pour on it a pint of boiling water, according to the degree of strength you desire, and then, having covered it, let it stand all night. In the morning pour it carefully from the dregs into a clean bottle; keep it for use. A tablespoonful of gum-water stirred into a pint of starch that has been made in the usual manner, will give lawns, either black or printed, a look of newness, when nothing else can restore them after washing. It is also good, much diluted, for thin white muslin and bobinet. ...

To Clean Black Ribbon. – Take an old kid glove, no matter how old, and boil it in a pint of water for a short time; then let it cool until the leather can be taken in the hand without burning; use the glove wet with the water to sponge off the ribbon. If the ribbon is very dirty, dip it into water and draw it through the fingers a few times before sponging. After cleaning, lay a piece of paper over the ribbon and iron; paper is better than cloth. The ribbon will look like new.

Starching Collars and Cuffs. – Always making up our own fine linen, we can highly recommend the following plan: Let the collars be washed, blued, and dried; then take two large tablespoonfuls of ordinary starch, and blend in cold water till there is about a breakfastcupful on it. Dip your collars through it without going to the sediment; wring dry, and lay them in a clean towel for two or three hours; then draw them, and iron them, and they will be stiff and glazed.

Peterson's Magazine, March 1873

To Clean a Silk Dress – Take one quarter of a pound of honey, one quarter of a pound of soft soap (buy the latter at a chemist's,) and a gill of gin or spirits of wine. Add to this two quarts of boiling soft water, and let it stand all night. With the mixture scrub the silk on a clean deal table with a small hard brush, putting each piece as it is cleaned through the water three times, and twice through soft water, and then through hard. Hang the pieces up somewhere to drain, and iron it while still wet, laying over it a fold of muslin to prevent the iron (which iron must be hot) from coming in contact with the silk. ...

To Wash White Alpaca and Mohair Garibaldis – Boiled white soap and lukewarm water must be used, (hot water will make the material yellow at once,) and after the alpaca has been washed in this, and the soap thoroughly removed by rinsing in cold water, it must pass through water with a very little blue in it, and afterward ironed while damp with a handkerchief or linen cloth over it.

To Remove Grease from Silk. – Mix fuller's-earth into a paste with water, and put it upon the spots. Rub it off when dry. The grease will be removed without injury to the silk.

Starch for Fine Muslin. – Isinglass is a very delicate starch for fine muslin, also rice. Some add a very little fine salt to starch.

Cleansing Black Lace. – Sponge the lace carefully with gin, or, if preferred, with green tea, and wind it round a bottle to dry, as if touched with an iron it would become glossy and have a flattened appearance. It must not be put near the fire, as it would lose its color, and look rusty.

To Restore Linen that has Long been Stained. – Rub the stains on each side with wet, brown soap. Mix some starch to a thick paste with cold water, and spread it over the soaped places. Then expose the linen to the sun and air; and if the stains have not disappeared in three or four days rub off the mixture, and repeat the process with fresh soap and starch. Afterward dry it, wet it with cold water, and put it in the wash.

Peterson's Magazine, October 1873

1874

As many are obliged now to practise economy, we will give some hints upon making over old dresses to look as well, or, as we have often heard it asserted, better than new. We doubt either of these assertions. The only way that can even be imagined is to compare them when finished with their appearance before they were remodelled. The change is sometimes so great as to make the exclamation possible, "They look like new!" We will begin with dresses. Suppose we have a shabby black silk and a French merino among our stock. The silk we first rip up; then rub each breadth carefully with a woollen cloth, to remove all dust; then sponge it all off with water in which one to two black kid gloves have been boiled – one quart of water for a pair of gloves; iron while wet with extremely hot iron, on the wrong side. For colored silks, the same colored gloves as the dress should be used. It is therefore advisable for persons to keep all their old gloves, so as to have a variety of colors to choose from. Another mode equally successful for black silk or ribbon (it might be injurious to colors) is to first rub off the dirt with a woollen cloth, as before mentioned; then mix an equal quantity of strong tea and vinegar, with which the silk is washed by rubbing it with a piece of flannel. It must be made very wet. Smooth the silk carefully, folding it, and in about fifteen minutes iron it on the wrong side with very hot irons. Then, if the skirt is long, cut it into walking length; this at once freshens up the edge. The bottom ruffle will have to be discarded, but it can be cut into folds, and a plaiting of Cashmere come below the second ruffle, in place of the one discarded. The overskirt can be made over by omitting the front breadth, and making deep pointed side widths and back, or if a polonaise, open down the front and trim with Cashmere, mixed with the silk; made a sleeveless basque of the Cashmere, trimmed with folds of silk made of the old ruffle, and if the sleeves are worn, make new ones out of the front breadth of the overskirt, which you took out. You have when completed a fashionable and entirely different looking dress. Now we come to the French merino; it is already *rasterre,* [the length of a walking skirt that just touches the ground] and so we must shorten it only to the extent of turning in the edge. Imagine it has a deep flounce, over which is a bias band; this we take off, and braid in black soutache, and replace. The polonaise we shorten into Louis XV. waistcoat fronts, cut square below to the waist, curved at the sides, and falling in deep points at the back. We then cut the material thus saved into bias bands of various widths, and trim the bodice with one-and-a-half-inch wide braided bands to simulate a jacket, and outline the pointed tails with the same trimming. The fronts or waistcoat portions should be covered with braiding, for which many designs given from time to time in this magazine are suitable. The front of the dress should be covered with three rows of graduated bands, braided. If the merino is colored, it should be braided in a darker shade, or with black; but a black merino must not be braided in colors. New dresses will, of course, be made up in the latest styles; but we do not think that they will look prettier than the above-mentioned toilets. Those ladies who have no serviceable dress left in a wearable state from last winter, can wear out the skirts only, with plain or spotted shirt bodices.

Godey's Lady's Book and Magazine, January 1874

1875

To Wash Calicos. – Dissolve half an ounce of alum in sufficient water to rinse two calico dresses. Dip them in, and when sure that every part is wet, wring them out; then have a warm soapsuds, in which wash quickly, and rinse in cold water. Then in second rinsing-water mix your starch, rinse, wring quickly, and hang to dry – not in the sun, but on a line where the wind will dry them quickly. Immediately they are dry enough, iron them, or if this is inconvenient, let them get quite dry, and iron them through a damp cloth. Calicos should never be sprinkled. ...

To Make Old Black Silk Look Like New. – Unpick the garment, and wash the pieces in hot soapsuds; rinse by dipping up and down in hot water, then dip in second water, prepared as follows: Boil two ounces of logwood chips in five quarts of water, add a quarter of an ounce of copperas; strain through an old bit of calico, and dip your silk into this dye. Let the silk be pinned on to a line by the corners, and hang until it is nearly dry. Then take it down and iron it between two pieces of old black silk. It will look like new.

Peterson's Magazine, February 1875

To Take Out Tea and Wine Stains. – A glass of white wine or a cup of tea, upset over a dress, would spoil it if allowed to dry. When an accident happens, immediately get some clean towels, and rub the dress till dry, and in most cases there will be no stain left. If the tea is very strong, sponge with a little cold water first. Port wine or claret stains are seldom got entirely out, but the stain may be lessened by sponging with cold water before the rubbing.

Peterson's Magazine, August 1875

1876

Some one inquires what she shall do with her rusty flat-irons. Put a little lump of bee's-wax or mutton-tallow in a soft rag and rub it over the face of the iron while warm. That will prevent rust. Then keep them hanging in a dry place, say on a row of nails under one of your pantry shelves, out of the way. In buying flat-irons, it pays best to get the large ones; small ones are not very serviceable, unless you have little boys and girls who can iron the towels and aprons, and assist you very materially that way. If you have, then get a couple of small four or five pound irons, and a cute little stand, and thus show that you appreciate the favor of having an assistant. When your ironing-sheets begin to grow scorched and dingy, cover them with a nice white, worn one, after you have taken the best end off it for a bed or pillow sham. The sham can have a wide hem on it, or ruffling of a lighter material. ...

There is no smell that seems more poisonous to me than that of a closet in which dirty clothes are kept. Other women have complained, and the subject has been talked over, but nothing arrived at which seems satisfactory. The plan of throwing soiled clothing on a line in an out-house or wood-shed has some good features, and yet it will not be adopted for fro a dozen reasons. Mice, unsightliness, carelessness, and other reasons, stand in the way. I like Ida's plan very well. She asked me one day if I would give her my little chest I used to keep my papers in to do as she pleased with it. I told her she was welcome to it; that I would be glad to see it put to some use, instead of standing an idle receptacle for old papers.

It is a neat, red chest, but rather heavy to move about when one is sweeping, and because of that it was stowed away in a closet. It was not long before I recognized my old acquaintance standing in an out-of-the-way corner of the summer kitchen mounted on castors, and filled with the week's washing that was fast accumulating. The wash-boiler hung above it, the clothes-frame stood behind it, and the bag of clothes-pins hung from the wall at one end.

I liked the new arrangement very much, and commended her, adding that she must never forget and put a damp towel or any wet thing into the chest, more especially in warm weather. ...

The clothes-line wound on a windlass and kept in the dry in a little box-house nailed up on a tree, or the side of an out-building, is a great convenience, and saves a woman putting out and taking in the line when her hands are wet or cold, or when she is hurried to get the wash out before dinner, or taken in before a shower. Any man can make this labor-saving convenience who knows enough to wipe his shoes, and if he don't do it he has the material in his nature of which villains are manufactured. ...

I believe I did tell you that if you have no ironing-board on which to iron dresses and skirts you should not rest until you have one. Let it be five or six feet long, wider at one end than the other, and heavy enough that it will lie firmly with one end on a table and the other on a window-sill, or some other convenient place. Have a hole in one end that it can be hung up out of the way. I used a board for year which I picked at the corn-crib, rough and weather-stained, but it answered very well until we got a real nice clean pine board purposely.

I was a little embarrassed, though, one time, when a woman sent her little girl to borrow it. She had never seen the naked board, and did not think that its first cousins lay all about her own back yard, and corn-crib, and carriage-house. I presented it to her with my complements.
Arthur's Illustrated Home Magazine, May 1876

Erasive Soap. – A genuine erasive soap that will remove grease and stains from clothing is made as follows: Two pounds of good castile soap; half a pound of carbonate of potash, dissolved in half a pint of hot water. Cut the soap in thin slices, boil it in the potash until it is thick enough to mould in cakes; add alcohol, half an ounce; camphor, half an ounce; color with half an ounce of pulverized charcoal. ...

To Remove Ink-Stains. – Ink-stains may easily be removed from cotton or linen by washing the spot that is stained in salt and water. This should be done previous to its being washed with soap, for soap sets the color.

To Cut Whalebone Easily. – Hold it in the flame of a lamp an instant, and you can cut it with the shears.

Colors Taken out by Acid. – Sal-volatile of hartshorn will restore colors taken out by acid.

To Remove Grease and Dirt from Cloth and Woollen Articles. – Place a cotton or woollen cloth, or better yet, a piece of blotting-paper, under the article to be cleansed, then rub upon the spots pure benzene, and the grease or dirt will disappear as if by magic. Be sure to place a cloth under the garment to be operated upon, otherwise a circular stain will remain, which can not be removed. The benzene drives the grease through the article to be cleaned, and is absorbed by the cloth placed under it. After the spot is removed, continue to rub with a dry cloth until the benzene is evaporated; this also is done to avoid a stain.

...

So to-day another wonderful invention, which will surely revolutionize that most dreaded washing-day in every family, is fighting and winning its way into public confidence. We refer to the Steam Washer. Probably there is not one in twenty of our readers who would or could believe the great fact of a steam engine before seeing it in operation. So there is not one in twenty of our readers, probably, who will or can fully believe the fact that the Steam Washer will do every particle of the labor of washing, except preparing the work to be done and wrinsing and drying the clothes after they have been washed, until they shall see the fact demonstrated by its operation. Hence we continue to send it on trial, with the provision that unless it shall give perfect satisfaction, it may be returned, in which case the money will be refunded. Thousands sent out on these terms are giving perfect satisfaction, and they are saving from twenty-five cents to one dollar per week in labor, besides much more in the wear of clothes, to every family using them.

...

The Protean Button-Hole Lancette.

This is an article which no lady, after becoming familiar with the manner of its application, and the many purposes for which it may be used, will be without. It is not only the most superior device ever invented for cutting button-holes, but serves equally well for ripping seams, cutting off hooks and eyes and buttons, erasing blots, opening letters, cutting leaves of books, etc.
Smith's Illustrated Pattern Bazaar, Fall 1876

1877

THE IRONING-TABLE.
By Helen Chauncey Warner.

Many a line washing is spoiled by carelessness or mismanagement in Ironing. In my own experience, I have rarely found that one person will perform both of these duties well, some giving the preponderance of their time and pains to the first, others to the last; in either case failing to accomplish the desired end. So many suggestions have been published relating to the best plans for washing, I will confine my own to the management of the ironing, supposing the former to have been accomplished.

It is desirable that the articles should be taken down from the line with care, and partially folded when laid in the basket, not gathered by the armful – as if a shower were coming on. On no account should any unnecessary creases be acquired. There is a certain stage in the drying process at which the clothes may be folded all ready for ironing, thus obviating the necessity of sprinkling, with the accompanying advantage of a freshness which is lost by the latter process. In sprinkling, much judgment should be exercised, lest the clothes be made too damp, which will chill the irons, and necessitate a longer airing than is desirable.

In articles which require folding, as table and bed-linen, etc., one-half of the labor may be saved by exactness of detail from the beginning. Always have *one* way of folding each article – lengthwise, until reduced to a convenient size, then crosswise.

Stockings, undershirts, etc., should be ironed on the wrong side, for convenience in mending, also all embroidery and braiding on children's dresses, etc.

Articles that are marked, should be folded so that this marking should be plainly seen, and those of a kind should be ironed at one time, though it is well to use a coarse towel or apron to cool the irons.

A provident housekeeper will see that her ironing-table or board is supplied with a clean, whole blanket, covered with a piece of coarse, unbleached muslin, which is much more suitable for the purpose than an old sheet, such as is generally used. Iron-holder, stand and wiping-cloth, are positive necessities for the accomplishment of the work in a neat and orderly manner, although a folded dish-towel, an old saucer and a piece of brown paper, have been used from time to time by some of our "professionals."

All articles to be ironed should be disposed of as quickly as may be consistent with thoroughness. They should be allowed to hang long enough to become thoroughly aired, but no longer, and in the summer a netting should be thrown over them to protect them from flies.

And, lastly, the laying away of the fresh, sweet linen should be done by the mistress of the household. I do insist that no "lady" can depute such delicate matters as this to a servant, with the hope of any degree of comfort, after having attended to it herself a few times. This should be a weekly exercise by every one who takes pride in chests and drawers of snowy, well-kept household linen.

Arthur's Home Magazine, January 1877

A LAUNDRY SECRET.

The following recipe for doing up shirts will be found of use to many housewives: Take two ounces of fine white gum arabic powder; put it into a pitcher and pour on it a pint or so of water; and then, having covered it up, let it stand all night. In the morning pour it carefully from the dregs into a clean bottle, and cork it and keep it for use. A tablespoonful of gum-water stirred into a pint of starch, made in the usual manner, will give to the lawns, either white or printed, a look of newness, when nothing else can restore them, after they have been washed.

Arthur's Home Magazine, February 1877

How To Wash Net – Wash it in a lather of fine soap and warm water, then dip in water very slightly blued, and again dip in either sugar and water, weak starch, or gum-arable and water. It must be pinned out to dry, after being well clapped with the hand. This clapping is one of the great secrets of clear-starching: nothing clears nets, muslins, etc., better, for it removes the sticky portion of the stiffening matter without lessening its crispness. Net should be ironed on the wrong side with a very hot iron, which brings up the stiffness; but ironing renders tarlatan limp. ...

The Art of Washing. – Hints. – In washing woollen things it is necessary to carry out the work rapidly, whether it be done by hand or in a machine. In a machine they are treated in much the same manner as other articles, save that no suds must on any account be used. For this reason flannels are generally washed first. Soft water is especially valuable for washing woollen things, the addition of soda being necessary to hard water in order to soften it. Pure Castile and curd soap are the best to use, as containing the least soda. They should always be used in the form of jelly. This should be prepared by the soap being cut up and boiled till it becomes of the proper consistency, after which it must be mixed with the water before the flannels are put in. The following are the main points to be attended to: They must always be washed by themselves. They must on no account be previously soaked. No suds should be used in washing them. Soap must never be rubbed on them; it must be used as a lather. They should be finished off at once, and never be left in the water during the course of washing, or be allowed to lie about damp. They must not be passed from hot to cold water. The waters used should each be hotter than the last. Cold water rather sets than removes the dirt, and makes them shrink.

The following mode of proceeding applies to almost every class of woollen things. Wash in two lathers of warm, soft water and soap jelly; rinse in another thinner lather, (slightly blued for white things;) wring thoroughly – and for this a wringer will be found most valuable, for the quicker the water can be wrung out, the better, and the twisting necessary in hand-wringing is bad for woollen things. Select a fine sunny day with a brisk wind; a rainy day is objectionable, for the drying should be done as quickly as possible in the open air. When this is impracticable, woollen things should not be put to dry too near the fire, which would tend to shrink and make them yellow; they should be well snapped and shaken before they are put on the line, and during the process of drying. Petticoats should be hung up by the bands, to prevent the water from settling in the gathers, and the bands of colored flannel petticoats should be dipped in salt, to avoid the color running into them. They should be taken down, when sufficiently damp for the ironing, which must be done at once. If any portion appears cockled, it should be well pulled out and straightened in preparing for ironing. The bands of petticoats, etc., should be subsequently ironed.

The following is a remedy for white flannels, which have become yellow: Pour over them water in which flour has been boiled, in the proportion of one tablespoonful to a quart; let them remain in this long enough for the water to cool, then rub them well in it, but use no soap; rinse subsequently in several warm waters. Repeat the process should it not at once prove effectual. Flannel will always shrink more or less in washing, and it is a good plan to have it shrunk before making up. To effect this, lay it in a tub of lukewarm soft water, take it out without squeezing as soon as it rises to the surface, hang it up to drain, and it will not have lost the appearance of newness. Another mode is to drain away the water in which it has been soaked, and then wash it through in a warm lather of curd soap. To prevent knitted articles shrinking, cut out in paper the exact shape of the article when new, and from this have a wooden frame made, with a ring attached to the top. After being washed, the garment should be slipped on it, and hung up by the ring to dry, by which means it will retain its original size and softness to the end.

Peterson's Magazine, February 1877

THIMBLES.

The name of this little instrument is said to have been derived from "thumb-bell," being first thumble, and afterward thimble. It is of Dutch invention, and was brought to England about the year 1605, by John Lofting, who commenced its manufacture at Islington, near London, and pursued it with great profit and success.

Formerly, iron and brass were used, but latterly steel, silver and gold have taken their places. In the ordinary manufacture, thin plates of metal are introduced into a die, and then punched into shape.

In Paris, gold thimbles are manufactured to a large extent. Thin sheets of sheet-iron are put into dies of about two inches in diameter. These being heated red-hot, are struck with a punch into a number of holes, gradually increasing in depth, to give them proper shape. The thimble is then trimmed, polished and indented around its outer surface with a number of little holes, by means of a small wheel.

It is then converted into steel by the cementation process, tempered, scoured and brought to a blue color.

Arthur's Home Magazine, April 1877

Washing Blankets, Merinos, Etc., Etc. – In our last number we gave some hints as to washing woolen things, such as flannels, etc. We now pursue the subject, treating, this month, of Shetland goods, blankets, etc.

Shetland goods must be washed in a lather of pure curd soap, which should be well worked up before they are placed in it. They must on no account be rubbed, but be passed up and down in the water, and drawn through the hand. When, by this gentle pressure, the dirt has been extracted, they are to be rinsed in soapy water, and as much of it as possible being pressed out of them, they should be well shaken to and fro. Shawls, and large pieces, must be pinned out straight and square on a sheet. This must be carefully done, and each strand of the fringe should be passed through the hand, straightened, and pulled out carefully. If they are required slightly stiffened, dip them in one pint and a half of warm water, in which one tablespoonful of gum-arabic has been dissolved, but they should not be made too stiff. Scarves, and other small articles in Shetland wool, may be dried by holding before the fire, pulling and shaking them out all the time. Stockings should be hung up by the toes to dry, and a wooden frame on which to stretch them will be found very useful.

Blankets should not be washed oftener than can be helped; they will remain clean much longer if, from time to time, they are hung up on lines in the open air, and the dust is well beaten out of them. In hand-washing, it is difficult to prevent their becoming sodden with water before the whole is washed, and this is apt to make them hard and lumpy; whereas, with a machine, the water, being always in action, effectually filters through them. When no machine is used, a stick will be found useful to shake them, and to press them well down in the water.

To wash white merino, alpaca, etc., if soap is used, the ordinary plan above described for ordinary woolen goods is pursued. The quicker the operation is carried out, the less danger will there be of the stuff becoming yellow. Bran is often used for this class of goods, instead of soap, a lather being made of one pound of bran, tied up in muslin, boiled in two gallons of water, blue being added to the rinsing water. Another plan is to grate three large potatoes in one pint of water, and let it stand some hours; then pour off the clear liquid, and sponge the material well with it, subsequently dipping it in fresh water. When these white materials are ironed, and not mangled, it must always be with muslin between, and they should be rolled in a cloth.

With regard to colored woolen things, the chief difference in the mode of washing is, that no blue is employed, and it is more than ever imperative that no soap be rubbed on them. They must be carefully dried in the shade; very delicate colors in the dark. The chief cause of color running is, that the things are allowed to lie about damp, and are not dried quickly enough. The usual method of fixing the color is to put a handful of salt in the tub of rinsing water, or a tablespoonful of ox-gall stirred in the lather, and a tablespoonful of vinegar in the rinsing water, will have the same effect. A tablespoonful of ammonia, or spirits of wine, mixed with the rinsing water, will answer the same purpose. White and colored flannels must on no account be washed together; woolen dresses, and also curtains, must be taken from the gathers before washing.

Peterson's Magazine, April 1877

WASHING AND SUNSHINE.

Faith Rochester, in one of her admirable articles in the *Agriculturist,* says: "Doubtless most of our readers have heard of the method of washing without boiling white clothes, by spreading the clothes fresh from the suds in which they were washed to bleach for an hour or so in the hot sunshine, then rinsing them in two clear waters, or 'sudsing' and rinsing them. This method saves both fuel and water in summer-time, provided you have green grass on which to spread your clothes."

The point in this brief extract to which we desire to call attention, says the *Herald of Health,* is the value of sunshine on our clothing and bedding, and to explain why the bleaching of clothing in the sun helps to clean them. From some experiments which we made last summer at Ocean Grove, to test the amount of ozone in the air, it was very evident that sunshine had powerful influence in its generation. The test paper under the full blaze of the sunshine always showed a sharper action than in the shade. Now, ozone possesses powerful oxygenizing, disinfecting properties, and when soiled linen is exposed to the powerful sun's rays, ozone is generated, and immediately acts on those impurities in our clothing which are unwholesome. It would be a most excellent thing if bedding and underclothing could be sunned every day. The ozone generated would rapidly clean it of most of its impurities. No doubt this same fact explains the greater healthfulness of sunny rooms. The ozone generated in them at once acts as nature's great disinfector, burning up such poisonous matter as is injurious.

Arthur's Home Magazine, May 1877

Washing Colored Fabrics. – "Before washing almost any colored fabrics," says the *Scientific American*, "it is recommended to soak them for some time in water, to every gallon of which is added a spoonful of ox-gall. A teacup of lye in a pail of water is said to improve the color of black goods, when it is necessary to wash them. A strong, clean tea of common hay will preserve the color of French linens. Vinegar in the rinsing water for pink or green, will brighten those colors, and soda answers the same end for both purple and blue."
Arthur's Home Magazine, July 1877

How To Clear Soapsuds. – It is well known that a little alum dissolved is very effective in clearing muddy water. But a short time since, some alum was applied in a manner which, from its novelty and valuable results, is worthy of notice. In a place where water is scarce, a little alum was dissolved in hot water, and thrown into a tub of thick soapsuds. In a short time the soap curdled, and, accompanied by the muddy particles, sank to the bottom, leaving the water above perfectly clear, pure and devoid of smell. This water was found very useful for washing clothing in again when poured off the sediment. A similar result was attained in a quick manner by filling a boiler with soapsuds, placing it on a fire, and throwing a bit of alum into it. When the suds boiled, the scum went over, and left the water clear, soft and as useful for washing clothes as it had originally been.
Arthur's Home Magazine, November 1877

To Wash Lace And Fine Things. – Lace and fine things should be washed in hot soft water. Well soap them and squeeze and shake out, but on no account rub them. Repeat the squeezing and shaking out again till they are clean. Rinse them in some more clean hot water and well soap them again and put them into a saucepan with enough hot water to cover them. Soft water is best, but if that cannot be procured, add a piece of soda – say a quarter of an ounce to half a gallon of water, according to the hardness of the water. Boil for half an hour. Then wash them out again and rinse in cold blue water. Hang them on a clothes horse till dry, when they can be starched. Lastly, roll them up in a dry cloth tor two hours, by which time they will be fit to iron.
Arthur's Home Magazine, December 1877

A PLEA FOR NEEDLES AND THREAD.

Nowadays, when newspapers teem with advertisements of sewing machines, foot and hand, lock and chain stitch, it may seem rather unnecessary to ask your attention to the benefits conferred on women by old-fashioned needlework. It is true that the new Board of Education are trying their best to revive its importance, and in so doing they are forwarding a good work; although it may be that children of the early age they suggest cannot be made skilful in hemming, running, stitching, felling, &c. &c. But that all these stitches, and others even more difficult, ought to be practically learned by girls before they are twelve is a thing much to be desired.

I remember what a very little thing I was when I was set down on a small footstool to my first task of "sewing" – *we* used to call it "overhand" in those days – which I was expected to complete before I moved. It was not more, perhaps, than a dozen or two of stitches, but I can still recall the way my little hot hands clutched the needle, and drove it by main force through the fourfold seam. It was a fancy my teacher had always to make us little ones sew with coloured thread, and I think the idea was good; it was so much easier to see the stitches one made with red on a white ground, than those worked with so-called white thread, which was generally a dirty grey by the time the task was finished. I can also recall the shame that I felt when a long, straggling red stitch made itself too conspicuous on the white foundation, and how vain I was when others saw, and I saw myself, the tiny red specks lying as close together, and as regular in length and in uprightness, as Miss G–'s own.

From that time I date not only my love for needlework, but for colour; and often have I thanked God for a gift which has stood me in good stead in my work-a-day life, and has helped to pass many a weary hour of sorrow and sickness.

I doubt whether a man can understand what needles and thread can do for a woman, spiritually as well as materially. Sewing-machines are among the marvels of the age; we can as little do without them now as we could do without railways, telegraphs, or gas; but while they, and other mechanical helps, *can* be done without, you cannot do without needles and thread. They are required to complete the most perfect of machine work; and there are a thousand trifles they can do which no machine can execute.

Besides, they are always at hand, whereas machines, either hand or foot, cannot be very easily carried about with one. Again, needlework rather assists than prevents pleasant talk, or reading aloud; but what conversation or reading can go on with the irritating whirr and clack-clack of a sewing-machine as an accompaniment? Then how many fragments of time needlework fills up usefully or pleasantly. The fate of ninety-nine women out of a hundred is to *wait* – wait for husband, children, brothers, sisters, friends, "'only a minute or two" perhaps; but those who acquire the habit of turning these lost minutes to account, get through an amount of work that would startle any one unaccustomed to gather up time's fragments; and such occupation saves many a fit of ill-temper. Waiting does not seem so long when we are occupied.

And this is true even in times of greater anxiety than those we have hinted at. The breadwinner of the household – father, brother, son – does not make his appearance at his usual hour of home-coming; everything is ready for him – the evening meal prepared, the fire burning brightly, we ourselves ready to greet him after the completion of his daily labour. But he does not come – and why? Has an accident happened to his train? Has some disaster befallen himself? We try to thrust aside the unwelcome thought, and forget it and ourselves in a book. We open it, but our eyes do not see the words on the page; they are wandering to the closed door, and our ears are listening vainly for the "footstep that has music in't coming up the stair." We cannot fix our thoughts on our studies, and lay down the book and listen. Not a sound! We rise slowly, and draw back the window-blind; the rain, it may be, is pattering against the panes, making us more wretched at the unusual detention of our dear one; or perhaps the cold, pure stars are looking down upon us as if indifferent to our anxiety, and we turn with a shiver from the outer world to our lonely room. Is there nothing we can do to pass the weary time? We cannot open that book again; and yet with what else can we occupy ourselves? Suddenly we remember some little bit of work we meant "some day" to do for him. Cannot we do it now? It seems as if it would do our heart good to have something for *him* to do; and we sit down to our task – a handkerchief to be hemmed, a shirt collar to be repaired—and insensibly are diverted from the too great strain on our thoughts. "Perhaps he will come before this button-hole is finished?" We start up – we hear the key turn in the lock – the familiar step come nearer and nearer. "He is safe – thank God!" And our hour of waiting is past.

Or we have been worried by some of those daily annoyances that pinprick the lives of most women, and we have a task of needlework to finish in a certain time which these worries have made scarcely sufficient. We sit down to it, feeling it is an aggravation of all that has gone before. Does it prove so in reality? Have you never felt the soothing effect of a long white seam upon your temper when ruffled? The steady regularity of the employment, the rhythmical click-click of the needle passing in and out of the stuff insensibly brings a change in our thoughts. It recalls perhaps the tune of an old song we used to lilt at our mother's knee, and before we are aware our thoughts are wafted back to those dear old times, we feel "the touch of a vanished hand," and hear "the sound of a voice that is still;" or we remember perhaps, as the material passes through our fingers, that we were busy with a somewhat similar task when we listened to words that were the turning-points of our lives. And thus insensibly associations are roused by our labour that make us forget the present and our worries together.

I do not mean to say that needlework can cure the heart sickness, but it helps – yes, believe me, it does help – to allay its bitterness. There is something in the "creative" faculty of needlework which has a marvellously healing influence upon those afflicted with sickness either of body or mind.

Often and often in the long, weary hours of solitary convalescence have I – and many besides me – thanked God for His merciful gift, the love of "work;" and, oh, how I have pitied those who can find no pleasure in it! Cultivate, then, the love of needlework in every way you can, both useful and fanciful. You little know how great a help it can be to you and to others. For myself, though it is not my profession, yet I believe I have tried as many varieties of needlework as most people, from stitching a shirt to embroidering a handkerchief – from art needlework to making carpets, cushions, chair covers, dresses, underlinen, &c. &c., even to a horsecloth and carriage lining. So I do not speak as one ignorant of what I write. And, as every new attempt has been to me a new pleasure, I wish I could make my sister women think as I do.

In spite of the "Song of the Shirt," and many a piteous and too true tale of the *abuse* of needlework, believe me that there is more – a thousand times more – to be said of its *use*. So let me entreat you to look upon it as a question of importance, and to cultivate it in all its branches. If you are well off, it is a graceful amusement; if ill off, you simply cannot exist without it. In short, it is a precious gift, and fills up a gap in woman's life which nothing else could do.

But now let us go from theory to practice.

SEWING-MACHINES.

I have said that to most people sewing-machines are a very valuable possession, and the question often asked is, Which is the best?

But the answer is difficult. It depends upon your own skill and management, and also on the use you intend to make of it. If you wish to make your living as a machinist, I suppose that Wheeler and Wilson's treadle machine is decidedly the best. But it is very expensive, and, if you only want a "machine" to run up an occasional seam, or to execute the little bits of work required in a family, I should advise a hand machine. It is less expensive, takes up less space, and the strain on the muscles of the back is not so great. For a delicate girl nothing is more hurtful than to sit all day at a treadle machine, but a short *stand* at a hand machine makes a good change from stooping too long over plain needlework. There are many new hand machines, both lock and chain stitch. If you are skilful, the lock stitch are the best; among others, Newton and Wilson's. Their chain stitch are also very good. I have had one of their "Cleopatras" for ten years, and it is still in good working condition.

Each machine has its printed form of directions, and, if you have no one to *show* you how to work it, you can by following them closely learn "'how to do it" very passably. But in most mechanical arts to see a thing used is a much easier way to understand its working than to do it by printed instructions. One thing, however, you must always keep in mind, and that is, that you must never use *force* with a sewing-machine. If it does not work properly, there must be a reason why. Either you don't know how to manage it, or something is amiss with the machine itself, and what that is you must try to discover before deciding against it. I have seen people abuse the working of the machine, when all that was wrong was that they had forgotten to drop the cloth presser before beginning to work, or had allowed a loose thread to twist itself round the driving wheel; or – in a lock stitch – had caught the tacking thread in the under wheel. So when there is a hitch look to these trifles, and do not attempt to ride roughshod over them, or you will come to grief.

The cotton you use depends on the machine. Some will only work with glazed thread, others with soft; and some of the lock-stitch machines require one sort for the upper and one for the under thread. See which is advised in your book of instructions.

In machines, as in needlework, the essentials are neatness, precision, regularity, and evenness of stitch. For both a steady hand and eye are required, and an earnest desire to do it as *well* as possible, not simply to get through the work anyhow. To insure this, careful tacking is required in machine work especially, for by this means only can a beginner secure a smooth surface to work upon, and have her mind relieved from the dread of the two pieces of stuff she is sewing together parting company just as they are within a stitch or two of the needle. With these anxieties removed, she has only to keep the work straight and regular, those two essentials in all neat work by whatever implements it is accomplished.

Another important matter both in needle and machine work is to begin and to finish off each seam neatly and securely. This is of vital importance in a chain-stitch machine, as otherwise the whole seam is apt to run down. Yet it is simple enough when once understood, for all that is required is to draw the end of the thread through the last loop of the chain, and fasten it off by one or two stitches with the needle.

...

To look well, a young woman, who is not rich, will have to be careful with her clothes – to keep them fresh, neat, and clean as long as she possibly can; never drop your clothes on the floor when you take them off; lift them over your head, and shake and fold them neatly.

Keep your drawers neat; have a place for everything, and everything in its place, so that you could find them in the dark, as people say. Do not leave your things about in the dust, though they should be taken out and aired occasionally. Never put away a dress the bottom of which is full of dust, brush or shake it clean first. If it is a silk dress, wipe it clean with a piece of soft flannel. White silk handkerchiefs should be kept in blue paper.

Keep your clothes in good repair by frequent mending. Remember, "A stitch in time saves nine." Do not put them away *damp;* air them first, as the moisture lying in them rots them.

It is economy to buy a new undergarment, or pair of stockings, every quarter, so that your stock may be well kept up, without any great outlay at one time.

Whenever you take off a nice bonnet, blow the dust off it before you put it away, and pull out the strings.

Take out your shawls or jackets every now and then, and air them, so that they may not get a frowsy smell. Never put them in the drawer directly you take them off; for the same reason, let them hang up in the air for a time.

Sew your gloves carefully and on the right side. When you take them off do not roll them up, but pull them straight, and lay one on the other.

If possible, wash your own collars and cuffs; they will last twice as long, and look twice as well, as they would do if sent to the laundress. *See* "The Laundress" for directions how to do them up, p. 76. [*below*]

To Clean Gloves. – Put them on the hands and wash them, *if very light,* with milk and white curd soap. If dark, wash them with spirit of turpentine till clean. Hang out to dry, and lose the smell. Benzoline also cleans gloves, but the smell must be well removed before using.

To Remove Stains from White Muslin or Linens. – Put less than half a teaspoonful of tartaric acid or salt of lemon into a tablespoonful of water, and mix it. Wet the stain with it, and lay it in the sun for an hour; wet it once or twice with cold water during the time. If the first time it is not removed, repeat the acid water, and lay it in the sun.

To Take out Ink Spots on Linen. – As soon as perceived put on them a little vinegar, and rub with the best hard soap.

To Remove Water Stains from Crape. – Spread the crape on the table, laying a weight of some sort on it to keep it steady. Put under it a piece of old black silk. Get a camel's-hair paintbrush, dip it in ink, and paint over the stain. Wipe off the too much ink with a little bit of old silk. When dry the mark will not show. Old limp crape may be stiffened by just wiping it over the wrong side with water in which potatoes have been scraped, and let stand; it must be pulled out.

To Take Grease out of Cloth. – Pour spirits of turpentine or common turpentine on it. Rub till quite dry with a piece of clean flannel. If not quite removed, repeat it; when the stain is out brush the place well, and hang in the open air to remove the smell.

To Clean Black Cloth Jacket Or Cloak. – Brush the cloth well and carefully. Boil four ounces of logwood in a copper containing two or three gallons of water for half an hour. Dip the cloth garment in warm water and squeeze it nearly dry; then boil it in the logwood and water in the copper for half an hour. Take it out and add three drams of sulphate of iron. Then put it back and boil for half an hour. Take it out, rinse it in three cold waters, dry it well, and brush it with a soft brush which has had a few drops of olive oil rubbed on its surface.

To Drive away Moths from Clothes. – Wrap them in, or cover them completely, in the coarsest brown paper, with a piece of camphor inside. Put a small open bottle of spirits of turpentine in the box or drawers with them. Take them out, occasionally shake them well, examine, and replace them.

To Restore Colours taken out by Acid. – Drop sal-volatile on the spot.

To Choose Calico. – Rub it to see that there is not much "dress" in it. If a quantity of white dust flies out do not buy it, as it is *really* thin, and will not wear well.

To Buy and Keep Cotton Stockings. – The best have a coloured thread or two – red or blue, run at the top of them. Inferior stockings have not this mark. It is a good plan to thicken the heels and toes of new stockings before wearing, by running them every alternate stitch in straight rows all over, leaving long loops. It makes them last as long again.

To Clean a Straw Bonnet. – Rub it all over with cut lemon, and wash the juice off carefully with water.

To Clean and Wash Black Crape. – Take some skimmed milk and water, with a little bit of glue in it. Make it scalding hot. Wash the crape with it. If then clapped and pulled out it will look as good as new.

To Take off Wax Candle Grease. – Scrape off the thick part with the back of a knife. Lay a piece of clean blotting-paper over the spot, and hold *close to it,* but *not on* it, a very hot iron. The grease will rise into the paper. Repeat with fresh paper till all is out.

To Dry an Umbrella. – Most people stand their umbrellas up on the point to dry. This is apt to rust the wires which secure the skeleton, and rot the silk. Stand it up *on its handle* after wiping it over.

To Take Out Paint Spots. – Drop spirits of turpentine on the spot. Let it stand for some time, and then rub it.

If the paint be wet, you can wash it off at once with spirits of turpentine.

To Clean an Old Silk Dress. – Unpick the dress and brush all dust off. Grate two potatoes into a quart of water, let it stand, and then drain off clean. Lay a breadth, outside upwards, on a clean cloth spread over an ironing blanket. Sponge the breadth well with the potato water. Do all the breadths thus; then iron them with a hot iron, laying a piece of linen or old handkerchief between the iron and the silk. This will prevent it from looking shiny.

To Take Grease Out of Silk. – Get some French chalk, scrape it fine, and mix it with water to the thickness of mustard. Put it on the spot and rub lightly with your fingers, and lay a sheet of blotting-paper on it, and press a hot iron on it. Repeat till out.

To Keep Silks. – Never fold a silk in white paper. The chloride of lime used in bleaching the paper is apt to spoil the colour of the silk.

...

THE LAUNDRESS.

Fuel and Soap. – Newcastle coal is considered the best, as it burns without making any dust and leaves very little residue; but it requires to be stirred often, or it cakes and goes out.

Silkstone is a good burner with a very little ash.

Coal contains a certain amount of water, some more, some less; it is therefore most economical to buy it in the hot, dry weather, when the coal is very dry. The price also is lower in summer. If possible, buy coals by the ton, as they come *much* cheaper than by the hundredweight – several shillings a ton less, in fact.

Soap. – This useful article should be bought in quantities; say, by the half-hundredweight or hundredweight at a time, if the washing be much; if little, it should be bought by the four bars at once. A bar contains about three pounds of soap. The reason for buying a quantity at once is that it hardens by keeping, and therefore does its work of cleansing without so much waste in the water. The bars should be cut into moderate-sized pieces for use with a fine twine; they will harden better than if it be left in the bar. Then put them in a drawer to dry and harden slowly, without being exposed to the air; for if soap were to dry quickly it would be likely to break when used.

Mottled soap is the most economical; the best yellow soap melts much more rapidly in water. Soft soap for washing linen is a saving of half the quantity; therefore it is economical, though dearer in price than hard soap.

Soda, by softening the water, saves soap.

One of the most useful soaps for washing linen is the St. Mungo Concentrated Soap. It combines the best properties of hard and soft soap, without the disagreeable smell of the soft soap. It does not damage fabrics in the slightest degree. In order to use it, it is dissolved in boiling water, and the clothes steeped in the solution will not require half the labour in rubbing them.

Soap is sold – yellow, at about 4 1/2*d.* per lb.; mottled, about 4*d.* per lb.

Carbolic soap is a valuable preparation, as it has great disinfecting powers, and should always be used in washing the linen of fever patients. It possesses also great cleansing power without injuring the material on which it is used. Its use is fatal to house insects. There is a carbolic toilette soap which is excellent in hot weather for the skin.

The following process for making soap is practised by emigrants: – Two or three gallons of clean water are poured upon about a bushel of wood ashes, thoroughly stirred, and the ash is allowed to subside. The liquid, which is now a lye, is drawn off and boiled for two or three hours with fat of any description. At the end of that time the fat will have assumed the consistency of soap. It is allowed to settle, and the liquor is then drawn off, being no longer of any use. The residue, although soft, will answer every purpose for which soap is used.

Starching. – Clear starching was introduced in the reign of James 1., and the first clear starchers were Dutch women. The yellow starch, introduced and made fashionable by the infamous Mrs. Turner, who was hung for assisting in the murder of Sir Thomas Overbury in the Tower, went out of fashion at her death, as she was hung in a yellow starched ruff.

Many vegetable substances afford starch – the chief are, wheat, rice and potatoes. Arrowroot also makes a delicate but expensive starch.

Potato starch is made by grating raw potatoes into a vessel full of clear water, and after sluicing it well, letting the mass settle. The water is poured off and fresh water added *three times;* the starch remains at the bottom of the vessel.

Arrowroot starch is made by simply pouring a little boiling water on the powder.

Starch will not dissolve in cold water; it requires boiling water. It should be kept in a jar, in a dry place.

Stone-blue. – Stone-blue is used, tied in a bag, to blue water into which washed linen or muslin is dipped. Powder-blue is smalt mixed with a very little starch.

Washing. – On Monday morning the soiled linen for the wash should be carefully examined. All rents mended and spots and stains taken out.

Ink spots are removed by dipping the part into hot water first; then spreading it smoothly over the back of the bowl of a spoon and pouring a few drops of salts of sorrel over the ink spot, rubbing and rinsing it in cold water till it disappears. Milk also removes ink stains.

Fruit and wine spots are removed by dipping the part stained into a solution of sal-ammoniac or spirits of wine, and then rinsing.

Next separate the clothes; put the table linen and sheets into one heap, the body linen into another, muslins into another, coloured cotton clothes into a fourth, woollens into a fifth, kitchen and greasy cloths into a sixth heap.

Place the sheets and table linen in a tub already half filled with lukewarm water, in which a little soda has been dissolved. Leave them to soak till the next morning.

In another tub put the body linen in the same kind of mixture – soda and water – and in another, the very dirty things and greasy cloths in very much stronger soda and water, and leave them to soak till the next morning, the soda and water covering the things when they are pressed down.

Copper and boiler should then be filled, and the fires laid ready to light.

The next morning light the fires, and as soon as you have hot water begin the washing. Do the sheets and table linen first.

Take each article out of the water in which it has soaked all night, rub, rinse, and wring it, and lay it aside. Empty the tub, and fill it with lukewarm water. Put the clothes in it, soap, and rub them well.

Then squeeze them out, pour away that water, and fill the tub with a second water, as hot as the hand can bear, and again soap and rub *well*. Now put them in the copper, and boil them in water in which soda has been dissolved, in the proportion of a teaspoonful to two gallons of water; stir frequently.

It is a good plan to boil the body linen when it has been washed in a cotton bag, to save it from the sides and scum of the copper.

When the clothes have boiled enough and been taken out, they should be rinsed, first in clean hot water, and next in an abundance of cold water, slightly tinged with blue, and then wrung out and hung out to dry.

The earlier they are hung out the whiter will be the linen.

The muslins must be done separately. *See* directions further on.

Greasy cloths, which have soaked all night in the strong soda-water, should then be washed out in *very* hot soap and water and rinsed in second water, then boiled for two hours in soda and water. When taken out, rinse them in cold water, and hang them out to dry.

Silk handkerchiefs should be washed alone, as must also be the collars, cuffs, &c .

Wash, blue, and dry the collars and cuffs; make a starch with one tablespoonful of starch, one teaspoonful of clear prepared gum, a lump of sugar, and one pinch of salt; mix it with cold water, stir till quite smooth, add sufficient boiling water, and make it clear and of the proper consistency, then stir a wax candle round it once or twice; dip the articles in the starch, squeeze them dry, roll them out in a cloth ten minutes, and then iron them.

Ordinary Starch. – Half a pint of cold water and one quart of boiling water to every two tablespoonfuls of starch.

Put the starch into a large basin, pour over it the cold water, and stir the mixture with a wooden spoon till it is quite smooth, then take the basin to the fire, and pour the water, when boiling, from the kettle on it, stirring it the whole time. The water must boil, or the starch will not thicken; if it does not, put it in a saucepan and boil it.

Strain it into a clean basin, and as soon as it is cool enough for you to bear your hand *in it,* starch the things. To make the starch very smooth and slimy, stir it round two or three times before you put in the things with a wax candle. This prevents the starch sticking to the iron.

After starching the things, squeeze them out, and clap any lace between the hands for a few times. Wrap the starched things in a towel, and let them lie for two or three hours, when they will be ready for ironing.

Ironing. – To iron well is a very difficult task, and requires practice. The ironing-cloth or blanket must be laid over the table, and the iron-stand placed on it.

Try if the iron is hot enough upon some rag of no value, and be sure the iron is quite clean. A box-iron is very nice for collars, lace, &c. &c., as it is sure to be clean.

Goffering-irons must be placed in a clear fire for a minute, then withdrawn, wiped with a clean coarse rubber, and their heat tried on a piece of paper before using them, lest they should scorch the muslin or lace.

The skirts of muslin dresses should be ironed on a skirt board covered with flannel, and the fronts of shirts also on a smaller board covered with flannel.

After things are mangled, they should be ironed in the folds and gathers; so should the bands of flannel petticoats, &c. &c.

Hints for the Laundress who Uses a Washing Machine. – Properly boiled suds are far better than soap for washing, particularly in the washing machine.

The Way to Prepare Suds.* – One pound of soap to one gallon of water. Add half a pound of soda. Put all in a large covered jar, and set it at the back of the kitchen range, or on the hob, till the soap is quite dissolved. Do it on Saturday evening, and the soap will be a smooth jelly ready to use by Monday morning.

* Suds are also best for washing by hand.

Unless linen is very much soiled, it will not require boiling more than every second time it is washed. Then boil it in the copper, putting in *(before the clothes)* two pints of soap jelly to a moderate-sized copperful of cold water. Put in the linen. Stir frequently to prevent them from burning, and only leave them in the copper ten minutes after the water begins to boil. Take them out, rinse them *well,* and blue them. To do this, use the best stone blue tied in a bag of thick flannel. Dip one article at a time into the blue-water, and do not let it fall to the bottom of the tub, as all the blue not in the water settles at the bottom, and if the linen touches it, it will get streaked and spoiled with blue, which is hard to get out. If you have tubs enough, *strain* the blue-water, and then you can throw in one article at a time without fear.

Our washerwomen use soda – as our receipt shows – but Dutch laundresses use borax instead, and they get up clothes beautifully: a handful of refined borax to ten gallons of boiling water. They save nearly half the quantity of soap, and borax does not injure even fine lace and cambric.

Borax Used in Washing. – Quarter of a pound of refined borax to five gallons of water; powder the borax; dissolve it in boiling water in the above proportion, and use. It is an excellent bleacher, and may be used for the most delicate laces even.

A little pipeclay dissolved in the hot water cleans very dirty linen with half the soap required without it.

To Bleach Linen. – Pour over a quarter of a pound of chloride of lime one gallon of boiling water. Let it stand two days, stirring it occasionally; then pour it clear off, and bottle it for use. When required, add half a pint to a quart or three pints of cold spring water. Wash your clothes well, and rinse it from the soap; then put it into the above, and let it steep for a few hours; pass it through clean water, and you will find the colour much improved.

Clothes Lines. – Gutta-percha clothes lines are stronger and much more durable than common cord. They can, moreover, be cleaned, and are not affected by wet. When the clothes line is done with, a little hot water will convert the material into a soap-bowl.

To Wash Coloured Muslins, Piques, &c. the French way. – Make a lather of soft water and the best white soap. Use it rather warm but not hot. Wash the dress quickly through, and do not let it soak. When the first lather is soiled, use a second for it. When it is thoroughly clean, rinse it in clean cold water, next in strained, *slightly blued* water. Squeeze it out – do not wring it, and hang it in a shady place, out of the sun, to dry. Any colour fades in sunshine.

A *very* little soda keeps the colour of lilac prints.

We have been told that a little alum in the water will keep in a green – but we cannot answer for this. We can for a piece of salt as big as an egg keeping the colour of stripes from running into the white ground or stripe. Salt will keep black stripes from running into white ones, and so on.

In getting-up muslins and piques, &c., the failure is, however, generally in the starching.

A good-sized panful of starch should be used, in which a good piece of wax candle has been melted while it was hot. The dress should be thoroughly squeezed from the starch, and folded wet between folds of old sheeting or table linen. It should then be passed beneath the rollers of the mangle, or through a wringing machine, to remove all lumps of starch.

To Wash Woollen Material Dresses. – Boil a pound of rice in a gallon of water for three hours. Wash the dress in part of it, rinse in cold water, then dip it in the remainder of the rice water, and hang it before the fire to dry. When dry enough to iron, use a *cool* iron. No soap must be used, and the dress must on no account *lie damp* for even an hour, or the colours will run. If parts of the dress get too dry to iron, damp them with a wet cloth while ironing.

To Wash Flannels. – Boil some good soap in soft water. Do not use boiling water with the suds, but only as hot as your hand can bear.

Flannel should not be soaped or rubbed, as rubbing knots the wool fabric and makes it shrink. Sluice the flannels up and down in plenty of suds, and afterwards squeeze – not wring – them out. The wringing machine is best for them. After rinsing, squeeze out the water, and dry quickly in the open air. Flannel should be shrank before it is made up.

To Wash Woollen Shawls. – Scrape one pound of soap, and boil it in sufficient water – *i.e.*, one gallon. When it is cooling beat it with the hand till it makes a sort of jelly. Add two tablespoonfuls of spirit of turpentine, and one of spirit of hartshorn. Add sufficient water, and wash the shawl thoroughly, rinse it in cold water till the soap is removed, then again in salt and water. Fold it between two sheets, taking care that the folds of the shawl do not touch each other. Mangle, and iron with a cool iron afterwards.

To Wash Coloured Prints, Cretonnes, &c. – Put a little bran into lukewarm water; wash quickly through; rinse *in cold* water also quickly. Hang to dry in a room without fire or sunshine. Iron with not *too* hot an iron. Use no soap.

The colour of mauve or violet may be preserved by putting a little soda in the water. Green can be kept by putting a little colloid in the water; ox-gall also preserves the colours. But if coloured prints continue wet *too* long, nothing can save the colours from running. They must be done quickly and not let lie in the water.

Washing Blond. – For blond use fine soap, very slightly; wash it gently in water in which a little stone blue is dissolved; when clean, dry it: then dip it in thin gum water; dry it again in linen, and iron it flat; if washed finally in water in which a lump of sugar is dissolved, it will have the face of new blond.

To Wash Lace. – Cover an ordinary wine bottle with flannel, stitch it firmly on. Tack the end of the lace to the flannel, and roll it smoothly round the bottle till you reach the other end. Sew it down. Cover over the lace with a piece of muslin, rub the whole gently with the soap jelly already described.

Hold the bottle under a running tap to clean the lace thoroughly of soap. Make some starch of arrowroot, in which is melted a little of the best white wax and a little loaf sugar.

Plunge the bottle two or three times into thin starch, pressing out the superfluous starch with the hand. Then clip the bottle into cold water, remove the muslin, fill the bottle with very hot water and put it in the sun to dry. When dry, take it carefully off the bottle and pick it out with the fingers.

Dissolve some salts of tartar in hot water. Put in the lace, and let it remain to soak for about half an hour. Then take it out of the water, and squeeze it dry.

The salts of tartar must be used when bought, to prevent them melting away.

Blond net or tulle may be washed in the same manner.

Black Lace (to Wash). – Wind the lace over flannel round a wine bottle. Make a lather of white soap and water, and then rub the lace with it in milkwarm water with great care. Rinse away the soap with clean milkwarm water, and let it gently dry. Next day make some good strong black tea, dissolve in it a little gum arabic, using as much powdered gum as you would sugar in the tea. Rinse the lace in this gum-tea several times. The tannin in the tea will restore the colour of the lace, the gum will stiffen it. Take it off the bottle when quite dry.

To Clean White Veils. – Make a solution of white soap; let the veil simmer in it for a quarter of an hour; squeeze in warm water and soap till it is clean; rinse it in cold water, in which put *a drop* of bluewater.

Pour boiling water on a teaspoonful of starch; run the veil through this, and clear by clapping it. Pin it out on a cloth or a cushion, very evenly, by the edges to dry.

To render Muslin, Lace, and Net Incombustible. – Mix with the starch half its weight of whiting. It answers also for lace flounces.

Or: – Dissolve half an ounce of sal-ammoniac in the rinsing water.

Alum also answers the purpose.

To render Muslins Uninflammable. – Tungstate of soda, prepared expressly for rendering fabrics non-inflammable, can be obtained by order of any chemist for about 1s. per pound. Directions for use: – To three parts of dry starch add one part of tungstate of soda, and use the starch in the ordinary way. If the material does not require starching, mix in the proportions of one pound of tungstate of soda to two gallons of water; well saturate the fabric with this solution, and dry it. The heat of the iron in no way affects the non-inflammability. Or, dip in a solution of chloride of zinc.

To Wash Brown Holland. – Use bran instead of soap, and lukewarm water; no soda. Iron on the *wrong* side.

To Wash Black Silk Stockings. – Wash them quickly in a good lather of soap and water, not too hot; rinse in clear lukewarm water, squeeze out the wet thoroughly, lay them on a clean cloth, and roll them up tight. When nearly dry smooth them out, and polish with a piece of flannel, rubbing always one way, on the right side. If obtainable, a handful of ivy leaves boiled in the water till quite dark helps to preserve the colour.

To Wash Black and White Striped Stockings. – Make a jelly, the night before it is wanted, of the best yellow soap; wash the stockings in warm water with a little salt in it, using the jelly instead of soap; rinse in clear water, also with a little salt in it; wring as dry as possible, and dry quickly.

To Remove Wine Stains from Linen. – Hold them in milk that is boiling on the fire, and they will soon disappear.

To Remove Stains made by Acids. – Wet the spots and lay on them some salt of sorrel, rub it, but do not wet it again. Then wash it out.

To Remove Ironmoulds. – Wet the spot; lay it over a hot-water plate, or strain it over a basin with hot water in it; put a little salts of lemon on the spot; wash it as soon as the spot is removed.

To take out Mildew. – Mix soft soap, powdered starch, half as much salt, and the juice of a lemon.

Paint both sides of the linen with a brush; put it out on the grass till the stain comes out.

Or when white linen becomes mildewed it should be washed in warm water, with a little borax, and then rinsed in clean water. After this, it must be put into a tub of water, containing a little hydrochloric acid; then rinsed and dried in the sun.

To restore Scorched or Discoloured Linen. – For discoloured linen or muslin, grass or seaside bleaching is always the best; but in town, mix a pound of bleaching-powder with six quarts of water, and put a portion of this into the tub where the articles are steeping.

To take out Fruit Stains with Chloride of Soda. – Wet first with cold soap and water, touch with chloride of soda. Wash again immediately.

Sheets. – Before the sheets are sent to the wash they should be carefully examined, and mended if they require repairs. If they have grown thin in the middle the centre seam must be unripped and the outside seams be turned inwards and sewn together; or if (as is now usually the case) the sheet is made the whole width, it must be cut very carefully and evenly by a thread, down the middle, and the sides joined inwards. In both cases the outsides must be neatly hemmed. When they are *again* worn in the centre they may be cut *across the length,* and the short ends sewn together in the middle.

A sheet quite worn out for the bed will still make pillow-cases, dusters, &c., and the pieces will be of use for cleaning lamps, candlesticks, &c.

To Wash Valuable Lace. – First dip it in white soap-suds, squeeze it and put it out in the open air to dry, wetting it constantly and letting it dry again until the colour is good. Then dip it into *thin clear* starch and pin it out most carefully on a board covered with linen, or on a heavy linen sheet folded several times. Small pins must be unsparingly used, stuck in upright, so as to make the lace dry in its proper form. Lace with a raised pattern, as old Brussels point, should be finished by raising the pattern with an ivory pin, rather like a good-sized bodkin with a round head.

Any ivory turner will supply it, and no lace cleaner should be without it.

If lace is very much discoloured, cover a bottle with flannel, wind the lace round it carefully, and just tack the ends; then fill the bottle with hot water and set it upright in a saucepan of suds made as described before (p. 77); let it boil for a few minutes, then take it out, let the tap run on it; starch and dry.

The Young Woman's Book, 1877

1878

It is a disputed question whether it is best to hang heavy silk dresses when not in use, or to fold them. Careful modistes who have elegant dresses to sell keep them packed in separate cases, or else in large trunks that are divided into many trays, putting a dress in each tray that it may not be crushed.

Harper's Bazar, March 2, 1878

But this heavy, wiry stuff [mohair] can be made into something useful, provided you are willing to take the time and trouble. It can be bleached out white, by the usual methods, such as soaking in sour milk, scalding in strong suds, scalding with lye; and, lastly, if you do not succeed satisfactorily, by putting it in a warm solution of oxalic acid, say six or eight cents' worth of the acid, dissolved in enough hot water to wet the goods thoroughly, then rinse in clean warm water. This liquid will be as hard on one's hands as moderately strong lye, so a clean stick must be used. Try and manage it without wringing; drain instead, for wringing breaks and creases it.

Arthur's Illustrated Home Magazine, March 1878

To Wash Book Muslins, Etc. – The following recipe may be used for lawn, book muslin dresses, fichus, etc. Boil two quarts of bran in water for half an hour, let it cool, then strain it, and mix the liquor with the water in which the things are to be washed. They will only require rinsing, as the bran will stiffen them sufficiently. For colored muslins, rice water is very good, as it helps to preserve the color; but, although it makes white muslins clear, it sometimes gives them a yellow tinge. When used, it should previously be boiled in the proportion of one pound of rice to one gallon of water. No soap is required.

Peterson's Magazine, March 1878

THE HOUSEKEEPER.

Washing Fine Things. – For ordinary muslin collars and cuffs, tuckers, dress handkerchiefs, gentlemen's white neckties, and other things which are not very much soiled, proceed as follows: Put them in soak overnight, in the morning wash them well with hot soap and water, rinse in cold water, slightly blued, dry them, and dip once more in cold water, wringing them well. This makes them clear, yet stiff. Fold them evenly, put them in a towel, and iron them. Babies' frocks, etc., which are more soiled, can be treated much in the same way, with the addition of a little borax in the soaking water to loosen the dirt, and they must be boiled after washing. Lace and muslin caps and other articles which are much worn sometimes become very dirty; in this case they should be put in a basin with shredded soap, and well covered with water, and allowed to stand from twenty to thirty minutes in a moderate oven. A plate should be laid over the basin to keep in the steam. After this they will require a great deal of rinsing to get rid of the dirt, and sometimes it may be necessary to put them in a pan full of cold water, and leave it on the fire till the water simmers. Snow water is invaluable to bleach fine things, or any white cotton or linen fabric.

Muslin curtains should first be soaked in cold water. In washing it is better to squeeze them with the hand rather than to rub them; they should then be rinsed in blue water, starched and dried. Many people pin them out carefully on a sheet stretched on the floor, and do not iron them, or they may be stretched on a frame, as is done by professional laundresses. If ironing is preferred, it is advisable to pin the upper end to the edge of the ironing table, so that in proceeding, the length can be let down double on a chair, which prevents the curtain getting creased. Two ironers should work simultaneously, and the thicker the ironing blanket the better; care should be taken to iron the edges evenly. For making thin muslin clear it will be found an excellent plan to beat up to a froth the lather in which it is to be washed, merely squeezing and pressing it with the hand, and not rubbing it; then, when quite dry, having passed it through thin starch, mixed with gum arable water, dry it once more, dip it into clear water, and clap it well with the hands to clear it until it is dry. If this be carefully done, the muslin will look equal to new, the gum arabic giving it a clear, bright appearance.

To prepare the gum water for mixing with starch, pour one pint of boiling water on two ounces of gum arabic; cover it, and let it stand twelve hours; pour it from the dregs, and bottle for use. This will be found useful for sprinkling washing dresses, which have to be ironed only, in course of wearing, and not washed. By rinsing muslin in alum water, or by mixing alum with the starch, it is rendered uninflammable. When muslin dresses are trimmed with plaitings, a piece of flannel is laid between the skirt and the flounce, so that they do not stick together in ironing.

Much of the success achieved by French laundresses is owing to the number of special appliances, various kinds of irons, they have for every branch of their work. Goffering tongs must never be put in the fire; when no stove is at hand, they can be warmed by placing them under a hot flat iron. The frill must be slightly wetted beforehand, and damped from time to time as required. The tongs should be held in the right hand like a pair of scissors, and the article taken between them; the point must be pushed well to the head of the frill, being steadied by the left hand, a half turn given with the right to settle the flute; the process must then be repeated. For the fashionable plaitings lying all one way, it is only necessary to pass an iron subsequently over these gofferings.

...

WARDROBE.

Various Modes of Preserving Furs. – 1. Lay up along with furs to be preserved a tallow candle. 2. Take out the furs from the drawer, etc., frequently, beat them well, expose them to the air, and scent the box where they are kept either with spirits of turpentine, camphor, Russia leather, or cedar wood. 3. Pepper them well before putting them away. 4. Wash them over with a very weak solution of corrosive sublimate. If this solution leaves a white powder on the fur when dry, it is too strong; ten grains to the pint will be enough.

To Clean Silk. – One pint and a fifth of gin or whiskey, four ounces soft soap, and six ounces honey; to be well mixed in an open dish. Lay the silk on a clean deal table, and rub it well on both sides with a sponge dipped in the above mixture. Have ready two pails filled with cold, soft water, and rinse the breadths separately, first in one bucket and then in the other, and put them in the open air upon a towel-horse to drain (a shady, cool place is best). When the silk is nearly dry, iron it on the wrong side. It will be of little use to turn a silk dress, without first removing all grease spots, as any marks very speedily work through.

A Hint. – Housekeepers should know that a small piece of paper or linen, moistened with spirits of turpentine, and put into a bureau or wardrobe, for a single day, two or three times a year, is a sufficient preservative against moths.

To Make Linen Collars and Cuffs Stiff and Bright. - Mix wheaten starch in cold water; dip in the articles, let them remain about ten minutes before ironing; they become glossy and stiff as new.

...

MISCELLANEOUS.

Stains of all Kinds. – If you have been picking or handling any acid fruit, and have stained your hands, wash them in clear water, wipe them lightly, and while they are yet moist strike a match, and shut your hands around it so as to catch the smoke, and the stains will disappear. If you have stained your muslin or gingham dress or your white apron with berries, before wetting with anything else, pour boiling water on the stains, and they will disappear. Before fruit juice dries, it can often be removed by cold water, using a sponge and towel if necessary. Rubbing the finger with the inside of the paring of apples will remove the most of the stain caused by paring. Ink, also, if washed out or sopped up from the carpet with milk, immediately when it is spilt, can be almost entirely removed. Ink spots on floors can be extracted by scouring with sand, wetted in oil of vitriol and water. When the ink is removed rinse with strong potash water.

Peterson's Magazine, April 1878

To Restore Color to Articles of Dress, etc. – When acid has been dropped on any article of clothing, apply liquid ammonia to kill the acid; then apply chloroform to restore the color. ...

To Wash Blankets. – For blankets, shawls, or clouds, or any white flannels, nothing should be used in washing them but plenty of soap and cold water. They then retain their color, and are soft and like new for years. The first water should be very strong with borax – about two ounces to a tub of warm water. Use soap sparingly on the soiled places only. The second water should be a weak suds. Rub in no soap, and use less borax. Rinse well in clear warm water. Wring very dry; shake well. Hang where they will dry quickly. The blankets will be as soft as new. ...

Wash your white zephyr shawl in tepid water into which you have previously put a teaspoonful of borax, and a little white castile soap. This will make a suds, in which was it clean, and then squeeze it out in clear cool water; stretch it on a mattress to dry, and do not iron it.

Demorest's Monthly Magazine, April, 1878

Starch for Fine Muslins. – A solution of gum-arabic in water makes a nice starch for lawns and thin muslins, giving them a new appearance. Dilute the dissolved gum until you find by experiment that you have it just right. It takes but a minute to rub a cloth in it, slightly dry and iron it, to test the strength of the gum-water. Lawns renewed in this way, after washing, not only look as though just made up, but retain their good appearance wonderfully well.

Arthur's Illustrated Home Magazine, August 1878

To Wash Red Flannel. – Make a warm suds; use very little soap (it hardens the flannel); add a tea-spoonful of pulverized borax to every pail of water; rub on the board, or, if possible, only with the hands; rinse in one plain warm water; wring or press very dry; shake well before hanging in a shady place to dry.
Arthur's Illustrated Home Magazine, September 1878

Any woman who reads, and thinks, and knows, or cares enough to put this and that together, must surely understand that hot soapsuds will "set" a stain or a soil instead of loosening it. In this day, it is known that by putting the washing to soak the night before, the dirt is loosened so that it washes out very readily; even soaking in clear, cold water is a great help, and facilitates the work amazingly. But tepid water is preferable; and if a spoonful of pulverized borax has been added, or a spoonful of turpentine stirred into the soap of which a weak suds is made, the labor of washing-day is very materially lightened of its burden. Women should all know what the detersives are, that the dreaded washing-day may be shorn of its terrors. Knowing this, she may use of the one she prefers. If she dislikes turpentine, let her use a little ammonia; if she dislikes the smell of ammonia, too, maybe she would prefer benzene; or, disliking this, let her use borax or sal-soda, or something that has no odor at all. Now, any of these things used with tepid water to soak the clothes over night, will rob the following day of the burdensome and tiresome task, and make it only a healthful exercise, one that starts perspiration and makes the sluggish blood flow faster. Any woman would welcome the cheerful toil for the recompense it brings in renewed vigor and awakened vitality. Many a woman, moping with the blues, having a hand-to-hand fight with the ugly old Apollyon, who attacks her nerves and makes her gloomy and dispirited, would find a sure retreat at the wash-tub. She could hide from him most effectively.

We can remember when the formula of washing-day was so much like the lesson in long division, that we puzzled our head not a little over the triple problems. So many tubs of suds and rinse-waters confused us. Now, instead of this old way of two suds, a boiling suds, an after-boiling suds, two rinses and the starch-water, the woman of the present day, the girl who takes time by the forelock, and leads him as a peasant lass would lead her kid, knows nothing of the way "my mother and my grandmother did." She dispenses with half the work by using detersives, or some of the modern soaps; she uses a washing-machine and a wringer, and saves her hands and her back, and her time and her strength. You would never dream, to look at those shapely hands gliding over the ivory keys, that they could so charmingly perform all the mysteries of housekeeping, doing it cheerfully and lovingly, and scouting the idea of calling these blessed tasks by the hateful name of "drudgery." She sees no drudgery in them. She soaks the clothes over night, and has her tubs and machine and everything convenient and ready; then she "rises with the lark," and has the work half done by the time her neighbor across the way has commenced hunting up her weekly washing. She, the neighbor, goes from room to room, searching behind trunks, between bedticks, on the floor, in closets, in dusty corners, in coat-pockets, and among garments hanging in divers places, for the work of the day.

If the clothes are a soak properly, one suds is sufficient before boiling, one afterward, and one good rinse-water, generally. But if soaking and using the best quality of modern soap – the kind we use – you will barely wring them out and put them on to boil in a suds made of this, then one suds after, and a rinse or two if you prefer. By consulting that large book published since the Centennial, looking among the awards for the best articles – best of everything – you will learn much indeed. It has been a great blessing to us, and will be to any person desiring to obtain the best articles in use, the labor-savers, the latest and best inventions, the greatest aids to the housewife.

...

If you have stained your muslin or gingham dress, or your white pants with berries, before wetting with anything else pour boiling water through the stains, and they will disappear.
Arthur's Illustrated Home Magazine, November 1878

1879

Washing Flannels. – A lady correspondent says: "I will give a little of my experience in washing flannels. I was taught to wash flannel in hot water, but it is a great mistake. In Italy my flannels were a wonder to me; they always came home from the wash so soft and white. I learned that the Italian women washed them in cold water. Many a time I have watched them kneeling in a box, which had one end taken out, to keep them out of the mud, by the bank of a stream, washing in the running water and drying on the bank or gravel, without boiling; and I never had washing done better, and flannels never half so well. I have tried it since, and find the secret of nice soft flannels to be the washing of them in cold or luke-warm water, and plenty of stretching before hanging out. Many recipes say 'Don't rub soap on flannels;' but you can rub soap on to the advantage of the flannels, if you will rinse it out afterward and use no hot water about them, not forgetting to stretch the threads in both directions before drying. Flannels so cared for will never become stiff, shrunken, or yellow."
Arthur's Illustrated Home Magazine, January 1879

I remember Josie made her old alpaca dress over, quite as good as new. She ripped it apart and turned it, cut off the worn and frayed edges, cleaned the soiled places with benzine, dampened and ironed it on the wrong side, made a new sham skirt, took the wide plaiting off from the bottom of it, turned, and put on fresh binding, cut the basque and overskirt into a long polonaise, trimmed with narrow bands of black silk, and, really, the dress is quite as good as new. She made over several old alpaca and cashmere dresses for us, into second-best. After a dress has been worn a good while, it will do nicely for winter-wear, if it has new, fresh, thick, good linings, but it will not be warm enough without these important changes. A dress becomes stretched and don't fit as snugly as at first, and for this reason it needs renovating. ...

My two dresses are both black. The old one was a jetty cashmere, that I bought when my husband died. It had become soiled in spite of me, and considerably worn about the bottom and under-side of the sleeves, and the button-holes had broken, and it was a mite too large at first. Esther and I had a deal between us, and to make it square, she proposed renovating my cashmere dress. She ripped it all to pieces, and took ten cents worth of soap-bark, which she bought at the drug-store in the city, boiled it in three pints of water, and strained it. Each piece of cashmere was dipped into this while the liquid was quite warm, well sponged and ironed between fold of muslin. This made it almost as good as new. New linings were used, and new trimmings and braid, and bows of gros-grain ribbon; the button-holes were newly worked, and the dress came out of Esther's hands just as good as new. It was trimmed with back bands of black silk, and the buttons were silk, gros-grain, covered.
Arthur's Illustrated Home Magazine, February 1879

Ladies' Patterns, such as Basques, Polonaise, Cloaks, etc., should be selected according to the bust measure. Pass a tape measure around the breast, just under the arms, and above the bust, as seen above, draw it *one inch tighter than the dress is to fit*; the number of inches ten ascertained is the size of the bust. Overskirts, Drawers, etc., should be selected according to the waist measure. The waist measure should be taken tight under the belt.
Bazar Glove-Fitting Patterns, 1879

Bibliography

Arthur's Lady's Home Magazine. July, 1872. Philadelphia, PA

Arthur's Illustrated Home Magazine. May, 1876. Philadelphia, PA

Arthur's Illustrated Home Magazine. January – December, 1878. Philadelphia, PA.

Arthur's Illustrated Home Magazine. January – December, 1879. Philadelphia, PA.

Arthur's Illustrated Home Magazine. January – December, 1880. Philadelphia, PA.

The Bazaar, The Exchange and Mart, and Journal of the Household. January-June, 1875. London, England

Bazar Glove-Fitting Patterns, No. 1-8, 1879. James McCall & Co.. New York, NY

The Christian Monitor, January – February, 1878. St. Louis, MO

The Christian Monitor, June – October, 1878. St. Louis, MO

Demorest's Monthly Magazine. June, 1870. W. Jennings Demorest. New York, NY

Demorest's Monthly Magazine. April & November, 1878. W. Jennings Demorest. New York, NY

Every Saturday, September 7, 1872. Boston, MA

The Female's Friend, and General Domestic Adviser. Robert Huish. London: George Virtue, 1837

Frank Leslie's Lady's Magazine. June, 1875. New York, NY

Godey's Lady's Book and Magazine. January – December, 1874. Philadelphia, PA.

Godey's Lady's Book and Magazine. January-December, 1878. Philadelphia, PA

Godey's Lady's Book and Magazine. February, 1879. Philadelphia, PA

Harper's Bazar, A Repository of Fashion, Pleasure, and Instruction. January 29, 1870. New York, NY

Harper's Bazar. March 25, 1871. New York, NY

Harper's Bazar. June 3, 1871. New York, NY

Harper's Bazar. October 7, 1871. New York, NY

Harper's Bazar. December 9, 1871. New York, NY

Harper's Bazar. June 1, 1872. New York, NY

Harper's Bazar. September 21, 1872. New York, NY

Harper's Bazar. July 25, 1874. New York, NY

Harper's Bazar. February 17, 1877. New York, NY

Harper's Bazar. August 11, 1877. New York, NY

Harper's Bazar. March 2, 1878. New York, NY

Harper's Bazar. January 25, 1879. New York, NY

Harper's Bazar. February 22, 1879. New York, NY

Harper's Bazar. April 5, 1879. New York, NY

Hints on Dress: or, What to Wear, When to Wear It, and How to Buy It. Ethel C. Gale. New York: G. P. Putnam & Sons, 1872

How to Dress on £15 a Year as a Lady. By a Lady. London: George Routledge & Sons, 1874

Madame Thérèse, Glossary and Phrase-book. Cambridge Local Examinations, Dec., 1870. John J. T. Jackson. Manchester: John Heywood, 1870

The Milliner and Dressmaker, and Warehouseman's Gazette. January – December, 1870. London, England

Peterson's Magazine, January – December, 1870. Philadelphia, PA

Peterson's Magazine, January – December, 1871. Philadelphia, PA

Peterson's Magazine, January – December, 1872. Philadelphia, PA

Peterson's Magazine, January – December, 1873. Philadelphia, PA

Peterson's Magazine. January – December, 1874. Philadelphia, PA.

Peterson's Magazine. January – December, 1875. Philadelphia, PA.

Peterson's Magazine. January – December, 1876. Philadelphia, PA.

Peterson's Magazine. January – December, 1877. Philadelphia, PA.

Peterson's Magazine. January – June, 1878. Philadelphia, PA.

Peterson's Magazine. January – December, 1879. Philadelphia, PA.

Smith's Illustrated Pattern Bazaar. Spring 1873. A. Burdette Smith. New York, NY.

Smith's Illustrated Pattern Bazaar. Fall 1876. A. Burdette Smith. New York, NY.

The Warehousemen and Drapers Trade Journal, July 29, 1876. London, England

World of Fashion, Fine Arts & Polite Literature. May 1876. A. Burdette Smith. New York, NY.

The Young Englishwoman. January & May 1875. London, England

The Young Woman's Book: a Useful Manual for Everyday Life. Mrs. Valentine. London: Frederick Warne and Co., 1877

About the Author

I adore nineteenth-century fashion magazines. I love Victorian-era sewing books even more.

Learning to sew in the loose-fitting fashions of the later twentieth century gave me no hint of the intricacies of structured clothing, or of the amazing things women were willing to put themselves through to trim their gorgeous dresses. This jeans and sweat-shirt girl quickly learned to appreciate the techniques those seamstresses employed. After many years of collecting, I wanted to share their original writings with other historical-dress enthusiasts.

I'm the owner (and sole employee) of The Mantua-Maker, quality historical sewing patterns for the modern sewing artist, established in 1993. I fell in love with costuming when my boyfriend took me to BayCon's Masquerade in 1886, and I've been making historical and fantastic clothing ever since.

My designs have won awards at World Con, Costume Con, WesterCon, and BayCon.

Please have a look at my previous books:

Elephant's Breath & London Smoke:
Historic Colour Names, Definitions & Uses

Fabric à la Romantic Regency:
A Glossary of Fabrics from Original Sources 1795 – 1836

Victorian Bathing and Bathing Suits:
The Culture of the Two-Piece Bathing Dress from 1837 – 1901

You can see more of my work at www.mantua-maker.com.

The Mantua-Maker Historical Sewing Patterns
Abbott, Texas
2014